AF869722

# The Political Economy of International Trade

333.45
MAN

## World Scientific Studies in International Economics

(ISSN: 1793-3641)

**Series Editor** Robert M. Stern, *University of Michigan and University of California-Berkeley, USA*

**Editorial Board** Vinod K. Aggarwal, *University of California-Berkeley, USA*
Alan Deardorff, *University of Michigan, USA*
Paul De Grauwe, *London School of Economics, UK*
Barry Eichengreen, *University of California-Berkeley, USA*
Mitsuhiro Fukao, *Keio University, Tokyo, Japan*
Robert L. Howse, *New York University, USA*
Keith E. Maskus, *University of Colorado, USA*
Arvind Panagariya, *Columbia University, USA*

---

Vol. 37 The Path of World Trade Law in the 21st Century
*by Steve Charnovitz (The George Washington University, USA)*

Vol. 38 International Trade, Distribution and Development: Empirical Studies of Trade Policies
*by Paul Brenton (The World Bank, USA)*

Vol. 39 Evolving Patterns in Global Trade and Finance
*by Sven W. Arndt (Claremont McKenna College, USA)*

Vol. 40 Shadow Banking Within and Across National Borders
*edited by Stijn Claessens (International Monetary Fund, USA), Douglas Evanoff (Federal Reserve Bank of Chicago, USA), George Kaufman (Loyola University Chicago, USA) & Luc Laeven (International Monetary Fund, USA)*

Vol. 41 Modeling Developing Countries' Policies in General Equilibrium
*by Jaime de Melo (FERDI, France & University of Geneva, Switzerland)*

Vol. 42 Developing Countries in the World Economy
*by Jaime de Melo (FERDI, France & University of Geneva, Switzerland)*

Vol. 43 Farm Policies and World Markets: Monitoring and Disciplining the International Trade Impacts of Agricultural Policies
*by Tim Josling (Stanford University, USA)*

Vol. 44 Non-Tariff Barriers, Regionalism and Poverty: Essays in Applied International Trade Analysis
*by L. Alan Winters (University of Sussex, UK)*

Vol. 45 Trade Law, Domestic Regulation and Development
*by Joel P. Trachtman (Tufts University, USA)*

Vol. 46 The Political Economy of International Trade
*edited by Edward D Mansfield (University of Pennsylvania, USA)*

The complete list of the published volumes in the series can be found at
http://www.worldscientific.com/series/wssie

46 World Scientific Studies in International Economics

# THE POLITICAL ECONOMY OF INTERNATIONAL TRADE

**Edward D. Mansfield**

University of Pennsylvania, USA

NEOMA Business School
LIBRARY
Campus de Rouen
1, rue du Maréchal Juin
BP 215 - Cedex
76825 Mont Saint Aignan
Tél : 02 32 82 57 00

World Scientific

NEW JERSEY • LONDON • SINGAPORE • BEIJING • SHANGHAI • HONG KONG • TAIPEI • CHENNAI

*Published by*

World Scientific Publishing Co. Pte. Ltd.
5 Toh Tuck Link, Singapore 596224
*USA office:* 27 Warren Street, Suite 401-402, Hackensack, NJ 07601
*UK office:* 57 Shelton Street, Covent Garden, London WC2H 9HE

**Library of Congress Cataloging-in-Publication Data**
The political economy of international trade / edited by Edward D. Mansfield.
pages cm. -- (World scientific studies in international economics, ISSN 1793-3641 ; 46)
Includes bibliographical references and index.
ISBN 978-9814644280 (hardcover) -- ISBN 9814644285 (hardcover)
1. International trade. 2. International economic relations. I. Mansfield, Edward D., 1962–
HF1379.P65 2015
382--dc23

2015009295

**British Library Cataloguing-in-Publication Data**
A catalogue record for this book is available from the British Library.

Copyright © 2015 by World Scientific Publishing Co. Pte. Ltd.

*All rights reserved. This book, or parts thereof, may not be reproduced in any form or by any means, electronic or mechanical, including photocopying, recording or any information storage and retrieval system now known or to be invented, without written permission from the publisher.*

For photocopying of material in this volume, please pay a copying fee through the Copyright Clearance Center, Inc., 222 Rosewood Drive, Danvers, MA 01923, USA. In this case permission to photocopy is not required from the publisher.

In-house Editor: Alisha Nguyen

Typeset by Stallion Press
Email: enquiries@stallionpress.com

To Katherine and Charlotte

## About the Author

Edward D. Mansfield is the Hum Rosen Professor of Political Science and Director of the Christopher H. Browne Center for International Politics at the University of Pennsylvania. His research focuses on international security and international political economy. He is the author of *Power, Trade, and War* (Princeton University Press, 1994), *Electing to Fight: Why Emerging Democracies Go to War* (with Jack Snyder) (MIT Press, 2005), and *Votes, Vetoes, and the Political Economy of International Trade Agreements* (with Helen V. Milner) (Princeton University Press, 2012). He is also the editor of fourteen books and journal special issues, and has published over ninety articles in the *American Political Science Review, British Journal of Political Science, Comparative Political Studies, International Organization, International Security, International Studies Quarterly, Journal of Conflict Resolution, World Politics*, and various other journals and books. The recipient of the 2000 Karl W. Deutsch Award in International Relations and Peace Research, Mansfield has been a National Fellow at the Hoover Institution and his research has been supported by grants from the Harry Frank Guggenheim Foundation, the Mershon Center, and the United States Institute of Peace. He is co-editor of the University of Michigan Press Series on International Political Economy and was an Associate Editor of the journal *International Organization*. He has been a Term Member of the Council on Foreign Relations, a member of the Graduate Record Examination Political Science Committee, and Program Co-Chair for the 2001 annual meeting of the American Political Science Association. Mansfield received his B.A., M.A., and Ph.D. from the University of Pennsylvania; and before joining the faculty there, he taught at Columbia University and Ohio State University.

## Contents

*About the Author* vii

*Introduction* xi

**Part I: Systemic Approaches to the International Trading System** **1**

Chapter 1. The Concentration of Capabilities and International Trade 3

Chapter 2. Power Politics and International Trade 37

Chapter 3. Alliances, Preferential Trading Arrangements, and International Trade 51

Chapter 4. International Institutions and the Volatility of International Trade 65

**Part II: The Political Economy of Trade Policy and Trade Attitudes** **97**

Chapter 5. The Political Economy of Nontariff Barriers: A Cross-National Analysis 99

Chapter 6. Free to Trade: Democracies, Autocracies, and International Trade 127

Chapter 7. Votes and Vetoes: The Political Determinants of Commercial Openness 145

Chapter 8. Support for Free Trade: Self-Interest, Sociotropic Politics, and Out-Group Anxiety 169

**Part III: The Political Economy of Preferential Trading Agreements 203**

Chapter 9. The Proliferation of Preferential Trading Arrangements 205

Chapter 10. Why Democracies Cooperate More: Electoral Control and International Trade Agreements 227

Chapter 11. Vetoing Co-operation: The Impact of Veto Players on Preferential Trading Arrangements 265

Chapter 12. Multilateral Determinants of Regionalism: The Effects of GATT/WTO on the Formation of Preferential Trading Arrangements 295

Chapter 13. The Expansion of Preferential Trading Arrangements 329

*Index* 343

# Introduction

Economists agree that free trade is beneficial. Open trade promotes growth, improves economic welfare, and fosters the efficient allocation of resources. Nonetheless, free trade has been the exception rather than the rule. Countries routinely impose barriers to trade, engage in disputes over trade, and try to manage the flow of trade. Politics is central to these deviations from openness, a longstanding realization that has generated a vibrant literature on the political economy of international trade. This volume contains a collection of the articles that various co-authors and I have written on this topic over the past twenty-five years.

The book is divided into three parts. Part I addresses the international political economy of trade. It includes three studies that analyze how the global trading system is influenced by the distribution of power among countries and by international institutions that were established to shape overseas commerce. The fourth study in Part I examines how international economic institutions influence the volatility of overseas commerce. Part II focuses on the domestic politics of trading partners, another core branch of research on the political economy of trade. The first article in Part II focuses on how domestic institutions and societal pressures interact to shape non-tariff barriers in a set of advanced industrial democracies. The following two articles analyze the effects on trade of a country's regime type and the extent to which power is fragmented within the national government. The final study in Part II examines what the mass public in the United States thinks about trade and why. Part III examines the political economy of international trade agreements. These agreements have become particularly widespread over the past half century and many observers argue that they have had a profound effect on the global trading system and trade relations between states. The five articles in Part III address the international and domestic politics driving the formation and expansion of trade agreements.

## Systemic Approaches to the International Trading System

A large and important body of research in the field of international relations is cast at the level of the international system. The 1970s and 1980s were marked by a particularly lively interest in systemic approaches. Led by Kenneth Waltz (1979), advocates of these approaches argued that the global context in which states operate is crucial to explaining patterns of international outcomes. This context is shaped primarily by the absence of any supranational authority (that is, the "anarchic" ordering principle of the system) and the distribution of power among the leading states in the system.

Scholars of the international political economy placed particular emphasis on one feature of the distribution of power, namely whether there exists a single, preponderantly powerful state that is both willing and able to exercise leadership. Various influential studies argued that the existence of a "hegemon" is necessary to ensure international economic stability and the openness of international trade (Kindleberger 1973; Gilpin 1975, 1981; Krasner 1976). These hegemonic stability theorists maintained that Great Britain played this role throughout the second half of the nineteenth century, underpinning an era of open international trade. In the aftermath of World War I, however, Britain was weakened and unable to serve as a hegemon. The United States, in contrast, was capable of taking up the mantle of global leadership, but was unwilling to bear the costs of doing so. The resulting dearth of international management contributed to the Great Depression and the beggar-thy-neighbor trade policies that marked the 1930s. In the aftermath of World War II and the devastation caused by the Depression, many influential observers in the U.S. expressed the view that the lack of American leadership had contributed to both of these events and that leading the global economy would allow the U.S. to establish policies and institutions that reflected its interests. Consequently, the U.S. assumed the role of hegemon, promoting the open multilateral regime that has characterized much of the past seventy years.

Despite the widespread interest prompted by hegemonic stability theory during the 1970s and 1980s, it was subjected to almost no statistical testing. In "The Concentration of Capabilities and International Trade," I attempted to help fill that gap in the literature. I argued that existing studies had done an inadequate job of defining and measuring hegemony, an especially important issue because observers do not agree on exactly which years have been marked by a hegemon. In fact, my results revealed that the effects of hegemony on trade depend heavily on how hegemony is defined and measured. An analysis based on classifications of hegemony developed by Robert Gilpin (1981, 1987) yielded support for hegemonic stability theory, whereas an analysis based on those generated by Immanuel Wallerstein (1983) did not. In addition, although extant systemic research on the international political economy had focused on hegemony, I explained that this was not the only feature of the distribution of power likely to affect international trade. The concentration of capabilities is equally — if not more — important. Moreover, while scholars had addressed whether there was a monotonic relationship between power relations and features of the trading system, I argued that the relationship between concentration and the openness of trade throughout the system was likely to have a U-shape. A series of statistical tests covering the $19^{th}$ and $20^{th}$ centuries strongly supported this hypothesis.

Although many observers consider the post-World War II trading system to be hegemonic, in terms of political-military relations the international system was bipolar, dominated by the U.S. and the Soviet Union. The U.S. promoted trade openness within its sphere of influence, especially among its political-military allies. Hegemonic stability theorists and many of their critics were focused only on this sphere. Joanne Gowa (1989), however, argued that this group of scholars had paid too little attention to how the broader context of global political-military relations influenced the trading system.

In "Power Politics and International Trade," Gowa and I analyzed these effects.

More specifically, we studied the effects of political-military alliances on international trade flows. Central to the effects of alliances on foreign commerce, we argued, are the efficiency gains from trade. As Albert Hirschman ([1945] 1980) points out, these gains yield increases in national income that can be used to augment a state's military power. Consequently, trade generates security externalities, which are uncompensated benefits or costs influencing a country's national security that arise from actions taken by other states. Gowa and I maintained that countries can address such externalities by trading more freely with their allies than with their (actual or potential) adversaries. Trade between allies enhances the security of both parties, since the gains from trade accrue to states with common security goals and bolster the aggregate political-military power of the alliance. In contrast, open trade between adversaries produces negative security externalities. A state that trades freely with an adversary augments the rival's national income and thereby jeopardizes its own security.

We also argued that the effects of major-power alliance on trade tend to be more pronounced during eras of bipolarity — when only two superpowers exist — than during eras of multipolarity — when there are more than two dominant powers. Alliances tend to be more fluid and alliance partners tend to have more exit options in multipolar than in bipolar systems. Consequently, countries in multipolar systems face a greater risk that trade with a current ally could adversely affect their national security if this state should reorient its foreign policy and enter a rival alliance.

We tested this hypothesis by using a "gravity model" to analyze the effects of alliances on bilateral trade flows involving seven major powers during the twentieth century. We focused on major powers because such states are likely to have sufficient market power to improve their terms of trade by imposing an optimal tariff. States with such power have little reason to liberalize trade with an adversary. However, liberalizing trade with an ally generates a positive security externality, strengthening the alliance as a whole.

The results supported our argument. Holding constant various economic influences on commerce, allies trade far more extensively than other states, an effect that is considerably larger during the bipolar period that followed World War II than during the preceding multipolar era.

In "Alliances, Preferential Trading Arrangements, and International Trade," Rachel Bronson and I analyzed whether the effects of alliances are heightened if the members of a security pact also belong to a preferential trading arrangement (PTA). PTAs are a broad class of international economic institutions that include free trade areas, customs unions, common markets, and economic unions. All of these agreements, however, aim to promote integration among member-states by improving and stabilizing the access that each member has to the markets of other participants. It is widely acknowledged that, on average, PTAs have spurred commerce among member-states (Frankel 1997; WTO 2011). In this study, Bronson and I argued that the combination of an alliance and a PTA provides multiple and reinforcing reasons for states to engage in open overseas commerce, creating an even greater impetus to trade than either type of institution alone.

Bronson and I also analyzed whether the presence of a major power conditions the effects of alliances on trade. My earlier work with Gowa focused on major-power alliances because major powers are particularly likely to be vested with sufficient market power to impose an optimal tariff. The effects of alliances on trade relations involving such states are expected to be especially pronounced. Furthermore, Bronson and I pointed out that alliances marked by a major-power member are likely to be more durable and stable, thereby reducing the risk that members will exit in the future and that free trade with today's ally will therefore strengthen a state that could become tomorrow's adversary.

To test these arguments, we estimated a gravity model of bilateral trade flows in 1960, 1965, 1970, 1975, 1980, 1985, and 1990. As expected, the results provided strong support for the argument that both alliances and PTAs promote trade, but that the combination of an alliance and a PTA generates far more overseas commerce among members than either type of institution alone. Finally, the effects of alliances are somewhat larger between states that include a major power than between other states. Even between smaller states, however, the effects of security pacts are marked.

During the past half-century, states have concluded a large number of international trade agreements. Some of these agreements undergird the multilateral trading regime, particularly the General Agreement on Tariffs and Trade (GATT) and its successor, the World Trade Organization (WTO). Many others have been PTAs. It is widely argued that states form trade agreements to enhance access to overseas markets and expand the flow of foreign commerce. In "International Institutions and the Volatility of International Trade," Eric Reinhardt and I claimed that such institutions are also designed to stabilize and reduce volatility in trade policy and trade flows, a function that has been largely overlooked by researchers.

More specifically, we maintained that governments aim to reduce the volatility of international trade and that participating in the GATT/WTO and PTAs can help achieve this goal. These institutions limit the ability of member-states to impose new trade barriers; they promote policy transparency and the cross-national convergence of policy instruments; and they alter markets in ways that generate stability in commercial transactions over time. International trade agreements also help to stabilize the price of traded goods, which has various benefits for firms and other economic actors. Consequently, these actors are likely to respond to lower trade variability between the country in which they are located and another country by increasing the flow of trade with that country. This implies that trade agreements which reduce the volatility of overseas commerce should enhance the volume of trade between member-states as well.

Reinhardt and I analyzed these hypotheses using data on exports for all pairs of countries from 1951 through 2001. The results strongly supported our arguments. Both PTAs and the GATT/WTO reduce the volatility of exports. In so doing, these institutions also contribute to an increase in the level of exports. Indeed, we found that much of the influence of trade agreements on the level of foreign commerce grows out of the reduction in commercial volatility they produce.

An important and underappreciated function of preferential and multilateral trade agreements is to promote the predictability of trade policy and flows.

## The Political Economy of Trade Policy and Trade Attitudes

In addition to research cast at the systemic or international level of analysis, there is a rich tradition of work on the domestic political economy of trade. Until the mid-1990s, most work on this topic emphasized how interest groups and other societal actors press government officials for trade policies that reflect their interests. Since then, however, growing interest has been expressed in the role that domestic institutions play in shaping trade and how these institutions filter societal interests. There has also been increased attention devoted to explaining societal attitudes about trade through the use of mass opinion surveys. This volume includes four studies that my co-authors and I have conducted on these topics.

The substantial body of research that emphasizes how interest groups affect trade policy by exerting political pressure on public officials generally views domestic institutions and policy makers as passive actors that supply the trade policies demanded by society's most influential groups.[1] Individuals and groups are central to these societal explanations. Such explanations therefore need to specify the factors that shape individuals' preferences about trade policy.

Since World War II, the effects of interest group pressure on trade policy have been treated most extensively in research referred to as "endogenous tariff theory." This theory is based on the assumption that trade policy is shaped primarily by demands reflecting the interests of various segments of society (Nelson 1988: 800; Rodrik 1995). Preferences for trade policy by particular societal actors can be inferred from the likely economic effects of trade policy on them, and their demands for trade policy will be based on these preferences.

[1]The classic statement is Schattschneider (1935).

While some work has focused on how sectoral conditions affect societal demands for trade policy, a considerable amount of research has instead focused on how macroeconomic fluctuations influence these demands. Central to this literature are the arguments that public officials must respond to demands made by broad segments of the populace in order to ensure their political survival and that public support for protectionism grows as domestic economic conditions degrade. Government officials therefore have reason to raise trade barriers when these conditions worsen in an effort to bolster their prospects of retaining office.

In "The Political Economy of Nontariff Barriers: A Cross-National Analysis," Marc Busch and I addressed the effects of unemployment and the exchange rate on cross-national patterns of nontariff barriers (NTBs). Extensive unemployment is likely to generate calls for protectionism by making it more difficult for workers to adjust to increases in imports. Individuals who lose their jobs due to rising import competition will find it harder to obtain alternative employment and are likely to be paid less once they become reemployed, if unemployment is widespread. These workers and others who fear that they may soon become unemployed have reason to press for relief from foreign competition. Variations in the exchange rate are another potent macroeconomic influence on trade policy (Dornbusch and Frankel 1987). Central to the effects of the exchange rate on societal demands for protectionism is the influence of the price of a state's currency on the competitiveness of its exports and import-competing products. An appreciated currency, by increasing the price of domestically produced goods, threatens to undermine both exports and import competing sectors. These developments are likely to stimulate pressure for protectionist measures.

Research on trade policy that infers societal demands for protection from macroeconomic conditions generally relies on the assumption that public officials respond to the societal pressures because these pressures influence the ability of leaders to retain power. In democracies — the countries on which the vast bulk of such work focuses — public officials can improve their electoral prospects by increasing trade barriers when unemployment rises or a country's currency appreciates since these actions are likely to be popular and to help blunt the short-term effects of economic downturns. In our study, Bush and I focused on explaining NTBs in fourteen advanced industrial democracies during the 1980s.

Although societal approaches to trade policy have been influential, they have also been criticized for placing too little emphasis on domestic institutions (Nelson 1988). Busch and I argued that societal and institutional accounts of trade policy should be treated as complementary and that more attention should be focused on the interaction between these factors. From an institutional standpoint, we argued that economically large countries with institutions that vest policymakers with autonomy and insulation from societal pressures are likely to enact protectionist trade policies. Economically large countries have the market power to benefit from the imposition an optimal tariff or its nontariff barrier equivalent. Institutions that insulate policymakers and enhance their autonomy provide a setting in which they can advance these state interests. We argued that insulation and autonomy are likely to be enhanced in democracies where electoral districts tend to be large and in proportional representation (PR) systems (Rogowski 1987).

Although various observers had suggested that the interaction between societal and institutional factors help to shape trade policy, ours was one of the first systematic empirical tests of this hypothesis. Consistent with our arguments, Busch and I found that NTBs are highest in countries that are: (1) marked by extensive unemployment and an appreciated exchange rate, (2) economically large, and (3) characterized by large electoral constituencies and PR systems. These results accord with our claim that NTBs flourish in countries where state and societal interests both favor protection and policymakers are vested with the institutional capacity to advance those interests.

Whereas Bush and I followed much of the existing literature on the domestic political economy of trade policy by analyzing democracies, the past twenty years has witnessed growing interest in whether the trade policies of democracies differ from those of other regime types. In "Free to Trade: Democracies, Autocracies, and International

Trade," Helen Milner, B. Peter Rosendorff, and I addressed this important issue. We developed a model in which the chief executive (that is, the president or prime minister) in a democracy requires the consent of a majority of the legislature to enact his or her preferred trade policy. In an autocracy, by contrast, the chief executive does not require a legislative majority to pass trade policy initiatives. We argued that this institutional difference contributes to a tendency for pairs of democratic countries to set lower trade barriers than pairs comprised of a democracy and an autocracy (that is "mixed" pairs). Furthermore, we show that whether pairs of autocratic countries liberalize trade more extensively than pairs of democracies or mixed pairs depends largely on the preferences of the autocratic leaders. Without knowledge of these preferences, we cannot make any firm predictions about the trade policies of autocratic pairs.

We can, however, evaluate the claim that democratic pairs of countries are more open with respect to overseas commerce than mixed pairs. To this end, we estimated a gravity model of bilateral trade using data drawn from the period 1960 to 1990. The results indicated that mixed pairs conducted significantly less commerce than democratic pairs and that this finding is robust to various measure of democracy.

In "Votes and Vetoes: The Political Determinants of Commercial Openness," Witold Henisz and I pursued two conclusions stemming from the two studies that were discussed above, namely that it is important to account for the institutional setting that filters societal preferences for trade policy and that regime type influences trade policy. Consistent with the argument that Busch and I advanced, Henisz and I argued that whereas societal demands and institutions are often regarded as having independent effects on such policy, it is more fruitful to view the influence of each type of factor as conditional on the other. More specifically, we claimed that deteriorating macroeconomic conditions are a potent source of protectionist demands throughout society, but that the extent to which such conditions reduce commercial openness hinges on two features of domestic institutions.

First, countries differ in the extent to which authority is concentrated within the national government. Central in this regard are the number of "veto points" or "veto players" that exist; that is, the number of independent partisan and institutional actor whose agreement is necessary to make policy. As the number of actors with veto power increases, authority becomes fragmented and it becomes harder to change existing policies since more actors can block such change. Consequently, Henisz and I argued that the effects of macroeconomic conditions on trade policy should be muted in countries with more veto points and heightened in countries with fewer veto points. Second, we argued that both fragmentation of power and societal pressures stemming from economic conditions should have a more pronounced impact on trade policy in democracies than in other regimes. The electoral constraints facing democratic leaders force them to respond to demands made by key segments of society, whereas autocrats depend on the support of a narrower portion of society. This narrower segment is less likely to base its support for the autocrat on macroeconomic conditions than on whether it generates economic rents from the government, regardless of the economy's overall performance.

The results of a set of tests based on the period from 1980 to 2000 supported these arguments. High levels of unemployment promote the closure of trade in democratic countries, but have far less influence in non-democratic states. Furthermore, the magnitude of unemployment's influence in democracies becomes attenuated as the number of veto points rises, making it harder to change trade policy.

Existing studies of societal and interest group preferences for trade policy — including those that I have conducted — frequently infer these preferences from macroeconomic conditions, sectoral conditions, or other factors. Recently, a small but growing body of literature has assessed these preferences directly through public opinion surveys. Much of this research addresses whether mass attitudes about trade can be explained by standard political economy models. Some cross-national studies, for example, have found that mass opinion about trade corresponds closely to predictions stemming from a factor endowments approach (O'Rourke and Sinnott 2002; Mayda and Rodrik 2005). Research on public attitudes toward trade in the U.S. has also generated support for this approach (Scheve and Slaughter 2001).

In "Support for Free Trade: Self-Interest, Sociotropic Politics, and Out-Group Anxiety," Diana Mutz and I offered a different perspective. Existing work on mass attitudes toward trade that relies on a political economy model (typically either a Heckscher-Ohlin or a Ricardo-Viner framework) assumes that individuals' opinions about overseas commerce are guided by material self-interest. More specifically, people form attitudes about trade based on how expanding or restricting foreign commerce would affect their income. Substantial research in other economic policy domains, however, has demonstrated that self-interest very rarely shapes the formation of policy opinions. Based on two surveys of Americans, Mutz and I found that the same holds true in the case of attitudes about trade policy. Our results provided little support for either a factor endowments or a specific factors model. Instead, perceptions about the effects of trade on the country as a whole — what are often referred to as "sociotropic" perceptions — play a substantial role in shaping attitudes about foreign commerce that is largely independent of self-interest. People who believe that trade is good for the U.S. tend to support open trade, whereas those who feel that trade is bad for the U.S. do not. Indeed, these perceptions are among the most important influences on opinions about trade.

Finally, Mutz and I found that trade policy attitudes are shaped in important ways by indicators of domestic ethnocentrism and foreign policy attitudes. There is little support for free trade among people who believe the U.S. should take an isolationist stance on international affairs more generally or among those who feel that members of other ethnic and racial groups are less praiseworthy than their own racial or ethnic group. Although such views have no direct bearing on the economic benefits of trade, they are far more predictive of trade preferences than indicators of economic self-interest.

## The Political Economy of Preferential Trading Agreements

The first section of this book includes a number of studies that address how PTAs influence both the flow and the volatility of trade. The final section of the book addresses the factors that drive the formation and expansion of these institutions. As I mentioned earlier, PTAs are a broad class of international agreements that include common markets, customs unions, free trade areas, and economic unions. All of these arrangements require members to mutually adjust their trade policies, granting each member preferential access to the others' markets.

Since World War II, PTAs have proliferated rapidly. Hundreds of them have formed over the past half-century and almost every country currently participates in at least one (WTO 2011). Why PTAs have spread and the effects of this development are issues that have generated considerable interest and controversy. A substantial amount of research has focused on explaining the effects of PTAs. It is widely argued, for example, that PTAs shape trade relations and trade flows (Frankel 1997). There is also evidence that they guide foreign investment (Büthe and Milner 2008). For over half a century, economists have debated whether PTAs promote or undermine the welfare of countries (Viner 1950). Similarly, scholars sharply disagree about whether the formation of these agreements will erode the multilateral trading system or foster multilateral openness and stability (Bhagwati 2008; Lawrence 1996). From a political standpoint, some have argued that PTAs can promote peace, enhance international environmental coordination, and improve human rights enforcement (Nye 1971; Mansfield and Pevehouse 2000; Limão 2005; Hafner-Burton 2009).

In light of the vast amount of research that has been conducted on the consequences of PTAs, the relative dearth of work on their origins is surprising. Even less work has been conducted on the political underpinnings of PTAs. In this book, I include five studies that aimed to help fill that void.

In "The Proliferation of Preferential Trading Arrangements," I addressed how various features of the international system have influenced the spread of PTAs. First, I mentioned earlier that many systemic accounts of the international trading system have emphasized the effects of hegemony. Some of these studies suggest that declining hegemony stimulates the formation of preferential agreements. Hegemonic stability theorists argue that the stability of the international trading system is a collective good, suboptimal amounts of which will be provided without a global leader. PTAs may be outgrowths of the economic instability fostered by the absence or the decline of such a country (Kindleberger 1973; Gilpin 1975, 1987; Krasner 1976). Alternatively, the erosion of hegemony may stimulate the creation and expansion of PTAs by a set of leading economic powers that feel these arrangements would assist them in managing the international economy (Yarbrough and Yarbrough 1992). Drawing smaller states into preferential arrangements with a relatively liberal cast toward third parties might reduce the capacity of these states to establish a series of more protectionist blocs, bind them to decisions about the system made by the leading powers, and contribute to the maintenance of an open global trading system.

Second, dips in the global business cycle may prompt the formation of PTAs. Governments may form these agreements during downturns in response to demands for protection from firms, since PTAs discriminate against the goods of third parties. At the same time, PTAs provide export opportunities to member-states and such opportunities might be especially valuable during economic downturns.

Third, it is widely argued that strategic interaction has guided the establishment and the spread of PTAs. The creation of a new PTA can prompt fears by third parties that it will undermine their competitiveness, thereby inducing them to form a rival bloc. Similarly, when a state joins an existing PTA it may provoke concern on the part of its economic rivals that they will be placed at a competitive disadvantage in international markets unless they respond in kind. Even if states are not economic rivals, the perception that a preferential agreement is benefitting members can lead other states that are anxious to reap similar gains to join a PTA (Pomfret

1988; Yarbrough and Yarbrough 1992). Finally, PTAs might form and expand in reaction to one another because they usually have more aggregate market power and thus more bargaining power than their constituent members (Fernández and Portes 1998).

I tested these hypotheses using data drawn from the period 1952 to 1994. The results confirmed that declining hegemony and recessions have contributed to the formation PTAs. They also provided ample evidence that strategic interaction has stimulated the establishment of PTAs. Finally, I found that members of the GATT/WTO have formed PTAs more frequently during multilateral negotiating rounds than in other periods.

In addition to international politics, domestic politics are likely to affect the establishment of PTAs. Like my research on trade policy and trade flows, the focus of my domestic analyses of PTAs has been on regime type and veto players.

In "Why Democracies Cooperate More: Electoral Control and International Trade Agreements," Helen Milner, B. Peter Rosendorff, and I argued that democratic leaders have especially strong incentives to form preferential agreements. Democratic leaders must stand for office in regular and competitive elections, whereas autocratic leaders must maintain the allegiance of small, select groups within society. Voters in democracies have difficulty distinguishing between adverse economic developments that are beyond the leader's control and adverse developments arising from the leader's poor performance in office. As a result, voters may remove a democratic head of state from office because they believe he or she has done a bad job when in fact this individual has not performed poorly. By entering a PTA, the chief executive in a democracy can guard against this possibility if these institutions furnish reliable information about the behavior of member-states. Countries that violate their commitments to the institution trip an alarm sounded by other members or the organization itself. By publicizing a democratic leader's actions, PTAs help him to avoid being turned out of office because voters mistakenly believe he has performed poorly. In non-democracies, electoral dynamics are far less important, giving leaders much less incentive to enter PTAs than their democratic counterparts.

Our empirical results — which cover the period from 1951 to 1992 — support the argument that democracies are more likely to form PTAs than other states. On average, the probability of a democracy entering a preferential agreement is roughly twice the probability of an autocracy doing so. Furthermore, the support for our argument is consistent across a number of leading measures of regime type.

A country's regime type is not the only political institution likely to affect PTA formation. In "Vetoing Cooperation: The Impact of Veto Players on Preferential Trading Arrangements," Helen Milner, Jon Pevehouse, and I address the impact of veto players. Recall that veto points or veto players (the terms tend to be used interchangeably) have the ability to block policy change and their assent is necessary to alter existing policies. These actors exist in all types of regimes, although democratic polities tend to have more of them than non-democratic regimes.

In most countries, the executive branch sets the agenda in foreign affairs and has the power to initiate foreign economic policy. However, veto players must ratify policy choices made by the executive, such as joining a trade agreement. Formally, the head of state in a democracy is often required by the national constitution to obtain the approval of the legislature for international agreements, including PTAs. He or she will therefore need to anticipate the legislature's (or any other veto player's) reaction to the proposed arrangement and ensure it is domestically acceptable.

Ratification can also be less formal. In dictatorships, shifts in foreign economic policy often require the support of groups like the military or local leaders. Implicitly these groups have ratified a trade agreement if they had the ability to veto it and chose not to. Informal ratification also occurs in democracies. If a leader needs to change a domestic law, norm, or practice in order to implement a PTA, even if no formal vote on the arrangement itself is required, a legislative vote on any necessary domestic change becomes a vote on the agreement.

Because of this ratification constraint, veto players affect the formation of PTAs. As the number of veto players increases, so does the likelihood that at least one such player will have a constituency that is adversely affected by the PTA and therefore will block its ratification.

There is ample support for this claim. Based on an analysis covering 1950 to 1999, Milner, Pevehouse, and I found that the odds of a country entering a PTA are inversely related to the number of veto players that exist. Even after controlling for the effects of regime type, veto players have a strong and sizable effect on PTA formation.[2]

It is noteworthy that the rapid proliferation of PTAs over the past half-century has been accompanied by the unprecedented growth of multilateral trade openness, spurred by the GATT and the WTO. It is not clear why states form preferential blocs when they belong to a successful multilateral trade regime. In "Multilateral Determinants of Regionalism: The Effects of GATT/WTO on the Formation of Preferential Trading Arrangements," Eric Reinhardt and I analyzed how the multilateral regime has conditioned the spread of PTAs.

We argued that the GATT/WTO has played a large role in stimulating the formation of PTAs. States frequently enter PTAs to increase their bargaining power in multilateral trade negotiations, to bolster their market power, and to insure against developments within the GATT/WTO that could threaten their economic interests. Conditions within the multilateral regime can create incentives for states to enhance their bargaining power, thereby leading them to form PTAs. First, the growth of GATT/WTO membership reduces each participant's leverage and fosters collective action problems within the regime. Entering a PTA composed of countries with similar economic interests can provide states with insurance against the emergence of these problems. Second, the multilateral trade negotiations sponsored by the GATT/WTO can prompt members to enter PTAs to insure against the possibility of the negotiations faltering and to bolster their bargaining position in the talks.

[2]For a more recent analysis of the effects of regime type and veto players on PTA formation, see Mansfield and Milner (2012).

Third, during GATT/WTO disputes, states may form PTAs with third parties to improve their leverage; and losing a GATT/WTO dispute may convince states to form PTAs with third parties to gain countervailing market access and added bargaining leverage.

To test these arguments, we analyzed PTA formation among members of the GATT/WTO. Consistent with our arguments, we found that parties to the multilateral regime are more likely to form a PTA when GATT/WTO membership increases, a multinational negotiating round is ongoing, and they have recently engaged in a GATT/WTO dispute, especially if they lost the dispute. These results indicate that while the GATT/WTO has made considerable headway in liberalizing trade, it has also created various incentives for member-states to seek PTAs as a means to obtaining greater benefits from the multilateral regime.

Over the past few decades, social scientists have exhibited rising interest in the factors that account for the formation of new PTAs. The proliferation of PTAs during the post-World War II era, however, has also been driven by existing agreements adding members. In general, very little is known about why some PTAs expand while others do not, an issue that Jon Pevehouse and I addressed in "The Expansion of Preferential Trading Arrangements."

In this study, we found that during the period from 1950 to 2007, bilateral PTAs (i.e., those comprised of two members that grant each other reciprocal preferences) and "hub and spoke" agreements (that is those in which one state or set of states grants unilateral preferences to other members that are not reciprocated) rarely added members, whereas over half of all multilateral PTAs (that is those comprised of more than two members, all of which grant the other participants reciprocal preferences) have expanded. Furthermore, we found that multilateral PTAs tend to enlarge when the existing members are particularly open with respect to trade, when the size distribution among members is relatively uniform, when the PTA is economically large (although this result is not overly robust), and in reaction to other PTAs expanding throughout the global system. Finally, our results indicated that, when PTAs expand, they tend to add members that are economically and politically similar to existing participants.

## Conclusion

It is widely acknowledged that politics affects trade. However, considerable disagreement exists about which aspects of politics are most important in this regard and the nature of their effects. The studies included in this volume represent the efforts that various co-authors and I have made to address these issues. They do not offer a single perspective on this topic. Aspects of trade are heavily influenced by features of the international system, bilateral relations between commercial partners, and the domestic politics of these states. The articles in this volume address all of these factors. Any comprehensive theory of the political economy of trade would need to coherently synthesize and integrate these factors. Is such a comprehensive theory possible? That question has not yet been answered but it could usefully guide future research on this important and enduring topic.

## References

Bhagwati, Jagdish. 2008. *Termites in the Trading System: How Preferential Agreements Undermine Free Trade.* New York: Oxford University Press.

Büthe, Tim, and Helen V. Milner. 2008. The Politics of Foreign Direct Investment into Developing Countries: Increasing FDI through International Trade Agreements? *American Journal of Political Science* 52 (4): 741–62.

Dornbusch, Rudiger, and Jeffrey A. Frankel. 1987. Macroeconomics and Protection. In Robert M. Stern, editor, *U.S. Trade Policies in a Changing World Economy*, pp. 77–130. Cambridge, MA: MIT Press.

Fernández, Raquel, and Jonathan Portes. 1998. Returns to Regionalism: An Analysis of Nontraditional Gains from Regional Trade Agreements. *World Bank Economic Review* 12 (2): 197–220.

Frankel, Jeffrey A. 1997. *Regional Trading Blocs in the World Economic System.* Washington, DC: Institute for International Economics.

Gilpin, Robert. 1975. *U.S. Power and the Multinational Corporation: The Political Economy of Foreign Direct Investment.* New York, NY: Basic Books.

Gilpin, Robert. 1981. *War and Change in World Politics.* New York, NY: Cambridge University Press.

Gilpin, Robert. 1987. *The Political Economy of International Relations.* Princeton, NJ: Princeton University Press.

Gowa, Joanne. 1989. Bipolarity, Multipolarity, and Free Trade. *American Political Science Review* 83 (4): 1245–56.

Hafner-Burton, Emilie M. 2009. *Forced to Be Good: Why Trade Agreements Boost Human Rights.* Ithaca, NY: Cornell University Press.

Hirschman, Albert O. 1980 [1945]. *National Power and the Structure of Foreign Trade.* Berkeley, CA: University of California Press.

Kindleberger, Charles P. 1973. *The World in Depression.* Berkeley, CA: University of California Press.

Krasner, Stephen D. 1976. State Power and the Structure of International Trade. *World Politics* 28 (3): 317–47.

Lawrence, Robert Z. 1996. *Regionalism, Multilateralism, and Deeper Integration.* Washington, DC: Brookings Institution.

Limão, Nuno. 2005. Trade Policy, Cross-Border Externalities and Lobbies: Do Linked Agreements Enforce More Cooperative Outcomes? *Journal of International Economics* 67 (1): 175–99.

Mansfield, Edward D., and Helen V. Milner. 2012. *Votes, Vetoes, and the Political Economy of International Trade Agreements.* Princeton, NJ: Princeton University Press.

Mansfield, Edward D., and Jon C. Pevehouse. 2000. Trade Blocs, Trade Flows, and International Conflict. *International Organization* 54 (4): 775–808.

Mayda, Anna Maria, and Dani Rodrik. 2005. Why Are Some People (and Countries) More Protectionist Than Others? *European Economic Review* 49 (6): 1393–430.

Nelson, Douglas. 1988. Endogenous Tariff Theory: A Critical Survey. *American Journal of Political Science* 32 (3): 796–837.

Nye, Joseph S. 1971. *Peace in Parts: Integration and Conflict in Regional Organization.* Boston, MA: Little, Brown.

O'Rourke, Kevin H., and Richard Sinnott. 2002. What Determines Attitudes Toward Protectionism? Some Cross-Country Evidence. In Susan M. Collins and Dani Rodrik, editors, *Brookings Trade Forum*, pp. 157–206. Washington, DC: Brookings Institution.

Pomfret, Richard. 1988. *Unequal Trade: The Economics of Discriminatory International Trade Policies.* Oxford, UK: Basil Blackwell.

Rodrik, Dani. 1995. The Political Economy of Trade Policy. In Gene Grossman and Kenneth Rogoff, editors, *Handbook of International Economics*, Vol. 3, pp. 1457–94. Amsterdam: Elsevier.

Rogowski, Ronald. 1987. Trade and the Variety of Democratic Institutions. *International Organization* 41 (2): 203–23.

Schattschneider, E. E. 1935. *Politics, Pressures and the Tariff.* New York, NY: Prentice Hall.

Scheve, Kenneth E., and Matthew J. Slaughter. 2001. What Determines Individual Trade-Policy Preferences? *Journal of International Economics* 54 (2): 267–92.

Viner, Jacob. 1950. *The Customs Union Issue.* New York, NY: Carnegie Endowment for International Peace.

Wallerstein, Immanuel. 1983. The Three Instances of Hegemony in the History of the Capitalist World Economy. *International Journal of Comparative Sociology* 24 (1–2): 100–8.

Waltz, Kenneth N. 1979. *Theory of International Politics.* Reading, MA: Addison-Wesley.

World Trade Organization (WTO). 2011. *World Trade Report 2011.* Geneva: WTO.

Yarbrough, Beth V., and Robert M. Yarbrough. 1992. *Cooperation and Governance in International Trade: The Strategic Organizational Approach.* Princeton, NJ: Princeton University Press.

# Part I:
# Systemic Approaches to the International Trading System

# The concentration of capabilities and international trade

Edward D. Mansfield

Over the course of the previous two decades, political scientists have become increasingly interested in the relationship between international politics and global trade. Much of the literature on this topic centers on the effects of a hegemonic distribution of power on commerce. Hegemonic stability theorists argue that hegemony is a necessary condition for the existence of a liberal economic order and that in the absence of a hegemon, a liberal international economy is particularly difficult to establish and maintain. However, a growing number of theoretical and empirical critiques have been leveled against hegemonic stability theory, and the issue of whether hegemony helps shape patterns of global trade continues to be the topic of heated debate.

Despite the interest that this debate has spawned, virtually no longitudinal statistical tests of the relationship between hegemony (or, more generally, the distribution of power) and international trade have been conducted. In this article, I conduct some of the first quantitative tests of the influence that both political and economic features of the international system have on trade. The results indicate that the distribution of power strongly affects international commerce but that the nature of the relationship is much different than is commonly thought.

Discussions of the systemic correlates of trade do not, however, revolve solely around the effects of hegemony. Some observers argue that war may be a more salient political influence on trade than is hegemony; others criticize hegemonic stability theorists for ignoring the effects of global economic conditions on trade. My results demonstrate the importance of each of these

An earlier version of this article was presented at the 1990 annual meeting of the American Political Science Association, San Francisco. I am grateful to David Baldwin, Jagdish Bhagwati, Eileen Crumm, Frederick Frey, Joanne Gowa, Robert Jervis, Stephen Krasner, Charles Kupchan, Arvid Lukauskas, Timothy McKeown, Helen Milner, Randall Schweller, David Spiro, and two anonymous reviewers for comments on this article. The research was supported by the Columbia University Council for Research in the Social Sciences.

*International Organization* 46, 3, Summer 1992
© 1992 by the World Peace Foundation and the Massachusetts Institute of Technology

factors: in addition to the distribution of power, both war and global income are strongly related to trade.

## Hegemony and trade

Hegemonic stability theorists agree that hegemony is associated with an open trading system, while the lack of a hegemon is associated with closure. Many of them also agree that because a liberal trading system takes on features of a public good, its creation and maintenance engender collective action problems.[1] Without a state that is willing and able to act as a privileged group and unilaterally provide a liberal trading order, the establishment of a system characterized by free trade is unlikely.

Hegemonic stability theorists disagree, however, on why hegemons provide a liberal trading system. On the one hand, Charles Kindleberger suggests that hegemons provide public goods largely for altruistic reasons.[2] He maintains that the central cause of the depression during the 1930s was the absence of a benevolent "stabilizer" to coordinate the international economy;[3] Great Britain was no longer able to assume this role as it had done in the nineteenth century, and the United States was not yet willing to assume the mantle of leadership. On the other hand, Robert Gilpin, Stephen Krasner, and David Lake argue that because the hegemon derives disproportionately greater gains from such a system, it has an incentive to create and sustain a liberal international economic order.[4] They maintain that the periods of relatively free trade during the nineteenth century and after World War II can be explained best by the benefits that accrued to Great Britain and the United States from an open trading system.[5]

1. See Mancur Olson, *The Logic of Collective Action: Public Goods and the Theory of Groups* (Cambridge, Mass.: Harvard University Press, 1971).

2. See the following works by Charles P. Kindleberger: *The World in Depression, 1929–1939* (Berkeley: University of California Press, 1973); and "Dominance and Leadership in the International Economy: Exploitation, Public Goods, and Free Riders," *International Studies Quarterly* 25 (June 1981), pp. 242–54.

3. In his original study on this topic, Kindleberger argued that a hegemon provides a source of countercyclical liquidity and a market for distressed goods, helps stabilize currencies, serves as a lender of last resort, and ensures an open international trading system. In a subsequent study, he indicated that hegemons also manage foreign exchange rates and coordinate domestic monetary policies. See ibid.

4. See Robert Gilpin, *U.S. Power and the Multinational Corporation: The Political Economy of Foreign Direct Investment* (New York: Basic Books, 1975); Robert Gilpin, *War and Change in World Politics* (New York: Cambridge University Press, 1981); Robert Gilpin, *The Political Economy of International Relations* (Princeton, N.J.: Princeton University Press, 1987); Stephen D. Krasner, "State Power and the Structure of International Trade," *World Politics* 28 (April 1976), pp. 317–47; and David A. Lake, *Power, Protection, and Free Trade: International Sources of U.S. Commercial Strategy, 1887–1939* (Ithaca, N.Y.: Cornell University Press, 1988).

5. Hegemonic stability theorists often posit that hegemony is a necessary, though not a sufficient, condition for the development of a liberal international economic order. For example, Gilpin

During the past decade, much has been written on the theoretical limitations of hegemonic stability theory. Many critics argue that systems need not be hegemonic in order to be open and, hence, no strong relationship exists between international trade on the one hand and a hegemonic or nonhegemonic system on the other. Because the theory of collective action does not preclude the provision of public goods by small (or *k*) groups,[6] certain nonhegemonic systems can also lead to a liberal trading order. The existence of a hegemon may ameliorate collective action problems when public goods such as a trade regime are initially supplied; but hegemony is not necessary for either their provision or their maintenance.[7] Others maintain that hegemony is unrelated to trade because hegemonic stability theory incorrectly identifies free trade as a public good. Since free trade does not meet the criterion of nonexcludability, a hegemon need not act as a privileged group to ensure its provision.[8]

Analysts have also argued that hegemony is related to trade but that the relationship is inverse rather than direct. They posit that nonhegemonic systems are likely to be relatively liberal because in the absence of a hegemon, no state possesses sufficient market power to influence world prices through the use of trade barriers. A hegemon, in contrast, has the market power necessary to improve its terms of trade by imposing an optimal tariff, and the noncooperative aspects of international commerce provide it with the incentive to take advantage of this ability.[9]

However, the extent to which the critiques described in this section undercut hegemonic stability theory remains open to question. Joanne Gowa recently argued that critics "have not deprived hegemonic stability theory of its analytic base: hegemons can reject the prescriptions of standard trade theory [to impose optimal tariffs]; . . . open international markets [often] do present public-good problems; and privileged groups enjoy a stronger advantage than small-group

---

argues that in addition to hegemony, a "liberal ideology [and] common interests [among the states in the system] must exist for the emergence and expansion of the liberal market system." See Gilpin, *The Political Economy of International Relations,* p. 73; and Gilpin, *War and Change in World Politics,* chap. 3.

6. See Olson, *The Logic of Collective Action.*

7. See Timothy J. McKeown, "Hegemonic Stability Theory and 19th-Century Tariff Levels in Europe," *International Organization* 37 (Winter 1983), pp. 73–91; Robert O. Keohane, *After Hegemony: Discord and Collaboration in the World Political Economy* (Princeton, N.J.: Princeton University Press, 1984); and Duncan Snidal, "The Limits of Hegemonic Stability Theory," *International Organization* 39 (Autumn 1985), pp. 579–614.

8. See John A. C. Conybeare, "Public Goods, Prisoners' Dilemmas and the International Political Economy," *International Studies Quarterly* 28 (March 1984), pp. 5–22; John A. C. Conybeare, *Trade Wars: The Theory and Practice of International Commercial Rivalry* (New York: Columbia University Press, 1987); Bruce Russett, "The Mysterious Case of Vanishing Hegemony; or, Is Mark Twain Really Dead?" *International Organization* 39 (Spring 1985), pp. 205–31, and Snidal, "The Limits of Hegemonic Stability Theory."

9. See Conybeare, "Public Goods, Prisoners' Dilemmas and the International Political Economy"; and Conybeare, *Trade Wars.*

advocates acknowledge."[10] Moreover, not all variants of this theory ascribe equal importance to the provision of public goods in the international political economy. Those analysts who place less weight on this aspect of hegemony are less susceptible to critiques that highlight either the absence of public goods in the international system or the ability of small groups to provide these goods. This suggests that the debate over the analytic underpinnings of hegemonic stability theory remains far from resolved. Also unresolved is the issue of what, if any, empirical relationship exists between hegemony and international trade.

## Empirical evidence and issues regarding hegemonic stability theory

In addition to the analytic critiques discussed above, hegemonic stability theory has also been challenged on empirical grounds. First, some analysts have argued that the relationship between hegemony and an open international trading system is weak. For example, John Conybeare found little cross-sectional or longitudinal evidence that hegemony is associated with national tariff levels, based on data from 1902 and 1971.[11] Similarly, Timothy McKeown concluded that no strong relationship exists between variables related to hegemony and national import levels (as a percentage of national income) of the advanced industrialized states from 1880 to 1987.[12]

Second, while others have conceded that hegemony may be associated with a relatively open trading system, they have challenged the causal linkages between hegemony and commerce. For example, Timothy McKeown, Arthur Stein, Giulio Gallarotti, and Susan Strange have maintained that a variety of international political and economic factors provide more satisfactory explanations for the existence of a liberal trading system during the nineteenth century than does British hegemony.[13] And Robert Keohane has argued that while the

10. See Joanne Gowa, "Rational Hegemons, Excludable Goods, and Small Groups: An Epitaph for Hegemonic Stability Theory?" *World Politics* 41 (April 1989), p. 322. In addition, Spiro argues that these critiques need not undermine hegemonic stability theory, since rather than expecting a relationship between hegemony and economic outcomes, we should expect variations in the nature of power that is exercised during different phases of hegemony. See David E. Spiro, "American Foreign Policy and International Finance," in Robert Art and Seyom Brown, eds., *American Foreign Policy After the Cold War* (New York: Macmillan, forthcoming).

11. John A. C. Conybeare, "Tariff Protection in Developed and Developing Countries: A Cross-Sectional and Longitudinal Analysis," *International Organization* 37 (Summer 1983), pp. 441–67.

12. Timothy J. McKeown, "A Liberal Trade Order? The Long-Run Pattern of Imports to the Advanced Capitalist States," *International Studies Quarterly* 35 (June 1991), pp. 151–72.

13. See McKeown, "Hegemonic Stability Theory and 19th-Century Tariff Levels in Europe"; Arthur A. Stein, "The Hegemon's Dilemma: Great Britain, the United States, and the International Economic Order," *International Organization* 38 (Spring 1984), pp. 355–86; Giulio M. Gallarotti, "Toward a Business Cycle Model of Tariffs," *International Organization* 39 (Winter 1985), pp. 155–87; and Susan Strange, "The Persistent Myth of Lost Hegemony," *International Organization* 41 (Autumn 1987), pp. 551–74.

empirical record from 1966 to 1977 is consistent with the predictions of hegemonic stability theory, the causal relationship between American hegemony and trade in manufactured goods is weak.[14]

Third, hegemonic stability theorists have been criticized for failing to measure adequately the distribution of power. This, in the opinion of some observers, has led them to choose incorrectly the cases of hegemony that they hold up as support for the theory. For example, Bruce Russett concluded that the theory mistakenly attributes hegemonic status to Great Britain during the nineteenth century and that, contrary to the position of many critics and adherents of the theory, American control over outcomes in the international political economy has not declined since the early 1970s.[15]

Three fundamental disagreements over the definition, measurement, and operationalization of hegemony underlie much of the controversy surrounding the empirical relationship between hegemony and trade. First, there is disagreement about the scope of hegemony—that is, disagreement about the aspects of international relations over which a state must wield preponderant power in order to be considered a hegemon.[16] Some scholars argue that hegemony is characterized by a situation in which a single state dominates and orders both economic and political relations.[17] Others, however, maintain that hegemony is characterized by a situation in which a single state dominates and orders international economic relations and possesses sufficient political power to ward off military threats to the international system.[18]

14. See Robert O. Keohane, "The Theory of Hegemonic Stability and Changes in International Economic Regimes, 1967–1977," in Ole R. Holsti, Randolph M. Siverson, and Alexander L. George, eds., *Change in the International System* (Boulder, Colo.: Westview Press, 1980), pp. 131–62. Gilpin also notes the inability of hegemonic stability theory "to demonstrate a close association between power and outcome." And Lake argues that because hegemonic stability theory "lacks a conception of process, or an explanation of how the constraints or interests derived from the international economic structure are transformed into decisions or political strategies within particular countries . . . the causal link between the system-level international economic structure and national-level policy is open to question." See Gilpin, *The Political Economy of International Relations,* p. 91; and David A. Lake, "International Economic Structure and American Foreign Economic Policy," *World Politics* 35 (July 1983), pp. 539–40. See also Joseph S. Nye, *Bound to Lead: The Changing Nature of American Power* (New York: Basic Books, 1990).

15. See Russett, "The Mysterious Case of Vanishing Hegemony." See also McKeown, "Hegemonic Stability Theory and 19th-Century Tariff Levels in Europe"; Keohane, *After Hegemony*; Nye, *Bound to Lead*; Strange, "The Persistent Myth of Lost Hegemony"; and Susan Strange, *States and Markets* (New York: Basil Blackwell, 1988).

16. See Russett, "The Mysterious Case of Vanishing Hegemony"; and Nye, *Bound to Lead.*

17. See, for example, Gilpin, *U. S. Power and the Multinational Corporation*; Gilpin, *War and Change in World Politics*; Gilpin, *The Political Economy of International Relations*; Russett, "The Mysterious Case of Vanishing Hegemony"; Immanuel Wallerstein, "Three Instances of Hegemony in the History of the Capitalist World-Economy," *International Journal of Comparative Sociology*, vol. 24, no. 1–2, 1983, pp. 100–108; and Paul M. Kennedy, *The Rise and Fall of the Great Powers: Economic Change and Military Conflict from 1500 to 2000* (New York: Random House, 1987).

18. See, for example, Krasner, "State Power and the Structure of International Trade"; Keohane, *After Hegemony*; and Lake, *Power, Protection, and Free Trade.* In addition, some scholars (particularly those who study war, rather than the international political economy) place less emphasis on economic power and define hegemony as a preponderance of political-military power. See Charles F. Doran and Wes Parsons, "War and the Cycle of Relative Power," *American Political*

Second, there is disagreement about the domain of a hegemon—that is, disagreement about the range of actors over which a state must wield preponderant power in order to be considered a hegemon.[19] Although hegemonic stability theory purports to explain *systemic* outcomes, as Stephan Haggard and Beth Simmons point out, "the relevant 'structure' is usually defined [by hegemonic stability theorists] as the distribution of power within the international capitalist system rather than within the world political system as a whole."[20]

Finally, there is no consensus regarding the inequality of power that is necessary for hegemony to obtain. While analysts agree that a hegemon is more powerful than the other actors in the system, most have been conspicuously silent on the fundamental issue of *how much more powerful* it needs to be in order to meet the requirements for hegemony.[21] A related problem is that analysts tend to treat as homogeneous all nonhegemonic distributions of power. However, the starkness of the dichotomy between hegemony and nonhegemony may mask the differential effects of various nonhegemonic distributions of power on outcomes in the international political economy.[22]

These disagreements over the definition, measurement, and operationalization of hegemony appear to influence substantially the empirical relationship between hegemony and trade. For example, Conybeare's and McKeown's

*Science Review* 74 (December 1980), pp. 947–65; Jack S. Levy, "The Polarity of the System and International Stability: An Empirical Analysis," in Alan Ned Sabrosky, ed., *Polarity and War* (Boulder, Colo.: Westview Press, 1985), pp. 41–66; George Modelski, "The Long Cycle of Global Politics and the Nation-State," *Comparative Studies in Society and History* 20 (April 1978), pp. 214–35; George Modelski and William R. Thompson, *Sea Power in Global Politics, 1494–1983* (Seattle: University of Washington Press, 1987); A. F. K. Organski, *World Politics* (New York: Knopf, 1958); and A. F. K. Organski and Jacek Kugler, *The War Ledger* (Chicago: University of Chicago Press, 1980). Still others differentiate between economic and political-military hegemony. See, for example, Joshua S. Goldstein, *Long Cycles* (New Haven, Conn.: Yale University Press, 1988). Hence, the types of power that are emphasized in the definition and operationalization of hegemony appear to be determined, in large measure, by the issue-area that is being studied. Further, some scholars of the international political economy argue that dimensions of hegemony other than political and economic power must also be considered. For example, Russett and Nye highlight the importance of cultural aspects of hegemony, and Ikenberry and Kupchan argue that hegemons exercise control by socializing elites in secondary states. See Russett, "The Mysterious Case of Vanishing Hegemony"; Nye, *Bound to Lead*; and G. John Ikenberry and Charles A. Kupchan, "Socialization and Hegemonic Power," *International Organization* 44 (Summer 1990), pp. 283–316. Despite their potential importance, these dimensions of hegemony are not considered in the present analysis because of the difficulty of operationalizing and measuring them.

19. For a more complete discussion of the importance of specifying the scope and domain of power in analyses of international relations, see David A. Baldwin, "Power Analysis and World Politics: New Trends Versus Old Tendencies," *World Politics* 31 (January 1979), pp. 161–94.

20. See Stephan Haggard and Beth A. Simmons, "Theories of International Regimes," *International Organization* 41 (Summer 1987), p. 503. See also Keohane, *After Hegemony*; Stein, "The Hegemon's Dilemma"; and Nye, *Bound to Lead.*

21. See McKeown, "Hegemonic Stability Theory and 19th-Century Tariff Levels in Europe"; Russett, "The Mysterious Case of Vanishing Hegemony"; and Frederick W. Frey, "The Distribution of Power in Political Systems," paper presented at the annual meeting of the American Political Science Association, Washington, D.C., 1986.

22. See Lake, *Power, Protection, and Free Trade.*

statistical results indicate that hegemony is largely unrelated to trade.[23] Alternatively, my own findings suggest that hegemony is associated with the level of global commerce: the relationship is direct when Robert Gilpin's data on hegemony are used, but it is inverse when Immanuel Wallerstein's data are used.[24] Moreover, even if hegemony had an unambiguous effect on the international trading system and no disagreements existed regarding how to define, measure, and operationalize it, hegemony is only one aspect of the distribution of power. Various other features of this distribution, not only hegemony, may have effects on trade; and it would be useful to analyze the effects of hegemony in conjunction with these other features of the distribution of power before assessing the extent to which hegemony can explain outcomes in the international political economy.

## The concentration of capabilities

In this study, I examine how the level of global trade as a percentage of global production is affected by hegemony and by the concentration of capabilities among the major powers in the international system. Despite disagreements over how to operationalize hegemony, most analysts agree that hegemony obtains when a sufficiently "large" disparity in power exists between the *two* most powerful states in the international system (and, by extension, between the largest state and every other state in the system). But whether or not the relative power disparity between the two most powerful states has or has not reached a particular threshold provides us with no information concerning how the remaining states in the system stand in relation to one another.

On the other hand, the index of concentration (*CON*) used in the present study[25] is a continuous measure of the distribution of power that takes on values ranging from 0 to 1 and measures the aggregate inequality of capabilities among all of the major powers. Hence, concentration is a measure of how *all* of the major powers stand in relation to one another. The index is as follows:

$$CON_t = \sqrt{\frac{\sum_{i=1}^{N_t} (S_{it})^2 - 1/N_t}{1 - 1/N_t}} \qquad (1)$$

23. See Conybeare, "Tariff Protection in Developed and Developing Countries"; and McKeown, "A Liberal Trade Order?"

24. See Edward D. Mansfield, "International Trade and the Onset of War," paper presented at the annual meeting of the American Political Science Association, Atlanta, Ga., 1989. The data are found in Gilpin's *War and Change in World Politics* and *The Political Economy of International Relations* and in Wallerstein's "Three Instances of Hegemony in the History of the Capitalist World-Economy."

25. The index of concentration used in my study is based on the work of Ray and Singer. See James Lee Ray and J. David Singer, "Measuring the Concentration of Power in the International System," *Sociological Methods and Research* 1 (May 1973), pp. 403–37.

LIBRARY
BP 215 - Cedex
76825 Mont Saint Aignan
Tél : 02 32 82 57 00
School

where $N_t$ is the number of major powers in the system in year $t$, and $S_{it}$ is the proportion of the capabilities possessed by all major powers that major power $i$ controls in year $t$.[26]

A recent study has shown that the level of concentration is a function of two variables: the number of major powers in the international system and the relative inequality of capabilities among the major powers.[27] In particular,

$$CON_t = \frac{V_t}{\sqrt{N_t - 1}} \qquad (2)$$

where $V_t$ is the coefficient of variation (standard deviation divided by the mean) of $S_{it}$ in year $t$. When $N_t$, the number of major powers in the international system, is held constant, $CON_t$ is proportional to $V_t$, the relative inequality of capabilities.

It is clear that concentration will increase if, holding $N$ (and the capabilities of all but the two largest major powers) constant, the relative disparity between the two largest major powers (and, hence, $V$) increases. In this sense, *CON* is related to hegemony. But concentration will also increase if: (1) holding $N$ constant, a "small" major power's capabilities decline relative to those of the other major powers in the system (since this will also increase $V$), even though no change occurs in the distribution of capabilities between the two largest states; or (2) holding $V$ constant, the number of major powers in the system decreases.[28] Thus, the distribution of power can be influenced by a variety of factors in addition to the relative position of the largest state in the international system. For this reason, I consider separately the effects of hegemony and concentration on the level of global commerce.

In addition to the richer typology of the distribution of power that is gained by examining features of both hegemony and the concentration of capabilities, there are a variety of other reasons to analyze the relationship between *CON* and trade. First, *CON* is jointly determined by $N$ and $V$; and there has been considerable interest in the effect of the interaction between these variables on outcomes in the international political economy.[29] But despite long-standing calls for empirical research on this topic,[30] few studies of this sort have been

26. Hence, *CON* measures the "standard deviation of the percentage shares [divided by] the maximum possible standard deviation in a system of size $N$." See Ray and Singer, ibid., p. 422.

27. See Edward D. Mansfield, "The Concentration of Capabilities and the Onset of War," *Journal of Conflict Resolution* 36 (March 1992), pp. 3–24.

28. Of course, this assumes that $V > 0$.

29. See Bruce M. Russett and John D. Sullivan, "Collective Goods and International Organization," *International Organization* 25 (Autumn 1971), pp. 845–65; Duncan Snidal, "Coordination Versus Prisoners' Dilemma: Implications for International Cooperation and Regimes," *American Political Science Review* 79 (December 1985), pp. 923–42; and Snidal, "The Limits of Hegemonic Stability Theory."

30. See, for example, Russett and Sullivan, "Collective Goods and International Organization."

conducted. By focusing on *CON*, it will be possible to assess empirically the influence of some aspects of the interaction between *N* and *V* on international trade.[31]

Second, one issue that is addressed in this study is the effect of market power on commerce. As Michael Waterson points out, economists "generally agree [that any measure of market structure] should be a one-dimensional measure, incorporating the two relevant aspects of industry structure, namely firm numbers . . . and size inequalities."[32] Conybeare suggests that for the purposes of measuring a hegemon's market power, "a Herfindahl index would be the best index of hegemony, since it would discriminate between situations where a country faced a large number of small powers or a small number of medium-sized countries."[33] Indeed, this index is widely used among economists to measure industry structure and market power. *CON* is closely related to the Hirschman-Herfindahl index; in fact, James Lee Ray and J. David Singer have demonstrated that it "is a perfectly predictable function of [the Hirschman-Herfindahl index], as long as we know the value of *N*."[34] But while *CON* is a

31. One reason for examining the interactive effects of these variables via concentration (rather than via some other variable that is a function of both *N* and *V*) is that although concentration has received little attention in studies of the international political economy, many analyses of war have used concentration to measure the distribution of power. See J. David Singer, Stuart Bremer, and John Stuckey, "Capability Distribution, Uncertainty, and Major Power Wars, 1820–1965," in Bruce M. Russett, ed., *Peace, War, and Numbers* (Beverly Hills, Calif.: Sage, 1972), pp. 19–48; Bruce Bueno de Mesquita, "Risk, Power Distributions, and the Likelihood of War," *International Studies Quarterly* 25 (December 1981), pp. 541–68; William R. Thompson, "Cycles, Capabilities, and War: An Ecumenical View," in William R. Thompson, ed., *Contending Approaches to World System Analysis* (Beverly Hills, Calif.: Sage, 1983), pp. 141–63; Bruce Bueno de Mesquita and David Lalman, "Empirical Support for Systemic and Dyadic Explanations of International Conflict," *World Politics* 41 (October 1988), pp. 1–20; and Mansfield, "The Concentration of Capabilities and the Onset of War." To my knowledge, the only study that analyzes the relationship between concentration and trade was conducted by McKeown. However, his analysis differs from the present study in a number of important ways. First, McKeown uses a different set of capabilities and major powers than I do to measure concentration. Second, his model is specified differently than mine. He examines the effects of the following on the ratio of imports to gross national product for industrialized capitalist countries: (1) the concentration of capabilities; (2) the percentage of global imports that the largest importer accounts for (*TCON*1); (3) the percentage of international imports that Great Britain, the United States, France, (West) Germany, and Japan account for (*TCON*5); (4) the ratio of *TCON*1 to *TCON*5; (5) the ratios of the nominal income of Great Britain and the United States, respectively, to that of the other leading states in the system; (6) time; (7) the growth of nominal income; and (8) a lagged dependent variable. See McKeown, "A Liberal Trade Order?"

32. See Michael Waterson, *Economic Theory of the Industry* (Cambridge: Cambridge University Press, 1984), pp. 166–67. See also F. M. Scherer, *Industrial Market Structure and Economic Performance*, 2d ed. (Chicago: Rand McNally, 1979), pp. 56–59.

33. Conybeare, *Trade Wars*, p. 287, fn. 4.

34. See Ray and Singer, "Measuring the Concentration of Power in the International System," p. 430. For the original derivation of the Hirschman-Herfindahl index (*HH*), see Albert O. Hirschman, *National Power and the Structure of Foreign Trade* (1945; reprint, Berkeley: University of California Press, 1980), pp. xviii–xx, 87–88, and 157–62). The equation for this index is as follows:

$$HH_t = \sum_{i=1}^{N_t} S_{it}^2$$

measure of market power, it is important to reiterate that neither it nor the Hirschman-Herfindahl index is technically a measure of hegemony, since they both measure the distribution of power among all major powers—not only the relative strength of the most powerful state. It is precisely for this reason that *CON* is a more comprehensive measure of aggregate market power than hegemony is and thus ought to be considered in a study of this sort. Hegemons are not uniquely able to impose optimal tariffs: large nonhegemonic states may also possess considerable market power vis-à-vis the remaining states in the system.

Third, *CON* possesses a number of properties that are particularly desirable for analyzing the problem at hand. For example, as I describe in more detail below, *CON* is measured by using economic and military (as well as demographic) capabilities, which are the same general indices of power that hegemonic stability theorists emphasize. Analyzing the effects on trade of both hegemony and concentration thus facilitates the comparison of different features of the distribution of power, holding constant the variables used to measure power.

The use of concentration also provides insights into a number of aspects of the relationship between the distribution of power and trade that hegemony is unable to provide. For example, while hegemonic stability theory is a theory of the international political economy, it is generally used to explain international relations among only the advanced industrialized countries. In contrast, *CON* measures the distribution of power among all of the major powers and, as a result, is closer than hegemony to a global measure of this distribution. Moreover, because *CON* is a continuous measure, it allows for the examination of the effects of different nonhegemonic distributions of power on trade and mitigates the problem of how to distinguish between hegemonic and nonhegemonic distributions of power.

## Relative inequality and trade

The preceding discussion indicates that the international distribution of power is a function of both the number of major powers and the relative inequality among them. Because of their effects via *CON* and for other reasons, each of these variables is likely to influence global trade when the other is held constant.

---

Hence,

$$CON_t = \sqrt{\frac{HH_t - 1/N_t}{1 - 1/N_t}}$$

It is clear that the primary difference between *HH* and *CON* is that the latter is somewhat less sensitive than *HH* to the size of *N*, since the lower bound of *CON* is 0, while the lower bound of *HH* is $1/N$.

Many theories about the international political economy focus primarily on the influence of the relative inequality of power in the system and place less emphasis on the size of the group. Most prominent among these explanations is hegemonic stability theory. The theory of hegemonic stability (as well as the theory of collective action) suggests that the effect of relative inequality on trade is direct. All other things being equal, greater relative inequality enhances the prospects for collective action;[35] as $V$ approaches its highest level, the prospects for collective action in the global trading system are greatest. Lake, for example, has found empirical support for this hypothesis. After measuring the structure of the system in terms of the relative inequality of power among a fixed group of major powers, he concluded that higher levels of inequality were associated with greater openness.[36]

Alternatively, the relationship between relative inequality and trade may be inverse. The argument that Conybeare advances rests on the premise that, all other things being equal, "the gains from . . . tariff[s] . . . are likely to be directly proportional to the countries' relative sizes."[37] When the relative inequality among the major powers is low, no major power possesses sufficient market power to influence its terms of trade. Hence, states have little economic incentive to impose tariffs or other trade barriers that would be expected to reduce global trade.[38] As relative inequality reaches higher levels, so too does the relative market power of the largest state (or states) in the system. Since this state (or group of states) has an incentive to exploit its market power by imposing an optimal tariff, relative inequality may be inversely related to the level of global trade.[39]

## Group size and trade

Another set of theories about the international political economy centers largely on the impact of group size and focuses less on the relative inequality among the states that comprise the group. Proponents of small group theory,

35. See Olson, *The Logic of Collective Action.*

36. In particular, Lake focuses on the United States, the United Kingdom, Germany, and France. Japan is also considered, beginning in 1950. See Lake, *Power, Protection, and Free Trade,* p. 33. For a critique of hegemonic stability theory that also centers on the effects of inequality, see Russett, "The Mysterious Case of Vanishing Hegemony."

37. Conybeare, *Trade Wars,* p. 26.

38. For a fuller discussion of this issue, see ibid.; Wilfred Ethier, *Modern International Economics* (New York: Norton, 1983); and Joanne Gowa, "Bipolarity, Multipolarity, and Free Trade," *American Political Science Review* 83 (December 1989), pp. 1245–56.

39. See Conybeare, "Public Goods, Prisoners' Dilemmas and the International Political Economy"; and Conybeare, *Trade Wars.* This, of course, assumes that a state's political power is roughly proportional to its market power—that is, to its ability to influence its terms of trade. The extent to which this is the case is an empirical question beyond the scope of this article. However, it is an assumption that is made often and one that seems reasonable for the purposes of a first cut at the problem.

for example, maintain that, all other things being equal, smaller groups are better able than larger groups to provide collective goods in international relations.[40] Thus, *N* may be inversely related to international trade when *V* is held constant.

Other scholars, however, imply that the number of major powers is directly associated with trade. Kenneth Waltz, for example, argues that as the number of major powers decreases, each major power is likely to be larger and more economically self-sufficient.[41] Since states in an anarchic system seek to reduce their dependence on one another, trade among major powers (which comprises a large portion of global trade) may be lowest when the number of major powers is small. Under these circumstances, major powers are best able to forgo commerce with, and limit their dependence on, one another. The number of major powers may also be directly related to trade if, as the size of the major power subsystem decreases, the market power of each major power increases vis-à-vis that of the remaining states in the system. Under these conditions, fewer major powers may be associated with higher overall tariff levels and thus with lower levels of global trade.

## Is the relationship between concentration and trade curvilinear?

It is also likely that *V* and *N* influence trade via their effects on concentration, as well as through other channels. With regard to their influence via concentration, I posit that the relationship between *CON* and trade is curvilinear. Specifically, I hypothesize that when *N* is held constant, this relationship is quadratic.

Conybeare suggests that when market power (and, hence, concentration) rises, trade falls. For low and moderate levels of concentration, this is likely to be the case. As *V* increases and *N* decreases (and *CON* increases), the market power of the dominant states rises, and these states are more likely to impose an optimal tariff. All other things being equal, less international commerce is expected to be conducted under these circumstances.[42]

40. See Keohane, *After Hegemony*; Robert Axelrod and Robert O. Keohane, "Achieving Cooperation Under Anarchy: Strategies and Institutions," *World Politics* 38 (October 1985), pp. 226–54; Russell Hardin, *Collective Action* (Baltimore, Md.: Johns Hopkins University Press, 1982); Charles Lipson, "International Cooperation in Economic and Security Affairs," *World Politics* 37 (October 1984), pp. 1–23; Kenneth A. Oye, "Explaining Cooperation Under Anarchy: Hypotheses and Strategies," *World Politics* 38 (October 1985), pp. 1–24; and Thomas C. Schelling, *Micromotives and Macrobehavior* (New York: Norton, 1978), pp. 211–43.

41. See the following works of Kenneth N. Waltz: "The Myth of National Interdependence," in Charles P. Kindleberger, ed., *The International Corporation* (Cambridge, Mass.: MIT Press, 1970), pp. 205–23; and *Theory of International Politics* (New York: Random House, 1979).

42. Of course, this assumes that larger states will not band together to deter each other from imposing optimal tariffs. Under these circumstances, the level of protectionism may remain relatively low.

However, this need not imply that the relationship between concentration and trade is always inverse. Beyond some level of concentration at which trade is minimized, I hypothesize that increases in *CON* will tend to increase commerce. Recent work by Gowa suggests why this may be the case.[43] States with little market power have few economic incentives to impose trade barriers; and as market power increases, so too does the economic incentive to impose an optimal tariff. But when concentration is highest, a rational, nonmyopic state with substantial market power may forgo the use of such an instrument in order to maintain its monopoly power in the international economy. And, as Gowa points out, even critics of hegemonic stability theory "acknowledge that hegemons which pursue political as well as economic goals may prefer free trade for political reasons."[44] For example, a hegemon that is interested in enhancing its political power may promote free trade in an effort to foster the dependence of smaller states.[45] A hegemon may also make commercial concessions and expand its trade with certain states in order to induce political concessions from these trading partners.[46]

This suggests that there is some level of concentration at which trade is minimized; but beyond this level, powerful states may abstain from the use of trade barriers for both political and economic reasons. Indeed, the level of global protectionism may be lowest and, hence, the level of trade may be greatest both when concentration is lowest *and* when concentration is highest. And the level of international trade may be minimized when concentration lies somewhere between its highest and lowest levels.[47] Thus, I hypothesize that a U-shaped (that is, quadratic) relationship exists between concentration and trade, since this is the simplest functional form of the relationship in which both of the extreme levels of concentration are associated with the highest levels of trade.

## Warfare and trade

Studies of the relationship between international politics and global trade often focus on the effects of the distribution of power. However, many

43. See Gowa, "Rational Hegemons, Excludable Goods, and Small Groups"; and Gowa, "Bipolarity, Multipolarity, and Free Trade."

44. See Gowa, "Rational Hegemons, Excludable Goods, and Small Groups," p. 311, fn. 12. See also Conybeare, "Public Goods, Prisoners' Dilemmas and the International Political Economy"; and Conybeare, *Trade Wars.*

45. See Hirschman, *National Power and the Structure of Foreign Trade.*

46. See Conybeare, "Public Goods, Prisoners' Dilemmas and the International Political Economy"; and McKeown, "Hegemonic Stability Theory and 19th-Century Tariff Levels in Europe."

47. Of course, I am only considering the range of variation of concentration found in the data. For example, if the world consisted entirely of two countries, one with few inhabitants, few resources, and little capital, and the other with the remainder of the world's population, resources, and capital, one would expect practically all trade to be intranational and the level of international commerce to be relatively small, even though the level of concentration might be quite high.

observers argue that nonstructural features of the international system also influence commerce. Since, among these features, the impact of war has been of particular interest, I examine the relationship between trade and the incidence of wars between major powers.[48] Specifically, I focus on the contemporaneous effect of war on trade.

On the one hand, if, as Susan Strange maintains, "nothing . . . has such a dampening effect on international trade as war,"[49] the incidence of war should be inversely related to trade. Wars may reduce commerce, since many resources that would otherwise have been exported by the antagonists are consumed in the war effort. Trade may also decline during wars if the combatants previously imported goods that are not essential to the war effort and are forgone during hostilities. Finally, wars may reduce trade by disrupting commercial transportation.

On the other hand, the relationship between war and trade may be direct. Nations that depend heavily on commerce in order to obtain the resources necessary to wage war may increase trade with allies or neutral states during war. If this increase more than offsets decreases in trade among adversaries, trade may be greater during wars than in the absence of hostilities.

## The economic determinants of global trade

Hegemonic stability theory has also been criticized for ignoring the effects of global market conditions (beyond the scope of the hegemon) on international economic outcomes.[50] Hence, aside from examining the impact of international politics on commerce, it is also important to consider the influence of economic

48. For discussions of the impact of war on trade, see Charles P. Kindleberger, *Foreign Trade and the National Economy* (New Haven, Conn.: Yale University Press, 1966); Edward E. Leamer and Robert M. Stern, *Quantitative International Economics* (Boston: Allyn & Bacon, 1970), p. 15; Krasner, "State Power and the Structure of International Trade"; Stein, "The Hegemon's Dilemma"; and Strange, *States and Markets.* Although I am unaware of any empirical research on the effect of war on trade at the systemic level, Brian Pollins found that among dyads of nations during the period after World War II, higher levels of conflict led to lower levels of trade. However, because wars constitute only a small subset of the conflict-events data that Pollins uses and because results at the dyadic level may diverge from those at the systemic level, it is worthwhile to examine this relationship further. See the following works of Brian M. Pollins: "Conflict, Cooperation, and Commerce: The Effect of International Political Interactions on Bilateral Trade Flows," *American Journal of Political Science* 33 (August 1989), pp. 737–61; and "Does Trade Still Follow the Flag?" *American Political Science Review* 83 (June 1989), pp. 465–80.

49. See Strange, *States and Markets,* p. 167. See also Stein, "The Hegemon's Dilemma."

50. See Peter F. Cowhey and Edward Long, "Testing Theories of Regime Change: Hegemonic Decline or Surplus Capacity," *International Organization* 37 (Spring 1983), pp. 157–88; Joanne Gowa, "Hegemons, IOs, and Markets: The Case of the Substitution Account," *International Organization* 38 (Autumn 1984), pp. 661–83; Stein, "The Hegemon's Dilemma"; Gallarotti, "Toward a Business Cycle Model of Tariffs"; James Cassing, Timothy J. McKeown, and Jack Ochs, "The Political Economy of the Tariff Cycle," *American Political Science Review* 80 (September 1986), pp. 843–62; Strange, "The Persistent Myth of Lost Hegemony"; and McKeown, "A Liberal Trade Order?" A number of hegemonic stability theorists have also concluded that more attention needs to be paid to the economic determinants of trade. See Krasner, "State Power and the Structure of International Trade"; and Gilpin, *The Political Economy of International Relations,* p. 91.

factors in order to compare the relative effects of each set of variables on patterns of global trade. Economists have tried in various ways to analyze what determines the amount of trade that is conducted, but they have focused primarily on the determinants of national and bilateral commerce rather than on total global trade. In this study, I seek to explain the ratio of global exports to global production.

Despite the relative dearth of economic analyses on this topic, a number of economic variables appear likely to influence the value of this ratio. First, the level of trade barriers throughout the system is likely to influence the value of the ratio of global exports to global production. All other things being equal, greater restrictions on trade are expected to reduce the level of international commerce. Second, technological advances are likely to have an effect on the percentage of international output that is exported.[51] For example, technological improvements that decrease transportation costs or improve communications would be expected to increase the value of the ratio of global exports to global production. Further, technological advances often give rise to new products; international trade is likely to increase more quickly than output if demand for these products increases rapidly among consumers who are unable to obtain these goods domestically. Third, the discovery of natural resources may increase the percentage of global output that is exported,[52] particularly if these resources are in great demand, have few substitutes, and are not distributed uniformly throughout the world.

Unfortunately, data on global levels of protectionism, technological advances, and the discovery of natural resources do not seem to be available for the period covered in this study.[53] However, data on global income, the fourth feature of the international economy that may influence the percentage of global output that is exported, do exist and I will therefore focus on the effect of this variable in my analysis.[54]

It is expected that global income is directly related to the value of the ratio of global exports to global production for the following reasons. First, some analysts have concluded that the business cycle has a large political influence on tariff levels.[55] They argue that during periods of prosperity, tariffs are likely to be lower (and, hence, trade is likely to be greater) than during depressions. Second, one determinant of the level of international trade is the income elasticity of demand. If, for example, the income elasticity of demand for

51. See Kindleberger, *Foreign Trade and the National Economy.*

52. See ibid.

53. It should be noted, however, that to the extent that $V$ and $N$ predict the level of global protectionism and that this variable, in turn, predicts the level of global trade, the level of global protectionism is endogenized. Under these circumstances, the lack of data on this variable does not pose a problem.

54. The data on global income are expressed in real terms and are adapted from Angus Maddison's *Phases of Capitalist Development* (New York: Oxford University Press, 1982). See my footnote 65, below, for a fuller explanation.

55. See Krasner, "State Power and the Structure of International Trade"; Gallarotti, "Toward a Business Cycle Model of Tariffs"; Cassing, McKeown, and Ochs, "The Political Economy of the Tariff Cycle"; and McKeown, "A Liberal Trade Order?"

manufactured and capital goods (which historically have comprised a particularly large percentage of global trade) is greater than unity, higher levels of global income are likely to be directly associated with higher levels of international trade as a percentage of total production.[56] Third, it is widely recognized that trade has increased more quickly than output over time.[57] Since it is also clear that there has been an increase in global income over time, global income should capture whatever secular trend exists in the value of the ratio of global exports to global production.[58] Increases in global income may be highly correlated with—and thus a good proxy for—decreases in transportation costs, improvements in communications, and the development of new products, all of which would be expected to increase the percentage of total output that is exported. Finally, to the extent that intra-industry trade comprises a large portion of global trade, higher levels of global income may lead to higher levels of global trade as a percentage of global production. As Jagdish Bhagwati argues, "Intra-industry trade in similar products . . . is an important characteristic of trade among industrialized countries. This alone could imply a higher rather than a lower ratio of trade to gross national product as incomes increase and consumption gets increasingly more diversified in terms of variety within broad industry groups while the trading countries continue to specialize in production of similar goods with differentiated characteristics."[59]

## The statistical model of trade

I therefore assume that trade is a function of the distribution of power, the incidence of warfare, and global income. The independent variables are defined and discussed below. The complete model is as follows:

$$Trade_t = A + B_1 Hegemony_{t-j} + B_2 Warfare_t + B_3 GDP_{t-1} + B_4 CON_{t-j} \quad (3)$$

$$+ B_5 CON^2_{t-j} + B_6 N_{t-j} + B_7 V_{t-j} + B_8 delta\ CON_{t-j} + B_9 MOVE_{t-j} + e_t$$

where $Trade_t$ is the annual level of global exports as a percentage of global

56. On this point, see Kindleberger, *Foreign Trade and the National Economy,* p. 89. Of course, as aggregate gross domestic product increases, the supply curves for imports may shift and this may be of consequence, too.

57. See ibid.; Thomas Kuczynski, "Have There Been Differences Between the Growth Rates in Different Periods of the Development of the Capitalist World Economy Since 1850?" in J. M. Clubb and E. K. Scheuch, eds., *Historical Social Research* (Stuttgart: Klett-Cotta, 1980), pp. 300–316; Maddison, *Phases of Capitalist Development*; and Alan V. Deardorff and Robert M. Stern, "Current Issues in Trade Policy: An Overview," in Robert M. Stern, ed., *U.S. Trade Policies in a Changing World Economy* (Cambridge, Mass.: MIT Press, 1987), pp. 15–68.

58. For a discussion of the increase in global income over time, see Maddison, *Phases of Capitalist Development.* I chose not to use both time and global income as independent variables, since they are highly collinear ($r^2$ = .82).

59. Jagdish Bhagwati, *Protectionism* (Cambridge, Mass.: MIT Press, 1988), pp. 5–6.

production in year $t$;[60] $Hegemony_t$ is a dummy variable that equals 1 if a hegemon exists and 0 if a hegemon does not exist in year $t$; $Warfare_t$ is the number of wars between major powers being conducted during year $t$; $GDP_{t-1}$ is the global gross domestic product in year $t-1$; $CON_t$ is the concentration of capabilities in year $t$; $N_t$ is the number of major powers in year $t$; $V_t$ is the coefficient of variation of the shares of the total capabilities that each major power possesses in year $t$; *delta* $CON_t$ is the average annual change in concentration in the five-year period from $t-5$ to $t$; $MOVE_t$ is the average annual movement in capabilities from $t-5$ to $t$; and $e_t$ is an error term. This model is estimated for the period from 1850 to 1965, since this is the only period in which data are available for all of the variables in equation 3. (See Appendix 1 for a description of some of these data.) Because data on *CON*, $CON^2$, *V*, *delta CON*, and *MOVE* are available only at five-year intervals (1850, 1855, . . . , 1960), these are the values of $t-j$ that are used. Since the effects of these variables are expected to occur with a lag, it is assumed in equation 3 that there is a lag of $j$ years.[61] In estimating this model, three values of $j$ are used: one, three, and five years.[62]

### *Definitions of the independent variables*

*Hegemony.* Because the results may depend on the classifications of hegemony that are chosen, both Gilpin's and Wallerstein's classifications of hegemony are used in the present analysis.[63]

60. Figures provided by Kuczynski are used for this purpose. See Kuczynski, "Have There Been Differences Between the Growth Rates in Different Periods of the Development of the Capitalist World Economy Since 1850?" p. 312. Since for the world as a whole exports must equal imports, this variable will provide an estimate of aggregate international commerce. It should be pointed out that hegemonic stability theorists do not agree as to whether the focus of this theory should be the explanation of trade (and other) outcomes in the international political economy or policy instruments and outcomes (such as tariffs, quotas, and subsidies). On this point, see McKeown, "A Liberal Trade Order?"; and David A. Lake, "The Theory of Hegemonic Stability: An Interim Report," paper presented at the Fifteenth World Congress of the International Political Science Association, Buenos Aires, 1991. I will restrict my attention to trade outcomes and, in particular, to the level of international trade, since there is little data on tariff levels and other policy instruments for much of the period analyzed in my study and since many noted experts agree with Hirschman's assertion that "international trade [is] the most important constituent of international economic relations." See Hirschman, *National Power and the Structure of Foreign Trade,* p. xvi. It is clear, however, that trade flows and trade policy need not move in tandem. Consequently, the results of my study may not apply uniformly to all variants of hegemonic stability theory.

61. The effects of hegemony and concentration are lagged because, as Hart points out, "the core propositions in . . . [hegemonic stability theory] state that a change in the distribution of power at time $t$ causes a change in international outcomes at time $t + 1$." See Jeffrey A. Hart, "Polarity, Hegemony and the Distribution of Power," paper presented at the annual meeting of the American Political Science Association, Washington, D.C., 1986, p. 15.

62. To illustrate this procedure, consider the data for 1900. In this case, *Hegemony, CON,* $CON^2$, *N,* and *V* are measured in 1900; and *delta CON* and *MOVE* are measured from 1895 to 1900. *Trade* is measured in 1901, 1903, and 1905 (one-year, three-year, and five-year lags); *Warfare* is measured in the same years as *Trade*; and *GDP* is measured in 1900 (when *Trade* is lagged by one year), 1902 (when *Trade* is lagged by three years), and 1904 (when *Trade* is lagged by five years).

63. Gilpin classifies the periods from 1815 to 1914 (Great Britain) and from 1945 to 1980 (the United States) as hegemonic. Gilpin does not actually date the end of U.S. hegemony, but this is

*Warfare.* Since wars between major powers would be expected to have the most pronounced effect on global trade, I will restrict my attention to the effects of these wars on trade, using Jack Levy's data set.[64] The coefficient of this variable will indicate whether (and if so, the extent to which) global trade is sensitive to the number of wars between major powers being conducted in the year that *Trade* is measured.

*GDP.* For the reasons mentioned above, there should be a direct relationship between global gross domestic product (the measure of global income used in the present study) and *Trade.* The data for this variable are adapted from data derived by Angus Maddison.[65]

*The concentration of capabilities.* Ray and Singer's index is used to measure the concentration of national population, urban population (in cities with more than 20,000 residents), energy consumption (from 1885 onward), iron and steel production, military personnel, and military expenditures among the major powers in the international system.[66] J. David Singer, Stuart Bremer,

not important for present purposes, since my study does not cover the period after 1965 and it is not until around 1980 that the ending date becomes an issue for Gilpin. Wallerstein classifies the periods from 1625 to 1672 (United Provinces of the Netherlands), from 1815 to 1873 (Great Britain), and from 1945 to 1967 (the United States) as hegemonic. Although this is only a sample of scholars who have conducted research on the effects of hegemony, it should provide some idea as to whether different definitions of hegemony produce different empirical results. See Gilpin, *War and Change in World Politics*; Gilpin, *The Political Economy of International Relations*; and Wallerstein, "Three Instances of Hegemony in the History of the Capitalist World-Economy."

64. See Jack S. Levy, *War in the Modern Great Power System, 1495–1975* (Lexington: University Press of Kentucky, 1983).

65. See Maddison, *Phases of Capitalist Development,* pp. 86 and 170. Maddison provides data on the annual change in the aggregate level of gross domestic product for sixteen leading countries from 1871 to 1981. These data are used to construct an index of the level of *GDP* by setting the level of *GDP* in 1870 equal to 100. The level of *GDP* is computed for each subsequent year $t$ by multiplying the value of the index in the preceding year $t - 1$ by the change in *GDP* from $t - 1$ to $t$. Maddison also provides data on the annual change in gross domestic product for some of the sixteen countries from 1850 to 1869. I determined the (unweighted) average annual rate of change for those countries for which data are available and used the procedure described above to compute the level of *GDP* from 1850 to 1869. It should be noted that if the rates of change in *GDP* among these sixteen countries differ markedly from those of the remaining states in the system, this index may not reflect global income. However, I am unaware of any more complete data on global income than those developed by Maddison.

66. Each of these components was weighted equally in arriving at values for concentration. For the iron and steel production component, iron was used until 1895; thereafter, steel was used. The index of Ray and Singer is described in their article "Measuring the Concentration of Power in the International System." Singer, Bremer, and Stuckey list the following nations as major powers: Austria-Hungary (1816–1918); Prussia/Germany (1816–1870, 1871–1918, and 1925–1945); Russia/Soviet Union (1816–1917 and 1922–present); France (1816–1940 and 1945–present); England (1816–present); Italy (1860–1943); Japan (1895–1945); the United States (1898–present); and China (1949–present). See Singer, Bremer, and Stuckey, "Capability Distribution, Uncertainty, and Major Power Wars, 1820–1965"; J. David Singer and Melvin Small, *The Wages of War, 1816–1965: A Statistical Handbook* (New York: Wiley, 1972); and Melvin Small and J. David Singer, *Resort to Arms: International and Civil Wars, 1816–1980* (Beverly Hills, Calif.: Sage, 1982).

and John Stuckey provide estimates of the annual level of *CON* (every five years) that are used in this analysis.[67] It is important to point out that the use of capabilities as measures of power poses a number of well-known problems. Since what James March refers to as "basic-force" models of power are context-specific and indicative of only the potential power of nations, the concentration of capabilities provides only a crude measure of the distribution of power.[68] The use of material capabilities as a proxy for power is, however, consistent with many previous analyses of the relationship between trade and the distribution of power, and capabilities are useful as first approximations of potential power.

*The coefficient of variation.* This variable, $V_t$, is the coefficient of variation of $S_{it}$. Equation 2 shows that $V_t$ and $N_t$ determine the level of concentration. As I argued above, there is reason to believe that both relative inequality and group size may have effects on *Trade* other than those via concentration. Hence, $V_t$ and $N_t$, as well as $CON_t$ (and $CON_t^2$), are included in equation 3.

*The change in concentration.* The equation for this variable is as follows:

$$delta\ CON_t = \frac{CON_t - CON_{(t-5)}}{t - (t-5)} \qquad (4)$$

where $CON_t$ is the level of concentration in year $t$ and $CON_{(t-5)}$ is the level of concentration in year $t-5$. Hegemonic stability theory suggests that a direct relationship exists between trade and the change in concentration. However, if nations abstain from protectionist measures in systems comprised of small states, while dominant states have incentives to use such measures in highly concentrated systems, the relationship may be inverse.

67. See Singer, Bremer, and Stuckey, "Capability Distribution, Uncertainty, and Major Power Wars, 1820–1965." In their analysis and in the present study, five-year periods were used in all cases except the following: 1910–1912, 1913–1919, 1935–1937, 1938–1945, and 1946–1949. These exceptions were made to avoid distorting the values of the indices by measuring the major powers' capabilities during World Wars I and II.

68. See James G. March, "The Power of Power," in David Easton, ed., *Varieties of Political Theory* (Englewood Cliffs, N.J.: Prentice-Hall, 1966), pp. 39–70. See also Robert A. Dahl, *Modern Political Analysis,* 3d ed. (Englewood Cliffs, N.J.: Prentice-Hall, 1976); Frederick W. Frey, "Comment: On Issues and Nonissues in the Study of Power," *American Political Science Review* 65 (December 1971), pp. 1081–1104; Frey, "The Distribution of Power in Political Systems"; David A. Baldwin, "Interdependence and Power: A Conceptual Analysis," *International Organization* 34 (Autumn 1980), pp. 471–506; Baldwin, "Power Analysis and World Politics"; and Keohane, *After Hegemony.* It should be noted that there are also potential drawbacks associated with using energy consumption and iron and steel production as indicators of economic strength. On these drawbacks, see Organski and Kugler, *The War Ledger*; William B. Moul, "Measuring the 'Balance of Power': A Look at Some Numbers," *Review of International Studies* 15 (April 1989), pp. 101–21; and John R. Oneal, "Measuring the Material Base of the Contemporary East–West Balance of Power," *International Interactions,* vol. 15, no. 2, 1989, pp. 177–96.

*The movement in the shares of capabilities among major powers.* The equation for this variable is as follows:

$$MOVE_t = \frac{\sum_{i=1}^{N_t} |S_{it} - S_{i(t-5)}|}{2(1 - S_{mt})} \qquad (5)$$

where $m$ is the major power with the lowest share of capabilities in year $t$. The regression coefficient of this variable will indicate the extent to which commercial relations are sensitive to stability in the relative amount of capabilities held by each major power.

*Estimates of the parameters*

Ordinary least squares regressions are used to estimate the parameters of equation 3.[69] The results, which are presented in Table 1, indicate that this equation fits better when *Hegemony, CON, CON*$^2$, *N,* and *V* are lagged by three or five years rather than by one year, and this in turn implies that *Trade* does not respond immediately to the distribution of capabilities. Regardless of whether Gilpin's or Wallerstein's periods of hegemony are used, the regression coefficients of the variables other than *Hegemony* are much the same; and when

69. In any regression analysis, two problems that might arise are autocorrelation of the residuals and heteroskedasticity. The Durbin-Watson statistics (shown in Table 1) indicate that there is no clear evidence that the disturbances are characterized by a first-order autoregressive [AR(1)] process. Rao and Griliches argue that for small samples, methods that correct for first-order autocorrelation will provide better estimates than will ordinary least squares when the absolute value of rho (the estimate of the first-order correlation among the residuals) is greater than or equal to 0.3. See Potluri Rao and Zvi Griliches, "Small-Sample Properties of Several Two-Stage Regression Methods in the Context of Auto-Correlated Errors," *Journal of the American Statistical Association* 64 (March 1969), pp. 253–72. The only instance in which the absolute value of rho is greater than or equal to 0.3 is when Gilpin's data on hegemony and a one-year lag are used. To correct for first-order autocorrelation in this case, generalized least squares estimates were generated. For a description of this procedure, see Douglas A. Hibbs, "Problems of Statistical Estimation and Causal Inference in Time-Series Regression Models," in Herbert L. Costner, ed., *Sociological Methodology, 1973–1974* (San Francisco: Jossey-Bass, 1974), pp. 252–308; Ronald Gallant and J. Jeffery Goebel, "Nonlinear Regression with Autocorrelated Errors," *Journal of the American Statistical Association* 71 (December 1976), pp. 961–67; Eric A. Hanushek and John E. Jackson, *Statistical Methods for Social Scientists* (New York: Academic Press, 1977), pp. 141–78; and A. C. Harvey, *The Econometric Analysis of Time Series* (Oxford: Halsted Press, 1981), pp. 189–220. While these results do not differ markedly from those in Table 1, the $t$-statistics of each coefficient are larger for the generalized least squares estimates than for the ordinary least squares estimates. Of particular interest is the increase in the value of the $t$-statistic of *Hegemony* from 1.56 ($p$ = .14) to 1.91 ($p$ = .08). To test for heteroskedasticity, the squares of the residuals were regressed on each of the independent variables and their squares, and an $F$-test of the regression was conducted. In no case was there any evidence of heteroskedasticity. For a description of this test, see Halbert White, "A Heteroskedasticity-Consistent Covariance Matrix Estimator and a Direct Test for Heteroskedasticity," *Econometrica* 48 (May 1980), pp. 817–38; G. S. Maddala, *Introduction to Econometrics* (New York: Macmillan, 1988), pp. 162–63; and Harry H. Kelejian and Wallace E. Oates, *Introduction to Econometrics: Principles and Applications,* 3d ed. (New York: Harper & Row, 1989), pp. 240–42. It should also be pointed out that there is little evidence of multicollinearity among the independent variables in equation 3, since the estimated coefficients are generally statistically significant and tend to remain stable when variables are omitted from the model.

lags of three and five years are used, the value of $\overline{R}^2$ is quite high—about .75. Thus, this simple model seems to explain about three-quarters of the variation in the ratio of global exports to global production.

Although the overall explanatory power of the model is not very sensitive to which classification of hegemony is used, the same cannot be said for the effect that *Hegemony* itself has on *Trade.* Instead, when Gilpin's data are used, *Hegemony* is directly related to *Trade* and the regression coefficient of *Hegemony* is statistically significant in two out of three cases.[70] *Hegemony* also has a relatively large quantitative effect on *Trade.* The existence of a hegemon is associated with an increase of about 0.034 in the ratio of global trade to output (which is substantial given that the ratio has varied by only about 0.124 during the period covered in this study). Further, if the other variables in equation 3 are held constant at their mean values, the percentage of output that is exported is about 25 percent greater when a hegemon exists than when a hegemon does not exist. But when Wallerstein's data are used, the results are much weaker. The sign of the regression coefficient of *Hegemony* depends upon the length of the lag, and in no case is it statistically significant.

Nevertheless, variables related to the concentration of capabilities appear to have both strong and consistent effects on *Trade.* The results indicate that the number of major powers and the relative inequality among them each influence *Trade* via concentration, as well as via other channels. The regression coefficient of $N$ is negative and the regression coefficient of $V$ is positive in all six cases; and both regression coefficients are statistically significant in four instances (although the results tend to be much stronger when Gilpin's data on hegemony are used). In order to assess the quantitative impact of each variable, it is necessary to consider both its direct effect on *Trade* and its indirect effect via concentration, holding constant the other variable. This can be accomplished by rewriting equation 3, using equation 2:

$$Trade_t = A + B_1 Hegemony_{t-j} + B_2 Warfare_t + B_3 GDP_{t-1} + B_4(V/\sqrt{N-1})_{t-j} + B_5[V^2/(N-1)]_{t-j} + B_6 N_{t-j} + B_7 V_{t-j} + B_8 delta\ CON_{t-j} + B_9 MOVE_{t-j} + e_t \quad (6)$$

Table 2 shows the predicted level of *Trade,* given the values of $N$ and $V$, holding constant *Warfare, GDP, delta CON,* and *MOVE* at their mean values, for periods of hegemony and nonhegemony.[71] The results indicate that,

70. When the model is corrected for first-order autocorrelation, the regression coefficient of *Hegemony* is also statistically significant (at the .10 level) using Gilpin's data and a one-year lag. See footnote 69, above.

71. The values of *Trade* in Table 2 were estimated using Gilpin's data and a three-year lag because this is the only specification of equation 3 in which all of the regression coefficients are statistically significant (see Table 1). The values of $N$ and $V$ in Table 2 correspond roughly to the range of values that they take on during the period covered in this study.

**TABLE 1.** *Regression of the level of global exports as a percentage of global production on hegemony (Gilpin's and Wallerstein's classifications), the number of wars between major powers currently in progress, global gross domestic product, CON, $CON^2$, N, V, delta CON, and MOVE, using one-year, three-year, and five-year lags, 1850–1965*[a]

| *Parameter* | *Gilpin's classifications of hegemony* | | | *Wallerstein's classifications of hegemony* | | |
|---|---|---|---|---|---|---|
| | *One-year lag* | *Three-year lag* | *Five-year lag* | *One-year lag* | *Three-year lag* | *Five-year lag* |
| Intercept | 1.88*<br>(4.31) | 1.47*<br>(4.68) | 1.62*<br>(5.22) | 1.45**<br>(2.44) | 1.07**<br>(2.29) | 1.66*<br>(3.78) |
| *Hegemony* | 0.0317<br>(1.56) | 0.0327**<br>(2.30) | 0.0345**<br>(2.55) | −0.0105<br>(−0.48) | −0.0057<br>(−0.36) | 0.0173<br>(1.11) |
| *Warfare* | −0.0024<br>(−0.25) | −0.0410*<br>(−4.29) | −0.0349*<br>(−5.32) | −0.0007<br>(−0.07) | −0.0460*<br>(−4.13) | −0.0367*<br>(−4.74) |
| *GDP* | 0.00008*<br>(3.10) | 0.00006*<br>(3.92) | 0.00005*<br>(3.79) | 0.00008**<br>(2.66) | 0.00006*<br>(3.10) | 0.00006*<br>(3.52) |
| *CON* | −13.77*<br>(−3.97) | −10.39*<br>(−4.10) | −11.33*<br>(−4.60) | −9.60***<br>(−2.08) | −6.47***<br>(−1.77) | −10.93*<br>(−3.21) |
| *$CON^2$* | 13.96*<br>(4.09) | 10.76*<br>(4.43) | 12.38*<br>(5.22) | 10.85**<br>(2.25) | 7.92***<br>(2.09) | 13.21*<br>(3.74) |
| *N* | −0.132*<br>(−3.13) | −0.098*<br>(−3.17) | −0.103*<br>(−3.38) | −0.080<br>(−1.72) | −0.047<br>(−1.27) | −0.081**<br>(−2.31) |
| *V* | 2.93*<br>(3.29) | 2.17*<br>(3.29) | 2.17*<br>(3.42) | 1.71<br>(1.75) | 0.97<br>(1.24) | 1.65**<br>(2.27) |

| | | | | | | |
|---|---|---|---|---|---|---|
| *delta CON* | −0.66<br>(−1.00) | −1.22**<br>(−2.70) | −0.74<br>(−1.68) | −0.79<br>(−1.13) | −1.37**<br>(−2.59) | −0.83<br>(−1.61) |
| *MOVE* | −1.61<br>(−1.17) | −1.84***<br>(−2.12) | −1.23<br>(−1.41) | −2.95**<br>(−2.52) | −3.08*<br>(−3.87) | −2.68*<br>(−3.34) |
| $\bar{R}^2$ | .54 | .79 | .81 | .46 | .70 | .74 |
| Durbin-Watson | 2.65 | 2.02 | 2.06 | 2.13 | 1.88 | 1.86 |

[a]One-tailed tests were conducted for the coefficient of *GDP* because its sign is specified by the model. Two-tailed tests were conducted for all other coefficients. For each regression, the number of observations equaled 23. *T*-statistics for each coefficient are reported in parentheses below the coefficient. Statistical significance is indicated as follows: $*p \leq .01$; $**p \leq .05$; and $***p \leq .10$.

*Sources.* For classifications of *Hegemony*, Robert Gilpin, *War and Change in World Politics* (New York: Cambridge University Press, 1981); Robert Gilpin, *The Political Economy of International Relations* (Princeton, N.J.: Princeton University Press, 1987); and Immanuel Wallerstein, "Three Instances of Hegemony in the History of the Capitalist World-Economy," *International Journal of Comparative Sociology*, vol. 24, no. 1–2, 1983, pp. 100–108. For data on *Warfare*, Jack S. Levy, *War in the Modern Great Power System, 1495–1975* (Lexington: University Press of Kentucky, 1983). For data on *GDP*, Angus Maddison, *Phases of Capitalist Development* (New York: Oxford University Press, 1982). For data on *CON*, *N*, *delta CON*, and *MOVE*, J. David Singer, Stuart Bremer, and John Stuckey, "Capability Distribution, Uncertainty, and Major Power Wars," in Bruce M. Russett, ed., *Peace, War, and Numbers* (Beverly Hills, Calif.: Sage, 1972), pp. 19–48. For data on *Trade*, Thomas Kuczynski, "Have There Been Differences Between the Growth Rates in Different Periods of the Development of the Capitalist World Economy Since 1850?" in J. M. Clubb and E. K. Scheuch, eds., *Historical Social Research* (Stuttgart: Klett-Cotta, 1980), pp. 300–316.

**TABLE 2.** *Predicted level of global exports as a percentage of global production, during periods of hegemony and nonhegemony, based on the number of major powers and the inequality of capabilities among them, using the regression equation in Table 1 with Gilpin's data and a three-year lag (and evaluating Warfare, GDP, delta CON, and MOVE at their mean values)*[a]

| | *Periods of hegemony* | | | | | *Periods of nonhegemony* | | | | |
|---|---|---|---|---|---|---|---|---|---|---|
| | *Coefficient of variation* | | | | | *Coefficient of variation* | | | | |
| *Number of major powers* | *.450* | *.500* | *.550* | *.600* | *.650* | *.450* | *.500* | *.550* | *.600* | *.650* |
| 5 | .198 | .176 | .166 | .171 | .188 | .166 | .143 | .134 | .138 | .155 |
| 6 | .238 | .217 | .206 | .207 | .218 | .205 | .184 | .174 | .174 | .186 |
| 7 | — | .231 | .222 | .222 | — | — | .198 | .189 | .189 | — |

[a]There are no observations for which 7 major powers exist and the coefficient of variation is approximately .450 or .650. Therefore, the predicted level of *Trade* was not computed.

*Sources.* See Table 1.

regardless of the level at which *V* is held constant, *N* is directly related to the predicted level of *Trade.* Further, when *N* equals 5 or 6, there is a U-shaped relationship between *V* and the predicted level of *Trade,* since the highest levels of *Trade* (in Table 2) obtain both when *V* equals .450 and when it equals .650.

As I hypothesized, holding *N* constant, there is a quadratic relationship between *CON* and *Trade:* in every case, the regression coefficient of *CON* is negative and statistically significant and the regression coefficient of $CON^2$ is positive and statistically significant. If *V* is expressed in terms of *N* and *CON* and if the derivative of equation 3 is taken with respect to *CON* and the result set equal to 0, the level of *CON* that minimizes *Trade,* according to equation 3, is determined. The level of *CON* that minimizes *Trade,* however, depends upon the value of *N.* In fact, this level becomes progressively lower as the number of major powers increases. If *N* equals 5, *Trade* is minimized when *CON* is approximately .282 using Gilpin's data and when it is about .287 using Wallerstein's data. If *N* equals 6, *Trade* is minimized when *CON* is approximately .259 using Gilpin's data and when it is about .271 using Wallerstein's data. And if *N* equals 7, *Trade* is minimized when *CON* is approximately .238 using Gilpin's data and when it is about .256 using Wallerstein's data.

In addition to static features of concentration, dynamic features of concentration also seem to influence *Trade.* As indicated in Table 1, the regression coefficient of *delta CON* is negative in each instance. And although it is statistically significant in only two cases, decreases in *CON* seem to be associated with higher levels of *Trade.* Further, there is evidence that greater movement in the relative shares of capabilities among the major powers discourages international trade, while stability in the relative shares of capabilities produces higher levels of commerce, since the regression coefficient of *MOVE* is negative in every instance and statistically significant in four cases.

With regard to the effect of war on trade, less trade is conducted during years in which wars between major powers are waged. Not only is the regression coefficient of *Warfare* negative in every case and statistically significant in four of them, but it is large enough that this effect is quantitatively, as well as statistically, significant. When three-year and five-year lags are used, a change from no war to one war decreases *Trade* by about 0.040. However, it is interesting to note that other features of war do not appear to have a particularly strong impact on *Trade.* For example, I also examined whether the termination of war between major powers influences *Trade* in subsequent years.[72] When this variable is introduced into equation 3, there is little evidence

72. After wars are concluded, it may take time for nations to reallocate resources from sectors of the economy that are vital for fighting a war to commercial sectors, and trade with former adversaries may not be quickly reestablished. As a result, the relationship between trade and the termination of war may be inverse. However, if nations rely on trade to help repair and revitalize their war-torn economies, the relationship may be direct.

that it has a non-zero effect on *Trade*.[73] This indicates that the influence of war on trade subsides rather quickly after hostilities end.

Finally, as expected, there is strong evidence of a direct relationship between global gross domestic product and *Trade*, since the regression coefficient of *GDP* is positive and statistically significant in all six cases. Further, like the political variables in this model, *GDP* has a strong quantitative effect on *Trade*. For example, when a three-year lag and Gilpin's classifications of hegemony are used, a change in *GDP* from its lowest to its highest level produces about a 40 percent increase in the level of *Trade* during periods of hegemony and about a 50 percent increase in *Trade* during periods of nonhegemony (holding constant the political variables in the model at their mean levels). This suggests that, not surprisingly, international economic conditions strongly affect the level of global commerce.

In addition to examining the influence of *GDP* on *Trade*, it is also possible to consider separately the effects on *Trade* of the secular trend in *GDP* over time and the deviations from that trend. And it is useful to do so in order to determine whether the observed relationship between *GDP* and *Trade* is due solely to an upward trend in both variables or whether the business cycle also has an independent effect on *Trade*. To this end, *GDP* is replaced in equation 3 with the following: (1) the year in which *Trade* is measured and (2) the residuals from a regression of the logarithm of *GDP* in year $t-1$ on year $t-1$ for each five-year period from 1850 to 1965 ($r^2$ = .99).[74] The results indicate that the respective influences of these variables on *Trade* are largely consistent with that of *GDP*. As expected, there is substantial evidence of an upward trend over time in *Trade*: the regression coefficient of year is positive and statistically significant in every case. And higher levels of trade are conducted in years following upswings in the business cycle: the regression coefficient of the residual is positive in five out of six cases, and it is statistically significant in three of these five instances. Hence, both time and the business cycle have individual effects on *Trade* which are much the same as their combined influence on *Trade* via *GDP*.

## Have the effects on trade of the distribution of capabilities, war, and GDP changed over time?

The final issue that is addressed in this article is whether the effects on trade of the distribution of capabilities, war, and gross domestic product have changed

73. The value of this variable, $Warfare_o$, is determined by the number of wars between major powers ending in the five years prior to the year in which *Trade* is measured.

74. Economists often use the deviation from the secular trend in gross domestic product as a measure of short-term fluctuations in the business cycle. See, for example, Robert Lucas, "Some International Evidence on Output-Inflation Tradeoffs," *American Economic Review* 63 (June 1973), pp. 326–34; Robert Lucas, *Studies in Business Cycle Theory* (Cambridge, Mass.: MIT Press, 1981); and Victor Zarnowitz, "Recent Work on Business Cycles in Historical Perspective: A Review of Theories and Evidence," *Journal of Economic Literature* 23 (June 1985), pp. 523–80. A one-year lag is used to avoid problems of simultaneity between *GDP* and *Trade*.

over time. In particular, I examine the stability of the model between the period prior to and the period subsequent to World War II.

Many analysts argue that the multipolar system that existed prior to World War II gave way to a bipolar system after the war.[75] Further, Waltz maintains that the polarity of the system influences the level of global interdependence (measured, in part, by aspects of international trade).[76] Since polarity and the level of concentration are likely to be at least loosely related,[77] it may be that the relationship between concentration and trade also changed after World War II. Further, the direct relationship between *GDP* and *Trade* almost certainly reflects (among other things) technological advances in transportation and communications. If the rate of technological change in these areas was more rapid after the war than it was before the war, one might expect that this would result in a change in the relationship between *GDP* and *Trade.*

McKeown found that his model of trade was unstable between the period before and the period after World War II.[78] To determine whether my model of trade is stable across this span of time, I conducted predictive tests of equation stability.[79] The results are shown in Table 3. My results, unlike McKeown's results, indicate that there is no evidence that any of the models are unstable between the period prior to and the period subsequent to World War II.[80] Thus, it is appropriate to pool the data, as I did in Table 1.

## Theoretical implications of the findings

The results of this study have a number of important implications for theories of the international political economy. Debates surrounding the merits of hegemonic stability theory have been at the forefront of research on the international political economy for some time. One reason why these debates

75. See, for example, Glenn H. Snyder and Paul Diesing, *Conflict Among Nations: Bargaining, Decision Making, and System Structure in International Crises* (Princeton, N.J.: Princeton University Press, 1977); and Waltz, *Theory of International Politics.*

76. See Waltz, "The Myth of National Interdependence"; and Waltz, *Theory of International Politics.*

77. For a discussion of the relationship between polarity and concentration, see Edward D. Mansfield, "Measuring the International Distribution of Power," paper presented at the Fifteenth World Congress of the International Political Science Association, Buenos Aires, 1991.

78. See McKeown, "A Liberal Trade Order?" p. 163.

79. This test (rather than, for example, an analysis-of-variance test) is appropriate because the number of observations after World War II (4) does not exceed $k + 1$ (10), where $k$ is the number of independent variables in the model. See Maddala, *Introduction to Econometrics,* pp. 134–36.

80. A number of points should be made concerning predictive tests of this sort. First, because the number of observations after World War II is less than $k + 1$, it may be more appropriate to think of these tests as tests of unbiasedness in prediction (in other words, tests of whether or not the prediction error has a mean equal to 0), rather than as tests of stability. Second, predictive tests of stability assume that the variance-of-error term for one period is equal to that for the other period. Finally, although these tests indicate that the model is stable over time, this does not deny the fact that the effects of some of the individual coefficients may have changed over time. For a fuller explanation of these points, see Maddala, *Introduction to Econometrics,* p. 136.

**TABLE 3.** *F-statistics based on (Chow) predictive tests for equation stability between the period prior to World War II (1850–1938) and the period subsequent to World War II (1946–1965)*[a]

| *Length of lag* | *Gilpin's classifications of hegemony* | *Wallerstein's classifications of hegemony* |
|---|---|---|
| One year | 0.66 | 2.24 |
| Three years | 1.06 | 2.93 |
| Five years | 1.13 | 2.94 |

[a]In the present case, the *F*-distribution has degrees of freedom equal to 4 (the number of observations in the period subsequent to World War II) and 9 (the number of observations in the period prior to World War II minus the number of independent variables in the model minus 1). The 5 percent significance level under these conditions is 3.63.

*Sources.* See Table 1.

remain unresolved is that scholars do not agree on how to define, measure, and operationalize hegemony and, hence, no consensus exists regarding the influence of hegemony on international relations. My findings clearly illustrate this problem. The extent to which the empirical relationship between hegemony and trade depends upon which data set is used (Gilpin's or Wallerstein's set) is both marked and troubling. For the periods covered in my study, the primary difference between the two data sets lies in the dating of the conclusion of British hegemony: Wallerstein dates its conclusion in 1873, while Gilpin dates its conclusion in 1914. Since trade levels were relatively high in the last decade of the nineteenth century and the portion of the twentieth century prior to World War I, it is not surprising that this disagreement produces substantial differences in the observed relationship between hegemony and trade.

These findings are of considerable theoretical, as well as methodological, importance. They strongly suggest that until the underlying conceptual ambiguities concerning hegemony are resolved, it will be extremely difficult to assess the usefulness of hegemonic stability theory.

But regardless of whether or not the relative inequality among the two largest major powers (hegemony) is associated with trade, more attention should be devoted to the effects of features of the distribution of capabilities among all of the major powers. When the total effects of *N* (both via *CON* and via other channels) are considered, the number of major powers is directly related to *Trade,* which is at odds with the predictions based on small group theories. It could be argued that since the number of major powers does not exceed 8 during the period covered in my study, even a large number of major powers constitutes a *k*-group. Under these circumstances, small groups may be able to provide an open international trading system. Even if this is the case, however, small group theory remains mute on why the value of $k$ should be directly, rather than inversely, related to the level of trade. Indeed, one of the major shortcomings of small group theory is that it fails to specify precisely *how small* a small group is.

Another reason why the results presented here are not consistent with expectations based on small group theories may be that small group theories draw their analytic foundation from the theory of collective action, and an open trading system is not a collective good. As such, neither a small group nor high levels of inequality are required for its provision. There is considerable evidence to support the position that many of the benefits derived from an open international economic order are quite excludable. The most obvious example of this is the Soviet Union and its allies, which, as many scholars have noted, had been systematically excluded from the benefits of free trade with the advanced industrialized countries since the conclusion of World War II.

One explanation for the direct relationship between group size and trade is that as $N$ increases, the market power of each major power declines. As a result, the ability of any major power to impose an optimal tariff may be lowest as $N$ approaches its maximum. These results may also reflect the fact that, all other things being equal, the smaller the number of major powers, the better able each major power is to provide for its own economic needs without engaging in commerce. And since there are security externalities associated with trade,[81] states may attempt to reduce their dependence on potential adversaries once they are self-sufficient enough to do so.

A related explanation for this finding inheres in the trade-offs between relative and absolute gains among states engaged in foreign trade. Neorealists have argued that cooperation in the international political economy is inhibited by concerns over how the gains from trade will be divided, since the distribution of these gains may influence the distribution of power among the participants in commerce.[82] However, Duncan Snidal has recently suggested that, under certain circumstances, the salience of concerns over relative gains is reduced as the number of major powers in the system increases.[83] Hence, the direct relationship between $N$ and *Trade* may reflect the tendency for states to worry less about the security implications of commerce, and therefore to become increasingly willing to engage in foreign trade, as $N$ increases.

In addition to the effect of the number of major powers, there is substantial evidence that the relative inequality among the major powers is also related to trade and that this relationship is U-shaped. Further, such a relationship exists between concentration and trade. To the extent that market power is a function of $V$, this is entirely consistent with my hypothesis. High levels of trade may

81. See Gowa, "Bipolarity, Multipolarity, and Free Trade."

82. See, for example, Waltz, *Theory of International Politics*; and Gilpin, *The Political Economy of International Relations*.

83. See Duncan Snidal, "Relative Gains and the Pattern of International Cooperation," *American Political Science Review* 85 (September 1991), pp. 701–26.

obtain when the level of relative inequality (and concentration) is low because under these conditions, market power is diffused among the states in the system. As the level of relative inequality (and concentration) increases, so too does the market power of the largest states in the system. This may lead these states to impose an optimal tariff, which would be expected to decrease global trade. But when market power is highest, states may choose to forgo the use of optimal tariffs for both economic and political reasons.[84]

Since hegemonic stability theorists are concerned primarily with the influence of relative inequality (and less with group size), the fact that higher levels of relative inequality are associated with higher levels of trade is consistent with their position. However, this relationship is much richer than they hypothesize, since there is considerable variation among nonhegemonic systems in the level of trade that is conducted. Systems in which the level of relative inequality is extremely high or extremely low are characterized by high levels of trade, whereas systems in which the level of relative inequality is intermediate are characterized by lower levels of trade.

Interestingly, the existence of a U-shaped relationship between relative inequality and trade is consistent with at least one variant of hegemonic stability theory. Krasner argues that while a preponderant state will favor an open trading system because it augments this state's political power, systems comprised of many small, highly developed states may also produce an open system because the opportunity costs of closure for states in such a system are quite large.[85] He adds, however, that "a system comprised of a few very large, but unequally developed states . . . is likely to lead to a closed system" because openness would create only moderate increases in these states' income and would engender social instability and political vulnerability.[86] Thus, Krasner suggests that the system is likely to be open when relative inequality is both highest and lowest. The results of my study are in accord with his position.

These results also suggest that critics of hegemonic stability theory are correct in arguing that shifts toward a more uniform distribution of capabilities need not be associated with closure, and that the prognosis offered by those analysts who predict that the decline in American power will undermine the liberal international economic order may be overly pessimistic. If, all other things being equal, $V$ is greater than the level that minimizes trade and is reduced, these fears may be warranted. But if, for example, Germany and Japan have already become or are becoming major powers, the combination of

84. Conybeare notes that dominant states often did not impose optimal tariffs during the nineteenth and twentieth centuries, but he argues that this era is exceptional in this regard. See Conybeare, *Trade Wars*, pp. 271–72.

85. See Krasner, "State Power and the Structure of International Trade." According to Krasner, the opportunity costs are so large because each state derives benefits from an open system and smaller powers have difficulty existing under conditions of autarky.

86. Ibid., pp. 321–22.

a decrease in relative inequality and an increase in the number of major powers may improve the prospects for freer trade.

The influence of dynamic features of the distribution of capabilities on trade is also apparent in the case of *MOVE*. The fact that *MOVE* is inversely related to *Trade* indicates that one precondition for the expansion of trade may be a relatively stable international system. Because when movement is high, nations whose relative capabilities are declining may feel that trade relations with states whose relative capabilities are growing will, as Gilpin maintains, "become a source for increasing the political power of the strong over the weak,"[87] weaker states may be hesitant to engage in commerce, thereby leading to lower levels of global trade.

Although there is considerable evidence that features of the distribution of capabilities help shape patterns in the international political economy, different features of the distribution of capabilities are related to the level of global trade in markedly different ways. Because much of the literature on the international political economy has focused exclusively on the effects of hegemony, studies of this topic have failed to uncover much of the relationship between the distribution of power and international commerce.

My findings also highlight the importance of examining features of the international system other than the distribution of capabilities in systemic analyses of trade. In particular, Stein and others are correct in arguing that among the "real dangers to a relatively liberal trading order are wars that destroy political relationships and disrupt economic ones, or major sustained downturns—real depressions in the global economy."[88] By focusing largely on the distribution of capabilities, neorealist explanations of the international political economy fail to capture important nonstructural influences on trade. However, it is not the case that war and global income are markedly more important determinants of trade than is the distribution of power. Instead, both structural and nonstructural factors need to be considered in studies of the international political economy.

## Conclusion

While many recent studies have attempted to determine whether international politics helps explain patterns of global trade, the virtual absence of statistical results regarding the political correlates of international commerce is a glaring gap in the literature. The purpose of my study has been to help fill this gap.[89]

87. Gilpin, *The Political Economy of International Relations*, p. 57.

88. Stein, "The Hegemon's Dilemma," p. 385.

89. It is clear, however, that this model of international trade suffers from a number of limitations. First, using material capabilities to measure power is admittedly crude, and the causal linkages between the concentration of capabilities and international trade are not clearly

My results indicate that it is important to distinguish among features of the distribution of capabilities, since various aspects of this distribution are related to trade in different ways. Whether or not there is a statistically significant relationship between hegemony and the level of global trade depends on how hegemony is defined, measured, and operationalized. However, this does not support the charge that the distribution of capabilities has an indeterminate effect on trade. On the contrary, there is substantial evidence that features of the concentration of capabilities are related strongly to the level of global commerce, although the relationship is more complex and richer than is usually thought.

Previous studies have analyzed only whether a monotonic relationship exists between trade and the distribution of power (perhaps because they have focused primarily on the effects of hegemony, which is often operationalized as a dichotomous variable). But it is important to recognize that the level of concentration depends on both the number of major powers and the relative inequality of their capabilities. When the number of major powers is held constant, there appears to be a U-shaped relationship between the relative inequality among the major powers in the international system and the level of trade. When the relative inequality of capabilities is held constant, there appears to be a direct relationship between the number of major powers and the level of trade. These tentative results suggest that it would be useful to broaden the range of both the features of the distribution of power and the nature of their effects that are commonly considered in studies of the international political economy.

Although political variables other than the distribution of capabilities have received scant attention in systemic analyses of trade, the contemporaneous incidence of war between major powers also determines the amount of commerce that is conducted. As might be expected, less trade is conducted during wars between major powers than during periods marked by the absence of such wars. Since war is obviously only one of a number of political variables that (in addition to the distribution of power) may influence the level of trade, it would be useful to conduct additional research examining the comparative effects of a broader array of political variables than are analyzed in the present study.

More generally, this study indicates that analysts of the international political economy and analysts of war could benefit from an expanded dialogue, particularly since specialists in both areas have expressed interest in the effects of many of the same aspects of the international system. Analysts of war have spent much time developing and refining measures of a number of these features (such as the measures of concentration used in the present study)

---

demonstrated. Second, no distinction is made between exports of manufactured goods and exports of agricultural goods. And, third, the model does not account for the effects of domestic factors on international trade. Although it is beyond the scope of this article to address these issues, it would be useful to consider them in future research on this topic.

which, while imperfect, may be of considerable use to scholars studying the international political economy.[90]

In addition, the results reported here strongly suggest that it would be useful to expand the interdisciplinary dialogue between economists and political scientists studying the international political economy. Both international economic and political variables appear to exert a substantial influence on global commerce. My simple model, which includes both political and economic variables, provides a remarkably good fit; in fact, it often explains about three-quarters of the variation in the level of international trade. Since economic models of trade often neglect the influence of international politics, the strength of these results indicates that economists might benefit from examining more carefully the effects of international politics in their analyses of trade.[91]

90. On this point, see Hart, "Polarity, Hegemony and the Distribution of Power."

91. For analyses that do take the influence of international politics into account, see John E. Roemer, "The Effect of Sphere of Influence and Economic Distance on the Commodity Composition of Trade in Manufactures," *Review of Economics and Statistics* 59 (August 1977), pp. 318–27; and Robert T. Green and James M. Lutz, *The United States and World Trade* (New York: Praeger, 1978). I am grateful to an anonymous reviewer for bringing these studies to my attention. For further discussions of the need to consider the influence of international politics on trade, see Benjamin J. Cohen, "The Political Economy of International Trade," *International Organization* 44 (Spring 1990), pp. 261–81; and John S. Odell, "Understanding International Trade Policies: An Emerging Synthesis," *World Politics* 43 (October 1990), pp. 139–67.

**APPENDIX.** *Data on trade, concentration, and hegemony, 1850–1965*

| *Year* | *Ratio of global exports to global production*[a] | *Concentration* | *Gilpin's classifications of hegemony* | *Wallerstein's classifications of hegemony* |
|---|---|---|---|---|
| 1850 | 0.124 | 0.260 | Hegemony | Hegemony |
| 1855 | 0.139 | 0.276 | Hegemony | Hegemony |
| 1860 | 0.155 | 0.280 | Hegemony | Hegemony |
| 1865 | 0.194 | 0.255 | Hegemony | Hegemony |
| 1870 | 0.200 | 0.233 | Hegemony | Hegemony |
| 1875 | 0.215 | 0.225 | Hegemony | Nonhegemony |
| 1880 | 0.235 | 0.226 | Hegemony | Nonhegemony |
| 1885 | 0.235 | 0.208 | Hegemony | Nonhegemony |
| 1890 | 0.218 | 0.203 | Hegemony | Nonhegemony |
| 1895 | 0.243 | 0.223 | Hegemony | Nonhegemony |
| 1900 | 0.217 | 0.202 | Hegemony | Nonhegemony |
| 1905 | 0.224 | 0.207 | Hegemony | Nonhegemony |
| 1910 | 0.244 | 0.212 | Hegemony | Nonhegemony |
| 1913 | 0.211 | 0.208 | Hegemony | Nonhegemony |
| 1920 | 0.212 | 0.371 | Nonhegemony | Nonhegemony |
| 1925 | 0.209 | 0.247 | Nonhegemony | Nonhegemony |
| 1930 | 0.213 | 0.241 | Nonhegemony | Nonhegemony |
| 1935 | 0.178 | 0.228 | Nonhegemony | Nonhegemony |
| 1938 | 0.169 | 0.217 | Nonhegemony | Nonhegemony |
| 1946 | 0.169 | 0.417 | Hegemony | Hegemony |
| 1950 | 0.192 | 0.293 | Hegemony | Hegemony |
| 1955 | 0.202 | 0.331 | Hegemony | Hegemony |
| 1960 | 0.217 | 0.303 | Hegemony | Hegemony |
| 1965 | 0.243 | — | Hegemony | Hegemony |

[a]These data pertain to the year after that shown in the first column. For example, the initial value (0.124) pertains to 1851, not 1850. This is because, according to equation 3, the effects of the distribution of capabilities on trade occur with a lag.

*Sources.* See Table 1.

# POWER POLITICS AND INTERNATIONAL TRADE

JOANNE GOWA *Princeton University*
EDWARD D. MANSFIELD *Columbia University*

*Recent literature attributes the relative scarcity of open international markets to the prisoner's dilemma structure of state preferences with respect to trade. We argue that the prisoner's dilemma representation does not reflect the most critical aspect of free trade agreements in an anarchic international system, namely, their security externalities. We consider these external effects explicitly. Doing so leads us to two conclusions: (1) free trade is more likely within, rather than across, political–military alliances; and (2) alliances are more likely to evolve into free-trade coalitions if they are embedded in bipolar systems than in multipolar systems. Using data drawn from an 80-year period beginning in 1905, we test these hypotheses. The results of the analysis make it clear that alliances do have a direct, statistically significant, and large impact on bilateral trade flows and that this relationship is stronger in bipolar, rather than in multipolar, systems.*

In the early 1970s, students of international relations began what would become a long and heated debate about the political correlates of open international markets. Recently, however, an important element of consensus has begun to emerge: most contributors to this debate now seem to agree that the prisoner's dilemma structure of state preferences with respect to trade explains the relative dearth of open international markets.[1]

Here, we argue that what has become the standard prisoner's dilemma representation neglects the most critical aspect of free-trade agreements in the anarchic international system, namely, their security externalities. We consider these external effects explicitly. In order to do so, we construct and analyze a simple game-theoretic model. The results of this analysis demonstrate that tariff games between allies differ systematically from those played between actual or potential adversaries.

These differences imply that free trade is more likely within, rather than across, political–military alliances. However, our analysis also suggests that the evolutionary prospects of alliances vary: those that are the products of bipolar systems are more likely to evolve into free-trade coalitions than are their multipolar counterparts. Less credible exit threats and clearer responsibilities for alliance stability explain the advantage of a bipolar system.

We test this argument using data drawn from an 80-year period beginning in 1905. The empirical analysis supports our argument. It demonstrates that alliances have a direct, statistically significant, and large effect upon bilateral trade. Moreover, it shows that on average, alliances have a much stronger effect on trade in a bipolar than in a multipolar world.[2]

## POWER, TRADE, AND TARIFFS

Unlike many arguments about the use of economic statecraft, ours is cast at the macroeconomic rather than at the microeconomic level. In other words, the argument we advance here is *not* about, for example, attempts to use economic statecraft to embargo exports of particular products or to inhibit the development of technologically advanced industries in other countries.[3] Instead, it is an argument that is based upon the effect of free trade on the real income and power potential of states.

We argue that the play of power politics is an inexorable element of any agreement to open international markets because trade produces security externalities.[4] These externalities arise because the source of gains from trade is the increased efficiency with which domestic resources can be employed. This increased efficiency itself frees economic resources for military uses (Baldwin 1985, 216; Hirschman 1980, 14; McKeown 1982, 225; idem 1984, 232; Root 1984, 75; Srinivasan 1987, 352). As a consequence, trade enhances the potential military power of any country that engages in it.

The anarchic structure of the international system, in turn, compels its constituent states to attend closely to the potential military power of both allies and potential or actual adversaries. It does so because the absence of any supranational authority in the international system enables a state to resort to force at any time to achieve its goals. The probability that a state will do so depends in part upon its power, which, in turn, depends partly upon its real income.

As a consequence, the real income gains that motivate free trade are also the source of the security externalities that can either impede or facilitate it: trade with an adversary produces a security diseconomy; trade with an ally produces a positive externality. In either case, agreements to open international markets create a divergence between the private and social costs of trade.[5] A socially suboptimal level of trade results, suggesting that government intervention in trade can be welfare-enhancing for the nation as a whole.

Figure 1 illustrates this situation. It shows the domestic market for a good that can also be imported at its world price, $P_w$, which is the private marginal

FIGURE 1

**Trade with an Adversary**

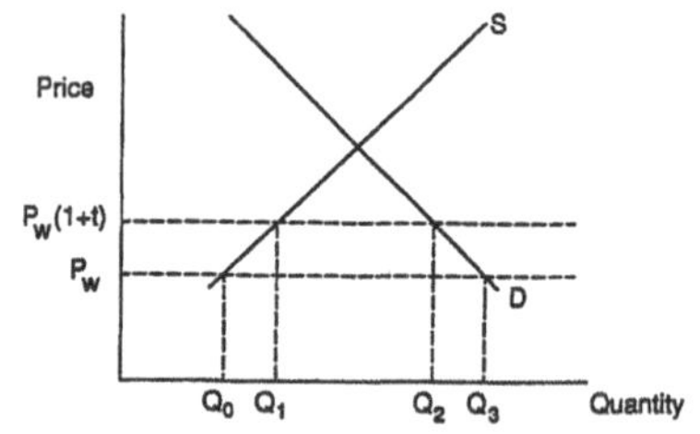


cost of imports. In the absence of government intervention, domestic output is $Q_0$; domestic demand is $Q_3$; and the amount imported is the difference between them ($Q_3 - Q_0$). Because of the external diseconomy that trade with actual or potential adversaries generates, however, the marginal social cost of imports is higher, $P_w(1 + t)$. This market failure can be eliminated by a tariff, t, which raises domestic output to $Q_1$, lowers domestic demand to $Q_2$, and reduces imports to $Q_2 - Q_1$.[6] Government intervention in trade to correct this distortion is, in addition, a first-best policy: the market failure in this instance does not originate in a domestic distortion but arises, instead, in trade itself.[7]

## OPTIMAL TARIFF GAMES

Successful intervention in trade to correct the security externalities associated with it depends upon the ability of a country to affect the real income of the state which is its target. Although any tariff will distort resource allocation in the target country and therefore decrease its real income, it will do so without imposing net costs on the home country only if the latter can affect its terms of trade.

Thus, in the absence of the requisite market power, a tariff will impose costs primarily upon the state that levies it. In its presence, a tariff will allow a state to increase its own real income at its adversary's expense. If a state can affect world prices, then, it can use a tariff to narrow the gap between the private and social costs of trade. Thus, a tariff can be welfare-superior to a policy of free trade for a state in an anarchic international political system.

This argument is, of course, a variant of the traditional optimal tariff argument. Its novelty inheres in the two conclusions that emerge from our discussion below: (1) tariff games between allies differ systematically from those played between adversaries; and (2) intraalliance free trade is more likely in a bipolar than in a multipolar system.

### The Standard Optimal Tariff Game

The payoff matrix of the standard optimal tariff game is shown in Figure 2. This game is a prisoner's dilemma in which T is the payoff that accrues to a state that unilaterally deploys an optimal tariff, R is the payoff that results if both states trade freely with each other, P is the return that accrues if both use optimal tariffs, and S is the payoff to unilateral free trade. As the matrix makes apparent, in a one-shot game, defection is a dominant strategy.[8] As a result, the inevitable outcome of this (or of a finite) game is bilateral tariffs.[9]

In contrast, in an infinite game or in a game in which states assume at every period that there is some positive probability that the game will continue, a variety of Pareto-improving outcomes, including that of free trade, can be realized.[10] This can occur if, for example, both states adhere to a "grim" strategy, that is, begin with free trade (i.e., cooperate); trade freely in every succeeding period if the outcome of the previous period was bilateral free trade; otherwise, deploy an optimal tariff (i.e., defect).[11]

This strategy will sustain cooperation in a prisoner's dilemma game if the discounted sum of cooperative payoffs, $R/(1 - \delta)$, is greater than the sum of the one-shot gain from defection, T, and the discounted sum of punishment payoffs, $\delta P/(1 - \delta)$.[12] Thus, cooperation can be sustained by a grim strategy if

FIGURE 2

**The Prisoner's Dilemma**

| | | Column: Cooperate | Column: Defect |
|---|---|---|---|
| Row | Cooperate | R,R | S,T |
| | Defect | T,S | P,P |

*Note*: T > R > P > S; Row's payoffs are listed first; $(T + S)/2 \leq R$.

FIGURE 3

**The Prisoner's Dilemma: Adversaries**

| | | State j | |
|---|---|---|---|
| | | Cooperate | Defect |
| State i | Cooperate | $R_i - w_{ij}R_j$, $R_j - w_{ji}R_i$ | $S_i - w_{ij}T_j$, $T_j - w_{ji}S_i$ |
| | Defect | $T_i - w_{ij}S_j$, $S_j - w_{ji}T_i$ | $P_i - w_{ij}P_j$, $P_j - w_{ji}P_i$ |

*Note:* This payoff matrix omits second-order effects.

$$R/(1 - \delta) \geq T + \delta P/(1 - \delta)$$

or

$$\delta \geq (T - R)/(T - P).$$

If this incentive compatibility constraint is satisfied, a grim strategy will enable free trade to emerge as the outcome of an infinite-horizon optimal tariff game. That this is possible not only in the abstract but also in the real world is suggested by the success of the General Agreement on Tariffs and Trade (GATT). Established in 1947, the GATT was created to, and did, enable states to avoid a replay of the tariff game that stymied trade among them in the interwar period.[13]

### Tariff Games Between Adversaries

The payoff matrix of the standard optimal tariff game assumes that there is no difference between private and social returns to interstate trade. Life in an anarchic international system, however, effectively alters the matrix of the standard game. Because interstate trade in such a system produces security externalities, it creates a divergence between private and social returns that any utility-maximizing state will take into account when it calculates its payoffs from trade.

Thus, the payoffs a state assigns to the outcomes of any given trade game differ from those of the standard optimal tariff game. In the case of trade with an adversary, a state incurs a marginal social cost that the standard matrix does not reflect. This transforms the standard matrix as shown in Figure 3. In each cell, the social cost that a state, i, incurs is represented as a fraction, $w_{ij}$, of the payoff that accrues to its adversary, j. Thus, $w_{ij}R_j$, for example, is the social cost or security diseconomy that accrues to state i when it trades freely with state j.

This cost is represented as an increasing function of the adversary's gains from trade. This representation is based in part on what Robert Powell has described as a "very simple, highly stylized assumption about the nature of warfare": that is, the "stronger a state is economically, the more likely it is to prevail in war" (1991, 1312). The functional dependence of social on private returns from trade also has a sector-specific component. The increase in domestic resource efficiency that results from trade frees economic resources for military uses and, therefore, increases an adversary's actual or potential military power.

The marginal social cost of trade is represented as a fraction, $w_{ij}$, of the adversary's gains from trade, partly because military power obviously does not depend only upon gross national product. It also depends, for example, on technology, skill, and the extractive potential of the state. In addition, military portfolios reflect the diversified interests of great powers. Because military resources are not completely fungible, not all additions to the military power of an adversary will weaken its trading partner. Thus, even if an adversary did divert all of its gains from trade to its military sector, its action would not necessarily inflict a social cost on its trading partner equal to the incremental addition to its military power.

When the returns from trade are adjusted to reflect its marginal social cost, the net effect is to make tariff games between adversaries more difficult to solve than is the standard optimal tariff game. Assuming that the game is iterated, free trade can be sustained in an optimal tariff game between adversaries if

$$(R_i - w_{ij}R_j)/(1 - \delta_i) \geq T_i - w_{ij}S_j + \delta_i\,(P_i - w_{ij}P_j)/(1 - \delta_i)$$

or

$$\delta_i^* \geq \frac{T_i - w_{ij}S_j - (R_i - w_{ij}R_j)}{T_i - w_{ij}S_j - (P_i - w_{ij}P_j)}.$$

This condition is more difficult to satisfy than the condition that emerges from an optimal tariff game among states with independent utility functions. In a prisoner's dilemma game with payoffs of (3, 2, 1, 0), for example, the minimum discount factor that would support free trade in the standard game is .50. In the modified game (with $w$ = .40), the analogous figure rises to .75.[14] Thus, the introduction of interdependent utility functions characteristic of adversarial states makes any given prisoner's dilemma more "severe" or difficult to solve. In addition, as $w$ increases, the severity of the game also increases.[15]

FIGURE 4

**The Prisoner's Dilemma: Allies**

| | | State j: Cooperate | State j: Defect |
|---|---|---|---|
| State i | Cooperate | $R_i + w_{ij}R_j, R_j + w_{ji}R_i$ | $S_i + w_{ij}T_j, T_j + w_{ji}S_i$ |
| | Defect | $T_i + w_{ij}S_j, S_j + w_{ji}T_i$ | $P_i + w_{ij}P_j, P_j + w_{ji}P_i$ |

*Note*: This payoff matrix omits second-order effects.

**Tariff Games Between Allies**

The gains of one state impose social costs on another only if the former is an actual or potential threat to the security of the latter. When a state trades with an ally, however, it realizes both private and social benefits. In the case of allies, the security externality that trade produces is positive. As in the case of trade between adversaries, a utility-maximizing state will take account of not only private but also social returns in calculating its payoffs from trade.

Thus, the standard matrix does not apply to this case either. The transformed prisoner's dilemma matrix is shown in Figure 4. In each cell, the social benefit that that a state, i, realizes as a consequence of trade with an ally is represented as some fraction, $w_{ij}$, of the payoff that accrues to its ally, j. This effectively internalizes the positive security externality associated with free trade between allies. The functional form is based on reasoning analogous to that which applies in the case of trade between adversaries. The applicable incentive compatibility constraint then becomes

$$(R_i + w_{ij}R_j)/(1 - \delta_i) \geq T_i + w_{ij}S_j + \delta_i\ (P_i + w_{ij}P_j)/(1 - \delta_i)$$

or

$$\delta_i^{**} \geq \frac{T_i + w_{ij}S_j - (R_i + w_{ij}R_j)}{T_i + w_{ij}S_j - (P_i + w_{ij}P_j)}.$$

This condition is more easily satisfied than is the condition that emerges from either the standard prisoner's dilemma or the transformed game among adversaries. Using the same values assigned in the example above, free trade can be sustained among allies when the discount factor is .13. In addition, if $w$ exceeds the larger of $(T - R)/(T - S)$ and $(D - S)/(T - S)$, free trade becomes the dominant strategy equilibrium. In short, tariff games between allies are easier to solve than tariff games between actual or potential adversaries.

**The Influence of Polarity**

While this model suggests that all alliances will influence trade barriers, it seems clear that alliances have exerted a stronger effect after, than before, World War II. Inspection of the incentive compatibility constraint that applies to the intraallied tariff game suggests one explanation of this difference. All other things being equal, the extent to which allies trade freely with each other depends upon the discount factor, $\delta$. The discount factor is a function of the risk of exit, which, in turn, is a function of systemic polarity (Gowa 1989).[16]

The risk of exit is the threat that an ally will abandon an existing alliance to join an alternative one. For several reasons, this risk is higher in multipolar than in bipolar systems.[17] First, while bipolar coalitions are the products largely of system structure, alliances in a multipolar system are the results of choice among several possible alternatives (Snyder 1984, 415). Second, in a bipolar system, realignment is impossible for either pole. By default, alliance stability is also the exclusive responsibility of each. Neither can expect any other state to prevent the defection of an ally from within its bloc (Snyder 1984). In a multipolar system, however, the interest in preserving alliance stability can be distributed across more than one pole. As a consequence, alliance stability can become problematic, as each pole seeks to transfer the burden of maintaining the alliance to another.

The implications of different exit risks for trade are clear. Any great-power member of a coalition in a multipolar world has strong incentives to discriminate among its allies in terms of its investment in them, because its allies confront divergent opportunity costs of exit. In contrast, the incentive to discriminate in a bipolar world is much weaker, since allies are much more uniformly and securely locked into coalitions. In a bipolar world, in other words, the gains from trade can be more easily privatized. As a consequence, investments in allies in a multipolar system are likely to be expressed in the form of discriminatory trade preferences; in a bipolar system, free trade is the more likely outcome.

In short, because the risk of exit is lower in a bipolar than in a multipolar system, the security externalities of any free-trade agreement are more likely to remain internalized within the alliances of the former than in those of the latter. As a result, allies in a multipolar system will tend to discount the future benefits accruing from open markets among them more heavily than will their bipolar counterparts. The greater stability of bipolar coalitions allows the value of future benefits to approximate present benefits more closely.

For any given structure of payoffs, then, free trade is more likely to emerge within the alliances of a bipolar than in those of a multipolar system. It is not surprising, therefore, that the effect of alliances on trade seems to have been greater after rather than before World War II. We shall now subject this and our more general hypothesis about the impact of alliances on trade to a systematic empirical test.

## THE RESEARCH DESIGN

Empirical analyses of the influence of political factors on bilateral trade are relatively rare. However, because several important studies do address closely related topics, we want to examine them briefly here. One group of studies examines the effects on bilateral trade of preferential trading arrangements (PTAs), such as customs unions and free-trade areas. Many of these analyses conclude that PTAs have done much to promote trade among member nations (Aitken 1973; Linnemann 1966; Pelzman 1977; Tinbergen 1962). Another group of studies uses events data to analyze the impact on bilateral trade of political conflict and cooperation. These analyses conclude that bilateral trade tends to be lower when the participants are engaged in conflicts than when political relations between them are relatively cooperative (Pollins 1989a, 1989b).

Our analysis differs from these studies in three ways. First, clear differences exist between alliances and economic arrangements that are explicitly designed to promote trade among their members. Moreover, since many PTAs have formed among political allies (Mansfield 1993), our model may at least partially endogenize their effects on bilateral trade. Second, it is unlikely that a very strong relationship exists between alliances and measures of conflict and cooperation based on events data: there may be a considerable degree of low-level conflict among members of an alliance and substantial cooperation among states that are not allied. Third, these studies examine the determinants of bilateral trade after 1945. To adequately test our model, we need to consider a much longer time period. Hence, while previous analyses have yielded important insights into the effects of certain aspects of international politics on trade, they do not analyze either the same dimension of international politics or the same period of time as we do here.[18]

Based on our argument, we expect that (1) fewer trade barriers will exist within than across alliances; and (2) intraalliance free trade will be more likely within bipolar than within multipolar systems. While we would prefer to test these hypotheses directly, it is not possible to do so. Reliable tariff data do not exist for all countries over the entire time span that we analyze. However, to the extent that alliance patterns explain tariffs and that tariffs, in turn, explain the volume of trade, tariffs are endogenized, and we can focus on the relationship between alliances and trade.[19] As a result, we examine the effects of alliances on bilateral trade flows.

Ideally, we would include in our sample all major powers and their allies. However, data limitations led us to focus on trade relations among the United States, Great Britain, France, Italy, Germany, the Soviet Union,[20] and Japan during the period from 1905 to 1985. Though this is clearly a limited sample, these states include most of the major powers in the international system during this period (Levy 1983; Small and Singer 1982). Moreover, since we expect the impact of alliances on trade to be most pronounced in cases of alliances involving major powers, this analysis will offer an important, though preliminary, test of our model.[21]

We also expect that bilateral alliances will affect trade flows more strongly than will multilateral alliances. While the *aggregate* flow of trade across a group of more than two states may be higher when these states are engaged in an alliance than when they are not, this need not imply that *all* bilateral trade flows among these states will be higher under these circumstances. For example, the existence of an alliance among states A, B, C, and D would be expected to produce an increase in the total trade among these states. This, however, would not necessarily lead to an increase in bilateral trade between A and B. Indeed, A and B may engage in less commerce during the course of this alliance than in the absence of the alliance (although they would be expected to offset this by trading more with C and/or D). But if our argument holds, bilateral alliances should be directly related to bilateral trade. Under these circumstances, the effects of alliances on aggregate intraalliance trade can be assessed directly by examining trade flows between the two partners.

## THE MODEL

In this section, we develop a simple model of the relationship between alliances and bilateral trade. It is clear that any analysis of this sort should incorporate economic, as well as political, determinants of trade. Among economists, gravity models of bilateral trade flows have been widely used (Aitken 1973; Anderson 1979; Deardorff 1984, 503–4; Frankel 1992; Leamer and Stern 1970, 145–70; Linnemann 1966; Pelzman 1977; Tinbergen 1962). In order to analyze the economic determinants of bilateral trade, we use a well-known variant of this model, which includes the gross national product (GNP) and the population of both the importer and the exporter, as well as the geographic distance between the two states. Consistent with previous research based on this model, we expect that the nominal value of bilateral trade will be directly related to the nominal GNP of both the importer and the exporter and inversely related to the population of both the importer and exporter and to the geographic distance between them.

In addition to GNP, population, and distance, we include two variables related to alliances in our model: one indicating whether a bilateral alliance exists between the trading partners and one indicating whether a multilateral alliance exists between these states. Finally, because we expect interstate wars to reduce trade among the belligerents, we also include a variable that indicates whether or not the importer and exporter are at war.

Hence, our model is

$$\begin{aligned}\log X_{ij(t)} &= \log A + B_1 \log Y_{i(t-1)} + B_2 \log Y_{j(t-1)} \\ &+ B_3 \log P_{i(t-1)} + B_4 \log P_{j(t-1)} \\ &+ B_5 \log D_{ij(t-1)} + B_6 \log BA_{ij(t-1)} \\ &+ B_7 \log MA_{ij(t-1)} + B_8 \log War_{ij(t-1)} + \log z_{ij}, \quad (1)\end{aligned}$$

where $\log X_{ij(t)}$ is the natural logarithm of the nominal value of exports (expressed in U.S. dollars) by state i to state j in year t,[22] $\log Y_{i(t-1)}$ is the natural logarithm of the nominal GNP (expressed in U.S. dollars) of state i in year $t - 1$,[23] $\log Y_{j(t-1)}$ is the natural logarithm of the nominal GNP (expressed in U.S. dollars) of state j in year $t - 1$, $\log P_{i(t-1)}$ is the natural logarithm of the population of state i in year $t - 1$,[24] $\log P_{j(t-1)}$ is the natural logarithm of the population of state j in year $t - 1$, $\log D_{ij(t-1)}$ is the natural logarithm of the geographic distance between states i and j in year t,[25] $\log BA_{ij(t-1)}$ is a dummy variable that equals 1 if an alliance exists between states i and j in year $t - 1$ that is comprised of no members except i and j (and 0 otherwise),[26] $\log MA_{ij(t-1)}$ is a dummy variable that equals 1 if an alliance exists between states i and j in year $t - 1$ that includes at least one additional member (and 0 otherwise), $\log War_{ij(t-1)}$ is a dummy variable that equals 1 if states i and j are engaged in a war in year $t - 1$ (and 0 otherwise),[27] and $\log z_{ij}$ is an error term. Note that in antilogarithmic form all dummy variables in this model take on values of e (the base of the natural logarithms) and one; the natural logarithms of these variables, therefore, take on values of one and zero. Since it is generally assumed that these variables exert a lagged effect on the value of exports and in order to avoid problems of simultaneity,[28] we assume a lag of one year in equation 1 for each variable. The log-linear specification of this model is used because it is consistent with many previous studies of trade that have used gravity models and because it has number of advantages relative to a linear specification (Leamer and Stern 1970).

Since we are interested in the relationship between alliances and trade at given points in time, as well as over time, equation 1 is estimated for a series of cross sections, beginning in 1905. Our analysis begins with 1905 (year t) because complete data for all of the independent variables in equation 1 are not available prior to 1904 (year $t - 1$). After 1905, the parameters in equation 1 are estimated for the first year of each subsequent ten-year interval. However, we do not estimate the model during World Wars I and II, since trade data are often not available for these years. Further, equation 1 is not estimated during the late 1940s because the occupation of Germany and Japan precluded both states from making autonomous decisions about trade policies or alliance partners. As a result, there are some cases in which the intervals are not ten years in length.

**Estimates of the Parameters**

Ordinary least squares estimates of the parameters in equation 1 are presented in Table 1. In each regression, at least one outlier was identified.[29] The results in Table 1 are estimated without these observations. However, it should be noted that very little difference exists between the results with these observations included and the results presented in Table 1.[30]

These findings indicate that on average, our model explains over 80% of the variation in the value of exports and that the overall fit of the model differs little across the nine years that are analyzed. Our results also indicate that the regression coefficients of GNP, population, geographic distance, and war usually point in the expected directions and are statistically significant. First, the regression coefficient of $\log Y_i$ is positive in nine cases and statistically significant in eight instances; and the regression coefficient of $\log Y_j$ is positive and statistically significant in all nine cases. Second, the regression coefficient of $\log P_i$ is negative in eight cases and statistically significant in seven instances; and the regression coefficient of $\log P_j$ is negative in nine cases and statistically significant in eight instances. Third, the regression coefficient of $\log D_{ij}$ is negative in eight cases and statistically significant in five instances. Finally, the regression coefficient of $\log War_{ij}$ is negative and statistically significant in one out of two cases.

These results also confirm the hypothesis that alliances are directly related to the value of exports. The regression coefficient of $\log BA_{ij}$ is positive in six out of nine cases and statistically significant in five instances; and the regression coefficient of $\log MA_{ij}$ is positive and statistically significant in six out of eight cases. Further, the mean of the nine regression coefficients of $\log BA_{ij}$ is about 1.09 and (assuming that these regression coefficients are statistically independent) the standard error of the mean is about .15.[31] The mean of the eight regression coefficients of $\log MA_{ij}$ is about .61, and the standard error of the mean is about .16.[32] On average, therefore, the relationships between bilateral alliances and multilateral alliances, on the one hand, and bilateral trade on the other seem to be direct and statistically significant.

Moreover, the quantitative impacts of both bilateral and multilateral alliances on the predicted value of bilateral trade are substantial. Even if the mean of the regression coefficients of $\log BA_{ij}$ was two standard errors less than 1.09, a change from the absence of a bilateral alliance to the existence of such an alliance would more than double the predicted value of exports.[33] And even if the mean of the regression

TABLE 1

**Regression of Exports on GNP, Population, Distance, Alliances, and War, 1905–85**

| | PERIOD OF MULTIPOLARITY | | | | | PERIOD OF BIPOLARITY | | | |
|---|---|---|---|---|---|---|---|---|---|
| PARAMETER | 1905 | 1913 | 1920 | 1930 | 1938 | 1955 | 1965 | 1975 | 1985 |
| Intercept | −4.57 | −8.79 | 57.21*** | 7.39 | 12.44* | 34.81*** | 5.69 | 6.29 | 12.14** |
| | (7.88) | (9.99) | (14.74) | (5.06) | (6.19) | (8.19) | (5.17) | (4.25) | (4.88) |
| log $GNP_i$ | .95*** | 1.68*** | 2.78*** | 1.53*** | 1.67*** | 1.12*** | .28 | .83*** | .96*** |
| | (.17) | (.23) | (.34) | (.14) | (.20) | (.26) | (.26) | (.20) | (.32) |
| log $GNP_j$ | 1.10*** | .90*** | 2.17*** | 1.25*** | 1.57*** | .93*** | .44** | .55*** | 1.19*** |
| | (.18) | (.25) | (.27) | (.14) | (.22) | (.25) | (.26) | (.21) | (.32) |
| log $Population_i$ | −.02 | −.95*** | −4.10*** | −1.21*** | −1.68*** | −1.88*** | .14 | −.68*** | −1.13*** |
| | (.33) | (.35) | (.83) | (.23) | (.34) | (.49) | (.39) | (.26) | (.42) |
| log $Population_j$ | −1.21*** | −.92*** | −4.83*** | −1.74*** | −2.27*** | −1.82*** | −.38 | −.45** | −1.42*** |
| | (.27) | (.31) | (.59) | (.23) | (.32) | (.49) | (.39) | (.25) | (.40) |
| log $Distance_{ij}$ | −.33*** | −.06 | .27 | −.35*** | −.06 | −.01 | −.12** | −.23*** | −.28*** |
| | (.09) | (.10) | (.13) | (.06) | (.09) | (.09) | (.06) | (.05) | (.07) |
| log Bilat. $alliance_{ij}$ | −.37 | −.57 | .20 | 1.04*** | −.30 | 3.02*** | 2.58*** | 2.07*** | 2.10*** |
| | (.31) | (.36) | (.77) | (.42) | (.40) | (.55) | (.39) | (.32) | (.43) |
| log Multilat. $alliance_{ij}$ | −.61 | −.31 | .96*** | —[a] | .48* | .86** | 1.65*** | .99*** | .84*** |
| | (.55) | (.72) | (.39) | | (.35) | (.46) | (.33) | (.18) | (.26) |
| log $War_{ij}$ | −7.12*** | —[b] | 1.55 | —[b] | —[b] | —[b] | —[b] | —[b] | —[b] |
| | (.61) | | (.72) | | | | | | |
| Adjusted $R^2$ | .92 | .71 | .83 | .86 | .80 | .78 | .82 | .82 | .80 |
| N | 39 | 39 | 37[c] | 40 | 37[d] | 41 | 40 | 41 | 41 |

*Note:* Entries are unstandardized regression coefficients with standard errors in parentheses. Years shown are year t in equation 1. For each year, there are 42 observations minus the number of outliers.
[a]No multilateral alliances existed among the major powers in 1929.
[b]No wars between major powers were conducted during these years.
[c]No data on the Soviet Union's exports to Germany are available for 1920.
[d]No data on Italian exports to the Soviet Union are available for 1938.
*$p \leq .10$ (one-tailed test); intercept $p \leq .10$ (two-tailed test).
**$p \leq .05$ (one-tailed test); intercept $p \leq .05$ (two-tailed test).
***$p \leq .01$ (one-tailed test); intercept $p \leq .01$ (two-tailed test).

coefficients of log $MA_{ij}$ was two standard errors less than .61, a change from the absence of a multilateral alliance to the existence of such an alliance would increase the predicted value of exports by more than one-third.[34]

As expected, the system's structure influences the strength and the magnitude of the effect of alliances on trade. The means of the regression coefficients of log $BA_{ij}$ and log $MA_{ij}$ have been substantially larger during periods of bipolarity than during periods of multipolarity; and the differences between these means are statistically significant (for log $BA_{ij}$, t = 6.26, $p < .005$; for log $MA_{ij}$, t = 2.34, $p < .05$). Thus, our results indicate that on average, the magnitude of the effects of alliances on trade has been considerably more pronounced during bipolar periods than during multipolar periods.

There is also some support for our hypothesis that bilateral alliances exert larger effects on trade than multilateral alliances, although the evidence is weaker than expected. When all years in Tables 1 are considered, the mean of the regression coefficients of log $BA_{ij}$ is almost twice as large as the mean of the regression coefficients of log $MA_{ij}$, but the difference between these means is not statistically significant. When only bipolar periods are examined, the mean of the regression coefficients of log $BA_{ij}$ is substantially larger than the mean of the regression coefficients of log $MA_{ij}$; and the difference between these means is statistically significant (t = 4.50, $p < .005$). But when only multipolar periods are analyzed, the mean of the regression coefficients of log $MA_{ij}$ is somewhat larger than the mean of the regression coefficients of log $BA_{ij}$; and, although the difference between these means is not statistically significant, this result is clearly at odds with our hypothesis. Hence, the extent to which our hypothesis concerning the effects of different types of alliances on trade is supported seems to depend in large measure on system structure.

## THE ROBUSTNESS OF THE RESULTS

In addition to estimating the effects of alliances on trade, it is also important to analyze the robustness of the results in Table 1. To this end, we address two issues. First, does the composition of the sample of states affect the results? More specifically, does the fact that we include the Soviet Union in our sample

TABLE 2

**Regression of Exports on Per Capita GNP, Distance, and Alliances, Excluding the Soviet Union, 1905–1985**

| | PERIOD OF MULTIPOLARITY | | | | PERIOD OF BIPOLARITY | | | |
|---|---|---|---|---|---|---|---|---|
| PARAMETER | 1905 | 1913 | 1920 | 1938 | 1955 | 1965 | 1975 | 1985 |
| Intercept | 9.57*** (2.54) | 3.60 (3.46) | 2.68 (2.95) | 3.17 (3.05) | 10.51*** (1.85) | 8.73** (3.48) | 8.33*** (2.79) | 7.78* (4.27) |
| log Per capita GNP$_i$ | 1.12*** (.23) | 1.76*** (.30) | 1.88*** (.29) | 1.41*** (.26) | .80*** (.21) | .79*** (.31) | .90*** (.21) | .69** (.30) |
| log Per capita GNP$_j$ | .96*** (.23) | .69*** (.32) | .94*** (.28) | 1.36*** (.26) | .51*** (.20) | .82*** (.30) | .78*** (.21) | 1.15*** (.30) |
| log Distance$_{ij}$ | −.26** (.11) | .06 (.14) | −.21** (.10) | −.18** (.10) | −.14* (.10) | −.17* (.11) | −.21*** (.06) | −.32*** (.09) |
| log Bilat. alliance$_{ij}$ | −.41 (.39) | −.11 (.42) | .58 (.66) | −.21 (.62) | 2.36*** (.49) | 2.41*** (.51) | 2.18*** (.32) | 1.92*** (.44) |
| log Multilat. alliance$_{ij}$ | −.61 (.63) | −.12 (.75) | 1.06** (.35) | .33 (.41) | 1.31*** (.53) | .93* (.55) | .97*** (.25) | .80*** (.31) |
| Adjusted $R^2$ | .75 | .63 | .74 | .78 | .87 | .80 | .85 | .81 |
| N | 28 | 28 | 28 | 28 | 29 | 30 | 28 | 28 |

*Note:* Entries are unstandardized regression coefficients with standard errors in parentheses. Years shown are year t in equation 2. For each year, there are 30 observations minus the number of outliers.
*$p \le .10$ (one-tailed test); intercept $p \le .10$ (two-tailed test).
**$p \le .05$ (one-tailed test); intercept $p \le .05$ (two-tailed test).
***$p \le .01$ (one-tailed test); intercept $p \le .01$ (two-tailed test).

enhance the influence of alliances on trade? Second, does the omission of certain variables that might be expected to influence both alliance patterns and trade flows account for the observed relationship between alliances and bilateral commerce?

### Estimates of the Parameters Excluding the Soviet Union

It is possible that including the Soviet Union in our sample may have exaggerated the impact of alliances on trade (in Table 1). The Soviet Union had both a command and a relatively autarkic economy during most of the twentieth century. It also concluded few alliances with other major powers in our sample after World War I. Thus, the strength of the observed relationship between alliances and trade might be due to the composition of our sample. In order to determine whether this is the case, ordinary least squares estimates of the parameters in equation 1 were obtained for those dyads that did not involve the Soviet Union.

These results (and auxiliary regressions based on these results) indicated that unlike our findings in Table 1, there was often considerable multicollinearity among log $Y_i$, log $Y_j$, log $P_i$, and log $P_j$ when dyads involving the Soviet Union were excluded from our analysis. One solution to this type of problem is to combine some of the explanatory variables (Fox 1991, 15–16). We, therefore, focus on the effects of the nominal per capita GNP (which is expressed as Y/P) of both the importer and the exporter, as well as distance and alliances, on nominal exports. This specification of our model is as follows:

$$\log X_{ij(t)} = \log A + B_1 \log (Y/P)_{i(t-1)} + B_2 \log (Y/P)_{j(t-1)} + B_3 \log D_{ij(t-1)} + B_4 \log BA_{ij(t-1)} + B_5 \log MA_{ij(t-1)} + \log z_{ij}, \quad (2)$$

where $\log (Y/P)_{i(t-1)}$ is the natural logarithm of the nominal per capita GNP of state i in year t − 1, $\log (Y/P)_{j(t-1)}$ is the natural logarithm of the nominal per capita GNP of state j in year t − 1, and the nominal per capita GNP of both states i and j is expected to be directly related to the nominal value of exports from i to j (Frankel 1992, Linnemann 1966). Since each of the wars we considered in our earlier analysis involved the Soviet Union, $War_{ij}$ is not included in this model. Further, because all alliances in 1929 involved the Soviet Union, it was not possible to estimate the effects of alliances on trade for this year.

Ordinary least squares estimates of the parameters of equation 2 are presented in Table 2 (with outliers deleted).[35] These results indicate that on average, our model continues to explain about 80% of the variation in exports and that the signs of the regression coefficients of per capita GNP and geographic distance are in the expected directions. In every case, the regression coefficients of $\log (Y/P)_i$ and $\log (Y/P)_j$ are positive and statistically significant; and the regression coefficient of $\log D_{ij}$ is negative and statistically significant in seven out of eight instances.

Of particular interest is the fact that the effects of both bilateral and multilateral alliances on bilateral trade are much the same, regardless of whether or not the Soviet Union is excluded from our sample of states. In no case does the sign of the regression coefficient of either $\log BA_{ij}$ or $\log MA_{ij}$ in Table 1 change when the Soviet Union is deleted; and in only one case (log $MA_{ij}$ in 1938) does the level of statistical significance of the regression coefficient of either log $BA_{ij}$ or log $MA_{ij}$ in Table 1 change when the composition of our sample of states is altered. Moreover, the means of the regression coefficients of both log $BA_{ij}$ (1.09) and log $MA_{ij}$ (.58) are virtually identical to those based on the results in Table 1.

On average, therefore, the relationships between both bilateral and multilateral alliances and bilateral trade continue to be direct and statistically significant. It should also be noted that on average, the magnitude of the effects of bilateral alliances on trade continues to be larger than that of multilateral alliances and that on average, the magnitude of the effects of both bilateral and multilateral alliances on bilateral trade continues to be significantly larger during periods of bipolarity than during periods of multipolarity.

### The Effects of Omitted Variables

We now turn to the issue of whether our results in Table 1 are robust with respect to the inclusion of variables that are omitted from equation 1 and that might account for the observed relationship between alliances and trade. First, as we have noted, many analysts have concluded that PTAs have promoted trade among their members. Further, since many of these arrangements have been embedded in alliances, it may be that PTAs are responsible for the observed relationship between alliances and trade.

In order to test this hypothesis, we conducted two separate analyses. Initially, we included a dummy variable in equation 1 that equalled 1 if states i and j were members of the European Economic Community in year t − 1, and 0 otherwise. Next, we included a dummy variable in equation 1 that equalled 1 if states i and j were members of the GATT in year t − 1, and 0 otherwise. In each case, we analyzed 1965, 1975, and 1985; and both analyses yielded quite similar findings.[36] In each analysis, the regression coefficient of the dummy variable was positive in all three cases (i.e., more trade has been conducted between states that were PTA members than between states that were not). But, in each case, only one regression coefficient was statistically significant; and the inclusion of this variable did not have a substantial effect on either the size or the level of statistical significance of any of the remaining regression coefficients in equation 1.

Second, in addition to wars, military disputes that do not escalate into wars may also influence bilateral trade relations. Further, the existence of military disputes may influence alliance patterns. In order to test whether military disputes account for the observed relationship between alliances and trade, we included in equation 1 a dummy variable that equalled 1 if states i and j were involved in a militarized dispute in year t − 1, and 0 otherwise. Among the years listed in Table 1, four were marked by military disputes, based on data developed by Gochman and Maoz (1984) and recently updated by the Correlates of War Project. Our findings indicated that the regression coefficient of this variable tended to be negative (i.e., the existence of a dispute involving states i and j tended to depress trade between them). But in no case was it statistically significant, nor did its inclusion in equation 1 substantially change either the size or the level of statistical significance of any of the remaining regression coefficients in our model.

Third, whether or not the states in our sample are democratic polities may account for the observed relationship between alliances and bilateral trade flows. Democratic states might, for example, trade more freely with each other than do either nondemocracies with democracies or nondemocracies with each other. This might occur because democratic states typically have relatively free market economies. Recent research also suggests that democracies have exhibited a disproportionate tendency to ally with one another during portions of the twentieth century (Siverson and Emmons 1991).

In order to determine whether the observed relationship between alliances and trade is due to regime type, a dummy variable was included in equation 1 that equalled 1 if both states i and j were democracies in year t − 1, and 0 otherwise, based on Doyle's (1986) data. Our results indicated that the sign of this regression coefficient varied substantially from year to year and that it was statistically significant in only one case. Moreover, the size and level of statistical significance of the remaining regression coefficients in equation 1 continued to be much the same as in Table 1.

Clearly, we are not suggesting that PTAs, military disputes, and regime type do not influence bilateral trade flows at all. But these factors do not seem to account for the observed relationship between alliances and trade among major powers during the twentieth century. Nor does the composition of the sample: our findings are also quite robust with respect to whether the Soviet Union is included in the analysis. Thus, while tentative, our results indicate that bilateral trade flows between major powers tend to be considerably higher when they are allies than when they are not.

## CONCLUSION

We have argued that a free-trade policy can be suboptimal for states in an anarchic international system. Under some conditions, an effort to induce trade to follow the flag can be welfare-enhancing. The results of our empirical analysis support the implications of our argument about the relationship between alliances and trade. They show that alliances exert a direct, statistically significant, and large effect on bilateral trade flows. They also show that the effects of alliances vary. Bilateral alliances sometimes influence trade flows more strongly than do multilateral alliances; and alliances embedded in bipolar systems have stronger effects upon trade than do their counterparts in multipolar systems.

The argument we develop here also suggests that there may be other sources of cross-alliance variation that our empirical analysis could not detect. One plausible source is differences across alliances with respect to the gains that would accrue from free trade and its associated externalities. According to the tenets of the Heckscher–Ohlin–Samuelson model of international trade, for example, gains from trade and differences in relative factor endowments are directly related. Thus, this model implies that allies with very different factor endowments will confront stronger incentives to trade freely with each other than will allies with more similar endowments.

The weight a state assigns to its ally will also affect the magnitude of the security externality that free trade generates. Cross-alliance variations in $w_{ij}$ might occur, for example, because of differences in the probability of war, the technology of weapons production, or the need (if any) for an ex ante coordination of forces. In addition, the magnitude of the external effects of trade depends upon the transaction costs of opening borders to trade. These costs might vary as a consequence, for example, of whether an alliance has been given formal institutional expression (Keohane 1984; Snidal 1985).

Because of these and other possible sources of cross-alliance variation, it is clear that we have not offered an exhaustive analysis of the impact of alliances on trade. Nonetheless, we have established the conditions under which it makes sense for states to attempt to tie trade to the flag. In addition, we show that alliances have influenced bilateral trade flows not only after, but also before, 1945. In doing so, we suggest that the end of the Cold War will precipitate changes in the play of power politics both in the political–military sphere and in the pattern of international trade.

## Notes

The alphabet determined the ordering of the authors' names. For their comments on earlier versions of this paper, we are grateful to Charles Cameron, Benjamin J. Cohen, Youssef Cohen, John A. C. Conybeare, Stephen M. Goldfeld, Robert O. Keohane, Timothy J. McKeown, Arvid Lukauskas, J. David Richardson, Robert Powell, and Beth V. Yarbrough. We are also grateful to Rachel Bronson, Matthias Kaelberer, and Hank Torbert for research assistance. In conducting this research, Gowa was assisted by awards from the Social Science Research Council of a MacArthur Foundation Fellowship in International Security and the Peter B. Lewis Family Fund and the Boesky Family Fund of the Center for International Studies at Princeton University; Mansfield was assisted by a grant from the Columbia University Council for Research in the Social Sciences.

1. Disagreement continues about the source of this preference ranking, however. Some attribute it to the public good character of international trade (e.g., Kindleberger 1973); others attribute it to the ability of states to exercise monopoly or monopsony power in world markets (Conybeare 1984). Still others contend that the trade game can be a coordination game (Snidal 1985).

2. Our argument and analysis are limited to the influence on trade of system-level variables. For incisive analyses of the domestic determinants of tariffs, see Frieden 1988; Magee, Brock, and Young 1989; and Ruggie 1982.

3. The voluminous literature on economic statecraft at the microeconomic level that now exists partly explains our decision to focus this analysis at the macroeconomic level. The decision, however, was also the product of the almost insuperable obstacles that confront any attempts at embargo, probably the most common form of microeconomic statecraft. For a good discussion, see Bayard, Pelzman, and Lopez 1983.

4. Externalities are uncompensated costs or benefits that an agent inflicts or confers on third parties.

5. This divergence arises because those whose actions generate externalities have no incentive to take these external effects into account. Thus, if an individual's actions produce diseconomies, for example, he will engage in them to a socially suboptimal extent. For a more detailed explanation, see Yeager and Tureck 1983/84, 661.

6. We use tariffs here as a substitute for several forms of government intervention in trade. Because of constraints imposed by the General Agreement on Tariffs and Trade, government intervention in trade now usually takes the form of nontariff barriers. As long as the home country captures the scarcity rents that accrue from trade barriers, the form in which intervention occurs does not affect the argument presented here.

7. The theory of the second best applies to most national security arguments for government intervention in trade: the latter usually imposes higher costs on national welfare than do policies that target the distortion directly. For example, if production in an import-competing industry is judged inadequate on national security grounds, the Pareto-optimal policy is a production subsidy (Corden 1986). The general principle, as Deardorff and Stern observe, "is that trade intervention, by introducing two distortions rather than one, may succeed in solving one problem but only at the same time that it causes another. Trade policy is like doing acupuncture with a fork: no matter how carefully you insert one prong, the other is likely to do damage" (1987, 39).

8. That is, a player is better off defecting regardless of what the other player does.

9. If incomplete information of a specific kind exists in a finite prisoner's dilemma game, however, it is possible for mutual cooperation to emerge on at least some plays of the game. See Kreps et al. 1982.

10. As the Folk theorem states, if the horizon is infinite and the actors are very patient, *any* individually rational outcome can be sustained (Fudenberg and Maskin 1986).

11. In a context in which deviations are perfectly observable, maximal punishment makes sense, because it never occurs on the equilibrium path. It is, therefore, costless (Tirole 1988, 252). Moreover, unlike Tit for Tat, a grim strategy is subgame perfect (i.e., it is rational for the players to follow the specified strategies if any defection occurs) (Rasmusen 1989, 91).

It is not, however, renegotiation-proof (i.e., if one player defects and the players have the opportunity to renegotiate, they will abandon the punishment strategy in favor of one that confers higher payoffs.) A Pareto-perfect or weakly renegotiation-proof strategy is a "penance" strategy: begin with cooperation; if a deviation occurs, the deviator cooperates and the other player defects; the players then revert to cooperation (Fudenberg and Tirole 1991, 179–82). We use a grim strategy here for two reasons: (1) it is more accessible; and more importantly, (2) our results do not change if a penance strategy is used.

12. The discount factor, $\delta$, is "the value in present payoff units of one payoff unit to be received one period from the present." It reflects both the rate of time preference, $\rho$, and the probability that the game will end, $\Theta$. The discount factor is $(1 - \Theta)/(1 + \rho)$ (Rasmusen 1989, 90). Thus, the discounted sum of an infinite series of payoffs, x, received at the beginning of each period is: (x) $(1 - \Theta)/(1 + \rho)$.

13. Even though much progress has been made, com-

pletely free trade remains elusive. Nonetheless, the GATT has clearly facilitated the process of lowering trade barriers among its member countries. Yarbrough and Yarbrough (1992) argue, however, that it is not grim strategies but third-party (i.e., U.S.) enforcement that has deterred states from defecting from GATT agreements. For a dramatic comparison of the postwar and interwar periods, see Oye 1992.

14. Adapted from Snidal 1991.

15. The game will remain a prisoner's dilemma as long as $0 \leq w < 1$.

16. We distinguish bipolar and multipolar systems here in terms of the number of great powers that exist in any given system (Snyder and Diesing 1977, 419–20; Waltz 1979). We do not mean to imply, however, that polarity is either the only, or necessarily the most important, aspect of the distribution of power. Other aspects, especially the concentration of power, might also influence the relationship between alliances and trade (Mansfield n.d.).

17. Empirical analyses support this assertion. See, e.g., Duncan and Siverson 1982.

18. It should be noted that Pollins's (1989a, 1989b) analyses take account of the effects of alliances on trade to the extent that a "major strategic alliance" is considered a cooperative "event" in the data that he uses (see Azar 1980; Polachek 1980, 58, n. 5). However, since Pollins's objective is to assess the effects of aggregate levels of conflict and cooperation on trade, he does not disaggregate the influence of various types of cooperative events, such as alliances.

19. Of course, trade barriers and trade flows need not always move in tandem. Tariffs, for example, may not be completely endogenized if demand is infinitely inelastic with respect to price. In addition, the 1970s witnessed the expansion of both trade barriers and trade flows. However, once we control for other determinants of trade, we would expect these variables to be directly related; and this approach should therefore provide a useful first cut at the problem.

20. For the period after World War II, we analyze West Germany; for the period before 1917, Russia. In order to simplify the presentation, however, we refer only to "Germany" and "the Soviet Union" in the text.

21. Small countries are excluded from this study, in addition, because they would not ordinarily be expected to be able to influence their terms of trade.

22. For the period from 1938 to 1985, all data on exports are taken from the International Monetary Fund's *Direction of Trade* for the years 1950, 1956, 1966, 1976, and 1986. For the period from 1905 to 1930, data are taken from Cacciapuoti 1928, 87–90; Clarke and Matko 1983, 62–73; France, Bureau de la Statistique Generale 1923, 236; League of Nations 1926, vol. 1, 218–39 and 1933, 328–48; Liesner 1989; Mitchell 1980, 1982, 1983; U.S. Bureau of the Census 1915, 330–37, 355–56; and U.S. Department of Commerce 1934—and also from the Commerce Department's *Foreign Commerce and Navigation of the United States* for 1914, 1921, and 1931 (pp. 7–8, 5–12, and 6–14, respectively) and the Japanese Finance Department's *Annual Return of the Foreign Trade of the Empire of Japan* for the years 1905 and 1920. In those cases where exports are not denominated in U.S. dollars, exchange rates are taken from Bidwell 1970; Liesner 1989, 54–55; and the Treasury Department's *Circulars* for the years 1904–5, 1912–13, and 1919–20.

It should also be pointed out that in some cases, exports by state i to state j are not available. However, in these cases, it is usually possible to find data on imports by j from i. Since these values should be equal, we convert imports in j's currency into U.S. dollars and use these data as measures of exports from i to j. When we do so, we should adjust the data to reflect the fact that the value of imports reported sometimes includes transportation costs. We do not do so, however, because our sources do not uniformly report on whether or not import data are net of transportation costs.

23. Data on nominal GNP for the period from 1904 to 1929 are taken from Gregory 1982; Liesner 1989; and Mitchell 1980, 1982, 1983. In certain cases, reliable data on Soviet and French GNP are not available. In these cases, GNP is estimated using data in Bairoch 1976; Gregory 1982; and Mitchell 1980. Data on nominal GNP and exchange rates for the period from 1937 to 1984 are taken from the United Nations' *Yearbook of National Account Statistics* for the years 1948, 1955, 1965, 1975, and 1985. For exchange rate data covering the period prior to 1937, see n. 22.

24. All data on national population are taken from Correlates of War Project 1991. It should be noted that since no data on West German population are available for 1954, we use data for 1955.

25. Data on geographical distances are found in Fitzpatrick and Modlin 1986 and the U.S. Hydrographic Office's *Table of Distances in Nautical and Statute Miles* for 1912 and 1936 and *Distance between Ports* for 1965 and 1989. For each pair of states, the shortest distance between ports or rail centers was used to measure the distance between states i and j.

26. Throughout this study, Small and Singer's (1969) data on alliances are used. We consider any defense pact, neutrality or nonaggression pact, or entente that is listed by Small and Singer to be an alliance. Because the purpose of Small and Singer's study was to explain war, they excluded all wartime alliances from their data. As they themselves observed, however, if their data are used for other purposes, the list of alliances should be amended correspondingly (p. 262). Thus, we also include as allies any states that fought on the same side of any interstate war, as listed by either Levy (1983) or Small and Singer (1982). For present purposes, this results in the inclusion of one multilateral alliance among Great Britain, France, Japan, and the United States in 1919, when these states participated in the Russian Civil War (Levy 1983). We also code the Japanese–United States Security Treaty (1951–60) and the subsequent Treaty of Mutual Cooperation and Security between these states (1960–present) as alliances. Among other things, these treaties called for the United States to come to the aid of Japan in the event that it was attacked (see Grenville 1974, 270, 286–87). As a result, they served much the same purpose as an alliance.

27. In this study, any war that is listed by either Levy (1983) or Small and Singer (1982) is analyzed. It might be expected that wars would exert a contemporaneous, as well as a lagged, effect on trade. Since both of the wars considered in this study were being waged in year t, as well as year $t - 1$, any contemporaneous effect these wars might have on trade will be captured by our model. Further, it should be noted that only one war (the Changkufeng War, 1938) would be added to our list of wars if we measured this variable in year t, rather than year $t - 1$.

28. While this strategy avoids potential problems of simultaneity, it is, of course, possible that the relationship between trade and alliances is multidirectional. Although it would also be useful to assess the effect of trade on alliance patterns, developing an adequate model of alliances is clearly beyond our scope here.

29. Outliers were identified based on the value of studentized residuals (see Fox 1991, 25–29; Maddala 1988, 412–17). Space limitations preclude us from presenting the results here both with and without outliers. The complete set of results for all the analyses in this paper can be found in Gowa (n.d.).

30. In regression analyses of this sort, it is important to ensure that the errors are not heteroscedastic. The results of White tests yielded no evidence of heteroscedasticity for any of estimates reported in this study. See Maddala 1988, 162–63; White 1980.

31. Assuming that this condition obtains, the standard error of the mean ($s(\bar{x})$) of the regression coefficients of log $BA_{ij}$ is estimated by

$$s(\bar{x}) = \sqrt{\frac{\sum_{i=1}^{n} s_i^2}{n^2}},$$

where $s_i^2$ is the estimated variance of the $i^{th}$ regression coefficient of log $BA_{ij}$ and n is the number of cross sections for which this regression coefficient is estimated.

32. See n. 31.

33. In antilogarithmic form, equation 1 can be expressed as

$$X_{ij(t)} = AY^{B1}_{i(t-1)}\, Y^{B2}_{j(t-1)}\, P^{B3}_{i(t-1)}\, P^{B4}_{j(t-1)}\, D^{B5}_{ij(t-1)}\, BA^{B6}_{ij(t-1)}\, MA^{B7}_{ij(t-1)}\, War^{B8}_{ij(t-1)}\, z_{ij},$$

where $BA_{ij(t-1)}$ is a dummy variable that equals e (the base of the natural logarithms) if a bilateral alliance exists between states i and j in year t − 1, and 1 otherwise. It is clear that if $BA_{ij(t-1)} = 1$ (and $\log BA_{ij(t-1)} = 0$), then

$$X_{ij(t)} = AY^{B1}_{i(t-1)}\, Y^{B2}_{j(t-1)}\, P^{B3}_{i(t-1)}\, P^{B4}_{j(t-1)}\, D^{B5}_{ij(t-1)}\, 1^{B6}\, MA^{B7}_{ij(t-1)}\, War^{B8}_{ij(t-1)}\, z_{ij}.$$

On the other hand, if $BA_{ij(t-1)} = e$ (and $\log BA_{ij(t-1)} = 1$), then

$$X_{ij(t)} = AY^{B1}_{i(t-1)}\, Y^{B2}_{j(t-1)}\, P^{B3}_{i(t-1)}\, P^{B4}_{j(t-1)}\, D^{B5}_{ij(t-1)}\, e^{B6}\, MA^{B7}_{ij(t-1)}\, War^{B8}_{ij(t-1)}\, z_{ij}.$$

As a result, the proportional increase in the predicted value of exports by state i if there exists a bilateral alliance between states i and j (rather than no bilateral alliance between them) is equal to $e^{B6}$ minus one. Since the mean of $B_6$ in Table 1 is about 1.09 and the standard error of the mean is about .15, if the mean was two standard errors less than 1.09, it would equal .79. And since $e^{.79} = 2.20$, the average effect of the change from the absence of a bilateral alliance between states i and j to the existence of such an alliance is to increase the predicted value of exports from i to j by 120%, when the remaining variables in the model are held constant.

34. See n. 33. This is the case, since $e^{.29} = 1.34$.

35. See n. 29.

36. For two reasons, we do not examine the effects of the GATT in 1955: (1) all of the states in our sample that were GATT members in 1954 (year t − 1) were also NATO members; and (2) for balance-of-payments reasons, several European members of the GATT had imposed quotas on imports from the dollar area.

## References


Aitken, Norman D. 1973. "The Effect of the EEC and EFTA on European Trade: A Temporal and Cross-Section Analysis." *American Economic Review* 63:881–92.

Anderson, James E. 1979. "A Theoretical Foundation for the Gravity Equation." *American Economic Review* 69:106–16.

Azar, Edward. 1980. "The Conflict and Peace Data Bank (COPDAB) Project." *Journal of Conflict Resolution* 24:143–52.

Bairoch, Paul. 1976. "Europe's Gross National Product, 1800–1975." *Journal of European Economic History* 5:273–340.

Baldwin, David A. 1985. *Economic Statecraft*. Princeton: Princeton University Press.

Bayard, Thomas O., Joseph Pelzman, and Jorge Perez Lopez. 1983. "Stakes and Risks in Economic Sanctions." *World Economy* 6:73–88.

Bidwell, R. L. 1970. *Currency Conversion Tables: A Hundred Years of Change*. London: Collings.

Cacciapuoti, Vincenzo. 1928. *Relazioni commerciali tra l'Italia e la Russia, 1878–1927*. Napoli: N. Jovenej.

Clarke, Roger A., and Dubravko J. I. Matko. 1983. *Soviet Economic Facts, 1917–1981*. 2d ed. New York: St. Martin's.

Conybeare, John A. C. 1984. "Public Goods, Prisoners' Dilemmas, and the International Political Economy." *International Studies Quarterly* 28:5–22.

Corden, Max. 1986. "The Normative Theory of International Trade." In *International Trade: Surveys of Theory and Policy*, ed. Ronald W. Jones. Amsterdam: North-Holland.

Correlates of War Project. 1991. *National Material Capabilities Data*. Ann Arbor: University of Michigan.

Deardorff, Alan V. 1984. "Testing Trade Theories and Predicting Trade Flows." In *Handbook of International Economics*, ed. Ronald W. Jones and P. B. Kenen. Amsterdam: North-Holland.

Deardorff, Alan V., and Robert M. Stern. 1987. "Current Issues in Trade Policy: An Overview." In *U.S. Trade Policies in a Changing World Economy*, ed. Robert Stern. Cambridge: Massachusetts Institute of Technology Press.

Doyle, Michael W. 1986. "Liberalism and World Politics." *American Political Science Review* 80:1151–69.

Duncan, George T., and Randolph M. Siverson. 1982. "Flexibility of Alliance Partner Choice in a Multipolar System: Models and Tests." *International Studies Quarterly* 26:511–38.

Fitzpatrick, Gary L., and Marilyn J. Modlin. 1986. *Direct-Line Distances*. Internat'l ed. Metuchen, NJ: Scarecrow.

Fox, John. 1991. *Regression Diagnostics*. Beverly Hills: Sage.

France. Bureau de la Statistique Generale. 1923. *Annuare statistique de la France*. Paris: Ministere du Commerce de l'Industy des Postes et des Telegraphs.

Frankel, Jeffrey A. 1992. "Is Japan Creating a Yen Bloc in East Asia and the Pacific?" Presented at the National Bureau of Economic Research conference, Japan and the United States in Pacific Asia, Del Mar, CA.

Frieden, Jeff. 1988. "Sectoral Conflict and U.S. Foreign Economic Policy." *International Organization* 42:59–90.

Fudenberg, Drew, and E. Maskin. 1986. "The Folk Theorem in Repeated Games with Discounting and Incomplete Information." *Econometrica* 52:87–100.

Fudenberg, Drew, and Jean Tirole. 1991. *Game Theory*. Cambridge: Massachusetts Institute of Technology Press.

Gochman, Charles S., and Zeev Maoz. 1984. "Militarized Interstate Disputes, 1816–1976: Procedures, Patterns, and Insights." *Journal of Conflict Resolution* 28:585–616.

Gowa, Joanne. 1989. "Bipolarity, Multipolarity, and Free Trade." *American Political Science Review* 83:1245–56.

Gowa, Joanne. N.d. *Allies, Adversaries, and International Trade*. Princeton: Princeton University Press. Forthcoming.

Gregory, Paul R. 1982. *Russian National Income, 1885–1913*. New York: Cambridge University Press.

Grenville, J. A. S. 1974. *The Major International Treaties 1914–1973*. London: Methuen.

Hirschman, Albert O. 1980. *National Power and the Structure of Foreign Trade*. Berkeley: University of California Press.

Keohane, Robert O. 1984. *After Hegemony: Cooperation and Discord in the World Political Economy*. Princeton: Princeton University Press.

Kindleberger, Charles P. 1973. *The World in Depression, 1929–1939*. Berkeley: University of California Press.

Kreps, David M., Paul Milgrom, John Roberts, and Robert Wilson. 1982. "Rational Cooperation in the Finitely Repeated Prisoners' Dilemma." *Journal of Economic Theory* 27:245–52.

League of Nations. 1926. *Memorandum on the Balance of Payments and Foreign Trade Balances, 1911–1925*. Geneva: League of Nations.

League of Nations. 1933. *International Trade Statistics, 1931 and 1932*. Geneva: League of Nations.

Leamer, Edward E., and Robert M. Stern. 1970. *Quantitative International Economics*. Boston: Allyn & Bacon.

Levy, Jack S. 1983. *War in the Modern Great Power System, 1495–1975*. Lexington: University Press of Kentucky.

Liesner, Thelma. 1989. *One Hundred Years of Economic Statistics*. Rev. ed. New York: Economist.

Linnemann, Hans. 1966. *An Econometric Study of International Trade Flows*. Amsterdam: North-Holland.

McKeown, Timothy J. 1982. "The Rise and Decline of the Open Trading Regime of the Nineteenth Century." Ph.D. diss. Stanford University.

McKeown, Timothy J. 1984. "Firms and Tariff Regime Change: Explaining the Demand for Protection." *World Politics* 36:215–33.

Maddala, G. S. 1988. *Introduction to Econometrics*. New York: Macmillan.

Magee, Stephen P., William A. Brock, and Leslie Young. 1989. *Black Hole Tariffs and Endogenous Policy Theory: Political Economy in General Equilibrium*. New York: Cambridge University Press.

Mansfield, Edward D. 1993. "The Effects of International Politics on Regionalism in International Trade." In *Regional Integration and the Global Trading System*. Eds. Kym Ander-

son and Richard Blackhurst. London: Harvester Wheatsheaf.
Mansfield, Edward D. N.d. *Power, Trade, and War*. Princeton: Princeton University Press. Forthcoming.
Mitchell, Brian R. 1980. *European Historical Statistics, 1750–1975*. London: Butler & Tanner.
Mitchell, Brian R. 1982. *International Historical Statistics: Africa and Asia*. New York: New York University Press.
Mitchell, Brian R. 1983. *International Historical Statistics: The Americas and Australia*. Detroit: Gale Research.
Oye, Kenneth A. 1992. *Economic Discrimination and Political Exchange: World Political Economy in the 1930s and 1980s*. Princeton: Princeton University Press.
Pelzman, Joseph. 1977. "Trade Creation and Trade Diversion in the Council of Mutual Economic Assistance: 1954–1970." *American Economic Review* 67:713–22.
Polachek, Solomon W. 1980. "Conflict and Trade." *Journal of Conflict Resolution* 24:55–78.
Pollins, Brian M. 1989a. "Does Trade Still Follow the Flag?" *American Political Science Review* 83:465–80.
Pollins, Brian M. 1989b. "Conflict, Cooperation, and Commerce: The Effects of International Political Interactions on Bilateral Trade Flows." *American Journal of Political Science* 33:737–61.
Powell, Robert. 1991. "Relative and Absolute Gains in International Relations." *American Political Science Review* 85: 1303–20.
Rasmusen, Eric. 1989. *Games and Information: An Introduction to Game Theory*. New York: Basil Blackwell.
Root, William A. 1984. "Trade Controls That Work." *Foreign Policy* 56:61–80.
Ruggie, John Gerard. 1982. "International Regimes, Transactions, and Change: Embedded Liberalism in the Postwar Economic Order." *International Organization* 36:379–415.
Siverson, Randolph M., and Juliann Emmons. 1991. "Birds of a Feather: Democratic Political Systems and Alliance Choices in the Twentieth Century." *Journal of Conflict Resolution* 35:285–306.
Small, Melvin, and J. David Singer. 1969. "Formal Alliances, 1816–1965: An Extension of the Basic Data." *Journal of Peace Research* 3:257–82.
Small, Melvin, and J. David Singer. 1982. *Resort to Arms: International and Civil Wars, 1816–1980*. Beverly Hills: Sage.
Snidal, Duncan. 1985. "Coordination Versus Prisoners' Dilemma: Implications for International Cooperation and Regimes." *American Political Science Review* 79:923–42.
Snidal, Duncan. 1991. "Relative Gains and the Pattern of International Cooperation." *American Political Science Review* 85:701–26.
Snyder, Glenn H. 1984. "The Security Dilemma in Alliance Politics." *World Politics* 36:461–95.
Snyder, Glenn H., and Paul Diesing. 1977. *Conflict among Nations: Bargaining, Decision Making, and System Structure in International Crises*. Princeton: Princeton University Press.
Srinivasan, T. N. 1987. "The National Defense Argument for Government Intervention in Foreign Trade." In *U.S. Trade Policies in a Changing World Economy*, ed. Robert M. Stern. Cambridge: Massachusetts Institute of Technology Press.
Tinbergen, Jan. 1962. *Shaping the World Economy: Suggestions for an International Economic Policy*. New York: Twentieth Century Fund.
Tirole, Jean. 1988. *Industrial Organization*. Cambridge: Massachusetts Institute of Technology Press.
U.S. Bureau of the Census. 1915. *Statistical Abstracts of the United States*. Washington: GPO.
U.S. Department of Commerce. 1934. *Foreign Commerce Yearbook, 1933*. Washington: GPO.
Waltz, Kenneth. 1979. *Theory of International Politics*. Reading: Addison-Wesley.
White, Halbert. 1980. "A Heteroskedasticity-Consistent Covariance Matrix Estimator and a Direct Test for Heteroskedasticity." *Econometrica* 48:817–38.
Yarbrough, Beth V., and Robert M. Yarbrough. 1992. *Cooperation and Governance in International Trade: The Strategic Organizational Approach*. Princeton: Princeton University Press.
Yeager, Leland B., and David G. Tureck. 1983/84. "Realism and Free-Trade Policy." *Cato Journal* 3:645–66.

Joanne Gowa is Professor of Politics, Princeton University, Princeton, NJ 08544.

Edward D. Mansfield is Assistant Professor of Political Science, Columbia University, New York, NY 10027.

# Alliances, Preferential Trading Arrangements, and International Trade

EDWARD D. MANSFIELD *Ohio State University*
RACHEL BRONSON *Columbia University*

*We analyze the effects of alliances and preferential trading arrangements on bilateral trade flows. Both factors are likely to promote trade among members, but we argue that the interaction between them is central to explaining patterns of commerce. The combination of an alliance, which creates political incentives for participants to engage in trade, and a commercial institution, which liberalizes trade among members, is expected to provide a considerable impetus to commerce among parties to both. The results of our quantitative analyses support these arguments. Both alliances and preferential trading arrangements strongly affected trade from 1960 to 1990, and allies that included a major power conducted considerably more trade than their nonmajor-power counterparts. Moreover, the interaction between alliances and preferential trading arrangements is fundamental to explaining patterns of bilateral commerce: Parties to a common preferential trading arrangement and a common alliance engage in markedly greater trade than do members of either type of institution but not both.*

Concerns about the stability of the international trading system have become widespread in recent years. Many observers feel that the relatively liberal system forged after World War II is being undermined by the proliferation of preferential trading arrangements. These concerns have spawned a great deal of empirical research, much of which has found that such arrangements exert a substantial effect on trade flows. Yet, these studies have neglected the role political-military alliances play in shaping patterns of commerce. This omission is important because there is ample reason to expect that alliances guide trade flows, and preferential trading arrangements often are comprised of allies. As a result, extant analyses risk confusing the effects of alliances and preferential trading arrangements on commerce and systematically overstating the effects of the latter.

In this study, we analyze the effects of alliances and preferential trading arrangements on bilateral trade flows. Both factors are likely to promote trade among members, but we argue that the interaction between them is central to explaining patterns of commerce. The combination of an alliance, which creates political incentives for participants to engage in trade, and a commercial institution, which liberalizes trade among members, is expected to provide a considerable impetus to commerce among parties to both.[1]

Our quantitative analysis supports these arguments. We find that both alliances and preferential trading arrangements strongly affected trade from 1960 to 1990, and that allies that included a major power conducted considerably more trade than their nonmajor-power counterparts. Moreover, the interaction between alliances and preferential trading arrangements is fundamental to explaining patterns of bilateral commerce: Parties to a common preferential trading arrangement and a common alliance engage in markedly greater trade than do members of either type of institution but not both.

## ALLIANCES AND TRADE

The effects of alliances on commerce emanate from the incentives of both governments and firms. Governments have an incentive to liberalize trade with allies because the efficiency gains from trade yield increases in national income that can be used to augment states' military power. As a result, trade generates security externalities (Gowa 1994).[2] Since the anarchic nature of the international system places pressure on states to attend to the power of others (Waltz 1979), they cannot ignore these security externalities without bearing substantial risks.

Open trade is much more likely to evolve among allies than among adversaries. Trade among allies is likely to enhance the security of all the parties; the gains from trade accrue to states with common security goals and bolster the aggregate political-military power of the alliance. In contrast, open trade among adversaries produces negative security externalities. A state that trades with an adversary augments the national income of its trading partner, thereby threatening to undermine its own security.[3] Especially among states

Edward D. Mansfield is Associate Professor of Political Science, Ohio State University, Columbus, OH 43210-1373. Rachel Bronson is a Ph.D. candidate in the Department of Political Science, Columbia University, New York, NY 10027.

Earlier versions of this paper were presented at the annual meeting of the American Political Science Association, September 1–4, 1994, New York, NY; and at seminars at several universities: Chicago (PIPES), Columbia, Cornell, Harvard, Ohio State, Pennsylvania, and Princeton. We are grateful to seminar participants and Jagdish Bhagwati, Xinyuan Dai, Jeffrey Frankel, Joanne Gowa, John Hartman, Arvid Lukauskas, Walter Mattli, Timothy McKeown, Helen Milner, Kenneth Oye, and Robert Shapiro for helpful comments; to Lynn Jacobsen, Salvatore Pittruzello, and Susan Zayak for computer programming assistance; and to Gina Marie Finan and Joe McGarvey for research assistance.

[1] By virtue of our focus on alliances and preferential trading arrangements, our analysis is cast at the systemic level. Although various studies emphasize the domestic determinants of trade (e.g., Cohen 1990, Frieden 1988, Rogowski 1989), it is beyond the scope of this paper to examine these factors.

[2] Security externalities are uncompensated benefits or costs that influence the security of one actor due to the actions of another actor. For a more extensive discussion of this issue, see Gowa 1994.

[3] A state may have an incentive to trade with an adversary if, for example, it anticipates realizing very large gains from trade or

with sufficient market power to influence their terms of trade, governments are expected to discriminate in their foreign economic policies between allies and adversaries (Gowa 1994).

Private traders and investors have incentives to behave in a manner consistent with these government policies. All other things being equal, trade barriers imposed on a product increase its local price, thereby reducing local demand for it by private traders and other consumers. Since governments are more likely to impose trade barriers on the goods of adversaries than on those of allies, local demand for adversaries' goods is likely to be less than that for allies' goods.

In addition, many investments by firms are relation specific, that is, they are made to support a particular transaction with a particular partner (Williamson 1985, 54; Yarbrough and Yarbrough 1992, 25). As Yarbrough and Yarbrough (1992, 28) have pointed out, investments in relation-specific assets "are common in international trade, because the process of specialization according to comparative advantage involves investment in increased productive capacity designed to service export markets." Many observers also argue that such investments have become increasingly pervasive.[4]

Among relation-specific investments related to international trade are those made in facilities designed to transport goods to a specific market, those made in dedicated assets to produce goods for a specific market, and those made to create vertically integrated production facilities across states. For example, a Japanese automobile manufacturer may invest in a plant or technology to meet the specific demands of U.S. consumers. Similarly, a firm located in one country that invests in raw materials may vertically integrate its production facilities by investing in a plant to process these materials that is located in a foreign country where the processing can be conducted most efficiently. In both cases, firms have undertaken investments to support a specific relationship. The costs of shifting the assets in which these firms have invested to their best alternative uses therefore are likely to be high, and their value depends in part on the continuity of the particular relationship for which they are designed (Williamson 1985, 55).

Particularly important for our purposes is the disproportionate susceptibility of relation-specific investments—and the trade flows they generate—to opportunistic behavior by foreign governments.[5] Investors face the risk that a foreign government will take actions, such as imposing new or raising existing trade barriers, which degrade the value of these investments.

Alliances can help regulate opportunism by foreign governments. Because open trade among allies promotes the security of members, governments have less incentive to behave opportunistically toward their allies' firms than toward firms of other states. Thus, private agents reduce the likelihood of opportunism—and enhance the expected profitability of investments—by investing in relation-specific assets to service allies' markets. Similarly, governments have incentives to engage in opportunistic behavior toward their adversaries' firms, since doing so helps to redress the security externalities arising from trade. Firms face heightened risks, including the possibility that a foreign government will raise its trade barriers or even expropriate dedicated assets located within its borders, if they make investments to service adversaries' markets.[6] Furthermore, as the experience of the Coordinating Committee for Multilateral Export Controls (COCOM) illustrates, firms' ability to conduct business abroad can be limited by government actions if they prefer to trade with an adversary (Mastanduno 1992). For these reasons, firms and private traders are expected to conduct more trade with agents located in states that are allies of their home government than with those located in states that are adversaries.

## PREFERENTIAL TRADING ARRANGEMENTS, MAJOR POWERS, AND TRADE

Two factors are likely to influence the magnitude of the relationship between alliances and trade. The first concerns whether allies also are members of a common preferential trading arrangement; the second concerns whether at least one of them is a major power.

That preferential trading arrangements are likely to facilitate trade among members is hardly controversial. Such arrangements refer to agreements stipulating that states impose lower levels of protection on members' goods than on the goods of third parties. These agreements may take the form of free trade areas, customs unions, common markets, and economic unions. While differences exist among these commercial arrangements, common to all of them is "the reciprocal nature of the preferential treatment which the participants accord to one another" (Anderson and Blackhurst 1993, 5).

Yarbrough and Yarbrough (1992) argue that preferential trading arrangements provide an institutional means of governing opportunism. Like alliances, preferential trading arrangements are likely to promote relation-specific investments by private agents, which in

promoting the competitiveness of domestic industries that are central to its security. Unless both this state and its adversary expect trade to have no influence on the distribution of power between them, however, the party that expects to gain less from trade (and therefore to experience a deterioration in its relative power) will have an incentive to limit commerce.

[4] For example, it has been argued that intrafirm trade is a good measure of trade involving relation-specific investments, and there is considerable evidence that intrafirm trade constitutes a substantial portion of international commerce and has been growing (McKeown 1991, 165–8; Yarbrough and Yarbrough 1992, 32).

[5] Of course, foreign firms also may engage in opportunistic behavior, an issue taken up by Williamson (1985) and Yarbrough and Yarbrough (1992, 34).

[6] This argument is consistent with the view that private traders are likely to "take account not only of price and quality of goods and services but of the place of origin of these products and the political relationship between them" (Pollins 1989a, 738). In addition, Pollins (1989a, 1989b) argues that private agents may prefer to reward actors in states that they perceive to be politically friendly and punish actors located in hostile states. This also suggests that trade will be greater between allies than adversaries.

turn spur commerce among participants. More generally, it seems clear that, all other things being equal, preferential treatment is likely to facilitate the flow of trade among members. Less clear, however, is the extent to which preferential arrangements foster trade and the relative importance of alliances and preferential trading arrangements in this regard.

In addition to the separate effects of alliances and preferential trading arrangements on commerce, there is reason to expect that trade will be especially open between states that are both allies and members of a preferential trading arrangement. To the extent that the latter facilitates the use of strategies of contingent cooperation, and since this type of arrangement often is explicitly designed to reduce trade barriers, the combination of an alliance and a preferential trading arrangement provides multiple and reinforcing incentives for states to liberalize commerce and for firms to make relation-specific investments to serve foreign markets, thereby generating greater trade among members than does either type of institution alone.

Besides preferential trading arrangements, the presence of a major power also is likely to influence the relationship between alliances and trade. As noted earlier, the effects of alliances on trade are expected to be heightened among states with the ability to impose an optimal tariff. States that can degrade the national income of an adversary have little incentive to liberalize trade with it, since doing so only serves to undermine their security. In contrast, such states do have an incentive to liberalize trade with an ally, since an optimal tariff redistributes the gains from trade to them but eliminates these gains altogether for their trading partner, thereby undermining the alliance's strength. Major powers are likely to possess some monopoly power in trade (Gowa 1994, Gowa and Mansfield 1993); hence, the effects on trade flows of alliances involving them are likely to be especially pronounced.

Alliances including major powers also are likely to enhance openness among members because these alliances tend to be more durable and stable than those comprised solely of weaker states. By virtue of major powers' disproportionate strength, alliances involving them often exhibit an especially skewed distribution of power, a characteristic that has been linked to heightened alliance durability and stability (e.g., Morrow 1990).

Consistent with this argument, Gaubatz (1996) found that alliances involving major powers were significantly more durable than other alliances from 1816 to 1965. The results of a preliminary test indicate that major-power alliances also have been more durable than other alliances during the period after World War II, the era on which we focus in this paper. The analyses of alliances and major powers conducted here are based on Small and Singer's (1969, 1982, 44–5) data and updates of them compiled by the Correlates of War (COW) Project. To assess the durability of major-power alliances after World War II, we code each alliance identified by Small and Singer that was formed during this era based on whether it includes at least one major power. We then compare the average duration of alliances that include a major power with the average duration of those that do not.[7] Our results indicate that major-power alliances tend to last about twice as long as other alliances and that this difference is statistically significant ($t = 4.33$, $p < .005$).

While all alliances are expected to promote trade among members, the disproportionate durability of major-power alliances is likely to bolster their effect on trade because members are likely to discount less heavily the future benefits arising from intraalliance trade than do members of other alliances. The relative longevity of major-power alliances and the dearth of such alliances among which members typically can relocate reduce the risk of exit by members. Consequently, these factors limit the likelihood that today's ally will become tomorrow's foe and turn its augmented power, derived from prior intraalliance trade, against its former confederates. These factors also limit the risks faced by investors that the governments of current allies will shift political alignments and threaten their relation-specific assets by engaging in opportunism in the near future. Alliances involving major powers therefore should be advantaged in their ability to promote trade among members.[8]

In sum, we expect that international trade is likely to be greater when trading partners are allies or members of a preferential trading arrangement than when neither of these conditions is met. We expect that commerce will be greater still when both of these conditions obtain and when trading partners are allies and include a major power. We expect that trade will be greatest among states that are allies, members of a preferential trading arrangement, and include a major power.

## PREVIOUS EMPIRICAL STUDIES

The existing empirical research bearing on these topics centers primarily on the effects of preferential trading arrangements on bilateral trade flows. Studies of this sort usually conclude that preferential trading arrangements increase the flow of trade among members, although the strength of these effects varies among commercial arrangements (Aitken 1973, Brada and Mendez 1983, Eichengreen and Irwin 1995, Frankel 1993, Linnemann 1966, Pelzman 1977, Pollins 1989a, Tinbergen 1962, Winters and Wang 1994). Yet, these studies rarely emphasize other "noneconomic" determinants of trade, which leads them to ignore the effects of alliances and other political factors. Since preferential trading arrangements often are comprised of allies (Mansfield 1993), these analyses risk confusing the

[7] Because many alliances are still in effect, it is not possible to measure their duration. For the purpose of this rough test, alliances still in effect as of 1993 (the last year for which data are available) are coded as ending in this year. Like Morrow's (1990, 921) analysis of alliance durability, "each alliance is treated as a whole and is not decomposed into dyads of allies."

[8] In addition, like the United States after World War II, major powers often have the economic capacity to provide aid and investment that may promote trade with weaker states (Freeland 1985).

effects of alliances and preferential trading arrangements. In so doing, they are likely to yield biased estimates of preferential trading arrangements' effects on trade flows and, hence, to offer a distorted view of the political economy of international trade.

Many empirical studies of the international political influences on trade focus on diplomatic cooperation and conflict between states. Polachek (1980, Gasiorowski and Polachek 1982), for example, argues that utility-maximizing actors tend to engage in cooperative relations with trading partners because of the opportunity costs associated with forgoing trade in the event of conflict. In the only studies bearing directly on this topic, Pollins (1989a, 1989b) examined the effects of preferential trading arrangements and diplomatic cooperation and conflict on bilateral trade flows. He found that cooperation promotes trade, but he also observed that his model may not account for variations in trade patterns between allies and adversaries or between major powers and other states (Pollins 1989a, 757). Indeed, since there is evidence that allies frequently engage in political conflicts (e.g., Bueno de Mesquita 1981), it is important to isolate the effects of alliances on trade rather than infer them from studies focusing on the effects of political cooperation and conflict.

A few studies have examined the effects of alliances on bilateral trade flows (Gowa 1994, Gowa and Mansfield 1993, Mansfield and Bronson 1997, Summary 1989), but they focused on trade involving major powers. As we argued above, it is important to determine the extent to which the strength and magnitude of the relationship between alliances and trade depend on whether the commercial partners are major powers. Furthermore, these studies did not examine the interactions among alliances, preferential trading arrangements, and major powers, an issue that is central to our analysis.

## THE MODEL

In order to test the hypotheses described earlier, we begin with a gravity model, which has become a standard framework for explaining patterns of bilateral trade (e.g., Aitken 1973; Anderson 1979; Deardorff 1984, 503–4; Frankel 1993; Gowa 1994; Gowa and Mansfield 1993; Leamer and Stern 1970, 145–70; Linnemann 1966; Pelzman 1977; Pollins 1989a; Tinbergen 1962; Winters and Wang 1994). The gravity model describes trade flows between a given pair of states in terms of factors that influence the supply of exports in one country, factors that affect the demand for imports in the other, and factors that impede or facilitate the flow of trade between them. This model usually takes on the following form:

$$X_{ij} = \beta_0 GDP_i^{\beta 1} GDP_j^{\beta 2} POP_i^{\beta 3} POP_j^{\beta 4} DIST_{ij}^{\beta 5} A_{ij}^{\beta 6} e_{ij}, \quad (1)$$

where $X_{ij}$ is the flow of trade between countries $i$ and $j$; $GDP_i$ and $GDP_j$ are the gross domestic product (GDP) of $i$ and $j$; $POP_i$ and $POP_j$ are the population (or, equivalently, the per capita GDP) of $i$ and $j$; $DIST_{ij}$ is the geographical distance between $i$ and $j$; $A_{ij}$ is a set of additional factors influencing trade between $i$ and $j$, often including preferential trading arrangements; and $e_{ij}$ is a lognormally distributed error term.

Different variants of this model have been advanced, and various theoretical justifications for it have been offered (Anderson 1979; Bergstrand 1985, 1989; Deardorff 1995; Helpman and Krugman 1985, chapter 8; Leamer and Stern 1970; Linnemann 1966; Tinbergen 1962).[9] But it is widely recognized that a state's capacity to supply exports is directly related to its GDP; so, too, is a state's demand for imports. Population often is included in this model as a proxy for a country's market size. Assuming economies of scale in production, the larger a country's population, the more goods for which it is likely to achieve the minimum scale needed for efficient production without relying on export markets (Aitken 1973, 882; Linnemann 1966, 11–4; Winters and Wang 1994, 12). A more populous country, therefore, is expected to produce less for export relative to its total production than is a less populous country. Similarly, a more populous country is expected to have a greater capacity to satisfy domestic demand with domestically produced goods, and thus a lower demand for imports, than is a less populous country.

Distance usually is included in the gravity model as a proxy for transportation and transaction costs. These costs are expected to rise, and hence bilateral trade flows are expected to decrease, as the distance between trade partners increases. For these and other reasons, the gravity model predicts that bilateral trade flows will be directly related to the GDP of $i$ and $j$ and inversely related to both the population of $i$ and $j$ and the distance between them.

In addition to GDP, population, and distance, we include in the following model variables related to whether both trading partners are members of a common alliance and a common preferential trading arrangement, whether either state is a major power, and the interactions among these factors.

As noted above, we use data on alliances and major powers compiled by the COW Project (Small and Singer 1969, 1982, 44–5) in this study. Furthermore, our analysis centers on the period since World War II, when the major powers have been the United States, the Soviet Union, Great Britain, France, and China. Although this list omits states that are major economic but not military powers—particularly West Germany and Japan—it seems appropriate in light of our emphasis on the relationship between political-military relations and trade. In order to assess the implications of excluding states that are solely economic powers from this list, however, we will analyze the sensitivity of

[9] A number of studies have attempted to provide a theoretical justification for the gravity model's multiplicative functional form (e.g., Anderson 1979; Bergstrand 1985, 1989; Deardorff 1995; Helpman and Krugman 1985, chapter 8). One reason to use a multiplicative rather than a linear specification of this model is that as the economic size—measured in terms of GDP and population—of either $i$ or $j$ approaches zero, so, too, should trade flows between them (Deardorff 1995, 4).

our empirical results to whether West Germany and Japan are considered major powers.

Also included in the following model are variables that measure whether the trading partners (1) are at war with one another, (2) are parties to the General Agreement on Tariffs and Trade (GATT), (3) had a prior colonial relationship, and (4) have command economies. First, it is important to control for the effects of war because it may influence patterns of both alliances and trade. A wide variety of studies have drawn links between alliances and warfare (e.g., Levy 1989, 228–30, 235–6); and the available evidence indicates that wars tend to dampen trade flows (Gowa 1994; Gowa and Mansfield 1993; Mansfield 1994; Pollins 1989a, 1989b). Second, the effects of the GATT on trade are analyzed since the GATT is widely viewed as having provided the global institutional framework for international trade during the post–World War II era, and there is evidence that it has promoted trade flows among members (e.g., Pollins 1989a). Since distinctions often are drawn between the GATT and preferential trading arrangements in both theoretical and empirical studies of international trade (e.g., Eichengreen and Irwin 1995; Pollins 1989a; Yarbrough and Yarbrough 1992, 5), we consider their effects separately.

Third, prior colonial relations are likely to influence trade flows (Kleiman 1976; Pollins 1989a, 741; Srivastava and Green 1986). Furthermore, omitting this variable from the model risks generating biased estimates of preferential trading arrangements' effects on trade, since a number of such arrangements (including the Lomé Convention and other preferential arrangements involving the European Community/European Union) are comprised of states that had a previous colonial relationship.

Finally, we include a variable pertaining to whether both trading partners have a command economy. Many pairs of countries with command economies also have been allied during the post–World War II era. It is important to ensure that any observed effect of alliances on trade is not due to the unusual ability of states with a command economy to direct trade toward allies and away from other states.

Thus, the model we will estimate is:

$$\begin{aligned}\log X_{ij(t)} &= \log \beta_0 + \beta_1 \log GDP_{i(t-1)} + \beta_2 \log GDP_{j(t-1)} \\ &+ \beta_3 \log POP_{i(t-1)} + \beta_4 \log POP_{j(t-1)} \\ &+ \beta_5 \log DIST_{ij(t-1)} + \beta_6 \log ALLY_{ij(t-1)} \\ &+ \beta_7 \log PTA_{ij(t-1)} + \beta_8 \log MP_{ij(t-1)} \\ &+ \beta_9 (\log ALLY_{ij(t-1)} \times \log PTA_{ij(t-1)}) \\ &+ \beta_{10} (\log ALLY_{ij(t-1)} \times \log MP_{ij(t-1)}) \\ &+ \beta_{11} (\log PTA_{ij(t-1)} \times \log MP_{ij(t-1)}) \\ &+ \beta_{12} \log GATT_{ij(t-1)} + \beta_{13} \log COL_{ij(t-1)} \\ &+ \beta_{14} \log COM_{ij(t-1)} + \beta_{15} \log WAR_{ij(t-1)} + \log e_{ij(t)}. \qquad (2)\end{aligned}$$

The dependent variable is the natural logarithm of the real value of exports from state $i$ to state $j$ in year $t$. The independent variables are defined as follows:

$\log GDP_{i(t-1)}$ and $\log GDP_{j(t-1)}$ are the natural logarithms of the real GDP of $i$ and $j$, respectively, in year $t-1$;

$\log POP_{i(t-1)}$ and $\log POP_{j(t-1)}$ are the natural logarithms of the national population of $i$ and $j$, respectively, in year $t-1$;

$\log DIST_{ij(t-1)}$ is the natural logarithm of the geographical distance between $i$ and $j$ in year $t-1$;

$\log ALLY_{ij(t-1)}$ is a dummy variable that equals one if $i$ and $j$ are allied in year $t-1$, zero otherwise;

$\log PTA_{ij(t-1)}$ is a dummy variable that equals one if $i$ and $j$ are party to a common preferential trading arrangement in year $t-1$, zero otherwise;

$\log MP_{ij(t-1)}$ is a dummy variable that equals one if either $i$ or $j$ is a major power in year $t-1$, zero otherwise;

$\log GATT_{ij(t-1)}$ is a dummy variable that equals one if both $i$ and $j$ are party to the GATT in year $t-1$, zero otherwise;

$\log COL_{ij(t-1)}$ is a dummy variable that equals one if $i$ and $j$ had a colonial relationship ending in or before year $t-1$ (provided that it concluded after the onset of World War II), zero otherwise;

$\log COM_{ij(t-1)}$ is a dummy variable that equals one if both $i$ and $j$ have a command economy in year $t-1$, zero otherwise;

$\log WAR_{ij(t-1)}$ is a dummy variable that equals one if $i$ and $j$ are at war with each other in year $t-1$, zero otherwise; and

$\log e_{ij(t)}$ is a stochastic error term.

The remaining variables are included in order to analyze whether, as we argued earlier, the interactions among alliances, preferential trading arrangements, and major powers help to explain patterns of bilateral trade.[10] A description of the data and coding procedures used in this analysis is provided in the Appendix.

In the following analysis, we include all pairs of countries for which complete data are available in 1960, 1965, 1970, 1975, 1980, 1985, or 1990 (years $t-1$). The data are pooled across these seven years. The parameters in equation 2 are estimated using ordinary least squares (OLS), after controlling for country-specific and year-specific fixed effects by including a dummy variable for each country and year in the sample (except the United States and 1990, which are the respective reference categories). Because White tests (Greene 1993, 392–3, 450; White 1980) yield evidence of heteroskedasticity in each cross-section, White heteroskedasticity-consistent standard errors are used in this analysis.

Furthermore, because there is reason to expect the disturbances to exhibit autocorrelation, we estimate the parameters in equation 2 after including a lagged endogenous variable in the model. Doing so also is

[10] It should be noted that in antilogarithmic form, all the dummy variables in equation 2 take on values of $e$ (the base of the natural logarithms) and one; as such, the logarithms of these variables take on values of one and zero.

useful since, if alliances, preferential trading arrangements, or other independent variables in equation 2 are influenced by prior trade flows, then omitting a lagged endogenous variable from the model will generate biased estimates of their effects (Eichengreen and Irwin 1995). The logarithm of the lagged value of exports, however, is likely to be correlated with the error term in equation 2, thereby generating inconsistent estimates. We therefore construct an instrument for the lagged endogenous variable, a well-known procedure for ameliorating this problem (Greene 1993, 435–6; Maddala 1988, 392–5).[11] Estimates of the parameters in equation 2 are shown in Table 1. The model estimated without the lagged endogenous variable is referred to as model 1; that estimated with the lagged endogenous variable is referred to as model 1A.

## ESTIMATES OF THE PARAMETERS

The results in Table 1 indicate that the variables in models 1 and 1A explain 55% of the variation in bilateral trade flows. Also, as expected, GDP is directly related to the value of exports, and population and distance are inversely related to the value of exports. The estimates of log $GDP_{i(t-1)}$ and log $GDP_{j(t-1)}$ are positive; the estimates of log $POP_{i(t-1)}$, log $POP_{j(t-1)}$, and log $DIST_{ij(t-1)}$ are negative; and each of them is statistically significant.

In addition, the results based on model 1A demonstrate that the lagged value of log $X_{ij(t)}$ is strongly related to its current value. Surprisingly, however, the estimate of this parameter is negative. Further analysis revealed that this result is due to collinearity between lagged log $X_{ij(t)}$ and the values of both GDP and population in year $t - 1$. To reduce the collinearity among these variables, we replace log $GDP_{i(t-1)}$ and log $GDP_{j(t-1)}$ with log $(GDP_{i(t-1)} \times GDP_{j(t-1)})$ and log $POP_{i(t-1)}$ and log $POP_{j(t-1)}$ with log $(POP_{i(t-1)} \times POP_{j(t-1)})$. This specification is referred to as model 1B in Table 1 and is closely related to that used in a number of previous studies (e.g., Eichengreen and Irwin 1995, Frankel 1993).[12] As expected, the estimate of log $(GDP_{i(t-1)} \times GDP_{j(t-1)})$ is positive, the estimate of log $(POP_{i(t-1)} \times POP_{j(t-1)})$ is negative, and both are statistically significant. Moreover, the estimate of lagged log $X_{ij(t)}$ based on model 1B is positive and significant, which accords with the findings of those studies that have included a lagged endogenous variable in a gravity model (e.g., Eichengreen and Irwin 1995).

It also is important to recognize that, as shown in Table 1, regardless of which model is analyzed, very

**TABLE 1. Regression of Exports on GDP, Population, Distance, Alliances, Preferential Trading Arrangements, Major-Power Status, GATT, Prior Colonial Ties, Command Economies, and War, 1960–90**

| | Model | | |
|---|---|---|---|
| Variable | 1 | 1A | 1B |
| log $\beta_0$ | 7.783* (3.156) | 2.462 (3.381) | 12.014** (3.373) |
| log $GDP_i$ | .687** (.041) | .781** (.047) | — |
| log $GDP_j$ | 1.322** (.040) | 1.608** (.076) | — |
| log $POP_i$ | −.872** (.079) | −.808** (.083) | — |
| log $POP_j$ | −.974** (.078) | −.959** (.083) | — |
| log ($GDP_i \times GDP_j$) | — | — | .527** (.044) |
| log ($POP_i \times POP_j$) | — | — | −.869** (.083) |
| log $DIST_{ij}$ | −.787** (.014) | −.790** (.014) | −.792** (.014) |
| log $ALLY_{ij}$ | .192** (.049) | .214** (.050) | .213** (.050) |
| log $PTA_{ij}$ | .499** (.038) | .490** (.039) | .466** (.039) |
| log $MP_{ij}$ | .631** (.133) | .652** (.124) | .642** (.124) |
| log $ALLY_{ij}$ × log $PTA_{ij}$ | .589** (.064) | .592** (.065) | .592** (.065) |
| log $ALLY_{ij}$ × log $MP_{ij}$ | .082 (.066) | −.005 (.063) | −.016 (.067) |
| log $PTA_{ij}$ × log $MP_{ij}$ | −.546** (.065) | −.548** (.067) | −.527** (.067) |
| log $GATT_{ij}$ | .071 (.037) | .050 (.040) | .042 (.040) |
| log $COL_{ij}$ | 1.812** (.083) | 1.800** (.089) | 1.791** (.089) |
| log $COM_{ij}$ | .791** (.102) | .760** (.110) | .841** (.113) |
| log $WAR_{ij}$ | −6.423** (.108) | −6.247** (.112) | −6.496** (.109) |
| lagged log $X_{ij}$ | — | −.293** (.066) | .913** (.014) |
| $\bar{R}^2$ | .55 | .55 | .54 |
| $N$ | 32,156 | 30,418 | 30,418 |

*Note:* Entries are unstandardized regression coefficients. Two-tailed tests are conducted for each regression coefficient. Figures in parentheses are White heteroskedasticity-consistent standard errors. Regressions include dummy variables for country-specific and year-specific fixed effects.
*$p \leq .05$; **$p \leq .001$.

[11] This instrument is created by regressing the lagged value of log $X_{ij(t)}$ on the lagged values of log $GDP_{i(t-1)}$, log $GDP_{j(t-1)}$, log $POP_{i(t-1)}$, log $POP_{j(t-1)}$, and a dummy variable for each year (except 1990) included in the analysis. Data on exports for 1956 and data on GDP and population for 1955 are used to generate values of the instrumental variable for 1961. The dearth of these data accounts for the decline in $N$ of 1,738 when the lagged endogenous variable is included in the model and (as noted in the Appendix) is one reason we restrict our analysis to the period beginning in 1960.

[12] Frankel (1993, 58; see also Helpman and Krugman 1985) points out that entering the GDP of the importer and exporter in product form is consistent with theories of international trade based on imperfect competition. One implication of this specification is that two states are expected to conduct more trade if both have a medium-sized economy than if one has a large economy and the other has a small economy.

little variation exists in the signs, sizes, or significance levels of the remaining variables in equation 2.

Turning to the remaining variables, there is considerable evidence that wars depress trade and that a former colonial relationship and the existence of a command economy on the part of both trade partners promote commerce. In every case, the estimate of log $WAR_{ij(t-1)}$ is negative, the estimates of log $COL_{ij(t-1)}$ and log $COM_{ij(t-1)}$ are positive, and all of them are statistically significant. In addition, there is some evidence that GATT membership facilitates trade. The coefficient of log $GATT_{ij(t-1)}$ is positive in each case, but it is never statistically significant.

## The Effects of Alliances and Preferential Trading Arrangements on Trade

The results in Table 1 also provide strong support for the arguments advanced earlier. They indicate that alliances and preferential trading arrangements each promote trade, that the effects of alliances are heightened if the trade partners include a major power, and that the combination of an alliance and a preferential trading arrangement generates more commerce than does either type of institution alone. The estimates of log $ALLY_{ij(t-1)}$, log $PTA_{ij(t-1)}$, and log $MP_{ij(t-1)}$ are positive and statistically significant based on all three models. Equally important for the purposes of testing the hypotheses described above, the estimates of log $ALLY_{ij(t-1)} \times$ log $PTA_{ij(t-1)}$ and log $PTA_{ij(t-1)} \times$ log $MP_{ij(t-1)}$ are significant in each instance, although there is no evidence that log $ALLY_{ij(t-1)} \times$ log $MP_{ij(t-1)}$ has a statistically significant effect on trade. Moreover, the quantitative effects of alliances, preferential trading arrangements, and major powers on the predicted value of exports tend to be quite large.

In antilogarithmic form and for a given pair of states, $i$ and $j$, in a given year, $t$, equation 2 can be expressed as:

$$X_{ij(t)} = C \times [ALLY_{ij(t-1)} \exp(\beta_6 + \beta_9 \log PTA_{ij(t-1)} + \beta_{10} \log MP_{ij(t-1)})] \times [PTA_{ij(t-1)} \exp(\beta_7 + \beta_{11} \log MP_{ij(t-1)})] \times [MP_{ij(t-1)} \exp(\beta_8)], \quad (3)$$

where

$$C = \beta_0 GDP_{i(t-1)}{}^{\beta 1} GDP_{j(t-1)}{}^{\beta 2} POP_{i(t-1)}{}^{\beta 3} \cdot POP_{j(t-1)}{}^{\beta 4} DIST_{ij(t-1)}{}^{\beta 5} GATT_{ij(t-1)}{}^{\beta 12} \cdot COL_{ij(t-1)}{}^{\beta 13} COM_{ij(t-1)}{}^{\beta 14} WAR_{ij(t-1)}{}^{\beta 15} e_{ij(t)}.$$

As noted earlier, $ALLY_{ij(t-1)}$, $PTA_{ij(t-1)}$, $MP_{ij(t-1)}$, $GATT_{ij(t-1)}$, $COL_{ij(t-1)}$, $COM_{ij(t-1)}$, and $WAR_{ij(t-1)}$ are dummy variables that take on values of $e$ and one; their natural logarithms therefore take on values of one and zero. For the purposes of analyzing the effects of alliances, preferential trading arrangements, and major powers on the predicted value of trade between a given pair of states in a given year, $C$ can be treated as a constant. The entries in Table 2 are derived by arbitrarily setting $C$ equal to 100. The estimates of $\beta_6 - \beta_{11}$ in Table 1 based on models 1, 1A, and 1B then are used to generate predicted values of $X_{ij(t)}$.[13] For each model, comparing the entries in Table 2 allows us to assess the proportional change in the predicted value of trade between a given pair of states in a given year if these states are allied rather than nonallied, are party to a common preferential trading arrangement rather than

**TABLE 2. Effects of Alliances, Preferential Trading Arrangements, and Major-Power Status on the Predicted Value of Exports, Based on Estimates in Table 1**

| Relationship between Countries *i* and *j* | Model 1 | Model 1A | Model 1B |
|---|---|---|---|
| A. Countries *i* and *j* include a major power | | | |
| Members of a preferential trading arrangement | | | |
| Allies | 425 | 403 | 394 |
| Not Allies | 179 | 181 | 179 |
| Not members of a preferential trading arrangement | | | |
| Allies | 247 | 237 | 231 |
| Not Allies | 188 | 192 | 190 |
| B. Countries *i* and *j* are not major powers | | | |
| Members of a preferential trading arrangement | | | |
| Allies | 360 | 365 | 356 |
| Not Allies | 165 | 163 | 159 |
| Not members of a preferential trading arrangement | | | |
| Allies | 121 | 124 | 124 |
| Not Allies | 100 | 100 | 100 |

*Note*: Entries are the predicted value of exports from country *i* to country *j*, based on equation 3, where *C* is set equal to 100.

[13] Rather than setting $C$ equal to 100, we could use the observed values of the variables in equation 3, the dummy variables pertaining to each country and year, and the estimates of their regression coefficients to obtain the predicted dollar value of trade for a given pair of countries in a given year. Note, however, that for this given pair of countries and year, doing so would yield the same proportional increases in trade as those derived using the entries in Table 2. Furthermore, doing so often generates predicted values of trade that deviate noticeably from their corresponding observed values. This problem is common in models estimated in double-log form. There is substantial variation about the regression lines estimated using models 1, 1A, and 1B, and this variation is magnified when the value of trade, rather than the logarithm of this value, is analyzed. Consider, for example, the twenty pairs of countries for which the logarithm of exports is closest to the sample mean. On average, the predicted log of exports based on model 1 deviates from the observed log of exports only by about 5%. This figure is only slightly higher for the twenty pairs of countries that conducted the most trade, but it is much higher for those pairs that conducted the least trade. Since the absolute values of these residuals often are relatively large, however, the differences between the predicted and observed values of exports based on this model are much more pronounced than those between the predicted and observed values of the logarithm of exports.

not, and include a major power rather than being composed solely of nonmajor powers, as well as the extent to which the quantitative effects of each factor are influenced by the other two factors.

The findings in Table 2 are consistent with the argument that alliances promote trade among members. A change from the absence to the existence of an alliance that does not include a major power increases the predicted value of trade between nonmajor powers by about 20% to 25% if these states are not members of a common preferential trading arrangement. If the trading partners include a major power and are not members of a preferential arrangement, a change from the absence to the existence of an alliance generates about a 20% to 30% increase in the predicted flow of exports. Furthermore, the predicted value of trade between allies that include a major power (and are not members of a common preferential trading arrangement) is roughly twice as large as the corresponding value between nonmajor-power allies.

That the effects of alliances are heightened if the trading partners are members of a common preferential trading arrangement also accords with our argument. Under these conditions, a change from the absence to the existence of an alliance yields an increase in the predicted value of trade of roughly 120% between nonmajor powers and of about 120% to 140% between states that include a major power.

Like alliances, preferential commercial arrangements exert a considerable influence on trade, but our results indicate they have a larger effect than alliances on trade flows between nonmajor powers, whereas the opposite holds for trade flows involving major powers. Instituting a preferential trading arrangement yields an increase of about 60% to 65% in the predicted value of exports between nonmajor powers that are not allied. Surprisingly, however, instituting such an arrangement decreases by about 5% the predicted value of trade between states that include a major power and are not allied.

As expected, the effects of a preferential trading arrangement are heightened if the members are allied. If allies establish a preferential commercial agreement, then the predicted value of exports increases by almost 200% between nonmajor powers and by roughly 70% between countries that include a major power.

These results provide strong support for our argument that the combination of an alliance and a preferential trading agreement generates a greater impetus to trade than does either of these institutions alone. As shown in Table 2, members of an alliance and a preferential trading arrangement conduct considerably more trade than do parties to either one or the other but not both. Moreover, allied preferential trading arrangement partners that include a major power engage in about 10% to 20% more trade than do their nonmajor-power counterparts. Indeed, the predicted value of trade for pairs of states that are allied, belong to a common preferential trading arrangement, and include a major power is the highest in Table 2 based on each model estimated, followed by that for nonmajor powers that are both allies and party to a common preferential trading arrangement, and that for major-power allies that are not members of a common preferential trading arrangement.

### Definition of a Major Power

It was noted earlier that our analysis of major powers is based on a definition that emphasizes political-military strength. Economic powers lacking sufficient military capabilities to meet this criterion, however, also may influence the commercial effects of alliances and preferential arrangements on trade. Japan and West Germany are obvious examples of such states, and we therefore estimate the parameters in models 1, 1A, and 1B after including them among the major powers.

The results of this analysis tend to be very similar to those in Table 1, with two notable differences. First, the estimate of log $MP_{ij(t-1)}$ is, on average, about 40% larger when Japan and West Germany are considered major powers than when they are not. This result is hardly surprising, since both countries have been especially active participants in the international trading system during the period examined here.

Second, the estimates of both log $ALLY_{ij(t-1)}$ × log $MP_{ij(t-1)}$ and log $PTA_{ij(t-1)}$ × log $MP_{ij(t-1)}$ are much smaller than their corresponding estimates in Table 1. Thus, for example, instituting an alliance between states that include a major power generates roughly a 15% smaller increase in the predicted value of trade when Japan and West Germany are considered major powers than when they are not. This suggests that political-military major powers augment the openness of alliances and preferential trading arrangements to a greater extent than do other economic powers, which is consistent with the argument advanced above.

## THE EFFECTS OF ALLIANCE FORMATION ON CHANGES IN TRADE

Thus far, we have examined the effects of preexisting alliances and preferential trading arrangements, on the level of trade among states. But it is important to ensure that our results are not undermined by simultaneity bias caused by any influence of trade on alliances or preferential arrangements. Various studies have suggested that high levels of trade can generate incentives for states to forge formal institutions, like preferential trading arrangements, that minimize future disruptions of commercial relations (e.g., Eichengreen and Irwin 1995, Yarbrough and Yarbrough 1992). We addressed this issue earlier by lagging the effects of the independent variables one year and by including the lagged value of exports in models 1A and 1B. We now examine whether the formation of alliances (and preferential trading arrangements) increases bilateral trade flows. We then examine the effects of trade flows and changes in them on the formation of alliances. Initially, we estimate the parameters in the following model:

$$\Delta X_{ij(t)} = \alpha_0 + \alpha_1 \Delta GDP_{i(t-1)} + \alpha_2 \Delta GDP_{j(t-1)}$$

**TABLE 3. Regression of Change in Exports on Changes in GDP, Population, Alliances, Preferential Trading Arrangements, GATT, Command Economies, and War, 1960–90**

| Variable | Model 2 | Model 2A |
|---|---|---|
| $\alpha_0$[a] | 917.833*** | 780.164*** |
| | (72.440) | (81.574) |
| $\Delta GDP_i$ | −.000521* | −.000361 |
| | (.000208) | (.000271) |
| $\Delta GDP_j$ | .000735 | .001613*** |
| | (.000431) | (.000459) |
| $\Delta POP_i$ | −2.403* | −1.683 |
| | (1.080) | (1.173) |
| $\Delta POP_j$ | −4.207*** | −3.767*** |
| | (1.044) | (1.046) |
| $\Delta ALLY_{ij}$[a] | 106.607 | 172.183 |
| | (56.109) | (125.577) |
| $\Delta PTA_{ij}$[a] | −63.376** | −87.851** |
| | (20.849) | (26.895) |
| $\Delta(ALLY_{ij} \times PTA_{ij})$[a] | 236.174*** | 430.848*** |
| | (67.700) | (101.215) |
| $\Delta(ALLY_{ij} \times MP_{ij})$[a] | 99.819 | 104.358 |
| | (115.261) | (227.728) |
| $\Delta(PTA_{ij} \times MP_{ij})$[a] | 174.900* | −96.825 |
| | (89.235) | (71.187) |
| $\Delta GATT_{ij}$[a] | −16.237 | −27.620 |
| | (12.309) | (15.662) |
| $\Delta COM_{ij}$[a] | 622.404*** | 301.254*** |
| | (184.746) | (64.213) |
| $\Delta WAR_{ij}$[a] | −130.052 | 67.431*** |
| | (76.238) | (17.161) |
| $\bar{R}^2$ | .06 | .06 |
| $N$ | 23,940 | 20,892 |

*Note:* Entries are unstandardized regression coefficients. Two-tailed tests are conducted for each regression coefficient. Figures in parentheses are White heteroskedasticity-consistent standard errors. Regressions include dummy variables for country-specific and year-specific fixed effects.
[a]Parameter estimate and standard error are divided by 1,000,000.
*$p \le .05$; **$p \le .01$; ***$p \le .001$.

$$+ \alpha_3 \Delta POP_{i(t-1)} + \alpha_4 \Delta POP_{j(t-1)} + \alpha_5 \Delta ALLY_{ij(t-1)}$$
$$+ \alpha_6 \Delta PTA_{ij(t-1)} + \alpha_7 \Delta(ALLY_{ij(t-1)} \times PTA_{ij(t-1)})$$
$$+ \alpha_8 \Delta(ALLY_{ij(t-1)} \times MP_{ij(t-1)}) + \alpha_9 \Delta(PTA_{ij(t-1)}$$
$$\times MP_{ij(t-1)}) + \alpha_{10} \Delta GATT_{ij(t-1)} + \alpha_{11} \Delta\, COM_{ij(t-1)}$$
$$+ \alpha_{12} \Delta WAR_{ij(t-1)} + \Delta z_{ij(t)}. \quad (4)$$

In this model, referred to as model 2 in Table 3, the change in exports between states $i$ and $j$ is measured from year $t-5$ to year $t$, the change in each independent variable is measured from year $t-6$ to year $t-1$, and $\Delta z_{ij(t)}$ is an error term. It is clear, however, that this specification may not completely alleviate any simultaneity between trade and the exogenous variables in the model. Changes in trade from year $t-5$ to year $t-1$ could, for example, lead to the formation of alliances or preferential trading arrangements during that time. We therefore estimate a second model, referred to as model 2A in Table 3, in which each independent variable is measured from year $t-11$ to year $t-6$. In this model, the effects of the independent variables are completely lagged, thereby further reducing any possibility of simultaneity bias.[14]

It should be noted that based on our sample of states and the period considered here, no changes occurred in the distance between states, the states that were major powers, and states that had a prior colonial relationship. These variables, therefore, are not included in equation 4.

As in our earlier analysis, OLS is used to derive estimates of the parameters in models 2 and 2A after pooling the observations over time and including dummy variables for each country and year in the sample (except the United States and 1960, which are the respective reference categories). Since evidence of heteroskedasticity exists in each cross-section, we continue to use White heteroskedasticity-consistent standard errors in our tests of statistical significance.

The results of this analysis are presented in Table 3. Particularly important is the fact that $\Delta ALLY_{ij(t-1)}$, $\Delta(ALLY_{ij(t-1)} \times MP_{ij(t-1)})$, and $\Delta(ALLY_{ij(t-1)} \times PTA_{ij(t-1)})$ are positive in each case.[15] These findings indicate that the formation of an alliance tends to increase trade among members. That this relationship is relatively weak, however, also is clear, since only the estimate of $\Delta(ALLY_{ij(t-1)} \times PTA_{ij(t-1)})$ is statistically significant based on either model.[16] In addition, the results in Table 3 indicate that the effects of alliance formation on trade tend to be larger in the five years after the alliance is formed than in the period during which it is formed. The estimate of $\Delta ALLY_{ij(t-1)}$ is

[14] It should be noted that the functional form of models 2 and 2A is linear rather than multiplicative, like models 1, 1A, and 1B. While a simpler linear model often has obvious advantages, under the present circumstances it could be argued that a multiplicative model is more appropriate. Hence, we also estimated the parameters in models 2 and 2A based on a multiplicative specification, whereby each variable was defined as the change in its natural logarithm. In only three cases—$\Delta GDP_{i(t-1)}$ and $\Delta(PTA_{ij(t-1)} \times MP_{ij(t-1)})$ based on model 2 and $\Delta WAR_{ij(t-1)}$ based on model 2A—did statistically significant estimates based on the linear specification (reported in Table 3) change signs but remain significant based on the multiplicative specification.

In addition, we included in equation 4 the level of exports from $i$ to $j$ in year $t$. The estimate of this variable was negative but insignificant based both on models 2 and 2A. Moreover, the signs, sizes, and significance levels of the remaining variables in equation 4 were not at all sensitive to the inclusion of this variable.

[15] One limitation of this analysis is that, based on the sample of states for which we have complete data, few pairs of countries changed from nonallies to allies during any of the five-year periods ($t-6$ to $t-1$ for model 2 and $t-11$ to $t-6$ for model 2A) in which the independent variables are measured. Indeed, most alliances and various preferential trading arrangements that existed during the era we examine were formed prior to its outset. As such, this and the following analysis only can be considered a preliminary first cut at the issues of whether the formation of alliances or preferential trading arrangements gives rise to changes in trade flows and whether trade flows contribute to their formation.

[16] The $p$-value of the estimate of $\Delta ALLY_{ij(t-1)}$ is .06 based on model 2 and .17 based on model 2A. Thus, the estimate based on model 2 would have been significant at the .05 level had we conducted a one-tailed rather than a two-tailed test.

about two-thirds larger and that of $\Delta(ALLY_{ij(t-1)} \times PTA_{ij(t-1)})$ is roughly three-quarters larger based on model 2A than model 2. The estimate of $\Delta(ALLY_{ij(t-1)} \times MP_{ij(t-1)})$, however, is virtually the same size regardless of whether the effects of alliance formation on changes in trade are fully lagged.

Whereas the formation of alliances between states that include a major power does not significantly increase trade flows, the formation of preferential trading arrangements between such states does. This increase, however, is realized only in the immediate aftermath of their formation. The estimate of $\Delta(PTA_{ij(t-1)} \times MP_{ij(t-1)})$ is positive and significant based on model 2 but is negative and not significant based on model 2A. Furthermore, the estimate of $\Delta PTA_{ij(t-1)}$ is negative and significant based on both models. In combination with our earlier results, these findings suggest that the trade-promoting effects of preferential arrangements that do not include allies or a major power occur only some time after they are formed.

The effects of GATT membership on trade seem to follow a similar pattern. Whereas our earlier results indicated that pairs of states belonging to the GATT conduct somewhat more trade than do other pairs, changes leading both trade partners to become partners to the GATT actually generate a mild decrease in trade. Indeed, the estimate of $\Delta GATT_{ij(t-1)}$ is negative, but small and insignificant, based on both models. There also is evidence that the onset of war depresses trade but that these effects are short-lived. The estimate of $\Delta WAR_{ij(t-1)}$ is negative and insignificant based on model 2 but positive and significant based on model 2A. In addition, changes leading both trade partners to have a command economy yield increases in trade: Both estimates of $\Delta COM_{ij(t-1)}$ are positive and significant. Finally, increases in the importer's GDP and decreases in the exporter's GDP and in the population of both trade partners give rise to increases in commerce. The estimate of $\Delta GDP_{j(t-1)}$ is positive, those of $\Delta GDP_{i(t-1)}$, $\Delta POP_{i(t-1)}$, and $\Delta POP_{j(t-1)}$ are negative, and five of the eight estimates are significant.

## THE EFFECTS OF TRADE ON ALLIANCE FORMATION

The preceding results indicate that allies conduct more trade than do nonallies and that the formation of alliances tends to generate increases in trade. To further ensure that our findings do not reflect the effects of trade flows or changes in trade on the formation of alliances, we conduct two additional analyses.

First, we define a variable that is equal to the log of the odds that states $i$ and $j$ form an alliance during the period from year $t + 1$ to year $t + 4$, where we observe one if an alliance is formed during this period and zero otherwise. Like our earlier analysis, trade flows between $i$ and $j$ are measured in year $t$ (where $t$ = 1956, 1961, 1966, 1971, 1976, 1981, and 1986). These data are pooled and a logistic regression is conducted to estimate the effects of trade flows on the probability of alliance formation. The results indicate that the maximum likelihood estimate of trade is positive but small ($9.29 \times 10^{-11}$) and not statistically significant ($t = .87$).

Second, we analyze whether the change in trade between $i$ and $j$ during the period from year $t - 5$ to year $t$ influences the probability that they form an alliance during the period from year $t + 1$ to year $t + 4$, using the same procedure described above. The maximum likelihood estimate of the change in trade also is positive but small ($2.94 \times 10^{-10}$) and not statistically significant ($t = 1.16$).

In addition, we introduced into these models other variables included in our earlier analyses and continued to find no evidence that trade flows or changes in them influence the formation of alliances. We also estimated these models using a multiplicative functional form and found no evidence that trade or changes in trade affect alliance formation, controlling for other variables (such as distance) included in our earlier analyses. These findings, therefore, provide no indication that our earlier results are undermined by problems of endogeneity.

## DISCUSSION AND CONCLUSION

The results of this study indicate that alliances and preferential trading arrangements both promote the flow of trade and that in combination they generate more commerce than does either alone. These findings are consistent with the argument that firms and private traders have incentives to reduce the risks of opportunism by foreign governments. Investing in relation-specific assets to service the market of an ally or a preferential trading arrangement partner reduces these risks. These risks are further reduced if such a partner is also an ally.

That alliances facilitate trade among members also accords with the argument that the security externalities fostered by commerce create incentives for states to trade more freely with allies than with adversaries. These incentives are especially pronounced for states with the ability to influence their terms of trade. Major powers are likely to have that ability, and this is consistent with our finding that pairs of allied states which include a major power conduct considerably more trade than allied pairs which do not. In addition, major-power alliances tend to be more durable and stable than those comprised solely of nonmajor powers. This tendency further reduces the risks of opportunism faced by investors in dedicated assets to service an ally's market. It also reduces the risk that a government's current allies will become adversaries in the near future and use the augmented political-military capacity derived from intraalliance trade to undermine its security.

Illustrative of the effects of major-power alliances is the case of the United States and South Korea. The United States has long sought to foster South Korean economic growth in order to bolster its security vis-à-vis North Korea and other potential adversaries. To this end, the United States pressured South Korea to adopt an export-led growth strategy and provided a market for a large portion of these exports (Haggard and Moon 1983). Indeed, it is widely acknowledged that these two countries have enjoyed a " 'special' . . . economic and trade relationship based primarily on strategic and other noneconomic factors" (Yang 1986, 34). The United States (and its allies) also has severely limited trade with North Korea in an attempt to undermine its security.

The heightened tendency for major powers to promote trade with allies at the expense of political rivals is not limited to this one example. Cohen argues that:

> from the start of the Cold War, official Washington's chief objective was to reconstruct the war-ravaged economies of Western Europe and Japan, and maintain the vigor of the undamaged Canadian economy, so that these countries could serve as effective barriers to communist expansion. . . . Toward this end, . . . the United States later encouraged an outflow of private investment from the United States, particularly to Canada but also to Europe, and it promoted through GATT a broad program of worldwide liberalization of industrial trade that frequently benefited its allies directly at its own expense (1991, 102; see also Gowa 1994).

In fact, U.S. policymakers seem to have recognized the contribution that free trade can make to the security of participants and the need to discriminate between friends and foes in this regard. As Dean Acheson argued in the late 1940s, "the preservation and development of sound trading relationships with other countries of the free world [that is, U.S. allies] is an essential and important element in the task of trying to build unity and strength in the free world" (quoted in Freeland 1985, 325).

Equally important in this regard was the denial of commercial benefits to adversaries of the United States and its allies. Chief among the efforts to achieve this end was COCOM, which was explicitly designed to stem the flow of commerce that might enhance the security of the Soviet Union and its allies (Mastanduno 1992). Due to its effect, "by the early 1950s, American trade with the East was negligible, while trade between Eastern and Western Europe continued but at much reduced levels" (Pollard and Wells 1984, 355–6).

These illustrations and our statistical results are consistent with the findings of most previous research on the effects of alliances on trade, almost all of which has analyzed commerce between or involving major powers (Gowa 1994, Gowa and Mansfield 1993, Mansfield and Bronson 1997, Summary 1989). But our results indicate that alliances comprised of nonmajor powers also promote trade and that the combination of an alliance and a preferential trading arrangement provides a particularly potent impetus to trade, important issues that have not been addressed to date.

Moreover, our results do not reflect the influence of war, command economies, prior colonial relations, or GATT membership. We controlled for the effects of each of these factors, and, except for the GATT, each has a strong influence on trade flows. That wars depress trade is consistent with various studies which have found that conflict inhibits trade, while cooperation promotes it (Polachek 1980; Pollins 1989a, 1989b). As we mentioned earlier, however, these studies did not analyze the effects of alliances on trade, and Pollins (1989a, 757) noted that these results might not account for variations in trade due to alliance relations. Our findings indicate that, in addition to conflict, alliances are salient influences on commerce.

The observed effects of command economies, prior colonial relations, and GATT membership on bilateral trade flows also accord with the existing literature (Kleiman 1976, Mansfield and Bronson 1997, Pollins 1989a, Srivastava and Green 1986), although the GATT's effect is somewhat weaker than expected. But alliances and preferential trading arrangements have strong and large influences on trade even after controlling for these factors. Thus, our findings pertaining to alliances and preferential trading arrangements are not, for example, due to the tendency for the Soviet Union to direct trade flows within the Warsaw Pact and the Council for Mutual Economic Assistance. Nor are they outgrowths of the tendency for some preferential trading arrangements and alliances to be comprised of states with a former colonial relationship or membership in the GATT.

Much research on the determinants of bilateral trade flows has focused on the effects of preferential trading arrangements. Consistent with the findings of this research, our results indicate that these arrangements had a marked influence on trade after World War II. As we mentioned earlier, however, very few studies have compared the effects of preferential trading arrangements with those of alliances; and no research has examined the extent to which the effects of preferential trading arrangements depend on whether commercial institutions include a major power or are comprised of allies.

Yet, these issues are centrally important. Based on our results, preferential trading arrangements have a larger influence than alliances on trade flows between nonmajor powers, whereas the opposite holds for states that include a major power. Furthermore, absent an alliance, the effects of preferential commercial treatment on trade depend very little on whether the trading partners include a major power. The predicted value of trade conducted by nonallied members of a preferential trading arrangement is about 10% larger if one partner is a major power than if both are not major powers. But regardless of major-power status, the effects of a preferential trading arrangement depend fundamentally on whether its members also are allies. Indeed, allied members of a preferential trading arrangement conduct roughly 120% to 140% more trade than do their nonallied counterparts (refer to Table 2).

Moreover, most studies of preferential trading arrangements omit alliances from the analysis; had we done so, too, substantial bias would have been introduced into our estimates of preferential trading arrangements' effects. For example, estimates of log $PTA_{ij(t-1)}$ based on models 1, 1A, and 1B increase by an average of about 50% when log $ALLY_{ij(t-1)}$, log $ALLY_{ij(t-1)}$ × log $MP_{ij(t-1)}$, and log $ALLY_{ij(t-1)}$ × log $PTA_{ij(t-1)}$ are deleted from these models. Since preferential trading arrangements often are comprised of political-military allies (Mansfield 1993), research that focuses solely on discriminatory commercial blocs therefore seems likely to confuse their effects with those of alliances and to systematically overstate the influence of preferential trading arrangements on commerce.

One central purpose of this paper was to analyze whether the combination of an alliance and a preferential trading arrangement provides a greater impetus to commerce than does either type of institution alone. Our results provide strong support for this argument. Nonmajor powers conduct roughly 120% to 200% more trade if they are party to both an alliance and a preferential trading arrangement than if they are either allies or members of such an arrangement (but not both). Allies that belong to a preferential trading arrangement and include a major power conduct about 70% more trade than do allies that include a major power but are not members of a preferential trading arrangement and roughly 125% more trade than nonallied members of such an arrangement that include a major power. Moreover, the predicted value of trade between states that are allies, members of a common preferential trading arrangement, and include a major power is greater than under any other set of conditions examined in this study, followed by the predicted value of trade between nonmajor powers that share both an alliance and a preferential trading arrangement (refer to Table 2).

These findings indicate that the interplay between alliances and preferential trading arrangements is fundamental to explaining patterns of international trade. It is clear that a wide variety of alliances and preferential trading arrangements exist and that different types of each may have different influences on trade. It is equally clear that our analysis is confined to the post–World War II period and that the effects of alliances and preferential commercial treatment during this era may not correspond to their effects during earlier periods. Our results strongly suggest, however, that the pursuit of power conditions the pursuit of plenty. In so doing, this paper provides considerable evidence that an understanding of international politics is central to the study of international trade.

## APPENDIX: DATA SOURCES AND CODING

Described here are the data used in this article and some coding issues pertaining to our analyses.

Data on exports are taken from the International Monetary Fund (IMF), *Direction of Trade* (various years). The IMF presents these data in nominal U.S. dollars. Following Eichengreen and Irwin (1995), we use the U.S. wholesale price index and producer price index to create real values of exports. Furthermore, the IMF often does not distinguish between pairs of countries for which so little trade is conducted that the trade flow is reported as zero and pairs of countries for which data are not available. As such, neither type of pair is included in any of our analyses.

Data on GDP and population are taken from the Mark 5.6 version of the Penn World Table (Summers and Heston 1991). In order to maintain consistency with the procedure for deflating the data on exports described above, we generate nominal values of GDP using the data provided in the Penn World Table on per capita GDP expressed in current prices and population. We then deflate these values using the U.S. wholesale price index and producer price index. This data set does not include values of per capita GDP and population for a number of countries in 1990. Where it is possible to do so, we substitute values of these variables in 1989 for missing values in 1990.

Consistent with previous studies using gravity models, we measure distance based on the shortest distance in nautical miles between ports in states $i$ and $j$. If at least one trading partner is land-locked, then we rely on land distances (either road or rail) to measure the distance between them. Data on geographical distances are taken from the Defense Mapping Agency, *Distances between Ports* (1985); Fitzpatrick and Modlin (1986); *The Times Atlas of the World* (1992); and *The Times Concise Atlas of the World* (1972).

Data on alliances are taken from Small and Singer (1969) and preliminary updates of these data provided by the COW Project, dated March 25, 1993. We consider all neutrality agreements, ententes, and defense pacts listed by Small and Singer to be alliances. Since they sought to explain wars, Small and Singer did not include wartime alliances in their compilation. They noted, however, that for other purposes it would be important to amend their list correspondingly, and previous studies of the relationship between alliances and trade have done so (Gowa 1994, Gowa and Mansfield 1993). We therefore include as allies all states fighting together in any interstate war listed by Small and Singer. In order to maintain consistency with the earlier studies of alliances and trade, we also include as allies the United States and Japan, even though this pair of countries is not included in Small and Singer's data set. This decision is made because the Japanese–United States Security Treaty (1951–60) and the Treaty of Mutual Cooperation and Security (1960–present) served much the same purpose as an alliance, including the stipulation that the United States come to Japan's assistance in the event it is attacked (Grenville 1974, 270, 286–7). However, the decision to code these states as allies has no bearing on any of our results.

Data on preferential trading arrangements are taken from Belous and Hartley (1990, 141–3), Schott (1989), and Hartland-Thunberg (1980). We also include the Council for Mutual Economic Assistance, the Southern African Development Coordination Conference, and the Eastern and Southern African Preferential Trade Area because various studies have identified them as preferential trading arrangements (Hanlon 1986, Kisanga 1991, Orimalade and Ubogu 1984, Pomfret 1988).

Data on major powers and wars are taken from Small and Singer (1982; Singer and Small 1994). It should be noted that only trade data between India and Pakistan are available for the pairs of states that were at war during the years $(t - 1)$ analyzed here.

Data on GATT membership are taken from various issues of GATT's *Basic Instruments and Selected Documents* (Geneva) and *International Trade* (Geneva). Data on prior colonial relations are taken from Kurian (1992). Data on command economies are taken from Kornai (1992, 6–7) for the period from 1960 to 1985 and from Staar et al. (1991) for 1990.

All the independent variables in equation 2 are measured at year $t - 1$. For each pair of states, $i$ and $j$, it should be noted that alliances, preferential trading arrangements, GATT membership, prior colonial relations, command economies, and war are coded based on the end of this year.

All pairs of countries for which complete data are available in 1960, 1965, 1970, 1975, 1980, 1985, or 1990—and that Small and Singer (1969, 1982; Singer and Small 1994) list as members of the interstate system—are included in our sample. Small and Singer only provide data on alliances and interstate wars for members of the interstate system; and, in some of the years mentioned above, their list of members excludes countries for which data on other variables analyzed here are available.

The number of dyads for which complete data exist ranges from 2,647 in 1960 to 5,667 in 1990. These differences arise because the number of members of the interstate system increased during this period, as did the availability of data on GDP and trade flows. Data on trade flows and GDP are quite limited for earlier years, especially for less developed countries and states with command economies. This is the primary reason we do not analyze periods prior to 1960, despite the obvious desirability of doing so if data on a wider range of countries were available.

## REFERENCES

Aitken, Norman D. 1973. "The Effect of the EEC and EFTA on European Trade: A Temporal and Cross-Section Analysis." *American Economic Review* 63 (December):881–92.

Anderson, James E. 1979. "A Theoretical Foundation for the Gravity Equation." *American Economic Review* 69 (March):106–16.

Anderson, Kym, and Richard Blackhurst. 1993. "Introduction and Summary." In *Regional Integration and the Global Trading System*, ed. Kym Anderson and Richard Blackhurst. London: Harvester Wheatsheaf.

Belous, Richard S., and Rebecca S. Hartley, eds. 1990. *The Growth of Regional Trading Blocs in the Global Economy*. Washington, DC: National Planning Association.

Bergstrand, Jeffrey H. 1985. "The Gravity Equation in International Trade: Some Microeconomic Foundations and Empirical Evidence." *Review of Economics and Statistics* 67 (August):474–81.

Bergstrand, Jeffrey H. 1989. "The Generalized Gravity Equation, Monopolistic Competition, and the Factor-Proportions Theory in International Trade." *Review of Economics and Statistics* 71 (February):143–53.

Brada, Josef C., and Jose A. Mendez. 1983. "Regional Economic Integration and the Volume of Intra-Regional Trade: A Comparison of Developed and Developing Country Experience." *Kyklos* 36 (4):589–603.

Bueno de Mesquita, Bruce. 1981. *The War Trap*. New Haven: Yale University Press.

Cohen, Benjamin J. 1990. "The Political Economy of International Trade." *International Organization* 44 (Spring):261–81.

Cohen, Benjamin J. 1991. *Crossing Frontiers: Explorations in International Political Economy*. Boulder, CO: Westview.

Deardorff, Alan V. 1984. "Testing Trade Theories and Predicting Trade Flows." In *Handbook of International Economics*, ed. Ronald W. Jones and Peter B. Kenen. Amsterdam: North-Holland.

Deardorff, Alan V. 1995. "Determinants of Bilateral Trade: Does Gravity Work in a Neoclassical World?" Paper presented at the National Bureau of Economic Research conference on Regionalization of the World Economy, Woodstock, Vermont.

Defense Mapping Agency. 1985. *Distances between Ports*. 5th ed. Washington, DC: Defense Mapping Agency.

Eichengreen, Barry, and Douglas A. Irwin. 1995. "The Role of History in Bilateral Trade Flows." Paper presented at the National Bureau of Economic Research conference on Regionalization of the World Economy, Woodstock, Vermont.

Frankel, Jeffrey, A. 1993. "Is Japan Creating a Yen Bloc in East Asia and the Pacific?" In *Regionalism and Rivalry: Japan and the United States in Pacific Asia*, ed. Jeffrey A. Frankel and Miles Kahler. Chicago: University of Chicago Press.

Freeland, Richard M. 1985. *The Truman Doctrine and the Origins of McCarthyism: Foreign Policy, Domestic Politics, and Internal Security 1946–1948*. New York: New York University Press.

Frieden, Jeff. 1988. "Sectoral Conflict and U.S. Foreign Economic Policy." *International Organization* 42 (Winter):59–90.

Fitzpatrick, Gary L., and Marilyn J. Modlin. 1986. *Direct-Line Distances*. International ed. Metuchen, NJ: Scarecrow.

Gasiorowski, Mark, and Solomon W. Polachek. 1982. "Conflict and Interdependence: East-West Trade and Linkages in the Era of Detente." *Journal of Conflict Resolution* 26 (December):709–29.

Gaubatz, Kurt Taylor. 1996. "Democratic States and Commitment in International Relations." *International Organization* 50 (Winter): 109–39.

Gowa, Joanne. 1994. *Allies, Adversaries, and International Trade*. Princeton: Princeton University Press.

Gowa, Joanne, and Edward D. Mansfield. 1993. "Power Politics and International Trade." *American Political Science Review* 87 (June): 408–20.

Greene, William H. 1993. *Econometric Analysis*. 2d ed. New York: Macmillan.

Grenville, J. A. S. 1974. *The Major International Treaties 1914–1973*. London: Methuen.

Haggard, Stephan, and Chung-in Moon. 1983. "The South Korean State in the International Economy: Liberal, Dependent, or Mercantile?" In *The Antinomies of Interdependence: National Welfare and the International Division of Labor*, ed. John Gerard Ruggie. New York: Columbia University Press.

Hanlon, Joseph. 1986. *Beggar Your Neighbor*. London: Villiers Publications.

Hartland-Thunberg, Penelope. 1980. *Trading Blocs, U.S. Exports, and World Trade*. Boulder, CO: Westview.

Helpman, Elhanan, and Paul Krugman. 1985. *Market Structure and Foreign Trade: Increasing Returns, Imperfect Competition and the International Economy*. Cambridge: Massachusetts Institute of Technology Press.

Kisanga, Eliawony J. 1991. *Industrial and Trade Cooperation in Eastern and Southern Africa*. Hong Kong: Avebury.

Kleiman, Ephraim. 1976. "Trade and the Decline of Colonialism." *Economic Journal* 86 (September):459–80.

Kornai, Janos. 1992. *The Socialist System: The Political Economy of Communism*. Princeton: Princeton University Press.

Kurian, George Thomas. 1992. *Encyclopedia of the Third World*, 4th ed. New York: Facts on File. Vols. 1–3.

Leamer, Edward E., and Robert M. Stern. 1970. *Quantitative International Economics*. Boston: Allyn and Bacon.

Levy, Jack S. 1989. "The Causes of War: A Review of Theories and Evidence." In *Behavior, Society, and Nuclear War*, ed. Philip E. Tetlock et al. New York: Oxford University Press.

Linnemann, Hans. 1966. *An Econometric Study of International Trade Flows*. Amsterdam: North-Holland.

Maddala, G. S. 1988. *Introduction to Econometrics*. New York: Macmillan.

Mansfield, Edward D. 1993. "Effects of International Politics on International Trade." In *Regional Integration and the Global Trading System*, ed. Kym Anderson and Richard Blackhurst. London: Harvester Wheatsheaf.

Mansfield, Edward D. 1994. *Power, Trade, and War*. Princeton: Princeton University Press.

Mansfield, Edward D., and Rachel Bronson. 1997. "The Political Economy of Major-Power Trade Flows." In *The Political Economy of Regionalism*, ed. Edward D. Mansfield and Helen V. Milner. New York: Columbia University Press.

Mastanduno, Michael. 1992. *Economic Containment: CoCom and the Politics of East-West Trade*. Ithaca: Cornell University Press.

McKeown, Timothy J. 1991. "A Liberal Trade Order? The Long-Run Pattern of Imports to the Advanced Capitalist States." *International Studies Quarterly* 35 (June):151–72.

Morrow, James D. 1990. "Alliances and Asymmetry: An Alternative to the Capability Aggregation Model of Alliances." *American Journal of Political Science* 35 (November):904–33.

Orimalade, Adeyinka, and R. E. Ubogu, eds. 1984. *Trade and Development in Economic Community of West African States*. Delhi, India: Vikas.

Pelzman, Joseph. 1977. "Trade Creation and Trade Diversion in the Council of Mutual Economic Assistance: 1954–1970." *American Economic Review* 67 (September):713–22.

Polachek, Solomon W. 1980. "Conflict and Trade." *Journal of Conflict Resolution* 24 (March):55–78.

Pollard, Robert A., and Samuel F. Wells, Jr. 1984. "1945–1960: The Era of American Economic Hegemony." In *Economic and World Power: An Assessment of American Diplomacy since 1789*, ed. William H. Becker and Samuel F. Wells, Jr. New York: Columbia University Press.

Pollins, Brian M. 1989a. "Conflict, Cooperation, and Commerce: The Effects of International Political Interactions on Bilateral Trade Flows." *American Journal of Political Science* 33 (August): 737–61.

Pollins, Brian M. 1989b. "Does Trade Still Follow the Flag?" *American Political Science Review* 83 (June):465–80.

Pomfret, Richard. 1988. *Unequal Trade: The Economics of Discriminatory International Trade Policies*. Oxford: Basil Blackwell.

Rogowski, Ronald. 1989. *Commerce and Coalitions: How Trade Affects Domestic Political Alignments*. Princeton: Princeton University Press.

Schott, Jeffrey J., ed. 1989. *Free Trade Areas and U.S. Trade Policy*. Washington, DC: Institute for International Economics.

Singer, J. David, and Melvin Small. 1994. *Correlates of War Project: International and Civil War Data, 1816–1992*. No. 9905. Ann Arbor: Inter-University Consortium for Political and Social Research.

Small, Melvin, and J. David Singer. 1969. "Formal Alliances, 1816–1965: An Extension of the Basic Data." *Journal of Peace Research* 6 (3):257–82.

Small, Melvin, and J. David Singer. 1982. *Resort to Arms: International and Civil Wars, 1816–1980*. Beverly Hills, CA: Sage.

Srivastava, Rajendra K., and Robert T. Green. 1986. "Determinants of Bilateral Trade Flows." *Journal of Business* 59 (October):623–40.

Staar, Richard F., et al., eds. 1991. *Yearbook on International Communist Affairs*. Stanford: Hoover Institution Press.

Summary, Rebecca M. 1989. "A Political-Economic Model of U.S. Bilateral Trade." *Review of Economics and Statistics* 71 (February): 179–82.

Summers, Robert, and Alan Heston. 1991. "The Penn World Table (Mark 5): An Expanded Set of International Comparisons." *Quarterly Journal of Economics* 106 (May):327–68.

*Times Atlas of the World*. 1992. 9th ed. New York: Times Books.

*Times Concise Atlas of the World*. 1972. New York: Times Books.

Tinbergen, Jan. 1962. *Shaping the World Economy: Suggestions for an International Economic Policy*. New York: The Twentieth Century Fund.

Waltz, Kenneth. 1979. *Theory of International Politics*. Reading, MA: Addison-Wesley.

White, Halbert. 1980. "A Heteroskedasticity-Consistent Covariance Matrix Estimator and a Direct Test for Heteroskedasticity." *Econometrica* 48 (May):817–38.

Williamson, Oliver E. 1985. *The Economic Institutions of Capitalism*. New York: Free Press.

Winters, L. Alan, and Zhen Kun Wang. 1994. *Eastern Europe's International Trade*. Manchester: Manchester University Press.

Yang, Jai-Hoon. 1986. "U.S.–Korean Economic and Trade Relations: Building a New 'Special Relationship.'" In *United States–Korea Relations*, ed. Robert A. Scalapino and Han Sung-joo. Research Papers and Policy Studies No. 19. Berkeley: Institute of East Asian Studies, University of California.

Yarbrough, Beth V., and Robert M. Yarbrough. 1992. *Cooperation and Governance in International Trade: The Strategic Organizational Approach*. Princeton: Princeton University Press.

# International Institutions and the Volatility of International Trade

Edward D. Mansfield and Eric Reinhardt

**Abstract** During the past half-century, states have established a large number of international trade institutions, both multilateral and regional in scope. The existing literature on this topic emphasizes that these agreements are chiefly designed to liberalize and increase the flow of overseas commerce. Yet such institutions have another function that has been largely ignored by researchers, namely, reducing volatility in trade policy and trade flows. Exposure to global markets increases the vulnerability of a country's output to terms of trade shocks. Governments seek to insulate their economies from such instability through membership in international trade institutions, particularly the World Trade Organization (WTO) and preferential trading arrangements (PTAs). We hypothesize that these institutions reduce the volatility of overseas commerce. We further hypothesize that, because market actors prefer price stability, trade institutions increase the volume of foreign commerce by reducing trade variability. This article conducts the first large-scale, multivariate statistical tests of these two hypotheses, using annual data on exports for all pairs of countries from 1951 through 2001. The tests provide strong support for our arguments. PTAs and the WTO regime significantly reduce export volatility. In so doing, these institutions also increase export levels.

During the past half-century, states have concluded a large number of international trade agreements. Some of these agreements have been multilateral in scope, particularly the General Agreement on Tariffs and Trade (GATT) and its successor, the World Trade Organization (WTO). Others have been bilateral or regional, most notably the preferential trading arrangements (PTAs) that have proliferated with striking speed in recent years. What do such trade institutions accom-

Earlier versions of this article were presented at the 2005 annual meeting of the American Political Science Association, Washington, D.C.; the 2006 annual meeting of the Midwest Political Science Association, Chicago; Emory University's Department of Political Science seminar series; and the Effectiveness of International Institutions Workshop, held at Princeton University. For helpful comments and suggestions, we are grateful to the participants in these seminars and to Marc Busch, Michael Gilligan, Joanne Gowa, David Leblang, Bumba Mukherjee, the editors of *International Organization*, and two anonymous reviewers.

*Note from the editors:* Since one of the authors is an associate editor of this journal, the editors handled this article outside of the normal editorial management system and put in place special procedures to ensure rigorous, double-blind peer review.

*International Organization* 62, Fall 2008, pp. 621–52
© 2008 by The IO Foundation.
doi:10.1017/S0020818308080223

plish, and why do states form them? The existing research on this topic emphasizes that trade agreements enhance market access for goods, services, and investment. In this view, they are chiefly designed to liberalize and increase the flow of overseas commerce.

Yet such institutions have another function that has been largely ignored by researchers. Specifically, in this article we argue that trade institutions are designed as much to stabilize and reduce volatility in trade policy and trade flows as they are to liberalize and expand foreign commerce. Exposure to global markets increases the vulnerability of a country's economic output to terms of trade shocks, and governments seek to insulate their economies from such instability. Various domestic institutions can serve this purpose, as recent studies underscore. However, international trade institutions—particularly the GATT/WTO and PTAs—can also reduce the volatility of overseas commerce. These institutions constrain member-states from introducing new trade barriers; they foster policy transparency and convergence in expectations, standards, and policy instruments; and they shift the structure of markets in ways that promote greater stability in commercial transactions over time.

Furthermore, by reducing the volatility of international trade, commercial agreements help stabilize the price of traded goods. Firms and other market actors have a strong preference for price stability. As such, they are likely to respond to lower trade variability between the country in which they are located and another state by expanding overseas commerce and investment with that state. If trade agreements do indeed reduce volatility, then they should correspondingly increase the amount of trade conducted among the contracting parties as well. This indirect effect of trade agreements on the flow of overseas commerce stands apart from any direct effect of the agreements on trade flows stemming from member-states' expanded access to foreign markets. In fact, this indirect effect is likely to be important even if agreements lock in rather than cut members' trade barriers. Studies of the relationship between trade institutions and trade flows that ignore their influence on the volatility of foreign commerce therefore risk arriving at misleading conclusions.

In this article, we conduct the first large-scale, multivariate statistical tests of these two hypotheses using annual data on exports for all pairs of countries from 1951 through 2001. The tests, which are based on four different measures of trade volatility, provide strong support for our arguments. Specifically, PTAs and the GATT/WTO significantly reduce export volatility. What is more, a part of the impact of trade agreements on trade levels stems from their tendency to dampen commercial volatility, rather than from their expansion of market access alone. Our results therefore indicate that a critical function of preferential and multilateral trade agreements is to make trade policy and trade flows more predictable.

Our study makes several important contributions to the literature on international institutions and the international political economy. First, a number of analyses of international regimes and institutions argue that these arrangements reduce the variance of international outcomes.[1] Ours is one of the first studies to test this argument. Second, our analysis helps to clarify limitations of prior empirical research on the links between trade institutions and trade flows. This research has been marked by stark disagreement about whether membership in the GATT/WTO, if not PTAs, promotes overseas trade.[2] These debates reflect the existing literature's predominant focus on the level—and its inattention to the volatility—of trade flows and policies. Once the volatility of trade is taken into account, there is clear evidence that trade agreements are beneficial. Finally, our analysis highlights an underappreciated function of international institutions of any stripe. Whereas many observers have argued that such institutions improve the status quo policies of member-states, their chief role may be to lock in and enhance the predictability of these policies.

## Theory

It is widely accepted that exposure to global markets increases the vulnerability of a country's business cycle, and thus its cross-border commercial and investment flows, to volatility in the terms of trade.[3] For workers, employment and wages become less secure.[4] For firms, profits and competitiveness in key markets are threatened.[5] Hence, as Frieden notes, private-market actors "with substantial cross-border contractual interests" prefer predictability in these flows.[6] Central to such predictability are government policies concerning trade, investment, and currencies, all of which affect relative international prices. "Business planners," Abbott observes, "generally prefer to operate under stable economic conditions under which the rules applicable to transactions are known in advance."[7] In an open economy, governments will thus face substantial pressure to insulate workers and firms from the vagaries of volatile global markets.

Recent studies have suggested a variety of domestic institutions and policies that states can use to reduce the volatility transmitted by increased exposure to the

1. See, for example, Martin and Simmons 1998, 753; and Braumoeller 2006.

2. See Rose 2003 and 2004; Gowa and Kim 2005; and Milner and Kubota 2005; but also see Özden and Reinhardt 2005a; and Goldstein, Rivers, and Tomz 2007.

3. See, for example, Rodrik 1998; and Easterly and Kraay 2000. Our argument is not that openness itself increases volatility. Rather, we simply observe that openness increases the percentage of economic output that is exposed to terms of trade shocks, linking a country's business cycle more closely with sources of external risk. On this issue, see Rodrik 1998; and Kim 2007.

4. Scheve and Slaughter 2004.

5. Aizenman 2003.

6. Frieden 2002, 839. Of course, hedging exchange-rate risk on the forward market is an essential part of any internationalized firm's global strategy. But hedging adds a significant transaction cost and few firms are fully hedged. For a small to medium-sized business, the potential downside from exchange-rate risk can dwarf any profits it may make from the actual sale of its product. See, for example, the discussion of the Markel Corporation in the *Wall Street Journal*, 7 February 2003, C1.

7. Abbott 2000, 528.

international economy.[8] Our argument is that international institutions can play a similar role, reducing the extent to which openness heightens the vulnerability of a country's output to terms of trade shocks. More specifically, trade institutions help stabilize trade policy and trade flows. Indeed, they help states lock in access to overseas markets even if they do not always lead member-countries to decrease trade barriers. This argument is hardly new, although it has been largely ignored in the empirical literature on international institutions and regimes. For example, Keohane points out that various international regimes—including the GATT—are explicitly designed to promote "orderly patterns of behavior among members," implying that they should enhance stability and reduce volatility in interactions among members.[9] For Martin and Simmons, international institutions "lock in a particular equilibrium, providing stability."[10] Abbott argues that trade agreements, at least those with "hard law," are adopted to reduce risk premia for private traders and investors.[11] Perroni and Whalley maintain that "countries see it in their interests to form insurance-based regional blocs, even if the barrier changes relative to the ... status quo are small."[12]

Governments themselves place considerable emphasis on the ability of trade institutions to reduce commercial volatility. As New Zealand argued in its third-party submission during Canada's 1984 *Newsprint* complaint against the European Community (EC), "the [GATT] disciplines and rules ... [should] be used in a way which would foster the stability and security of international trade."[13] Going further, Brazil's WTO representative pointed out that the Uruguay Round had done little to improve Brazil's access to foreign markets, but that WTO membership was nonetheless beneficial because the "rules-based multilateral trading system ensured predictability, stability, and security to its economic agents."[14] Indeed, this function is emphasized in the WTO treaty itself: Article 3.2 of the Dispute Settlement Understanding (DSU) defines its primary purpose as "providing security and predictability."[15]

PTAs also aim to reduce the volatility of trade policies and the flow of overseas commerce between members. These institutions include agreements that partially liberalize commerce, free trade areas (FTAs), customs unions, common markets,

8. See Rodrik 1998; Quinn and Woolley 2001; Adserà and Boix 2002; and Bernhard and Leblang 2006.
9. Keohane 1983, 167.
10. Martin and Simmons 1998, 746.
11. Abbott 2000, 528–29.
12. Perroni and Whalley 2000, 3. On this point, see also Koremenos, Lipson, and Snidal 2001, 782; and Mansfield and Reinhardt 2003.
13. GATT 1984, 12.
14. WTO 2000, 5.
15. In a decision that has since been cited frequently as precedent, the WTO's Appellate Body ruling in the *Computer Equipment* case (DS 62/67/68) broadens the legal reference for this objective, concluding that "the security and predictability of 'the reciprocal and mutually advantageous arrangements...' is an object and purpose of the WTO Agreement," not just of the DSU per se. See WTO 1998, para. 82.

and economic unions. All PTAs vest each member with preferential access to the markets of the other participants.[16] Members also recognize, however, that such arrangements can reduce the volatility of international trade. For example, two chief objectives of the 2003 Singapore-Australia FTA, as stated in its Article 1, were to "create a predictable ... trading environment" and to "establish a framework of transparent rules to govern trade and investment."[17] The preamble to the 2001 Mexico-European Free Trade Area states that its goals are "to create an expanded and *secure* market for goods and services" and "to ensure a stable and predictable environment for investment."[18] Similarly, the Chile-European Union (EU) Association Agreement strives to enhance the transparency of trade and customs "procedures ... in order to reduce costs and increase predictability for economic operators."[19]

Despite its *prima facie* grounding in existing trade agreements, this volatility-reducing function has received little attention in studies of trade institutions. Bagwell and Staiger, for instance, maintain that the purpose of trade agreements is to allow states with market power to reach more efficient market access exchanges.[20] In their view, reciprocity and nondiscrimination—key features of institutions such as the GATT/WTO—promote such exchanges. Other scholars have emphasized different institutional features that also serve to increase market access. For example, Davis points to an institution's ability to facilitate linkage bargaining.[21]

This perspective, however, is at odds with recent evidence that many PTAs and the WTO itself do not actually induce members to lower their trade barriers.[22] Various post-Communist countries, for example, liberalized trade unilaterally prior to the implementation of the WTO's Uruguay Round agreements; their WTO bindings remain far higher than their applied tariff levels.[23] Furthermore, Japan left its heavily protected rice market entirely off the table in its 2005 FTA talks with Thailand and Malaysia, leading critics to claim that these FTAs "fall well short of promoting real free trade."[24] Indeed, most trade accords include exceptions designed to maintain protection for politically sensitive sectors that, if liberalized, would

16. We restrict our attention to reciprocal PTAs, in which all parties make concessions, as opposed to nonreciprocal arrangements, such as the Generalized System of Preferences (GSP), which are granted and removed unilaterally.

17. Available at ⟨http://www.dfat.gov.au/trade/negotiations/safta/chapter_1.pdf⟩. Accessed 27 June 2008.

18. Available at ⟨http://www.sice.oas.org/Trade/mexefta/mexefta1.asp#PREAMBLE⟩. Accessed 27 June 2008. Emphasis added.

19. Available at ⟨http://www.sice.oas.org/Trade/chieu_e/chieu1_e.asp⟩. Accessed 27 June 2008. Article 79, para. 3(d).

20. Bagwell and Staiger 2002.

21. Davis 2004. The recent empirical debate about whether the GATT/WTO actually increases trade also implicitly accepts this market-access-centric view of the institution's functions. See Rose 2003 and 2004; Gowa and Kim 2005; and Goldstein, Rivers, and Tomz 2007.

22. See Foroutan 1998; and Rose 2004.

23. See Finger, Ingco, and Reincke 1996; and Drabek and Bacchetta 2004.

24. *Financial Times*, 18 January 2005, 9.

generate especially sizable gains from trade. To be sure, swapping market access in areas of complementary comparative advantage is a defining objective of trade agreements. But, as the preceding examples illustrate, some agreements do not make much headway in that direction. This suggests that trade agreements are designed for other purposes as well, including the reduction of volatility in trade policy and trade flows. With that in mind, our study makes one of the first efforts to determine whether international institutions designed to regulate trade actually dampen the volatility of overseas commerce.

*Three Mechanisms*

We argue that trade institutions reduce the variability of trade flows in three complementary ways. First, institutions help enforce existing market-access commitments and deter the erection of new protectionist barriers that could otherwise precipitate fluctuations in trade. Second, trade institutions foster transparency and policy convergence among member-states. Third, such institutions change certain characteristics of markets, stimulating responses by private traders that reduce the volatility of cross-border transactions.

One of the most important functions of trade agreements is to constrain member-states from introducing new protectionist policies. As long as members view the costs of violating the agreement as fairly high, locking in trade policies through this sort of external mechanism can help governments to "tie their hands" and resist protectionist pressures from domestic groups.[25]

In addition, trade institutions serve as informational clearinghouses, sometimes even autonomously monitoring members' trade policies. Such information helps focus reputational or retaliation costs on members that abrogate their treaty commitments by introducing trade barriers. These costs may arise domestically if the institution reveals that a government has imposed such barriers or other rent-seeking policies and citizens punish the government as a result.[26] These costs may also arise internationally if, for instance, member-states bring grievances against participants that violate their treaty obligations. The WTO's highly legalized dispute settlement procedures have long been considered the gold standard in this regard, but most PTAs also contain such provisions.[27] If one member introduces a protectionist policy, the affected member-state can initiate a dispute settlement proceeding to collect damages.

25. See Finlayson and Zacher 1981, 600; Krueger 1999, 118; and Abbott 2000.

26. See Keefer and Stasavage 2002; and Mansfield, Milner, and Rosendorff 2002.

27. See Hudec 1993; and Jackson 2001. No comprehensive data yet exists on variation across PTAs in specific provisions for dispute settlement. The best available data, from Smith, covers sixty-two of the most prominent PTAs. See Smith 2000. Only eighteen of these contain no provisions for formal dispute settlement of any type, and all but five of the remainder incorporate legally binding third-party review procedures. More recent agreements, in particular, tend to have more clearly defined provisions for dispute settlement.

How much does the threat of these proceedings prevent the introduction of protection by parties to a trade agreement? Little research has been conducted on this issue. However, there is evidence that even a country with as much market power as the United States is deterred from imposing antidumping (AD) duties against WTO members, regardless of the target's countervailing market power.[28] That such procedures weigh heavily on states tempted to introduce protection is also implied by the outcomes of GATT/WTO disputes. For example, economically powerful states often settle disputes prior to official rulings, and small countries have frequently succeeded in using dispute settlement procedures to induce large countries to remove protectionist barriers.[29] Further, Desai and Hines show that the stock prices of protected firms drop after a WTO complaint is filed against the barriers shielding them from foreign competition.[30] Hence, market actors seem to believe that this enforcement mechanism is politically credible. More generally, trade agreements can help states commit to a given level of market access, decreasing the chances they will take actions that degrade that access over time. By reducing the probability of new protectionist barriers, trade institutions reduce the volatility of trade flows.

Anecdotal evidence in support of this proposition is easy to locate. Australia's trade minister acknowledged in 2001 that a chief motivation for establishing the U.S.-Australian FTA was to create an "insurance policy" that limited the possibility of increases in U.S. trade barriers.[31] Facing a proliferation of unfair trade actions initiated by the United States, Canada had a similar objective in forming its free trade agreement with the United States.[32] Chile's agreement with Mercosur was also designed to secure its existing level of market access in the Southern Cone.[33] Likewise, a central reason for China's desire to join the WTO was to guarantee access to the U.S. market; heretofore, the extent of this access had been subject to annual and highly politicized congressional reviews.[34] States thus view trade institutions as devices to secure their existing access to their partners' markets, even if additional access is not forthcoming.

The second way that trade agreements reduce volatility is by fostering transparency and policy convergence among contracting parties. Trade agreements increase transparency—that is, the ease with which governments and private actors can monitor policy developments—by clarifying the obligations of each participant (for example, by establishing precise schedules of tariff bindings). Equally, these agreements create clearinghouses for members' notifications about policy devel-

28. See Blonigen and Bown 2003; and Busch, Raciborski, and Reinhardt 2007. Francois and Niels (2004) demonstrate the same finding as applied to Mexico's AD investigations.
29. See Reinhardt 2001; and Busch and Reinhardt 2003.
30. Desai and Hines 2004.
31. *Australian*, 26 June 2001, 15.
32. Mansfield and Reinhardt 2003, 846.
33. *Financial Times*, 8 December 1995, 7.
34. Drabek and Bacchetta 2004, 1091.

opments, and they specify procedures for addressing disputes. "Transparency," as one GATT committee chairman emphasized, "is not an end in itself. It is a means to build confidence in and provide security and stability to the multilateral trading system, to minimize trade restriction and distortion, to assist private market operators to adjust to changing trade policies. . . ."[35] For this reason, Canada insisted on increasing the precision of the rules of origin regarding automobiles and auto parts during negotiations over the North American Free Trade Agreement (NAFTA). The prior rules had been vague and susceptible to reinterpretation by the U.S. government, thereby deterring foreign firms from locating investments in Canada for the purpose of producing finished goods for sale in the United States.[36]

Convergence occurs as regulatory instruments, practices, and procedures grow increasingly similar across member-states. Trade agreements circumscribe the range of protectionist policies that participants can impose, thereby channeling protection to a common set of instruments, the domestic implementation of which draws on harmonized international standards and regulations. As such, trade agreements cause signatories to protect their markets in similar and more transparent ways.[37] A classic example is the Uruguay Round's effort to convert diverse trade protection schemes into tariff equivalents. International institutions and their bureaucrats may "teach norms" or act as "purveyor[s] of global policy knowledge."[38] The transparency they provide helps members emulate one another's apparently successful practices.[39] For instance, the widely observed spread of AD actions is partly attributable to their acceptability (under tightly defined conditions) based on WTO law.[40] As Martin and Simmons put it, "once policy is delegated to an international institution, state behavior will converge: members will tend to adopt similar monetary, trade, or defense policies."[41] Blackhurst, Finlayson, and Zacher, and others, concur with this assessment, maintaining that the reduction of policy-related uncertainty through the establishment of rules and procedures guiding trade relations has been the GATT/WTO's chief accomplishment.[42]

35. GATT 1994, 9.
36. Abbott 2000, 528–29.
37. Botcheva and Martin (2001) usefully highlight the potential for international institutions to encourage *divergence* rather than convergence where cross-state externalities in the relevant domain are low. Trade protection, however, has well-known and very high cross-state externalities, which make institutions in our setting strongly suited to promote convergence rather than the opposite.
38. See Finnemore 1993; and Morrissey and Nelson 2001.
39. Simmons and Elkins 2004, 179.
40. See Morrissey and Nelson 2001, 21–24; and Kucik and Reinhardt 2008.
41. Martin and Simmons 1998, 752.
42. See Blackhurst 1998, 44; and Finlayson and Zacher 1981, 602. Many observers have argued that domestic institutions can help filter or reroute international sources of pressure for generalized policy convergence. We do not take issue with this claim, because it emphasizes international integration's spillover effects on traditionally domestic policy domains, such as old-age pension schemes and welfare systems. Our point is that international trade agreements cause states to converge on a common set of policy instruments, practices, and standards in the international domain specifically covered by the agreements.

Transparency and convergence in policy instruments reduce the volatility of trade flows by stabilizing the expectations of private traders. With trade institutions in place, private actors have less difficulty obtaining information about trade policy and monitoring the behavior of member governments. Private actors also have clearer avenues of recourse in disputes over members' regulatory actions. In an environment of greater and more reliable information, private actors are thus less likely to exhibit herd behavior, overreacting to the inevitable vicissitudes in global markets. By fostering transparency and convergence, international trade institutions should dampen boom-and-bust cycles in international commercial and investment flows.

The third mechanism through which trade institutions reduce trade volatility is by restructuring investment and commerce in ways that promote greater long-term predictability. A trade agreement invites greater foreign direct investment (FDI) in member-states where firms might otherwise rely on arms-length trade to serve these markets, since the agreement bolsters investors' confidence that member-governments will not engage in predatory activities that jeopardize their assets.[43] Commerce driven by such fixed-cost investments tied to a global production network is less variable than that resulting from a continual search for the lowest-cost foreign supplier.

Besides increasing FDI, trade institutions also shift the nature of the investment a country attracts. Specifically, trade agreements promote export-platform and vertical FDI to a greater extent than FDI aimed at increasing sales in the host market.[44] The latter type of investment is often designed to circumvent a host country's trade barriers. Once firms make such investments, they then have a stake in supporting that country's protectionist policies, which place them at an advantage over their competitors located abroad. Firms engaged in vertical or export-platform FDI, in contrast, should lobby the host to forego increased protectionism that would raise transaction costs within their global production network. Through this domestic mechanism, a trade agreement's impact on the type of investment a country attracts reinforces the institution's ability to provide secure market access, thereby stabilizing commercial flows.

Finally, by increasing the range of products that are granted preferential market access, trade agreements generally help countries diversify their portfolio of exports. There is evidence that greater concentration of exports heightens the volatility of a country's terms of trade.[45] Conversely, export diversification is likely to decrease terms-of-trade volatility and accordingly the volatility of commercial flows.[46] Thus, by changing characteristics of the market itself, trade agreements are likely to reduce trade volatility.

43. Yarbrough and Yarbrough 1992.
44. See Hanson, Mataloni, and Slaughter 2001, 262; Markusen and Maskus 2001, 35; and Aizenman 2003.
45. Razin, Sadka, and Coury 2003.
46. Hausmann, Panizza, and Rigobon 2004, 14.

*Hypotheses*

The three mechanisms described above form the basis for our primary hypothesis:

*H1: Joint membership in a reciprocal trade agreement—a PTA or the GATT/WTO—should decrease the volatility of a country's exports to a trade partner.*

From a theoretical standpoint, we are agnostic about whether PTAs will have a larger or smaller effect on volatility than the GATT/WTO. One possibility is that, since PTAs have many fewer members and less diffuse trade structures than the multilateral regime, participants in PTAs might more easily detect protectionist policies and might have a greater incentive to punish states that enact such measures.[47] If so, PTAs might be better able than the GATT/WTO to deter spikes in protectionism by members and thereby dampen trade volatility. On the other hand, PTAs are a diverse group of organizations. Some are highly institutionalized and should be especially effective at performing the functions described in the previous section. Others are poorly institutionalized and have far less ability to perform these functions. It is difficult to predict whether, on average, PTAs will perform these functions more or less effectively than the GATT/WTO.

Our argument has an important corollary concerning the level of trade. It is widely argued that volatility in relative prices reduces the profitability of cross-border commerce and thus dampens trade.[48] As noted earlier, cross-border contracting arrangements are more costly for firms if they are uncertain about prices. By reducing this uncertainty and promoting predictability in economic relations, trade agreements should indirectly increase the volume of trade. Moreover, this effect should be realized even if the trade agreement does not significantly lower protectionist barriers. Increasing the stability of economic actors' expectations may prompt them to engage in more foreign commerce, regardless of whether trade barriers change. This argument gives rise to a secondary hypothesis:

*H2: Greater expected volatility of exports from a given country to a trade partner should decrease the level of those bilateral exports.*

Figure 1 shows the theoretical relationships among trade agreements, volatility, and flows. The arrows at the top show the "direct" effect of a trade agreement on commerce, which stems from reciprocal trade barrier reductions among members. Our argument is not based on this topmost causal path. Instead, we focus on the "indirect" effect of trade agreements on trade flows. This indirect effect is repre-

47. Fernández and Portes 1998.

48. Klein and Shambaugh 2004. Volatility may have a stronger dampening effect on trade in differentiated goods, which presumably have lower pass-through, and whose producers must therefore continue to sell at the local price even when relative price movements are disadvantageous. On this point, see Frieden 2002, 839.

sented by the thick causal arrows in the lower portion of the figure, which correspond to our hypotheses H1 and H2, on the left and right, respectively. Together, these two hypotheses imply that, even without expanding market access, trade agreements can promote heightened foreign commerce by reducing volatility. Our argument is silent on the relative weights of the direct (protection-reducing) versus indirect (volatility-reducing) effects of trade agreements on trade levels. We suspect, however, that the substantive impact of volatility is considerable. As far as we are aware, the following results are the first to bear directly on this important issue.

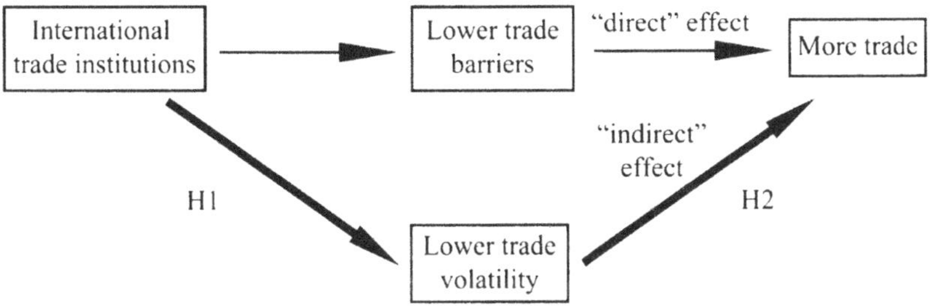


**FIGURE 1.** *Diagram of the theoretical relationships*

## Research Design

To test our hypotheses, we construct a data set with one observation per ordered pair ("directed dyad") of states, *i* and *j*, for each year, *t*, from 1951 to 2001. We include Hong Kong and Macao, in addition to all country-years on the Correlates of War (COW) interstate system membership list, version 2002.1.[49] This yields a total of 1,082,652 possible directed-dyad-years; however, gaps in trade data for some countries reduce the sample that is actually analyzed below to about half of this size, or 527,883 observations.[50] This sample includes 162 countries and a panel of 21,167 unique ordered pairs, for an average of 24.9 years each.

49. Correlates of War Project 2003.

50. Note that the observations excluded due to missing (trade) data are similar in many important respects to those included in the regression sample. The two sets of observations have nearly identical values of (1) GDP growth rates and growth volatility, (2) military conflict participation, and (3) landlocked geography. There appears to be virtually no difference in the years covered in the missing and nonmissing observations as well. However, the missing observations tend to involve somewhat less democratic states (on average, a 2-point difference on the 21-point scale described below) with slightly lower average per capita incomes ($4,481 compared to $6,027 for the states included in the sample, where these values are expressed in constant 1995 U.S. dollars). Our subsequent analyses (in Models

*Dependent Variable: Volatility*

There is no universally accepted measure of volatility and little precedent in the existing literature for scoring volatility in trade. Studies of the impact of exchange rate volatility on trade tend to operationalize volatility as the variance within a time series of yearly observations of trade for a given country or pair of countries.[51] This technique, however, conflates predictable changes in trade with unexpected shocks.[52] It is also unable to furnish time-specific values of volatility within, not merely across, series.

We consider four different measures of volatility, none of which suffer from these limitations. Our measures are applied to the goods exports of state $i$ to state $j$ in year $t$ ($X_{i,j,t}$), expressed in constant 1995 U.S. dollars.[53] The last of these is the most direct indicator of volatility used in this study. However, we first present three somewhat simpler and more intuitive measures. Analyzing all four variables should increase confidence in the robustness of our results.

Our first measure, used in Model A, is the absolute value of the change in the logged value of real exports from state $i$ to state $j$, between years $t - 1$ and $t$.[54]

$$Abs(\Delta \text{ LOG EXPORTS})_{i,j,t} = |\ln X_{i,j,t} - \ln X_{i,j,t-1}| \qquad (1)$$

One advantage of this measure is that it varies from year to year within the export series for each country-pair. As a result, we can control for time-varying factors

A–C) reveal no systematic relationship between democracy or per capita income, on one hand, and trade volatility, on the other. Hence, the nature of the missing data is unlikely to bias our findings on the relationship between international institutions and the volatility of commerce.

51. See Devereux and Lane 2003; IMF 2004, 30; and Rose 2005.

52. To illustrate this distinction, consider two hypothetical time series, each with ten observations. Series A is a linear increase from 1 to 10. Series B is a normally-distributed random variable with the same mean (5.5) and a variance of 8. Despite the fact that Series A is entirely predictable, whereas B's series oscillates widely and totally randomly, A's variance of 8.25 is greater than B's. A measure of volatility covering a long period of time needs to distinguish between these two different situations.

53. We obtain data on (goods) exports, $X_{i,j,t}$, from a hierarchical set of sources, including, from highest to lowest priority, the *United Nations Commodity Trade Statistics Database* (COMTRADE), the Organization for Economic Cooperation and Development's (OECD's) *Monthly Statistics of International Trade*, Statistics Canada's *World Trade Analyzer*, and the International Monetary Fund's (IMF's) *Direction of Trade Statistics*. Where these sources, after compilation, did not report a value for $i$'s exports to $j$ in year $t$, but did provide a value for $j$'s imports from $i$ (as reported by state $j$) in that year ($M_{j,i,t}$), we fill in $X_{i,j,t} = M_{j,i,t}$. Trade data are often subject to reporting errors. Volatility scores could be greatly affected by such errors. Hence we screened the data by identifying the directed-dyads that contained the 2000 largest annual percent changes in exports. We then compared the orders of magnitude reported in the multiple sources above, and where an obvious disagreement existed, we used the source with the more reasonable order of magnitude. In no case did we fill in or average data; every observation of $X$ is from one of the above sources. We convert $X_{i,j,t}$ from the source units, current U.S. dollars, to constant 1995 U.S. dollars using the U.S. Consumer Price Index. See the category "All-Urban," at ⟨www.bls.gov⟩.

54. In those cases where the annual volume of exports is zero, we follow the common practice of adding $1000 to this value before taking the log. See, for example, Eichengreen and Irwin 1995.

affecting the level of trade, thereby enhancing our ability to isolate the effects of trade agreements. Larger values of this measure represent wider fluctuations from year to year and thus greater trade volatility. Of course, analyzing the logarithm of exports compresses high values, so that the same real deviations would appear smaller at higher levels of trade than at lower ones. We address this issue by controlling for the prior level of exports ($\ln X_{i,j,t-1}$).

Our second measure of volatility, used in Model B, is the absolute value of the change in the supplier's export share in the importer's market, expressed as a percentage.

$$Abs(\Delta \text{ EXPORT SHARE})_{i,j,t} = 100 \times \left| \left( \frac{X_{i,j,t}}{GDP_{j,t}} \right) - \left( \frac{X_{i,j,t-1}}{GDP_{j,t-1}} \right) \right| \quad (2)$$

This measure scales exports by the importing country's gross domestic product (GDP).[55]

Our third measure, EXPORT $\text{DROP}_{i,j,t}$, used in Model C, is dichotomous. It equals 1 if state $i$'s real exports to state $j$ drop by 50 percent or more from year $t-1$ to year $t$, that is, if $[100 \times (X_{i,j,t} - X_{i,j,t-1})/X_{i,j,t-1}] \leq -50$. It equals zero otherwise. Fifteen percent of the observations in our sample experience such a dip. (We can alternatively draw the cutoff at 10 or 25 percent with no consequence for the following results.) Unlike the previous two measures of volatility, this variable taps the direction of trade volatility. Doing so is important because we expect trade institutions to reduce the probability of year-to-year collapses in the flow of exports.

Our final technique for assessing the links between trade agreements and export volatility is the most direct. We begin by assuming that the level of exports from one state to another in year $t$ is given by:

$$\ln X_{i,j,t} = \beta_0 + \beta_1 WTO_{i,j,t-1} + \beta_2 PTA_{i,j,t-1} + \mathbf{Z}_{i,j,t}\boldsymbol{\varphi} + \mu_{i,j} + \delta_t + \varepsilon_{i,j,t} \quad (3)$$

where $\mathbf{Z}$ is a vector of control variables with $\boldsymbol{\varphi}$ as their coefficients, $\mu_{i,j}$ is a directed-dyad-specific fixed effect, $\delta_t$ is a year-specific fixed effect, and $\text{PTA}_{i,j,t-1}$ and $\text{WTO}_{i,j,t-1}$ are dummy variables indicating whether countries $i$ and $j$ are, respectively, members of the same PTA or the GATT/WTO in year $t-1$. We also assume

55. Normalizing by the size of the importer's GDP captures the overall revealed market access granted by the importer country to the supplier country. Normalizing by the importing country's total imports would only address the extent to which the supplier was the target or beneficiary of changes in discrimination across suppliers (that is, relative rather than absolute levels of market access). This is not the issue addressed by our theory.

that the error term, $\varepsilon_{i,j,t}$, follows a normal distribution with mean zero and, crucially, observation-specific variance, $\sigma^2_{i,j,t}$. Higher error variance in a given case indicates that the deviations in the actual levels of exports are greater. This error variance, then, is the embodiment of observation-specific volatility.

To capture the impact of trade agreements on volatility, we estimate a heteroskedastic regression, Model D, which parameterizes the variance function as:

$$\sigma^2_{i,j,t} = \exp(\alpha_0 + \alpha_1 \ln X_{i,j,t-1} + \alpha_2 PTA_{i,j,t-1} + \alpha_3 WTO_{i,j,t-1} + \mathbf{W}_{i,j,t}\boldsymbol{\gamma} + \tau_t) \tag{4}$$

where $\mathbf{W}$ is a vector of control variables and $\tau_t$ is a year-specific fixed effect. Our argument will be supported if $\alpha_2, \alpha_3 < 0$, indicating that trade agreements reduce the variance in export levels. As with the first measure of volatility, this procedure uses a logarithmic scale; accordingly, to correct for the compression at high values, we control in the variance equation for the level of exports from country $i$ to country $j$ in year $t - 1$.

*Estimating the Direct and Indirect Effects of Trade Agreements on Export Levels*

Model D does not differentiate between the direct and indirect impact of trade agreements on export levels, which are merged into single coefficients in equation (3)—$\beta_1$ or $\beta_2$, the coefficients of $\text{WTO}_{i,j,t-1}$ and $\text{PTA}_{i,j,t-1}$, respectively. Indirectly, trade institutions can boost export flows by stabilizing policies even if they do not directly increase market access, since economic actors are expected to engage in more cross-border trade when relative prices are less volatile. To separate these direct and indirect effects of trade agreements on export levels, we estimate an ARCH-in-mean model. Model E generalizes the heteroskedastic regression framework by adding the observation-specific conditional error variance term, $\sigma^2_{i,j,t}$, as a causal variable in our model of the level of exports (ARCH.M) and by allowing for first-order autoregressive-conditional heteroskedasticity (ARCH.1) in the variance equation. Specifically, underlining what has been added to equations (3) and (4),

$$\ln X_{i,j,t} = \beta_0 + \beta_1 WTO_{i,j,t-1} + \beta_2 PTA_{i,j,t-1} + \underline{\beta_3 \sigma^2_{i,j,t}} + \mathbf{Z}_{i,j,t}\boldsymbol{\varphi} + \mu_{i,j} + \delta_t + \varepsilon_{i,j,t} \tag{5}$$

and

$$\sigma_{i,j,t} = \exp(\alpha_0 + \alpha_1 \ln X_{i,j,t-1} + \alpha_2 WTO_{i,j,t-1} + \alpha_3 PTA_{i,j,t-1} + \mathbf{W}_{i,j,t}\boldsymbol{\gamma} + \tau_t) + \underline{\alpha_4 \varepsilon^2_{i,j,t-1}} \tag{6}$$

Model E further allows for first-order autocorrelation (AR.1), such that $Cov(\varepsilon_{i,j,t}, \varepsilon_{i,j,t-1}) \neq 0$. A simpler version of this modeling technique was devised by Engle, Lilien, and Robins to analyze volatility in financial markets.[56] To our knowledge, it has not been used in studies of international trade, although it is ideally suited to our purposes. It is important to recognize, however, that our version explicitly adapts to the panel data context by including directed-dyad-specific fixed effects ($\mu_{i,j}$) in equation (5).[57]

Trade agreements have a positive *indirect* impact on export levels to the extent that, simultaneously, $\alpha_2, \alpha_3 < 0$ in equation (3) and $\beta_3 < 0$ in equation (5). Trade agreements have a positive *direct* effect on exports to the extent that $\beta_1$, $\beta_2 > 0$ in equation (5).[58]

### *Independent Variables: Trade Agreements*

Our two primary explanatory variables are $\text{PTA}_{i,j,t-1}$ and $\text{WTO}_{i,j,t-1}$. These dummy variables indicate, respectively, that the pair of countries, *i* and *j*, are members of the same PTA or of the GATT/WTO, at some point in year $t - 1$. For convenience, subsequent references to these variables often omit subscripts, but note that they are always lagged by one year. PTA takes account of partial scope accords, FTAs, customs unions, common markets, and economic unions, but not general cooperation agreements unless they include a schedule of trade-liberalizing commitments with specific products, amounts, and timetables. This variable is restricted to agreements that are reciprocal in nature; accordingly, the Generalized System of Preferences and the EC's Lome Convention are not included. For hub-and-spoke agreements (such as the EC's Arusha II accord with Kenya, Tanzania, and Uganda), PTA is coded as 1 only for those bilateral relationships covered by the agreement, not for the relations among the "spokes" (unless, of course, they were covered by a separate PTA).[59] This variable equals 1 in 9 percent of the sample's observations, reflecting about 250 distinct PTA treaties, depending on how one counts successor or extension treaties. WTO equals 1 in 47 percent of our sample.

56. See Engle, Lilien, and Robins 1987; Engle 2001; Leblang and Mukherjee 2004; and Hausmann, Panizza, and Rigobon 2004.

57. To make estimation feasible, we have had to assume that the ARCH.1, AR.1, and ARCH.M terms are common across panels (though this is hardly an unusual assumption, given the conventional constraint, in such pooled analyses, that the other coefficients are constant across cross-sections as well).

58. Further, one year's volatility is positively related to the next year's if the ARCH.1 coefficient, 4, is greater than zero.

59. To code PTA, we assembled various lists of preferential trade arrangements, working chiefly from official WTO documents (Mansfield and Reinhardt 2003). We also used extensive records maintained unofficially by WTO Secretariat staff to keep track of PTAs not formally notified to the WTO as well as those consisting of countries not belonging to the WTO (available on request). Finally, we consulted the available internet home pages of the relevant agreements. This variable incorporates information in these sources about dates of official termination or practical cessation of the agreement. Instances of a revised PTA succeeding a predecessor with no interruption, however, manifest themselves in this variable as a continuous stretch in which $PTA = 1$.

*Control Variables*

To adequately assess the effects of these explanatory variables, it is important to control for various other factors that previous studies have identified as likely influences on bilateral trade flows and on membership in trade agreements.[60] All of these variables are measured in year $t - 1$. Gravity models emphasize that trade flows between states $i$ and $j$ are influenced by each state's GDP and per capita GDP (or equivalently, national population).[61] We also control for the existence of a currency union between states $i$ and $j$.[62] In addition, we include three dummy variables measuring political-military conflict. The first indicates whether state $i$ was the site of an armed conflict (either civil or international); the second indicates whether state $j$ was such a site; and the third indicates whether $i$ and $j$ were antagonists in an armed conflict.[63] Finally, we include a 21-point measure of each state's regime type based on the Polity IV data set that ranges from $-10$ for the most autocratic countries to 10 for the most democratic ones.[64] Table 1 provides descriptive statistics on all of our independent variables, as well as our measures of trade volatility.[65]

All five models incorporate fixed effects specific to each ordered pair of countries, $i$ and $j$, as well as year-specific fixed effects. The latter capture system-wide trade shocks felt by all pairs of states. The former control for unobserved sources of pairwise heterogeneity. We include such fixed effects because a number of recent studies have argued that omitting them can dramatically bias coefficient estimates in models of international trade.[66] As a consequence of using this method, how-

60. See Eichengreen and Irwin 1995; Frankel 1997; Mansfield, Milner, and Rosendorff 2000 and 2002; Glick and Rose 2002; Mansfield and Reinhardt 2003; Rose 2003, 2004, and 2005; Gowa and Mansfield 2004; and Goldstein, Rivers, and Tomz 2007.

61. GDP is expressed in trillions of constant 1995 U.S. dollars. Per capita GDP is expressed in thousands of constant 1995 U.S. dollars. Data on these variables are from a hierarchy of sources, starting with the World Bank's *World Development Indicators*, the OECD's *Monthly Statistics of International Trade*, UNCTAD's *Handbook of Statistics On-Line*, the IMF's *World Economic Outlook*, the Penn World Table version 6.1, and the IMF's *International Financial Statistics*. The source for any given observation is available on request.

62. We code currency unions using data in Glick and Rose, which we updated using their sources and definition (Glick and Rose 2002, 1128–29). We discovered a small number of apparent discrepancies between their data and the material contained in the original IMF documents, which we corrected to fit their stated definition.

63. These are from the International Peace Research Institute's (PRIO's) Armed Conflict Dataset, version 2.1. Gleditsch et al. 2002.

64. See Jaggers and Gurr 1995; and Marshall and Jaggers 2005.

65. These various measures of volatility are not highly correlated. In particular, the measure normalized by the partner's GDP exhibits virtually zero correlation with all the others, while the dummy variable measuring a large drop in exports, the absolute change in log exports, and the fitted estimate of the conditional variance, $\hat{\sigma}^2_{i,j,t}$, in Models D and E, have bivariate correlations ranging from 0.08 to 0.15, 0.34, 0.38, and 0.40. Since these operational measures of volatility diverge widely in practice, we should infer support for our hypotheses only if the results from each variable's separate regression are largely in agreement.

66. See Anderson and van Wincoop 2003; and Baltagi, Egger, and Pfaffermayr 2003. The debate over Rose's finding that the GATT/WTO does not increase trade flows has revolved in part around the

**TABLE 1.** *Descriptive statistics*

| *Variables* | *Mean* | *Standard deviation* | *Minimum* | *Maximum* |
|---|---|---|---|---|
| LOG EXPORTS$_{i,j,t}$ | −0.63 | 4.73 | −9.33 | 12.27 |
| ABS(Δ LOG EXPORTS)$_{i,j,t}$ | 1.15 | 2.06 | 0 | 17.92 |
| ABS(Δ EXPORT SHARE)$_{i,j,t}$ | 0.14 | 4.39 | 0 | 1310.0 |
| EXPORT DROP$_{i,j,t}$ | 0.17 | 0.38 | 0 | 1 |
| LOG EXPORTS$_{i,j,t-1}$ | −0.74 | 4.77 | −9.33 | 12.27 |
| DEMOCRACY$_{i,t-1}$ | 0.91 | 7.73 | −10 | 10 |
| DEMOCRACY$_{j,t-1}$ | 0.86 | 7.73 | −10 | 10 |
| CONFLICT$_{i,j,t-1}$ | 0.001 | 0.033 | 0 | 1 |
| CONFLICT$_{i,t-1}$ | 0.25 | 0.43 | 0 | 1 |
| CONFLICT$_{j,t-1}$ | 0.24 | 0.43 | 0 | 1 |
| LOG GDP$_{i,t-1}$ | 23.98 | 2.03 | 17.73 | 29.79 |
| LOG GDP$_{j,t-1}$ | 23.91 | 2.05 | 17.73 | 29.79 |
| LOG INCOME$_{i,t-1}$ | 7.79 | 1.43 | 3.90 | 11.05 |
| LOG INCOME$_{j,t-1}$ | 7.78 | 1.44 | 3.90 | 11.05 |
| CURRENCY UNION$_{i,j,t-1}$ | 0.02 | 0.13 | 0 | 1 |
| WTO$_{i,j,t-1}$ | 0.47 | 0.50 | 0 | 1 |
| PTA$_{i,j,t-1}$ | 0.09 | 0.28 | 0 | 1 |

*Notes:* $N$ = 527,883 (the sample used in Models A, B, D, and E). $N$ = 473,797 for EXPORT DROP, which is used only in Model C. Number of countries = 162. Number of country-pairs (dyads) = 11,194. Number of ordered country-pairs (directed dyads) = 21,167. Average number of years per directed dyad = 24.9.

ever, we cannot estimate the impact of factors that are constant over time within an ordered pair of countries. Some factors of this sort—especially bilateral distance, border contiguity, and past colonial relationships—are often included in gravity models that omit pairwise fixed effects. Similarly, such a tiny fraction of country pairs change their alliance status over our sample period that we are not able to control for that variable either. However, excluding these covariates does not introduce bias since their effects are fully absorbed into the cross-sectional fixed effects.[67]

### *The Models*

Models A, B, and C include PTA$_{i,j,t-1}$, WTO$_{i,j,t-1}$, the control variables described above, and the lagged export level, $\ln X_{i,j,t-1}$. Models D and E—the heteroskedas-

issue of whether to include country-specific or pair-specific fixed effects in the estimation. See Rose 2003; Goldstein, Rivers, and Tomz 2007; and Subramanian and Wei 2007. Yet the results we report below, on the negative impact of GATT/WTO and PTA membership on trade volatility, become much stronger, not weaker, if we exclude fixed effects from our estimation. Not surprisingly, tests of the collective significance of the sets of cross-sectional and year-specific fixed effects validate their inclusion, with $p < .001$ in each model.

67. Of the pairs in our sample, forty-three (21 percent) experience at least one change in GATT/WTO or PTA membership, respectively. As such there is considerable within-dyad as well as across-dyad variation in our central independent variables.

tic regression and ARCH-in-mean model—include $\text{PTA}_{i,j,t-1}$, $\text{WTO}_{i,j,t-1}$, all the control variables, and $\ln X_{i,j,t-1}$ in their export levels equations (3 and 5, above).[68] Their variance equations (4) and (6) incorporate $\text{PTA}_{i,j,t-1}$, $\text{WTO}_{i,j,t-1}$, $\ln X_{i,j,t-1}$, year-specific fixed effects, and $\text{CURRENCY UNION}_{i,j,t-1}$. We add the latter variable because participation in a currency union is likely to stabilize prices.

## Results

The regression estimates for Models A to C (the three different year-on-year change measures), Model D (heteroskedastic regression), and Model E (ARCH-in-mean) are shown in Tables 2, 3, and 4, respectively. All five models provide strong and consistent support for our hypotheses. Both PTAs and the GATT/WTO reduce the volatility of exports in a substantively meaningful and statistically significant fashion. This finding does not depend on which measure of volatility is analyzed, and it is quite robust statistically, as we describe below. Moreover, the Model E results—which parse out the direct and indirect effects of trade agreements on export levels—show that some of the beneficial impact these agreements have on export levels stems from their ability to reduce volatility rather than from increased market access alone.

### *Models A to D*

Models A to D provide a good overall fit.[69] Moreover, in Models A, B, and C, and in Model D's variance equation, the estimated coefficients of PTA and WTO are negative and statistically significant, as we expected. Trade agreements reduce absolute changes in exports, whether logged or as a share of the partner's market, and they decrease the chances of a collapse in bilateral exports. They also reduce the instantaneous variance of export flows, as evidenced in Model D's variance function.

68. We incorporate the ordered pair-specific fixed effects in the levels equations of Models D and E through the technique of de-meaning. Doing so makes estimation of these already computationally demanding models feasible, with no consequence for the estimates reported below.

69. The fact that these models explain a relatively small proportion of the sample variance, however, is to be expected. While there are identifiable institutional determinants of volatility, a large fraction of the variation in volatility is due to chance. It is also important to note that our results are not threatened by some common regression assumption violations. Multicolinearity is not sizable, with a maximum variance inflation factor (VIF) of 2.7. While tests reveal the presence of heteroskedasticity in these models—not surprisingly, since this is the central theoretical focus of Models D and E—we base tests of statistical significance on heteroskedastic-consistent standard errors that address this problem. Furthermore, we address potential serial correlation in the data by controlling for the lagged value of exports in all models, including Model D's variance equation. What is more, Maddala-Wu panel unit root tests (with trend and constant) reject the null hypothesis of nonstationarity in any of the ordered pairs' series, with $p < .001$, for the dependent variables in all five models. See Maddala and Wu 1999.

**TABLE 2.** *Trade volatility models*

| | Model A | | Model B | | Model C | |
|---|---|---|---|---|---|---|
| *Estimation* | *OLS* | | *OLS* | | *Conditional logit* | |
| *Dependent variable* | ABS(Δ LOG EXPORTS)$_{i,j,t}$ | | ABS(Δ EXPORT SHARE)$_{i,j,t}$ | | EXPORT DROP$_{i,j,t}$ | |
| *Units* | *Log 1995 \$ millions* | | *% of partner's GDP* | | *Cutoff: > 50 % drop* | |
| | *Coefficient* | *Standard error* | *Coefficient* | *Standard error* | *Coefficient* | *Standard error* |
| *Constant* | 2.760** | (1.009) | 11.125** | (2.993) | — | - |
| LOG EXPORTS$_{i,j,t-1}$ | −0.038** | (0.003) | 0.028** | (0.008) | 0.495** | (0.004) |
| DEMOCRACY$_{i,t-1}$ | 0.000 | (0.001) | 0.001 | (0.003) | −0.001 | (0.002) |
| DEMOCRACY$_{j,t-1}$ | 0.000 | (0.001) | 0.003* | (0.002) | −0.005** | (0.002) |
| CONFLICT$_{i,j,t-1}$ | 0.113 | (0.178) | −0.101 | (0.088) | 1.608** | (0.235) |
| CONFLICT$_{i,t-1}$ | 0.032** | (0.011) | 0.078** | (0.019) | 0.059** | (0.018) |
| CONFLICT$_{j,t-1}$ | 0.055** | (0.011) | 0.149** | (0.046) | 0.138** | (0.018) |
| LOG GDP$_{i,t-1}$ | 0.032 | (0.039) | −0.191* | (0.095) | −0.062 | (0.070) |
| LOG GDP$_{j,t-1}$ | −0.091** | (0.034) | −0.358** | (0.090) | −0.768** | (0.068) |
| LOG INCOME$_{i,t-1}$ | −0.114** | (0.035) | 0.283** | (0.089) | −0.334** | (0.067) |
| LOG INCOME$_{j,t-1}$ | 0.055 | (0.031) | 0.008 | (0.037) | 0.451** | (0.066) |
| CURRENCY UNION$_{i,j,t-1}$ | −0.014 | (0.060) | 0.025 | (0.027) | −0.368** | (0.105) |
| WTO$_{i,j,t-1}$ | −0.060** | (0.016) | −0.066** | (0.020) | −0.166** | (0.028) |
| PTA$_{i,j,t-1}$ | −0.111** | (0.019) | −0.068* | (0.028) | −0.379** | (0.037) |
| *N* | 527,883 | | 527,883 | | 473,797 | |
| *Model test* | $F = 43.1^{**}$ | | $F = 8.1^{**}$ | | $\chi^2 = 15005.9^{**}$ | |
| *Fit to sample* | Adj. $R^2 = .149$ | | Adj. $R^2 = .160$ | | Pseudo-$R^2 = .195$ | |

*Notes:* All tests of statistical significance are two-tailed. Robust standard errors clustered by dyad are in parentheses. All models include year-specific as well as directed-dyad-specific fixed effects. OLS = ordinary least squares. $*p < .05$; $**p < .01$.

The volatility-reducing impact of PTA and GATT/WTO membership is substantively as well as statistically significant. Figure 2 compares the predicted values of the volatility measures, based on the estimates of Models A to E, given the absence and presence of PTA and GATT/WTO membership, respectively, holding all other variables at their sample means. In combination, these institutions reduce volatility by about a third, though that value ranges from 14 to 76 percent, depending on the measure used.[70] As shown in the figure, whether membership in GATT/WTO or the average PTA has a greater effect in reducing the volatility of trade likewise varies across the models.[71] Note that this comparison is with the average PTA; the difference may be attenuated when comparing the GATT/WTO to, say, the EU, or the handful of other PTAs with comparably strong institutions and dispute settlement regimes.

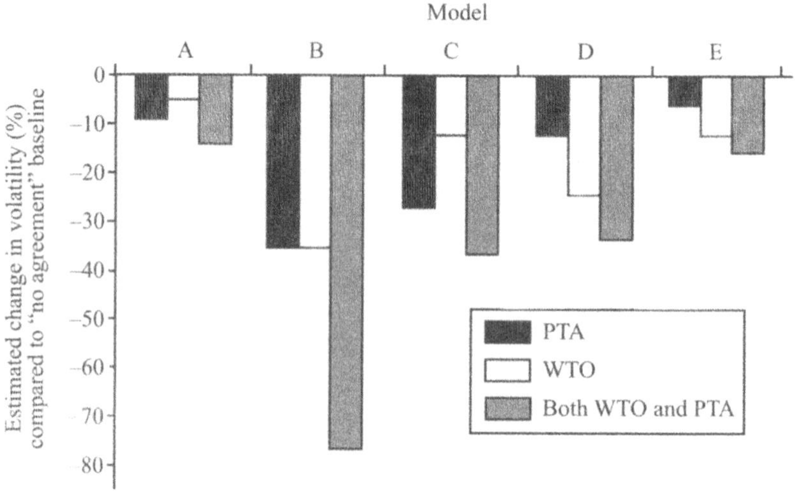


**FIGURE 2.** *Estimated impact of trade institutions on trade volatility*

What is the impact of PTAs and WTO membership on trade levels in Model D? As shown in the first column of Table 3, both PTAs and the GATT/WTO strongly

70. Recall that the logarithmic scale of the dependent variable in Models A, D, and E compresses these apparent differences. In real dollar terms, the percentages would be higher.

71. We can reject the null hypothesis that the estimated coefficients of $PTA_{i,j,t-1}$ and $WTO_{i,j,t-1}$ are equal in all cases except Model B ($p < .05$). $PTA_{i,j,t-1}$ has a stronger effect than $WTO_{i,j,t-1}$ in Models A and C; but the reverse is true in the variance equations for Models D and E.

boost the level of bilateral exports, while simultaneously reducing trade volatility (see the table's third column).

**TABLE 3.** ***Heteroskedastic regression model of trade levels and volatility***

| | *Model D* | | | |
|---|---|---|---|---|
| *Dependent variable* | LOG EXPORTS$_{i,j,t}$ | | LOG VARIANCE$_{i,j,t}$ | |
| *Units* | *Log 1995 $ millions* | | | |
| | *Coefficient* | *Standard error* | *Coefficient* | *Standard error* |
| *Constant* | — | — | 1.741** | (0.014) |
| LOG EXPORTS$_{i,j,t-1}$ | — | — | −0.098** | (0.001) |
| DEMOCRACY$_{i,t-1}$ | 0.018** | (0.001) | — | — |
| DEMOCRACY$_{j,t-1}$ | 0.016** | (0.001) | — | — |
| CONFLICT$_{i,j,t-1}$ | −2.606** | (0.211) | — | — |
| CONFLICT$_{i,t-1}$ | −0.180** | (0.011) | — | — |
| CONFLICT$_{j,t-1}$ | −0.129** | (0.010) | — | — |
| LOG GDP$_{i,t-1}$ | 1.394** | (0.026) | — | — |
| LOG GDP$_{j,t-1}$ | 1.723** | (0.022) | — | — |
| LOG INCOME$_{i,t-1}$ | −0.835** | (0.024) | — | — |
| LOG INCOME$_{j,t-1}$ | −1.165** | (0.020) | — | — |
| CURRENCY UNION$_{i,j,t-1}$ | 0.806** | (0.044) | 0.421** | (0.022) |
| WTO$_{i,j,t-1}$ | 0.217** | (0.012) | −0.284** | (0.006) |
| PTA$_{i,j,t-1}$ | 0.417** | (0.014) | −0.128** | (0.013) |
| *N* | 527,883 | | | |
| *Model test* | $\chi^2 \rightarrow p < .001$ | | $\chi^2 \rightarrow p < .001$ | |

*Notes:* All tests of statistical significance are two-tailed. Robust standard errors are in parentheses. Both equations include year-specific fixed effects, and the export levels equation includes directed-dyad-specific fixed effects. *$p < .05$; **$p < .01$.

The volatility-reducing effects of PTAs and the GATT/WTO in Models A to D are robust to a wide variety of statistical challenges. First, the effects hold for all four measures of export volatility. Second, these effects persist even after dropping observations where the value of the dependent variable is extremely large.[72] Third, the results are unchanged if we add three variables indicating whether the exporter, the importer, or the pair are members of the EC; or if we add the GDP growth rate of each country to the models. Fourth, the coefficient estimates of PTA and WTO remain negative and statistically significant in Model C, even if we reduce the threshold at which EXPORT DROP equals 1 from 50 percent to 25 percent or 10

72. Specifically, the findings apply if we drop cases where $Abs(\Delta \text{LOG EXPORTS})_{i,j,t}$ exceeds 10.

percent. Fifth, the results are also unchanged if we employ Newey-West standard errors that are robust to first-order autocorrelation as well as heteroskedasticity. Sixth, the two trade institution variables retain their effects if we recode the conflict variables using a higher threshold of violence ("war") or if we add a variable indicating whether either state in the dyad had a contiguous neighbor participating in a war in year $t - 1$. Seventh, the results are robust to the inclusion of a variable measuring the past year's bilateral exchange rate variability.[73]

Two other sensitivity tests deserve special attention. First, some recent studies have argued that only the most powerful states in the global system benefit from the protections afforded by trade agreements.[74] Gowa and Kim, in particular, find that GATT membership boosts trade flows only among pairs of industrial nations.[75] Could our findings about the trade-stabilizing effects of trade agreements likewise be driven by patterns unique to dyads of powerful states? To find out, we re-estimated Models A, B, and C, after excluding all industrial country pairs (20,288 observations), based on Gowa and Kim's list of industrial states.[76] The resulting coefficient estimates of PTA and WTO are virtually identical to those in Table 2: they remain negative, statistically significant, and sizable. Trade agreements decrease the volatility of commerce for all types of member-states, not just for the most powerful countries.

Second, it is useful to address the possibility that the effects of trade agreements vary over time. Could a trade agreement actually raise the volatility of trade when it is initially implemented, as the market adjusts to recent trade barrier reductions? In fact, there is reason to expect that this will not be the case. Most PTAs and most cases in which states accede to the GATT/WTO involve prolonged negotiations over at least a few years, with every development being widely reported. Then there is usually a delay for ratification and for the ratified deal to take effect. Consequently, the impact of the ensuing changes in trade barriers among members should be widely foreseen. Firms and other economic actors, in turn, are likely to start adjusting to these changes well in advance of the trade agreement's implementation, thereby limiting any increase in volatility during its initial stages.

To address this issue further, we re-estimated Models A to C after adding two dichotomous variables. The first indicated whether the country-pair had recently established a PTA; the second indicated whether the pair had recently become joint parties to the GATT/WTO. For each variable, we coded recent membership in three different ways: as less than one year in duration, as less than three years,

73. The variable in question is the (absolute value of the) percentage drop from year $t - 1$ to year $t$ of the nominal bilateral exchange rate, expressed in terms of the side losing its value (from the IMF's *International Financial Statistics*). Joint membership in either type of trade agreement is virtually unrelated to bilateral exchange rate volatility across our sample: this variable has a bivariate correlation with PTA and WTO of less than $|0.02|$.

74. See, for example, Bagwell and Staiger 2002; and Blonigen and Bown 2003.

75. Gowa and Kim 2005.

76. Ibid., 468.

and as less than five years. Regardless of how we coded these variables, however, none of the associated coefficient estimates were positive and statistically significant. Furthermore, including these variables had no bearing on the remaining results. Trade agreements therefore reduce the volatility of bilateral trade when they are new as well as when they have matured.

*Model E: ARCH-in-Mean*

As shown in Table 4, Model E also provides a good fit to the data. Moreover, the parameters that distinguish it from Model D—the ARCH-in-mean (ARCH.M), ARCH.1, and AR.1 terms—are statistically significant, indicating that this is an appropriate generalization of heteroskedastic regression with which to analyze our data.[77] It is therefore particularly noteworthy that this model yields the same basic results as the earlier models: PTA membership and GATT/WTO membership both decrease the instantaneous variance in real exports. These findings are statistically and substantively significant. Figure 2 shows the variance as estimated in Model E, holding all other variables at their sample means, and including the average ARCH.1 component of the variance, for different combinations of PTA and GATT/WTO membership. Compared to a baseline predicted variance if no agreements were in place, a PTA reduces variability by 6.1 [3.6, 8.5] percent; the GATT/WTO reduces variability by 12.3 [11.2, 13.4] percent; and both agreements together reduce variability by 16.2 [14.3, 18.1] percent (where the figures in brackets form a 95 percent confidence interval around these point predictions). That this is the weakest substantive effect among our five models probably stems from the apparent ARCH.1 process at work. Volatility spills over from one year to the next, a dynamic that should not be attributed to the impact of trade institutions.

However, as we mentioned earlier, the ARCH-in-mean model allows us to parse out the direct and indirect impact of trade agreements on the level of exports. The results are striking. First, the negative and statistically significant coefficient of the ARCH.M term in the export levels model indicates that heightened volatility itself reduces exports. This is consistent with the argument that private traders and investors respond rapidly to expected volatility by decreasing their commerce with the affected market.

Second, by reducing volatility, trade agreements indirectly boost export levels. Of course, since the estimated coefficients of WTO and PTA are positive and statistically significant in the export levels equation, both kinds of agreements directly increase the volume of bilateral trade. Compared to an otherwise-average reference point with no agreements in place, and ignoring the impact of reduced vari-

77. However, even a simple ARCH-in-mean model such as that reflected in equations (5) and (6), applied to this large data set is exceptionally time consuming to estimate and would be unlikely to converge if we extended it further. The estimates in Table 4 were generated in Stata 9.1 SE using "arch . . . , noconstant arch(1/1) archm(1) het(. . .) robust difficult," which successfully converged at the default tolerance in 214 iterations.

**TABLE 4.** *ARCH-in-mean model of trade levels and volatility*

| | *Model E* | | | |
|---|---|---|---|---|
| *Dependent variables* | LOG EXPORTS$_{i,j,t}$ | | LOG VARIANCE$_{i,j,t}$ | |
| *Units* | *Log 1995 \$ millions* | | | |
| | *Coefficient* | *Standard error* | *Coefficient* | *Standard error* |
| *Constant* | — | — | 0.959** | (0.035) |
| LOG EXPORTS$_{i,j,t-1}$ | — | — | −0.178** | (0.003) |
| DEMOCRACY$_{i,t-1}$ | 0.012** | (0.002) | — | — |
| DEMOCRACY$_{j,t-1}$ | 0.006** | (0.002) | — | — |
| CONFLICT$_{i,j,t-1}$ | −0.723* | (0.320) | — | — |
| CONFLICT$_{i,t-1}$ | −0.049** | (0.013) | — | — |
| CONFLICT$_{j,t-1}$ | −0.051** | (0.012) | — | — |
| LOG GDP$_{i,t-1}$ | 1.319** | (0.078) | — | — |
| LOG GDP$_{j,t-1}$ | 1.526** | (0.055) | — | — |
| LOG INCOME$_{i,t-1}$ | −0.914** | (0.076) | — | — |
| LOG INCOME$_{j,t-1}$ | −1.064** | (0.052) | — | — |
| CURRENCY UNION$_{i,j,t-1}$ | 0.434** | (0.067) | 0.601** | (0.078) |
| WTO$_{i,j,t-1}$ | 0.161** | (0.021) | −0.439** | (0.020) |
| PTA$_{i,j,t-1}$ | 0.290** | (0.030) | −0.195** | (0.044) |
| $\sigma^2_{i,j,t}$ (ARCH.M) | −0.020** | (0.001) | — | — |
| $\rho$ (AR.1) | 0.484** | (0.005) | | |
| $\varepsilon^2_{i,j,t-1}$ (ARCH.1) | — | — | 0.799** | (0.010) |
| *N* | 527,883 | | | |
| *Model test* | $\chi^2 \rightarrow p < .001$ | | $\chi^2 \rightarrow p < .001$ | |

*Notes:* All tests of statistical significance are two-tailed. Robust standard errors are in parentheses. Both equations include year-specific fixed effects, and the export levels equation includes directed-dyad-specific fixed effects. *$p < .05$; **$p < .01$.

ance, joint membership in the GATT/WTO, a PTA, or both types of agreements directly boosts export levels by 17 [13, 22], 34 [26, 42], or 57 [45, 69] percent, respectively. Going beyond this direct effect, because trade agreements reduce the variance of trade, they also increase commercial flows indirectly, when the predicted variance is multiplied by the ARCH.M term in the levels equation. Specifically, through this channel, joint membership in the GATT/WTO, a PTA, or both types of agreements enhances exports by another 1.5 [1.3, 1.8], 0.9 [0.5, 1.2], and 2.7 [2.2, 3.2] percent, respectively.

Although these are relatively modest additions, they are nonetheless substantively meaningful, especially for the GATT/WTO. We can see this more clearly by expressing the findings somewhat differently. Absent a trade agreement, high volatility acts as a substantial "tax" on commerce, reducing the expected value of exports by an estimated 9.9 [8.6, 11.2] percent. With the GATT/WTO and a PTA in place, this volatility tax on the average pair's exports shrinks to 8.4 [7.3, 9.5] percent. Consequently, the gain in exports from the two agreements working together to reduce volatility is comparable to the gain achieved by cutting the average nominal tariff by 1.5 percent. That is equal to about half of the tariff cut (3.2 percent) made by high-income countries in the Uruguay Round for all merchandise products, and the Uruguay Round tariff reductions corresponded to a 35 percent, 1.2 trillion dollar, real increase in goods imports by those countries (comparing 1990 imports with those in 2000).[78] A volatility tax cut of 1.5 percent should thus affect the volume of foreign trade very substantially indeed.

### *Control Variables*

Before concluding, we should also summarize the effects of the control variables. While these factors are not central to our analysis, little empirical work has been conducted on the political economy of trade volatility, so the results should be of interest. A few variables exert a strong and a fairly uniform influence, regardless of which measure of volatility is analyzed. Military conflict is associated with greater volatility in overseas commerce and exports to countries with large markets are less volatile. However, the remaining variables do not have a consistent impact on trade volatility.[79]

In addition, there is some evidence that currency unions increase export volatility (at least in Models D and E). Very little research has been accumulated on this issue, but Rose finds that monetary unions have no systemic effect on trade volatility.[80] As shown by our Models D and E, however, a number of related studies conclude that currency unions promote the flow of trade among members.[81] How can these findings be reconciled? One insight with venerable roots is that countries in currency unions generally have higher output volatility; conversely, more flexible exchange rate arrangements help insulate a country against terms-of-trade shocks. Trade volatility is a likely byproduct of output volatility and macroeconomic fluctuations, which affect production and demand for traded goods. Consistent with this point, Edwards and Levy-Yeyati and Broda report that terms-of-trade shocks have a significantly greater impact on real GDP in countries with

78. Finger, Ingco, and Reincke 1996, 47.

79. It should also be noted that most of the estimates in the models of export levels (the first columns of Tables 3 and 4) accord with our expectations. That GDP is positively related to trade is consistent with predictions based on the gravity model (Frankel 1997). Furthermore, like previous studies, we find that (1) democracy and currency unions promote the flow of trade; (2) military conflict inhibits commerce; and (3) the level of exports exhibits temporal dependence. If per capita GDP has an unexpected sign here, that is because of the inclusion of pair-specific fixed effects, which absorb the major contrasts in trade levels evident when comparing rich pairs with poor ones. See Eichengreen and Irwin 1995; Frankel 1997; Mansfield, Milner, and Rosendorff 2000; Glick and Rose 2002; Mansfield and Reinhardt 2003; Rose 2003 and 2004; and Gowa and Mansfield 2004.

80. Rose 2005.

81. See Glick and Rose 2002; and Klein and Shambaugh 2004. In no case do our results regarding CURRENCY UNION change if we use Glick and Rose's exact coding, with the attendant restrictions that are placed on the sample.

a nominally fixed exchange rate regime.[82] Edwards and Magendzo, and Levy-Yeyati and Sturzenegger also find that countries with fixed currencies experience more volatility in the rate of economic growth.[83] Glick and Rose's measure of currency unions focuses only on the nominal currency regime, and only on the most extreme form of regime.[84] More recent work on exchange rates has emphasized *de facto* exchange rate regime classifications, with a wider range of types represented.[85] Perhaps this distinction between *de jure* and *de facto* currency regimes is empirically significant for trade. Future studies might address this puzzle by examining the relationships among the exchange rate regime, trade volatility, and trade levels with these richer data on currency policies.

## Discussion

Our results offer strong evidence that PTAs and the GATT/WTO reduce the volatility of exports. Moreover, there is ample reason to be confident in this finding. We have analyzed the largest possible sample of cases, indeed, the entire population of independent countries since World War II. We have measured trade volatility using a number of different indices and techniques. Our findings are robust with respect to a range of statistical challenges and estimation methods.

Not only do trade agreements reduce the volatility of exports, lower export volatility itself increases the level of exports. By addressing this issue, we have been able to identify the direct and the indirect influence of such agreements on export levels. Our findings indicate that indirect effects are indeed at work: the boost in export levels associated with PTA and GATT/WTO membership stems in part from the tendency for these institutions to reduce trade volatility, rather than solely from their ability to increase market access. These results accord with the conventional wisdom that private traders and investors prefer stability in (cross-border) relative prices. Moreover, private-market actors seem to respond to the assurance of such stability, which is promoted by trade agreements, by increasing their overseas commerce and investment.

Nevertheless, another possibility is that our results reflect a tendency to form commercial agreements on the part of states that, for whatever reason, already have stable trade relations. If so, then the effect of PTAs would be spurious to a pre-existing harmony of interests.[86] However, further analysis, based on our earlier study of PTA formation among GATT/WTO members, allows us to refute this possibility.[87] We add (one at a time) the various volatility measures from our cur-

82. See Edwards and Levy-Yeyati 2003; and Broda 2004.
83. See Edwards and Magendzo 2003; and Levy-Yeyati and Sturzenegger 2003.
84. Glick and Rose 2002.
85. See Levy-Yeyati and Sturzenegger 2003; and Klein and Shambaugh 2004.
86. Downs, Rocke, and Barsoom 1996.
87. Mansfield and Reinhardt 2003.

rent article, lagged by one year, to the three models of PTA formation reported in Table 2 of our earlier study.[88] Model A's and Model B's measures of volatility have no impact on the establishment of PTAs. Model C's measure is inversely related to PTA formation, whereas the observation-specific variance estimated from Models D and E is positively associated with the formation of PTAs. Taken together, these results provide no evidence that trade volatility has a clear, systematic influence on preferential arrangements. Furthermore, to the extent that volatility does affect these arrangements, the results based on the measures in Models D and E indicate that country-pairs experiencing extensive trade volatility are especially likely to enter PTAs—no doubt for the reasons we have advanced in this article. These findings suggest that the estimates of Models D and E in Tables 3 and 4 actually may underestimate the impact of PTAs on trade volatility.

Consider the example of Germany's exports to Finland, Sweden, and Austria in the wake of their accession to the EU in 1995. Not surprisingly, the level of German exports to those three countries increased after accession. The volatility of its exports to them decreased considerably at the same time. Specifically, the average absolute percentage change in the real value of exports to these three countries dropped from 12.1 to 5.7, comparing the five years before and after 1995. Alternatively, Germany's comparable figure averaged over all other developed GATT/WTO member-states actually rose from 15.5 to 17.4 over the same two periods. This case illustrates the independent role that PTAs play in reducing trade volatility.

Our results also bear on an interesting and important debate over whether the GATT/WTO promotes international trade. This debate was stimulated in large measure by a series of studies in which Rose found that GATT/WTO membership does not increase the volume of trade conducted by country-pairs.[89] As shown in the first column of Tables 3 and 4, our results point in the opposite direction since the GATT/WTO directly increases bilateral trade flows. Of greater importance for present purposes, however, is the divergence between Rose's conclusion that the GATT/WTO does not dampen trade volatility and our finding that this institution markedly reduces such volatility.[90]

In part, this divergence stems from how trade volatility is measured. In contrast to our dependent variables, Rose measures volatility as the variation within a time series (of observations of $X_{i,j,t}$) for a given country measured over 25-year periods. However, as we have argued, his approach ignores period-to-period variation and conflates predictable changes in trade with unexpected fluctuations. Our measures of volatility, though rough in some ways, do not suffer from these limitations.

Furthermore, our results cast doubt on his conclusion that the multilateral trade regime has little overall bearing on international trade. Rose does not account for the effect of trade volatility on trade flows. We do so and find that the GATT/

88. Ibid., 849.
89. Rose 2003 and 2004.
90. Rose 2005.

WTO regime does indeed boost trade levels indirectly, by reducing volatility. This could be the case even if it did not do so directly by expanding market access.

As Rose argues, the GATT/WTO has not done as much as might be expected to reduce trade barriers.[91] After all, the Generalized System of Preferences and other nonreciprocal schemes undermine the multilateral regime's applicability.[92] Likewise, many countries have far higher Uruguay Round bindings than applied tariffs, suggesting that the GATT/WTO does not universally operate to reduce trade barriers reciprocally.[93] Nonetheless, the GATT/WTO's impact on exports is not trivial. Apart from reducing trade barriers, this institution secures and binds policies, locking them in place at their status quo level, whatever that may be. Such stability and security reduces the "volatility tax" that otherwise dampens international commerce, thereby promoting trade among the contracting parties to the multilateral trade regime.

The issues addressed in this article raise various questions for future research. For instance, we have argued that trade institutions reduce volatility in relative international prices and, consequently, variability in trade flows. Whereas we have focused attention on the volatility of trade, it would be useful to analyze more directly whether participation in such institutions reduces terms-of-trade volatility. Similarly, we have argued that trade institutions deter members from introducing new protectionist barriers on the products of other participants. As with most of the studies in this area, however, we do not measure trade policy directly since reliable data of this sort are in very short supply. There is a pressing need for more and better data on trade policy, as well as for samples that include new instances of trade protection and "noncases" where protection is merely contemplated but not imposed.[94] Furthermore, not all trade agreements are alike. Do differences across agreements in the breadth and depth of market access concessions, dispute settlement institutions, heterogeneity of membership, and organizational development condition how much they reduce trade volatility? There is reason to think so, based on the argument presented here, and future research could usefully explore this issue. Finally, we have argued that trade institutions reduce volatility by stabilizing the expectations of private traders and investors. It would be useful to analyze this micro-causal mechanism more directly in a study cast at the level of individual firms' responses to trade agreement formation.

## Conclusions

In this article, we have presented some of the first systemic evidence that international institutions stabilize and reduce the volatility in international outcomes.

91. Rose 2004; see also Milner and Kubota 2005.
92. Özden and Reinhardt 2005b.
93. Finger, Ingco, and Reincke 1996.
94. Busch, Raciborski, and Reinhardt 2007.

Despite the voluminous literature that has been generated on international institutions, remarkably little emphasis has been placed on exactly how they operate to affect state behavior and what sorts of behavior they influence. The studies that have addressed this issue place virtually no emphasis on the ability of such institutions to reduce the volatility of outcomes, focusing instead on whether the level of a given outcome rises in the presence of an international institution. We have shown, however, that ignoring the volatility-reducing effects of international institutions and regimes risks both significantly underestimating their impact on global outcomes and presenting a distorted picture of how these institutions affect international relations.

Our analysis also helps to clarify why recent empirical research has been characterized by such heated debate about the effect of the GATT/WTO on trade. These debates stem partly from the emphasis that existing studies place on the level of trade without also considering its volatility. Once we take trade volatility into account, the beneficial impact of trade agreements becomes particularly apparent. Finally, our results show that international institutions can benefit members as much by locking in the status quo as by improving it. Such institutions have an important effect on the international economy, but for reasons quite different than those advanced in most of the existing literature on this topic.

## References

Abbott, Frederick M. 2000. NAFTA and the Legalization of World Politics: A Case Study. *International Organization* 54 (3):519–47.

Adserà, Alicia, and Carles Boix. 2002. Trade, Democracy, and the Size of the Public Sector: The Political Underpinnings of Openness. *International Organization* 56 (3):229–62.

Aizenman, Joshua. 2003. Volatility, Employment, and the Patterns of FDI in Emerging Markets. *Journal of Development Economics* 72 (2):585–601.

Anderson, James E., and Eric van Wincoop. 2003. Gravity with Gravitas: A Solution to the Border Puzzle. *American Economic Review* 93 (1):170–92.

Bagwell, Kyle, and Robert W. Staiger. 2002. *The Economics of the World Trading System*. Cambridge, Mass.: MIT Press.

Baltagi, Badi H., Peter Egger, and Michael Pfaffermayr. 2003. A Generalized Design for Bilateral Trade Flow Models. *Economics Letters* 80 (3):391–97.

Bernhard, William, and David Leblang. 2006. *Democratic Processes and Financial Markets: Pricing Politics*. New York: Cambridge University Press.

Blackhurst, Richard. 1998. The Capacity of the WTO to Fulfill Its Mandate. In *The WTO as an International Organization*, edited by Anne O. Krueger, 31–58. Chicago: University of Chicago Press.

Blonigen, Bruce A., and Chad P. Bown. 2003. Antidumping and Retaliation Threats. *Journal of International Economics* 60 (2):249–73.

Botcheva, Liliana, and Lisa L. Martin. 2001. Institutional Effects on State Behavior: Convergence and Divergence. *International Studies Quarterly* 45 (1):1–26.

Braumoeller, Bear F. 2006. Explaining Variance: Or, Stuck in a Moment We Can't Get Out of. *Political Analysis* 14:268–90.

Broda, Christian. 2004. Terms of Trade and Exchange Rate Regimes in Developing Countries. *Journal of International Economics* 63 (1):31–58.

Busch, Marc L., Rafal Raciborski, and Eric Reinhardt. 2007. Does the WTO Matter? US Antidumping Investigations and the Rule of Law. Unpublished manuscript, Department of Political Science, Emory University, Atlanta, Ga.

Busch, Marc L., and Eric Reinhardt. 2003. Developing Countries and GATT/WTO Dispute Settlement. *Journal of World Trade* 37 (4):719–35.

Correlates of War Project. 2003. State System Membership List Version 2002.1. Available at ⟨http://correlatesofwar.org⟩. Accessed 26 February 2008.

Davis, Christina L. 2004. International Institutions and Issue Linkage: Building Support for Agricultural Trade Liberalization. *American Political Science Review* 98 (1):153–69.

Desai, Mihir A., and James R. Hines Jr. 2004. Market Reactions to Export Subsidies. NBER Working Paper 10233. Cambridge, Mass.: National Bureau of Economic Research.

Devereux, Michael B., and Philip R. Lane. 2003. Understanding Bilateral Exchange Rate Volatility. *Journal of International Economics* 60 (1):109–32.

Downs, George W., David M. Rocke, and Peter N. Barsoom. 1996. Is the Good News About Compliance Good News About Cooperation? *International Organization* 50 (3):379–406.

Drabek, Zdenek, and Marc Bacchetta. 2004. Tracing the Effects of WTO Accession on Policy-Making in Sovereign States: Preliminary Lessons from the Recent Experience of Transition Countries. *World Economy* 27 (7):1083–125.

Easterly, William, and Aart Kraay. 2000. Small States, Small Problems? Income, Growth, and Volatility in Small States. *World Development* 28 (11):2013–27.

Edwards, Sebastian, and Eduardo Levy-Yeyati. 2003. Flexible Exchange Rates as Shock Absorbers. NBER Working Paper 9867. Cambridge, Mass.: National Bureau of Economic Research.

Edwards, Sebastian, and I. Igal Magendzo. 2003. A Currency of One's Own? An Empirical Investigation on Dollarization and Independent Currency Unions. NBER Working Paper 9514. Cambridge, Mass.: National Bureau of Economic Research.

Eichengreen, Barry, and Douglas A. Irwin. 1995. Trade Blocs, Currency Blocs, and the Reorientation of World Trade in the 1930s. *Journal of International Economics* 38 (1–2):1–24.

Engle, Robert F. 2001. GARCH 101: The Use of ARCH/GARCH Models in Applied Econometrics. *Journal of Economic Perspectives* 15 (4):157–68.

Engle, Robert F., David M. Lilien, and Russell P. Robins. 1987. Estimating Time Varying Risk Premia in the Term Structure: The Arch-M Model. *Econometrica* 55 (2):391–407.

Fernández, Raquel, and Jonathan Portes. 1998. Returns to Regionalism: An Analysis of Nontraditional Gains from Regional Trade Agreements. *World Bank Economic Review* 12 (2):197–220.

Finger, J. Michael, Merlinda D. Ingco, and Ulrich Reincke. 1996. *The Uruguay Round: Statistics on Tariff Concessions Given and Received*. Washington, D.C.: World Bank.

Finlayson, Jock A., and Mark W. Zacher. 1981. The GATT and the Regulation of Trade Barriers: Regime Dynamics and Functions. *International Organization* 35 (4):561–602.

Finnemore, Martha. 1993. International Organizations as Teachers of Norms: The United Nations Educational, Scientific, and Cultural Organization and Science Policy. *International Organization* 47 (4):565–97.

Foroutan, Faezeh. 1998. Does Membership in a Regional Preferential Trade Arrangement Make a Country More or Less Protectionist? *World Economy* 21 (3):305–35.

Francois, Joseph, and Gunnar Niels. 2004. Political Influence in a New Anti-Dumping Regime: Evidence from Mexico. CEPER Discussion Paper 4297. London: Centre for Economic Policy Research.

Frankel, Jeffrey A. 1997. *Regional Trading Blocs in the World Economic System*. Washington, D.C.: Institute for International Economics.

Frieden, Jeffrey A. 2002. Real Sources of European Currency Policy: Sectoral Interests and European Monetary Integration. *International Organization* 56 (4):831–60.

General Agreement on Tariffs and Trade (GATT). 1984. *Panel on Newsprint—Report of the Panel*. L/5680. Geneva: GATT.

———. 1994. Report by Ambassador H. Ukawa (Japan), Chairman of the Group on Environmental Measures and International Trade, to the 49th Session of the Contracting Parties. L/7402. Geneva: GATT.

Gleditsch, Nils Petter, Peter Wallensteen, Mikael Eriksson, Margareta Sollenberg, and Håvard Strand. 2002. Armed Conflict 1946–2001: A New Dataset. *Journal of Peace Research* 39 (5): 615–37.

Glick, Reuven, and Andrew K. Rose. 2002. Does a Currency Union Affect Trade? The Time-Series Evidence. *European Economic Review* 46 (6):1125–51.

Goldstein, Judith L., Douglas Rivers, and Michael Tomz. 2007. Institutions in International Relations: Understanding the Effects of the GATT and the WTO on World Trade. *International Organization* 61 (1):37–67.

Gowa, Joanne, and Soo Yeon Kim. 2005. An Exclusive Country Club: The Effects of the GATT on Trade, 1950–94. *World Politics* 57 (4):453–78.

Gowa, Joanne, and Edward D. Mansfield. 2004. Alliances, Imperfect Markets, and Major-Power Trade. *International Organization* 58 (4):775–805.

Hanson, Gordon H., Raymond J. Mataloni Jr., and Matthew J. Slaughter. 2001. Expansion Strategies of U.S. Multinational Firms." In *Brookings Trade Forum: 2001*, edited by Dani Rodrik and Susan Collins, 245–82. Washington, D.C.: Brookings Institution Press.

Hausmann, Ricardo, Ugo Panizza, and Roberto Rigobon. 2004. The Long-Run Volatility Puzzle of the Real Exchange Rate. NBER Working Paper 10751. Cambridge, Mass.: National Bureau of Economic Research.

Hudec, Robert E. 1993. *Enforcing International Trade Law: The Evolution of the Modern GATT Legal System*. Salem, N.H.: Butterworth Legal Publishers.

International Monetary Fund (IMF). 2004. Exchange Rate Volatility and Trade Flows—Some New Evidence. Washington, D.C.: IMF.

Jackson, John H. 2001. The Role and Effectiveness of the WTO Dispute Settlement Mechanism. In *Brookings Trade Forum: 2000*, edited by Susan M. Collins and Dani Rodrik, 179–236. Washington, D.C.: Brookings Institution Press.

Jaggers, Keith, and Ted Robert Gurr. 1995. Tracking Democracy's Third Wave with the Polity III Data. *Journal of Peace Research* 32 (4):469–82.

Keefer, Philip, and David Stasavage. 2002. Checks and Balances, Private Information, and the Credibility of Monetary Commitments. *International Organization* 56 (4):751–74.

Keohane, Robert O. 1983. The Demand for International Regimes. In *International Regimes*, edited by Stephen D. Krasner, 141–71. Ithaca, N.Y.: Cornell University Press.

Kim, So Young. 2007. Openness, External Risk, and Volatility: Implications for the Compensation Hypothesis. *International Organization* 61 (1):181–216.

Klein, Michael W., and Jay C. Shambaugh. 2004. Fixed Exchange Rates and Trade. NBER Working Paper 10696. Cambridge, Mass.: National Bureau of Economic Research.

Koremenos, Barbara, Charles Lipson, and Duncan Snidal. 2001. The Rational Design of International Institutions. *International Organization* 55 (4):761–99.

Krueger, Anne O. 1999. Are Preferential Trading Arrangements Trade-Liberalizing or Protectionist? *Journal of Economic Perspectives* 13 (4):105–24.

Kucik, Jeffrey, and Eric Reinhardt. 2008. Does Flexibility Promote Cooperation? An Application to the Global Trade Regime. *International Organization* 62 (3):477–505.

Leblang, David, and Bumba Mukherjee. 2004. Presidential Elections and the Stock Market: Comparing Markov-Switching and Fractionally Integrated GARCH Models of Volatility. *Political Analysis* 12 (3):296–322.

Levy-Yeyati, Eduardo, and Federico Sturzenegger. 2003. To Float or to Fix: Evidence on the Impact of Exchange Rate Regimes on Growth. *American Economic Review* 93 (4):1173–93.

Maddala, G. S., and Shaowen Wu. 1999. A Comparative Study of Unit Root Tests with Panel Data and a New Simple Test. *Oxford Bulletin of Economics and Statistics* 61 (S1):631–52.

Mansfield, Edward D., Helen V. Milner, and B. Peter Rosendorff. 2000. Free to Trade: Democracies, Autocracies, and International Trade. *American Political Science Review* 94 (2):305–21.

———. 2002. Why Democracies Cooperate More: Electoral Control and International Trade Agreements. *International Organization* 56 (3):477–513.

Mansfield, Edward D., and Eric Reinhardt. 2003. Multilateral Determinants of Regionalism: The Effects of GATT/WTO on the Formation of Preferential Trading Arrangements. *International Organization* 57 (4):829–62.

Markusen, James R., and Keith E. Maskus. 2001. General Equilibrium Approaches to the Multinational Firm: A Review of Theory and Evidence. NBER Working Paper 8334. Cambridge, Mass.: National Bureau of Economic Research.

Marshall, Monty G., and Keith Jaggers. 2005. Polity IV: Political Regime Characteristics and Transitions, 1800–2004. Center for International Development and Conflict Management, University of Maryland.

Martin, Lisa L., and Beth A. Simmons. 1998. Theories and Empirical Studies of International Institutions. *International Organization* 52 (4):729–57.

Milner, Helen V., and Keiko Kubota. 2005. Why the Move to Free Trade? Democracy and Trade Liberalization in the Developing Countries. *International Organization* 59 (1):107–43.

Morrissey, Oliver, and Douglas Nelson. 2001. The Role of the WTO in the Transfer of Policy Knowledge on Trade and Competition. Paper presented at the Conference on Innovation, Competition and Regulation in the Global Economy, September, Margaret River, Australia.

Özden, Caglar, and Eric Reinhardt. 2005a. First Do No Harm: The Effect of Trade Preferences on Developing Country Exports. Unpublished manuscript, Department of Political Science, Emory University, Atlanta, Ga.

———. 2005b. The Perversity of Preferences: GSP and Developing Country Trade Policies, 1976–2000. *Journal of Development Economics* 78 (1):1–21.

Perroni, Carlo, and John Whalley. 2000. The New Regionalism: Trade Liberalization or Insurance? *Canadian Journal of Economics* 33 (1):1–24.

Quinn, Dennis P., and John T. Woolley. 2001. Democracy and National Economic Performance: The Preference for Stability. *American Journal of Political Science* 45 (3):634–57.

Razin, Assaf, Efraim Sadka, and Tarek Coury. 2003. Trade Openness, Investment Instability, and Terms-of-Trade Volatility. *Journal of International Economics* 61 (2):285–306.

Reinhardt, Eric. 2001. Adjudication without Enforcement in GATT Disputes. *The Journal of Conflict Resolution* 45 (2):174–95.

Rodrik, Dani. 1998. Why Do More Open Economies Have Bigger Governments? *Journal of Political Economy* 106 (5):997–1032.

Rose, Andrew K. 2003. Do We Really Know That the WTO Increases Trade? *American Economic Review* 94 (1):98–114.

———. 2004. Do WTO Members Have More Liberal Trade Policy? *Journal of International Economics* 63 (2):209–35.

———. 2005. Does the WTO Make Trade More Stable? *Open Economies Review* 16 (1):7–22.

Scheve, Kenneth, and Matthew J. Slaughter. 2004. Economic Insecurity and the Globalization of Production. *American Journal of Political Science* 48 (4):662–74.

Simmons, Beth A., and Zachary Elkins. 2004. The Globalization of Liberalization: Policy Diffusion in the International Political Economy. *American Political Science Review* 98 (1):171–89.

Smith, James McCall. 2000. The Politics of Dispute Settlement Design: Explaining Legalism in Regional Trade Pacts. *International Organization* 54 (1):137–80.

Subramanian, Arvind, and Shang-Jin Wei. 2007. The WTO Promotes Trade, Strongly but Unevenly. *Journal of International Economics* 72 (1):151–75.

World Trade Organization (WTO). 1998. *European Communities—Customs Classification of Certain Computer Equipment—Report of the Appellate Body*. WT/DS68/AB/R. Geneva: WTO.

———. 2000. Trade Policy Review—Brazil—Minutes of Meeting. WT/TPR/M/75. Geneva: WTO.

Yarbrough, Beth V., and Robert M. Yarbrough. 1992. *Cooperation and Governance in International Trade: The Strategic Organizational Approach*. Princeton, N.J.: Princeton University Press.

# Part II:

# The Political Economy of Trade Policy and Trade Attitudes

# The political economy of nontariff barriers: a cross-national analysis

Edward D. Mansfield and Marc L. Busch

Much research on the determinants of trade policy has focused on the efficacy of societal and statist approaches. Societal theories typically attribute patterns of protection to variations in demands made by pressure groups, whereas statist theories emphasize the effects of the "national interest" and domestic institutions in determining the level of protection. While both approaches have gained considerable currency, debates concerning their relative merits have been heated and long-standing. Yet very little quantitative evidence has been brought to bear on this topic.

In this article, we provide some of the first results of this sort. Our findings indicate that although societal and statist approaches often are considered mutually exclusive, it is more fruitful to view them as complementary. Moreover, the interaction between factors that give rise to demands for protection and those that regulate the provision of protection by policymakers has not been treated adequately in the literature on foreign economic policy. This gap in the literature is fundamentally important, since our results indicate that the interaction between these factors is a central determinant of trade policy. Thus, analyses of commercial policy that fail to consider both societal and statist variables and the interaction between them are likely to be inadequate.

Our analysis centers on explaining cross-national patterns of nontariff barriers (NTBs). Scholars have conducted little cross-national research on trade policy and virtually none with a focus on NTBs. Instead, single-country studies of tariffs comprise much of the existing literature on the political

Earlier versions of this article were presented at the 1993 annual meeting of the American Political Science Association, Washington, D.C., 2–5 September 1993; and the University of Southern California's Workshop on International Relations Theory, Los Angeles, March 1994. We are grateful to Vinod Aggarwal, Jagdish Bhagwati, Youssef Cohen, Eileen Crumm, David Epstein, Joanne Gowa, Robert Keohane, David Lake, Arvid Lukauskas, Helen Milner, Sunita Parikh, Sharyn O'Halloran, John Odell, Dani Rodrik, John Ruggie, Robert Shapiro, Jack Snyder, David Spiro, Hendrick Spruyt, Robert Uriu, and two anonymous reviewers for comments on this article.

*International Organization* 49, 4, Autumn 1995, pp. 723–49
© 1995 by The IO Foundation and the Massachusetts Institute of Technology

NEOMA Business School LIBRARY Campus de Rouen 1, rue du Maréchal Juin BP 215 - Cedex 76825 Mont Saint Aignan Tél : 02 32 82 57 00 economy of commercial policy. Yet the usefulness of societal and statist theories of foreign economic policy hinges on the ability of these theories to explain variations in protection across states, and NTBs have become increasingly pervasive among the advanced industrial countries. Because the General Agreement on Tariffs and Trade (GATT) and the World Trade Organization (WTO) limit the ability of contracting parties to impose tariffs, policymakers who view protection as an attractive means by which to meet the demands of pressure groups or advance state interests are likely to rely primarily on NTBs. Many observers have suggested that this is occurring with increasing regularity and that the recent proliferation of NTBs has done much to offset the gains in liberalization made during successive rounds of the GATT. A fuller understanding is therefore needed of the factors that account for variations in NTBs across states.

## Societal approaches to trade policy

Societal (or pluralist) approaches to the study of foreign economic policy focus primarily on the effects of demands for protection by pressure groups. Societal explanations consider trade policy to be the product of competition among pressure groups and other nonstate actors that are affected by commerce. The impact of these groups on policy depends largely on their ability to organize for the purpose of articulating their demands and on the amount of electoral influence they possess. Societal approaches attribute little importance to policymakers and political institutions for the purposes of explaining trade policy. As G. John Ikenberry, David Lake, and Michael Mastanduno point out, societal theories view the state as "essentially passive; it acts as a disinterested referee for competing groups, and supplies policies to satisfy the demands of successful domestic players."[1]

Societal approaches to the study of trade policy characterize much of the literature on endogenous protection.[2] Empirical studies of this sort infer the demands for protection based on macroeconomic and/or sectoral fluctuations. Most analyses of endogenous protection conducted by political scientists have been cast at the sectoral level. A large and growing body of literature, however,

1. The quotation is drawn from pp. 7–8 of G. John Ikenberry, David A. Lake, and Michael Mastanduno, "Introduction: Approaches to Explaining American Foreign Policy," *International Organization* 42 (Winter 1988), pp. 1–14. See also Jeffry A. Frieden, "Sectoral Conflict and U.S. Foreign Economic Policy," *International Organization* 42 (Winter 1988), pp. 59–90.

2. For excellent reviews of this literature, see Douglas Nelson, "Endogenous Tariff Theory: A Critical Survey," *American Journal of Political Science* 32 (August 1988), pp. 796–837; Edward John Ray, "Empirical Research on the Political Economy of Trade," in Colin A. Carter, Alex F. McCalla, and Jerry A. Sharples, eds., *Imperfect Competition and Political Economy: The New Trade Theory in Agricultural Trade Research* (Boulder, Colo.: Westview, 1990), pp. 175–214; and Dani Rodrik, "What Does the Political Economy Literature on Trade Policy (Not) Tell Us that We Ought to Know?" working paper no. 4870, National Bureau of Economic Research, Cambridge, Mass., 1994.

centers on the macroeconomic determinants of protection. Much of this research supports the view advanced by certain societal theories that macroeconomic fluctuations strongly influence pressures for protection.[3] Therefore we focus our societal analysis of NTBs on macroeconomic factors.

Chief among the macroeconomic variables that these studies emphasize are unemployment and the real exchange rate. It is widely accepted by analysts of trade policy that high levels of unemployment contribute to demands for protection. Indeed, according to C. Fred Bergsten and William Cline, "Conventional wisdom suggests that high levels of unemployment are the single most important source of protectionist pressures."[4] Widespread unemployment increases the costs to workers of adjusting to rising import levels. Workers who

3. See Robert E. Baldwin, "U.S. Trade Policy: Recent Changes and Future U.S. Interests," *American Economic Association Papers and Proceedings* 79 (May 1989), pp. 128–33; C. Fred Bergsten et al., *From Rambouillet to Versailles: A Symposium* (Princeton, N.J.: Princeton Essays in International Finance, No. 149, 1982); C. Fred Bergsten and William R. Cline, "Trade Policy in the 1980s: An Overview," in William R. Cline, ed., *Trade Policy in the 1980s* (Washington, D.C.: Institute for International Economics, 1983), pp. 59–98; C. Fred Bergsten and John Williamson, "Exchange Rates and Trade Policy," in Cline, *Trade Policy in the 1980s,* pp. 99–120; Jagdish Bhagwati, *The World Trading System at Risk* (Princeton, N.J.: Princeton University Press, 1991); Alok K. Bohara and William H. Kaempfer, "A Test of Tariff Endogeneity in the United States," *American Economic Review* 81 (September 1991), pp. 952–60; W. Max Corden, "The Revival of Protectionism in Developed Countries," in Dominick Salvatore, ed., *Protectionism and World Welfare* (New York: Cambridge University Press, 1993), pp. 54–79; William R. Cline, "Macroeconomic Influences on Trade Policy," *American Economic Association Papers and Proceedings* 79 (May 1989), pp. 123–27; Cletus C. Coughlin, Joseph V. Terza, and Noor Aini Khalifah, "The Determinants of Escape Clause Petitions," *Review of Economics and Statistics* 71 (May 1989), pp. 341–47; Alan V. Deardorff and Robert M. Stern, "Current Issues in Trade Policy: An Overview," in Robert M. Stern, ed., *U.S. Trade Policies in a Changing World Economy* (Cambridge, Mass.: MIT Press, 1987), pp. 15–68; I. M. Destler, *American Trade Politics,* 2d ed. (Washington, D.C.: Institute for International Economics, 1992); Rudiger Dornbusch and Jeffrey A. Frankel, "Macroeconomics and Protection," in Stern, *U.S. Trade Policies in a Changing World Economy,* pp. 77–130; Susan Feigenbaum and Thomas D. Willett, "Domestic Versus International Influences on Protectionist Pressures in the United States," in Sven W. Arndt, Richard J. Sweeny, and Thomas D. Willett, eds., *Exchange Rates, Trade, and the U.S. Economy* (Cambridge, Mass.: Ballinger, 1985), pp. 181–90; Susan Feigenbaum, Henry Ortiz, and Thomas D. Willett, "Protectionist Pressures and Aggregate Economic Conditions: Comment on Takacs," *Economic Inquiry* 23 (January 1985), pp. 175–82; Grant W. Gardner and Kent P. Kimbrough, "The Behavior of U.S. Tariff Rates," *American Economic Review* 79 (March 1989), pp. 211–18; Stephen P. Magee, William A. Brock, and Leslie Young, *Black Hole Tariffs and Endogenous Policy Theory: Political Economy in General Equilibrium* (New York: Cambridge University Press, 1989); Stephen P. Magee and Leslie Young, "Endogenous Protection in the United States, 1900–1984," in Stern, *U.S. Trade Policies in a Changing World Economy,* pp. 145–95; Dominick Salvatore, "Import Penetration, Exchange Rates, and Protectionism in the United States," *Journal of Policy Modeling* 9 (Spring 1987), pp. 125–41; Wendy E. Takacs, "Pressures for Protectionism: An Empirical Analysis," *Economic Inquiry* 19 (October 1981), pp. 687–93; and Wendy E. Takacs, "More on Protectionist Pressure and Aggregate Economic Conditions: A Reply," *Economic Inquiry* 23 (January 1985), pp. 183–84.

4. Bergsten and Cline, "Trade Policy in the 1980s," p. 77. It should be noted that seeking protection via trade relief measures need not be considered protectionist. Ruggie has argued that such measures are the domestic adjustment mechanism of international liberalization and that domestic intervention and economic liberalism went hand in hand during much of the period after World War II. See John Gerard Ruggie, "International Regimes, Transactions, and Change: Embedded Liberalism in the Postwar Economic Order," in Stephen D. Krasner, ed., *International Regimes* (Ithaca, N.Y.: Cornell University Press, 1983), pp. 195–231.

are displaced by imports will find it progressively more difficult to obtain alternative employment, and when they do, downward pressure will be placed on their wages. Together these factors promote pressures to restrict the flow of imports.[5]

In addition to unemployment, variations in the exchange rate are expected to give rise to protectionist pressures. In fact, Rudiger Dornbusch and Jeffrey Frankel argue that "hypotheses concerning the exchange rate may be the most important macroeconomic theories of protection."[6]

Central to the effects of the exchange rate on demands for protection is the influence of the price of a state's currency on the competitiveness of its exports and its import-competing products. An appreciated currency, by increasing the price of domestically produced goods, threatens to undermine both exports and import-competing sectors of the economy. As C. Fred Bergsten and John Williamson point out in a related context, these developments are likely to contribute to "pressure that is generated for protectionist measures. Export- and import-competing firms and workers will tend to seek help from their governments to offset these distortions, which undermine their ability to compete, with some degree of legitimacy since the distortions are accepted—in some cases, even fostered—by those governments. Coalitions in support of trade restrictions will be much easier to form, and much broader in their political clout, because no longer will only the most vulnerable firms and workers be seeking help—and no longer will the countervailing pressures from successful exporters be as effective."[7]

Public officials in liberal democracies are expected to meet demands for protection that arise due to high levels of unemployment and an appreciated currency because these variables influence the voting behavior of constituents. There is evidence that voters cast ballots on the basis of their personal economic circumstances, especially if they are recently unemployed.[8] However, substantial evidence also indicates that voters cast ballots on the basis of macroeconomic conditions, regardless of whether they are directly affected by these conditions.[9] In fact, some studies have concluded that macroeconomic factors are more salient determinants of voting behavior than are personal economic circumstances. Other survey research further suggests that public

5. See Bergsten and Cline, "Trade Policy in the 1980s," p. 79; and Takacs, "Pressures for Protectionism."

6. Dornbusch and Frankel, "Macroeconomics and Protection," p. 100.

7. Bergsten and Williamson, "Exchange Rates and Trade Policy," pp. 101–2.

8. See D. Roderick Kiewiet, *Macroeconomics and Micropolitics: The Electoral Effects of Economic Issues* (New Haven, Conn.: Yale University Press, 1983).

9. See ibid.; Donald R. Kinder and D. Roderick Kiewiet, "Economic Discontent and Political Behavior: The Role of Personal Grievances and Collective Economic Judgments in Congressional Voting," *American Journal of Political Science* 23 (August 1979), pp. 493–527; Gerald H. Kramer, "Short-Term Fluctuations in U.S. Voting Behavior, 1896–1964," *American Political Science Review* 65 (March 1971), pp. 131–43; and Michael S. Lewis-Beck, *Economics and Elections: The Major Western Democracies* (Ann Arbor: University of Michigan Press, 1988).

support for protection increases during downturns in the economy and when domestic industries are under severe pressure from foreign competition.[10] As a result, public officials seeking to enhance their electoral fortunes have incentives to impose protection during periods of high unemployment and currency appreciation because such measures are likely to be popular and may blunt the short-term effects of macroeconomic pressures. These analyses therefore lead us to expect a direct relationship to exist between both the level of unemployment and the real exchange rate, on the one hand, and the incidence of NTBs, on the other hand.

## Statist approaches to trade policy

While societal approaches have been especially influential in the field of political economy, they also have been criticized on a number of grounds. Especially important is the charge leveled by statists and others that societal approaches systematically underestimate the effects of two factors that regulate the provision of protection: state interests with respect to trade policy and domestic institutions.[11] Analyses that emphasize state interests generally focus on the roles of politicians and policymakers in the formation of trade policy, holding constant societal pressures. Further, as Ikenberry, Lake, and Mastanduno note, these analyses presume that the preferences of public officials "are partially, if not wholly, distinct from the parochial concerns of either societal groups or particular government institutions, and are tied to conceptions of the 'national interest' or the maximization of some social welfare function."[12]

Many statists conclude that the ability of policymakers to advance the national interest depends in large measure on the extent to which domestic political institutions render them susceptible to demands by pressure groups

10. See Robert Y. Shapiro and Benjamin I. Page, "Foreign Policy and Public Opinion," in David A. Deese, ed., *The New Politics of American Foreign Policy* (New York: St. Martin's, 1994), p. 225.

11. See Judith Goldstein, "Ideas, Institutions, and American Trade Policy," *International Organization* 42 (Winter 1988), pp. 179–218; Peter Gourevitch, *Politics in Hard Times: Comparative Responses to International Economic Crises* (Ithaca, N.Y.: Cornell University Press, 1986); Joanne Gowa, "Public Goods and Political Institutions: Trade and Monetary Policy Processes in the United States," *International Organization* 42 (Winter 1988), pp. 15–32; G. John Ikenberry, "Conclusion: An Institutional Approach to American Foreign Economic Policy," *International Organization* 42 (Winter 1988), pp. 219–43; Peter J. Katzenstein, "Conclusion: Domestic Structures and Strategies of Foreign Economic Policy," in Peter J. Katzenstein, ed., *Between Power and Plenty: Foreign Economic Policies of Advanced Industrial States* (Madison: University of Wisconsin Press, 1978), pp. 295–336; Stephen D. Krasner, *Defending the National Interest: Raw Materials Investments and U.S. Foreign Policy* (Princeton, N.J.: Princeton University Press, 1978); Stephen D. Krasner, "United States Commercial and Monetary Policy: Unravelling the Paradox of External Strength and Internal Weakness," in Katzenstein, *Between Power and Plenty*, pp. 51–87; and David A. Lake, *Power, Protection, and Free Trade: International Sources of U.S. Commercial Strategy, 1887–1939* (Ithaca, N.Y.: Cornell University Press, 1988).

12. Ikenberry, Lake, and Mastanduno, "Introduction," p. 10.

and other nonstate actors.[13] Policymakers who are poorly insulated from, and lack autonomy with respect to, pressure groups will face difficulty advancing the national interest unless (as discussed further below) it converges with the preferences of societal groups. Thus, one hypothesis we will test is that institutional factors that foster the insulation and autonomy of public officials bolster the ability of states to pursue trade policy consistent with the national interest.

*Relative size*

Clearly, the national interest with respect to trade is likely to vary across states; and it is not possible to assess adequately the influence of institutional factors on trade policy from a statist perspective unless each state's interest can be specified. On this score, many analysts have argued that a state's economic size governs its national interest with respect to trade policy.

There is ample reason to expect that larger states will display a more pronounced interest in protection than their smaller counterparts. First, international trade theory suggests that this should be the case. By virtue of their size, large states are likely to be vested with disproportionate market power.[14] They can exploit their monopoly power through the use of tariffs, as well as quotas and other NTBs that duplicate a tariff's effect.[15] If the imposition of an optimal quota elicits retaliation, the welfare of both parties will suffer.[16] This, however, only limits the incentives for a large state to impose NTBs against a state of similar size, since only states with some monopoly power have an incentive to retaliate in response to the imposition of protection. Large states retain an incentive to target small states, since the latter have no incentive to retaliate. In contrast, small states are unlikely to possess the market power necessary to benefit from optimal protection and face the prospect of retaliation by trade partners (thereby reducing foreign commerce on which they tend to be highly dependent) if they impose NTBs. Hence, on average, we expect larger states to display a greater preference for NTBs than their smaller counterparts.

Second, state size is likely to be directly related to patterns of protection due to the time period analyzed in this article. As discussed further below, the empirical analysis conducted in this study is based on the mid-1980s. In the

13. See Katzenstein, "Conclusion"; Krasner, *Defending the National Interest;* Krasner, "United States Commercial and Monetary Policy"; Gourevitch, *Politics in Hard Times;* and Lake, *Power, Protection, and Free Trade.*

14. On this point, see Rudiger W. Dornbusch, "The Case for Bilateralism," in Salvatore, *Protectionism and World Welfare,* pp. 180–99.

15. For a seminal analysis of the conditions under which tariffs and quotas are equivalent, see Jagdish N. Bhagwati, "On the Equivalence of Tariffs and Quotas," in Robert E. Baldwin et al., eds., *Trade, Growth, and the Balance of Payments* (Chicago: Rand McNally, 1965), pp. 53–67.

16. See, for example, Carlos Alfredo Rodriguez, "The Non-equivalence of Tariffs and Quotas Under Retaliation," *Journal of International Economics* 4 (November 1974), pp. 295–98.

opinion of many scholars, this was a period characterized by a moderately skewed distribution of power among a few relatively large nonhegemonic states. A number of studies have concluded that systems of this sort—as well as ones in which hegemony is declining—provide incentives for the dominant states to behave in a commercially predatory manner.[17] Based on these considerations, we expect that economic size will be directly related to the incidence of NTBs.

We measure a state's relative economic size in two ways: the ratio of its imports to total global imports and the ratio of its gross domestic product (GDP) to total global GDP. The first variable has been used repeatedly as a measure of economic size.[18] The second is also important because states with relatively large GDPs are likely to possess greater market power and to be better able to forgo commerce than are states with relatively small GDPs.[19]

Although it is clear that these two measures of relative size should be highly correlated, analyzing both allows us to determine whether our empirical results are sensitive to the measure that is used. Moreover, analyzing both measures of size is important because the ratio of national imports to global imports is closely related to the measure of trade dependence used by Ronald Rogowski; and his analysis implies that any observed effect on NTBs of those domestic institutions on which we focus here (and that are discussed below) might be due to the effects of trade dependence on both domestic institutions and NTBs. Further, including national GDP as a percentage of global GDP is important because Wendy Takacs links the level of national product to macroeconomic cycles that give rise to demands for protection. Contrary to the hypothesis discussed above, however, she finds that national product is inversely related to escape clause investigations and (to a lesser degree) to positive findings by the U.S. International Trade Commission in such cases. Including both measures of size allows us to examine each of these issues.[20]

### *Domestic institutions*

From a statist viewpoint, NTBs should be most prevalent in large states characterized by high degrees of institutional insulation and autonomy, since

17. See Robert Gilpin, *The Political Economy of International Relations* (Princeton, N.J.: Princeton University Press, 1987); Stephen D. Krasner, "State Power and the Structure of International Trade," *World Politics* 28 (April 1976), pp. 317–47; Edward D. Mansfield, *Power, Trade, and War* (Princeton, N.J.: Princeton University Press, 1994), chap. 5; and Duncan Snidal, "Relative Gains and the Pattern of Economic Cooperation," *American Political Science Review* 85 (September 1991), pp. 701–26.

18. See, for example, Krasner, "State Power and the Structure of International Trade"; and Lake, *Power, Protection, and Free Trade.*

19. Of course, the aggregate size of a state's economy may not correspond to its ability to forgo trade in all products. However, since we adopt a macroeconomic and macropolitical approach in this study, the use of aggregate measures of size seems appropriate.

20. See Ronald Rogowski, "Trade and the Variety of Democratic Institutions," *International Organization* 41 (Spring 1987), pp. 203–23; and Takacs, "Pressures for Protectionism," respectively.

these conditions provide policymakers with an economic incentive to impose NTBs and vest them with the capacity to advance those interests.

Our analysis of institutions draws heavily on an important study by Rogowski.[21] He argues that "insulation from regional and sectoral pressure in a democracy . . . is most easily achieved with large electoral districts. . . . [This argument is] easily defended, in part because institutional theorists have almost universally accepted it . . ., but more because it is almost self-evident. When automakers or dairy farmers entirely dominate twenty small constituencies and are a powerful minority in fifty more, their voice will be heard in a nation's councils. When they constitute but one or two percent of an enormous district's electorate, representatives may defy them more freely."[22]

Rogowski therefore relies on the (natural logarithm of the) number of parliamentary constituencies in the most powerful legislative body (or, in those cases where the most powerful body is not obvious, the chamber with the most members) of each democratic state as a measure of institutional insulation and autonomy. It is expected that insulation and autonomy will be inverse functions of the number of constituencies in any democracy. All other things being equal, a larger number of constituencies reduces the size of the average constituency in each state. The smaller is this average size, the more homogeneous is each district, the fewer is the number of special interests that are likely to exist per constituency, and the greater will be the political influence of each pressure group in that district.

As a result, small electoral districts encourage patronage and pork-barrel politics.[23] Since legislators representing small districts are likely to be beholden to a few influential pressure groups, they are likely to attempt to provide those groups with benefits, including trade policies that reflect their preferences. Yet in polities composed of many small constituencies, no single legislator has the capacity to provide these benefits. As Barry Weingast and William Marshall argue, "This, in combination with the diversity of interests they represent, generates a gain from exchange and cooperation among legislators."[24] The logrolling to which this situation gives rise is likely to yield trade policy that covers more types of goods and services than would be the case in a country characterized by large electoral districts and less influential interest groups.

21. Rogowski, "Trade and the Variety of Democratic Institutions."

22. Ibid., p. 200.

23. On pork-barrel or "distributive" politics, see Theodore J. Lowi, "American Business, Public Policy, Case-Studies, and Political Theory," *World Politics* 16 (July 1964), pp. 677–715; Kenneth A. Shepsle, "Institutional Equilibrium and Equilibrium Institutions," in Herbert Weisberg, ed., *Political Science: The Science of Politics* (New York: Agathon, 1986), pp. 51–82; Kenneth A. Shepsle and Barry R. Weingast, "Political Preferences for the Pork Barrel: A Generalization," *American Journal of Political Science* 25 (February 1981), pp. 96–111; Kenneth A. Shepsle and Barry R. Weingast, "Positive Theories of Congressional Institutions," *Legislative Studies Quarterly* 19 (May 1994), pp. 149–79; and Barry R. Weingast and William J. Marshall, "The Industrial Organization of Congress; or, Why Legislatures, Like Firms, Are Not Organized as Markets," *Journal of Political Economy* 96 (February 1988), pp. 132–63.

24. Weingast and Marshall, "The Industrial Organization of Congress," p. 137.

In addition to the number of parliamentary constituencies, another important institutional feature of democracies concerns whether a list-system proportional representation (PR) or a winner-take-all system exists. Rogowski maintains that the autonomy of public officials in democratic states is bolstered by both large constituencies and the existence of a list-system PR regime. As he notes, "Pressure groups are restrained where campaign resources or the legal control of nominations are centralized in the hands of party leaders. Of course, such control is achieved quite effectively in rigid list-system PR."[25]

We begin the following analysis by focusing on the effects of the number of parliamentary constituencies on NTBs. We then analyze the effects of both the number of constituencies and whether a state's electoral system is winner-take-all or PR. We take this tack to determine whether our results are robust with respect to the inclusion of PR in our model. Doing so is useful because some studies have found that differences exist in the autonomy of policymakers among various PR systems and that, in certain cases, public officials in PR systems may be vested with less autonomy than their counterparts in winner-take-all systems.[26]

## Effects of the interaction between societal and statist factors on trade policy

Although the relative merits of societal and statist approaches to the study of foreign economic policy have been hotly debated, quantitative comparisons of them have been rare. Rarer still have been empirical analyses of the impact of the interaction between societal and statist factors on trade policy.[27] The few previous studies of this sort have focused almost exclusively on U.S. commercial policy.[28] Additionally, much of their effort has been directed at explaining

25. Rogowski, "Trade and the Variety of Democratic Institutions," p. 209.

26. See, for example, Rein Taagepera and Matthew Soberg Shugart, *Seats and Votes: The Effects and Determinants of Electoral Systems* (New Haven, Conn.: Yale University Press, 1989).

27. On the need for further research of this sort, see Benjamin J. Cohen, "The Political Economy of International Trade," *International Organization* 44 (Spring 1990), pp. 261–81; and John S. Odell, "Understanding International Trade Policies: An Emerging Synthesis," *World Politics* 43 (October 1990), pp. 139–67.

28. See, for example, Robert E. Baldwin, *The Political Economy of U.S. Import Policy* (Cambridge, Mass.: MIT Press, 1985); John A. C. Conybeare, "Voting for Protection: An Electoral Model of Tariff Policy," *International Organization* 45 (Winter 1991), pp. 57–81; I. M. Destler and John S. Odell, *Anti-protection: Changing Forces in United States Trade Policies* (Washington, D.C.: Institute for International Economics, 1987); Krasner, "United States Commercial and Monetary Policy"; Lake, *Power, Protection, and Free Trade;* Susanne Lohmann and Sharyn O'Halloran, "Divided Government and U.S. Trade Policy: Theory and Evidence," *International Organization* 48 (Autumn 1994), pp. 595–632; Magee and Young, "Endogenous Protection in the United States, 1900–1984"; and Stanley D. Nollen and Dennis P. Quinn, "Free Trade, Fair Trade, Strategic Trade, and Protectionism in the U.S. Congress, 1987–1988," *International Organization* 48 (Summer 1994), pp. 491–525.

tariffs, rather than NTBs.[29] However, its unusual size and institutional structure may limit how broadly conclusions based on studies of U.S. trade policy can be applied.[30] Further, it is widely recognized that successive rounds of the GATT limited the ability of member states to respond to demands for protection or to advance state interests by imposing tariffs. Since the states we examine are all contracting parties to the GATT, our focus on explaining NTBs (rather than tariffs) is especially important. Indeed, the need to analyze the effects of factors that govern demands for and the provision of protection—as well as the interactions among them—on cross-national patterns of NTBs is a glaring gap in the literature, and one that we seek to redress.[31]

We focus on two related issues concerning the interaction between societal and statist factors. As noted above, some statists argue that the policies of states in which policymakers are poorly insulated from societal pressures tend to reflect the interests of societal groups rather than the national interest. There is also reason to expect increases in societal demands for protection during cyclical downturns in the economy and when macroeconomic conditions undermine the competitiveness of a state's goods. Thus, one hypothesis we will examine is that the incidence of NTBs tends to be greatest in states characterized by (1) high levels of unemployment and appreciated currencies and (2) domestic institutions that undermine the insulation and autonomy of public officials with respect to pressure groups.

A second hypothesis we will test is that the incidence of NTBs is greatest in cases where both state and societal actors display a preference for protection. Although much of the literature bearing on the interaction between statist and societal factors has focused on the effects of divergent preferences between state and societal actors, the possibility that their preferences might converge has been raised in a number of studies, although it has not been analyzed in sufficient detail.[32] If such a convergence is an important determinant of

29. Several previous studies have examined the effects of macroeconomic factors and changes in U.S. trade legislation on patterns of escape clause filings in the United States, but none has examined the interaction between macroeconomic and institutional factors. Moreover, we are interested in analyzing a wider variety of both NTBs and countries than considered earlier. For examples of studies of this sort, see Coughlin, Terza, and Khalifah, "The Determinants of Escape Clause Protection"; Feigenbaum and Willett, "Domestic Versus International Influences on Protectionist Pressures in the United States"; Feigenbaum, Ortiz, and Willett, "Protectionist Pressures and Aggregate Economic Conditions"; and Salvatore, "Import Penetration, Exchange Rates, and Protectionism in the United States."

30. For example, it is well-known that the United States' geographically based, winner-take-all electoral system limits both the ability of parties to control the votes of legislators and their insulation from constituent pressures for protection. In this respect, the United States stands in contrast to PR systems, among other types of regimes. For examinations of these and other variations that are likely to influence trade policy, see Destler, *American Trade Politics;* and Rogowski, "Trade and the Variety of Democratic Institutions."

31. Among the few studies that address this topic, see Katzenstein, "Conclusion"; Gourevitch, *Politics in Hard Times;* and Helen V. Milner, *Resisting Protectionism: Global Industries and the Politics of International Trade* (Princeton, N.J.: Princeton University Press, 1988).

32. See, for example, Krasner, *Defending the National Interest;* Krasner, "United States Commercial and Monetary Policy"; Lake, *Power, Protection, and Free Trade;* Edward D. Mansfield,

NTBs, then their incidence should be greatest in large states characterized by (1) high levels of unemployment and appreciated currencies and (2) political institutions that bolster the insulation and autonomy of public officials with respect to pressure groups. As noted above, deteriorating macroeconomic conditions elicit demands for protection, and public officials who fail to respond to these demands may suffer accordingly in subsequent elections. Further, in contrast to small states, large states often have an incentive to impose protection; and public officials that are well-insulated and vested with considerable autonomy will be in a position to act on those incentives, and would be expected to do so.

A high degree of institutional insulation and autonomy is essential in this regard. Although we expect high levels of unemployment and appreciated currencies to yield widespread demands for protection, some societal groups are likely to retain an interest in lower trade barriers. These groups include multinational corporations, industries that depend on or are highly sensitive to the price of imports, and industries that depend on exports and fear either that increases in protection by their government will elicit retaliation by foreign governments or that protection will reduce foreign exports and hence the ability of foreign consumers to purchase their imports.[33] Moreover, in a study of U.S. trade policy, I. M. Destler and John Odell found that the political pressure exerted by these antiprotectionist forces increased during those periods when macroeconomic downturns led to broad-based societal pressures for protection.[34] Their influence, like that of other societal groups, depends on the structure of domestic institutions. Thus, large states characterized by high levels of unemployment and appreciated currencies should experience a higher incidence of NTBs when institutions insulate policymakers from those groups that prefer lower trade barriers than when porous institutions enhance the influence of these groups on trade policy.

## The relationship between tariffs and NTBs

In addition to the hypotheses described above, we also examine the effects of preexisting tariff levels on NTBs. Doing so is important because preexisting tariff levels may influence both the strength of societal demands for NTBs and the willingness of public officials to meet these demands. Groups already well

---

"International Institutions and Economic Sanctions," *World Politics* 47 (July 1995), pp. 575–605; and Edward John Ray, "Changing Patterns of Protectionism: The Fall in Tariffs and the Rise in Non-tariff Barriers," *Northwestern Journal of International Law and Business* 8 (Fall 1987), pp. 285–325.

33. See Jagdish Bhagwati, *Protectionism* (Cambridge, Mass.: MIT Press, 1988); Destler and Odell, *Anti-protection;* and Milner, *Resisting Protectionism.*

34. Destler and Odell, *Anti-protection.*

protected by tariffs may bring less pressure for new NTBs and face more governmental resistance to their demands than less well protected groups. This suggests that tariffs and NTBs are substitutes, which is consistent with the view expressed by some economists that NTBs are often used to protect industries that have lost tariff protection due to successive rounds of the GATT. Jagdish Bhagwati refers to this dynamic as the "law of constant protection." As he points out, "The evidence of increased nontariff barriers and administered protection just as tariffs had been reduced to new lows suggests the intriguing possibility that there may be a Law of Constant Protection: If you reduce one type of protection, another variety simply pops up elsewhere. (You then have a Displacement Effect, not evidence of any increase in protectionist pressure.)"[35]

In contrast to this view, another prominent position holds that tariffs and NTBs are complements. Those who advance this argument maintain that NTBs are often used to protect those industries that are also the beneficiaries of high tariffs, while states avoid using NTBs to shield industries that receive little tariff protection. Edward John Ray, for example, mentions that U.S. NTBs may be concentrated in industries least affected by the Kennedy Round of the GATT.[36] In contrast to the law of constant protection, a direct relationship between tariffs and NTBs might suggest that NTBs are used to counter new foreign challenges to important sectors that are already the beneficiaries of tariff protection. Indeed, the results of a number of single-country analyses seem to support this position.[37] Cross-national studies, however, have produced more ambiguous evidence on this score.[38]

A related reason to include tariffs in our model is that they might account for any observed relationship between societal and statist variables, on the one hand, and the incidence of NTBs, on the other hand. Various studies have found that the unemployment rate, the exchange rate, economic size, and institutional factors are related to patterns of tariffs; and the research discussed in this section links tariffs to patterns of NTBs. It is therefore important to determine whether tariffs influence the effects of macroeconomic and institutional factors on NTBs.

35. Bhagwati, *Protectionism*, p. 53.

36. Edward John Ray, "Empirical Research on the Political Economy of Trade." See also Edward John Ray and Howard P. Marvel, "The Pattern of Protection in the Industrial World," *Review of Economics and Statistics* 66 (August 1984), pp. 452–58.

37. See Edward John Ray, "The Determinants of Tariff and Nontariff Restrictions in the United States," *Journal of Political Economy* 89 (February 1981), pp. 105–21; and Ray, "Empirical Research on the Political Economy of Trade." On the other hand, based on an analysis of the relationship between tariffs and escape clause filings in the United States, Salvatore concludes that tariffs and NTBs are substitutes. See Salvatore, "Import Penetration, Exchange Rates, and Protectionism in the United States."

38. Ray and Marvel, "The Pattern of Protection in the Industrial World."

## A model of nontariff barriers to trade

Our initial model, then, is:

$$NTB_{t+1} = A + B_1 SIZE_t + B_2(\log CONST)_t + B_3(SIZE \cdot \log CONST)_t + \quad (1)$$
$$B_4 UNEM_t + B_5(UNEM \cdot \log CONST)_t + B_6(UNEM \cdot SIZE \cdot \log CONST)_t$$
$$+ B_7 REER_t + B_8(REER \cdot \log CONST)_t + B_9(REER \cdot SIZE \cdot \log CONST)_t$$
$$+ B_{10} TARIFF_t + e_t.$$

The dependent variable, $NTB_{t+1}$, is the proportion of imports subject to NTBs in each state in year $t + 1$ based on the United Nations Conference on Trade and Development's (UNCTAD) "inventory list" of NTBs. As Sam Laird and Alexander Yeats observe, this list includes "Variable import levies and product specific charges (excluding tariff quotas); Quotas; Prohibitions (including seasonal prohibitions): non-automatic import authorisations including restrictive import licensing requirements; quantitative 'voluntary' export restraints; and trade restraints under the Multifibre Arrangement."[39] It is, of course, difficult to gauge the extent of NTB protection within or across states. Unlike tariffs, NTBs have no natural measure of intensity, and calculations of ad valorem equivalents of NTBs have proven to be unreliable.[40] Some analysts have treated NTBs as a dichotomous variable based on whether or not a given sector is protected by them. Others have estimated the level of NTBs based on the difference between the predicted and observed openness of an economy.[41]

In contrast to these approaches, we examine the incidence of NTBs. This measure is chosen because the UNCTAD trade coverage ratios are viewed by many experts as the most reliable estimates of NTBs across states and because it is the most appropriate variable with which to test our theory.[42] For example, polities characterized by many (and therefore small) parliamentary constituencies may be especially prone to pork-barrel politics. Under these conditions, logrolling is likely to be pervasive and the preferences of many different interest groups are therefore likely to be reflected in trade policy. Since the extent and variety of interest-group demands reflected in trade policy bear directly on the

39. Sam Laird and Alexander Yeats, *Quantitative Methods for Trade-Barrier Analysis* (New York: New York University Press, 1990), p. 90.

40. See ibid., p. 121; and Julio J. Nogues, Andrzej Olechowski, and Alan Winters, "The Extent of Nontariff Barriers to Imports of Industrial Countries" World Bank staff working paper no. 789, Washington, D.C., 1986, p. 9.

41. Magee, Brock, and Young, *Black Hole Tariffs and Endogenous Policy Theory*, p. 236.

42. On the merits of the UNCTAD trade coverage ratios, see Edward E. Leamer, "The Structure and Effects of Tariff and Nontariff Barriers in 1983," in Ronald W. Jones and Anne O. Krueger, eds., *The Political Economy of International Trade* (New York: Basil Blackwell, 1990), pp. 224–60; and Nogues, Olechowski, and Winters, "The Extent of Nontariff Barriers to Imports of Industrial Countries," p. 9.

incidence of protection, we focus on explaining the incidence of NTBs. The coverage ratios that we analyze measure the proportion of a state's imports that are subject to NTBs.[43]

Turning to the independent variables, $SIZE_t$ is the economic size of each state in year $t$. It was pointed out earlier that both the ratio of national imports to total global imports and the ratio of national GDP to global GDP are used to measure relative state size. Thus, we estimate the parameters in equation (1) using both variables.[44] In addition, log $CONST_t$ is the natural logarithm of the number of parliamentary constituencies in each state in year $t$ based on Rogowski's data; $UNEM_t$ is the unemployment rate in each state in year $t$; $REER_t$ is an index of the real exchange rate in each state in year $t$; $TARIFF_t$ is the average national post–Tokyo Round offer rate for each state; and $e_t$ is an error term.[45] The remaining variables are included in order to determine whether, as we hypothesized above, the interaction between factors that regulate the provision of protection ($SIZE \cdot \log CONST$), and the interaction between factors that govern demands for protection and those that regulate its supply, are important determinants of cross-national patterns of NTBs.

Data limitations led us to focus on explaining NTBs in 1983 and 1986. UNCTAD provides data on NTBs for fourteen advanced industrial states in these years. The fourteen states are: Belgium-Luxembourg, Denmark, Finland, France, Greece, Ireland, Italy, Japan, the Netherlands, Norway, Switzerland, the United Kingdom, the United States, and West Germany.[46] Although

43. These data, as well as an extensive overview of the methods used to measure NTBs, are presented in Laird and Yeats, *Quantitative Methods for Trade-Barrier Analysis.*

44. Data on GDP are expressed in real terms and are taken from Robert Summers and Alan Heston, "The Penn World Table (Mark 5): An Expanded Set of International Comparisons, 1950–1988," *Quarterly Journal of Economics* 106 (May 1991), pp. 327–68, and the computer diskette supplement to that article, dated 15 June 1993. Data on imports are taken from the International Monetary Fund (IMF), *International Financial Statistics* (Washington, D.C.: IMF, various years).

45. On log *CONST,* see Rogowski, "Trade and the Variety of Democratic Institutions," p. 215. Rogowski analyzes the natural logarithm of the number of national constituencies because there exist a few countries with a very large number of constituencies in his sample. It should be noted, however, that the results reported below are relatively robust with respect to whether log *CONST* or *CONST* is analyzed. Data on *UNEM* are taken from Organization for Economic Cooperation and Development (OECD), *Employment Outlook* (Paris: OECD, various years). Data on *REER* are taken from IMF, *International Financial Statistics Yearbook* (Washington, D.C.: IMF, 1988). This is an index of the real effective exchange rate, the base year of which is 1980. Data on *TARIFF* are taken from Alan V. Deardorff and Robert M. Stern, *The Michigan Model of World Production and Trade* (Cambridge, Mass.: MIT Press, 1986), p. 49, for all states except Greece. Leamer reports that average Greek tariffs for 1983 were about 1 percent; and the average nominal tariff for Greece in 1986 was also about 1 percent, based on data in United Nations, *National Account Statistics: Analyses of Main Aggregates* (New York: United Nations, various years). As a result, we use this value for Greek tariffs in the following analysis. See Leamer, "The Structure and Effects of Tariff and Nontariff Barriers in 1983." Data used in this analysis are available upon request from the authors.

46. Belgium and Luxembourg are treated as a single state for the purposes of this analysis because the Belgium-Luxembourg Economic Unit stipulates that the two states maintain parity between their currencies, share in integrated foreign trade and balance of payment policies, and maintain a joint central bank. On this point, see The Economist Intelligence Unit, *Belgium, Luxembourg Country Profile 1992–93* (London: The Economist Intelligence Unit, 1992).

UNCTAD also provides NTB data for New Zealand, our results indicated that this country was a statistical outlier.[47] We therefore excluded New Zealand and focus on the aforementioned fourteen states in the following analysis. Because NTBs are measured in 1983 and 1986 (years $t + 1$), the independent variables in equation (1) (except for *TARIFF*) are measured in 1982 and 1985 (years $t$). The observations for 1983 and 1986 are initially pooled; however, the extent to which the incidence of NTBs varied between 1983 and 1986 is also examined below.

It should be noted at the outset that all of the states analyzed in this study are advanced industrial countries. This precludes, for example, an assessment of whether our findings vary depending on a state's level of economic development. It is also clear that caution must be exercised when offering generalizations based on an analysis of such a limited time period. But since the tendency for advanced industrial countries to rely on NTBs became increasingly pervasive during the 1980s and virtually no quantitative cross-national research has been conducted on the issues addressed here, our results should provide a useful first cut at the hypotheses presented above.[48]

### *Estimates of the parameters*

We used ordinary least squares (OLS) to estimate the parameters in equation (1). These findings indicate that our model explains about 80 percent of the variation in NTBs. They also indicate that unemployment, the real exchange rate, economic size, and domestic institutions each exert a strong effect on the incidence of NTBs. Further, the nature and strength of the results in Table 1 are extremely robust with respect to the measure of economic size that is used.

The results in Table 1 bear out the statist hypotheses discussed above. First, there is evidence that economic size is directly related to the incidence of NTBs, since the regression coefficient of *SIZE* is positive and statistically significant. Second, our results indicate that the number of parliamentary constituencies exerts a strong influence on the incidence of NTBs, since the regression coefficient of log *CONST* is positive and statistically significant.

Third, in addition to their individual effects, the interaction between the number of constituencies and economic size helps to shape patterns of NTBs. More specifically, the regression coefficient of *SIZE* · log *CONST* is negative and statistically significant. These results indicate that NTBs are most pervasive in economically large states characterized by a small number of (and, hence,

47. This is not surprising, since New Zealand's economy is considerably different from the other states in our sample. For a discussion of the unique features of New Zealand's economy, see Economist Intelligence Unit, *New Zealand: Country Profile 1992–93* (London: Economist Intelligence Unit, 1992), p. 8.

48. See Bhagwati, *Protectionism*, chap. 3; and Laird and Yeats, *Quantitative Methods for Trade-Barrier Analysis*.

**TABLE 1.** *Regression of the incidence of nontariff barriers on economic size, number of parliamentary constituencies, unemployment, real exchange rate, existence or absence of a proportional representation system, and tariffs, based on pooled data for fourteen states in 1983 and 1986*[a]

| | *Measure of Relative Size* | | | |
|---|---|---|---|---|
| | *Imports* | | *GDP*[b] | |
| *Parameter* | *Equation (1)* | *Equation (2)* | *Equation (1)* | *Equation (2)* |
| *INTERCEPT* | −0.984***<br>(−3.27) | −1.279***<br>(−5.42) | −0.844**<br>(−2.58) | −1.128***<br>(−4.28) |
| *SIZE* | 2.499**<br>(2.76) | 2.539***<br>(3.80) | 0.0036***<br>(3.37) | 0.0035***<br>(4.29) |
| log *CONST* | 0.334***<br>(4.11) | 0.400***<br>(6.34) | 0.312***<br>(3.58) | 0.369***<br>(5.28) |
| *SIZE* · log *CONST* | −1.311*<br>(−2.07) | −1.252**<br>(−2.68) | −0.0016***<br>(−3.01) | −0.0014***<br>(−3.34) |
| *UNEM* | 3.192***<br>(5.14) | 3.884***<br>(7.21) | 3.538***<br>(5.26) | 3.708***<br>(6.20) |
| *UNEM* · log *CONST* | −1.022***<br>(−4.44) | −1.173***<br>(−6.13) | −1.107***<br>(−4.98) | −1.072***<br>(−5.52) |
| *UNEM* · *SIZE* · log *CONST* | 3.342**<br>(2.13) | 2.944**<br>(2.28) | 0.0034**<br>(2.43) | 0.0021*<br>(1.79) |
| *REER* | 0.0085***<br>(3.38) | 0.0095***<br>(4.96) | 0.0068**<br>(2.32) | 0.0081***<br>(3.58) |
| *REER* · log *CONST* | −0.0023***<br>(−3.45) | −0.0025***<br>(−4.94) | −0.0020**<br>(−2.50) | −0.0022***<br>(−3.65) |
| *REER* · *SIZE* · log *CONST* | 0.0056*<br>(1.90) | 0.0053**<br>(2.45) | 0.0000063**<br>(2.51) | 0.0000055**<br>(2.87) |
| *PR* | — | 0.184**<br>(2.78) | — | 0.262***<br>(3.74) |
| *PR* · log *CONST* | — | −0.025*<br>(−1.93) | — | −0.043***<br>(−3.34) |
| *TARIFF* | −1.430***<br>(−3.14) | −2.575***<br>(−5.62) | −1.301***<br>(−3.31) | −2.859***<br>(−5.68) |
| Adjusted $R^2$ | .84 | .91 | .79 | .88 |

*$p \leq 0.10$. **$p \leq 0.05$. ***$p \leq 0.01$.

[a]*T*-statistics are reported in parentheses below each regression coefficient. Two-tailed tests were conducted for each coefficient.

[b]Abbreviations are as follows: GDP = gross domestic product; *SIZE* = economic size; log *CONST* = the natural logarithm of the number of parliamentary constituencies; *UNEM* = unemployment rate; *REER* = index of real exchange rate; *PR* = proportional representation system; *TARIFF* = tariffs. Equations (1) and (2) are defined in the text.

*Sources.* For data on NTBs, Sam Laird and Alexander Yeats, *Quantitative Methods for Trade-Barrier Analysis* (New York: New York University Press, 1990). For data on imports, the International Monetary Fund (IMF), *International Financial Statistics* (Washington, D.C.: IMF, various years). For data on GDP, Robert Summers and Alan Heston, "The Penn World Table (Mark 5): An Expanded Set of International Comparisons, 1950–1988," *Quarterly Journal of Economics* 106 (May 1991), pp. 327–68. For data on *CONST* and *PR*, Ronald Rogowski, "Trade and the Variety of Domestic Institutions," *International Organization* 41 (Spring 1987), pp. 203–23. For data on *UNEM*, the Organization for Economic Cooperation and Development (OECD), *Employment Outlook* (Paris: OECD, various years). For data on *REER*, IMF, *International Financial Statistics Yearbook* (Washington, D.C.: IMF, 1988). For data on *TARIFF*, Alan V. Deardorff and Robert M. Stern, *The Michigan Model of World Production and Trade* (Cambridge, Mass.: MIT Press, 1986), and the additional sources in our footnote 45.

large) constituencies. Under these circumstances, the predicted incidence of NTBs is about one-third greater than the incidence based on any other combination of economic size and domestic institutions, holding constant the remaining variables in equation (1) at their mean values.

The results in Table 1 also provide support for the societal hypothesis that high rates of unemployment and appreciated currencies are strongly linked to a high incidence of NTBs, since the regression coefficients of *UNEM* and *REER* are both positive and statistically significant.

Further, our findings yield substantial evidence that the interaction between factors related to demands for and the provision of protection is a centrally important influence on NTBs. The interactions between the number of constituencies and both unemployment (*UNEM* · log *CONST*) and the real exchange rate (*REER* · log *CONST*) are strongly related to NTBs. So, too, are the interactions among the number of constituencies, economic size, and both unemployment (*UNEM* · *SIZE* · log *CONST*) and the real exchange rate (*REER* · *SIZE* · log *CONST*). Indeed, the regression coefficient of each of these variables is statistically significant and quantitatively large.

The results based on equation (1) demonstrate that the highest (lowest) values of *NTB* obtain when: (1) states are largest (smallest); (2) policymakers are well (poorly) insulated from societal pressures and most (least) autonomous; and (3) domestic pressures for protection are most (least) pronounced. More specifically, the predicted incidence of NTBs is at least 35 percent greater when *SIZE* and both *UNEM* and *REER* attain their highest observed values and log *CONST* attains its lowest observed value than when any other combination of these values is assessed. These findings are therefore consistent with the hypothesis that the incidence of *NTB* is greatest when state and societal interests converge regarding the desirability of protection and policymakers are vested with the institutional capacity to advance these interests.

The strength of our results depends fundamentally on the inclusion of factors concerning demands for and the provision of protection, as well as the interaction between them. Equation (1) explains substantially more of the cross-national variation in NTBs than do models utilizing *TARIFF* and (1) *UNEM* and *REER*, (2) *SIZE*, log *CONST*, and *SIZE* · log *CONST*, and (3) all of these variables, but not any other interaction term. These models explain between 1 and 50 percent of the variation in NTBs, depending on whether or not both societal and statist variables are included and the particular measure of economic size that is used. Thus, our model of NTBs is considerably more powerful than a societal model, a statist model, or a model that includes both types of factors but neglects the interaction between them.

Another purpose of this study is to assess the impact of tariffs on NTBs. The results in Table 1 provide considerable evidence of an inverse relationship between tariffs and NTBs, since the regression coefficient of *TARIFF* is negative and statistically significant. Moreover, tariffs exert a large quantitative effect on NTBs: for every 1 percent reduction in tariffs, the share of imports subject to NTBs rises by about 1.4 percent, holding constant the remaining variables in the model. Thus, tariffs and NTBs seem to be substitutes.

### *Proportional representation and NTBs*

In addition to the number of parliamentary constituencies, whether the state is PR or not also influences the autonomy of public officials. In order to analyze the effects of PR systems on NTBs, we include in equation (1) a dummy variable that takes on a value of 1 if the state in question was classified by Rogowski as a PR regime and 0 otherwise.[49] Further, because it has been argued that the autonomy of public officials is bolstered in PR systems characterized by large average-sized parliamentary constituencies, we also include a variable designed to capture the interaction between these institutional factors (*PR* · log *CONST*) in our model.[50] (It should be noted that we also examined whether the interactions between *PR* and *SIZE, UNEM,* and *REER,* respectively, contributed to cross-national variations in NTBs. However, because we found no evidence that this was the case, these interaction effects are not analyzed below.)

Our extended model, which is referred to as equation (2) in Table 1, explains about 90 percent of the variation in the incidence of NTBs across the states considered here. Further, in addition to the factors discussed above, whether or not a PR system exists is an important influence on the incidence of NTBs: the regression coefficient of *PR* is positive and the regression coefficient of *PR* · log *CONST* is negative, and both coefficients are statistically significant. Based on the findings presented in Table 1, the predicted value of *NTB* is greatest (lowest) when *SIZE* and both *UNEM* and *REER* attain their highest (lowest) observed levels, log *CONST* is lowest (greatest), and a (non) PR system exists. Holding constant *SIZE, UNEM,* and *REER* (respectively) at their highest values, log *CONST* at its lowest value, and *TARIFF* at its mean value, the effect of changing from a winner-take-all to a PR system is to increase the predicted value of *NTB* by about 25 percent. Moreover, the predicted value of *NTB* obtained under these circumstances is at least twice that obtained in any other set of circumstances, given the results in Table 1. Thus, these results continue to support the hypothesis that the incidence of NTBs is greatest when the imposition of protection is in both the national interest and the interest of many pressure groups, and when public officials possess the institutional means necessary to advance those interests.

It should be noted that only the regression coefficient of *TARIFF* changes in any substantial way because of the inclusion of *PR* and its interaction with log *CONST* in the model. The size of this coefficient doubles, however, when these variables are included. Based on the estimates of equation (2), the effect of

49. Rogowski, "Trade and the Variety of Democratic Institutions," p. 213.
50. For a discussion of this issue, see ibid.

allowing *TARIFF* to vary from its highest to its lowest observed value is to double the predicted value of *NTB* in the case of both PR and winner-take-all systems (holding constant the remaining variables at their mean values).

### *Regression diagnostics*

Before proceeding, a number of issues regarding the regression results presented in Table 1 need to be addressed. First, in a cross-sectional analysis such as that conducted here, one concern is that the errors in the regression ($e_t$) will not have a common variance. Under these circumstances, the OLS estimates will be heteroscedastic and therefore inefficient. White tests yielded no evidence of heteroscedasticity in the present case.[51]

Second, as noted above, it is important to ensure that our decision to pool data across 1983 and 1986 was appropriate. It is obvious that if the effects of the independent variables in equations (1) and (2) on NTBs vary over time, this procedure would be inappropriate. However, analysis-of-variance tests yielded no evidence that the model is unstable between 1983 and 1986, and Chow tests also yielded no evidence that any of the individual regression coefficients is unstable across time.[52]

Third, the use of OLS might be inappropriate because the value of the dependent variable (*NTB*) is a proportion (and therefore is bounded by zero and one). Under these conditions, OLS estimates may be inefficient and predict proportions of *NTB* that exceed one or are less than zero. Since it is well-known that a Tobit model can be used to deal with these problems, we estimated the parameters in equations (1) and (2) using that model.[53] The results were virtually identical to those in Table 1. Apparently, the fact that the dependent variable is truncated poses no problem here.

Fourth, we should examine the extent to which our results are sensitive to influential observations. To this end, we estimated the parameters in equations

51. For descriptions of this test, see William H. Greene, *Econometric Analysis,* 2d ed. (New York: Macmillan, 1993), pp. 392–93; and Halbert White, "A Heteroskedasticity-Consistent Covariance Matrix Estimator and a Direct Test for Heteroskedasticity," *Econometrica* 48 (May 1980), pp. 817–38. This test involves regressing the squared residuals from equations (1) and (2) on each independent variable, the square of each independent variable, and their cross products. Because the number of degrees of freedom is negative in the present case, we omitted the cross products for the purposes of conducting this test. On this procedure, see Harry H. Kelejian and Wallace E. Oates, *Introduction to Econometrics: Principles and Applications,* 3d ed. (New York: Harper and Row, 1989), p. 242.

52. On these tests, see Gregory C. Chow, "Tests of Equality Between Subsets of Coefficients in Two Linear Regression Models," *Econometrica* 28 (July 1960), pp. 591–605; and Greene, *Econometric Analysis,* pp. 211–14.

53. On the Tobit model, see Greene, *Econometric Analysis,* pp. 694–706; G. S. Maddala, *Limited-Dependent and Qualitative Variables in Econometrics* (New York: Cambridge University Press, 1983), pp. 151–62; and James Tobin, "Estimation of Relationships for Limited Dependent Variables," *Econometrica* 26 (January 1958), pp. 24–36.

(1) and (2) after deleting observations one at a time.[54] Our findings indicated that the signs and statistical significance of the regression coefficients in Table 1 are quite robust with respect to the deletion of individual observations. Regardless of which measure of economic size was used, there was no case in which the sign of a regression coefficient changed, and in fewer than 5 percent of the cases did a regression coefficient fail to remain significant once any observation was removed from the sample. Indeed, this number of changes would be expected by chance alone.

Fifth, it is important to ensure that our results are not vitiated by multicollinearity. The results of bivariate correlations and auxiliary regressions indicated that all of those few cases in which multicollinearity might be a problem involved *PR* and *TARIFF.* To determine whether the effects of the remaining variables in the model were sensitive to the inclusion of *PR* and *TARIFF,* we deleted these variables (as well as *PR* · *SIZE*) from the model individually and in combination. The signs, sizes, and levels of statistical significance of the remaining variables in equations (1) and (2) were quite robust with respect to the inclusion or omission of these variables.[55]

Finally, it is useful to consider the possibility that variables omitted from our model may influence the findings in Table 1. Particularly important in this regard is whether the extent of government intervention in the economy influences the rate of unemployment and its propensity to impose NTBs. We therefore included in equations (1) and (2) the ratio of government expenditures to GDP in year *t*, which is a measure of government intervention.[56] The results of this analysis indicate that the regression coefficient of this variable is negative and statistically significant in every case. This may reflect the tendency for states characterized by high levels of government spending to buffer and compensate societal groups disproportionately, thereby reducing demands for protection from groups that are adversely affected by imports. It is important to note, however, that the inclusion of this variable in our models has no effect on the sign or level of statistical significance of any remaining variable, including *UNEM, UNEM* · log *CONST,* and *UNEM* · *SIZE* · log *CONST.* Nor are the quantitative effects of the variables in equations (1) and (2)—and, hence, the conditions that maximize and minimize the incidence of NTBs—influenced in any substantial way by its inclusion.[57]

54. On this procedure, see David A. Belsley, Edwin Kuh, and Roy E. Welsch, *Regression Diagnostics: Identifying Influential Data and Sources of Collinearity* (New York: Wiley, 1980).

55. Although some sectoral analyses of tariffs and NTBs have examined whether these variables are jointly determined, such an approach is unwarranted here. There is, for example, little reason to expect that the incidence of NTBs in 1983 and 1986 should have influenced tariff levels agreed to during the Tokyo Round of the GATT, which concluded in 1979. See Ray, "The Determinants of Tariff and Nontariff Trade Restrictions in the United States"; and Daniel Trefler, "Trade Liberalization and the Theory of Endogenous Protection: An Econometric Study of U.S. Import Policy," *Journal of Political Economy* 101 (February 1993), pp. 138–60.

56. These data are taken from Summers and Heston, "The Penn World Table (Mark 5)."

57. Our analysis of this issue was conducted too recently to include these results in Table 1. The results are available upon request from the authors. We are grateful to Robert O. Keohane for suggesting that we conduct these tests related to the ratio of government expenditures to GDP.

## Some illustrations of the statistical findings

Having tested our model, it is useful to illustrate how the societal and statist variables on which we focused affected trade policy in the countries considered here. While detailed case studies are beyond the scope of this article, anecdotal evidence suggests that these variables were salient influences on commercial policy during the 1980s.

Consider, for example, the role that the exchange rate played in United States trade policy. Between 1983 and 1986, the incidence of U.S. NTBs rose by over 25 percent. Much of this rise seems to be due to a significant appreciation in the dollar. While the values of the other independent variables in our model changed relatively little from 1982 to 1985 in the case of the United States, the value of *REER* increased dramatically. The societal view that this appreciation should precipitate an increase in demands for protection accords with a number of accounts of exchange-rate politics in the United States during this period.[58] I. M. Destler and C. Randall Henning note that, by the early 1980s, many sectors of U.S. industry had concluded that the dollar's strength was degrading their competitiveness.[59] By 1985, their opposition to the dollar's strength reached a peak. Imports were flooding into the United States at a rate unprecedented during the post–World War II era and Destler and Henning maintain that "most [industries] considered the prime source of their problems [to be] the sky-high dollar."[60] They also argue that "[w]hen the strong dollar triggered a flood of imports, a rise in protectionist bills was a predictable result."[61] U.S. industry and labor petitioned the Reagan administration and Congress to remedy the dollar appreciation. With no direct control over exchange-rate policy, Congress responded by "generat[ing] a veritable explosion of trade legislation initiatives" in 1985.[62] It is also noteworthy that the period from 1982 to 1985 witnessed a rapid surge in the number of petitions for trade-policy relief by U.S. industry and a turn toward managed-trade policies by the United States. These developments both led directly to an increase in the incidence of NTBs and, in the opinion of J. David Richardson, were largely attributable to the dollar's appreciation.[63]

58. See Robert E. Baldwin, "Changes in the Global Trading System: A Response to Shifts in National Economic Power," in Salvatore, *Protectionism and World Welfare*, pp. 80–98; I. M. Destler and C. Randall Henning, *Dollar Politics: Exchange Rate Policymaking in the United States* (Washington, D.C.: Institute for International Economics, 1989); Destler, *American Trade Politics;* and J. David Richardson, "U.S. Trade Policy in the 1980s: Turns—and Roads Not Taken," in Martin Feldstein, ed., *American Economic Policy in the 1980s* (Chicago: University of Chicago Press, 1994), pp. 627–58.

59. Destler and Henning, *Dollar Politics*, pp. 36–40. See also Destler, *American Trade Politics*, pp. 123–24 and 188.

60. Destler and Henning, *Dollar Politics*, p. 119. See also Destler, *American Trade Politics*, p. 123.

61. Destler and Henning, *Dollar Politics*, p. 104.

62. Ibid., p. 39. See also Destler, *American Trade Politics*, p. 83; and Richardson, "U.S. Trade Policy in the 1980s," pp. 646–47.

63. Richardson, "U.S. Trade Policy in the 1980s," pp. 636–37 and 642–43.

The effects of unemployment on NTBs are illustrated by the case of West Germany during the 1980s. From 1983 to 1986 the incidence of West German NTBs rose by approximately 15 percent; and from 1982 to 1985, the level of West German unemployment rose by about 25 percent, while the remaining independent variables in our model experienced only very modest fluctuations. Kathleen Thelen points out that throughout the post–World War II era, "the [West German] government sought first and foremost to maintain a stable currency and hold inflation in check, even if it meant higher unemployment."[64] By 1983, the West German economy had deteriorated to the point where unemployment had reached its highest level since the end of World War II. Of particular importance for present purposes was the structural nature of West German unemployment. In 1983, over a quarter of those West Germans without jobs had been unemployed for more than one year.[65] The Bundesbank reported that "[t]he prospects for bringing unemployment down quickly to a more bearable level are admittedly slim; this will certainly not happen in the short term."[66] Labor problems reached a peak in 1984 with the metal workers' strike, which was designed in part to reduce unemployment.[67] It is interesting that the Organization for Economic Cooperation and Development reported in 1986 that West German NTBs were most pervasive in those sectors where tariffs had been reduced and that among these were sectors in which metal workers were employed in large numbers (such as steel).[68] This suggests that the government responded to mounting unemployment by increasing the incidence of NTBs in 1986. Given the political strength of organized labor, the traditional unwillingness of the government to enact macroeconomic policies to counter unemployment at the risk of undermining monetary stability, and Germany's mounting unemployment problems, West Germany's course of action is not surprising.[69]

Further, it is interesting to compare the effects of institutional variations between Japan and the United States on their respective propensities to impose NTBs. It is often argued that Japan is a "strong" state in which policymakers are extremely well-insulated and autonomous with respect to interest groups.[70] The United States, on the other hand, is often portrayed as a "weak" state in which policymakers lack both insulation and autonomy.[71] Yet

64. Kathleen A. Thelen, *Union of Parts: Labor Politics in Postwar Germany* (Ithaca, N.Y.: Cornell University Press, 1991), pp. 107–8.

65. OECD Economic Surveys, *Germany* (Paris: OECD, 1984), p. 12.

66. *Report of the Bundesbank for the Year 1983* (Frankfurt: Johanes Weisbecker, 1984), p. 13.

67. Peter J. Katzenstein, *Policy and Politics in West Germany: The Growth of a Semisovereign State* (Philadelphia: Temple University Press, 1987), p. 354.

68. OECD Economic Surveys, *Germany* (Paris: OECD, 1986), p. 26.

69. On organized labor's political strength, see Katzenstein, *Policy and Politics in West Germany,* p. 356.

70. See, for example, Chalmers Johnson, *MITI and the Japanese Miracle* (Stanford, Calif.: Stanford University Press, 1982); and Katzenstein, "Conclusion."

71. See, for example, Katzenstein, "Conclusion"; Krasner, *Defending the National Interest;* and Krasner, "United States Commercial and Monetary Policy."

both of these countries are characterized by a relatively large number of parliamentary constituencies based on our sample of states. This suggests that public officials in both countries are likely to be susceptible to societal pressures (although not necessarily to the same extent); and it jibes with the view expressed in a number of recent studies that Japanese policymakers are far less autonomous and less insulated from interest groups than is implied by those who characterize it as a strong state.[72] As Kent Calder argues, "Japan's system of medium-size electoral districts forces as many as five members of the largest political parties . . . to run against one another in the same electoral district. . . . As a result, . . . legislators tend to be highly sensitive to constituency pressure, especially from relatively well-organized grassroots pressure groups such as agriculture and small business."[73] A primary foreign policy interest of these groups is the prevention of the loss of domestic markets to imports, and this has led them to form alliances with politicians and bureaucrats that are likely to undermine the insulation and autonomy of these state actors.[74]

Going a step further, it is useful to consider the results presented in Table 1 in light of this discussion of Japanese and U.S. institutions. In 1986, for example, Japan and the United States were the two largest states in our sample, both countries had appreciated currencies and relatively little unemployment, and neither state's electoral system was PR. From the standpoint of our model, the primary difference between them was that the United States had noticeably more constituencies than did Japan. As a result, it would be expected on the basis of this model that Japanese policymakers would be somewhat better insulated and more autonomous than their American counterparts, and that this institutional feature would better enable them to pursue the national interest. It, therefore, is not surprising that the incidence of NTBs was greater in Japan than in the United States during 1986. At the same time, however, both Japanese and U.S. NTBs were relatively high in 1986 based on the sample of countries considered here. This is consistent with the view described above that, while Japanese policymakers are vested with greater institutional capacity (and therefore are better able to advance the national interest as they see it) than their American counterparts, the institutional characteristics of Japan and the United States are more similar than is often recognized.[75]

72. See Kent E. Calder, "Japanese Foreign Economic Policy Formation: Explaining the Reactive State," *World Politics* 40 (July 1988), pp. 515–41; Peter F. Cowhey, "Domestic Institutions and the Credibility of International Commitments: Japan and the United States," *International Organization* 47 (Spring 1993), pp. 299–326; Gerald L. Curtis, *The Japanese Way of Politics* (New York: Columbia University Press, 1988); Samuel Kernell, "The Primacy of Politics in Economic Policy," in Samuel Kernell, ed., *Parallel Politics: Economic Policymaking in Japan and the United States* (Washington, D.C.: The Brookings Institution, 1991), pp. 325–78; J. Mark Ramseyer and Frances McCall Rosenbluth, *Japan's Political Marketplace* (Cambridge, Mass.: Harvard University Press, 1993); and Robert M. Uriu, *Troubled Industries: The Political Economy of Industrial Adjustment in Japan* (Ithaca, N.Y.: Cornell University Press, forthcoming).

73. Calder, "Japanese Foreign Economic Policy Formation," pp. 530–31.

74. Ibid., pp. 528–32.

75. Kernell, "The Primacy of Politics in Economic Policy."

Clearly, the cases presented in this section can be taken as no more than suggestive of the ways in which societal and statist factors influence trade policy. Yet these examples do illustrate why the variables emphasized in our model are so strongly related to cross-national patterns of NTBs.

## Implications and conclusions

Our results have a number of implications for studies of the political economy of trade policy. In recent years, one of the most persistent sources of debate among both economists and political scientists has centered on the relative merits of societal and statist explanations of foreign economic policy. Our findings lend support for the societal argument that macroeconomic fluctuations contribute to demands for protection, which are in turn central determinants of trade policy. Consistent with societal theories, high levels of unemployment and appreciated currencies are strongly related to a high incidence of NTBs. In addition to their effects on NTBs, both of these macroeconomic factors also have been linked to cross-national patterns of tariffs. What is often referred to as the "new" protection (i.e., NTBs) may therefore be newer in form than in cause: it appears to be the product of many of the same factors that explain the "old" protection (i.e., tariffs).

While factors emphasized by societal approaches are strongly related to cross-national patterns of NTBs, factors highlighted by statist approaches also are centrally important in this regard. As statist analyses predict, economic size (which, in the opinion of many statists, helps to shape the preferences of policymakers with respect to trade policy) is strongly related to the incidence of NTBs. Large states have a greater incentive to impose protection than their smaller counterparts, and our findings indicate that they do in fact impose NTBs more widely than small states. It is curious that, despite the clear importance of this factor, it has been considered so rarely in empirical research on trade policy. Our results indicate that this omission is likely to yield incomplete and potentially misleading conclusions regarding the determinants of commercial policy.

So, too, is the failure to consider cross-national variations in domestic institutions in analyses of trade policy. Even though studies of political economy increasingly emphasize the need to understand the effects of institutions, few attempts have been made to assess the quantitative impact of institutions on trade policy. Further, no previous study has attempted to link cross-national variations in domestic institutions to patterns of NTBs. We find considerable evidence that institutions help to shape differences in NTBs. Particularly important in this regard is their effect on the relationships between macroeconomic variables and size, respectively, and NTBs.

Our findings bear out the position that the provision of NTBs is at least partially governed by economic size, domestic institutions, and the interaction between these factors. More specifically, NTBs are highest in large states that are characterized by high levels of institutional insulation and autonomy. Thus, states are most likely to impose NTBs when economic incentives to do so exist and when strong domestic institutions insulate policymakers from interest-group pressures, thereby allowing them to advance the national interest unencumbered by those pressure groups that display preferences for freer trade.

In addition to the interaction between variables that regulate the provision of NTBs, the interaction between these variables and those related to domestic pressures for protection also exerts a significant influence on trade policy. A number of political scientists and economists have argued that this should be the case, but little empirical evidence bearing on this fundamental topic has been accumulated.[76] Our results indicate that an understanding of the interaction between these factors is crucial for the purposes of explaining cross-national patterns of NTBs. All other things being equal, the incidence of NTBs is greatest when deteriorating macroeconomic conditions generate widespread demands for protection, a state is sufficiently large to give policymakers incentives to impose protection, and public officials are vested with the institutional capacity necessary to act on these preferences and resist pressures exerted by groups with an interest in lower trade barriers.

These findings stand in stark contrast to predictions based on either societal or statist models of foreign economic policy alone. Societal models—including most endogenous models of protection—emphasize factors related to societal demands for protection, but systematically neglect the factors that regulate the provision of trade barriers. Statist models place considerable emphasis on factors that account for the provision of protection, but often fail to address adequately the influence of pressure groups on trade policy. Each of these approaches correctly emphasizes one type of factor, while giving short shrift to the other type. Rather than considering these approaches as mutually exclusive, it is more fruitful to view them as complementary.

Many studies of foreign economic policy imply that protection is likely to be most pervasive in states characterized by vehement demands for protection articulated by well-organized groups and state institutions that fail to insulate policymakers from the brunt of these demands. This is particularly prevalent in the "state–society" literature that has been the topic of much heated controversy among scholars of foreign economic policy.[77] Our findings indicate that these debates have been miscast. Rather than viewing protection as an

76. See, for example, Bhagwati, *Protectionism;* Gourevitch, *Politics in Hard Times;* Krasner, *Defending the National Interest;* Krasner, "United States Commercial and Monetary Policy"; Lake, *Power, Protection, and Free Trade;* Milner, *Resisting Protectionism;* and Nelson, "Endogenous Tariff Theory."

77. See, for example, Gourevitch, *Politics in Hard Times;* Gowa, "Public Goods and Political Institutions"; Ikenberry, Lake, and Mastanduno, "Introduction"; Katzenstein, "Conclusion"; Krasner, *Defending the National Interest;* and Milner, *Resisting Protectionism.*

outcome whereby pressure groups run roughshod over public officials who are inherently liberal with respect to trade, NTBs are greatest when the interests of state and societal actors converge. Similarly, much of the recent disagreement among analysts of foreign economic policy has centered on whether societal demands for protection or domestic institutions that regulate the provision of protection should be emphasized. This debate has served to create a false dichotomy. The issue is not which factor should be emphasized, since both are centrally important determinants of NTBs. Rather, the central issue is how to integrate both factors in a comprehensive manner. Although it is obvious that our results should be taken as tentative, their strength is striking. These findings strongly indicate that it would be fruitful to further integrate societal models—especially models of endogenous protection—and statist models, and that this research strategy is likely to generate new and important insights concerning the determinants of trade policy.

Finally, our results yield substantial evidence that tariffs are strongly related to the incidence of NTBs, and that these forms of protection are substitutes.[78] This finding is consistent with the law of constant protection. Among the states considered here, new tariffs could not easily have been imposed due to GATT restrictions. States with low tariff levels that wish to augment their trade barriers therefore have had reason to rely on NTBs for this purpose. Further, states characterized by high tariff levels are likely to be sufficiently well-protected that they need not supplement tariffs with NTBs. Our findings suggest the possibility that many of the tariff reductions made by the GATT during the Tokyo Round may not have had the intended effect of reducing protection. Instead, these cuts seem to have produced countervailing increases in the incidence of NTBs.

In addition to the implications of this study, it is also important to address its limitations. One limitation of this sort concerns the available data on NTBs. While the coverage ratios on which we relied are viewed by many as the best data of their kind, NTBs are inherently difficult to measure. Further, these data are available for only a few years during the 1980s, and the determinants of NTBs may vary over time. Another limitation concerns the sample of states that was analyzed. As noted earlier, we chose the fourteen states examined in this study because they were the only states for which all of the necessary data were available. It is obvious, however, that these states do not comprise a representative sample for the global economy as a whole. Of central importance in this regard is the fact that they are all advanced industrial and democratic states. The processes that account for NTBs in such countries may differ considerably from those in less developed and/or authoritarian and

78. As noted throughout, our focus has been on explaining the incidence on NTBs. Other studies have focused on the level of NTBs and argued that NTBs and tariffs are complements. It is clear that our results and those based on the level of NTBs need not be incompatible. For one leading attempt to assess the relationship between tariffs and NTB levels, see Magee, Brock, and Young, *Black Hole Tariffs and Endogenous Policy Theory*, pp. 236–41.

newly emerging democratic states. A state's factor endowments or level of economic development may also contribute to the nature of its political institutions and patterns of protection.[79] Our focus on advanced industrial states clearly limits our ability to examine this issue, since little variation exists in the capital abundance or the level of economic development among the countries analyzed here. Nonetheless, we believe that this study has shed new light on the conditions that explain cross-national variations in NTBs among these countries.

79. For two perspectives on this possibility, see Carlos F. Diaz-Alejandro, *Trade, Development and the World Economy* (New York: Basil Blackwell, 1988; ed., Andres Velasco), chap. 14; and Ronald Findlay, "Trade, Development, and the State," in Gustav Ranis and T. Paul Schultz, eds., *The State of Development Economics: Progress and Perspectives* (New York: Basil Blackwell, 1988), pp. 78–95. We are grateful to an anonymous reviewer for bringing this point to our attention.

# Free to Trade: Democracies, Autocracies, and International Trade

EDWARD D. MANSFIELD *Ohio State University*
HELEN V. MILNER *Columbia University*
B. PETER ROSENDORFF *Georgetown University and University of Southern California*

*Relatively little research has focused on whether countries' political institutions affect their international trade relations. We address this issue by analyzing the relationship between regime type and trade policy. In a formal model of commercial policy, we establish that the ratification responsibility of the legislature in democratic states leads pairs of democracies to set trade barriers at a lower level than mixed country-pairs (composed of an autocracy and a democracy). We test this hypothesis by analyzing the effects of regime type on trade during the period from 1960 to 1990. The results of this analysis accord with our argument: Democratic pairs have had much more open trade relations than mixed pairs.*

The effects of domestic political institutions on trade policy have long been a source of controversy among social scientists. Despite the widespread interest that this debate has prompted, however, remarkably few studies have addressed the links between political regime type and commercial policy.[1] Most work on the political economy of trade policy that examines institutional factors focuses only on variations in policy among democracies and avoids comparing democracies with other types of regimes. Moreover, many analyses of trade barriers—especially those by economists—ignore the effects of domestic political institutions. In light of the recent interest expressed in how regime type influences various aspects of foreign policy (e.g., Doyle 1986; Farber and Gowa 1995; Russett 1993; Siverson and Emmons 1991), a systematic analysis of the links between regime type and trade policy seems long overdue.

Here, we examine whether groups of democracies are better able to liberalize trade than are groups of autocracies or groups comprised of both democracies and autocracies. By providing one of the first assessments of whether patterns of commercial protection depend on regime type, we help shed light on whether there is a "democratic difference" in foreign economic policy. Our study also should contribute to a broader understanding of the political economy of trade policy. One recent analysis concludes: "Theoretical and empirical work relating [domestic] institutional contexts to trade policy outcomes is in its infancy but should be a promising area of research" (Rodrik 1995, 1485). We seek to help fill this important gap in the literature.

We develop a formal model that emphasizes the role of domestic legislatures in democracies. Central to this model is that the chief executive (i.e., prime minister or president) in a democracy needs the approval of a legislative majority to enact her preferred trade policies.[2] Absent such approval, the legislature's preferred policy becomes law. We argue that legislative "ratification" of commercial policy occurs in both parliamentary and presidential systems. In parliamentary systems, ratification is often ex ante; the potential prime minister must negotiate an acceptable trade policy with her legislative majority before taking office. This internal bargain is enforced afterward because the majority can call for a vote of (no) confidence if the prime minister strays from the accepted position in international economic negotiations. In presidential systems, major changes in trade policy usually require legislative ratification ex post.

By contrast, autocracies vest the chief executive with much more authority than democracies. Autocrats do not need a legislative majority to pass their trade policy initiatives; either a legislature does not exist or it rubber-stamps executive proposals. We claim that this institutional difference contributes to a greater tendency for pairs of democratic countries to agree upon lower trade barriers than pairs comprised of a democracy and an autocracy (i.e., mixed pairs). We further demonstrate that whether pairs of autocracies liberalize trade more extensively than either pairs of democracies or mixed pairs depends on the preferences of the

Edward D. Mansfield is Associate Professor of Political Science, Ohio State University, Columbus, OH 43210 (mansfield@polisci.sbs.ohio-state.edu). Helen V. Milner is Professor of Political Science, Columbia University, New York, NY 10027 (hvm1@columbia.edu). B. Peter Rosendorff is Associate Professor in the School of International Relations, University of Southern California, Los Angeles, CA 90089, and in the Department of Economics and the School of Foreign Service, Georgetown University, Washington, DC 20057 (bpeter@usc.edu).

Earlier versions of this paper were presented at the 1997 annual meeting of the American Political Science Association, Washington, DC, and at seminars at the University of Chicago (PIPES), Georgetown University, Stanford University, the University of Southern California, and Yale University. We are grateful to participants in these seminars, to David Baldwin, Marc Busch, James Fearon, Jeffry Frieden, Joanne Gowa, Dean Lacy, David Lake, Charles Lipson, John McLaren, John Odell, Robert Pahre, Mohan Penubarti, Ronald Rogowski, Seth Sanders, and Duncan Snidal for helpful comments, and to Joe McGarvey and Jon C. Pevehouse for research assistance. In conducting this research, Mansfield was assisted by a grant from the Ohio State University Office of Research and by the Hoover Institution at Stanford University, where he was a National Fellow during 1998–99. Rosendorff was assisted by a grant from the James H. Zumberge Faculty Research and Innovation Fund at the University of Southern California.

[1] For a few exceptions, see Bliss and Russett 1998, Dixon and Moon 1993, and Morrow, Siverson, and Tabares 1998.

[2] We are not arguing that autocracies do not need domestic political support. Our point is that autocrats do not require the majority approval of a legislature elected by the public to represent its interests. Autocrats may well depend on the support of such actors as the military or industrialists, but these groups do not represent the voting public.

political decision makers involved, as well as on institutional differences between their regime types. Hence, we can make no prediction about the trade barriers of autocratic pairs relative to mixed pairs or democratic pairs without knowledge of the respective executives' trade policy preferences.

Our focus differs sharply from studies that address how institutional variations among countries with the same regime type affect trade policy. Crucial to the following analysis is that the institutional feature which distinguishes democracies from autocracies is the existence of a popularly elected legislature with the capacity to constrain a country's chief executive. We assume that legislatures are more protectionist than executives in democracies and show that, even so, pairs of democracies are more likely than mixed pairs to liberalize commerce.[3] Our focus, then, is on differences across regime types not within them.

The results of an empirical analysis based on the period 1960–90 are consistent with these predictions. Holding constant various economic and political factors, democratic dyads tend to trade more freely than dyads composed of a democracy and an autocracy. Furthermore, no significant difference exists in the openness of commerce within autocratic pairs and within democratic pairs.

## THE MODEL

### The Actors and Their Preferences

A key difference between an autocracy and a democracy is that the latter is vested with a legislature that has de jure and de facto ratification power over the chief executive's proposals. Because no such institution exists or has such powers in an autocracy, it is modeled as a unitary actor; it has only an executive, who is effectively a dictator and is labeled $A$. In contrast, a democracy is characterized by two actors: an executive, who may be the president or prime minister, $P$, and a legislature, represented by the median legislator, $C$. In what follows, we consider the case in which two countries enter into negotiations to reduce trade barriers between them. The labels $A$, $P$, and $C$ refer to the "home" country in these negotiations, whereas $A^*$, $P^*$, and $C^*$ refer to the "foreign" country.

In the home country, each of the aforementioned actors tries to maximize its utility by obtaining the greatest possible level of electoral support. That support depends on the trade policy chosen. Every actor wants to enact the level of trade barriers that will maximize its political support (i.e., its ideal point). But each one must strike a balance among the conflicting preferences of its constituents to determine the ideal level. Actors receive political support from a variety of domestic groups. Some groups prefer that the home country lowers trade barriers (e.g., consumers, exporters, users of imported inputs, owners of relatively abundant factors), and others prefer that it raises barriers (e.g., import-competing firms, owners of scarce factors). All groups, however, prefer that the foreign country's trade barriers be as low as possible, an outcome that benefits consumers, exporters, and import-competing firms alike. Ceteris paribus, all domestic groups will increase their electoral support for policymakers in the home country if these officials negotiate very low levels of protection abroad.[4] We refer to the home country's trade barriers as $t$ and those of the foreign country as $t^*$.

The political support function of each actor, $U_i$, can be expressed as a simple loss function. Every actor has an ideal level of trade barriers at home and abroad, denoted $(t_i, t_i^*)$, that $i$ would choose if it were not constrained by any of the other actors. All domestic actors prefer the elimination of foreign trade barriers; hence, $t_i^* = 0$ for $i = P, C, A$, and $t_i = 0$ for $i = P^*, C^*, A^*$. Each actor maximizes its utility by minimizing the difference between the level of protection that it prefers both at home and abroad and the level that actually obtains. For the home country, $i$'s utility function is

$$U_i(t, t^*) = -(t - t_i)^2 - t^{*2} \quad \text{for } i = P, A, C. \tag{1}$$

For the foreign country, its actors attempt to maximize

$$U_i(t, t^*) = -t^2 - (t^* - t_i^*)^2 \quad \text{for } i = P^*, A^*, C^*. \tag{1*}$$

These utility functions imply that the actors' indifference curves are circles. Their utility decreases symmetrically as changes occur in any direction away from their ideal level of trade barriers at home and abroad. Such utility functions are very common to spatial models (e.g., Enelow and Hinich 1984).[5]

Our approach to the making of trade policy is consistent with behavior in both democracies and autocracies. For instance, it captures the notion that democratically elected politicians are motivated by a desire to be reelected, the chances of which grow larger in the face of both rising welfare experienced by voters

[3] If legislatures are not more protectionist than executives, then the results depend on the actors' preferences. Differences in trade policy will depend on both institutions and preferences in that case. We focus instead on the case in which the effect of institutional variation is robust to any preference ordering among the players.

[4] This formulation of the objective functions bears some similarity to Krugman's GATT-think (Ethier 1998; Krugman 1997), in which trade negotiators are motivated by mercantilist notions: Exports are good, imports are bad, and an equal increase in exports and imports is good.

[5] As implied above, the objective functions 1 and 1* can be seen as the reduced form of a model that combines elements of the underlying economy with a political game of policymaking. For instance, if political support (as in Hillman 1982) is a function of consumer surplus (CS), tariff revenue (T), profits of the import-competing firms ($\text{Profits}_\text{I}$), and profits of the exporting firms ($\text{Profits}_\text{E}$), then for the home country, $(t_i, t_i^*) = \text{argmax } F(\text{CS}(t, t^*), \text{Profits}_\text{I}(t), \text{Profits}_\text{E}(t^*), \text{ and T}(t))$ for $i = P, C, A$, where $F$ is increasing in each argument (Hillman, Long, and Moser 1995). The exact form of the function $F$ and the weights placed on each term depend on the underlying market demand and supply conditions, the relative political pressure that each group can bring to bear, and the political institutions that mediate this pressure. This approach is consistent with Grossman and Helpman (1994), who posit that the government cares about a weighted average of social welfare and campaign contributions. Then equations 1 and 1* would be the second-order approximations of a political support function around the ideal points.

and increasing campaign contributions (or lobbying activity undertaken) by organized lobbies, such as industry groups. Hence, trade policies that raise consumer surplus and firm profits increase the political support that a politician receives. Consumers are made better off by a rise in their surplus; and because they vote according to their pocketbooks, their support for the government grows. In addition, as firms' profits rise, they distribute higher profits to consumers (who are also stockholders) and make larger contributions to (or exercise greater influence over) politicians. Note that the government responds to the pressures of both its import-competing and exporting firms. We assume that the government does not have a direct instrument to benefit the exporting sector (such as a subsidy), but it can reduce trade barriers abroad through negotiations and reciprocal concessions, thereby benefiting local exporting industries.

In autocracies, the executive must also maintain political support. The extent of the support provided by consumers and firms often depends on economic conditions. For example, a recent analysis notes that, in the wake of Deng Xiaoping's death, China's autocratic leaders "are acutely aware that a vibrant, flourishing, and progressing economy is the core of their legitimacy" (*New York Times*, February 21, 1997, A15). Again, trade policy has a direct influence on consumer surplus and firms' profits. Greater consumer surplus means higher real incomes, fewer incentives to riot and rebel, and thus more support for autocratic leaders. Similarly, greater firm profits mean higher incomes for at least some groups (the firm owners), implying increased political support for the autocrat. Whether autocrats care more about consumers and the overall state of the economy or the special interests of firms depends on a number of factors that do not concern us here.

The trade policy preferences of autocrats relative to those of democratic leaders are of central concern. It is unclear whether, on average, autocrats are more protectionist than democratic heads of state. Freed from the need to finance expensive electoral campaigns, autocrats may be more attentive to the economy's performance and hence less protectionist than their democratic counterparts. Yet, if autocrats depend only on the support of a small group of powerful interests, they may be more willing to extract economic rents (through trade barriers and other means) from those sectors of the economy in which these interests do not operate. We handle this difficult issue by varying the preferences of the autocrat relative to those of the democratic executive and assessing how changes in their relative preferences combined with the institutional differences between these two regime types affect our results.

In a democracy, the two main political actors often do not agree on the ideal level of home trade barriers; that is, $t_P$ and $t_C$ are unlikely to be identical. The executive and the median legislator may weigh consumer surplus and firm profits differently in their electoral calculus. Legislators, who represent smaller constituencies than the chief executive, are more easily captured by special interests than the executive (Mansfield and Busch 1995; Rogowski 1987). We assume that the median legislator cares more about the profits of import-competing firms than about consumer surplus and holds more protectionist preferences than the democratic executive (Lohmann and O'Halloran 1994; Rosendorff 1996). Thus, we assume that $t_P < t_C$ and $t_{P*} < t_{C*}$.[6]

All domestic agents prefer that, ceteris paribus, foreign barriers be as low as possible. Ideal values for the domestic trade barriers do vary, however. The median voter theorem is therefore applicable: Single-peaked objective functions over a single dimension imply the median voter is decisive (Black 1958). This similarity of preferences allows us to avoid the cycles associated with median voter models in larger dimensions. We can identify the median legislator as that member who holds the median value for the level of domestic trade barriers, and the legislature as represented by this median legislator.

Each player receives the maximum utility when its ideal trade barrier combination is adopted. Maximum feasible utility for each player is $U^P(t_P, 0)$, $U^C(t_C, 0)$, $U^A(t_A, 0)$, $U^{P^*}(0, t^*_{P*})$, $U^{C^*}(0, t^*_{C*})$, $U^{A^*}(0, t^*_{A*})$.

### The Noncooperative Trade Barrier Setting Game: The Trade War

In the absence of any agreement on mutual trade policy concessions, each country is free to set trade barriers only in its own country. Each country sets its trade policy *simultaneously*, taking the actions of the other as given. The Nash equilibrium to this noncooperative trade barrier-setting game can be considered the "trade war" outcome, which is what we assume occurs when countries do not agree to mutually acceptable trade barrier concessions. Political leaders at home have authority over $t$. Foreign barriers ($t^*$) are controlled by the foreign government. When both countries are autocratic (denoted $AA^*$), each executive determines the level of trade barriers in her country. Consider the problem facing the home autocrat, $A$, who maximizes equation 1 taking $t^*$ as given. $A$'s reaction function is independent of $t^*$ and hence is vertical at $t_A$.[7] Similarly, $A^*$'s reaction function is independent of $t$ and hence horizontal at $t^*_{A*}$. The Nash equilibrium is the pair of preferred trade barrier levels ($t_A$, $t^*_{A*}$) chosen by the home and the foreign autocrat. In Figure 1, this point is labeled $N_{AA^*}$. Note that both parties could be made better off if they could negotiate to a point on or closer to the Pareto frontier, $t_A t^*_{A*}$.

When one or both countries are democracies, we assume that the legislature ($C$ or $C^*$) has the final say on domestic trade policy.[8] Again, each domestic play-

[6] Throughout, we assume that there is a meaningful difference between their preferences; we assume that $t_C > 2t_P$ and $t^*_{C*} > 2t^*_{P*}$.

[7] This follows from the additive separability of $t$ and $t^*$ in the objective functions in equations 1 and 1*.

[8] This assumption is not necessary for our results. If the legislature simply has some ability to force the executive to take its preferences into account in the event of the trade war outcome, then our results

**FIGURE 1. Trade Barriers Set by Two Autocracies**

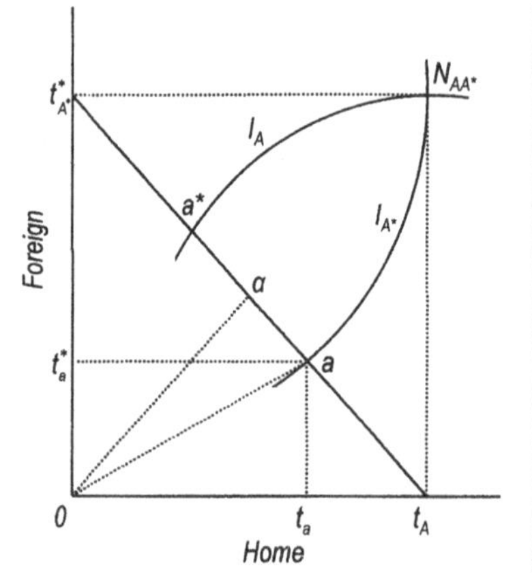


er's ideal domestic policy is independent of the actions of the foreign player (and vice versa). When the home country is a democracy and the foreign one is an autocracy (denoted $DA^*$), the best-response functions call for $C$ to implement $t_C$ for any value of $t^*$ and for $A^*$ to play $t^*_{A^*}$, irrespective of $t$. The noncooperative game between home and abroad has as its equilibrium $N_{DA^*} = (t_C, t^*_{A^*})$, as labeled in Figure 2A, B, and C. Realized returns to $C$, $P$, and $A^*$ are $C(t_C, t^*_{A^*})$, $P(t_C, t^*_{A^*})$, and $A^*(t_C, t^*_{A^*})$. These returns are lower than the respective optima $C(t_C, 0)$, $P(t_P, 0)$, and $A^*(0, t^*_{A^*})$. Pareto improvements are possible; if $C$, $P$, and $A^*$ can agree to mutually reduce trade barriers (slightly) from $(t_C, t^*_{A^*})$, all could gain.

Finally, when both countries are democracies ($DD^*$), the Nash equilibrium is set by the two legislatures. In this case, failure to find mutual concessions leads to point $N_{DD^*} = (t_C, t^*_{C^*})$ in Figure 3.

In all three cases, the Nash equilibrium to this simultaneous game of trade barrier setting is the defect-defect outcome in the prisoners' dilemma. If the countries do not cooperate, they will choose a level of trade barriers at home that is ideal, but that results in a higher level abroad than they ideally desire. Since both countries make such a choice, they end up at the noncooperative Nash equilibrium, which is not welfare maximizing. If they coordinate their trade policies, then they can both achieve welfare gains. As such, the problem facing political leaders is to reach a pair of trade barrier levels closer to their optima, and this necessarily involves mutual concessions.

are maintained. The legislature's preferences must simply affect a democracy's unilateral, noncooperative choice of barriers.

## The Negotiation Game: TILI

Consider the simplest bargaining game, in which we assume that the actors have perfect information. The players' ideal trade barrier levels at home and abroad are common knowledge, as is the structure of the game. We consider two bargaining structures. In the first game, the home country—by virtue of having the first move—is chosen to make a take-it-or-leave-it (TILI) offer to the foreign country. The latter can either accept and implement this offer or reject it, thereby inducing a reversion to the trade war outcome, that is, the Nash equilibrium. Then we switch the identity of the first mover and consider the same TILI game; that is, the foreign country makes the first move, and bargaining power is reversed. Under either bargaining structure, neither country can dictate the levels of trade barriers that both choose. Both countries know they can gain from making mutual concessions, and they know that everyone must be left at least as well off as they would be in the trade war outcome. We establish that the results are robust to this change in the bargaining structure, and we infer that any structure in which bargaining power is distributed in a less extreme fashion between the players will yield similar results.

For instance, if the parties agree to split evenly the gains from any mutual reductions in trade barrier levels —an approach consistent with the symmetric Nash Bargaining Solution (Nash 1950)—then they will generate outcomes that lie somewhere between that of TILI when the home executive proposes and TILI when the foreign executive proposes. Thus, our results are general to a variety of bargaining structures.

In the TILI game, the moves of the players occur in two steps. First, the home executive, whether democratic or not, makes an offer, specifying a mutually reduced level of home and foreign trade barriers. If both countries are autocracies, then the foreign leader is asked to agree. If home is a democracy and foreign is an autocracy, then the home executive puts her offer to both the foreign autocrat and the domestic legislature. Either player has veto power, which induces a reversion to the trade war outcome. If both countries are democracies, then the home executive picks an offer, which must be acceptable to the foreign executive and both legislatures.[9] Failure to obtain legislative ratification in the latter two cases leads to the trade war, or Nash equilibrium, either $N_{DA^*}$ or $N_{DD^*}$. It is assumed that *no player* will ever take an action that is dominated: They will not reject an offer that is better than that which will be received in the trade war. The elimination of dominated strategies is equivalent (in this game) to requiring the equilibrium to be subgame perfect.

Note that the structure of preferences in the countries is symmetric. That is, the optimal level of trade barriers preferred by $A$ is the same as that preferred by $A^*$, and similarly for $P$ and $P^*$ as well as $C$ and $C^*$. We

[9] In fact, we require that the international negotiators choose a ratifiable offer that lies on their Pareto frontier when such an agreement exists.

**FIGURE 2. Trade Barriers Set by an Autocracy and a Democracy**

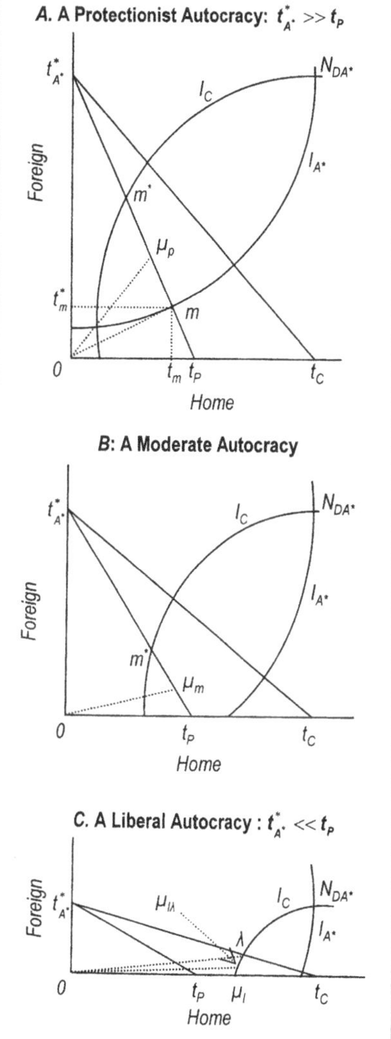


make this assumption because our focus is on differences *between* regime types, not within each regime type. This assumption, however, has two implications. First, we do not model what happens when a protectionist autocrat faces an autocrat who prefers to liberalize trade, an interesting issue but one that departs from our focus on variations across regime types.

Second, the symmetry assumption implies that the distance between the democratic executive and its legislature is the same at home and abroad for all democratic dyads. Again, we make this assumption because we are interested in variations between regime types, not within them. Both our model and our data analysis treat each type of regime as homogeneous. Democracies are distinct from autocracies because they have a legislature that exercises ratification power, regardless of its preferences. The differences among regime types rest on institutional features and not on the policy preferences of decision makers. Varying the difference in the ideal policies of $P$ and $C$ does not alter the degree of democracy present; it only changes the extent to which government is divided within democracies. Furthermore, whether a government is divided or unified has no bearing on the degree to which a country is democratic. Hence, examining the influence of such divisions (i.e., as the ideal points of $P$ and $C$ diverge or converge) does not inform us about democracies versus autocracies, only about more divided versus less divided democracies.[10] Our model is capable of deriving outcomes when such symmetry of preferences is relaxed, but we have neither the space nor the data in this article to explore these variations within democracies.

Figures 1–3 show the central results. We measure the aggregate level of trade barriers by the sum of the two countries' levels of trade barriers. The indifference curves for the actors $C$, $C^*$, $A$, and $A^*$ through $N$ have been drawn and are labeled $I_C$, $I_{C^*}$, $I_A$, and $I_{A^*}$, respectively. These curves mark the boundary of the set of mutual reductions in trade barriers that are preferred by each player (respectively, $C$, $C^*$, or/and $A$, $A^*$) to the noncooperative Nash equilibrium outcome. The solution to the bargaining must lie in this feasible set, often termed the "win set." In addition, the contract curve between the executives $A^*$ (or $P^*$) and $A$ (or $P$) has been drawn. It is a straight line between the executives' ideal points (since the indifference curves are circles). The contract curve between $C$ and $P$ (or $C^*$ and $P^*$) can be thought of as that part of the horizontal (vertical) axis that lies between $t_C$ and $t_P$ ($t^*_{C^*}$ and $t^*_{P^*}$). More generally, the contract curve refers to the set of points where the two actors' indifference curves are tangent, that is, the set of trade barriers that both actors mutually prefer to any other set of barriers. Note, however, that movements along

[10] This is why comparative statics are less helpful. They ask what happens when the executive moves slightly closer to the legislature, or vice versa, and thus examine how divisions in government matter for trade policy. We believe that research on how democracies vary among themselves is vitally important, but we leave for another study an exploration of such intrademocracy divisions. See Lohmann and O'Halloran 1994, Milner and Rosendorff 1996, and O'Halloran 1994 for the effects of changes in the degree of divided government on trade policy.

**FIGURE 3. Trade Barriers Set by Two Democracies**

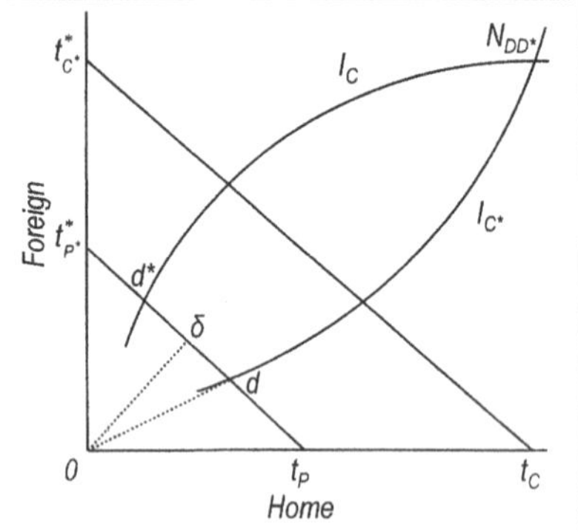


the contract curve cannot make one actor better off without making the other worse off.

In Figure 1, two autocracies must agree on mutual concessions about trade barriers. Home will offer a mutual reduction of barriers to point $a$ on the contract curve; this is the point on the Pareto frontier that leaves foreign indifferent between accepting and rejecting, thus allowing home to earn all the surplus. The level of bilateral trade barriers under TILI is measured by the sum of the home and foreign trade barriers. These aggregate barriers are $0t_a + 0t^*_a$.

Figure 2 presents the results of bargaining within mixed pairs, while varying the relative preferences of the autocrat and the democratic executive. In Figure 2A, a democracy seeks to find mutually acceptable trade concessions with a protectionist autocrat. The democratic executive, $P$, has freer trade inclinations than the autocratic leader, $A^*$. $P$ must offer a set of trade barriers inside the area between the two indifference curves, $I_C$ and $I_{A^*}$, in order for $C$ and $A^*$ to accept it. In addition, $P$ will offer a point on the contract curve between $t_P$ and $t^*_{A^*}$. Although $P$ optimally wants to choose her ideal point, $t_P$, she is constrained by $A^*$. Thus, $P$ must choose the point at which $A^*$'s indifference curve through the no-agreement point intersects the Pareto frontier, that is, point $m$.

In Figure 2B, a moderate autocrat seeks mutual trade concessions with a democracy. Now $P$'s ideal point is in the win set. Naturally, $P$ chooses this as the offer $(t_P, 0)$, which both the foreign autocrat and the democratic home legislature accept.

In Figure 2C, a liberal autocrat attempts to find mutual trade concessions with a democracy. The democratic executive is much more protectionist than the autocrat. The outcome in this case also must lie within the win set created by the legislature's indifference curve through the Nash trade war equilibrium, $I_C$, and the autocrat's indifference curve through this point, $I_{A^*}$. The legislature exercises the major constraint here. The democratic executive and the autocrat will choose a point as close as possible to their ideal points that is still acceptable to the legislature; that is, one lying along the legislature's indifference curve. Hence, their choice is bounded by the legislature's preference in this case. Since $P$ makes the offer, $P$ chooses $\mu_l = t_C - t^*_{A^*}$, which is accepted by $A^*$ as well as by $C$.[11]

In Figure 3, two democracies with symmetric preferences try to find mutually acceptable trade concessions. The executives must choose a set of trade barriers within the win set formed by the indifference curves of the median legislators through the Nash equilibrium, that is, between $I_C$ and $I_{C^*}$. Again, the contract curve between the two executives inside the win set is the line segment $d^*d$. $P$ chooses the point on that line segment closest to her ideal point, $t_P$. The offer is at point $d$, which is accepted by the foreign executive and both legislatures.

## Levels of Trade Barriers and Regime Type

Can we compare the levels of trade barriers across the three types of regime pairs?

PROPOSITION: *Aggregate trade barriers are lower within democratic pairs than within pairs composed of an autocracy and a democracy.*

A complete proof for both bargaining structures is given in the Appendix (propositions 1 and 2). Although we measure the aggregate barriers by the sum of the two countries' trade barriers in the proofs, intuitive use can be made of the length of the ray from the origin to the agreement point. Figure 4 shows all the possible outcomes in a single diagram. When home makes the offer, the bilateral trade barrier level in the democratic pair is measured by the length of the ray $0d$. In the case of the protectionist autocracy in the mixed pair, the ray has length $0m$; in the moderate case, the length is $0t_P$; in the liberal case, the ray has length $0\mu_l$. In all these cases, the ray corresponding to the democratic pair $(0d)$ is smaller than that corresponding to the mixed pair $(0m$, $0t_P$, or $0\mu_l)$.

A democracy lowers its trade barriers more when it seeks mutually acceptable concessions with another democracy than when it deals with an autocracy, no matter what the relative preferences of the two leaders. Why? When both are democracies and home makes the initial proposal, it is the pressure of the foreign legislature that forces the home country to compromise or else end up in a trade war. The Nash equilibrium is worse for both countries in the case of two democracies $(N_{DD^*})$ than in the autocracy-democracy case $(N_{DA^*})$, which induces the democratic executives to agree to liberalize trade more than otherwise.[12] The threat of a legislative veto in both countries moves the executives

[11] Recall that $P$ is required to offer to $A^*$ a point on their Pareto frontier; in Figure 2C, no point on the line $t^*_{A^*}t_P$ is ratifiable. In this case, $P$ offers $\mu_l$, which is ratifiable.

[12] As Axelrod (1970, 56) observes, a worsening of the no-agreement point can induce greater cooperation between the actors under certain circumstances.

**FIGURE 4. TILI Outcomes with Liberal and Protectionist Autocrats**

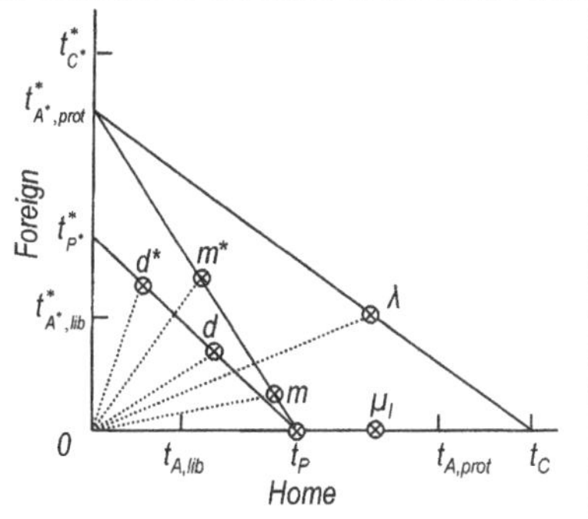


to a freer trade equilibrium than in the case of a mixed pair. Paradoxically, then, a protectionist legislature forces democracies to lower their trade barriers more than otherwise.

In contrast, whether such barriers will be higher within democratic pairs than within autocratic pairs depends on the preferences of the leaders in the different regimes. When autocrats are more (less) protectionist than democratic executives, mutual reductions in trade barriers will be smaller (greater) between autocracies than between democracies (proposition 3 in the Appendix). Institutional differences alone do not distinguish between the outcomes; the structure of preferences is also important. The same is true for mixed pairs relative to autocratic pairs. When the preferences of the autocrats are protectionist relative to those of the legislature in a democracy, the pair of autocracies will be unable to lower barriers as much as the mixed pair (proposition 4 in the Appendix). Because the two autocrats do not have to contend with a legislature that is more protectionist than they are, they do not have to compromise as much. This reinforces our counterintuitive claim that a protectionist legislature may actually promote freer trade among countries.

In the Appendix we also show what happens when the foreign country is able to make the first offer. On the whole, the results reported above continue to hold. As the first mover, however, the foreign government has greater bargaining power. In each case, the equilibrium outcome now lies closer to the foreign government's ideal point. In Figure 1, for instance, the outcome is $a^*$ instead of $a$. When $A^*$ proposes, she knows that $A$ will accept any point on the contract curve at or below the intersection of her indifference curve through the Nash trade war equilibrium, $I_A$. Thus, $A^*$ proposes the set of trade barriers closest to her ideal point that $A$ will also accept, that is, point $a^*$. In Figure 2A, the outcome is $m^*$; in Figure 2B, it is also $m^*$. In Figure 2C, the outcome is now $\lambda$, since this is the point at which the highest indifference curve of the foreign autocrat, $I_{A^*}$, is tangent to the home legislature's indifference curve.[13] In the case of two democracies, as in Figure 3, $P^*$ proposes $d^*$, which both the home executive and the two legislatures accept. In effect, changing the proposer moves the outcome along the contract curve closer to the proposer's ideal point, which improves the outcome for the proposer at the expense of the other country. These outcomes, displayed in Figure 4, show that the ray $0d^*$ (aggregate barriers under joint democracy) is shorter than the rays $0m^*$ (aggregate barriers under the mixed case with a protectionist or a moderate autocrat) and $0\lambda$ (aggregate barriers in the mixed case with a liberal autocrat).

As pointed out above, the equilibrium outcome of any game in which the two countries divide the concessions equally (which we call the SPLIT game) is always in the middle of the range of the contract curve bounded by the maximum value that each can get when she proposes. In the case of two democracies (Figure 3), the SPLIT outcome is in the middle of the portion of the contract curve bounded by $d^*$ and $d$, labeled $\delta$. The outcomes in the other cases under SPLIT are labeled $\alpha$, $\mu_p$, $\mu_m$, and $\mu_{l\lambda}$ in figures 1, 2A, 2B, and 2C, respectively. Inspection of the lengths of the rays in Figure 5 establishes that $0\delta < \min\{0\mu_P, 0\mu_m, 0\mu_{l\lambda}\}$.

In sum, regime type is likely to exert an important influence on trade policy. Our model predicts that pairs of democracies should trade more freely than mixed pairs, a result that arises from the tendency for a protectionist legislature to enhance the prospects of trade barrier reductions. Yet, our model is silent on whether commerce will be more open within autocratic pairs than within either democratic or mixed pairs, an issue that hinges on the trade policy preferences of decision makers.

Our model is also silent on the effects of variations within regime types. It does not yield predictions about how institutional differences either among autocracies or among democracies (e.g., whether the government is presidential or parliamentary) affect trade policy, issues that have been addressed elsewhere (e.g., Mansfield and Busch 1995; Milner 1997; Milner and Rosendorff 1996, 1997; Pahre 1997). We focus solely on the institutional differences between autocracies and democracies. Central to our analysis is the assumption that, unlike autocracies, democracies are marked by a legislature that can effectively constrain the chief executive and that is more protectionist than the executive.

Following lemma 2 in the Appendix, it is clear that, given our symmetry assumption in the case of two democracies, aggregate barriers are $t_P$ irrespective of the location of $t_C$. Hence, it is a direct consequence of lemma 2 that variations in the degree of division between the executive and the legislature in the democracies will have no effect on the outcome when two democracies bargain. Therefore, our claim that democratic dyads prefer lower trade barriers than mixed

[13] As in note 11, no point on the Pareto frontier between the ideal points of $A^*$ and $P$ is ratifiable in Figure 2C. In this instance, $A^*$ offers $\lambda$, which is acceptable to both $C$ and $P$.

**FIGURE 5. SPLIT Outcomes with Liberal and Protectionist Autocrats**

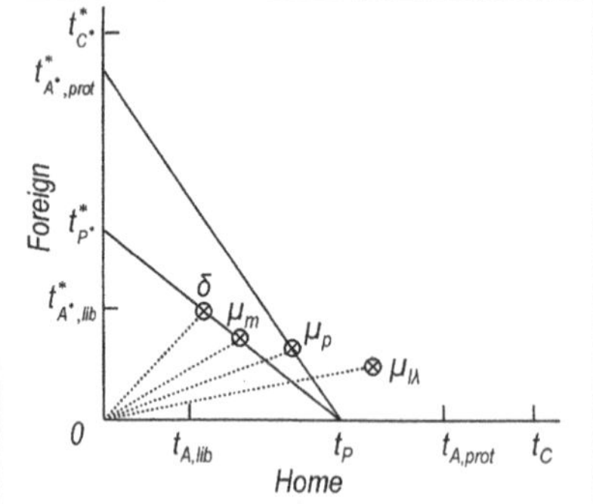


pairs is preserved, even if the legislatures in the democratic dyad case become more protectionist. Put more formally as a corollary to lemma 2 and proved in the Appendix:

COROLLARY. *Irrespective of which country makes the first offer, as the legislatures become more protectionist, the aggregate level of barriers on which a pair of democracies agree is unchanged.*

## EMPIRICAL ANALYSIS

We now turn to an empirical analysis of the hypotheses derived from the model. Our central hypothesis is that trade barriers should be lower between two democracies than between an autocracy and a democracy. It is not possible to test this proposition directly, since reliable data on bilateral trade barriers are not available for many of the countries analyzed here, but data on bilateral trade flows are readily available for most countries and can serve as a proxy for trade policy. Various studies have found that, other things being equal, there is an inverse relationship between the height of trade barriers and the volume of interstate trade (e.g., Harrigan 1993; Leamer 1988; Rodrik 1994, 72; Trefler 1993). We therefore test the propositions stemming from our model by analyzing the effects of regime type on bilateral trade flows and controlling for various other known influences on interstate commerce.

### The Statistical Model

To this end, we begin with a gravity model of bilateral trade, which predicts the amount of commerce that should occur between two countries in the absence of trade barriers. It includes the national income and population of both trading partners, as well as the geographic distance between them. Existing research indicates that the gravity framework—which can be derived from a broad class of international trade models—is quite successful in explaining the flow of interstate commerce (Anderson 1979; Bergstrand 1985, 1989; Deardorff 1998; Eichengreen and Irwin 1995; Feenstra, Markusen, and Rose 1998; Frankel 1993; Frankel, Stein, and Wei 1995; Gowa 1994; Helpman and Krugman 1985; Linnemann 1966; Mansfield and Bronson 1997; Pollins 1989). We extend the gravity model in the following way:

$$\log(X_{ij}) = \log \beta_0 + \beta_1 \log(GDP_i \times GDP_j) + \beta_2 \log(POP_i \times POP_j) + \beta_3 \log(DIST_{ij}) + \beta_4 MIXED_{ij} + \beta_5 AUT_{ij} + \beta_6 OTHER_{ij} + \beta_7 ALLY_{ij} + \beta_8 PTA_{ij} + \beta_9 MP_{ij} + \beta_{10}(ALLY_{ij} \times PTA_{ij}) + \beta_{11}(ALLY_{ij} \times MP_{ij}) + \beta_{12}(PTA_{ij} \times MP_{ij}) + \beta_{13} GATT_{ij} + \beta_{14} COL_{ij} + \beta_{15} COM_{ij} + \beta_{16} WAR_{ij} + \beta_{17} \text{lagged} \log(X_{ij}) + \log z_{ij}. \quad (2)$$

In equation 2, $X_{ij}$ is the value of exports from state $i$ to state $j$ in year $t$. $GDP_i$ and $GDP_j$ are these states' respective gross domestic products in year $t - 1$, $POP_i$ and $POP_j$ are their respective populations in $t - 1$, and $DIST_{ij}$ is the geographical distance between them.[14] We take the natural logarithm of each variable because the gravity model's underlying functional form is multiplicative (Anderson 1979; Bergstrand 1985, 1989; Deardorff 1998). Entering the trading partners' national incomes and populations (or, equivalently, their per-capita incomes) in product form is common and accords with theories of international trade based on models of imperfect competition (Eichengreen and Irwin 1995; Frankel 1993; Frankel, Stein, and Wei 1995; Helpman and Krugman 1985).[15] These theories indicate that $\beta_1$ should be positive and that $\beta_2$ and $\beta_3$ should be negative.

Ideally, we would use a measure of regime type that directly captures the extent to which countries have a legislature that can constrain the chief executive and affect trade policy. choices. Because such a measure does not exist, we rely on a well-known index of regime type developed by Gurr and his colleagues (Jaggers and Gurr 1995; Gurr, Jaggers, and Moore 1989). This measure, which has been used repeatedly in studies of international relations (e.g., Farber and Gowa 1995; Mansfield and Snyder 1995; Oneal and Rusett 1997; Russett 1993), emphasizes five institutional factors that

[14] Per-capita income is sometimes included in gravity models instead of national population, but doing so yields equivalent results. Data on exports are taken from the International Monetary Fund's *Direction of Trade* (various years); those on GDP and population are taken from the Mark 5.6 version of the Penn World Table (Summers and Heston 1991) and from Maddison 1995. All data on GDP and exports are expressed in U.S. dollars and in real terms; they are deflated using the U.S. wholesale price index and producer price index. Distance is measured based on the closest ports between $i$ and $j$ or, if the countries are landlocked, the shortest land or rail distance between them. These data are taken from the Defense Mapping Agency 1985, Fitzpatrick and Modlin 1986, *Times Atlas of the World*, and *Times Concise Atlas of the World*.

[15] The effects of regime type on trade reported below do not depend on whether we introduce the GDPs and populations of the trading partners in product form.

distinguish democracies from autocracies: (1) the competitiveness of the process through which a country's chief executive is selected, (2) the openness of that process, (3) the extent to which there are institutional constraints on a chief executive's decision-making authority, (4) the competitiveness of political participation within a country, and (5) the degree to which binding rules govern political participation within it.

One element of this measure is directly related to our central argument: States are coded as increasingly democratic as the chief executive faces greater institutional constraints, including those emanating from the legislature. But its other components are important as well. If political leaders are not elected competitively, then the legislature will be in a much weaker position vis-à-vis the executive. As Shumpeter (1942) observed, unless leaders can lose office, democratic constraints on their behavior—including those imposed by the legislature—are likely to be ineffective. The competitiveness of elections and political participation, then, are telling indicators of the extent to which institutions such as legislatures can constrain the head of state. Since Gurr's data do not directly tap whether the chief executive needs legislative ratification to enact policies, the following analysis provides only an indirect test of our model. We are unaware, however, of any data that more directly measure legislative control over the head of state. Moreover, this index seems appropriate for distinguishing between regimes with no legislature or an ineffective one and regimes with a popularly elected legislature that can constrain the executive.

To measure regime type, Jaggers and Gurr (1995) create an 11-point measure of a state's democratic characteristics (*DEMOC*) and an 11-point measure of its autocratic characteristics (*AUTOC*).[16] They then derive a variable, $REG = DEMOC - AUTOC$, which takes on values ranging from $-10$ to 10. Initially, we define countries for which $REG \geq 6$ as coherent democracies, those for which $REG \leq -6$ as coherent autocracies, and all remaining regimes as incoherent. After generating an initial set of estimates, we also assess the robustness of our results to this coding procedure. Relying on these criteria, we code each state in the sample as democratic, autocratic, or incoherent in year $t - 1$.

In equation 2, $MIXED_{ij}$ is a dummy variable that equals one if $i$ and $j$ include a democracy and an autocracy, zero otherwise; $AUT_{ij}$ equals one if both $i$ and $j$ are autocracies, zero otherwise; and $OTHER_{ij}$ equals one if either $i$ or $j$ is an incoherent polity, zero otherwise. The reference category is a pair of democratic countries. Since our model indicates that greater trade liberalization should occur between democratic dyads than between mixed pairs, we expect $\beta_4$ to be negative. Our model, however, yields no determinate prediction about the sign of either $\beta_5$ or $\beta_6$.

Besides addressing the influence of national income, population, distance, and regime type, it is also important to take account of variables that might be responsible for any observed relationship between regime type and bilateral trade. As we explain in more detail below, our analysis centers on the period after World War II. This era was marked by the existence of two major blocs, one made up of autocracies (the Warsaw Pact) and the other composed almost entirely of democracies (the North Atlantic Treaty Organization). To ensure that our results do not simply reflect Cold War rivalries, we include an array of international political variables in equation 2. For instance, there is evidence that democracies were especially likely to ally with one another during the Cold War (Siverson and Emmons 1991). Furthermore, various studies have found that alliances promote trade, which suggests that alliances may account for any observed effects of regime type on trade flows (Gowa 1994; Mansfield and Bronson 1997). In the same vein, recent research indicates that, since World War II, pairs of democracies have been much more likely to establish preferential trading arrangements (PTAs) than other pairs (Mansfield, Milner, and Rosendorff 1998); and it is widely recognized that such arrangements tend to promote the flow of commerce between member states (Frankel 1993; Frankel, Stein, and Wei 1995; Gowa 1994; Linnemann 1966; Mansfield and Bronson 1997; Pollins 1989). To control for the effects of alliances and PTAs, we include $ALLY_{ij}$ and $PTA_{ij}$. The former equals one if $i$ and $j$ are allied in year $t - 1$, zero otherwise. The latter equals one if $i$ and $j$ belong to the same PTA in $t - 1$, zero otherwise.

Previous studies also have found that states trade more extensively if they are members of the General Agreement on Tariffs and Trade (GATT), if they include a major power, if they have command economies, if they are not involved in a war, and if they had a colonial relationship (Gowa 1994; Kleiman 1976; Mansfield and Bronson 1997; Pollins 1989). As such, we include the following dummy variables, each of which is measured in $t - 1$: $MP_{ij}$ equals one if either $i$ or $j$ is a major power, zero if neither state is a major power; $GATT_{ij}$ equals one if both $i$ and $j$ are parties to the GATT, zero otherwise; $COL_{ij}$ equals one if $i$ and $j$ had a colonial relationship that concluded in or before $t - 1$ (and after World War II's onset), zero otherwise; $COM_{ij}$ equals one if both $i$ and $j$ have command economies, zero if they do not; and $WAR_{ij}$ equals one if $i$ and $j$ are at war, zero if they are not.[17] By including all these variables, we control for the most likely international political influences on trade relations during the Cold War.

Earlier research indicates that states belonging to

[16] To compute these measures, we rely on the coding rules set forth in Gurr, Jaggers, and Moore 1989.

[17] Data on alliances are taken from Small and Singer 1969 and from updates of their list provided by the Correlates of War Project and dated March 25, 1993. Data on PTAs are taken from de Melo and Panagariya 1993, Hartland-Thunberg 1980, Pomfret 1988, and the World Trade Organization 1995. See Singer and Small (1994) for data on major powers and wars, selected issues of the GATT's *International Trade* and *Basic Instruments and Selected Documents* for data on GATT membership, Kornai (1992, 6–7) for data on command economies from 1960 to 1985, Staar et al. (1991) for these data in 1990, and Kurian (1992) for data on colonial relations. See Mansfield and Bronson (1997, esp. 105–6) for more on all the data used in this study, except those on regime type.

the same alliance and the same PTA conduct more trade than countries that are either allies or PTA members, but not both. Furthermore, there is evidence that allies and PTA members trade more extensively if at least one state is a major power (Mansfield and Bronson 1997). We thus introduce $ALLY_{ij} \times PTA_{ij}$, $ALLY_{ij} \times MP_{ij}$, and $PTA_{ij} \times MP_{ij}$ in equation 2. To account for any temporal dependence in bilateral trade flows, we include an instrument for the lagged value of $\log X_{ij}$.[18] We also account for any country-specific or year-specific effects on trade by including dummy variables for all but one country and for all but one year analyzed here. Finally, $\log z_{ij}$ is a stochastic error term.

Our sample consists of all pairs of states listed as members of the interstate system by the Correlates of War Project (Singer and Small 1994) in 1960, 1965, 1970, 1975, 1980, 1985, or 1990 for which complete data are available. The independent variables in our model are measured in these years ($t - 1$), and the value of exports from $i$ to $j$ is measured one year hence (in years $t$, which are 1961, . . . , 1991) to minimize any potential problems of simultaneity. We do not analyze years before 1960 because data on GDP and exports are especially limited for many autocracies until that point. Including the available data for these years could bias our results by systematically underrepresenting dyads that are not jointly democratic. After pooling these data, ordinary least squares was used to generate estimates of the parameters in equation 2. Tests of statistical significance are based on White (1980) heteroskedasticity-consistent standard errors.[19]

## Estimates of the Parameters

Our initial results, which are reported in the first column of Table 1, accord with the central proposition advanced earlier. The estimate of $MIXED_{ij}$ is negative and statistically significant, which indicates that trade flows between democratic states tend to be greater than trade flows between democracies and autocracies. Moreover, the predicted difference in trade between democratic pairs and mixed pairs is relatively large: On average, a democracy and an autocracy engage in roughly 15% to 20% less commerce than a dyad composed of two democracies.[20]

As noted earlier, our model does not yield determinate predictions about whether trade will be more open within autocratic pairs than within either democratic or mixed pairs. The results in the first column of Table 1 provide little evidence that the flow of commerce between autocracies differs markedly from the flow between democracies, since the estimate of $AUT_{ij}$ is not statistically significant. Yet, autocratic pairs trade much more extensively than mixed pairs. The estimate of $AUT_{ij}$ is considerably larger than the estimate of $MIXED_{ij}$, and the difference between them is significant ($t = 5.79$). Finally, the estimate of $OTHER_{ij}$ is negative. Pairs that include an incoherent polity conduct significantly less trade than democratic or autocratic dyads, although they engage in significantly more commerce than mixed pairs.[21]

To assess the robustness of these results, we conduct a number of additional tests. First, our model emphasizes how domestic legislatures constrain the trade policy choices of executives in democracies. But in fledgling democracies, legislative institutions are often weak and poorly developed (e.g., Haggard and Kaufman 1995; Haggard and Webb 1994). Hence, trade policy between mature democracies may differ from that between countries that include a nascent democracy with a weakly institutionalized legislature. To address this issue, we include $DEMZ_{ij}$ in equation 2. It equals one if either $i$ or $j$ experienced a democratic transition between years $t - 6$ and $t - 1$ (i.e., if either state is not a coherent democracy in $t - 6$ and if both states are democratic in $t - 1$), zero otherwise. For present purposes, $AUT_{ij}$, $MIXED_{ij}$, and $OTHER_{ij}$ are set equal to zero if $DEMZ_{ij}$ equals one.

As shown in the second column of Table 1, pairs with a fledgling democracy conduct significantly less trade than pairs composed of two mature democracies, since the estimate of $DEMZ_{ij}$ is negative and statistically significant. Furthermore, when $DEMZ_{ij}$ is included in the analysis, there is even stronger evidence that democratic pairs trade more extensively than mixed pairs. The estimate of $MIXED_{ij}$ continues to be statistically significant, and its absolute value is noticeably larger than before.

Second, we address the robustness of the preceding results with respect to the coding of democratic and autocratic regimes. Thus far, we have coded states as democratic if $REG \geq 6$, and we have coded them as autocratic if $REG \leq -6$. These operational definitions have been used in other studies, but they are clearly somewhat arbitrary, and it is important to determine if relaxing them affects our findings. We therefore estimate equation 2 after redefining these thresholds as: (a) 5 and −5, (b) 4 and −4, (c) 3 and −3, (d) 2 and −2, and (e) 1 and −1.

Table 2 shows the estimates of $MIXED_{ij}$, $AUT_{ij}$, and $OTHER_{ij}$ for each set of thresholds. (The estimates of the remaining parameters are not presented to conserve space.) These results provide a further indication that our earlier findings are quite robust. The estimate of $MIXED_{ij}$ is negative and statistically significant

[18] We use an instrument for the lagged value of $\log X_{ij}$, rather than its observed value, because the natural logarithm of the lagged value of exports is likely to be correlated with the error term in equation 2, which would yield inconsistent estimates. This instrument is generated by regressing the lagged value of the natural logarithm of exports on the lagged values of the natural logarithms of $GDP_i$, $GDP_j$, $POP_i$, and $POP_j$, as well as a dummy variable for each year but one in the sample. Note that we use data on exports from 1956 and data on GDP and population from 1955 to derive estimates of the lagged value of $\log X_{ij}$ for 1961.

[19] All of the statistical analyses in this article are conducted using STATA version 5.0.

[20] More precisely, the estimated change in the predicted volume of trade for a mixed pair compared to a democratic pair is $e^{\beta_4} - 1$. From column 1 of Table 1, $\beta_4 = -0.188$; and $e^{-0.188} - 1 = -0.17$.

[21] Note that, like the difference between democratic pairs and dyads with an incoherent polity shown in Table 1, the differences between $OTHER_{ij}$, on the one hand, and both $MIXED_{ij}$ and $AUT_{ij}$, on the other, are statistically significant ($t = 3.07$ and 3.52, respectively).

**TABLE 1. Regression of Trade on GDP, Population, Distance, Regime Type, Alliances, Preferential Trading Arrangements, Major Power, GATT, Prior Colonial Ties, Command Economies, and War, 1960–90, Using Different Measures of Regime Type**

| | Measure of Regime Type | | | |
|---|---|---|---|---|
| | Jaggers and Gurr (1995) | | Alvarez et al. (1996) | |
| Variable | (1) | (1A) | (2) | (2A) |
| log $\beta_0$ | 17.274*** (3.058) | 17.688*** (3.057) | 22.550*** (3.166) | 23.263*** (3.175) |
| $\log(GDP_i \times GDP_j)$ | .512*** (.039) | .512*** (.039) | .580*** (.044) | .582*** (.044) |
| $\log(POP_i \times POP_j)$ | −.937*** (.080) | −.943*** (.080) | −1.211*** (.083) | −1.232*** (.084) |
| $\log(DIST_{ij})$ | −.759*** (.014) | −.758*** (.014) | −.778*** (.014) | −.777*** (.014) |
| $MIXED_{ij}$ | −.188*** (.035) | −.233*** (.039) | −.111*** (.025) | −.134*** (.027) |
| $AUT_{ij}$ | .098 (.065) | .036 (.069) | −.053 (.051) | −.075 (.052) |
| $OTHER_{ij}$ | −.088* (.039) | −.141*** (.043) | — | — |
| $DEMZ_{ij}$ | — | −.142** (.053) | — | −.120** (.043) |
| $ALLY_{ij}$ | .119* (.052) | .115* (.052) | .184*** (.051) | .180*** (.051) |
| $PTA_{ij}$ | .527*** (.039) | .521*** (.039) | .473*** (.040) | .470*** (.040) |
| $MP_{ij}$ | .548*** (.136) | .548*** (.135) | .618*** (.136) | .620*** (.137) |
| $ALLY_{ij} \times PTA_{ij}$ | .535*** (.066) | .537*** (.067) | .618*** (.066) | .620*** (.066) |
| $ALLY_{ij} \times MP_{ij}$ | .179** (.068) | .182** (.068) | .052 (.067) | .050 (.067) |
| $PTA_{ij} \times MP_{ij}$ | −.476*** (.068) | −.483*** (.068) | −.518*** (.068) | −.522*** (.068) |
| $GATT_{ij}$ | .074 (.038) | .072 (.038) | .126** (.040) | .125** (.040) |
| $COL_{ij}$ | 1.682*** (.085) | 1.684*** (.085) | 1.780*** (.087) | 1.787*** (.087) |
| $COM_{ij}$ | 1.033*** (.095) | 1.031*** (.095) | .855*** (.117) | .847*** (.117) |
| $WAR_{ij}$ | −6.463*** (.107) | −6.447*** (.107) | −6.556*** (.110) | −6.562*** (.110) |
| lagged $\log(X_{ij})$ | .855*** (.014) | .855*** (.014) | .946*** (.014) | .946*** (.014) |
| $\bar{R}^2$ | .53 | .53 | .55 | .55 |
| $N$ | 33,116 | 33,116 | 30,480 | 30,480 |

*Note*: Entries are unstandardized regression coefficients. Figures in parentheses are White heteroskedasticity-consistent standard errors. One-tailed tests are conducted for the regression coefficient of $MIXED_{ij}$, since its sign is specified by the model. Two-tailed tests are conducted for the remaining coefficients. Regressions include dummy variables for country-specific and year-specific fixed effects. *$p \leq .05$, **$p \leq .01$, ***$p \leq .001$.

regardless of which set of thresholds is used, and its size does not vary much. Furthermore, the estimate of $AUT_{ij}$ continues to be positive, and there is only one case in which it is statistically significant. The estimate of $OTHER_{ij}$ continues to be negative, and it is significant in two instances.

**TABLE 2. Estimated Effects of Regime Type on Trade, Based on Different Operational Definitions of Democracy and Autocracy, 1960–90**

| Operational Definition of | | Regression Coefficient | | |
|---|---|---|---|---|
| Democracy | Autocracy | $MIXED_{ij}$ | $AUT_{ij}$ | $OTHER_{ij}$ |
| $REG \geq 5$ | $REG \leq -5$ | −.171*** (.034) | .109 (.064) | −.110** (.043) |
| $REG \geq 4$ | $REG \leq -4$ | −.184*** (.034) | .100 (.063) | −.119** (.046) |
| $REG \geq 3$ | $REG \leq -3$ | −.141*** (.034) | .128* (.063) | −.060 (.053) |
| $REG \geq 2$ | $REG \leq -2$ | −.138*** (.034) | .093 (.063) | −.047 (.058) |
| $REG \geq 1$ | $REG \leq -1$ | −.143*** (.033) | .053 (.062) | −.193 (.104) |

*Note:* Entries are unstandardized regression coefficients based on equation 2 and using the Jaggers and Gurr (1995) measure of regime type. Figures in parentheses are White heteroskedasticity-consistent standard errors. One-tailed tests are conducted for the regression coefficient of $MIXED_{ij}$, since its sign is specified by the model. Two-tailed tests are conducted for the remaining coefficients. Regressions include dummy variables for country-specific and year-specific fixed effects. *$p \leq .05$, **$p \leq .01$, ***$p \leq .001$.

Besides altering the thresholds that distinguish between regime types when the Jaggers and Gurr (1995) measure (*REG*) is used, we examined whether our results differ if another measure of regime type is used. Various alternative measures exist, but very few cover the range of countries and years analyzed here.[22] Alvarez et al. (1996), however, have coded the regime type of most countries in our sample on an annual basis during the period from 1950 to 1990. Unlike Jaggers and Gurr, Alvarez et al. identify each state as either democratic or autocratic in every year. Relying on their measure has certain advantages, since we do not need to establish quantitative thresholds to code regime type. From our standpoint, however, this measure also has certain drawbacks, especially Alvarez et al.'s (1996, 5) intentionally narrow definition of democracy, which centers solely on the competitiveness of the political process. In their view, democracy exists when there are competitive elections for the head of state and the legislature; otherwise, the regime is autocratic. As noted above, the competitiveness of the political process helps shape whether the legislature can effectively constrain the chief executive. In contrast to Jaggers and Gurr, however, Alvarez et al. do not directly measure our key variable of interest: the legislature's role in constraining the executive.

Nonetheless, it is useful to analyze the Alvarez et al. data in order to assess the robustness of our initial results. To this end, we reestimated equation 2 after using their data to code $MIXED_{ij}$, $AUT_{ij}$, and $DEMZ_{ij}$. Note that $OTHER_{ij}$ is not included in this analysis, since Alvarez et al. code each state as either a democracy or an autocracy. The results are presented in the third column (omitting $DEMZ_{ij}$) and the fourth column (including $DEMZ_{ij}$) of Table 1. Clearly, there is considerable agreement between these findings and those generated using the Jaggers and Gurr data. Particularly important for present purposes is that the estimate of $MIXED_{ij}$ continues to be negative and statistically significant, although its absolute value is somewhat smaller when we rely on the Alvarez et al. data rather than the Jaggers and Gurr data. Furthermore, we again find that democratic transitions dampen trade, since the estimate of $DEMZ_{ij}$ is negative and significant. It is also noteworthy that no statistically significant difference exists between the flow of trade within autocratic pairs and democratic pairs. As in the first two columns in Table 1, the estimate of $AUT_{ij}$ is not significant, although it is negative when the Alvarez et al. data are used, and it is positive when the Jaggers and Gurr data are employed. In sum, our results are quite robust with respect to the coding of regime type.[23]

Third, it is useful to ensure that our statistical design does not mask any substantial intertemporal variation in the effects of regime type on trade. In a preliminary effort to address this issue, we conducted separate analyses of each decade in our sample; we pooled the observations for 1960 and 1965, for 1970 and 1975, and for 1980 and 1985, and we analyzed 1990 alone. For each set of observations, we estimated equation 2 using the same operational measure of regime type that was used to generate our original results (i.e., states are coded as democratic if $REG \geq 6$, autocratic if $REG \leq -6$).[24] Table 3 presents the estimated coefficients of $MIXED_{ij}$, $AUT_{ij}$, and $OTHER_{ij}$. (As in Table 2, the remaining coefficient estimates are not reported to

[22] For example, the Political Regime Change data set developed by Gasiorowski (1996) is restricted to 97 less developed countries, a much different sample of countries than ours.

[23] Note that we have included country-specific fixed effects in all the preceding analyses, but we also analyzed whether replacing them with pair-specific fixed effects has any bearing on our results. To this end, we reestimated the models shown in the second and fourth columns of Table 1 after accounting for pair-specific fixed effects and found that doing so has little influence on the estimates.

[24] To estimate equation 2 for the 1960s, the 1970s, and the 1980s, a dummy variable for the first year in each decade (1960, 1970, and 1980, respectively) is included. Note that the following results are quite similar if the Alvarez et al. (1996) data on regime type are used instead of the Jaggers and Gurr data.

**TABLE 3. Estimated Effects of Regime Type on Trade by Decade, 1960–90**

| | Regression Coefficient | | |
|---|---|---|---|
| Years | $MIXED_{ij}$ | $AUT_{ij}$ | $OTHER_{ij}$ |
| 1960 and 1965 | −.191* | .182 | .029 |
| | (.083) | (.156) | (.117) |
| 1970 and 1975 | .015 | .147 | .147 |
| | (.083) | (.149) | (.119) |
| 1980 and 1985 | −.294*** | −.036 | .006 |
| | (.081) | (.153) | (.119) |
| 1990 | −.494*** | −.547* | −.274 |
| | (.126) | (.256) | (.155) |

*Note:* Entries are unstandardized regression coefficients based on equation 2 and using the Jaggers and Gurr (1995) measure of regime type. Figures in parentheses are White heteroskedasticity-consistent standard errors. One-tailed tests are conducted for the regression coefficient of $MIXED_{ij}$, since its sign is specified by the model. Two-tailed tests are conducted for the remaining coefficients. Regressions include dummy variables for country-specific and (in the first three regressions shown above, year-specific) fixed effects. $^*p \leq .05$, $^{***}p \leq .001$.

conserve space.) In three of the four decades we assess, the estimate of $MIXED_{ij}$ is negative and statistically significant, which indicates that the tendency for trade to be more open within democratic pairs than within mixed pairs is relatively stable over time. Also, it is interesting that any tendency for autocratic pairs to trade more extensively than their democratic counterparts has become attenuated over time, an issue that warrants attention in future research.

Our sample includes all countries for which we were able to obtain data for the variables in equation 2. For various countries, however, data on GDP, trade, or both are missing in certain years analyzed here. Since a number of these are autocracies that are unlikely to trade extensively due to their severely distorted economies (e.g., Albania, Cambodia, Cuba, Laos, Libya, North Korea, and Sudan), we ran a series of Heckman selection models to ensure that there was no bias in our earlier findings (Greene 1993, 706–14). We found no evidence of such a bias.[25] In addition to the countries in our sample with missing data for certain years, there are other countries for which we were unable to obtain any economic data. These (e.g., Afghanistan, Bangladesh, Burundi, Liberia, Rwanda, Somalia, Uganda, Yemen) were excluded from our sample altogether. Virtually all of them are autocracies with highly distorted economies. Such distortions are likely to hamper commerce, so there is ample reason to expect that our results understate the actual extent to which democratic dyads trade more freely and extensively than mixed dyads. Equally, the omission of these countries probably helps explain why, for example, the estimate of $AUT_{ij}$ is positive in Table 1 when the Jaggers and Gurr measure of regime type is considered.

Finally, we address whether our results are robust with respect to the inclusion of various factors omitted from equation 2. Of chief importance in this regard are economic growth and the level of economic development. It is possible, for example, that democratic pairs conduct more trade than mixed pairs because democracies experience higher growth than autocracies, and growth promotes trade. Similarly, democracies may be more highly developed economically, and more highly developed states may engage in more trade than less developed countries. Our results do not accord with either of these possibilities; democratic pairs trade more extensively than mixed pairs, but so do autocratic pairs. Nonetheless, as a further test of the robustness of the results, we included in equation 2 the real per-capita GDP of both $i$ and $j$ in year $t - 1$. We then replace per-capita GDP with various other factors that have been used as measures of economic development in studies of international trade (e.g., Polachek 1980), including the number of highway vehicles per capita, per-capita school enrollment, per-capita university enrollment, and electrical production per capita. Finally, to examine the effects of growth, we include the change in per-capita GDP of both $i$ and $j$ between year $t - 6$ and year $t - 1$.[26] It should be noted that, for some of these variables, complete data are available for only a fraction of the states and years we analyzed, so the estimates generated after including them in equation 2 are not directly comparable to those in Table 1. But our findings indicate that including these variables has no substantive influence on the estimates in Table 1. Most important for present purposes, the estimate of $MIXED_{ij}$ is negative and statistically significant in each of these analyses.

Turning to the remaining variables in equation 2, the effects of GDP, population, and distance accord with expectations based on the gravity model. As shown in Table 1, the estimate of $\log(GDP_i \times GDP_j)$ is positive and statistically significant, and the estimates of both $\log(POP_i \times POP_j)$ and $\log(DIST_{ij})$ are negative and significant. In addition, the estimates of $ALLY_{ij}$, $PTA_{ij}$, $MP_{ij}$, $ALLY_{ij} \times PTA_{ij}$, and $ALLY_{ij} \times MP_{ij}$ are positive; and the estimate of $PTA_{ij} \times MP_{ij}$ is negative. All these estimates are statistically significant when the Jaggers and Gurr data are used, and all but the estimate of $ALLY_{ij} \times MP_{ij}$ is significant based on the Alvarez et al. data. These results indicate that alliances, PTAs, and the presence of a major power each promotes commerce. Moreover, countries that belong to the same alliance and the same PTA conduct more trade than countries that are either allies or parties to the same PTA, but not both. Alliances provide a much greater impetus to trade between states that include a major power than between other states. PTAs yield marginally more commerce between trading partners that include a major power than between other countries.

Our results also indicate that a former colonial relationship heightens bilateral trade flows, that states with command economies trade extensively with each

[25] The estimate of ρ (which is the correlation between the error term in the selection equation and the error term in equation 2) is quite small, and we found no evidence that it is significantly different from zero.

[26] These data are taken from Banks 1995, Maddison 1995, and Summers and Heston 1991.

other, and that warfare depresses commerce. The estimates of $COL_{ij}$ and $COM_{ij}$ are positive, the estimate of $WAR_{ij}$ is negative, and all these results are statistically significant. GATT membership, however, has a weaker effect on bilateral trade flows. The estimate of $GATT_{ij}$ is positive, which suggests that trade flows between parties to the GATT tend to be somewhat larger than trade flows between nonmember states. But this estimate is relatively small, and it is not statistically significant when the Jaggers and Gurr data on regime type are used.

In sum, the results of this empirical analysis support the central prediction of our formal model. Holding constant a large number of economic and political factors—including variables pertaining to the dynamics of the Cold War—we find that pairs of democracies have conducted considerably more trade than mixed pairs since World War II. Furthermore, although our model generates no definitive predictions about autocratic pairs, it is noteworthy that, based on our sample, no systematic difference exists in trade relations between these pairs and democratic dyads.

## CONCLUSION

It is frequently argued that the foreign policies of democracies are distinctive, but few studies have focused on the trade policy choices made by such states. Moreover, most work on trade policy overlooks the effects of regime type. By addressing the effects of regime type on trade policy, this article contributes to the literature on the links between democracy and foreign policy as well as that on the political economy of trade policy.

The model we developed highlights the legislature's role in making trade policy in democracies. Having a legislature that ratifies the chief executive's trade proposals may create a credible threat that allows executives in democracies to arrive at freer trade outcomes than would otherwise occur. The possible veto of a trade deal by one or both legislatures in the dyad may lead the executives to search for lower mutually acceptable levels of trade barriers. This, in turn, may explain why pairs of democracies are better able to lower their trade barriers than mixed pairs.

Our analysis focuses on variations between democracies and autocracies, not on variations within either regime type. Both our model and the data analysis treat each type of regime as homogeneous. Democracies are distinct from autocracies because they have a legislature that exercises ratification power, regardless of its preferences. The differences among regime types rest on institutional features, not on the policy preferences of decision makers. Varying the trade policy preferences of the executive and legislature does not alter the degree of democracy present; it only changes the extent to which government is divided within democracies. Furthermore, whether a government is divided or unified has no bearing on the degree to which a country is democratic. Hence, examining the influence of such divisions (i.e., as the trade policy preferences of the executive and legislature diverge or converge) does not facilitate comparisons between democracies and autocracies, only between more divided and less divided democracies. Our model is capable of deriving outcomes when such changes occur, but in this article we have neither the space nor the data to explore such variations within democracies. It is interesting to note, however, the finding of others that increasing divisions in the preferences of executives and legislatures may result in more protectionism for a single country and less possibility of trade-barrier-reducing agreements between countries (e.g., Lohmann and O'Halloran 1994; Milner and Rosendorff 1996). Our results differ from but are not inconsistent with those earlier findings. We show that having a protectionist legislature with ratification powers may help democracies arrive at lower levels of trade barriers in their dealings with one another.

Our theoretical model generates two central predictions. First, aggregate trade barriers will be lower between democracies than between a democracy and an autocracy. Since a trade war between two protectionist legislatures is worse than a trade war involving just one such legislature, two democratic executives will choose significant trade liberalization. Our empirical results accord with this proposition. They indicate that trade between democracies tends to be more extensive than commerce within mixed pairs. On average, dyads composed of a democracy and an autocracy engage in roughly 15% to 20% less commerce than those composed of two democracies. Interestingly, this result seems to strengthen over time. By the 1990s, as Table 3 shows, the average volume of trade between a democracy and an autocracy was roughly 40% less than that of democratic dyads.

Our data overlap the bipolar period extensively. To control for any Cold War influences that might account for the effects of regime type on trade, we analyzed various international political factors. The Cold War was marked by the existence of two camps, with democracies concentrated in one and autocracies in the other. It could be that democratic pairs trade more because they tend to be allies, because they belong to the same commercial institutions (the GATT or PTAs), or because they are not involved in military conflicts. Even when we control for these factors, however, we find that trade flows are significantly greater within democratic dyads than within mixed dyads.

Second, whether the level of aggregate trade barriers will be higher within autocratic pairs than within either democratic or mixed pairs depends on the relative trade preferences of the actors involved. Although it was not possible to incorporate the preferences of political actors directly into our empirical analysis, our results conform with this conclusion. By and large, no significant difference exists between the volume of trade conducted within autocratic pairs and within democratic pairs, which suggests that both domestic institutions and the preferences of decision makers help shape trade policy.

Our model uses a very general institutional characteristic to distinguish democratic and autocratic regimes: the presence or absence of a legislature that can effectively constrain the executive. This simplified approach is appropriate given our purpose, but it may mask variations in trade policy within both democracies (e.g., among presidential and parliamentary systems) and autocracies (e.g., those governed by military leaders as opposed to those governed by hereditary monarchs). Examining the influence of such factors is an important step for future research. It is striking, however, that notwithstanding the institutional distinctions within each regime type, broadly defined differences across regime types exert a noticeable effect on trade relations. Exploring such broad institutional differences across autocracies and democracies, we believe, is an important and prior step toward examining the effect of differences within these two regime types.

Although our analysis hinges on one institutional feature assumed to be common among democracies (i.e., a legislature with the power to ratify executive proposals), it is obvious that many other institutional distinctions can be drawn between autocracies and democracies. These institutional differences may also influence international trade. Our empirical tests pick up the effect of the legislature as well as that of these other differences, so we cannot rule out the possibility that other elements of democracy are important factors. Measures of democracy that isolate the effect of the legislature simply do not exist, however, and given our large, longitudinal sample of countries, they would be prohibitive to construct. Moreover, our evidence and our model reinforce each other, lending credibility to our claims. Abstracting away from preferences and other institutional factors, the presence of popularly elected legislatures that must ratify policies may be an important difference between democracies and other regime types in international trade. Paradoxically, the protectionist threat provided by the legislature in democracies can result in more open trade, rather than less.

## APPENDIX

Let the two executives who bargain internationally be identified as $i$ and $j$.

LEMMA 1. *The Pareto frontier between* i *and* j *is* $t^* = -t(t_j^*/t_i) + t_j^*$.

*Proof:* Maximizing $U_i(t, t^*)$ subject to $U_j(t, t^*) \geq \bar{U}$ and $(t, t^*) \geq 0$ yields the result. *Q.E.D.*

### The TILI Game with Home Offers

In the case of the democratic pair, we require the home executive to offer the foreign executive an agreement that lies on their Pareto frontier (as given by lemma 1).

LEMMA 2. *When two democracies negotiate under TILI, the agreement point is* $(-1/2\, t_C + 1/2\, t_P + 1/2\sqrt{(t_C^2 + 2t_Ct_P - t_P^2)}, 1/2\, t_P + 1/2\, t_C - 1/2\sqrt{(t_C^2 + 2t_Ct_P - t_P^2)})$, *and aggregate barriers are* $t_P$.

*Proof:* The no-agreement point is $(t_C, t_{C^*}^*)$. Under TILI, with home making the offer, home's problem is max $U_P(t, t^*)$ subject to $U_C(t, t^*) \geq U_C(t_C, t_{C^*}^*)$, $U_{C^*}(t, t^*) \geq U_{C^*}(t_C, t_{C^*}^*)$, $U_{P^*}(t, t^*) \geq U_{P^*}(t_C, t_{C^*}^*)$, $t^* = t_{P^*}^* - t(t_{P^*}^*/t_P)$ and $t, t^* \geq 0$. The solution lies at point $d$ in Figure 3, where foreign's indifference curve intersects the Pareto frontier. The second constraint binds; we solve $t^* = t_{C^*}^* - \sqrt{t_C^2 - t^2}$ and (from lemma 1) $t^* = t_{P^*}^* - t(t_{P^*}^*/t_P)$ for $t, t^*$. Recalling that we study only the symmetric case $t_P = t_{P^*}^*$, $t_C = t_{C^*}^*$ and solving, we get the solution above. *Q.E.D.*

In the case of the mixed pair, the home executive will offer the foreign autocrat a point on the Pareto frontier when such a point is ratifiable. If no such point exists, then $P$ chooses the nearest point to its ideal point that is preferred by both $A^*$ and $C$ to the status quo.

LEMMA 3. *When a mixed pair negotiate under TILI, the agreement point is*

1. $(t_Pt_C/\sqrt{t_P^2 + t_{A^*}^{*2}}, t_{A^*}^*(\sqrt{t_P^2 + t_{A^*}^{*2}} - t_C)/\sqrt{t_P^2 + t_{A^*}^{*2}})$, *and aggregate barriers are* $t_{A^*}^* + t_C(t_P - t_{A^*}^*)/\sqrt{t_P^2 + t_{A^*}^{*2}}$ *when* $t_C^2 - t_P^2 < t_{A^*}^{*2}$.
2. $(t_P, 0)$ *and aggregate barriers are* $t_P$ *when* $t_C^2 - t_P^2 \geq t_{A^*}^{*2} \geq (t_C - t_P)^2$.
3. $(t_C - t_{A^*}^*, 0)$ *and aggregate barriers are* $t_C - t_{A^*}^*$ *when* $t_{A^*}^{*2} < (t_C - t_P)^2$.

*Proof:* The no-agreement point is $(t_C, t_{A^*}^*)$. Under TILI, with home, the democracy, making the offer, home's problem is max $U_P(t, t^*)$ subject to $U_C(t, t^*) \geq U_C(t_C, t_{A^*}^*)$, $U_{A^*}(t, t^*) \geq U_{A^*}(t_C, t_{A^*}^*)$, and $t, t^* \geq 0$.

At point $m$ in Figure 2A, the foreign indifference curve binds, as does the constraint that $t^* \geq 0$. We solve $t^* = t_{A^*}^* - \sqrt{t_C^2 - t^2}$ and (from lemma 1) $t^* = t_{A^*}^* - t(t_{A^*}^*/t_P)$ for $t, t^*$, and the condition that $t^* \geq 0$ is $t_C^2 - t_P^2 < t_{A^*}^{*2}$. Where $t_C^2 - t_P^2 \geq t_{A^*}^{*2} \geq (t_C - t_P)^2$ neither constraint binds, and the solution is at the point $(t_P, 0)$. When $t_{A^*}^{*2} < (t_C - t_P)^2$, the domestic legislature's constraint binds, leading to the solution at point $(t_C - t_{A^*}^*, 0)$. *Q.E.D.*

We assume that there is a meaningful difference between the ideal points of $C$ and $P$ (and $C^*$ and $P^*$).

ASSUMPTION. $t_C > 2t_P$ *and* $t_{C^*}^* > 2t_{P^*}^*$.

PROPOSITION 1. *Under TILI (when home makes the offers), the mixed dyad has at least as high aggregate barriers as does the democratic dyad.*

*Proof:* Let $B^D$, $B^M$, and $B^A$ denote the aggregate barriers for the democratic dyad, the mixed dyad, and the autocratic dyad, respectively. Then $B^D = t_P$, and

$$B^M = \begin{cases} \dfrac{t_C(t_P - t_{A^*}^*)}{\sqrt{t_P^2 + t_{A^*}^{*2}}} + t_{A^*}^* & \text{if } t_C^2 - t_P^2 < t_{A^*}^{*2} \\ t_P & \text{if } t_C^2 - t_P^2 \geq t_{A^*}^{*2} \geq (t_C - t_P)^2 \\ t_C - t_{A^*}^* & \text{if } t_{A^*}^{*2} < (t_C - t_P)^2 \end{cases} \qquad \text{(A-1)}$$

Suppose $t_C^2 - t_P^2 < t_{A^*}^{*2}$ which implies $B^D - B^M = (t_P - t_{A^*}^*)((\sqrt{t_P^2 + t_{A^*}^{*2}} - t_C)/\sqrt{t_P^2 + t_{A^*}^{*2}})$. Now $t_C^2 - t_P^2 < t_{A^*}^{*2} \Rightarrow \sqrt{t_P^2 + t_{A^*}^{*2}} - t_C > 0$. By the assumption, $t_C > 2t_P > \sqrt{2}t_P \Rightarrow t_C^2 > 2t_P^2$. Then $t_C^2 - t_P^2 > t_P^2$. Now $t_C^2 - t_P^2 < t_{A^*}^{*2}$, so $t_P < t_{A^*}^*$, and $B^D - B^M < 0$. Suppose that $t_C^2 - t_P^2 \geq t_{A^*}^{*2} \geq (t_C - t_P)^2$. Then $B^D - B^M = 0$. If $t_{A^*}^{*2} < (t_C - t_P)^2$, then $t_{A^*}^* < t_C - t_P$ or $t_P < t_C - t_{A^*}^*$. Hence, $B^D - B^M = t_P - (t_C - t_{A^*}^*) < 0$. *Q.E.D.*

### TILI When Foreign Makes the Offer

Once again we compare the democratic dyad case with the mixed case. Home is in both cases the democracy. Foreign in the first case is a democracy and in the second an autocracy. We now let foreign make the offers. Foreign offers the home executive an agreement; if the home executive agrees, then the offer is put to the legislature for a possible veto.

PROPOSITION 2. *Under TILI (when foreign makes the offer), the mixed dyad has higher aggregate barriers as does the democratic dyad.*

*Proof:* In the democratic dyad the outcome is at point $d^*$ in figures 3 and 5; $B^D = t_P$. In the mixed dyad the outcome is at $m^*$ in Figure 2A and B and at point λ in Figure 2C.

$$B^M = \begin{cases} -[-t_C t_P^2 - t_P t_{A\cdot}^{*2} \\ \quad + t_{A\cdot}^*(t_P - t_{A\cdot}^*)\sqrt{2t_C t_P + t_{A\cdot}^{*2} - t_C^2} & \text{if } t_{A\cdot}^{*2} > (t_C - t_P)^2 \\ \quad - t_P^2 t_{A\cdot}^* + t_C t_{A\cdot}^* - t_P]/(t_P^2 + t_{A\cdot}^{*2}) & \\ t_C + t_{A\cdot}^* \dfrac{t_C - t_{A\cdot}^{*2}}{\sqrt{t_C^2 + t_{A\cdot}^{*2}}} & \text{if } t_{A\cdot}^{*2} \le (t_C - t_P)^2 \end{cases} \quad \text{(A-2)}$$

Suppose $t_{A\cdot}^2 > (t_C - t_P)^2$. Then $B^D - B^M = (t_P - t_{A\cdot}^*)(t_P^2 - t_C t_P + t_{A\cdot}^*\sqrt{2t_C t_P + t_{A\cdot}^{*2} - t_C^2})/(t_P^2 + t_{A\cdot}^{*2})$. Now $(t_P^2 - t_C t_P + t_{A\cdot}^*\sqrt{2t_C t_P + t_{A\cdot}^{*2} - t_C^2})/(t_P^2 + t_{A\cdot}^{*2}) > 0$, and $t_{A\cdot}^2 > (t_C - t_P)^2 = t_C(t_C - 2t_P) + t_P^2 > t_P^2$ by the assumption. Then $t_P < t_{A\cdot}^*$ and $B^D - B^M < 0$. If $t_{A\cdot}^{*2} \le (t_C - t_P)^2$ then $t_C - t_P \ge t_{A\cdot}^* > t_{A\cdot}^*(t_{A\cdot}^* - t_C)/\sqrt{t_{A\cdot}^{*2} + t_C^2}$ since $(t_{A\cdot}^* - t_C)/\sqrt{t_{A\cdot}^{*2} + t_C^2} < 1$. Then $t_P < t_C - t_{A\cdot}^*(t_{A\cdot}^* - t_C)/\sqrt{t_{A\cdot}^{*2} + t_C^2}$, and $B^D - B^M < 0$. *Q.E.D.*

PROPOSITION 3. $B^D \le B^A \Leftrightarrow t_P \le t_{A\cdot}^*$.

*Proof:* This follows from $B^D = t_P$ and $B^A = t_{A\cdot}^*$. *Q.E.D.*

## The Effect of More Divided Democracies

COROLLARY. *Irrespective of which country makes the first offer, as the legislatures become more protectionist (or less), the aggregate level of barriers to which a pair of democracies agree is unchanged.*

*Proof:* Aggregate barriers are always $t_P$ in the joint democracy case which is unaffected by changes in $t_C$. *Q.E.D.*

## Comparing Barriers of Joint Autocracies and the Mixed Pair

The outcomes here are not independent of the preferences of the players.

PROPOSITION 4. *Under TILI, when home (foreign) makes the offer,* $B^A \le B^M$ *when* $2t_A \le t_C (t_A \le t_C - t_P)$.

*Proof:* Note that in the autocracy case, $t_A = t_{A\cdot}^*$. (a) When home makes the offer, $B^A = t_A$, and $B^M$ is as in equation A-1 above. If $2t_A \le t_C$, then $2t_A - t_C \le 0 < t_C - 2t_P$ (by the assumption), which means $t_A < (t_C - t_P)$ and equivalently $t_A^2 < (t_C - t_P)^2$. From equation A-1, $B^M = t_C - t_A$ when $t_A^2 < (t_C - t_P)^2$. Then $B^A - B^M = 2t_A - t_C \le 0$ when $2t_A \le t_C$. If $2t_A > t_C$, then either (1) $t_A^2 < (t_C - t_P)^2$, or (2) $t_C^2 - t_P^2 \ge t_A^2 \ge (t_C - t_P)^2$, or (3) $t_C^2 - t_P^2 < t_A^2$. In the first instance, $B^A - B^M = 2t_A - t_C > 0$; in the second instance, $B^A - B^M = t_A - t_P$. By the assumption that $2t_P < t_C$, we have $t_A^2 \ge (t_C - t_P)^2 > t_P^2$. So $B^A - B^M > 0$. In the third instance, $B^A - B^M = -[t_C(t_P - t_A)/\sqrt{t_P^2 + t_A^2}]$. Again, $t_A^2 \ge t_C^2 - t_P^2 > t_P^2$, so $B^A - B^M > 0$. (b) When foreign makes the offer, $B^A = t_A$ and $B^M$ is as in equation A-2 above. If $t_A > t_C - t_P$, then $B^A - B^M = [(t_A - t_P)(t_A^2 + t_C t_P - t_A\sqrt{t_A^2 + t_C t_P - t_C^2})]/(t_A^2 + t_P^2)$; it is straightforward to show that $t_A^2 + t_C t_P - t_A\sqrt{t_A^2 + t_C t_P - t_C^2} > 0$. By the assumption that $2t_P < t_C$, we have $t_A^2 > (t_C - t_P)^2 > t_P^2$. So $B^A - B^M > 0$. If $t_A \le t_C - t_P$, then $B^A - B^M = (t_A - \sqrt{t_A^2 + t_C^2})[(t_C - t_A)/\sqrt{t_A^2 + t_C^2}]$. Now $(t_A - \sqrt{t_A^2 + t_C^2}) < 0$, and $t_A \le t_C - t_P \Rightarrow t_A \le t_C$, and, hence, $B^A - B^M \le 0$. *Q.E.D.*

## REFERENCES


Alvarez, Mike, José Antonio Cheibub, Fernando Limongi, and Adam Przeworski. 1996. "Classifying Political Regimes." *Studies in Comparative International Development* 31 (Summer): 3–36.

Anderson, James E. 1979. "A Theoretical Foundation for the Gravity Equation." *American Economic Review* 69 (March): 106–16.

Axelrod, Robert. 1970. *Conflict of Interest*. Chicago: Markham.

Banks, Arthur. 1995. *Cross-National Time-Series Data Archive*. Binghampton, NY: Center for Social Analysis, SUNY-Binghampton.

Bergstrand, Jeffrey H. 1985. "The Gravity Equation in International Trade: Some Microeconomic Foundations and Empirical Evidence." *Review of Economics and Statistics* 67 (August): 474–81.

Bergstrand, Jeffrey H. 1989. "The Generalized Gravity Equation, Monopolistic Competition, and the Factor-Proportions Theory in International Trade." *Review of Economics and Statistics* 71 (February): 143–53.

Black, Duncan. 1958. *The Theory of Committees and Elections*. Cambridge: Cambridge University Press.

Bliss, Harry, and Bruce Russett. 1998. "Democratic Trading Partners: The Liberal Connection, 1962–1989." *Journal of Politics* 60 (November): 1126–47.

de Melo, Jaime, and Arvind Panagariya, eds. 1993. *New Dimensions in Regional Integration*. New York: Cambridge University Press.

Deardorff, Alan V. 1998. "Determinants of Bilateral Trade: Does Gravity Work in a Neoclassical World?" In *The Regionalization of the World Economy*, ed. Jeffrey A. Frankel. Chicago: University of Chicago Press. Pp. 7–22.

Defense Mapping Agency. 1985. *Distance Between Ports*. 5th ed. Washington, DC: Defense Mapping Agency.

Dixon, William, and Bruce Moon. 1993. "Political Similarity and American Foreign Trade Patterns." *Political Research Quarterly* 46 (March): 5–25.

Doyle, Michael. 1986. "Liberalism and World Politics." *American Political Science Review* 80 (December): 1151–69.

Eichengreen, Barry, and Douglas A. Irwin. 1995. "Trade Blocs, Currency Blocs and the Reorientation of Trade in the 1930s." *Journal of International Economics* 38 (February): 1–24.

Enelow, James, and Melvin Hinich. 1984. *The Spatial Theory of Voting: An Introduction*. New York: Cambridge University Press.

Ethier, Wilfred J. 1998. "Unilateralism in a Multilateral World." University of Pennsylvania. Mimeograph.

Farber, Henry S., and Joanne Gowa. 1995. "Polities and Peace." *International Security* 20 (Fall): 123–46.

Feenstra, Robert C., James Markusen, and Andrew Rose. 1998. "Understanding the Home Market Effect and the Gravity Equation." Working Paper no. 6804. Cambridge, MA: National Bureau of Economic Research.

Fitzpatrick, Gary L., and Marilyn J. Modlin. 1986. *Direct-Line Distances*. International ed. Metuchen, NJ: Scarecrow.

Frankel, Jeffrey A. 1993. "Is Japan Creating a Yen Bloc in East Asia and the Pacific?" In *Regionalism and Rivalry: Japan and the United States in Pacific Asia*, ed. Jeffrey A. Frankel and Miles Kahler. Chicago: University of Chicago Press. Pp. 53–87.

Frankel, Jeffrey, Ernesto Stein, and Shang-jin Wei. 1995. "Trading Blocs and the Americas: The Natural, the Unnatural, and the Super-Natural." *Journal of Development Economics* 47 (June): 61–95.

Gasiorowski, Mark. 1996. "An Overview of the Political Regime Change Dataset." *Comparative Political Studies* 29 (August): 469–83.

Gowa, Joanne. 1994. *Allies, Adversaries, and International Trade*. Princeton, NJ: Princeton University Press.

Greene, William H. 1993. *Econometric Analysis*. 2d ed. New York: Macmillan.

Grieco, Joseph M. 1990. *Cooperation among Nations: Europe, Amer-*

*ica, and Non-Tariff Barriers to Trade*. Ithaca, NY: Cornell University Press.
Grossman, Gene M., and Elhanan Helpman. 1994. "Protection for Sale." *American Economic Review* 84 (September): 833-50.
Gurr, Ted Robert, Keith Jaggers, and Will H. Moore. 1989. *Polity II: Political Structures and Regime Change, 1800-1986*. ICPSR Codebook (Study #9263). Ann Arbor, MI: Inter-University Consortium for Political and Social Research.
Haggard, Stephan, and Robert R. Kaufman. 1995. *The Political Economy of Democratic Transitions*. Princeton, NJ: Princeton University Press.
Haggard, Stephan, and Steven B. Webb, eds. 1994. *Voting for Reform: Democracy, Political Liberalization, and Economic Adjustment*. New York: Oxford University Press.
Harrigan, Keith. 1993. "OECD Imports and Trade Barriers in 1983." *Journal of International Economics* 35 (August): 91-111.
Hartland-Thunberg, Penelope. 1980. *Trading Blocs, U.S. Exports, and World Trade*. Boulder, CO: Westview.
Helpman, Elhanan, and Paul Krugman. 1985. *Market Structure and Foreign Trade: Increasing Returns, Imperfect Competition and the International Economy*. Cambridge, MA: MIT Press.
Hillman, Arye L. 1982. "Declining Industries and Political-Support Protectionist Motives." *American Economic Review* 72 (December): 1180-90.
Hillman, Arye L., Ngo Van Long, and Peter Moser. 1995. "Modeling Reciprocal Trade Liberalization: The Political-Economy and National-Welfare Perspectives." *Swiss Journal of Economics and Statistics* 131 (September): 503-15.
Jaggers, Keith, and Ted Robert Gurr. 1995. "Tracking Democracy's Third Wave with the Polity III Data." *Journal of Peace Research* 32 (November): 469-82.
Kleiman, Ephraim. 1976. "Trade and the Decline of Colonialism." *Economic Journal* 86 (September): 459-80.
Kornai, Janos. 1992. *The Socialist System: The Political Economy of Communism*. Princeton, NJ: Princeton University Press.
Krugman, Paul. 1997. "What Should Trade Negotiators Negotiate About?" *Journal of Economic Literature* 35 (March): 113-20.
Kurian, George Thomas. 1992. *Encyclopedia of the Third World*. 4th ed. Vols. 1-3. New York: Facts on File.
Leamer, Edward. 1988. "Cross-Section Estimation of the Effects of Trade Barriers." In *Empirical Methods for International Trade*, ed. Robert C. Feenstra. Cambridge, MA: MIT Press. Pp. 51-82.
Linnemann, Hans. 1966. *An Econometric Study of International Trade Flows*. Amsterdam: North-Holland.
Lohmann, Susanne, and Sharyn O'Halloran. 1994. "Divided Government and U.S. Trade Policy: Theory and Evidence." *International Organization* 48 (Autumn): 595-632.
Maddison, Angus. 1995. *Monitoring the World Economy, 1820-1992*. Paris: Development Centre of the Organisation for Economic Co-operation and Development.
Mansfield, Edward D., and Rachel Bronson. 1997. "Alliances, Preferential Trading Arrangements, and International Trade." *American Political Science Review* 91 (March): 94-107.
Mansfield, Edward D., and Marc L. Busch. 1995. "The Political Economy of Nontariff Barriers: A Cross-National Analysis." *International Organization* 49 (Autumn): 723-49.
Mansfield, Edward D., Helen V. Milner, and B. Peter Rosendorff. 1998. "Why Democracies Cooperate More: Electoral Control and International Trade Agreements." Paper presented at the annual meeting of the American Political Science Association, Boston.
Mansfield, Edward D., and Jack Snyder. 1995. "Democratization and the Danger of War." *International Security* 20 (Summer): 5-38.
Milner, Helen V. 1997. *Interests, Institutions and Information: Domestic Politics and International Relations*. Princeton, NJ: Princeton University Press.
Milner, Helen V., and B. Peter Rosendorff. 1996. "Trade Negotiations, Information and Domestic Politics: The Role of Domestic Groups." *Economics and Politics* 8 (July): 145-89.
Milner, Helen V., and B. Peter Rosendorff. 1997. "Democracy and International Trade Negotiations." *Journal of Conflict Resolution* 41 (February): 117-46.
Morrow, James D., Randolph M. Siverson, and Tressa E. Taberes. 1998. "The Political Determinants of International Trade: The Major Powers, 1907-1990." *American Political Science Review* 92 (September): 649-61.
Nash, John F. 1950. "The Bargaining Problem." *Econometrica* 18 (April): 155-62.
O'Halloran, Sharyn. 1994. *Politics, Process, and American Trade Policy*. Ann Arbor: University of Michigan Press.
Oneal, John R., and Bruce M. Russett. 1997. "The Classical Liberals Were Right: Democracy, Interdependence, and Conflict, 1950-1985." *International Studies Quarterly* 41 (June): 267-93.
Pahre, Robert. 1997. "Endogenous Domestic Institutions in Two Level Games." *Journal of Conflict Resolution* 41 (February): 147-74.
Polachek, Solomon William. 1980. "Conflict and Trade." *Journal of Conflict Resolution* 24 (March): 55-78.
Pollins, Brian M. 1989. "Conflict, Cooperation, and Commerce: The Effects of International Political Interactions on Bilateral Trade Flows." *American Journal of Political Science* 33 (August): 737-61.
Pomfret, Richard. 1988. *Unequal Trade: The Economics of Discriminatory International Trade Policies*. Oxford: Basil Blackwell.
Rodrik, Dani. 1994. "The Rush to Free Trade in the Developing World. Why So Late? Why Now? Will It Last?" In *Voting for Reform: Democracy, Political Liberalization, and Economic Adjustment*, ed. Stephan Haggard and Steven B. Webb. New York: Oxford University Press. Pp. 61-88.
Rodrik, Dani. 1995. "The Political Economy of Trade Policy." In *Handbook of International Economics*, ed. Gene M. Grossman and Kenneth Rogoff. Amsterdam: Elsevier Science BV. Vol. III. Pp. 1457-94.
Rogowski, Ronald. 1987. "Trade and the Variety of Democratic Institutions." *International Organization* 41 (Spring): 203-24.
Rosendorff, B. Peter. 1996. "Endogenous Trade Restrictions and Domestic Political Pressure." In *The Political Economy of Trade Policy: Essays in Honor of Jagdish Bhagwati*, ed. Robert C. Feenstra, Gene M. Grossman, and Douglas Irwin. Cambridge, MA: MIT Press. Pp. 245-64.
Russett, Bruce. 1993. *Grasping the Democratic Peace: Principles for a Post-Cold War World*. Princeton, NJ: Princeton University Press.
Schumpeter, Joseph. 1942. *Capitalism, Socialism and Democracy*. New York: Harper & Row.
Singer, J. David, and Melvin Small. 1994. *Correlates of War Project: International and Civil War Data, 1816-1992* [computer file] (Study #9905). Ann Arbor, MI: J. David Singer and Melvin Small [producers], 1993. Ann Arbor, MI: Inter-University Consortium for Political and Social Research [distributor], 1994.
Siverson, Randolph M., and Juliann Emmons. 1991. "Birds of a Feather: Democratic Political Systems and Alliance Choices in the Twentieth Century." *Journal of Conflict Resolution* 35 (June): 285-306.
Small, Melvin, and J. David Singer. 1969. "Formal Alliances, 1816-1965: An Extension of the Basic Data." *Journal of Peace Research* 6 (3): 257-82.
Staar, Richard F., et al., eds. 1991. *Yearbook on International Communist Affairs*. Stanford, CA: Hoover Institution Press.
Summers, Robert, and Alan Heston. 1991. "The Penn World Table (Mark 5): An Expanded Set of International Comparisons." *Quarterly Journal of Economics* 106 (May): 327-68.
*Times Atlas of the World*. 1992. 9th ed. New York: Times Books.
*Times Concise Atlas of the World*. 1972. New York: Times Books.
Trefler, Daniel. 1993. "Trade Liberalization and the Theory of Endogenous Protection." *Journal of Political Economy* 101 (February): 138-60.
White, Halbert. 1980. "A Heteroskedasticity-Consistent Covariance Matrix Estimator and a Direct Test for Heteroskedasticity." *Econometrica* 48 (May): 817-38.
World Trade Organization. 1995. *Regionalism and the World Trading System*. Geneva: World Trade Organization.

*International Studies Quarterly* (2006) **50**, 189–211

# Votes and Vetoes: The Political Determinants of Commercial Openness

WITOLD J. HENISZ AND EDWARD D. MANSFIELD
*University of Pennsylvania*

Some theories of foreign economic policy stress the importance of domestic interest groups, whereas others focus on the effects of domestic institutions. Debates between advocates of these approaches are long-standing, but little systematic empirical research has been brought to bear on the relative merits of these theories. We argue that while interest group demands and institutions are often regarded as having independent and competing effects, it is more fruitful to view the influence of each type of factor as conditional on the other. As explanations emphasizing societal interests contend, deteriorating macroeconomic conditions are a potent source of protectionist sentiment. The extent to which such conditions reduce commercial openness, however, depends centrally on a country's political institutions, especially the number of veto points in a country's policy-making structure and its regime type. We expect the effects of macroeconomic conditions on trade policy to become weaker as the number of veto points increases. We also expect both veto points and the societal pressures stemming from the economy to have a more potent impact on trade policy in democracies than in other regimes. The results of our statistical tests covering almost 60 countries during the period from 1980 to 2000 strongly support these arguments.

Much of the recent literature on the political economy of trade policy emphasizes the role of domestic politics. Some theories of foreign economic policy stress the importance of domestic interest groups, whereas others focus on the effects of domestic institutions. Debates between advocates of these approaches are long-standing, but little systematic empirical research has been brought to bear on the relative merits of these theories. Moreover, most extant research addresses trade policy in stable, mature, and wealthy democracies, a tack that places important restrictions on the range of both interest group pressures and domestic political institutions that are analyzed, and thereby hampers efforts to undertake comparisons of the two approaches.

In this article, we analyze the domestic determinants of commercial openness for democracies and non-democracies at all stages of economic development. Our core argument is that while interest group demands and institutions are often regarded as having independent and competing effects, it is more fruitful to view the influence of each type of factor as conditional on the other. More specifically, as

*Authors' note*: For very helpful comments on earlier versions of this article, we are grateful to Marc Busch, Mark Hallerberg, David Leblang, Helen Milner, Dennis Quinn, Daniel Treisman, and the anonymous reviewers. We also thank Todor Enev and Matthew Tubin for research assistance, and the Christopher H. Browne Center for International Politics for financial support.

© 2006 International Studies Association.
Published by Blackwell Publishing, 350 Main Street, Malden, MA 02148, USA, and 9600 Garsington Road, Oxford OX4 2DQ, UK.

explanations emphasizing societal interests contend, deteriorating macroeconomic conditions are a potent source of protectionist sentiment. The extent to which such conditions reduce commercial openness, however, depends centrally on the domestic political institutions through which interest group pressures must filter to influence policy.

Two institutional features stand out in this regard. First, countries vary substantially in the degree to which authority is concentrated within the government. In states marked by greater fragmentation of authority and more "veto points," it is harder to change existing policies because any number of actors can block such a change. Consequently, we expect the effects of macroeconomic conditions on trade policy to be weaker in fragmented states (i.e., those with more veto points) than in those characterized by a highly centralized government (i.e., those with fewer veto points).[1] Second, we expect both fragmentation and interest group pressures stemming from the economy to have a more potent impact on commercial openness in democracies than in other regimes. The electoral constraints facing democratic leaders force them to respond to demands made by key segments of society. While autocrats can more easily change policy than democratic leaders, regardless of how concentrated authority is in a democracy, autocrats depend on a narrower set of groups for political power than their democratic counterparts. This set of groups is less likely to base their political support on broad macroeconomic conditions than on whether they benefit from the government's economic policy, regardless of the economy's overall performance.

Taken as a whole, we therefore expect deteriorating macroeconomic conditions to impede commercial openness, but the effect of these conditions is likely to hinge on the extent of institutional fragmentation. Equally, we expect macroeconomic factors to have a more pronounced influence on trade policy in democracies than in other countries. The results of our statistical tests—covering almost 60 countries during the period from 1980 to 2000—strongly support these arguments.

## Societal Interests and Trade Policy

Various studies emphasize how interest groups affect trade policy by exerting political pressure on public officials.[2] These studies generally view domestic institutions and policy makers as passive actors that supply the trade policies demanded by the most influential groups in society (Ikenberry, Lake, and Mastanduno 1988). Societal demands for protection are frequently inferred from macroeconomic conditions, a research strategy that has contributed to a burgeoning literature on the links between aspects of national economic performance and foreign commerce (e.g., Bergsten and Cline 1983; Deardorff and Stern 1987; Dornbusch and Frankel 1987; Baldwin 1989; Cline 1989; Gardner and Kimbrough 1989; Magee, Brock, and Young 1989; Bhagwati 1991; Bohara and Kaempfer 1991; Destler 1992; Corden 1993).

Central to this literature is the argument that public officials must respond to demands made by broad segments of the populace in order to ensure their political survival. There is considerable evidence that voters pay attention to overall macroeconomic conditions as well as their own economic circumstances when casting ballots (Kinder and Kiewiet 1981; Lewis-Beck 1988; Colton 2000). Furthermore, survey research indicates that public support for protectionism rises as domestic economic conditions degrade (Shapiro and Page 1994). Government officials

[1] As long as the policy preferences by political actors across "veto points" are not perfectly correlated and they encounter some positive decision costs in reaching a consensus, the response to a given shock or change in environmental circumstance will, on average, be muted for a country with multiple veto points as compared with one characterized by a single veto point.

[2] The classic statement is Schattschneider (1935).

therefore have reason to raise trade barriers when these conditions worsen in an effort to bolster their prospects of retaining office.

It is widely argued that, among the macroeconomic determinants of trade policy, unemployment is crucial. In fact, as Bergsten and Cline (1983:77) point out, "conventional wisdom suggests that high levels of unemployment are the single most important source of protectionist pressures." Similarly, an International Monetary Fund study concludes that "perhaps the most crucial factor—and the one most likely to influence policy choices toward protection—is the extent and duration of existing unemployment" (Nowzad 1978:35). Various other studies have arrived at the same conclusion (Hughes and Waelbroeck 1981; Wallerstein 1987).

High levels of unemployment are expected to generate calls for protectionism by making it more difficult for workers to adjust to increases in imports. Workers who lose their jobs because of rising import competition will find it harder to obtain alternative employment and are likely to be paid less once they become reemployed. These workers and others who fear that they may soon become unemployed have reason to press for relief from foreign competition (Bradford 2003). So do firms that depend on consumption by these workers. High levels of unemployment stimulate workers, investors, and other interest groups adversely affected by open trade to overcome collective action problems and mobilize to press for policies that reduce openness (Olson 1983).

The "dual" of this relationship would be a positive association between the political strength of groups that benefit from free trade and increases in commercial openness. We offer no such prediction because of a lack of internationally comparable, time-varying, and exogenous measures of the strength of the free trade lobby. It is important to recognize, however, that the lack of an explicit measure of the strength of this lobby does not bear on our expectation that an inverse relationship will exist between unemployment and changes in trade openness. The marginal effect of high unemployment on openness (while all other factors are held constant) should be negative, regardless of the unobserved free trade lobby's political potency.

## Veto Points and Trade Policy

Approaches that stress the importance of interest groups in shaping trade policy usually give short shrift to the domestic political institutions that filter demands made by these groups and set policy. Crucial in this regard are the extent of fragmentation within a country's government and its regime type (Garrett and Lange 1996).

The fragmentation of power within a government depends on the number of independent partisan and institutional actors whose agreement is necessary to make policy. These actors include competing branches of government and coalitions within a given branch. As the number of independent actors with such veto power—or veto points—increases, groups in society have greater difficulty pressing for a change in policy (Henisz 2000; Tsebelis 2003).

In the trade policy arena, any actor with the authority to set policy understands that the final outcome must lie within a range of policies that satisfies all veto points. To the extent that the preferences of actors with veto power differ, institutional structures with more veto points limit the range of feasible trade policy choices. As a result, "the potential for policy change decreases with the number of veto players, the lack of congruence (dissimilarity of policy positions among veto players), and the cohesion (similarity of policy positions among the constituent units of each veto player) of these players" (Tsebelis 1995:289). Various cross-national studies that link policy stability to the number of veto points support these theoretical insights (Haggard and Kaufman 1995; Milner 1997; Hallerberg and Basinger 1998; Franzese 1999; Treisman 2000; MacIntyre 2001; Kastner and Rector 2003; Tsebelis 2003; Mansfield, Milner, and Pevehouse 2005).

In a similar vein, we argue that governments will be less responsive to societal pressures as the number of veto points rises in policy-making structures (Frieden and Rogowski 1996:43; Garrett and Lange 1996:66). More specifically, we expect that a high level of unemployment will stimulate interest group demands for policies to decrease unemployment at the cost of more expensive imports, including reductions in commercial openness. However, we also expect that more fragmented policy-making structures will reduce the sensitivity of government actors to such societal pressures. When a large number of veto points exists, there is more likely to be an actor in control of a veto point who is hostile to raising trade barriers and who can use this control to frustrate societal demands for protection. As the number of veto points declines, it becomes easier to change the existing trade regime as the actors controlling veto points are more likely to have relatively homogeneous interests (Henisz 2000). We therefore anticipate that adverse macroeconomic conditions will stimulate a larger decline in external trade linkages as countries become more institutionally centralized.

As we mentioned earlier, it is not possible to observe the corresponding moderating role that veto points have on the positive relationship between the strength of the free trade lobby and changes in openness, as reliable, cross-national data on this lobby are unavailable. Comparing the relationship between the estimated change in openness when the unemployment rate is zero and few veto points exist with this relationship when a large number of veto points exist, however, will be informative in this regard. In the hypothetical absence of unemployment, only the unobserved lobby for free trade should pressure the government over commercial policy. A larger number of veto points should moderate the positive association between the strength of this lobby and the estimated change in openness. We therefore expect that where the unemployment rate is relatively low, the predicted increase in the level of openness will be smaller as the number of veto points grows larger.

Relatively few studies have addressed the effects of veto points on trade policy. But Lohmann and O'Halloran (1994) find that divided government has impeded trade liberalization by the United States. Unified government (i.e., one with few veto points), by contrast, has promoted liberalization. In a study of post-Communist countries during the 1990s, however, Frye and Mansfield (2003) find that trade has reform becomes more likely as the number of veto points increases, especially in non-democratic states. This result, they argue, stems from the autarkic trade regimes put in place by these countries during the Cold War and the tendency for an increase in the number of veto players during the era since the collapse of the Berlin Wall to expand the range of economic interests shaping foreign economic policy, bringing groups with an interest in trade liberalization onto the political stage and leading to more open overseas commerce.

The difference between the effects of veto points in these two studies may be an outgrowth of variations in the status quo policy that the authors consider. In the situation analyzed by Lohmann and O'Halloran, the status quo trade policy is relatively open and was put in place by a comparable set of political actors to those currently holding power. A reduction in the number of veto points thus allows a subset of political actors to overcome opposition and push through a change in the status quo policy, leading to trade liberalization. In the case of post-Communist countries, by contrast, the status quo trade policy is highly protectionist and nations differ substantially in the extent to which the existing political actors and veto points are the same as or closely related to those that promoted closure. Where veto points are more numerous, political regime change has brought new political actors to the table, fostering a new coalition that endorses trade liberalization. Where few veto points exist, it is more likely that the same political actors that supported autarky remain in power. This interpretation of these conflicting findings highlights the need to control for the status quo trade policy and to explore the impact of the nature of the political regime.

## Regime Type and Trade Policy

Our analysis adds to the burgeoning literature on the political economy of foreign trade by addressing the combined effects of interest group pressures generated by macroeconomic conditions and institutional fragmentation on political actors' incentives and ability to change trade policy. Of course, the need for leaders to respond to such pressures differs markedly depending on whether the populace is able to monitor their behavior and penalize them for being unresponsive. In democracies, the populace is able to do so. Indeed, the hallmark of democracy is the existence of regular, open, and fair elections involving candidates who compete for the votes of a large portion of the adult population (e.g., Schumpeter 1942; Huntington 1991:5–13; Przeworski et al. 2000). Furthermore, a free press and the relatively free flow of information about governmental activities keep constituents apprised of changes in foreign economic policy and leaders' behavior. If democratic leaders do not take overt steps to cushion the effects of macroeconomic downturns—by increasing trade barriers among other measures—they face audience costs, including the prospect of being turned out of office by voters.

Non-democratic governments, by contrast, are less susceptible to broad-based societal demands. The absence of electoral pressures and checks on their power by an independent and representative legislature give non-democratic leaders less incentive to respond to demands for protection arising from higher levels of unemployment than their democratic counterparts. Like democratic leaders, autocrats rely on the support of various interest groups to maintain power. However, the segment of society to which an autocrat must appeal to retain office is typically much narrower and therefore less motivated by aggregate macroeconomic conditions than in a democracy. Instead, an autocrat's key constituents tend to focus greater attention on how resources are distributed within society and their share of these resources than on national economic performance. Autocrats, therefore, should be relatively insensitive to the societal pressures generated by adverse macroeconomic conditions (Frieden and Rogowski 1996; Garrett and Lange 1996; Wintrobe 1998; Brooker 2000; Acemoglu and Robinson 2005).

In sum, then, we expect commercial openness to dip as the level of unemployment rises, and we anticipate that the influence of unemployment will grow larger as the number of veto points declines. In addition, while democracies are generally marked by a higher number of veto points than non-democracies, we expect the impact of unemployment and veto points to be more pronounced in democratic regimes.[3]

Anecdotal evidence points to the effect that veto points can have on trade policy. Consider the cases of Chile and Peru. In Chile, a democratically elected government came to power in 1989 and subsequently cut the tariff rate to 11 percent in 1991 (Lederman 2001:226–227). Based on our data, the number of veto points in Chile rose substantially during the early 1990s. Consistent with our argument, the Chilean government succeeded in warding off demands for protection during this decade despite adverse economic conditions. As Saez, Salazar, and Vicuña (1995:49) point out, in the early 1990s, the government faced "pressures to raise the level of protection" but "these pressures were not fruitful." Nor were such pressures effective at the end of this decade, despite an unemployment rate that rose to almost 10 percent (Lederman 2001). Again, the maintenance of Chile's open trade policy accords with our claim that deteriorating macroeconomic conditions

[3] It is important to recognize that regime type and veto points tap different, although somewhat related, aspects of domestic politics. The extent of veto points varies considerably among democracies and non-democracies alike (the mean among stable democracies is 0.60 and the standard deviation is 0.26 while among other nations the mean is 0.09 and the standard deviation 0.20). Furthermore, while democracies tend to have more veto points than other countries, the correlation between regime type and veto points is not overwhelmingly high (0.63 or 0.46, depending on which measure of veto points is analyzed; see Table 1).

are less likely to yield heightened trade barriers in democracies with a wider range of veto points.

In Peru's emerging democracy, unemployment rose dramatically during the early 1980s, reaching a rate of about 60 percent by 1984. During that time, Wise (1989:170) reports, constitutional changes and other developments precipitated a "greater concentration of power in the executive." As such, the number of veto points declined during the first half of the 1980s. Hence, it is not surprising that Peru abandoned its export-led growth strategy and increased trade barriers during these years (Wise 1989:170; Nogues and Gulati 1994:487). We would expect that demands for protection spurred by heightened unemployment would have a greater effect on trade policy as the number of veto points declines.

Of course, these are only illustrations of our argument, but they suggest that the factors we emphasize may have influenced trade policy. To test the argument more fully, we now turn to a set of quantitative analyses. These analyses depart from the existing empirical work on the domestic politics of trade in various ways. First, very few studies have addressed the effects of veto points on trade policy. None that we are aware of have addressed how veto points influence the relationship between interest group pressures and foreign commerce, even though it is widely recognized that domestic institutions and societal pressures are likely to have an interactive effect on trade policy (Mansfield and Busch 1995; Garrett and Lange 1996; Gilligan 1997; Milner 1997; Grossman and Helpman 2002). Instead, most empirical studies assume that interest group demands and policy structures operate independently of each other. Our model, by contrast, explicitly accounts for the moderating role of policy-making structures and political regimes. Second, the vast bulk of the empirical studies of trade policy have focused on democratic, advanced industrial countries. Although there has been widespread interest in whether variations in regime type are linked to patterns of commercial openness, systematic research on this topic has been relatively scarce (Bliss and Russett 1998; Mansfield, Milner, and Rosendorff 2000; Frye and Mansfield 2003; Milner and Kubota 2005). Equally, the work that has been conducted has not addressed whether societal influences on trade policy vary between democracies and non-democracies. Our analysis—covering almost 60 countries between 1980 and 2000—will provide some of the first quantitative results bearing on this important issue.

## Model and Measures

To test our argument, we begin by estimating the following model:

$$\begin{aligned}\Delta IMPORTS_{i,t} &= \beta_1 UNEMPL_{i,t-1} + \beta_2 VP_{i,t-1} + \beta_3 UNEMPL_{i,t-1} \times VP_{i,t-1} \\ &+ \beta_4 IMPORTS_{i,t-1} + \beta_5 REER_{i,t-1} + \beta_6 \Delta REER_{i,t-1} + \beta_7 \Delta TOT_{i,t-1} + \beta_8 RES_{i,t-1} \\ &+ \beta_9 GPCF_{i,t-1} + PTA_{i,t-1}\boldsymbol{\beta} + COUNTRY_i\boldsymbol{\beta} + YEAR_t\boldsymbol{\beta} + \varepsilon_{i,t}\end{aligned}$$

Our dependent variable is the annual percentage change in import penetration. For each country, $i$, import penetration is defined as the value of imports in domestic currency divided by the nation's gross domestic product (GDP) in a given year ($t$), using data drawn from the World Bank's *World Development Indicators*. The dependent variable is the percentage change in import penetration from year $t-1$ to year $t$. For the period covered in our analysis (1980–2000), the mean value of the dependent variable is 3 percent with a standard deviation of 21 percent, indicating both a slight tendency for countries to expand their imports over time and substantial variation in this regard within the sample.

Of course, this measure of trade policy is not ideal as aggregate shifts in import penetration could reflect various factors other than policy decisions (Leamer 1988; O'Rourke and Williamson 1999). However, the alternative measures that have been developed cover only a fraction of the countries included in our sample. Moreover, they exclude many autocracies and numerous developing countries, rendering them inappropriate for our purposes.[4] To test our argument, it is especially important to analyze a sample of countries with as wide a range of political institutions and macroeconomic conditions as possible. Furthermore, protectionist trade policies should generally reduce imports and trade liberalization should generally increase them. Consequently, while we consider the robustness of our results to an alternative measure of openness that is based on a gravity model of trade and discussed further below (Hiscox and Kastner 2002), there is ample reason to use $\Delta IMPORTS_{i,t}$ in our core specification.

### *Independent Variables*

The central variables in our model are the unemployment rate (*UNEMPL*) and the extensiveness of veto points in each country. All of the independent variables are measured in year $t-1$, reflecting the fact that trade policy does not respond immediately to either societal pressures or institutional conditions, and helping to address the possibility of endogeneity in the model.

As we mentioned earlier, existing studies frequently infer demands for protection from the unemployment rate. The *World Development Indicators* reports the unemployment rate that is given by each country's national statistical agency. These data cover the widest possible range of countries and years, rendering them especially useful in light of our objectives.[5] Prior to 1980, however, unemployment data for developing countries are not compiled using a comparable methodology, making cross-national comparisons very difficult to conduct. As such, our analysis covers the period from 1980 to 2000.

The key institutional factor included in the model is the extent of the constraints faced by government officials in each country (VP). We measure the level of veto points in terms of the structure of a country's formal political institutions and the degree of partisan heterogeneity within and among these institutions. We used two veto points measures: the Political Constraints Index (*POLCON*) developed by Henisz (2000) and the *CHECKS* index developed by Beck et al. (2001).

The first step in the construction of *POLCON* is identifying the number of independent branches of government (executive, lower and upper legislative chambers, judiciary, and sub-federal institutions) with veto power over policy change in each country.[6] Countries lacking any formal veto points are assigned a score of 0. For all other countries, the majority preference of each of these branches and the status quo policy are then assumed to be independently and identically drawn from a uniform, one-dimensional policy space [0, 1]. This assumption facilitates the derivation of a quantitative measure of institutional constraints using a simple spatial model of political interaction.

This initial measure is then modified to take into account the extent of alignment across branches of government using data on the party composition of the executive and legislative branches. Alignment across branches increases the feasibility of policy change, thereby reducing the level of political constraints. The measure is then further modified to capture the extent of preference heterogeneity within each legislative branch. Greater within-branch heterogeneity increases (decreases) the costs of overturning policy for aligned (opposed) branches. Scores for the final

[4] For an overview of these measures, see Edwards (1993).

[5] Data from the International Labor Office offer equal coverage to the World Bank data set and are drawn from the same national sources.

[6] Note that the following results are quite similar when we replace this variant of *POLCON* with one that excludes the judiciary and sub-federal institutions. The data and codebook for these measures are available from http://www-management.wharton.upenn.edu/henisz/POLCON/ContactInfo.html

measure of political constraints can range from zero (least constrained) to one (most constrained).

Countries with the most veto points in the formal policy-making apparatus are federal states with strong independent judiciaries and either presidential regimes or those with proportional representation electoral rules that tend to yield coalition governments, such as the United States, Germany, and Switzerland. Political constraints decrease as the number of veto points declines or as their preferences become more homogeneous, as is the case in moving to a mixed Parliamentary–Presidential system, typified by France and Brazil, to heavily fractionalized Parliamentary systems like those of Belgium, Israel, and the Netherlands, or to Westminster Parliamentary systems with winner-take-all districts, such as the United Kingdom. Non-democratic countries and those with transitional political regimes have the lowest levels of political constraints because the formal institutional structures in these states provide tremendous discretion to policy makers.

The alternative measure—the logarithm of *CHECKS*—"count[s] the number of veto players in a political system, adjusting for whether these veto players are independent of each other, as determined by the level of electoral competitiveness in a system, their respective party affiliations, and the electoral rules" (Beck et al. 2001:170). This index yields a minimum score of 0 when a country lacks an effective legislature. The score then increases linearly with the addition of subsequent veto points whose political preferences are closer to that of the opposition than they are to the average government preference, based on a three-point scale calculated using a different methodology for Presidential and Parliamentary systems.

For Presidential systems, the opposition is defined as the largest opposition party. The index's value increases by one point for each legislative chamber and for the president, unless elections are held under closed lists and the president's party is the largest one in a particular chamber, in which case the president is not considered a check. For Parliamentary systems, the opposition is defined as the three largest opposition parties. The index's value increases by one point for the prime minister and for each party in the government coalition, including that of the prime minister, unless elections are held under closed lists.

In our sample, the correlation between *POLCON* and *CHECKS* is 0.72. The greatest divergence between the two measures is in their treatment of broad coalition governments. As *CHECKS* treats each party as a veto point, countries such as India, Pakistan, Turkey, and France have the highest level of veto points by this measure. Alternatively, *POLCON* indicates that countries such as Germany, Switzerland, Belgium, and the United States have the highest level of veto points.

As our argument is that the impact of societal forces on trade policy will be moderated as the number of veto points rises, we analyze *UNEMPL* × *POLCON* and *UNEMPL* × *CHECKS* in addition to *POLCON* and *CHECKS*.

Another key aspect of our argument is that the effects of veto points and broad societal pressures for protection should be qualitatively different in stable democracies than in other political regimes. We therefore generate three sets of parameter estimates: one for the full sample, a second for the stable remaining democratic states in the sample, and a third for the remaining states.[7] We distinguish between democratic and non-democratic regimes using two different sources of data. First, we use the Polity IV data set (Marshall and Jaggers 2001), which contains separate 11-point indices of each state's democratic (*DEM*) and autocratic (*AUT*) characteristics in each year. The difference between these indices (*DEM* −*AUT* = *REGIME*) yields an overall measure of regime type ranging from −10 to 10 (Jaggers and

[7] In our robustness tests, we further address this issue by pooling the democratic and non-democratic states in the sample and including a democracy indicator variable as described in further detail below. We chose to split our data into these two subsamples on the basis of a Wald test that suggested statistically significant ($p$ = .003) differences in the full set of coefficient estimates as opposed to merely a change in the intercept.

Gurr 1995). Following much of the existing literature, we define stable democratic regimes as those where *REGIME* is greater than or equal to 6 for 5 consecutive years.[8] Later, however, we assess the robustness of the results by fluctuating this cutoff point for democracy, and by using data from Freedom House (2005) on Political Rights and Civil Liberties within a country.

As our dependent variable is the percentage change in import penetration, it is important to include the level of import penetration as well. There are practical limits on the extent of import penetration that countries can achieve. Those that are already relatively open with respect to trade may find it difficult to increase import penetration much, whereas those that are relatively closed will face strong economic incentives to liberalize their trade regimes. Controlling for initial conditions in this manner will also help to isolate the differing mechanisms that led to conflicting theoretical arguments and empirical evidence regarding the impact of veto points in earlier research on trade policy (Lohmann and O'Halloran 1994; Frye and Mansfield 2003).

Although our primary interest is in the interaction between societal pressures and domestic institutions, it is obviously important to account for various additional factors that might influence foreign commerce. To this end, we include the following: (1) the level of and change in each country's real effective exchange rate (*REER* and Δ*REER*), which alters the relative price of imports and thus demand for them; (2) the change in each state's terms of trade (Δ*TOT*), which captures relative price movements particular to a country's imports or exports that may not be fully reflected in its exchange rate (e.g., the effect of an oil price shock on oil importers or oil exporters in a fixed exchange rate regime); (3) the government's supply of foreign exchange reserves as a percentage of imports (*RES*), which is positively associated with its ability to withstand a run on its currency and is negatively associated with the likelihood that it will liberalize trade as part of a multilateral program to restore financial stability; (4) gross private capital formation (*GPCF*), which plays a role similar to reserves in shaping trade policy; and (5) a vector of time-varying dummy variables indicating whether a country is a member of each of the 50 preferential trade agreements (PTA) that may require, encourage, or solicit membership from those countries that are more likely to expand their overseas economic linkages (Ingram, Robinson, and Busch, forthcoming). Further, we include dummy variables indicating whether each country was a member of the Organization of Petroleum Exporting Countries or the Council for Mutual Economic Cooperation, as a heavy dependence on oil exports and a command economy are likely to influence the evolution of trade policy.

Finally, to capture any unmeasured country-specific but time-invariant or time-specific but country-invariant heterogeneity in the data, we include country-specific and year-specific fixed effects. The inclusion of these fixed effects implies that our coefficient estimates are identified by within-country variation in the independent variables that is not common to all countries in a given year. For example, the inclusion of time-invariant characteristics of a country—such as its land area—would confer no additional explanatory power to our model as variables of this kind are already captured by the country's fixed effect. Similarly, cross-country variation in the mean level of our independent variables—including veto points and unemployment—are also subsumed within the country's fixed effect.

## Results

We estimate the model described in the previous section using ordinary least squares (OLS) with panel-corrected standard errors. These standard errors are

[8] The same country may appear in both subsamples in different time periods. For example, a country that was an autocracy from 1980 to 1990 and then became a stable democracy would appear in the stable democracy subsample after 1995, but in the other subsample from 1980 to 1995.

TABLE 1. Summary Statistics

| *Variable* | # | *1* | *2* | *3* | *4* | *5* | *6* | *7* | *8* | *9* | *10* | *11* | *12* | *13* | *14* | *15* | *16* |
|---|---|---|---|---|---|---|---|---|---|---|---|---|---|---|---|---|---|
| *N* | | 4,368 | 2,620 | 4,489 | 2,703 | 5,108 | 3,280 | 1,173 | 1,162 | 1,512 | 1,437 | 4,105 | 2,856 | 3,033 | 4,275 | 3,843 | 4,533 |
| Mean | | 0.03 | 0.01 | 34.21 | 30.58 | 0.26 | 0.62 | 8.17 | 4.53 | 32.77 | 0.01 | 0.01 | 13.09 | 3.48 | 0.11 | 52.42 | 59.17 |
| Standard deviation | | 0.21 | 0.12 | 22.74 | 10.39 | 0.33 | 0.67 | 5.71 | 3.93 | 984.30 | 0.26 | 0.15 | 34.37 | 2.93 | 0.13 | 540.07 | 623.42 |
| Minimum | | −0.69 | −1.00 | 0.69 | 0.00 | 0.00 | 0.00 | 0.10 | 0.00 | 0.18 | −1.00 | −1.13 | 0.00 | −0.09 | 0.00 | −13.05 | −29.17 |
| Maximum | | 3.54 | 2.55 | 223.64 | 66.27 | 0.89 | 2.89 | 42.20 | 18.72 | 37,969 | 7.92 | 3.20 | 688.64 | 24.66 | 1.71 | 23,773 | 26,762 |
| Change in import penetration | 1 | | | | | | | | | | | | | | | | |
| Change in Hiscox/Kastner indicator | 2 | −0.25 | | | | | | | | | | | | | | | |
| Level of import penetration | 3 | 0.24 | −0.15 | | | | | | | | | | | | | | |
| Level of Hiscox indicator | 4 | −0.10 | 0.10 | −0.55 | | | | | | | | | | | | | |
| Political constraints | 5 | −0.10 | −0.12 | 0.23 | −0.32 | | | | | | | | | | | | |
| Log checks | 6 | −0.03 | −0.04 | 0.13 | −0.16 | 0.67 | | | | | | | | | | | |
| Unemployment rate | 7 | −0.08 | 0.17 | −0.14 | −0.13 | 0.04 | 0.11 | | | | | | | | | | |
| Political constraints × unemployment rate | 8 | −0.10 | −0.06 | 0.03 | −0.14 | 0.83 | 0.62 | 0.44 | | | | | | | | | |
| Real effective exchange rate index/1,000 | 9 | −0.23 | 0.35 | −0.28 | 0.24 | −0.25 | −0.31 | −0.10 | −0.23 | | | | | | | | |
| Change in real effective exchange rate index | 10 | −0.40 | −0.08 | 0.07 | −0.14 | 0.07 | 0.02 | 0.09 | 0.09 | 0.03 | | | | | | | |
| Change in terms of trade/GDP | 11 | −0.11 | −0.02 | −0.03 | −0.31 | −0.11 | −0.07 | −0.04 | −0.21 | 0.06 | −0.12 | | | | | | |
| Gross private capital formation/GDP | 12 | −0.13 | 0.13 | 0.10 | −0.36 | 0.16 | 0.15 | 0.16 | 0.13 | −0.10 | 0.08 | 0.10 | | | | | |
| Gross international reserves/imports | 13 | −0.09 | 0.02 | −0.43 | 0.07 | 0.24 | 0.15 | 0.10 | 0.32 | 0.03 | −0.06 | −0.03 | 0.22 | | | | |
| Gross international reserves/GDP | 14 | −0.05 | −0.13 | 0.24 | −0.35 | 0.43 | 0.24 | 0.03 | 0.35 | −0.16 | 0.07 | −0.01 | 0.38 | 0.72 | | | |
| Inflation (CPI) | 15 | 0.63 | −0.09 | 0.36 | −0.18 | −0.13 | −0.02 | 0.04 | −0.08 | −0.33 | 0.17 | −0.26 | −0.06 | −0.16 | −0.01 | | |
| Inflation (GDP deflator) | 16 | 0.76 | −0.08 | 0.35 | −0.18 | −0.14 | −0.02 | 0.02 | −0.10 | −0.31 | −0.02 | −0.22 | −0.06 | −0.16 | −0.04 | 0.96 | |
| Log inflation (CPI) | 17 | 0.47 | −0.03 | 0.34 | −0.23 | −0.08 | 0.05 | 0.10 | −0.01 | −0.41 | 0.27 | −0.28 | 0.03 | −0.12 | 0.04 | 0.94 | 0.89 |
| Log inflation (GDP deflator) | 18 | 0.49 | −0.02 | 0.35 | −0.23 | −0.09 | 0.04 | 0.10 | −0.01 | −0.41 | 0.22 | −0.27 | 0.03 | −0.12 | 0.02 | 0.93 | 0.90 |
| Inflation indicator (≥ 33% < 100%) | 19 | −0.07 | 0.05 | −0.02 | −0.14 | 0.30 | 0.32 | 0.10 | 0.34 | −0.33 | −0.09 | −0.10 | 0.26 | 0.12 | 0.08 | −0.06 | −0.06 |
| Inflation indicator (≥ 100% < 1,000%) | 20 | −0.02 | −0.03 | −0.11 | −0.09 | 0.04 | 0.12 | 0.02 | 0.05 | −0.16 | 0.03 | 0.13 | 0.06 | 0.09 | 0.01 | −0.01 | −0.01 |
| Inflation indicator (≥ 1,000%) | 21 | 0.43 | −0.01 | 0.40 | −0.19 | −0.13 | −0.03 | 0.09 | −0.07 | −0.31 | 0.29 | −0.30 | −0.02 | −0.18 | 0.01 | 0.91 | 0.87 |
| Log real gross domestic product ($b) | 22 | −0.19 | −0.03 | −0.38 | 0.60 | −0.09 | −0.03 | −0.06 | −0.04 | 0.21 | −0.14 | −0.04 | −0.04 | 0.24 | 0.04 | −0.43 | −0.41 |
| Log real gross domestic product per capita ($) | 23 | −0.13 | −0.01 | 0.04 | −0.51 | 0.56 | 0.31 | 0.24 | 0.48 | −0.18 | −0.07 | 0.24 | 0.44 | 0.50 | 0.64 | −0.28 | −0.27 |
| Gross foreign direct investment/GDP | 24 | −0.06 | −0.17 | 0.45 | −0.31 | 0.34 | 0.23 | −0.10 | 0.15 | −0.18 | −0.04 | 0.23 | 0.27 | −0.04 | 0.34 | −0.17 | −0.16 |
| Net foreign direct investment/GDP | 25 | −0.06 | −0.13 | 0.50 | −0.29 | 0.37 | 0.26 | −0.09 | 0.17 | −0.14 | −0.01 | 0.23 | 0.19 | −0.08 | 0.31 | −0.15 | −0.15 |
| Portfolio investment/GDP | 26 | −0.04 | −0.03 | −0.08 | 0.04 | 0.14 | 0.17 | 0.05 | 0.18 | −0.09 | −0.02 | −0.14 | 0.60 | 0.27 | 0.23 | −0.02 | −0.02 |
| Government budget balance/GDP | 27 | −0.31 | 0.08 | −0.16 | −0.13 | 0.17 | 0.08 | 0.14 | 0.20 | −0.01 | −0.28 | 0.25 | 0.18 | 0.30 | 0.20 | −0.64 | −0.53 |
| Debt service/GDP | 28 | −0.10 | 0.11 | 0.27 | −0.33 | 0.21 | 0.00 | 0.28 | 0.21 | −0.08 | 0.16 | 0.05 | 0.38 | −0.11 | 0.17 | −0.07 | 0.00 |
| Debt service/exports | 29 | −0.09 | 0.24 | −0.17 | −0.09 | −0.03 | −0.09 | 0.36 | 0.07 | 0.10 | 0.16 | −0.01 | 0.23 | −0.02 | −0.07 | −0.07 | 0.00 |
| Stable democracy—Polity (0, 1) | 30 | −0.06 | 0.02 | −0.24 | −0.03 | 0.63 | 0.46 | 0.20 | 0.66 | −0.09 | −0.03 | −0.21 | 0.03 | 0.23 | 0.05 | −0.13 | −0.13 |
| Stable democracy—Freedom House (0, 1) | 31 | −0.08 | 0.01 | −0.22 | −0.21 | 0.66 | 0.60 | 0.16 | 0.64 | −0.15 | −0.03 | 0.03 | 0.13 | 0.30 | 0.15 | −0.14 | −0.14 |

| Variable | # | 17 | 18 | 19 | 20 | 21 | 22 | 23 | 24 | 25 | 26 | 27 | 28 | 29 | 30 | 31 |
|---|---|---|---|---|---|---|---|---|---|---|---|---|---|---|---|---|
| N | | 3,843 | 4,533 | 5,247 | 5,247 | 5,247 | 4,465 | 4,465 | 2,826 | 3,336 | 2,654 | 2,572 | 2,643 | 2,308 | 5,247 | 5,247 |
| Mean | | 4.78 | 4.78 | 0.07 | 0.03 | 0.01 | 23.36 | 7.44 | 2.41 | 1.42 | 0.00 | −3.68 | 5.27 | 18.78 | 0.32 | 0.23 |
| Standard deviation | | 0.38 | 0.41 | 0.25 | 0.17 | 0.09 | 2.16 | 1.60 | 3.86 | 2.88 | 0.03 | 6.12 | 5.30 | 14.73 | 0.47 | 0.42 |
| Minimum | | 4.48 | 4.26 | 0.00 | 0.00 | 0.00 | 18.54 | 4.34 | 0.00 | −25.78 | −0.30 | −64.49 | 0.00 | 0.00 | 0.00 | 0.00 |
| Maximum | | 10.08 | 10.20 | 1.00 | 1.00 | 1.00 | 29.79 | 10.87 | 56.01 | 39.86 | 0.45 | 58.71 | 107.45 | 180.85 | 1.00 | 1.00 |
| Change in import penetration | 1 | | | | | | | | | | | | | | | |
| Change in Hiscox/Kastner indicator | 2 | | | | | | | | | | | | | | | |
| Level of import penetration | 3 | | | | | | | | | | | | | | | |
| Level of Hiscox indicator | 4 | | | | | | | | | | | | | | | |
| Political constraints | 5 | | | | | | | | | | | | | | | |
| Log checks | 6 | | | | | | | | | | | | | | | |
| Unemployment rate | 7 | | | | | | | | | | | | | | | |
| Political constraints × unemployment rate | 8 | | | | | | | | | | | | | | | |
| Real effective exchange rate index/1,000 | 9 | | | | | | | | | | | | | | | |
| Change in real effective exchange rate index | 10 | | | | | | | | | | | | | | | |
| Change in terms of trade/GDP | 11 | | | | | | | | | | | | | | | |
| Gross private capital formation/GDP | 12 | | | | | | | | | | | | | | | |
| Gross international reserves/imports | 13 | | | | | | | | | | | | | | | |
| Gross international reserves/GDP | 14 | | | | | | | | | | | | | | | |
| Inflation (CPI) | 15 | | | | | | | | | | | | | | | |
| Inflation (GDP deflator) | 16 | | | | | | | | | | | | | | | |
| Log inflation (CPI) | 17 | | | | | | | | | | | | | | | |
| Log inflation (GDP deflator) | 18 | 1.00 | | | | | | | | | | | | | | |
| Inflation indicator (≥ 33% < 100%) | 19 | 0.07 | 0.08 | | | | | | | | | | | | | |
| Inflation indicator (≥ 100% < 1,000%) | 20 | 0.07 | 0.07 | −0.05 | | | | | | | | | | | | |
| Inflation indicator (≥ 1,000%) | 21 | 0.97 | 0.97 | −0.08 | −0.02 | | | | | | | | | | | |
| Log real gross domestic product ($b) | 22 | −0.51 | −0.51 | −0.17 | −0.06 | −0.47 | | | | | | | | | | |
| Log real gross domestic product per capita ($) | 23 | −0.22 | −0.22 | 0.25 | 0.19 | −0.32 | −0.03 | | | | | | | | | |
| Gross foreign direct investment/GDP | 24 | −0.20 | −0.20 | −0.03 | −0.13 | −0.18 | 0.16 | 0.30 | | | | | | | | |
| Net foreign direct investment/GDP | 25 | −0.20 | −0.20 | −0.06 | −0.12 | −0.17 | 0.15 | 0.28 | 0.92 | | | | | | | |
| Portfolio investment/GDP | 26 | 0.00 | 0.00 | 0.24 | 0.01 | −0.03 | 0.09 | 0.13 | −0.01 | −0.04 | | | | | | |
| Government budget balance/GDP | 27 | −0.47 | −0.44 | 0.14 | 0.08 | −0.47 | 0.10 | 0.44 | 0.22 | 0.17 | 0.04 | | | | | |
| Debt service/GDP | 28 | 0.08 | 0.11 | 0.03 | 0.02 | 0.14 | −0.13 | 0.25 | 0.12 | 0.10 | 0.05 | 0.27 | | | | |
| Debt service/exports | 29 | 0.09 | 0.13 | −0.04 | 0.06 | 0.14 | −0.08 | 0.09 | −0.16 | −0.18 | −0.03 | 0.26 | 0.80 | | | |
| Stable democracy—Polity (0, 1) | 30 | −0.07 | −0.07 | 0.22 | 0.15 | −0.15 | −0.07 | 0.38 | 0.06 | 0.05 | 0.08 | 0.23 | −0.01 | 0.08 | | |
| Stable democracy—Freedom House (0, 1) | 31 | −0.06 | −0.06 | 0.37 | 0.14 | −0.16 | −0.13 | 0.46 | 0.09 | 0.07 | 0.12 | 0.23 | −0.01 | 0.05 | 0.73 | |

calculated assuming that the disturbances in the cross-sectional time series data are heteroscedastic across panels (i.e., grouped by country) and autocorrelated within panels (i.e., disturbances in a given country in a given year are correlated with disturbances in that country in the previous year) (Beck and Katz 1995). The procedure involves generating Prais–Winsten coefficient estimates conditional on the estimated autocorrelation parameter. The variance–covariance matrix of these coefficients is then estimated using feasible generalized least squares (FGLS). In the presence of incorrectly specified covariance structures, Prais–Winsten estimates improve the efficiency of both the coefficient estimates and their variance–covariance matrix when compared with FGLS (Beck and Katz 1995). We assume that the autocorrelation parameter (ρ) is constant across panels. Table 1 provides summary statistics and a correlation matrix for the variables included in our analysis.

The least-squares estimates are displayed in Table 2. In the first three columns, we use *POLCON* as a measure of veto points; in the last three columns, we use *CHECKS*. Within each set of findings, we give the results for the full sample, the subsample of stable democracies, and the subsample of other countries. When using *POLCON* as our measure of veto points and analyzing the entire sample, we find a negative relationship between the unemployment rate and the change in import penetration that is moderated by the extent of veto points. The coefficient estimate of *UNEMPL* is negative, the estimate of *UNEMPL* × *POLCON* is positive, and both are statistically significant (although the estimate of *UNEMPL* is only marginally so). As expected, the effects of these variables are both stronger and quantitatively larger when we focus on the subsample of stable democracies. They are much weaker when we focus on non-democratic states. We find a similar pattern when using *CHECKS* as our measure of veto points, although the coefficient

TABLE 2. Effects of Unemployment and Veto Points on Trade Policy, 1980–2000

| | (1) | (2) | (3) | (4) | (5) | (6) |
|---|---|---|---|---|---|---|
| *N* | 731 | 587 | 144 | 723 | 583 | 140 |
| # countries | 58 | 44 | 26 | 58 | 45 | 25 |
| $R^2$ | 0.72 | 0.39 | 0.90 | 0.72 | 0.38 | 0.90 |
| Sample | All | Stable democracies | Other countries | All | Stable democracies | Other countries |
| Source of democracy data | | Polity ≥ 6 | Polity < 6 | | Polity ≥ 6 | Polity < 6 |
| Level of import penetration | −0.007 | −0.009 | −0.013 | −0.007 | −0.010 | −0.012 |
| | 0.000 | 0.000 | 0.000 | 0.000 | 0.000 | 0.000 |
| Veto points | −0.136 | −0.273 | −0.055 | −0.048 | −0.061 | −0.015 |
| | 0.014 | 0.000 | 0.628 | 0.047 | 0.060 | 0.751 |
| Unemployment rate | −0.005 | −0.023 | −0.001 | −0.005 | −0.010 | 0.005 |
| | 0.087 | 0.001 | 0.749 | 0.160 | 0.086 | 0.433 |
| Veto points × unemployment rate | 0.012 | 0.034 | −0.013 | 0.006 | 0.009 | −0.008 |
| | 0.007 | 0.000 | 0.235 | 0.029 | 0.019 | 0.231 |
| Real effective exchange rate | 0.000 | −0.001 | 0.000 | 0.000 | −0.001 | 0.000 |
| | 0.000 | 0.164 | 0.000 | 0.000 | 0.067 | 0.000 |
| Change in real effective exchange rate | −0.031 | −0.102 | 0.027 | −0.034 | −0.104 | 0.018 |
| | 0.450 | 0.117 | 0.586 | 0.416 | 0.118 | 0.731 |
| Change in terms of trade | 0.721 | 0.626 | 1.247 | 0.662 | 0.636 | 1.500 |
| | 0.001 | 0.007 | 0.004 | 0.002 | 0.007 | 0.010 |
| Gross private capital formation/GDP | 0.001 | 0.001 | −0.002 | 0.001 | 0.001 | −0.002 |
| | 0.013 | 0.026 | 0.479 | 0.009 | 0.012 | 0.412 |
| Gross international reserves/imports | 0.014 | 0.012 | 0.026 | 0.012 | 0.010 | 0.027 |
| | 0.000 | 0.001 | 0.003 | 0.000 | 0.003 | 0.002 |

*Notes:* Entries are ordinary least-squares coefficient estimates above corresponding *p*-values, based on panel-corrected standard errors. Coefficient estimates for PTA, country, and year indicator variables are not reported to conserve space. As we included PTA, country, and year indicator variables, we do not include a constant term.

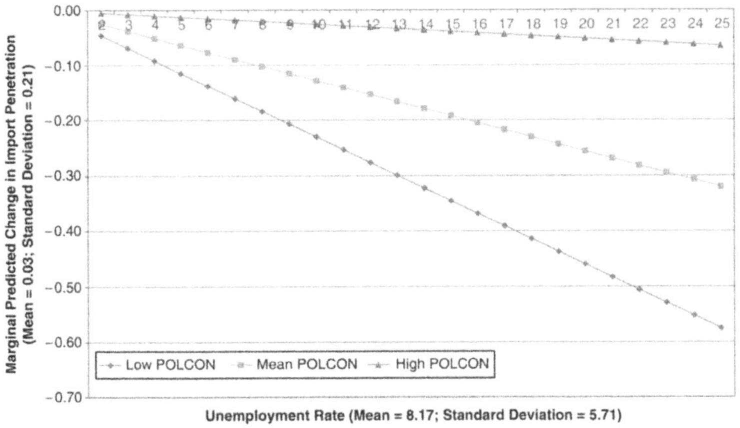


FIG. 1. How Political Constraints Moderate Societal Pressures for Protectionism

estimate for the unemployment rate is only marginally significant ($p = .086$) when stable democracies are analyzed. Further, regardless of the measure of veto points, in the hypothetical case where the unemployment rate equals zero, openness to trade is lower where more veto points exist, suggesting that extensive veto points moderate the ability of the unobserved free trade lobby to secure greater trade openness.

To address the substantive significance of these results, Figure 1 plots the predicted marginal effect of a given level of unemployment on the change in import penetration for a stable democracy having a given level of veto points, based on the results in the second column of Table 2 (i.e., the coefficient estimate of *UNEMPL* multiplied by the unemployment rate plus the coefficient estimate of *UNEMPL* × *POLCON* multiplied by the unemployment rate and the level of veto points). The figure does not show the predicted impact of unemployment on changes in openness for a specific or even a hypothetical county. In order to generate the total predicted change in trade policy, it is necessary to combine the partial effects displayed in Figure 1 with the other relevant variables for a specific country-year, including the omitted country, PTA, and time indicator variables, a task that we do not undertake here.

The downward-sloping schedules in Figure 1 show that, *ceteris paribus*, higher unemployment is associated with a reduction in import penetration and hence increased protectionism. Consistent with our argument, this effect becomes stronger as the number of veto points declines. For example, in a stable democracy where the number of veto points is approximately one standard deviation below the mean for stable democracies (0.3) and the unemployment rate is 10 percent, the predicted change in external trade linkages is 10 percentage points lower than if the unemployment rate was 2 percent (a predicted reduction of 13 percentage points instead of 3 percentage points) and 7 percentage points lower than if the unemployment rate was a more realistic 5 percent (a predicted reduction of 13 percentage points instead of 6 percentage points). This relationship, however, is influenced by the number of veto points. For example, if political constraints are held at approximately their mean level for stable democracies (0.6), the impact of having an unemployment rate of 10 percent instead of 2 (5) percent falls from a decline of 10 (7) percentage points to a decline of 2.1 (1.3) percentage points.

As expected, the estimate for the initial level of import penetration is large and negative, indicating that relatively open countries are less likely to expand their external trade linkages than countries that are relatively closed. In addition, there is evidence that preferential trade agreements are positively associated with changes in import penetration (although we do not present these parameter estimates to conserve space). Increases in the terms of trade, the availability of local capital, and the stock of reserves are each associated with rising import penetration. So, too, is a higher real exchange rate, although changes in this rate have little effect on openness. Finally, the year-specific and country-specific indicator variables are jointly significant. Note that the use of these fixed effects is a less restrictive means of capturing the impact of a time trend, national size, coastline, or distance from other countries, variables that, if entered independently, would impose linear or other functional restrictions on each of the effects.

## Robustness Checks

Having generated some initial estimates of the model, it is important to assess the robustness of these results to alternate measures of the key variables, alternate approaches to modeling time series cross-section error structures, the use of changes in unemployment instead of levels, and potentially omitted independent variables. To conserve on space, the following tests rely on Henisz's measure of veto points, although it should be noted that the results rarely change much when Beck et al.'s measure is used instead.

First, we analyze a different measure of trade policy that was constructed by Hiscox and Kastner (2002). This measure involves using estimates of fixed country-year effects in a gravity model of trade flows to assess each state's trade policy in a given year.[9] In Table 3, we replicate our initial results after replacing our original dependent variable with Hiscox and Kastner's measure. In interpreting these results, it is important to recognize that higher values of their measure indicate greater protectionism, whereas larger increases in import penetration indicate greater liberalization. As such, we expect the signs of the coefficient estimates in our model to be reversed when focusing on Hiscox and Kastner's measure, an expectation that is borne out by the results in Table 3. Indeed, the effects of unemployment and veto points in all countries and in stable democracies do not depend in any significant way on which measure of trade policy we analyze, even though there is a substantial reduction in the sample size (particularly among non-democracies) when Hiscox and Kastner's measure is used.[10]

Second, we assess whether our results depend on how stable democracies are defined and measured. Recall that we have coded a country as democratic if the value of *REGIME*—the 21-point Polity index that ranges from −10 to 10—for this country is 6 or higher for the past 5 consecutive years. To begin, we redefine stable democracies as those country-years where this index is greater than or equal to 7 for the past 5 consecutive years. These results, which are reported in Table 4 (models 1 and 2), are qualitatively similar to the base specifications in Table 2 (models 2 and 3). Next, we redefine stable democracies using the average of the Freedom House (2005) score for political rights and civil liberties. Following Freedom House's procedures, we code each state for which this average is less than 3 as

[9] More specifically, they regressed the ratio of annual imports by country *i* from country *j* to *i*'s annual GDP on *j*'s annual GDP, *j*'s annual per capita GDP, the geographical distance between *i* and *j*, the yearly difference in *i*'s and *j*'s endowments of labor and capital, and fixed country-year effects. All of the continuous variables in the model are expressed in logarithmic form.

[10] Our results are also unchanged when we replace the percentage change in import penetration with the absolute change in import penetration or with the percentage or absolute change in overall trade openness (i.e., the sum of a country's imports and exports divided by its gross domestic product).

Table 3. Effects of Unemployment and Veto Points on the Hiscox and Kastner Measure of Trade Policy, 1980–2000

| | *(1)* | *(2)* | *(3)* |
|---|---|---|---|
| *N* | 375 | 299 | 76 |
| # countries | 38 | 30 | 11 |
| $R^2$ | 0.37 | 0.37 | 0.78 |
| Sample | All | Stable democracies | Other countries |
| Source of democracy data | | Polity $\geq 6$ | Polity < 6 |
| Level of Hiscox and Kastner Residual | −0.023 | −0.027 | −0.018 |
| | 0.000 | 0.000 | 0.000 |
| Veto points | 0.186 | 0.769 | 0.165 |
| | 0.099 | 0.025 | 0.028 |
| Unemployment rate | 0.008 | 0.033 | 0.005 |
| | 0.010 | 0.106 | 0.014 |
| Veto points × unemployment rate | −0.038 | −0.076 | −0.028 |
| | 0.005 | 0.016 | 0.015 |
| Real effective exchange rate | 0.000 | 0.001 | 0.000 |
| | 0.671 | 0.155 | 0.542 |
| Change in real effective exchange rate | −0.021 | −0.164 | 0.005 |
| | 0.349 | 0.086 | 0.728 |
| Change in terms of trade | −0.013 | −0.077 | −0.357 |
| | 0.960 | 0.839 | 0.259 |
| Gross private capital formation/GDP | 0.000 | 0.000 | −0.001 |
| | 0.878 | 0.876 | 0.727 |
| Gross international reserves/imports | −0.001 | 0.003 | −0.191 |
| | 0.725 | 0.592 | 0.234 |

*Notes:* Entries are ordinary least-squares coefficient estimates above corresponding *p*-values, based on panel-corrected standard errors. Coefficient estimates for PTA, country, and year indicator variables are not reported to conserve space. The value of the Hiscox and Kastner measure is inversely correlated with the degree of trade openness.

a "free" country or stable democracy (models 3 and 4). We also analyze the entire sample of countries and enter an indicator variable for stable democracies using both the original (6 and greater) and modified (7 and greater) Polity thresholds as well as the Freedom House threshold (less than 3). Doing so yields no substantive changes in the results of theoretical interest (see Table 4, models 5–7). These results suggest that democracy's effect on changes in import penetration is conditional on the structure of a nation's political institutions and societal pressures.

Third, to address the possibility that our earlier results are driven by the endogeneity of our independent variables, we undertake two additional tests. To begin, we conduct a variant of the Granger causality test designed for panel data (Marvell and Moody 1996) to assess whether unemployment is endogenous. This might be the case if rising trade openness leads to a reallocation of capital and labor from those sectors that are relatively uncompetitive in international markets to sectors that are more competitive and if it takes time for individuals who lose jobs in uncompetitive sectors to become reabsorbed into the workforce.[11] The results indicate that we can reject the null hypothesis that unemployment does not Granger cause changes in import penetration ($F[3,518] = 3.84$, $p = .01$; $\chi^2[3] = 13.58$, $p = .004$). However, we are unable to reject the null hypothesis that changes in import penetration do not Granger cause unemployment ($F[3,518] = 0.51$, $p = .68$; $\chi^2[3] = 1.80$, $p = .62$). Consequently, there is no evidence that unemployment is endogenous.

[11] We are grateful to an anonymous reviewer for raising this point.

TABLE 4. Effects of Unemployment and Veto Points on Trade Policy, 1980–2000 Using Alternate Measures of Democracy

| | *(1)* | *(2)* | *(3)* | *(4)* | *(5)* | *(6)* | *(7)* |
|---|---|---|---|---|---|---|---|
| *N* | 570 | 161 | 571 | 160 | 731 | 731 | 731 |
| # countries | 40 | 28 | 43 | 25 | 58 | 58 | 58 |
| $R^2$ | 0.37 | 0.88 | 0.36 | 0.88 | 0.72 | 0.72 | 0.72 |
| Sample | Stable democracies | Other countries | Stable democracies | Other countries | All | All | All |
| Definition of democracy | Polity $\geqslant 7$ | Polity $< 7$ | Freedom House $< 3$ | Freedom House $> 3$ | Polity $\geq 6$ | Polity $\geq 7$ | Freedom House |
| Level of import penetration | −0.010 | −0.010 | −0.008 | −0.009 | −0.007 | −0.007 | −0.007 |
| | 0.000 | 0.000 | 0.000 | 0.000 | 0.000 | 0.000 | 0.000 |
| Veto points | −0.320 | −0.151 | −0.280 | −0.057 | −0.143 | −0.138 | −0.121 |
| | 0.000 | 0.173 | 0.001 | 0.655 | 0.011 | 0.014 | 0.036 |
| Unemployment rate | −0.033 | −0.001 | −0.026 | −0.005 | −0.005 | −0.005 | −0.005 |
| | 0.001 | 0.797 | 0.008 | 0.153 | 0.082 | 0.087 | 0.083 |
| Veto points × unemployment rate | 0.045 | 0.005 | 0.039 | 0.007 | 0.012 | 0.012 | 0.012 |
| | 0.001 | 0.629 | 0.004 | 0.442 | 0.007 | 0.007 | 0.006 |
| Real effective exchange rate | −0.001 | 0.000 | 0.000 | 0.000 | 0.000 | 0.000 | 0.000 |
| | 0.218 | 0.000 | 0.766 | 0.000 | 0.000 | 0.000 | 0.000 |
| Change in real effective exchange rate | −0.119 | −0.005 | −0.134 | −0.001 | −0.029 | −0.031 | −0.032 |
| | 0.079 | 0.919 | 0.034 | 0.984 | 0.468 | 0.452 | 0.439 |
| Change in terms of trade | 0.620 | 0.933 | 0.525 | 1.349 | 0.702 | 0.715 | 0.733 |
| | 0.009 | 0.025 | 0.029 | 0.000 | 0.001 | 0.001 | 0.001 |
| Gross private capital formation/GDP | 0.001 | 0.003 | 0.001 | −0.001 | 0.001 | 0.001 | 0.001 |
| | 0.034 | 0.287 | 0.015 | 0.810 | 0.015 | 0.013 | 0.013 |
| Gross international reserves/imports | 0.012 | 0.027 | 0.010 | 0.026 | 0.013 | 0.014 | 0.014 |
| | 0.001 | 0.002 | 0.005 | 0.001 | 0.000 | 0.000 | 0.000 |
| Stable democracy—(0, 1) | | | | | 0.033 | 0.010 | −0.026 |
| | | | | | 0.123 | 0.659 | 0.335 |

*Notes:* Entries are ordinary least-squares coefficient estimates above corresponding *p*-values, based on panel-corrected standard errors. Coefficient estimates for PTA, country, and year indicator variables are not reported to conserve space. Models (1), (2), and (5) define stable democracies using a threshold of 7 on the Polity scale. Models (5)–(7) include an indicator variable for stable democracies and analyze the full sample.

To further address the possibility of endogeneity in the model, we implement the dynamic panel estimator of Arrelano and Bond (1991). Caselli, Esquivel, and Lefort (1996) argue that OLS estimators, such as the ones we use in our primary specification, are biased and inconsistent for two reasons. First, the country-specific effects—including any omitted variables—are necessarily correlated with the other independent variables. Second, the control variables are likely to be endogenous to some extent. Ignoring this relationship will lead to upwardly biased coefficient estimates because the endogenous variable, in reality, appears on the right-hand side of the estimating equation. Furthermore, the estimators will be inconsistent as the regressors are correlated with the error term.

A common practice in the literature is to use lagged variables as an instrument for potentially endogenous regressors in a three-stage least-squares regression. While this procedure addresses the endogeneity problem discussed above, it neglects the bias and inconsistency generated by the omitted variable or fixed effect. Nor does it take into account any time-specific shocks or time trends.

By contrast, Casseli et al. (1996) demonstrate that a generalized method of moments (GMM) estimator is consistent if three identifying assumptions are satisfied: (1) there is no second-order serial correlation, (2) "stock" variables in the model are predetermined at time $t-2$, and (3) "flow" variables are not predetermined at time $t-2$ but are predetermined at time $t-1$. The process involves first differencing the data to remove random effects and using lagged levels and differences of the dependent and strictly exogenous independent variables to construct a large instrument matrix. To calculate the GMM estimator, we follow the two-step process suggested by Arellano and Bond (1991). A first-step estimate is generated using the assumption of independently and identically distributed error terms. Consistent but inefficient (assuming heteroscedasticity) estimates of the error terms are computed and then used in a second-stage regression in which the assumption of homoskedasticity imposed in the first stage is relaxed.

Using the GMM two-step estimator, the Sargan test statistic fails to reject the null hypothesis that the overidentifying restrictions are valid, and we similarly fail to reject the null hypothesis that there is no second-order autocorrelation. In the full sample, the Sargan test statistic is weakly significant, suggesting potential heteroscedasticity. But once we divide the sample into stable democracies and other countries, the test statistic is not significant, providing an additional reason to focus our analysis on these two subsamples. As shown in Table 5, the results for stable democracies are largely unchanged, indicating that these results are quite robust. In the pooled sample and the subsample of non-democratic countries, there are some noticeable differences in the results. Nonetheless, consistent with our argument, we continue to find that the influence of unemployment on trade policy grows larger as the number of veto points declines in stable democracies, but that these factors have relatively little bearing on commercial policy in other regimes.

Fourth, our use of country-specific fixed effects implies that the identification of the coefficients of *UNEMPL* and *UNEMPL* × *POLCON* is driven by within-country changes in unemployment. Nonetheless, it is still possible that the structural rate of unemployment across countries varies substantively in our sample across time, and that we should therefore focus on either the change in unemployment or on both the level of and the change in unemployment. Models (1) and (2) of Table 6 present these results. After replacing the level of unemployment with the change in unemployment, we continue to find support for our hypotheses, as the estimate of $\Delta$*UNEMPL* is negative, the coefficient estimate of $\Delta$*UNEMPL* × *POLCON* is positive, and both are statistically significant (see model 1). However, when we include both the level of unemployment and the change in unemployment, we find that the coefficient estimate of the former variable and its interaction with veto points remain significant, whereas that of the latter variable and its interaction with veto

TABLE 5. Effects of Unemployment and Veto Points on Trade Policy, 1980–2000, Using a Dynamic Panel Estimator

| | *(1)* | *(2)* | *(3)* |
|---|---|---|---|
| *N* | 661 | 550 | 111 |
| # countries | 53 | 42 | 21 |
| Log likelihood | 4,437.01 | 6,353.74 | 6,307.80 |
| Sample | All | Stable democracies | Other countries |
| Level of import penetration | −0.007 | −0.009 | −0.015 |
| | 0.001 | 0.000 | 0.015 |
| Veto points | −0.189 | −0.331 | −0.021 |
| | 0.082 | 0.000 | 0.912 |
| Unemployment rate | −0.005 | −0.034 | 0.001 |
| | 0.318 | 0.000 | 0.875 |
| Veto points × unemployment rate | 0.012 | 0.048 | −0.033 |
| | 0.093 | 0.000 | 0.078 |
| Real effective exchange rate | 0.000 | −0.001 | 0.000 |
| | 0.000 | 0.244 | 0.000 |
| Change in real effective exchange rate | −0.025 | −0.153 | 0.056 |
| | 0.765 | 0.011 | 0.490 |
| Change in terms of trade | 0.798 | 0.648 | 1.047 |
| | 0.004 | 0.000 | 0.031 |
| Gross private capital formation/GDP | 0.001 | 0.001 | 0.005 |
| | 0.141 | 0.125 | 0.806 |
| Gross international reserves/imports | 0.013 | 0.012 | 0.026 |
| | 0.008 | 0.008 | 0.031 |
| Sargan test of over-identifying restrictions | $p = .072$ | $p = .916$ | $p = .999$ |
| H0: no 2nd order autocorrelation | $p = .607$ | $p = .153$ | $p = .455$ |

*Notes*: Entries are ordinary least-squares coefficient estimates above corresponding *p*-values, derived using Arellano and Bond's (1991) dynamic panel estimator. Coefficient estimates for PTA, country, and year indicator variables are not reported to conserve space.

points are not significant.[12] As such, in a specification like ours that includes country-specific fixed effects, the change in unemployment provides no additional explanatory power in predicting trade policy beyond that furnished by the level of unemployment.

Finally, we examine a range of macroeconomic variables and country characteristics suggested by the literature as potential determinants of openness to ensure that they do not account for the observed effects of unemployment and veto points on trade policy. First, we use an alternate normalization for international reserves, the ratio of these reserves to GDP instead of imports. Second, we analyze five different measures of inflation: (1) as derived from the consumer price index (CPI), (2) as derived from the GDP deflator, (3) the logarithm of the CPI-derived measure, (4) the logarithm of the GDP deflator-derived measure, and (5) indicator variables for inflation levels in excess of 33 and 100 percent, respectively. High levels of inflation could signal an impending financial crisis, stimulating commercial reform (Krueger 1993; Rodrik 1996). Third, we analyze real GDP. Economically large states may have the ability to impose an optimal tariff and they are likely to produce

[12] We also explored the possibility that the effect of the level of unemployment on changes in import penetration could be nonlinear and found some evidence in support of this hypothesis. The magnitude of the change in the predicted value of the dependent variable generated by this nonlinearity, however, is relatively small. For example, at an unemployment rate of 5 percent for political constraint scores of 0.3 and 0.6, the predicted changes in import penetration using the linear specification are −6.4 and −1.3 percent, respectively. Using the nonlinear specification, the corresponding figures are −8.7 and −3.2 percent. Increasing the unemployment rate to 15 percent yields predicted changes in import penetration of −19.2 and −3.9 percent in the linear specification, and −22.1 and −4.9 percent in the nonlinear specification.

TABLE 6. Effects of Unemployment and Veto Points on Trade Policy, 1980–2000, Controlling for Potentially Omitted Variables

| | (1) | (2) | (3) | (4) | (5) | (6) | (7) | (8) | (9) | (10) | (11) | (12) | (13) | (14) | (15) | (16) | (17) |
|---|---|---|---|---|---|---|---|---|---|---|---|---|---|---|---|---|---|
| *N* | 558 | 558 | 587 | 585 | 587 | 585 | 587 | 587 | 587 | 587 | 581 | 557 | 581 | 557 | 538 | 555 | 549 |
| # countries | 43 | 43 | 44 | 44 | 44 | 44 | 44 | 44 | 44 | 44 | 44 | 43 | 44 | 43 | 41 | 43 | 42 |
| $R^2$ | 0.40 | 0.41 | 0.37 | 0.39 | 0.39 | 0.39 | 0.39 | 0.39 | 0.39 | 0.39 | 0.39 | 0.39 | 0.39 | 0.39 | 0.39 | 0.40 | 0.40 |
| Level of | −0.010 | −0.010 | −0.010 | −0.009 | −0.009 | −0.009 | −0.009 | −0.010 | −0.010 | −0.010 | −0.010 | −0.011 | −0.010 | −0.011 | −0.009 | −0.009 | −0.010 |
| import penetration | 0.000 | 0.000 | 0.000 | 0.000 | 0.000 | 0.000 | 0.000 | 0.000 | 0.000 | 0.000 | 0.000 | 0.000 | 0.000 | 0.000 | 0.000 | 0.000 | 0.000 |
| Veto points | −0.081 | −0.275 | −0.258 | −0.274 | −0.261 | −0.274 | −0.254 | −0.265 | −0.246 | −0.249 | −0.245 | −0.304 | −0.244 | −0.306 | −0.251 | −0.293 | −0.268 |
| | 0.124 | 0.000 | 0.000 | 0.001 | 0.001 | 0.000 | 0.001 | 0.000 | 0.001 | 0.001 | 0.001 | 0.000 | 0.001 | 0.000 | 0.001 | 0.000 | 0.000 |
| Unemployment rate | | −0.213 | −0.022 | −0.022 | −0.021 | −0.022 | −0.021 | −0.022 | −0.022 | −0.022 | −0.021 | −0.027 | −0.021 | −0.027 | −0.024 | −0.021 | −0.023 |
| | | 0.005 | 0.001 | 0.002 | 0.005 | 0.002 | 0.004 | 0.002 | 0.002 | 0.001 | 0.002 | 0.000 | 0.002 | 0.000 | 0.001 | 0.003 | 0.001 |
| Veto points | | 0.032 | 0.033 | 0.033 | 0.033 | 0.034 | 0.032 | 0.034 | 0.032 | 0.031 | 0.032 | 0.040 | 0.032 | 0.040 | 0.037 | 0.033 | 0.034 |
| × unemployment rate | | 0.002 | 0.000 | 0.001 | 0.002 | 0.001 | 0.001 | 0.001 | 0.001 | 0.002 | 0.001 | 0.000 | 0.001 | 0.000 | 0.000 | 0.001 | 0.000 |
| Real effective | −0.001 | −0.001 | −0.001 | −0.001 | −0.001 | −0.001 | −0.001 | −0.001 | −0.001 | −0.001 | −0.001 | −0.001 | −0.001 | −0.001 | −0.001 | −0.001 | −0.001 |
| exchange rate | 0.063 | 0.135 | 0.161 | 0.169 | 0.187 | 0.170 | 0.231 | 0.237 | 0.105 | 0.179 | 0.099 | 0.184 | 0.101 | 0.176 | 0.072 | 0.165 | 0.100 |
| Change in real effective | −0.126 | −0.132 | −0.103 | −0.099 | −0.106 | −0.099 | −0.108 | −0.099 | −0.088 | −0.096 | −0.091 | −0.119 | −0.092 | −0.117 | −0.088 | −0.107 | −0.088 |
| exchange rate | 0.068 | 0.058 | 0.124 | 0.134 | 0.109 | 0.134 | 0.103 | 0.130 | 0.190 | 0.190 | 0.179 | 0.070 | 0.176 | 0.070 | 0.186 | 0.067 | 0.215 |
| Change in terms of trade | 0.729 | 0.762 | 0.653 | 0.624 | 0.624 | 0.624 | 0.622 | 0.629 | 0.684 | 0.649 | 0.697 | 0.755 | 0.712 | 0.733 | 0.700 | 0.702 | 0.628 |
| | 0.003 | 0.001 | 0.006 | 0.008 | 0.008 | 0.008 | 0.008 | 0.007 | 0.005 | 0.010 | 0.005 | 0.003 | 0.005 | 0.005 | 0.005 | 0.002 | 0.008 |
| Gross private | 0.001 | 0.001 | 0.001 | 0.001 | 0.001 | 0.001 | 0.001 | 0.001 | 0.001 | 0.001 | 0.001 | 0.001 | 0.001 | 0.001 | 0.001 | 0.001 | 0.001 |
| capital formation/GDP | 0.060 | 0.063 | 0.030 | 0.023 | 0.027 | 0.023 | 0.029 | 0.034 | 0.043 | 0.025 | 0.099 | 0.007 | 0.106 | 0.004 | 0.090 | 0.009 | 0.011 |
| Gross international | 0.013 | 0.014 | | 0.012 | 0.012 | 0.012 | 0.012 | 0.012 | 0.012 | 0.012 | 0.012 | 0.012 | 0.012 | 0.012 | 0.012 | 0.009 | 0.012 |
| reserves/imports | 0.001 | 0.000 | | 0.001 | 0.001 | 0.001 | 0.001 | 0.001 | 0.001 | 0.001 | 0.001 | 0.001 | 0.002 | 0.001 | 0.001 | 0.011 | 0.001 |
| Rotated variables | −0.037 | −0.018 | 0.200 | 0.000 | 0.000 | 0.002 | 0.025 | 0.029 | 0.000 | 0.000 | 0.000 | 0.000 | 0.001 | −0.003 | 0.000 | −0.002 | −0.050 |
| (see notes) | 0.025 | 0.274 | 0.022 | 0.967 | 0.739 | 0.960 | 0.461 | 0.282 | 0.384 | 0.157 | 0.966 | 0.407 | 0.768 | 0.444 | 0.685 | 0.867 | 0.078 |
| | 0.046 | 0.019 | | | | | | 0.038 | | | | 0.090 | | 0.080 | | 0.001 | −0.185 |
| | 0.041 | 0.402 | | | | | | 0.331 | | | | 0.623 | | 0.669 | | 0.961 | 0.366 |
| | | | | | | | | | | | | | | | | | 0.002 |
| | | | | | | | | | | | | | | | | | 0.938 |

*Notes*: Entries are ordinary least-squares coefficient estimates above corresponding *p*-values, based on panel-corrected standard errors. Coefficient estimates for PTA, country, and year indicator variables are not reported to conserve space. In model number (1), we use the change in unemployment instead of the level of unemployment. In model numbers (2)–(17), we rotate in the following variables in the noted model number: (2) change in unemployment and its interaction with veto points; (3) gross international reserves/GDP (4) inflation, CPI; (5) inflation, GDP; (6) log inflation, CPI; (7) log inflation, GDP; (8) inflation indicator variables; (9) real GDP; (10) real per capita GDP; (11) gross FDI inflows; (12) gross FDI inflows and portfolio inflows; (13) net FDI inflows; (14) net FDI inflows and portfolio flows; (15) government budget balance; (16) chief executive is left or right; and (17) electoral system is single member, open list proportional representation, or close list proportional representation.

domestic alternatives to many imported goods, thereby impeding trade liberalization. Fourth, we analyze real per capita GDP. Heightened economic development could enhance liberalization as a country increasingly trades in differentiated industrial products.[13] Next, we address four measures of inward capital flows: (1) gross foreign direct investment (FDI), (2) gross FDI and portfolio investment, (3) net FDI, and (4) net FDI and portfolio investment. We also analyze the government budget balance. These are additional measures of financial stability that should promote trade liberalization. Finally, we consider the ideology of a country's chief executive and its type of electoral system, factors that some recent research has linked to trade policy (Milner and Judkins 2004).[14]

Models (3)–(17) of Table 6 report the results from these supplementary analyses for the subsample of stable democracies. The findings indicate that, with the exception of the alternate measure of gross international reserves, none of these variables is statistically significant. Nor does their introduction into the primary specification substantively alter the empirical support for our hypotheses. Taken as a whole, then, the tests described in this section offer considerable evidence that our results are quite robust.

## Conclusions

The remarkable expansion of global trade since World War II has stimulated a large and important literature, much of which stresses the effects of domestic politics on trade policy. This literature, however, has miscast certain aspects of the domestic determinants of trade policy. Whereas interest groups and political institutions are usually viewed as having independent and competing influences, these factors actually have an interactive effect on trade policy. Deteriorating macroeconomic conditions give rise to societal demands for protectionism. But the extent to which these demands are met and barriers to trade are put in place depends on the domestic institutions through which interest group pressures are filtered.

Various studies have raised the possibility that the interaction between societal demands and institutions is central to shaping trade policy, but remarkably little empirical research has directly confronted this possibility (Mansfield and Busch 1995; Garrett and Lange 1996; Gilligan 1997; Milner 1997; Grossman and Helpman 2002). Our findings indicate that the effects of unemployment depend heavily on the number of veto points that constrain decision makers and whether a country is democratic or not. High unemployment leads to protectionist trade policies in stable democracies marked by few veto points. As expected, however, the magnitude of this relationship becomes attenuated as the number of veto points rises, making it more difficult to change the existing trade regime and increasing the heterogeneity of the points' interests. Equally, macroeconomic fluctuations have a much more pronounced influence on the trade regime in stable democracies than other countries, reflecting the need for democratic leaders to be more responsive to demands made by the general population than in other countries.

Our results also bear heavily on recent debates about the relationship between regime type and economic reform. Virtually all of the literature on this topic ignores the effects of institutional variations within both democracies and nondemocracies alike. Such variations, however, are crucial to explaining changes in trade policy, especially in democracies. Holding macroeconomic conditions constant, the trade regime changes less within democracies as the number of veto points increases. Furthermore, societal calls for protectionism precipitated by

[13] In the same vein, we also excluded members of the Organization for Economic Cooperation and Development (OECD) from the sample and reestimated the model. The results were virtually unchanged.

[14] Data on these variables are taken from Beck et al. (2001).

adverse macroeconomic conditions are increasingly likely to be met as the number of veto points declines. Equally, a thriving economy—marked by very low levels of unemployment—creates a substantial constituency for expanding commercial openness. Such an expansion is most likely to occur in countries with few veto points. Not only do these results indicate that regime type is just one of the institutional influences on trade policy, they also point to the importance of veto points, a factor that has been underemphasized in existing studies of trade policy.

Similarly, we find that within democracies, changes in import penetration are more likely to occur as the number of veto points declines. However, whether such changes lead to greater protection or liberalization hinges on the demands being issued by interest groups. When the economy is faltering, giving rise to calls for protection, a small number of veto points tends to promote greater closure; when the economy is flourishing, a small number of these points foster greater openness. Our results offer important qualifications to studies of foreign economic policy that make unconditional comparisons between either domestic political concentration and fragmentation or democracy and autocracy (Haggard 1990; Wade 1990; Haggard and Kaufman 1995). Just as the effects of societal forces depend on domestic institutions, the effects of institutions are contingent on societal forces. Our findings also suggest that whether spreading democracy throughout the world will promote prosperity and free trade—as many observers have argued—depends on institutional factors within democracies, global and local macroeconomic conditions, and the patterns of domestic interest group competition. A better understanding of these factors and how they operate is crucial to improving our understanding of the political economy of trade policy.

## References


Acemoglu, Daron, and James Robinson. (2005) *The Economic Origins of Dictatorship and Democracy: Economic and Political Origins*. New York: Cambridge University Press.

Arellano, Manuel, and Stephen Bond. (1991) Some Tests of Specification for Panel Data: Monte Carlo Evidence and an Application to Employment Equations. *Review of Economic Studies* 58: 277–298.

Baldwin, Robert. (1989) US Trade Policy: Recent Changes and Future U.S. Interests. *American Economic Review* 79:128–133.

Beck, Nathaniel, and Jonathan N. Katz. (1995) What to Do (and Not to Do) with Time-Series-Cross-Section Data in Comparative Politics. *American Political Science Review* 89:634–647.

Beck, Thorsten, George Clarke, Alberto Groff, Philip Keefer, and Patrick Walsh. (2001) New Tools and New Tests in Comparative Political Economy: The Database of Political Institutions. *World Bank Economic Review* 15:165–176.

Bergsten, C. Fred, and William R. Cline. (1983) "Trade Policy in the 1980s: An Overview." In *Trade Policy in the 1980s*, edited by William R. Cline. Washington: Institute for International Economics.

Bhagwati, Jagdish. (1991) *The World Trading System at Risk*. Princeton: Princeton University Press.

Bliss, Harry, and Bruce Russett. (1998) Democratic Trading Partners: The Liberal Connection, 1962–1989. *Journal of Politics* 60:1126–1147.

Bohara, Alok K., and William H. Kaempfer. (1991) A Test of Tariff Endogeneity in the United States. *American Economic Review* 81:952–960.

Bradford, Scott. (2003) *Protection and Unemployment*. Available from http://www.nottingham.ac.uk/economics/leverhulme/conferences/june_2003/Bradford.pdf

Brooker, Paul. (2000) *Non-Democratic Regimes: Theory, Government and Politics*. New York: Palgrave Macmillan.

Caselli, Francesco, Gerardo Esquivel, and Fernando Lefort. (1996) Reopening the Convergence Debate: A New Look at Cross-Country Growth Empirics. *Journal of Economic Growth* 1:363–390.

Cline, William R. (1989) Macroeconomic Influences on Trade Policy. *American Economic Review* 79:123–127.

Colton, Timothy. (2000) *Transitional Citizens: Voters and What Influences Them in the New Russia*. Cambridge, MA: Harvard University Press.

Corden, W. Max. (1993) "The Revival of Protectionism in Developed Countries." In *Protectionism and World Welfare*, edited by Dominick Salvatore. New York: Cambridge University Press.

Deardorff, Alan V., and Robert M. Stern. (1987) "Current Issues in Trade Policy: An Overview." In *U.S. Trade Policies in a Changing World Economy*, edited by Robert M. Stern. Cambridge, MA: MIT Press.

Destler, I. M. (1992) *American Trade Politics*. 2nd ed. Washington: Institute for International Economics.

Dornbusch, Rudiger, and Jeffrey A. Frankel. (1987) "Macroeconomics and Protection". In *U.S. Trade Policies in a Changing World Economy*, edited by Robert M. Stern. Cambridge, MA: MIT Press.

Edwards, Sebastian. (1993) Openness, Trade Liberalization, and Growth in Developing Countries. *Journal of Economic Literature* 31:1358–1393.

Franzese Jr., Robert J. (1999) *The Positive Political Economy of Public Debt: An Empirical Examination of the OECD Postwar Debt Experience*. Unpublished manuscript, Department of Political Science, University of Michigan.

Freedom House. (2005) *Freedom in the World*. Downloaded from http://www.freedomhouse.org/ratings/index.htm

Frieden, Jeffry A., and Ronald Rogowski. (1996) "The Impact of the International Economy on National Policies: An Overview." In *Internationalization and Domestic Politics*, edited by Robert O. Keohane and Helen V. Milner. New York: Cambridge University Press.

Frye, Timothy, and Edward D. Mansfield. (2003) Fragmenting Protection: The Political Economy of Trade Policy in the Post-Communist World. *British Journal of Political Science* 33:633–657.

Garrett, Geoffrey, and Peter Lange. (1996) "Internationalization, Institutions, and Political Change." In *Internationalization and Domestic Politics*, edited by Robert O. Keohane and Helen V. Milner. New York: Cambridge University Press.

Gardner, Grant W., and Kent P. Kimbrough. (1989) The Behavior of U.S. Tariff Rates. *American Economic Review* 79:211–218.

Gilligan, Michael J. (1997) Lobbying as a Private Good with Intra-Industry Trade. *International Studies Quarterly* 41:455–474.

Grossman, Gene M., and Elhanan Helpman. (2002) *Interest Groups and Trade Policy*. Princeton: Princeton University Press.

Haggard, Stephan. (1990) *Pathways from the Periphery: The Politics of Growth in the Newly Industrializing Countries*. Ithaca: Cornell University Press.

Haggard, Stephan, and Robert Kaufman. (1995) *The Political Economy of Democratic Transitions*. Princeton: Princeton University Press.

Hallerberg, Mark, and Scott Basinger. (1998) Internationalization and Changes in Tax Policy in OECD Countries: The Importance of Domestic Veto Players. *Comparative Political Studies* 31:321–352.

Henisz, Witold Jerzy. (2000) The Institutional Environment for Economic Growth. *Economics and Politics* 12:1–31.

Henisz, Witold Jerzy. (2004) Political Institutions and Policy Volatility. *Economics and Politics* 16:1–27.

Hiscox, Michael J., and Scott L. Kastner. (2002) *A General Measure of Trade Policy Orientations: Gravity-Model-Based Estimates for 82 Nations 1960–92*. Unpublished manuscript, Department of Government, Harvard University.

Hughes, Helen, and Jean Waelbroeck. (1981) Can Developing-Country Exports Keep Growing in the 1980s? *World Economy* 4:127–147.

Huntington, Samuel P. (1991) *The Third Wave: Democratization in the Late Twentieth Century*. Norman: University of Oklahoma Press.

Ikenberry, G. John, David A. Lake, and Michael Mastanduno. (1988) Introduction: Approaches to Explaining American Foreign Policy. *International Organization* 42:59–90.

Ingram, Paul, Jeffrey Robinson, and Marc Busch. (forthcoming) The Interstate Institutional Network: IGO Connectedness, Governance and Embeddedness in World Trade. *American Journal of Sociology*.

Jaggers, Keith, and Ted Robert Gurr. (1995) Tracking Democracy's Third Wave with the Polity III Data. *Journal of Peace Research* 32:469–482.

Kastner, Scott L., and Chad Rector. (2003) International Regimes, Domestic Veto Players, and Capital Controls Policy Stability. *International Studies Quarterly* 47:1–22.

Kinder, Donald R., and D. Roderick Kiewiet. (1981) Sociotropic Politics: The American Case. *British Journal of Political Science* 11:129–161.

Krueger, Anne O. (1993) *Political Economy of Policy Reform in the Developing Countries*. Cambridge, MA: MIT Press.

Leamer, Edward E. (1988) "Measures of Openness." In *Trade Policy Issues and Empirical Analysis*, edited by Robert E. Baldwin. Chicago: University of Chicago Press.

LEDERMAN, DANIEL. (2001) *The Political Economy of Protection: Theory and the Chilean Experience*. Washington: World Bank.

LEWIS-BECK, MICHAEL S. (1988) *Economics and Elections: The Major Western Democracies*. Ann Arbor: University of Michigan Press.

LOHMANN, SUSANNE, AND SHARYN O'HALLORAN. (1994) Divided Government and U.S. Trade Policy: Theory and Evidence. *International Organization* 48:595–632.

MACINTYRE, ANDREW. (2001) Institutions and Investors: The Politics of the Financial Crisis in Southeast Asia. *International Organization* 55:81–122.

MAGEE, STEPHEN P., WILLIAM A. BROCK, AND LESLIE YOUNG. (1989) *Black Hole Tariffs and Endogenous Policy Theory*. New York: Cambridge University Press.

MANSFIELD, EDWARD D., AND MARC L. BUSCH. (1995) The Political Economy of Nontariff Barriers: A Cross-National Analysis. *International Organization* 49:723–749.

MANSFIELD, EDWARD D., HELEN V. MILNER, AND JON PEVEHOUSE. (2005) *Vetoing Cooperation: The Impact of Veto Players on International Trade Agreements*. Paper presented at the Annual Meeting of the American Political Science Association, Washington, DC, September 1–4.

MANSFIELD, EDWARD D., HELEN V. MILNER, AND B. PETER ROSENDORFF. (2000) Free to Trade: Democracies, Autocracies, and International Trade. *American Political Science Review* 94:305–321.

MARSHALL, MONTY, AND KEITH JAGGERS. (2001) *Polity IV*. Integrated Network for Societal Conflict Research (INSCR) Program, Center for International Development and Conflict Management, University of Maryland.

MARVELL, THOMAS B., AND CARLISLE E. MOODY. (1996) Specification Problems, Police Levels, and Crime Rates. *Criminology* 34:600–645.

MILNER, HELEN V. (1997) *Interests, Institutions, and Information: Domestic Politics and International Relations*. Princeton: Princeton University Press.

MILNER, HELEN V., AND BENJAMIN JUDKINS. (2004) Partisanship, Trade Policy, and Globalization: Is There a Left-Right Divide on Trade Policy? *International Studies Quarterly* 48:95–119.

MILNER, HELEN V., WITH KEIKO KUBOTA. (2005) Why the Move to Free Trade? Democracy and Trade Liberalization in the Developing Countries. *International Organization* 59:107–143.

NOGUES, JULIO, AND SUNIL GULATI. (1994) Economic Policies and Performance under Alternative Trade Regimes: Latin America during the 1980s. *World Economy* 17:467–496.

NOWZAD, BAHRAM. (1978) *The Rise of Protectionism. Pamphlet Series*, Vol. 24. Washington: International Monetary Fund.

OLSON, MANCUR. (1983) "The Political Economy of Comparative Growth Rates." In *The Political Economy of Growth*, edited by Dennis Mueller. New Haven: Yale University Press.

O'ROURKE, KEVIN, AND JEFFREY G. WILLIAMSON. (1999) *Globalization and History: The Evolution of a Nineteenth-Century Atlantic Economy*. Cambridge, MA: MIT Press.

PRZEWORSKI, ADAM, MICHAEL E. ALVAREZ, JOSÉ CHEIBUB, AND FERNANDO LIMONGI. (2000) *Democracy and Development: Political Institutions and Well-Being in the World, 1950–1990*. Cambridge: Cambridge University Press.

RODRIK, DANI. (1996) Understanding Economic Policy Reform. *Journal of Economic Literature* 34:9–41.

SAEZ, SEBASTIAN, JUAN SALAZAR, AND RICARDO VICUÑA. (1995) Antecedentes y resultados de la estrategia comercial del Gobierno Aylwin. *Colección de Estudios CIEPLAN* 40:41–66.

SCHATTSCHNEIDER, ELMER E. (1935) *Politics, Pressures and the Tariff: A Study of Free Private Enterprise in Pressure Politics, as Shown in the 1929–1930 Revision of the Tariff*. New York: Prentice-Hall.

SCHUMPETER, JOSEPH. (1942) *Capitalism, Socialism and Democracy*. London: G. Allen & Unwin Ltd.

SHAPIRO, ROBERT Y., AND BENJAMIN I. PAGE. (1994) "Foreign Policy and Public Opinion." In *The New Politics of American Foreign Policy*, edited by David A. Deese. New York: St. Martin's Press.

TREISMAN, DANIEL. (2000) Decentralization and Inflation: Commitment, Collective Action or Continuity. *American Political Science Review* 94:837–857.

TSEBELIS, GEORGE. (1995) Decision-Making in Political Systems: Veto Players in Presidentialism, Parliamentarism, Multicameralism and Multipartyism. *British Journal of Political Science* 25:289–325.

TSEBELIS, GEORGE (2003) *Veto Players: How Political Institutions Work*. Princeton: Princeton University Press.

WADE, ROBERT. (1990) *Governing the Market: Economic Theory and the Role of the Government in East Asian Industrialization*. Princeton: Princeton University Press.

WALLERSTEIN, MICHAEL. (1987) Unemployment, Collective Bargaining, and the Demand for Protection. *American Journal of Political Science* 31:729–752.

WINTROBE, RONALD. (1998) *The Political Economy of Dictatorship*. New York: Cambridge University Press.

WISE, CAROL. (1989) "Democratization, Crisis, and the APRA's Modernization Project in Peru." In *Debt and Democracy in Latin America*, edited by Barbara Stallings and Robert Kaufman. Boulder: Westview.

# Support for Free Trade: Self-Interest, Sociotropic Politics, and Out-Group Anxiety

Edward D. Mansfield and Diana C. Mutz

**Abstract** Although it is widely acknowledged that an understanding of mass attitudes about trade is crucial to the political economy of foreign commerce, only a handful of studies have addressed this topic. These studies have focused largely on testing two models, both of which emphasize that trade preferences are shaped by how trade affects an individual's income. The factor endowments or Heckscher-Ohlin model posits that these preferences are affected primarily by a person's skills. The specific factors or Ricardo-Viner model posits that trade preferences depend on the industry in which a person works. We find little support for either of these models using two representative national surveys of Americans. The only potential exception involves the effects of education. Initial tests indicate that educational attainment and support for open trade are directly related, which is often interpreted as support for the Heckscher-Ohlin model. However, further analysis reveals that education's effects are less representative of skill than of individuals' anxieties about involvement with out-groups in their own country and beyond. Furthermore, we find strong evidence that trade attitudes are guided less by material self-interest than by perceptions of how the U.S. economy as a whole is affected by trade.

The politics of international trade has been a long-standing puzzle for social scientists. Among economists, there is widespread agreement that free trade is beneficial.[1] Open trade and cross-national market integration help to allocate factors of production efficiently and to promote the welfare of countries and the world as

Earlier versions of this article were presented at the 2006 annual meeting of the American Political Science Association, Philadelphia; seminars at the University of Chicago (Harris School), Emory University, Harvard University, and the University of Virginia; and a conference on Domestic Preferences and Foreign Economic Policy, held at Princeton University. We are grateful to Marc Busch, Jens Hainmueller, So Young Kim, Richard Valelly, the editors of *International Organization*, and two anonymous reviewers for helpful comments; to Rumi Morishima, Matthew Tubin, and Carmela Aquino for research assistance; and to the Christopher H. Browne Center for International Politics and the Institute for the Study of Citizens and Politics for financial assistance.

*Note from the editors:* Since one of the authors is an associate editor of this journal, the editors handled this article outside of the normal editorial management system and put in place special procedures to ensure rigorous, double-blind peer review.

1. Alston, Kearl, and Vaughan 1992.

*International Organization* 63, Summer 2009, pp. 425–57
© 2009 by The IO Foundation.
doi:10.1017/S0020818309090158

a whole. Historically, however, open trade has been the exception rather than the rule.

Studies of the political economy of trade often attribute variations in trade preferences to the distributional implications of overseas commerce. Despite the economic benefits that a given country would accrue from open trade, some individuals suffer economic harm as a result. If these individuals form a politically potent constituency, they may be able to pressure policymakers to increase trade barriers even if doing so is economically counterproductive for the country as a whole. If, on the other hand, the individuals who derive welfare gains from trade are particularly influential, then an open trade regime is likely to take hold. Recent research indicates that, in democratic countries, constituency opinion on trade plays a central role in influencing the policy positions of public officials.[2]

There are two principle ways of assessing the distributional consequences of trade. First, the factor endowments approach emphasizes that, in a given country, trade benefits those individuals who own factors of production that are in abundant supply relative to the remainder of the world, and harms owners of factors that are in scarce supply. In countries such as the United States, which has a skilled labor force, free trade benefits highly skilled workers and harms less skilled workers. Second, the specific factors approach predicts that an individual's attitudes toward trade will reflect characteristics of the industry in which he or she works. People employed in industries that depend on overseas markets should be more supportive of open trade than people working in industries that face considerable competition from imports.

A small but growing number of studies have evaluated the strength of these explanations for trade policy preferences. We extend this body of research using two representative national surveys of Americans and more comprehensive measures of industries and occupations than previous studies had available to them. In addition, we link the study of trade preferences to the more extensive body of theory and empirical research on how self-interest enters into the formation of domestic economic policy preferences.

Substantial research in other economic policy domains has demonstrated that self-interest rarely shapes the formation of policy opinions because people have a difficult time understanding the connection between personal economic well-being and government policy. By mounting the most thorough individual-level examination to date of the effects of industry and skill on individual trade preferences, we seek to determine whether trade is, indeed, one of those rare exceptions in which personal experiences are successfully politicized. Alternatively, if attitudes about trade are formed in a manner similar to attitudes about domestic economic domains such as unemployment, then trade policy preferences will be based on how people believe a policy affects the country collectively rather than on narrowly defined self-interest. Importantly, the analysis of aggregate-level data—the

2. See Fordham and McKeown 2003; and Kono 2008.

approach used by most previous studies of trade preferences—cannot differentiate between these two possibilities. Thus, uniquely, this study simultaneously examines both how personal economic self-interest and perceptions of the collective national interest influence trade preferences.

Our findings indicate that accounting for perceptions of how the U.S. economy is affected by trade is important to modeling trade preferences. Consistent with previous research on the impact of self-interest on policy attitudes, our data show little support for either the factor endowments or the specific factors model. By contrast, perceptions of how trade affects the country as a whole—what are often referred to as "sociotropic" perceptions—play a substantial role in shaping attitudes about foreign commerce, a role that is largely independent of self-interest. Indeed, these perceptions are among the most important influences on opinions about trade.

Finally, we further improve our understanding of mass trade preferences by incorporating into our model indicators of domestic ethnocentrism and foreign policy attitudes. There is little support for free trade among people who believe the United States should take an isolationist stance on international affairs more generally or those who feel that members of other ethnic and racial groups are less praiseworthy than their own racial or ethnic group. Although such views have no direct bearing on the economic benefits of trade, they are far more predictive of trade preferences than indicators of economic self-interest.

Taken as a whole, the results of this article cast doubt on the ability of standard political economy models to explain trade preferences. Furthermore, the fact that sociotropic perceptions and out-group anxiety are such powerful predictors of these preferences indicates that research on trade policy would benefit by developing psychologically based models that address how individuals process information about the economy, and how they form attitudes about people and places beyond their borders.

## The Origins of Trade Preferences

Much of the existing research on trade preferences has been guided by two models. The factor endowments, or Heckscher-Ohlin, model assumes that all factors of production within a country are mobile across sectors, that markets are perfectly competitive, and that there are constant returns to scale in production. Based on these assumptions, Stolper and Samuelson showed that, in a given country, open trade benefits owners of factors of production that are abundant, relative to the remainder of the world, and harms owners of scarce factors.[3] Consequently, in the United States—a country endowed with an abundance of highly skilled and well-educated labor relative to the rest of the world—free trade benefits highly skilled workers

3. Stolper and Samuelson 1941.

and damages less-skilled individuals.[4] Open trade increases the demand for skilled workers, since the United States has a comparative advantage in the production of goods that use this input intensively. As the demand for such workers rises, so do their wages. Conversely, heightened trade decreases the demand for low-skilled labor in the United States and depresses its wage rate since goods produced using such labor intensively can be produced more efficiently abroad.[5] The factor endowments approach therefore predicts that highly skilled workers in the United States should be protrade, whereas other workers should hold more protectionist views.

Empirical studies of trade policy attitudes have generated a fair amount of support for this theory. In a set of cross-national analyses, O'Rourke and Sinnott and Mayda and Rodrik find that mass opinion about trade corresponds closely to predictions stemming from the factor endowments approach.[6] Scheve and Slaughter provide some additional support for this approach, based on an analysis of public attitudes in the United States; and Balistreri concludes that this model helps to explain Canadian attitudes toward the Canadian–U.S. Free Trade Agreement.[7] Nonetheless, a number of recent studies have raised questions about the fit between trade preferences and the factor endowments model.[8] A key assumption in the Heckscher-Ohlin model is that factors of production can move quickly and easily from one sector to another. In the long run, this assumption is not difficult to justify. In the short run, however, it can be difficult for people (not to mention other factors of production) to change the sector in which they are employed.[9]

The specific factors, or Ricardo-Viner, model is an alternative framework that assumes that, at least in the short run, certain factors of production cannot be shifted across sectors. If workers cannot easily move from one sector to another, then they will base their trade preferences on how changes in trade policy are expected to affect the industry in which they are currently employed. This model suggests that individuals who work in export-oriented sectors of the economy will support open trade because they personally benefit from it, while those in import-competing sectors will be more protectionist. Equally, an individual employed in a nontraded sector of the economy should be more protrade than someone employed in an industry that faces substantial competition from foreign imports.

Few studies have tried to evaluate whether trade preferences correspond to the specific factors model, primarily due to a lack of data on individuals' industry of

4. Leamer 1984.

5. The human capital model makes similar predictions about the attitudes of highly skilled workers in countries with a highly skilled labor force. In this model, however, the reason highly skilled workers should support open trade is that they can more easily shift occupations and industries, and thus adapt successfully to economic change. See Gabel 1998; Baker 2003 and 2005; Kaltenthaler, Gelleny, and Ceccoli 2004; and Kocher and Minushkin 2006.

6. See O'Rourke and Sinnott 2002; and Mayda and Rodrik 2005.

7. See Balistreri 1997; and Scheve and Slaughter 2001.

8. See Baker 2003; and Hainmueller and Hiscox 2006.

9. The model may still prove useful if citizens use a relatively long time frame to evaluate the impact of trade policies. On this point, see Mayda and Rodrik 2005.

employment in most extant surveys. Mayda and Rodrik try to infer respondents' industry from occupational data; but this is an imperfect solution, with many individuals assigned to multiple overlapping sectors because of inadequate information.[10] Nonetheless, Mayda and Rodrik find evidence that is broadly consistent with the specific factors model. In a similarly motivated analysis, Scheve and Slaughter compare the factor endowments and specific factors models, using educational attainment and the average yearly earnings for the respondent's occupation as indicators of skill, and the comparative advantage or disadvantage of the respondent's industry of employment as specific factors indicators.[11] Their study provides evidence for the factor endowments model, but none supportive of the specific factors model.

Notably, the underlying premise in both models described above is that attitudes toward trade are largely a function of who is personally helped or hurt by trade policies. As Mayda and Rodrik note, "to the extent that individuals are motivated by material self-interest, these models provide important hints about an individual's likely attitudes toward trade depending upon his/her factor type or sector of employment."[12] Unfortunately, the explanatory value of these models has been quite limited to date, and even simple demographics often explain more about trade preferences than variables linked to either model.

Beyond these two dominant theoretical frameworks, existing studies have also produced a set of empirical findings that remain in need of a theoretical framework. For example, Mayda and Rodrik find that social status, relative incomes, and values play a more important role than variables highlighted by either economic model.[13] Upper-class people are more likely to be protrade as are those with higher relative incomes. In addition, older people appear to be more protectionist than younger generations.

In the same vein, although educational attainment tends to be highly correlated with support for trade, the appropriate interpretation of this relationship remains unclear.[14] If education is simply serving as a proxy for skill level, then this relationship can be interpreted as support for the factor endowments model. This, in fact, is how these results are typically viewed.

But there are many other plausible explanations for why education might relate to trade preferences. Well-educated people are different from their less-educated counterparts in numerous ways, including levels of tolerance for out-groups (such as foreigners), risk preferences, levels of dogmatism, and preferences for immediate versus delayed gratification. To the extent that trade preferences are driven by

10. Ibid.
11. Scheve and Slaughter 2001.
12. Mayda and Rodrik 2005, 1394.
13. Mayda and Rodrik 2005.
14. For studies that have found such a correlation, see Bauer, Pool, and Dexter 1963, chap. 6; Scheve and Slaughter 2001; O'Rourke and Sinnott 2002; Kaltenthaler, Gelleny, and Ceccoli 2004; and Mayda and Rodrik 2005.

characteristics such as ethnocentricism, out-group hostility, or isolationist foreign policy tendencies, education's influence may have little to do with economic self-interest.

Hainmueller and Hiscox argue that education represents something other than skill level.[15] They find that the effect of education on trade preferences is much the same for Americans who are not currently employed as for those who are working. Equally, there is no distinguishable difference in the effects of education between working individuals and retirees, a subset of nonworking individuals who are unlikely to re-enter the labor force. In their view, the fact that education's impact is not contingent on whether an individual is receiving wages for using his or her skills casts doubt on the factor endowments model. Rather than serving as a proxy for skill, they argue that education represents the effects of exposure to economic ideas among the college-educated. Because mainstream economists generally favor open trade, college-educated individuals will have more exposure to arguments about the economic benefits of foreign commerce than those with less formal education.

This claim is consistent with Hainmueller and Hiscox's findings that college-educated individuals have especially protrade attitudes, but these individuals are distinctive from their less educated counterparts in many other ways as well. As Nie, Junn, and Stehlik-Barry point out, education is a powerful predictor of many civic virtues.[16] Unfortunately, it is poorly understood why education is linked to these outcomes. Empirical research suggests that education affects political preferences in at least two ways: (1) through occupational prominence and position in social networks, and (2) through cognitive proficiency and analytical ability.[17] If education serves as a proxy for skill level, then it falls into the first of these categories. Under these circumstances, education influences trade preferences because of where schooling locates people in socioeconomic strata. But since education also contributes to tolerance of different cultures and countries, as well as a belief on the part of Americans that the United States should be more actively engaged in foreign affairs, it remains to be seen if exposure to arguments about the virtues of international trade is driving Hainmueller and Hiscox's results.[18]

Furthermore, the expected trade attitudes of retirees are far from clear. That education's impact on such attitudes is indistinguishable between workers and retirees could reflect a tendency for trade preferences to persist over the course of a lifetime, rather than changing suddenly at retirement. Thus, based on this analysis alone, it is difficult to determine whether skill level influences the formation of trade preferences.

The common finding that women are more protectionist than men, even after controlling for educational differences, also has been attributed to a college edu-

15. Hainmueller and Hiscox 2006.
16. Nie, Junn, and Stehlik-Barry 1996.
17. Ibid.
18. See Bauer, Pool, and Dexter 1963, chap. 6; Erikson and Tedin 2005; and Fordham 2008.

cation, in this case to differences in the kinds of courses taken by men and women. Burgoon and Hiscox, for example, maintain that college-educated men are more likely than college-educated women to be exposed to mainstream economic arguments about the gains from trade. They argue that the gender gap in trade policy attitudes stems from the fact that protrade ideas reach more men than women through their college coursework.[19]

More generally, Burgoon and Hiscox and Hainmueller and Hiscox make the important point that the kind of information to which citizens are exposed is likely to play a crucial role in shaping trade preferences.[20] To extend their argument beyond the educational environment, it is easy to see how if a person is a union member, they will be exposed to a different kind of information about the impact of free trade policies than a nonunion worker. As new concerns about globalization arise, organizations regularly communicate with their members to encourage certain policy preferences and to inform them about how they think people will be affected by particular policies. Likewise, members of the retiree organization AARP may receive regular information about the perils of financial insecurity in today's global economy, thus cultivating the impression of risk and volatility that could drive perceptions of the need for protectionist policies. Particularly in the current highly specialized media environment, different people receive different information.[21]

Whether this information variability is an outgrowth of the college courses they took, of newsletters, or of the daily newspaper, it helps shape perceptions that may or may not have a basis in the individual's personal economic reality. We refer to this collection of models emphasizing information differences as a source of variance in trade preferences as information-based models.

Intuitively, information of the kind one might be exposed to in college or in a daily newspaper would seem to pale in comparison to the hard reality of economic risk faced by a worker in a given occupation or industry. Surely threats to one's livelihood would seem to be a more potent influence on policy preferences. Surprisingly, the literature on economic policy preferences suggests that self-interest is unlikely to play an influential role in shaping attitudes toward free trade.[22] A large body of research demonstrates that self-interest enters into the formation of policy opinions only under very special and rare circumstances.[23]

Because of the counterintuitive nature of this claim, social scientists have searched extensively for instances in which economic self-interest played a significant role in the formation of policy preferences, but with little success. Evidence suggests that the economic impact of policies on individual families has little, if any, influence on their policy preferences.[24] The lack of self-interested policy pref-

19. Burgoon and Hiscox 2004.
20. See Burgoon and Hiscox 2004; and Hainmueller and Hiscox 2006.
21. Prior 2007.
22. For a review of this literature, see Kiewiet 1983.
23. Sears and Funk 1990.
24. Ibid.

erences occurs not out of a mass tendency toward altruism, but rather because citizens have a difficult time linking their personal economic situations to public policies. Furthermore, this pattern is not restricted to the economic realm. The list of failed attempts to observe the influence of self-interest in the formation of policy preferences is by now quite lengthy.[25] Exceptions to this general rule have received a great deal of attention, if only because of their rarity.[26]

But this is not to say that economic conditions are unrelated to policy preferences. Instead, because people tend to formulate policy preferences on the basis of collective, national-level information (that is, perceptions of how a given policy has affected the nation as a whole), economic conditions can influence these preferences, but through a fundamentally different process than what has been suggested by theories emphasizing self-interest. Even something as personally jarring as losing a job has far less impact on political preferences than the perception that unemployment is worsening as a collective, national problem.[27] Thus, to the extent that trade preferences are similar to attitudes toward other aspects of economic policy, they will stem from people's perceptions of the collective impact that trade policy has on the nation. This pattern has been dubbed sociotropic influence because of the tendency it suggests for relying on collective-level information rather than personal experience.[28]

Sociotropic models are, at root, information-based explanations. They are rooted in people's perceptions (or misperceptions) derived from any number of sources of information, beyond personal life experience. Most interestingly, such perceptions are not mere generalizations from personal experience. The two kinds of information that have been found to influence national-level collective perceptions are: (1) local information, such as information about the local economy, and (2) mass media coverage of economic issues. Citizens tend to process personal-level experiences and concerns in a fashion that compartmentalizes them from the political world.[29] Collective-level information, on the other hand, is more easily linked to government policy. An unemployed person is unlikely to blame the government for his or her personal situation, but people who are aware of rising joblessness in their country or community are likely to hold the government accountable for this development, regardless of their employment status. In the case of trade preferences, if available information convinces a person that many in the United States are being adversely affected by free trade, even if he is not, it

25. For a full review, see ibid.

26. Green and Gerken, for example, found that smoking-related policy preferences were significantly influenced by whether a person was a smoker. The few exceptions are simple policies with straightforward effects on individuals, such as the effects of nonsmoking policies on smokers. As complex, difficult to understand agreements, trade policies would not naturally fall into this category of policies in which one would expect self-interest to affect political preferences. See Green and Gerken 1989.

27. See Sears and Funk 1990; and Mutz 1992.

28. Kinder and Kiewiet 1981.

29. See, for example, Brody and Sniderman 1977; and Mutz 1994.

will be the former, sociotropic perception that shapes his trade policy preferences rather than how trade has influenced his personal economic well-being.

To summarize, research on the role of economic well-being on political preferences would warn against the assumption of self-interest as the driving force behind attitudes toward trade. Studies of mass opinion have repeatedly shown that individuals rarely form political preferences on the basis of economic self-interest. Although early studies of U.S. voting behavior attributed the surge enjoyed by incumbent parties in good economic times, and the anti-incumbent preferences in bad economic times, to so-called "pocketbook" voting, once these studies moved beyond aggregates to the individual level of analysis, it became clear that self-interest was not the mechanism driving economic accountability. The people helped or hurt by the economy were not those rewarding and punishing accordingly; instead, accountability rested on citizens' perceptions of how the nation as a whole was faring—perceptions that might or might not be accurate.

In some ways, this account is quite consistent with the relatively poor performance of the leading political economy models in explaining individuals' trade policy attitudes. Effects have appeared weak to nonexistent in many studies or have been derived from measures such as education, the interpretation of which remains ambiguous. Moreover, because many studies have used aggregate-level measures of preferences and impact, and none have asked about sociotropic perceptions, previous research has not been able to distinguish these various sources of trade preferences.

In this study, we use individual-level data that include multiple measures of attitudes toward trade. To date, few analyses of trade preferences have utilized data gathered at the individual level.[30] In all but a handful of studies, trade attitudes have been inferred from aggregate vote results, patterns of campaign contributions, or the outcomes of the policy debates themselves. Importantly, aggregate-level data can produce evidence of self-interested attitudes toward trade policies that is impossible to distinguish from preferences formed on a sociotropic basis, that is, on the basis of how people think the collective as a whole is influenced.

In addition, previous individual-level studies have generally relied on single-item indicators. Individual questions tend to be unreliable and sensitive to question wording and to the framing of options, problems that are easily avoided if responses across a variety of measures produce a reliable index.[31] We also use these data to expand the potential ways in which self-interest might enter into these policy preferences, beyond skill levels and industry impact.

Interestingly, most research on this topic has not viewed trade as a political issue. Instead, the emphasis in explaining trade attitudes has been on how trade

30. These studies include Bauer, Pool, and Dexter 1963; Balistreri 1997; Scheve and Slaughter 2001; Baker 2003 and 2005; Burgoon and Hiscox 2004; Kaltenthaler, Gelleny, and Ceccoli 2004; Mayda and Rodrik 2005; Hays, Ehrlich, and Peinhardt 2005; Hainmueller and Hiscox 2006; Hiscox 2006; and Kocher and Minushkin 2006.

31. See Bauer, Pool, and Dexter 1963, 84–85; Worldviews 2002; and Hiscox 2006.

positively or negatively affects individuals economically. With these data, we examine not only the dominant political economy models, but also the sociotropic hypothesis, which is the preference formation model most widely documented in public opinion research on economic policy preferences. In so doing, we not only improve our overall understanding of the origins of attitudes toward trade, we also reveal the importance of the kind of political information that reaches citizens in explaining American preferences in this policy domain.

## Study Design

Using two representative national surveys, we attempt to move beyond ecological inferences and the limitations of previous individual-level surveys by asking working and temporarily unemployed Americans about their attitudes toward trade and related matters. One was a telephone survey conducted as part of the National Annenberg Election Study (NAES) during the summer of 2004.[32] The other was a survey conducted via Internet or Web TV by Knowledge Networks (KN) in summer 2007.

We focus on the attitudes of Americans for various reasons. First, the United States has been the dominant country in the global trading system for more than half a century. As a result, social scientists have expressed substantial interest in the factors driving U.S. trade policy. The attitudes of Americans toward trade are likely to influence outcomes in this policy arena.[33] Second, a number of key studies of trade attitudes center on the United States.[34] Focusing on the attitudes of Americans should enhance the comparability of our results to these previous analyses.

### *The Dependent Variables*

Two survey questions served to construct the dependent variables in the analyses based on the NAES survey:

1. *As you may know, international trade has increased substantially in recent years. This increase is due to the lowering of trade barriers between countries, that is, tariffs or taxes that make it more difficult or more expensive to buy and sell things across international borders. Do you think government should try to encourage international trade or to discourage international*

32. The conservative AAPOR Response Rate 1 calculation was 23 percent, which represents a minimum possible response rate.

33. Fordham and McKeown 2003.

34. See, for example, Bauer, Pool, and Dexter 1963; Scheve and Slaughter 2001; Burgoon and Hiscox 2004; and Hainmueller and Hiscox 2006, 474–81, 487–91.

*trade? Do you think the government should [encourage/discourage] this a lot or only a little?*

2. *I'm going to read you some actions the federal government in Washington can take on a variety of issues. For each one please tell me whether you favor or oppose the federal government doing it.... How about the federal government negotiating more free trade agreements like NAFTA? Do you favor or oppose the federal government doing this? Is that strongly [favor/oppose] or only somewhat [favor/oppose]?*

Each item was scored on a five-point scale, or a four-point scale in the KN survey.[35] The highest (lowest) score was assigned to respondents who believed that the government should encourage (discourage) international trade a lot and who strongly favored (opposed) the government negotiating free trade agreements, respectively.[36]

Our first dependent variable is the mean score for these two items. The second dependent variable is an ordered trichotomous measure that equals 1 if a respondent opposes free trade agreements and believes that international trade should be discouraged, and 3 if he or she favors free trade agreements and believes that international trade should be encouraged. All other respondents were scored as 2. This variable therefore groups individuals based on whether they have a consistent preference for open trade or protectionism, or whether their preferences are inconsistent.[37]

Five survey questions were used to generate the dependent variable for the analysis based on the KN survey. The first two questions were identical to those described earlier, but three additional items were asked as well:

3. *Do you believe that globalization, especially the increasing connections of our economy with others around the world, is good or bad for the United States?*

4. *Should foreign companies be encouraged or discouraged from investing in the United States, for example, by building their factories in this country?*

5. *Do you have a very favorable, somewhat favorable, somewhat unfavorable, or very unfavorable opinion of the WTO, the World Trade Organization?*

Each of these items was scored on a four-point scale. The highest (lowest) score was assigned to respondents who believed that the government should strongly

35. These two items are especially useful because one segment of the literature on trade policy preferences focuses on free trade agreements and another segment addresses more general attitudes toward trade. On this first segment, see, for example, Balistreri 1997; and Baker 2003.

36. For the first item, individuals who expressed no opinion or refused to answer were assigned to a middle category; for the second item, such individuals were grouped with respondents who neither favored nor opposed free trade agreements.

37. Combining these two items has various advantages, chiefly that the dependent variable is a more reliable measure and less prone to problems associated with idiosyncratic wording or measurement error than if we analyzed each item separately. On this issue, see Baker 2003, 444, fn. 35.

encourage (discourage) international trade, who strongly favored (opposed) the government negotiating free trade agreements, who felt that globalization is very good (bad) for the United States, who strongly encouraged (discouraged) foreign investment in the United States, and who had a very favorable (unfavorable) opinion of the WTO. The mean of the responses to these five items is our third dependent variable.

Although these items clearly do not address exactly the same issues, it is noteworthy just how consistent people's preferences were across the questions. Experts on these issues might anticipate that people would have different attitudes on the North American Free Trade Agreement (NAFTA) than on free trade more generally, or toward direct foreign investment than toward the World Trade Organization (WTO). Nonetheless, responses to these five questions indicated a very high degree of internal consistency, with a Cronbach's alpha of greater than 0.80 and a Cramer's V that averages about 0.80 for pairs of the items. In short, people's attitudes are very consistent across these facets of international economic relations, so much so that it would be inaccurate to describe them as anything other than a single underlying protrade or antitrade preference.

### *The Independent Variables*

Our key independent variables fall into three broad categories: (1) indicators of the individual characteristics suggested by the factor endowments and specific factors models, (2) indicators of respondents' perceptions of how trade influences their family's financial conditions as well as the country as a whole, and (3) indicators tapping potential noneconomic influences on trade preferences, including nationalism, ethnocentrism, and attitudes toward intervention in the affairs of other countries.

To analyze self-interest within the first category of models, we include measures of a respondent's skill level and features of his or her industry of employment. Economic studies typically use the average annual wage for an individual's occupation and the extent of an individual's formal education to measure skill, a tack that has been followed in much of the research on trade attitudes.[38] In both surveys, we therefore asked individuals, "In your current (or most recent) job, what kind of work do you do?" Each respondent's occupation was then coded using the U.S. Department of Labor's Standard Occupational Classification (SOC) system. We used data compiled by the Department of Labor's Bureau of Labor Statistics to calculate AVERAGE ANNUAL WAGE in 2003 (for the 2004 survey) and in 2006 (for the 2007 survey) for each occupation in our sample.[39] We also asked

38. See Attewell 1990, 425; Spenner 1990, 407; Balistreri 1997; Scheve and Slaughter 2001; Hays, Ehrlich, and Peinhardt 2005; and Mayda and Rodrik 2005.

39. The data on occupation and wages are taken from U.S. Department of Labor 2008a and 2008b, respectively.

each respondent about his or her formal education and created three dummy variables based on this information. The first, SOME COLLEGE, indicates whether the person graduated from a technical school or a two-year college, or whether the respondent attended but did not graduate from a four-college. The second, COLLEGE GRADUATE, indicates whether he or she graduated from a four-year college; and the third, GRADUATE SCHOOL, indicates whether the person attended graduate school. The reference category is someone who did not receive any formal education beyond high school.

To test the specific factors model using the NAES survey, we asked open-ended questions of each respondent about the industry in which they work, as well as details about their occupations. Because the full range of occupations and industries cannot easily be coded in real time, respondents were probed at length for details. Based on audio recordings of their responses, they were later assigned to one of the U.S. Census Bureau's three-digit North American Industry Codes (NAIC).[40] In the KN survey, we presented respondents with a list of the three-digit NAIC categories and asked them to select the one that best described the industry in which they work or most recently worked. For each industry represented in our sample, $i$, we constructed one measure of export orientation and another measure of import competition. EXPORT ORIENTATION is defined as the natural logarithm of $(X_i/Y_i)$ and IMPORT COMPETITION is defined as the natural logarithm of $(M_i/Y_i)$, where $X_i$ is sector $i$'s total exports, $M_i$ is the volume of imports in sector $i$, and $Y_i$ is this sector's total output. These variables are derived using 2003 data for the NAES survey and 2006 data for the KN survey.[41] Various industries in our sample are nontradable and therefore do not export or import goods. Since the natural logarithm of zero is undefined, we arbitrarily add 0.01 to both $X_i$ and $M_i$. The specific factors model predicts that individuals employed in industries that export a substantial portion of output should support open trade, whereas those working in sectors that face extensive competition from imports should be especially hostile to overseas commerce.

To distinguish evidence of self-interested policy preferences from sociotropic ones, an item in both surveys asked how respondents thought the nation as a whole had been influenced by trade. Respondents answered using a five-point scale ranging from "helped a lot" (5) to "hurt a lot" (1).[42] A parallel item asked about the

40. For a list of the three-digit industry classifications, see U.S. Census Bureau 2008a. Note that our sample is representative of the distribution of workers across industries in the U.S. population as a whole. We compared the distribution of respondents across industries in our sample to the distribution in the U.S. population, using data provided by U.S. Census Bureau 2008b. For each industry, the percentage of respondents in our sample is much the same as the percentage of the U.S. workforce.

41. Data on exports and imports are taken from U.S. International Trade Commission 2008. We used version 2.7.4 of the data when analyzing the NAES survey and version 2.8.4 of the data when analyzing the KN survey. Data on output are taken from U.S. Department of Commerce 2008 (Bureau of Economic Analysis).

42. People who refused to answer this question or who said they did not know the answer were grouped together with people who answered that trade neither hurts nor helps the economy.

perceived effect of trade on the financial situation of the person's family. Although the latter variable might appear to be an indicator of subjectively assessed self-interest, it is included to take into account however much slippage may occur between actual self-interest and what people perceive to be in their economic interests. These perceptions are inevitably a function of personal experience, but they also reflect information that causes people to attribute a particular economic situation to international trade.

As shown in Figure 1, both surveys demonstrate a slight skew toward perceptions that trade has adversely affected the economy. The NAES survey produced a roughly uniform distribution across the five response categories from "helped a lot" to "hurt a lot," whereas the KN results are more bimodal, with most respondents feeling that trade has either helped or hurt the economy "a little."

Importantly, both distributions deviate starkly from the distribution on this same scale for the American public's perceived effects of trade on their family's financial well being. Based on both surveys, there is a striking tendency for respondents to claim that trade has not affected their family's financial situation. Indeed, "no effect" is the modal response when people are asked to assess trade's perceived effects on their personal economic situation, which is consistent with the fact that most Americans are employed in nontradable sectors of the economy.

In the KN survey, we also included three indexes designed to help clarify the role of education in shaping trade preferences. Toward this end, we added items addressing three well-studied orientations that are known to be a function of education and that also are potentially linked to attitudes toward foreign commerce. First, regardless of context, well-educated people tend to favor a more activist role for the United States in foreign policy matters. Such individuals, for example, hold more favorable views of the United Nations, are more willing to normalize relations with Cuba, are more likely to favor signing international treaties, and generally endorse a more active role for the United States in foreign affairs than less-educated individuals.[43] Thus, protrade preferences among the well-educated may be a function of the same underlying tendency to involve one's self in affairs beyond national borders. Second, the poorly educated tend to have a stronger sense of nationalism, which might also account for their hostility to open overseas commerce. Finally, ethnocentrism—that is, the tendency to think less of those who are racially or ethnically different from one's own group—is tied to education and may also promote antitrade preferences. To the extent that the observed effects of education stem from any of these factors, it puts a different cast on what drives attitudes toward trade.

Our first index, ISOLATIONISM, is comprised of five widely used items tapping the extent to which respondents believe the United States should adopt an isolationist or an activist stance on international affairs. Notably, these items do not address economic relations between countries so much as whether the United States should

43. See Bauer, Pool, and Dexter 1963, chap. 6; Erikson and Tedin 2005; and Fordham 2008.

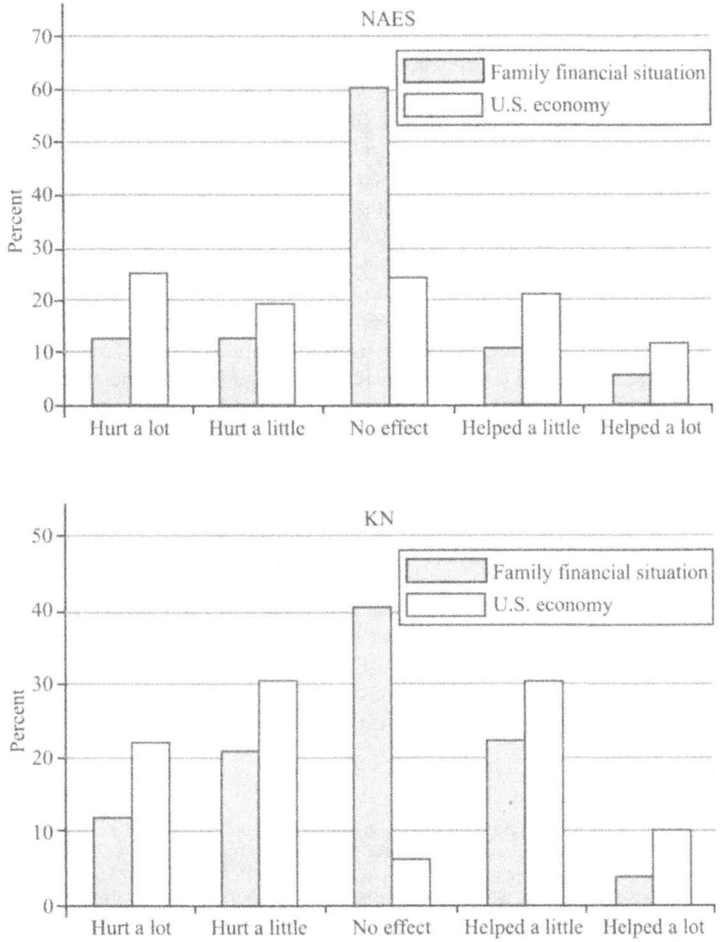


**FIGURE 1.** ***The perceived impact of trade on respondents' families and on the U.S. economy***

intervene to prevent human rights abuses abroad, cooperate with foreign countries to solve global problems, and so forth.[44] The second index, NATIONALISM, draws

44. See Wittkopf and Maggiotto 1983, Maggiotto and Wittkopf 1981; and Herrmann, Tetlock, and Diascro 2001. These five items are as follows. "Please tell us whether you agree or disagree with each of the following statements: [RANDOMIZED ORDER] (1) The U.S. needs to play an active role in

on three previously used questions to assess whether respondents believe that the United States is culturally superior to other countries.[45] The third index, ETHNOCENTRISM, taps "prejudice, broadly conceived."[46] Ethnocentrism scales are designed to measure the "commonplace inclination to divide the world into in-groups and out-groups, the former characterized by virtuosity and talent, the latter by corruption and mediocrity."[47] By asking an individual about some positive and some negative human characteristics with reference to the in-group as well as what are out-groups for that given person, we obtain an indicator of the extent to which the person employs an in-group/out-group mode of thinking.[48] To construct these measures, we use the same racial and ethnic in-groups and out-groups as previous studies (blacks, whites, and Hispanics). Each of these three indexes was highly reliable, with Cronbach's alphas greater than 0.80. All were standardized, with a mean of zero, and coded such that larger positive (negative) values of these variables reflect views that are more (less) isolationist, nationalistic, and ethnocentric, respectively.

In addition, our models include measures of party identification (one variable indicating whether respondents describe themselves as a Democrat and another indicating whether they describe themselves as Republican, with the reference category being someone without a partisan affiliation), whether anyone in the home belonged to a union, whether the respondent was currently unemployed or laid off, age, gender (which equals 1 if the respondent is male and 0 if she is female), and family income.

In the following tests, we use ordinary least squares (OLS) to analyze our nine-point measure of trade policy preferences based on the NAES survey and our measure based on the KN survey, since both of them have a roughly normal distribution. To analyze the ordered trichotomous measure of the consistency of trade policy preferences across the two items, we use an ordered logit specification. All tests

---

solving conflicts around the world; (2) The U.S. government should just try to take care of the well-being of Americans and not get involved with other nations; (3) It is essential for the United States to work with other nations to solve problems, such as overpopulation, hunger, and pollution; (4) It will be best for the future of the country if we stay out of world affairs; (5) The United States has the responsibility to play the role of 'world policeman,' that is, to fight violations of international law and aggression wherever they occur."

45. Rankin 2001. These three items are as follows. "To what extent do you agree or disagree with each of these statements? [RANDOMIZED ORDER]: (1) In the United States, our people are not perfect, but our culture is superior to others; (2) I would rather be a citizen of America than of any other country in the world; (3) The world would be a better place if people from other countries were more like Americans."

46. Levinson 1949, 19.

47. Kam and Kinder 2007, 321. All respondents are asked about their racial ethnic group as well as two out-groups. Ethnocentrism is the difference between the mean for positive-negative characteristics attributed to the in-group and the same characteristics attributed to the out-group. "Next are some questions about various groups in our society. Below are seven-point scales on which you can rate characteristics of people in different groups. Where would you rate physicians in general on this scale? Where would you rate [BLACKS/WHITES/HISPANIC-AMERICANS] in general on these scales?" The scales range from 1 to 7, anchored by Hard Working-Lazy, Efficient-Wasteful, and Trustworthy-Untrustworthy.

48. Levinson 1949.

of statistical significance are based on robust standard errors, which account for any heteroskedasticity in the data and which are clustered by the state in which the respondent resides.

## Results

Table 1 shows the results based on the NAES nine-point index of trade opinions, Table 2 reports the results based on the NAES trichotomous index, and Table 3 presents the results based on the mean of the five items on trade opinions from the KN survey. In each table, we start by estimating a model to test the factor endowments and specific factors hypotheses. This model includes occupational wages, education, the industry of employment's exposure to trade, and the control variables. Then we supplement this baseline model with additional variables to evaluate the impact of perceptions of trade's influence on the national economy and to assess the robustness of our results.

Our initial findings offer some apparent support for the factor endowments hypothesis. For each dependent variable, the coefficient estimates of SOME COLLEGE, COLLEGE GRADUATE, and GRADUATE SCHOOL are positive and jointly statistically significant. Furthermore, the results in each table indicate that respondents become increasingly supportive of open trade as they obtain more formal education. The estimated coefficient of SOME COLLEGE is always the smallest among these three variables and the coefficient estimate of GRADUATE SCHOOL is always the largest. Individuals who attended graduate school are much more supportive of open trade than both people with only a high school education and those with some college education. Each coefficient estimate of GRADUATE SCHOOL is statistically significant. Additional analyses of the incremental effect of each additional level of education furnish mixed results.[49] In the KN survey, each additional level of achievement—from high school to some college, and from some college to a four-year college degree—contributes to greater support for trade. Graduate school, on the other hand, does not contribute additional support beyond what one receives by virtue of having completed a four-year college degree. In the NAES study, by contrast, a graduate school education has a statistically significant impact on trade support beyond receiving a four-year degree, whereas prior levels of educational achievement (some college and a college degree) do not contribute significantly.

Whereas education exerts a strong influence on attitudes about trade, the effect of occupational wages is weak. The coefficient estimate of AVERAGE ANNUAL WAGE is positive, which is consistent with the factor endowments approach, but it is

49. The additional analyses to test the incremental effect of each level of educational achievement were conducted by coding education as a set of nested dummy variables. All people with graduate degrees were coded as also having four-year degrees and some college, all who had four-year degrees were coded as also having completed some college, and so forth.

**TABLE 1.** *The determinants of trade preferences, based on the NAES nine-point index*

| *Variables* | *Model 1* | *Model 2* | *Model 3* | *Model 4* | *Model 5* |
|---|---|---|---|---|---|
| SOME COLLEGE | 0.068 | −0.024 | −0.041 | −0.025 | −0.070 |
| | (0.089) | (0.082) | (0.074) | (0.082) | (0.070) |
| COLLEGE GRADUATE | 0.164 | 0.111 | 0.131+ | 0.110 | 0.060 |
| | (0.122) | (0.087) | (0.071) | (0.087) | (0.069) |
| GRADUATE SCHOOL | 0.377*** | 0.304** | 0.319*** | 0.305** | 0.248** |
| | (0.100) | (0.089) | (0.082) | (0.089) | (0.078) |
| AVERAGE ANNUAL WAGE | 0.000 | 0.000 | | 0.000 | |
| | (0.000) | (0.000) | | (0.000) | |
| EXPORT ORIENTATION | −0.174 | −0.033 | 0.089 | | 0.076 |
| | (0.170) | (0.133) | (0.114) | | (0.114) |
| IMPORT COMPETITION | 0.129 | 0.011 | −0.097 | | −0.090 |
| | (0.163) | (0.126) | (0.108) | | (0.109) |
| TARIFF RATE | | | | −0.025 | |
| | | | | (0.021) | |
| PERCEIVED EFFECT OF TRADE ON U.S. | | 0.361*** | 0.380*** | 0.363*** | 0.297*** |
| | | (0.024) | (0.020) | (0.024) | (0.020) |
| PERCEIVED EFFECT OF TRADE ON SELF | | | | | 0.247*** |
| | | | | | (0.033) |
| UNION MEMBERSHIP | −0.443*** | −0.331*** | −0.338*** | −0.331*** | −0.325*** |
| | (0.079) | (0.070) | (0.055) | (0.070) | (0.053) |
| UNEMPLOYED | −0.168 | 0.034 | 0.030 | 0.033 | 0.085 |
| | (0.186) | (0.183) | (0.174) | (0.183) | (0.158) |
| REPUBLICAN | 0.014 | −0.047 | −0.018 | −0.047 | −0.074 |
| | (0.065) | (0.069) | (0.068) | (0.068) | (0.066) |
| DEMOCRAT | −0.173+ | −0.082 | −0.078 | −0.080 | −0.090 |
| | (0.097) | (0.088) | (0.069) | (0.088) | (0.070) |
| MALE | 0.211* | 0.128 | 0.076 | 0.123 | 0.064 |
| | (0.101) | (0.084) | (0.068) | (0.083) | (0.066) |
| AGE | −0.003 | −0.002 | −0.002 | −0.002 | −0.003 |
| | (0.003) | (0.003) | (0.002) | (0.003) | (0.002) |
| INCOME | 0.017 | 0.000 | −0.014 | −0.000 | −0.014 |
| | (0.026) | (0.024) | (0.019) | (0.024) | (0.017) |
| *Constant* | 2.992*** | 2.201*** | 2.334*** | 2.184*** | 1.927*** |
| | (0.212) | (0.204) | (0.166) | (0.220) | (0.155) |
| *R-square* | 0.077 | 0.253 | 0.263 | 0.252 | 0.293 |
| *Adjusted R-square* | 0.062 | 0.240 | 0.254 | 0.240 | 0.284 |
| *N* | 851 | 851 | 1084 | 851 | 1084 |

*Notes:* Entries are ordinary least squares regression estimates with robust standard errors, clustered by the respondent's state of residence, in parentheses. Two-tailed tests of statistical significance are conducted for all coefficient estimates. Statistical significance is indicated as follows: + $p < .10$; * $p < .05$; ** $p < .01$; *** $p < .001$.

small and far from statistically significant. Furthermore, the results offer no support for the specific factors hypothesis since neither EXPORT ORIENTATION nor IMPORT COMPETITION has a statistically significant impact on trade preferences.

There is little evidence that individuals form attitudes about trade based on how trade affects their income. But as shown in the second columns of Tables 1, 2, and 3, there is strong evidence that these attitudes are formed in response to perceptions of how trade affects the U.S. economy. Respondents who feel that trade benefits the economy as a whole are significantly more likely to favor open trade than

**TABLE 2.** *The determinants of trade preferences, based on the NAES trichotomous index*

| *Variables* | *Model 1* | *Model 2* | *Model 3* | *Model 4* | *Model 5* |
|---|---|---|---|---|---|
| SOME COLLEGE | 0.111 | −0.004 | −0.003 | −0.006 | −0.049 |
| | (0.154) | (0.163) | (0.152) | (0.163) | (0.150) |
| COLLEGE GRADUATE | 0.256 | 0.216 | 0.247 | 0.215 | 0.130 |
| | (0.220) | (0.179) | (0.151) | (0.180) | (0.151) |
| GRADUATE SCHOOL | 0.598** | 0.596** | 0.507** | 0.597** | 0.388* |
| | (0.187) | (0.190) | (0.166) | (0.191) | (0.163) |
| AVERAGE ANNUAL WAGE | 0.000 | 0.000 | | 0.000 | |
| | (0.000) | (0.000) | | (0.000) | |
| EXPORT ORIENTATION | −0.280 | −0.056 | 0.172 | | 0.156 |
| | (0.299) | (0.261) | (0.223) | | (0.234) |
| IMPORT COMPETITION | 0.209 | 0.020 | −0.181 | | −0.175 |
| | (0.282) | (0.244) | (0.209) | | (0.221) |
| TARIFF RATE | | | | −0.038 | |
| | | | | (0.044) | |
| PERCEIVED EFFECT OF TRADE ON U.S. | | 0.639*** | 0.669*** | 0.641*** | 0.536*** |
| | | (0.051) | (0.042) | (0.050) | (0.043) |
| PERCEIVED EFFECT OF TRADE ON SELF | | | | | 0.429*** |
| | | | | | (0.071) |
| UNION MEMBERSHIP | −0.626*** | −0.493*** | −0.487*** | −0.493*** | −0.474*** |
| | (0.120) | (0.132) | (0.098) | (0.132) | (0.097) |
| UNEMPLOYED | −0.287 | 0.020 | 0.040 | 0.018 | 0.132 |
| | (0.340) | (0.402) | (0.379) | (0.402) | (0.369) |
| REPUBLICAN | 0.036 | −0.086 | −0.047 | −0.086 | −0.141 |
| | (0.139) | (0.151) | (0.137) | (0.150) | (0.136) |
| DEMOCRAT | −0.276 | −0.159 | −0.192 | −0.155 | −0.219 |
| | (0.185) | (0.195) | (0.161) | (0.194) | (0.161) |
| MALE | 0.393* | 0.290+ | 0.185 | 0.280+ | 0.167 |
| | (0.164) | (0.154) | (0.135) | (0.155) | (0.136) |
| AGE | −0.004 | −0.002 | −0.005 | −0.002 | −0.006 |
| | (0.005) | (0.005) | (0.004) | (0.005) | (0.004) |
| INCOME | 0.024 | −0.009 | −0.031 | −0.010 | −0.030 |
| | (0.040) | (0.042) | (0.031) | (0.042) | (0.029) |
| *Cut_1* | −1.247*** | 0.003 | −0.348 | 0.020 | 0.353 |
| | (0.359) | (0.400) | (0.290) | (0.429) | (0.299) |
| *Cut_2* | 1.125** | 2.710*** | 2.362*** | 2.725*** | 3.124*** |
| | (0.378) | (0.409) | (0.295) | (0.439) | (0.313) |
| *Pseudo log likelihood* | −829.509 | −759.039 | −969.012 | −759.390 | −953.927 |
| *Pseudo R-square* | 0.030 | 0.113 | 0.114 | 0.112 | 0.128 |
| *N* | 851 | 851 | 1084 | 851 | 1084 |

*Notes:* Entries are ordered logit estimates with robust standard errors, clustered by the respondent's state of residence, in parentheses. Two-tailed tests of statistical significance are conducted for all coefficient estimates. Statistical significance is indicated as follows: + $p < .10$; * $p < .05$; ** $p < .01$; *** $p < .001$.

those who believe that trade is economically harmful, providing considerable support for sociotropic arguments about overseas commerce. Including PERCEIVED EFFECT OF TRADE ON U.S. substantially strengthens the model's explanatory power, increasing the adjusted coefficient of variation ($R^2$) by about fourfold in Table 1 and by roughly sevenfold in Table 3. In addition, doing so weakens the effects of gender, partisanship, and age.

Our initial results—in the first column of Tables 1, 2, and 3—provide clear evidence of a gender gap, with women holding more protectionist attitudes than men.[50] There is also evidence of a partisan split, although the nature of this split differs across the two surveys. Based on the findings in Table 1, Democrats are more protectionist than either unaffiliated individuals or Republicans. Based on the findings in Table 3, there is no difference between the estimated coefficients of DEMOCRAT and REPUBLICAN, but Republicans are more protectionist than unaffiliated voters. Equally, the results in Table 3 indicate that people become more protectionist as they grow older. All of these relationships except the split between Republicans and unaffiliated voters in Table 3, however, become attenuated once we add the sociotropic variable to the model. Including this variable also reduces the magnitude of education's impact on preferences about overseas commerce, especially when analyzing the KN index.

Consistent with existing research, Tables 1 and 2 further indicate that union membership affects an individual's attitude toward trade.[51] Respondents who either were a union member or had a union member in their family were much less likely to be protrade than those without a union affiliation. However, income seems to have no bearing on trade preferences. In addition, what little evidence there is that unemployment influences these preferences (see the second and third columns of Table 3) becomes much weaker once we account for respondents' perceptions of how trade has influenced their family financial situation (see the fourth column of Table 3).

Taken together, our results indicate that perceptions of how trade affects the U.S. economy, union membership, and education strongly influence mass opinion about trade. To further analyze the impact of these factors, we estimate the effects of a change in each factor on the predicted probability that our trichotomous dependent variable equals 1 (consistent opposition to trade) and 3 (consistent support for trade), respectively. These predicted probabilities are generated using Stata's *prvalue* program, based on the model in the second column of Table 2, and setting the remaining continuous variables to their sample means and the remaining discrete variables to their modal categories.[52]

The results indicate that the perception of trade's effects on the U.S. economy has a sizable impact on trade preferences. A change from not being sure whether trade benefits the U.S. economy (a score of 3) to the view that trade has helped the economy "a little" (a score of 4) yields about a 50 percent increase in the probability that a respondent consistently supports free trade; a change to the belief that trade helps the economy "a lot" (a score of 5) yields roughly a 100 percent increase in this probability.

50. See O'Rourke and Sinnott 2002; Burgoon and Hiscox 2004; Baker 2005; Hays, Ehrlich, and Peinhardt 2005; and Mayda and Rodrik 2005.

51. See Balistreri 1997; and Mayda and Rodrik 2005.

52. On this program, see Long and Freese 2005. Note that these results are virtually identical if we rely on the estimates in the third or fourth columns of Table 2.

**TABLE 3.** ***The determinants of trade preferences, based on the KN index***

| *Variables* | *Model 1* | *Model 2* | *Model 3* | *Model 4* | *Model 5* | *Model 6* |
|---|---|---|---|---|---|---|
| SOME COLLEGE | 0.146*<br>(0.061) | 0.072<br>(0.051) | 0.073<br>(0.050) | 0.069<br>(0.050) | 0.050<br>(0.048) | 0.027<br>(0.048) |
| COLLEGE GRADUATE | 0.284***<br>(0.061) | 0.155***<br>(0.044) | 0.158***<br>(0.043) | 0.143**<br>(0.043) | 0.107*<br>(0.043) | 0.056<br>(0.043) |
| GRADUATE SCHOOL | 0.338***<br>(0.063) | 0.177**<br>(0.051) | 0.181***<br>(0.051) | 0.153**<br>(0.054) | 0.121*<br>(0.057) | 0.031<br>(0.050) |
| AVERAGE ANNUAL WAGE | 0.000<br>(0.000) | −0.000<br>(0.000) | −0.000<br>(0.000) | −0.000<br>(0.000) | −0.000<br>(0.000) | −0.000<br>(0.000) |
| EXPORT ORIENTATION | 0.030<br>(0.051) | −0.017<br>(0.026) | | −0.043<br>(0.027) | −0.038<br>(0.029) | −0.029<br>(0.026) |
| IMPORT COMPETITION | −0.032<br>(0.045) | 0.017<br>(0.024) | | 0.040<br>(0.025) | 0.035<br>(0.027) | 0.030<br>(0.025) |
| TARIFF RATE | | | 0.007<br>(0.009) | | | |
| PERCEIVED EFFECT OF TRADE ON U.S. | | 0.300***<br>(0.010) | 0.300***<br>(0.010) | 0.257***<br>(0.011) | 0.254***<br>(0.011) | 0.249***<br>(0.012) |
| PERCEIVED EFFECT OF TRADE ON SELF | | | | 0.101***<br>(0.015) | 0.100***<br>(0.016) | 0.075***<br>(0.018) |
| UNION MEMBERSHIP | −0.001<br>(0.053) | 0.045<br>(0.043) | 0.046<br>(0.043) | 0.052<br>(0.043) | 0.054<br>(0.043) | 0.066<br>(0.048) |
| UNEMPLOYED | −0.126<br>(0.090) | −0.128*<br>(0.062) | −0.130*<br>(0.063) | −0.089<br>(0.063) | −0.089<br>(0.063) | −0.075<br>(0.070) |
| REPUBLICAN | −0.118*<br>(0.052) | −0.095*<br>(0.041) | −0.096*<br>(0.041) | −0.113**<br>(0.042) | −0.110*<br>(0.042) | −0.123*<br>(0.047) |
| DEMOCRAT | −0.081<br>(0.061) | −0.032<br>(0.039) | −0.034<br>(0.039) | −0.034<br>(0.038) | −0.032<br>(0.039) | −0.044<br>(0.048) |
| MALE | 0.100**<br>(0.032) | 0.035<br>(0.030) | 0.033<br>(0.030) | 0.034<br>(0.030) | 0.024<br>(0.029) | 0.009<br>(0.031) |
| AGE | −0.004*<br>(0.002) | −0.002<br>(0.001) | −0.002<br>(0.001) | −0.002<br>(0.001) | −0.001<br>(0.001) | −0.002<br>(0.001) |
| INCOME | 0.010<br>(0.012) | 0.010<br>(0.010) | 0.010<br>(0.010) | 0.006<br>(0.010) | 0.003<br>(0.009) | 0.005<br>(0.009) |
| ECONOMICS CLASS | | | | | 0.044<br>(0.026) | 0.056+<br>(0.030) |
| ECONOMISTS' VIEW OF TRADE | | | | | 0.062*<br>(0.026) | 0.055+<br>(0.027) |
| ISOLATIONISM | | | | | | −0.099***<br>(0.011) |
| ETHNOCENTRISM | | | | | | −0.029**<br>(0.010) |
| NATIONALISM | | | | | | −0.023<br>(0.019) |
| *Constant* | 2.723***<br>(0.087) | 1.902***<br>(0.084) | 1.936***<br>(0.090) | 1.754***<br>(0.076) | 1.759***<br>(0.077) | 1.886***<br>(0.087) |
| *R-square* | 0.070 | 0.446 | 0.446 | 0.463 | 0.466 | 0.480 |
| *Adjusted R-square* | 0.064 | 0.442 | 0.442 | 0.458 | 0.461 | 0.474 |
| *N* | 1995 | 1995 | 1995 | 1995 | 1992 | 1822 |

*Notes:* Entries are ordinary least squares regression estimates with robust standard errors, clustered by the respondent's state of residence, in parentheses. Two-tailed tests of statistical significance are conducted for all coefficient estimates. Statistical significance is indicated as follows: + $p < .10$; * $p < .05$; ** $p < .01$; *** $p < .001$.

Union membership also has a considerable influence on the probability of supporting trade. People with a union member in their household are about 35 percent more likely to oppose trade than other individuals. At first blush, it is tempting to interpret the effect of union membership as an indicator of self-interested preferences. This might be the case if union members work in industries that are adversely affected by trade or are relatively low-skilled workers. However, we have already accounted for the industry of employment and skill level, suggesting that union membership is not simply a feature of self-interest. Instead, unions probably influence attitudes on trade by disseminating information: most major unions oppose trade liberalization and free trade arrangements, and promote such views among their rank and file. Interestingly, most union members in our surveys work in nontradable sectors, such as primary, secondary, and higher education. There is no reason why trade would harm these individuals.

Education also has a marked effect on trade preferences. People with a graduate school education, for example, are about 65 percent more likely to consistently support trade than people with either a high school education or some college education but not a four-year degree. All of these effects are statistically significant.[53]

It is worth considering whether sociotropic perceptions of how trade affects the nation as a whole are potentially rationalized from pre-existing policy opinions. In other words, might people have a priori opinions on trade from some other influence and then rationalize from those issue preferences to an evaluation of how trade affects the nation's economy?

In using sociotropic perceptions of trade's impact as a predictor of trade preferences, we did not assume that such perceptions were completely exogenous. Indeed, previous work suggests that sociotropic perceptions of closely related issues such as unemployment and national economic decline are spawned by media coverage as well as by local economic conditions.[54] Moreover, there is some evidence to suggest that the same pattern of origins is true of trade perceptions.[55] Whereas media coverage may alter sociotropic perceptions, it generally has no direct effect on opinions, thus implying that the ordering we have suggested must be largely correct. Information sources alter collective-level perceptions, and these in turn alter policy preferences.[56]

Importantly, it is obvious from our results that inclusion of the sociotropic variable has no bearing on whether the variables representing self-interest demon-

53. Recall that, based on the results in Table 3, there is also evidence of a split between Republicans and unaffiliated individuals. However, the magnitude of this split is quite modest. A change in party affiliation from unaffiliated to Republican yields less than a 4 percent reduction in the predicted value of the KN index, holding constant the continuous variables in our model at their sample means and the remaining discrete variables at their modal categories.

54. See, for example, Erbring, Goldenberg, and Miller 1980; Conover, Feldman, and Knight 1986; and Mutz 1998.

55. See Busch and Reinhardt 2000; and Mansfield and Mutz 2006.

56. Mutz 1992.

strate influence. Regardless of ordering, we find little evidence that self-interest forms the basis of trade preferences. But if sociotropic perceptions were merely rationalizations of pre-existing issue attachments, one would expect panel data to show null effects from changing sociotropic perceptions over time. However, as in our results, panel analyses show that sociotropic perceptions have a strong and significant influence on political preferences.[57]

## The Robustness of the Results

Having generated some initial estimates of our models, we now assess the robustness of our results. First, in coding the data on occupation based on the NAES survey, it was not possible to assign every respondent an SOC code. Consequently, the size of our sample in Tables 1 and 2 is reduced when including AVERAGE ANNUAL WAGE in the model. Since this variable has little impact on trade preferences and to ensure that the effects of the remaining variables remain stable when we analyze the largest possible sample, we estimate the models using the NAES data after dropping AVERAGE ANNUAL WAGE. As shown in the third column of Tables 1 and 2, this change in the model's specification has no bearing on any variable except COLLEGE GRADUATE, which now has a marginally significant effect in Table 1, and MALE, which no longer has a statistically significant effect in Table 2.

Second, our initial findings do not support the specific factors hypothesis. One reason might be the measures we used to test this hypothesis. In addition to measuring the export orientation and import competition of a respondent's industry of employment, a few studies have analyzed whether the tariff rate of this industry affects his or her trade preferences.[58] Hence, we replace the variables tapping export orientation and import competition with a measure of his or her industry's 2003 (for the NAES survey) or 2006 (for the KN survey) tariff rate.[59] Like Scheve and Slaughter, we estimate the effective tariff rate by taking the natural logarithm of the ratio of customs revenue to total imports in each sector, using data compiled by the U.S. International Trade Commission.[60] Nontradable sectors are assigned a tariff rate of zero. Since the natural logarithm of zero is undefined, we arbitrarily add 0.01 to each (unlogged) tariff rate, thereby retaining all of our original observations.

57. See, for example, Kiewiet 1983.

58. See, for example, Scheve and Slaughter 2001.

59. We do not include export orientation, import competition, and the tariff rate in the same model because the first two variables are fairly highly correlated with the latter variable.

60. Scheve and Slaughter 2001. The data are available at U.S. International Trade Commission 2008. We used version 2.7.4 of the data when analyzing the NAES survey and version 2.8.4 of the data when analyzing the KN survey.

Scheve and Slaughter argue that industries marked by extensive protection are likely to be at a comparative disadvantage.[61] As such, the specific-factors model predicts individuals in such industries should be hostile to open trade and should press for protectionism. Our tests, however, continue to provide no support for this approach. As shown in the fourth columns of Tables 1 and 2 and the third column of Table 3, the coefficient estimate of TARIFF RATE is always small and far from statistically significant.

Third, to bolster assessment of self-interest beyond the factor endowments and specific factors measures, respondents in the NAES survey also were asked direct questions about the extent to which their place of work is involved in importing and exporting. They were asked whether their workplace: (1) exports products, (2) imports products, (3) supplies products or services to companies that import or export, or (4) outsources some of its work to other countries. None of these measures of how trade affects their place of employment had a significant bearing on trade preferences. Nor did including these variables have any impact on the remaining results.

To further address whether the effects of trade on an individual's personal life influences or his or her trade preferences, we included in the model respondents' perceptions of how they and their family had been influenced by open trade, as illustrated in Figure 1. Including this variable in our models of trade preferences is particularly important because we want to ensure that the observed effect of people's attitudes about how trade affects the nation is not simply an outgrowth of their attitudes about how trade has influenced them on a personal level. The results in the final column of Tables 1 and 2 and the fourth column of Table 3 show that people who feel that trade has helped them and their family support trade.[62] In all three tables, the coefficient estimate of PERCEIVED EFFECT OF TRADE ON SELF is positive and statistically significant. These estimates are also fairly large. For example, a change from not being sure whether trade benefits a respondent (a score of 3) to holding the opinion that trade helps him or her "a little" (a score of 4) yields about a 40 percent increase in the probability that a respondent consistently supports free trade; a change to the belief that trade helps the person "a lot" (a score of 5) yields roughly a 90 percent increase in this probability. Nonetheless, the effect of this variable is somewhat less than that of the sociotropic variable, whose coefficient is only marginally smaller than in our earlier analysis, and this difference is statistically significant based on the results in Table 3. Even after accounting for subjective perceptions of how trade affects a respondent, perceptions of how trade influences the nation have a strong and sizable impact on whether people support open trade.

Finally, a number of previous studies have included the effects of marital status, race, urban-rural residence, and religiosity in models of trade preferences. To

61. Scheve and Slaughter 2001.

62. We present the results without AVERAGE ANNUAL WAGE to maximize the sample size, but the results do not change when this variable is included.

assess the robustness of our results, we included these variables one at a time and in combination. There is no case in which any of these factors strongly influences trade preferences and including them had no bearing on the remaining results.

## Interpreting the Effects of Education

We have found that as Americans obtain more formal education, they become increasingly likely to prefer free trade. Most studies have viewed education as a proxy for skill and therefore interpret findings such as these as supportive of the factor endowments approach. As noted earlier, Hainmueller and Hiscox have challenged this interpretation, maintaining that a college education affects trade opinions, above and beyond increasing human capital and skill, by exposing people to theories about the benefits of trade.[63] This exposure, rather than the occupational skills acquired in the classroom, is why education is positively associated with preferences for open trade in the United States. To test their argument, Hainmueller and Hiscox compared the effects of education (especially a college education) on trade attitudes for people in the workforce and for retirees. If education is a proxy for skill, they reasoned, the factor endowments approach predicts that it should have a much greater influence on the trade policy attitudes of people in the workforce than on retirees. Their results provided no evidence of this sort; nor do ours.

First, we added retirees who were included in the NAES survey to our sample of respondents. We then added four variables to our model: (1) an indicator variable for whether the respondent was retired or in the workforce, and (2) the interaction between this variable and SOME COLLEGE, COLLEGE GRADUATE, and GRADUATE SCHOOL, respectively.[64] (We dropped AVERAGE ANNUAL WAGE, EXPORT ORIENTATION, IMPORT COMPETITION, and UNEMPLOYED since these do not apply to retirees.) Our results indicate that, for any given amount of formal education, the difference in the predicted value of each dependent variable between individuals in and out of the workforce is less than three percent. Clearly, the effects of education do not vary in any meaningful way between these sets of people.

Second, in order to directly test Hainmueller and Hiscox's argument, we included two items on the KN survey. The first asked whether respondents had taken an economics course. The second asked whether economists believe that free trade is good or bad for the economy. We included the latter item to determine whether an understanding of the basic principles of international economics affects trade attitudes, regardless of whether someone has taken an economics course. We then created two dummy variables. ECONOMICS CLASS equals 1 if a respondent has taken such a course, 0 otherwise. ECONOMISTS' VIEW OF TRADE equals 1 if a respondent

63. Hainmueller and Hiscox 2006.
64. Note that retirees make up about 19 percent of the sample in this analysis.

understands that economists believe that free trade is good for the economy, 0 otherwise. If Hainmueller and Hiscox are correct, then the estimated coefficients of these variables should be positive and statistically significant. The coefficients of SOME COLLEGE, COLLEGE GRADUATE, and GRADUATE EDUCATION, however, should not be significant.

The results shown in the fifth column of Table 3 provide some support for Hainmueller and Hiscox's thesis. The estimated coefficients of the two variables tapping exposure to ideas about the benefits of trade are both positive. ECONOMISTS' VIEW OF TRADE has a statistically significant effect, whereas the influence of ECONOMICS CLASS is marginally significant ($p = .105$). Nonetheless, economic knowledge has a small impact on trade attitudes: taking an economics class or understanding that economists argue that free trade is beneficial increases the predicted value of the KN dependent variable by only 2 to 3 percent, holding constant the remaining variables in the model. Equally, the estimated coefficients of SOME COLLEGE, COLLEGE GRADUATE, and GRADUATE SCHOOL, although somewhat smaller than before, remain jointly significant; and the coefficients of the latter two variables remain positive and statistically significant. The impact of education on trade attitudes stems from far more than a knowledge of basic economic principles.

What, then, underlies the influence of education? To gain a better understanding of this issue, we turn to an analysis of noneconomic influences, including ETHNOCENTRISM, NATIONALISM, and ISOLATIONISM, indexes drawn from the KN survey that we described earlier and that are likely to be closely tied to educational attainment. The effects of these variables are reported in the final column of Table 3. The coefficient estimates of all three variables are negative, indicating that there is little support for free trade among people who believe the United States is superior to other countries, hold isolationist views, and exhibit evidence of prejudice toward groups unlike themselves. The effects of isolationist attitudes and ethnocentrism are statistically significant. These effects are also relatively large. A change from the most globally interventionist attitudes registered by respondents to the most isolationist attitudes reduces the predicted value of our measure of trade attitudes by almost 20 percent. A shift from the least ethnocentric views to the most ethnocentric views reduces this predicted value by about 12 percent. Both of these changes are statistically significant.

Not only do ISOLATIONISM and ETHNOCENTRISM have a strong bearing on preferences about trade, they also account for the effects of education. After including ISOLATIONISM, ETHNOCENTRISM, and NATIONALISM in the model, the estimated coefficients of SOME COLLEGE, COLLEGE GRADUATE, and GRADUATE SCHOOL become substantially smaller. Moreover, none of these coefficients are even close to statistically significant and they are no longer jointly significant. The smaller and weaker effects of education stem from the impact of ISOLATIONISM and ETHNOCENTRISM, rather than NATIONALISM. If we exclude ISOLATIONISM and ETHNOCENTRISM but include NATIONALISM, the effects of education grow larger and stronger. In fact, the coefficients of the variables pertaining to education are almost identical to the corresponding coefficients in the fifth column of Table 3, a finding that accords with previous research on the relationship between nationalism and trade attitudes.[65] Consequently, the effects of education reflect differences in attitudes about the extent to which the United States should take an activist stance in international affairs and a general tendency to think less of out-groups relative to in-groups.

At one level, these results might seem curious. Why, for example, does a belief that the United States should play the role of "world policeman" in preventing human rights abuses in other countries have anything to do with trade preferences? Why should how blacks feel about whites and Hispanics (or vice-versa) have anything to do with trade liberalization? Activist foreign policy attitudes, a positive attitude toward out-groups, and a preference for open trade, however, all reflect a sense of cosmopolitanism and inclusion. Isolationism, a negative attitude toward out-groups, and antipathy toward open trade all reflect a sense of insularity and separatism. In short, trade preferences are driven less by economic considerations and more by an individual's psychological worldview.

## Conclusion

It is widely acknowledged that any complete model of the political economy of trade must account for the preferences of the mass public.[66] These preferences influence trade policy because government officials need to attend to constituent interests to retain office.[67] Despite the obvious importance of understanding the factors that influence attitudes about trade, however, there have been only a handful of studies on this topic.

Much of the research to date emphasizes that trade preferences are shaped by how overseas commerce affects an individual's income. The factor endowments or Heckscher-Ohlin framework posits that these preferences are affected primarily by a person's skills. In a country such as the United States, highly skilled individuals will benefit economically from open trade and therefore should prefer the expansion of foreign commerce, while less skilled individuals should oppose it. The specific factors or Ricardo-Viner framework posits that people who work in import-competing industries should oppose open trade because foreign competition is likely to degrade their income and threaten their jobs, whereas those who are employed in export-oriented industries should support it.

As with most existing studies of attitudes toward trade, we find limited support for either approach. Occupational wages, a widely used measure of skill, have no

65. See O'Rourke and Sinnott 2002; and Mayda and Rodrik 2005. Note that our measure of nationalism is virtually identical to the measures used in these earlier studies.

66. See Rodrik 1995; Scheve and Slaughter 2001; and O'Rourke and Sinnott 2002.

67. Fordham and McKeown 2003.

effect on attitudes about trade. On the other hand, highly educated Americans are much more likely to support open trade than are less-educated individuals. Some previous studies have interpreted this result as support for the factor endowments approach. However, we have found that that there is reason to be wary of this interpretation. In this study, we conducted the first systematic analysis of the influence of isolationism and ethnocentrism on trade attitudes. Our findings reveal that the observed effects of education reflect negative attitudes toward out-groups, as well as views about whether U.S. foreign policy should be isolationist or interventionist. Isolationism and domestic ethnocentrism are strongly linked to hostility toward free trade. People who have less formal education also hold more negative attitudes toward those different from themselves. Although there are several theories as to how and why education increases tolerance and promotes more cosmopolitan worldviews, there is little doubt that these factors are closely linked. After accounting for the effects of isolationism and ethnocentrism, we find that education has no direct effect on trade attitudes, thus suggesting that its effects represent out-group anxiety rather than economic self-interest.

In addition, we find no support for the specific factors approach. The revealed comparative (dis)advantage of the industry in which an individual is employed does not influence his or her opinions in the way that this approach predicts. Nor does the tariff level of the industry in which he or she works. In short, despite our efforts to gather detailed information on industry of employment and on individual skill levels, the self-interest hypothesis has little explanatory power when it comes to understanding attitudes toward trade.

Besides out-group anxiety, we find that opinions on trade are driven by perceptions of trade's impact on the nation as a whole. While at one level this finding may seem obvious, because existing studies have emphasized that trade preferences are shaped by self-interest, they have largely ignored the influence of the information that drives perceptions of trade's collective-level impact on the nation. We argue that this oversight is a significant shortcoming. Americans' attitudes about trade are guided in powerful ways by whether they believe that trade harms or benefits the national economy, and this perception is not a mere extension of their personal self-interest. If sociotropic perceptions were merely personal interests projected onto the country at large, then we would not expect the impact of perceptions to be consistently strong and influential in shaping trade attitudes in models that simultaneously demonstrate little, if any, impact from indicators of objective self-interest.

The fact that sociotropic perceptions powerfully shape trade attitudes begs the question of where these perceptions originate. Although a thorough analysis of this question is beyond the scope of this study, scholars studying the origins of sociotropic perceptions in other economic policy arenas have identified three likely sources. First, many have found that mass media coverage of the economy plays an important role in forming these perceptions. To the extent that negative economic indicators and downturns are stressed in press coverage, perceptions of the economy also tend to become more negative, regardless of whether people are personally experiencing these downturns.[68] Likewise, when unemployment is emphasized in local and national media, individuals' perceptions of the state of unemployment also become more negative.[69] Any tendency for the press to place greater emphasis on the harmful impact of trade and less emphasis on the beneficial impact might help to account for the negatively skewed sociotropic perceptions shown in Figure 1.

In addition to mass media, local economic conditions that individuals learn about through interpersonal contact and casual conversations also influence their perceptions of the direction of national economic change. Although evidence is less extensive on this point, even those individuals who are not personally affected by trade policies can form impressions of its impact based on acquaintances who have been personally influenced.[70] In the case of trade, formal coursework in economics and related disciplines may also shape perceptions of whether trade is good or bad for the U.S. economy. Finally, perceptions of national-level conditions could be affected by personal experience, although most available evidence suggests that this relationship is fairly weak since people tend to compartmentalize personal-level and collective-level information.[71] Overall, our findings suggest that a better understanding of trade preferences among the mass public requires that we account for the broader information environment in which policy attitudes are formed, as well as the psychological predispositions of individuals.

The strong implication of our study is that standard political economy models are limited in what they can explain about trade preferences. Self-interest accounts for at best only a small portion of the variance in attitudes about trade. Incorporating the effects of sociotropic perceptions, isolationism, and out-group anxiety substantially increases the explanatory power of models of such attitudes. These results conform to what public opinion research has shown about how people form economic policy preferences more generally. Moreover, they point to the need for studies of trade policy to focus more attention on the development of psychologically informed models addressing how people process economic information, and whether political leaders are accurately held accountable for the effects of trade policies.

In one sense our findings were foreshadowed by research almost half a century ago, although this approach did not become dominant in explaining trade preferences. As early as 1963, Bauer, Pool, and Dexter noted that education's importance in shaping attitudes toward foreign trade in the United States exceeded even that of the economic characteristics of a respondent.[72] Unfortunately, they lacked the kind of specific information we have accumulated on individual skill levels

68. See, for example, Adoni and Cohen 1978; Erbring, Goldenberg, and Miller 1980; MacKuen and Coombs 1981; and Behr and Iyengar 1985.
69. Mutz 1992.
70. Conover, Feldman, and Knight 1986.
71. See Tyler 1980 and 1984; and Tyler and Cook 1984.
72. Bauer, Pool, and Dexter 1963.

and industries, and thus they could not differentiate between various explanations as to why education was so influential. These same scholars were also prescient in recognizing the role of communications in shaping perceptions of trade's impact, noting that press coverage in the 1950s was probably what changed public perceptions of whether trade was beneficial for the country. Finally, Bauer, Pool, and Dexter argued, as we have, that attitudes toward trade were driven in part by more general attitudes toward isolationism and internationalism.[73]

The implications of out-group anxiety for trade policy are particularly worrisome because anxiety toward out-groups is such a widespread reaction to what is unfamiliar. Although our findings are limited to a sample of Americans, we suspect that they generalize to other nations as well, precisely because fear of outsiders is so commonplace. Although the structure of economies differs greatly from country to country, human psychology tends to cross national borders easily. The origins of ethnocentric worldviews have been extensively studied, thus enabling some understanding of its origins.

Moreover, our findings may help to explain why previous studies have found that education is positively associated with support for trade liberalization, even in countries in which skilled labor is a scarce factor.[74] To the extent that education promotes cosmopolitanism and reduces out-group anxiety, its effects should be in the same direction in a wide variety of countries. Future approaches to explaining trade preferences will inevitably need to integrate the impact of information about how trade is perceived to affect the economy as well as the symbolic, psychological threat posed by U.S. involvement in foreign markets.

## References

Adoni, Hannah, and Akiba A. Cohen. 1978. Television Economic News and the Social Construction of Economic Reality. *Journal of Communication* 28 (4):61–70.

Alston, Richard M., J. R. Kearl, and Michael B. Vaughan. 1992. Is There a Consensus Among Economists in the 1990's? *American Economic Review* 82 (2):203–9.

Attewell, Paul. 1990. What Is Skill? *Work and Occupations* 17 (4):422–48.

Baker, Andy. 2003. Why Is Trade Reform So Popular in Latin America? A Consumption-Based Theory of Trade Policy Preferences. *World Politics* 55 (3):423–55.

———. 2005. Who Wants to Globalize? Consumer Tastes and Labor Markets in a Theory of Trade Policy Beliefs. *American Journal of Political Science* 49 (4):924–38.

Balistreri, Edward J. 1997. The Performance of the Heckscher-Ohlin-Vanek Model in Predicting Endogenous Policy Forces at the Individual Level. *Canadian Journal of Economics* 30 (1):1–17.

Bauer, Raymond A., Ithiel de Sola Pool, and Lewis Anthony Dexter. 1963. *American Business and Public Policy: The Politics of Foreign Trade*. New York: Atherton.

Beaulieu, Eugene, Michael Benarroch, and James Donald Gaisford. 2004. Intra-Industry Trade Liberalization, Wage Inequality and Trade Policy Preferences. Unpublished manuscript, Department of Economics, University of Calgary, Canada.

73. Ibid., 96–99.
74. See Beaulieu, Benarroch, and Gaisford 2004; and Beaulieu, Yatawara, and Wang 2005.

Beaulieu, Eugene, Ravindra A. Yatawara, and Wei Guo Wang. 2005. Who Supports Free Trade in Latin America? *World Economy* 28 (7):941–58.

Behr, Roy L., and Shanto Iyengar. 1985. Television News, Real World Cues, and Changes in the Public Agenda. *Public Opinion Quarterly* 49 (1):38–57.

Brody, Richard A., and Paul M. Sniderman. 1977. From Life Space to Polling Place: The Relevance of Personal Concerns for Voting Behavior. *British Journal of Political Science* 7 (3):337–60.

Burgoon, Brian A., and Michael J. Hiscox. 2004. The Mysterious Case of Female Protectionism: Gender Bias in Attitudes Toward International Trade. Unpublished manuscript, Department of Government, Harvard University, Cambridge, Mass.

Busch, Marc L., and Eric Reinhardt. 2000. Geography, International Trade, and Political Mobilization in U.S. Industries. *American Journal of Political Science* 44 (4):703–19.

Conover, Pamela Johnston, Stanley Feldman, and Kathleen Knight. 1986. Judging Inflation and Unemployment: The Origins of Retrospective Evaluations. *Journal of Politics* 48 (3):565–88.

Erbring, Lutz, Edie N. Goldenberg, and Arthur H. Miller. 1980. Front-Page News and Real-World Cues: A New Look at Agenda-Setting by the Media. *American Journal of Political Science* 24 (1):16–49.

Erikson, Robert S., and Kent L. Tedin. 2005. *American Public Opinion: Its Origin, Content and Impact.* 7th ed. New York: Pearson-Longman.

Fordham, Benjamin O. 2008. Economic Interests and Public Support for American Global Activism. *International Organization* 62 (1):163–82.

Fordham, Benjamin O., and Timothy J. McKeown. 2003. Selection and Influence: Interest Groups and Congressional Voting on Trade Policy. *International Organization* 57 (3):519–49.

Gabel, Matthew J. 1998. *Interests and Information: Market Liberalization, Public Opinion, and European Union.* Ann Arbor: University of Michigan Press.

Green, Donald P., and Ann E. Gerken. 1989. Self-Interest and Public Opinion toward Smoking Restrictions and Cigarette Taxes. *Public Opinion Quarterly* 53 (1):1–16.

Hainmueller, Jens, and Michael J. Hiscox. 2006. Learning to Love Globalization: Education and Individual Attitudes Toward International Trade. *International Organization* 60 (2):469–98.

Hays, Jude C., Sean D. Ehrlich, and Clint Peinhardt. 2005. Government Spending and Public Support for Trade in the OECD: Am Empirical Test of the Embedded Liberalism Thesis. *International Organization* 59 (2):473–94.

Herrmann, Richard K., Philip E. Tetlock, and Matthew N. Diascro. 2001. How Americans Think About Trade: Reconciling Conflicts Among Money, Power, and Principles. *International Studies Quarterly* 45 (2):191–218.

Hiscox, Michael J. 2006. Through a Glass and Darkly: Attitudes Toward International Trade and the Curious Effects of Issue Framing. *International Organization* 60 (3):755–80.

Kaltenthaler, Karl C., Ronald D. Gelleny, and Stephen J. Ceccoli. 2004. Explaining Citizen Support for Trade Liberalization. *International Studies Quarterly* 48 (4):829–52.

Kam, Cindy, and Donald R. Kinder. 2007. Terror and Ethnocentrism: Foundations of American Support for the War on Terrorism. *Journal of Politics* 69 (2):320–38.

Kiewiet, D. Roderick. 1983. *Macroeconomics and Micropolitics: The Electoral Effects of Economic Issues.* Chicago: University of Chicago Press.

Kinder, Donald R., and D. Roderick Kiewiet. 1981. Sociotropic Politics: The American Case. *British Journal of Political Science* 11 (2):129–61.

Kocher, Matthew A., and Susan Minushkin. 2006. Trade and Investment Policy Preferences and Public Opinion in Mexico. Paper presented at the 47th Annual Convention of the International Studies Association, March, San Diego, Calif.

Kono, Daniel Y. 2008. Does Public Opinion Affect Trade Policy? *Business and Politics* 10 (2): Article 2. Available at ⟨http://www.bepress.com/bap/vol10/iss2/art2⟩. Accessed 31 March 2009.

Leamer, Edward E. 1984. *Sources of International Comparative Advantage.* Cambridge, Mass.: MIT Press.

Levinson, Daniel J. 1949. An Approach to the Theory and Measurement of Ethnocentric Ideology. *Journal of Psychology* 28 (1):19–39.

NEOMA Business School
LIBRARY
Campus de Rouen
1, rue du Maréchal Juin
BP 215 - Cedex
76825 Mont Saint Aignan
Tél : 02 32 82 57 00

Long, J. Scott, and Jeremy Freese. 2005. *Regression Models for Categorical Outcomes Using Stata*. 2d ed. College Station, Tex: Stata Press.

MacKuen, Michael Bruce, and Stephen Lane Coombs. 1981. *More Than News: Media Power in Public Affairs*. Beverly Hills, Calif.: Sage Publications.

Maggiotto, Michael A., and Eugene R. Wittkopf. 1981. American Public Attitudes toward Foreign Policy. *International Studies Quarterly* 25 (4):601–31.

Mansfield, Edward D., and Diana C. Mutz. 2006. What Determines Perceptions of Trade's Influence on the US Economy? Paper presented at the 102d Annual Meeting of the American Political Science Association, August-September, Philadelphia.

Mayda, Anna-Maria, and Dani Rodrik. 2005. Why Are Some People (and Countries) More Protectionist Than Others? *European Economic Review* 49 (6):1393–430.

Mutz, Diana C. 1992. Mass Media and the Depoliticization of Personal Experience. *American Journal of Political Science* 36 (2):483–508.

———. 1994. Contextualizing Personal Experience: The Role of Mass Media. *Journal of Politics* 56 (4):689–714.

———. 1998. *Impersonal Influence: How Perceptions of Mass Collectives Affect Political Attitudes*. New York: Cambridge University Press.

Nie, Norman H., Jane Junn, and Kenneth Stehlik-Barry. 1996. *Education and Democratic Citizenship in America*. Chicago: University of Chicago Press.

O'Rourke, Kevin H., and Richard Sinnott. 2002. The Determinants of Individual Trade Policy Preferences: International Survey Evidence. In *Brookings Trade Forum, 2002*, edited by Susan M. Collins and Dani Rodrik, 157–206. Washington, D.C.: Brookings Institution.

Prior, Markus. 2007. *Post-Broadcast Democracy: How Media Choice Increases Inequality in Political Involvement and Polarizes Elections*. New York: Cambridge University Press.

Rankin, David M. 2001. Identities, Interests, and Imports. *Political Behavior* 23 (4):351–76.

Rodrik, Dani. 1995. Political Economy of Trade Policy. In *Handbook of International Economics*. Vol. 3, edited by Gene M. Grossman and Kenneth Rogoff, 1457–94. Amsterdam: Elsevier.

Scheve, Kenneth F., and Matthew J. Slaughter. 2001. What Determines Individual Trade-Policy Preferences? *Journal of International Economics* 54 (2):267–92.

Sears, David O., and Carolyn L. Funk. 1990. Self-Interest in Americans' Political Opinions. In *Beyond Self-Interest*, edited by Jane J. Mansbridge, 147–70. Chicago: University of Chicago Press.

Spenner, Kenneth I. 1990. Skill: Meanings, Methods, and Measures. *Work and Occupations* 17 (4): 399–421.

Stolper, Wolfgang Friedrich, and Paul A. Samuelson. 1941. Protection and Real Wages. *Review of Economic Studies* 9:58–73.

Tyler, Tom R. 1980. Impact of Directly and Indirectly Experienced Events: The Origins of Crime-Related Judgments and Behaviors. *Journal of Personality and Social Psychology* 39 (1):13–28.

———. 1984. Assessing the Risk of Crime Victimization: The Integration of Personal Victimization Experience and Socially Transmitted Information. *Journal of Social Issues* 40 (1):27–38.

Tyler, Tom R., and Fay L. Cook. 1984. The Mass Media and Judgments of Risk: Distinguishing Impact on Personal and Societal Level Judgments. *Journal of Personality and Social Psychology* 47 (4): 693–708.

U.S. Census Bureau. 2008a. North American Industry Classification System (NAICS). Available at ⟨http://www.census.gov/epcd/www/naics.html⟩. Accessed 31 March 2009.

———. 2008b. DP-3, Profile of Selected Economic Characteristics: 2000. Available at ⟨http://factfinder.census.gov/servlet/QTTable?_bm=y&-geo_id=01000US&-qr_name=DEC_2000_SF3_U_DP3&-ds_name=DEC_2000_SF3_U&-_lang=en&-_caller=geoselect&-state=qt&-format=⟩. Accessed 30 April 2009.

U.S. Department of Commerce. 2008. Industry Economic Accounts. Bureau of Economic Analysis. Available at ⟨http://www.bea.gov/industry/gdpbyind_data.htm⟩. Accessed 30 April 2009.

U.S. Department of Labor. 2008a. Standard Occupational Classification. Bureau of Labor Statistics. Available at ⟨http://www.bls.gov/soc/⟩. Accessed 30 April 2009.

———. 2008b. Occupational Employment Statistics. Bureau of Labor Statistics. Available at ⟨http://www.bls.gov/oes/oes_dl.htm⟩. Accessed 30 April 2009.

U.S. International Trade Commission. 2008. USITC Interactive Tariff and Trade DataWeb. Available at ⟨http://dataweb.usitc.gov/scripts/user_set.asp⟩. Accessed 30 April 2009.

Wittkopf, Eugene R., and Michael A. Maggiotto. 1983. Elites and Masses: A Comparative Analysis of Attitudes Toward America's World Role. *Journal of Politics* 45 (2):303–34.

Worldviews. 2002. American Public Opinion and Foreign Policy. Chicago Council on Foreign Relations. Available at ⟨http://www.worldviews.org/detailreports/usreport.pdf⟩. Accessed 30 April 2009.

# Part III:

# The Political Economy of Preferential Trading Agreements

# The Proliferation of Preferential Trading Arrangements

EDWARD D. MANSFIELD
*Department of Political Science*
*Ohio State University*

This article examines some international factors contributing to the recent spread of preferential trading arrangements (PTAs). PTAs help states to ensure against future disruptions of commerce with key trade partners. When stress is placed on the international trading system, the threat of such disruptions rises. Both hegemonic decline and global recessions raise the specter of commercial closure, and therefore each factor may stimulate the proliferation of PTAs. Furthermore, strategic interaction among both PTAs and countries is likely to guide the growth of preferential arrangements. As PTAs become increasingly pervasive, states that are not covered by one have strong incentives to enter such an arrangement. Doing so reduces the prospect that their access to important markets will be curtailed and that their competitiveness abroad will be undermined. The findings of this article conform with these arguments. In general, eroding hegemony, global recessions, and strategic interdependence have accelerated the pace of commercial regionalism since World War II.

Preferential trading arrangements (PTAs) have long been important features of the international political economy, but recently they have become increasingly pervasive. Over 50 have been formed since the conclusion of World War II, and almost every member of the World Trade Organization (WTO) is currently party to at least one. These developments have prompted heated debates about whether the proliferation of PTAs will generate conflicts between trade blocs and fragment the multilateral economic system or facilitate cooperation, thereby bolstering the multilateral system.[1] Equally heated are debates about why PTAs have proliferated. But, although numerous empirical studies have analyzed the effects of preferential commercial arrangements on international relations, very little empirical research has focused on the international factors affecting the growth of these arrangements.[2] The latter issue is centrally important, and the purpose of this article is to provide some preliminary quantitative evidence bearing on it.

AUTHOR'S NOTE: I am grateful to Marc Busch, Joanne Gowa, Timothy Groseclose, Helen Milner, Jon Pevehouse, Brian Pollins, Beth Yarbrough, and two anonymous referees for helpful comments. I would also like to thank David Bearce, Joe McGarvey, and Kathy Powers for research assistance.

1. For various perspectives on this debate, see Bhagwati (1991, 1993), Bhagwati and Panagariya (1996), Krugman (1991, 1993), Lawrence (1996), Oye (1992), Pomfret (1988), and Westhoff, Yarbrough, and Yarbrough (1994).

2. Among the many empirical studies of PTAs' effects on international economic relations are Aitken (1973), Frankel (1993), Frankel, Stein, and Wei (1995), Mansfield and Bronson (1997), and Winters and Wang (1994).

JOURNAL OF CONFLICT RESOLUTION, Vol. 42 No. 5, October 1998 523-543
© 1998 Sage Publications, Inc.

PTAs accord preferential commercial access to members' products and include free trade areas, common markets, and customs unions (Anderson and Blackhurst 1993; Bhagwati and Panagariya 1996; de Melo and Panagariya 1993; Pomfret 1988). Because these commercial arrangements are often composed of members located in the same geographic region, their growth has led many observers to conclude that the international economy is experiencing a wave of regionalism.[3] The results of this study will help to identify some factors contributing to any such wave.

I argue that a key reason why states enter PTAs is to ensure that commerce with trade partners will not be disrupted in the future. When stress is placed on the international trading system, the threat of such disruptions rises. Both hegemonic decline and global recessions raise the specter of commercial closure, and therefore each factor may stimulate the proliferation of PTAs. Strategic interaction among trade blocs and among countries is likely to guide the growth of preferential arrangements as well. On the heels of an increase in regionalism, states that are not covered by a PTA have strong incentives to create new and join existing preferential arrangements. Doing so reduces the prospect that their access to important markets will be curtailed and that their competitiveness abroad will be undermined. The findings of this article conform with these arguments. In general, eroding hegemony, global recessions, and strategic interdependence have accelerated the pace of commercial regionalism since World War II.[4]

## INTERNATIONAL POLITICAL AND ECONOMIC INFLUENCES ON PTA FORMATION

Here, I address two aspects of regionalism's growth—the rate at which PTAs form and the rate at which states join PTAs. Because much contemporary research on this topic emphasizes the rising number of both preferential commercial arrangements and parties to them (e.g., de Melo and Panagariya 1993; Fernández 1997), analyzing each rate is appropriate.

3. Indeed, the terms regionalism and PTAs are often used interchangeably, and I will do so as well, although it is important to recognize that not all PTAs are made up of states located in the same geographic region (e.g., the United States-Israel Free Trade Area). Following various other studies, I refer to regionalism as a political process whereby states grant commercial preferences to particular trade partners. I distinguish it from regionalization, an economic process whereby trade or investment flows increase more quickly between a given group of countries than they do between this group of countries and the rest of the world. On this distinction, see Fishlow and Haggard (1992), Frankel (1993), Haggard (1997, 48 n. 1), and Yarbrough and Yarbrough (1997, 160 n. 1). Note that although regionalism and regionalization are likely to be related, the causal links between them are not clear (Fishlow and Haggard 1992). For analyses of political factors influencing regionalization, see Chadwick and Deutsch (1973) and McKeown (1991).

4. Because my focus is on explaining global patterns of PTA formation, the following analysis is cast at the systemic (or international) level. This systemic focus obviously directs attention away from domestic and regional factors that also may contribute to the establishment of PTAs. But the advantages of assessing the extent to which systemic features explain patterns of international relations before focusing on domestic or regional variables are widely recognized (Keohane 1986; Waltz 1979). For analyses of the domestic and regional factors affecting the formation of PTAs, see Busch and Milner (1994), de Melo, Panagariya, and Rodrik (1993), Grieco (1997), Grossman and Helpman (1995), Haggard (1997), Milner (1997), and Pomfret (1988).

States often form and join PTAs to improve their access to foreign markets. By reducing trade barriers among participants and restricting members' ability to subsequently raise these barriers, PTAs provide insurance against future disruptions of commerce with selected economic partners (Perroni and Whalley 1994; Whalley 1998; Yarbrough and Yarbrough 1992). PTAs are especially useful instruments in this regard because states tend to have a greater capacity to make binding commitments to open their markets in regional than in multilateral settings (Bagwell and Staiger 1997; Bond and Syropoulos 1996).

Some recent studies have concluded that, when the stability of the global trading system is threatened, the incentives increase for states to ensure against future commercial disruptions by establishing preferential arrangements (Perroni and Whalley 1994; Whalley 1998). If the trading system were to become closed, then commercial relations with important trade partners would be jeopardized. The prospect of closure heightens the risks faced by states that depend on international trade and raises the value of striking agreements that guarantee preferential access to foreign markets. Thus, the factors that threaten to undermine the global trading system are likely to stimulate the formation of PTAs. Because the erosion of hegemony and global recessions are two such factors, part of my analysis centers on their influence on the frequency of PTA formation and the frequency with which states join these arrangements.

## HEGEMONY AND THE GLOBAL BUSINESS CYCLE

For more than two decades, economists and political scientists have debated whether commercial openness is affected by hegemony, a condition marked by the existence of a single country that is powerful enough and willing to manage the international system (e.g., Gilpin 1975, 1987; Gowa 1994; Keohane 1984; Kindleberger 1973; Krasner 1976; Lake 1988; Mansfield 1994). Many scholars have argued that establishing and maintaining an open trading system is a collective good that will be underprovided absent a stable hegemon.[5] By virtue of its size, a hegemon, like a privileged group, has incentives to provide collective goods regardless of the contributions made to them by other states.[6] Although analysts who advance this argument disagree about the nature of these incentives, they agree that hegemonic decline reduces this state's contribution to the stability of the global trading system.

To the extent that eroding hegemony increases the likelihood of systemic closure, it may prompt states to seek insurance against this contingency by establishing and joining PTAs. This position corresponds with the conclusions reached in various analyses (Gilpin 1975, 1987; Kindleberger 1973; Krasner 1976) but diverges from the views of others who argue that hegemony has little effect on regionalism (McKeown 1991; Oye 1992; Yarbrough and Yarbrough 1992).

Despite the widespread and heated debates about the effects of hegemony on the stability of the international economic system, few empirical studies have addressed

5. See Gilpin (1975, 1987) and Kindleberger (1973). See also Krasner (1976), who argues that hegemonic decline stimulates regionalism but does not emphasize the provision of collective goods in the international system.

6. On privileged groups, see Olson (1965).

its influence on regionalism.[7] I am aware of none that has analyzed hegemony's effect on the incidence of PTA formation. Numerous observers identify declining U.S. leadership in the General Agreement on Tariffs and Trade (GATT)/ WTO and its waning commitment to multilateralism as central sources of the contemporary growth of PTAs (Baldwin 1993; Bhagwati 1993; Bhagwati and Panagariya 1996; Gilpin 1987; Krugman 1991, 1993). However, an earlier wave of regionalism began during the 1960s, a period widely regarded as the apex of U.S. hegemony (Gilpin 1975, 1987; Krasner 1976). In light of the dearth of systematic evidence on this issue and the interest expressed in it, an analysis of the relationship between hegemony and the proliferation of PTAs seems long overdue.

Besides hegemony, global recessions can threaten the stability of the international trading system by depressing the demand for goods and services, thereby squeezing firms' profits, reducing employment, and creating incentives for import-competing firms and other segments of society to press for protection.[8] But, like hegemony, little empirical work has been conducted on whether fluctuations in the global business cycle influence the formation of PTAs.

Recessions may lead states to form or join a PTA comprising countries whose principal industries do not rival each other. Doing so is one way a government can address domestic pressures for protection by restricting imports from third parties. Responding to these demands by forming or joining a PTA rather than imposing unilateral trade barriers affords particular advantages to members of the GATT/WTO. As Pomfret (1988, 158) points out, "if a country intends to raise MFN [most favored nation] tariffs or introduce import quotas, it is both contravening GATT and risking retaliation. A bilaterally negotiated discriminatory trade barrier is a way to sidestep GATT obligations without an open breach."[9]

At the same time, states may enter PTAs during an economic downturn to create commercial opportunities abroad in the face of depressed global demand. Countries may also establish and join preferential arrangements during a recession to ensure that export opportunities will not be jeopardized should the recession stimulate protectionist pressures in key trade partners. The benefits of acceding to a PTA under these conditions are likely to rise if participating in such an arrangement allows firms to realize economies of scale by expanding their access to members' markets, to integrate regional production, or to reduce the risks of making relation-specific investments to service foreign markets (Haggard 1997; Milner 1997; Yarbrough and Yarbrough 1992).

7. Among the studies that have been conducted on this topic are McKeown (1991), Oye (1992), and Yarbrough and Yarbrough (1992).

8. On the relationship between recessions and societal demands for protection, see Corden (1993, 55), Mansfield and Busch (1995), and McKeown (1991).

9. Alternatively, global recessions may depress the rate of PTA formation. Import-competing firms that expect intrabloc liberalization to heighten domestic import penetration are likely to resist a PTA's formation, especially during global recessions when downward pressure is already being placed on profits. Furthermore, global expansions tend to spur global trade, and some studies have concluded that rising commerce among a group of countries can foster the establishment of a PTA to help insulate the flow of trade from future disruptions (see Yarbrough and Yarbrough 1992).

**STRATEGIC INTERACTION**

As countries form and join PTAs at a rising pace, states that are not parties to these arrangements can face incentives to respond in kind. Various theoretical analyses suggest that, due to these incentives, the creation of a PTA tends to beget the development of additional PTAs and that countries joining these arrangements encourage other states to do likewise (e.g., de Melo and Panagariya 1993, 5-6; Fernández 1997; Oye 1992; Pomfret 1988; Yarbrough and Yarbrough 1992). A PTA's creation, for example, may prompt fears by countries located outside the commercial union that it will degrade their competitiveness, thereby leading them to form a rival bloc. So, too, a state joining a PTA may generate concern by its economic rivals (outside the bloc) that this state's preferential access to an expanded market will furnish it with a competitive advantage, thus inducing its rivals to join this or other PTAs to obtain similar benefits.[10]

In the same vein, positive contagion in the rates of PTA formation or states' involvement in these arrangements may be due to a demonstration effect: the appearance that a PTA is benefiting members can foster the creation of additional commercial unions by countries eager to realize similar gains (Pomfret 1988; Yarbrough and Yarbrough 1992). Furthermore, PTAs heighten members' market power vis-à-vis third parties and hence their bargaining power (Fernández 1997; Oye 1992). Preferential arrangements are likely to form in reaction to one another, and states are likely to join PTAs in response to one another, because the proliferation of these arrangements erodes the bargaining power of states that remain uncovered by them.

Consistent with the view that strategic interaction has influenced the growth of PTAs, it is often argued that deepening European integration contributed to the formation of the North American Free Trade Agreement (NAFTA) (Bhagwati 1991, 72; Fernández 1997, 16-19), and that NAFTA spurred the development of, and agreements to establish future, bilateral economic arrangements within both the Western Hemisphere and the Asia-Pacific region (Serra et al. 1997, 8-9). Also in accord with this view, many observers have pointed out that the recent spate of PTAs has led various developing countries to join preferential agreements to ensure that their access to important foreign markets will not be curtailed (e.g., Bhagwati 1991, 72; de Melo and Panagariya 1993, 5-6; Fernández 1997, 16-19; Perroni and Whalley 1996).

These illustrations are suggestive, but very little systematic evidence has been accumulated on whether PTAs' growth has been marked by positive contagion. This study's focus on the international system obviously limits my ability to assess directly the extent to which strategic interdependence guides the formation and expansion of PTAs. However, the following results will be among the first on this topic and therefore should be of interest.

Before turning to an analysis of the hypotheses just advanced, two qualifications should be noted. First, these hypotheses rest on the heightened incentives for states to safeguard market access as the threat of systemic closure rises. My argument is that hegemonic decline and global recessions can affect the magnitude of this threat.

10. Of course, the fact that countries have incentives to join PTAs need not imply that parties to existing PTAs always prefer to grant them membership (Bhagwati and Panagariya 1996).

But whether these factors actually lead to closure is neither well established nor critical for present purposes.

Second, this analysis does not address the welfare effects of PTAs. One reason is that substantial differences seem to exist between preferential arrangements in this regard. Central to a PTA's welfare implications is whether it creates more trade among participants than it diverts from efficient producers located elsewhere (Viner 1950). There is ample evidence that many commercial arrangements have been trade diverting, especially those formed among less developed countries and among communist states (Bhagwati 1993; Bhagwati and Panagariya 1996; de Melo and Panagariya 1993; Pomfret 1988). Particularly in recent years, however, other PTAs seem to have been trade creating (Eichengreen and Frankel 1995; Frankel and Wei 1998). Thus, as Frankel and Wei (1998, 216) conclude, "The pattern is mixed. . . . Apparently regionalism can, depending on the circumstances, be associated with either more or less general liberalization." Equally important is that the welfare implications of PTAs do not directly bear on the hypotheses advanced earlier. Although declining hegemony, dips in the global business cycle, and strategic interdependence are each likely to accelerate the pace of regionalism, there is little reason to expect that these factors systematically promote either trade-creating or trade-diverting PTAs.

## MODELS AND ESTIMATION PROCEDURES

To test the hypotheses previously discussed, the following models are estimated:

$$\text{FORM PTA}_t = \beta_0 + \beta_1\text{HEGEMONY}_{t-1} + \beta_2\text{PTA}_{t-1} + \beta_3\Delta\text{GNP}_{t-1} + \beta_4\text{YEAR}_t + \beta_5\text{FORM PTA}_{t-1} + e_t \quad (1)$$

$$\text{JOIN PTA}_t = \alpha_0 + \alpha_1\text{HEGEMONY}_{t-1} + \alpha_2\text{COUNTRY PTA}_{t-1} + \alpha_3\Delta\text{GNP}_{t-1} + \alpha_4\text{YEAR}_t + \alpha_5\text{JOIN PTA}_{t-1} + z_t. \quad (2)$$

FORM $\text{PTA}_t$ is the number of PTAs that form in year $t$, and JOIN $\text{PTA}_t$ is the number of countries joining a PTA in year $t$.[11] $\text{HEGEMONY}_{t-1}$ is the percentage of total global

11. The primary source of data for these variables is the list of PTAs notified to the GATT under Article XXIV and the Enabling Clause, which is reported in World Trade Organization (1995, 77-91). Because the WTO lists only PTAs formed by its members and those of the GATT, I supplement these data by including the PTAs listed in Hartland-Thunberg (1980). I also include the Council on Mutual Economic Assistance (CMEA), the Southern African Customs Union, the Economic Community of West African States, the Southern African Development Coordination Conference, and the Eastern and Southern African Preferential Trade Area, since various studies have identified each of these groupings as PTAs. For example, see de Melo and Panagariya (1993), Foroutan (1993, 246-51), Hanlon (1986), Kisanga (1991), Orimalade and Ubogu (1984), and Pomfret (1988).

All PTAs listed by the WTO—and when it is possible to obtain this information, those listed in the other sources mentioned above—are coded as beginning in the year they enter into force. The original members of each PTA are coded as joining it in this year as well. If the year a PTA entered into force is unavailable, its onset is dated as the year the negotiations leading to its formation were concluded. The GATT/WTO lists only PTAs whose members are parties to the GATT and does so only when these agreements are trade (the sum of imports and exports) conducted by the state engaging in the most commerce in year $t-1$ and is a widely used measure of hegemony in studies of the international political economy (Krasner 1976; Lake 1988; Mansfield and Busch 1995; McKeown 1991).[12]

$PTA_{t-1}$ is the number of existing PTAs in year $t-1$, and COUNTRY $PTA_{t-1}$ is the percentage of countries involved in at least one PTA in year $t-1$.[13] The latter variables are included because the rates at which PTAs form and states join them may depend on how many preferential arrangements already exist and the portion of countries that are already parties to a commercial bloc. Either rate, for example, may be characterized by a ceiling or saturation effect. When the number of PTAs or the percentage of countries involved in a PTA is sufficiently large, few countries will be left uncovered by such an arrangement. This, in turn, may reduce the number of states seeking PTA membership, thus depressing the rates at which PTAs form and states join them. If so, a quadratic relationship might exist between the number of existing PTAs and the frequency of PTA formation, as well as between the percentage of countries involved in a PTA and the frequency with which states join PTAs. To address this possibility, $PTA^2_{t-1}$ and COUNTRY $PTA^2_{t-1}$ are introduced in models (1) and (2), respectively, after initially estimating each model. In addition, $\Delta GNP_{t-1}$ is the change in global income from year $t-2$ to year $t-1$ and measures the global business cycle;[14] and $YEAR_t$ is $t$, which I include to directly assess whether there has been a secular increase in regionalism.

Finally, FORM $PTA_{t-1}$ and JOIN $PTA_{t-1}$ are lagged endogenous variables that are included because the rates of PTA creation and states' accession to PTAs may be characterized by temporal dependence. As discussed below, their coefficients also bear on the extent to which PTA formation and expansion are marked by strategic

officially notified to it. Thus, for some PTAs, the date of initiation given by the WTO differs from that given by the other sources listed above. In these cases, I use the earliest date.

I do not consider agreements strengthening or superseding an existing PTA to be new PTAs. Nor do I consider the formation of hub-and-spoke agreements between an existing PTA (e.g., the European Economic Community [EEC]) and a state or group of states (e.g., the African, Carribean, and Pacific [ACP] states) to be a new PTA. I do, however, code states that join hub-and-spoke agreements with existing PTAs as having joined a PTA in the year the agreement went into effect. Thus, for example, none of the many association agreements between the EEC/European Community (EC) and European, Middle Eastern, and African countries is coded as a new PTA. But all countries that form such an agreement are coded as having joined a PTA.

To distinguish countries from extrasovereign entities entering a PTA, I generally require that actors be members of the United Nations in the year they joined a PTA to be coded as having acceded to it. The only exceptions to this coding rule are South Korea and Switzerland, which did not join the United Nations, and the members of the CMEA, which did not join the United Nations until after this PTA formed.

12. See Lake (1988) for a discussion of this measure's merits in studies of the international trading system. For each year analyzed here, the United States conducts more trade than any other state. Consequently, for each year, $t-1$, this measure is derived by summing U.S. imports and exports and dividing this total by the sum of global imports and exports. Data on these variables are expressed in U.S. dollars and are taken from the International Monetary Fund, *International Financial Statistics* (Washington, DC: International Monetary Fund, various years).

13. For a description of the data and the coding procedures used to measure these variables, see note 11. Countries that are not members of the United Nations when they join a PTA but subsequently become members are coded as parties to the PTA starting in the year they join the United Nations.

14. Data on global income are derived by merging two indices (each of which is expressed in real terms) obtained from the GATT. The first covers the period from 1950 to 1985; the second covers the period from 1986 to 1994. See General Agreement on Tariffs and Trade (1986, 139; 1996, 135).

TABLE 1
Descriptive Statistics for the Variables in Models (1) and (2), 1952-1994

| Variable | Mean | Standard Deviation |
|---|---|---|
| PTAs formed | 1.256 | 1.733 |
| Countries joining PTAs | 7.442 | 9.305 |
| Hegemony | 0.143 | 0.011 |
| Number of existing PTAs | 21.744 | 12.760 |
| Percentage of countries in PTAs | 0.624 | 0.270 |
| Change in GNP | 3.605 | 2.301 |
| Year | 1973 | 12.557 |
| Instrument for lagged number of PTAs formed | 1.230 | 1.312 |
| Instrument for lagged number of countries joining PTAs | 7.108 | 5.150 |

interdependence over time. These variables, however, are likely to be correlated with $e_t$ and $z_t$, respectively, which are stochastic error terms, thereby generating biased parameter estimates. Therefore, an instrument for each lagged endogenous variable is used instead.[15]

These tests cover the period from 1952 to 1994 because much of the literature on regionalism focuses on this era, and data for some variables in models (1) and (2) are unavailable in earlier years.[16] Descriptive statistics for the variables in both models based on this time frame are presented in Table 1.

The following results are generated using two related discrete regression models.[17] I assume that the processes giving rise to the formation of PTAs and states' involvement in them are unobservable, but that a count of each outcome is observed at the end of each year, $t_1, \ldots, t_n$, where $n$ is the number of years in the sample. Various studies of international relations have used event count models in which the underlying process generating the events is assumed to have a Poisson distribution (e.g., Martin 1992; Pollins 1996). Based on a Poisson model,

$$Y_t \sim f(y_t|\lambda_t) = \frac{(\lambda_t)^{y_t} e^{-\lambda_t}}{y_t!}. \qquad (3)$$

In the present case, $Y_t$ refers to FORM PTA$_t$ in model (1) and JOIN PTA$_t$ in model (2); $\lambda_t$ is the annual rate of PTA formation for model (1) and the annual rate at which

15. These instruments are the predicted counts of FORM PTA and JOIN PTA in year $t-1$. They are created by estimating a Poisson regression of FORM PTA in $t-1$ on HEGEMONY, PTA, (the level of) GNP, FORM PTA, and YEAR in $t-2$, and by estimating a negative binomial regression of JOIN PTA in $t-1$ on HEGEMONY, COUNTRY PTA, (the level of) GNP, JOIN PTA, and YEAR in $t-2$. Except for YEAR and the lagged endogenous variables, each of these independent variables is measured by regressing its value on time and using the residual of this regression as a measure of the variable. These variables and measurement procedures clearly differ somewhat from the variables and measurement procedures in models (1) and (2). But the resulting instruments are closely related to the actual dependent variables, and relatively little collinearity exists between these instruments and the independent variables in both models.

16. As noted in note 14, the first year that complete data are available for global income is 1950. But because the instruments for the lagged endogenous variables in models (1) and (2) are generated using data in year $t-2$, 1952 is the first year included in the following analysis.

17. On these models, see King (1989) and Maddala (1983).

countries join PTAs for model (2); and $y_t$ is the observed event count at year $t$. The expected value of $Y$ at $t$ is $E(Y_t) = \lambda_t = \exp(X_t\beta)$, where $X_t$ is a vector of independent variables and $\beta$ is a vector of parameters.

Central to the Poisson distribution is the assumption that the probability of an event occurring in a given period of time is independent of prior events in that period and that the rate at which events occur during this period, $\lambda_t$, is constant (or does not depend on prior events).[18] This assumption, however, may be violated in the present case if, as discussed above, decisions to form or join PTAs are characterized by strategic interdependence. Poisson regression will not be appropriate for estimating models (1) and (2) if the formation of a PTA or a country's decision to join a PTA in a given year influences the probability that another PTA will form or another state will join a PTA in the same year.

One feature of the Poisson distribution is that the variance of $Y_t$, $\text{Var}(Y_t) = E(Y_t) = \lambda_t = \exp(X_t\beta)$. The extent to which the independence of events occurring at a given time is violated can be assessed by expressing the variance of $Y_t$ as $\text{Var}(Y_t) = \lambda_t\exp(\delta)$ and testing the hypothesis that $\delta = 0$ (King 1989, 126-27; Martin 1992, 78-79). If this hypothesis is not rejected, the Poisson distribution is the appropriate basis for the event count model. If it is rejected, the events are characterized by contagion (or $\lambda_t$ is characterized by heterogeneity), and a negative binomial model should be used (King 1989, 52, 126).

## ESTIMATES OF THE PARAMETERS

Initially, I focus on estimating the parameters in model (1). The results of a likelihood ratio test indicate that the null hypothesis that $\delta = 0$ cannot be rejected ($p > .99$), so Poisson regression is used to estimate these parameters. The results are reported in the first two columns of Table 2. I will focus on those in the first column, which are derived without $\text{PTA}^2_{t-1}$, because there is no evidence of a quadratic relationship between the number of existing preferential arrangements and the rate of PTA formation. Instead, the frequency with which PTAs are created decreases as the number of existing PTAs rises, since the estimate of $\text{PTA}_{t-1}$ is negative and statistically significant. Underlying this finding could be that as the number of PTAs increases, so does the proportion of countries that belong to at least one such arrangement; and any tendency for states to react to a trade bloc's creation by establishing a rival bloc might be attenuated if they are already parties to a commercial arrangement. But more is at work here. I also included the percentage of countries that are members of at least one PTA in year $t-1$ ($\text{COUNTRY PTA}_{t-1}$) in model (1) and found no evidence that it has a significant bearing on $\text{FORM PTA}_t$.

18. See King (1989, 50-51). More precisely, the Poisson distribution occurs if (1) the probability of an event occurring in a short period of time is proportional to the period's length, (2) the probability is zero that multiple events occur in a given period, (3) the events occurring in a given period are independent of each other, and (4) the probability that an event occurs in a very short period of time is invariant to when the period starts.

TABLE 2

Regressions of the Annual Number of PTAs That Form and Countries That Join PTAs, Based on Models (1) and (2), 1952-1994

| *Variable* | *Model (1)* | | *Model (2)* | |
|---|---|---|---|---|
| Intercept | –238.601** | –239.954** | 58.706 | –86.443 |
| | (–2.18) | (–2.11) | (1.06) | (–1.30) |
| Hegemony | –48.764** | –19.683 | –69.447*** | –74.483*** |
| | (–2.17) | (–0.62) | (–2.95) | (–3.67) |
| Existing PTAs | –0.150** | –0.041 | | |
| | (–2.56) | (–0.39) | | |
| Existing PTAs$^2$ | | –0.002 | | |
| | | (–1.23) | | |
| % Countries in PTAs | | | –0.089 | 12.034*** |
| | | | (–0.09) | (3.44) |
| % Countries in PTAs$^2$ | | | | –14.172*** |
| | | | | (–3.78) |
| Change in GNP | –0.124* | –0.169** | –0.058 | –0.037 |
| | (–1.95) | (–2.29) | (–0.73) | (–0.57) |
| Year | 0.126** | 0.124** | –0.024 | 0.050 |
| | (2.24) | (2.13) | (–0.84) | (1.45) |
| Lagged PTAs formed | 0.473*** | 0.588*** | | |
| | (5.12) | (4.45) | | |
| Lagged countries joining PTAs | | | 0.062* | –0.012 |
| | | | (1.69) | (–0.38) |
| Log likelihood | –51.04 | –50.26 | –119.64 | –113.54 |
| $\chi^2$ | 46.53*** | 48.10*** | 23.61*** | 35.80*** |

NOTE: The parameters in model (1) are estimated using Poisson regression; those in model (2) are estimated using negative binomial regression. Figures in parentheses are *t* statistics. For each regression, $N = 43$.
*$p < .10$; **$p < .05$; ***$p < .01$ (two-tailed).

Consistent with the hypotheses advanced earlier, the negative and statistically significant estimates of $\text{HEGEMONY}_{t-1}$ and $\Delta\text{GNP}_{t-1}$ indicate that hegemony's erosion and global recessions have each spawned a rise in the development of PTAs. There has also been a secular increase in the incidence of PTA formation during the post–World War II era, since the estimate of $\text{YEAR}_t$ is positive and significant. Finally, although the creation of PTAs is not guided by positive contagion in a given year, it does seem to be guided by positive feedback from one year to the next. The estimate of FORM $\text{PTA}_{t-1}$ is positive and statistically significant.

Having analyzed the factors contributing to the rate of PTA formation, I now turn to those influencing the rate at which states join PTAs. These factors differ in a number of respects. Because, in contrast to the results based on model (1), the estimate of $\delta$ is positive and statistically significant ($p < .001$), negative binomial regression is used to estimate the parameters in model (2). One obvious reason why positive contagion marks the rate at which states join PTAs is that any PTA's formation involves a joint decision by a group of countries to simultaneously become members. However, as discussed below, these findings probably reflect strategic interaction among countries competing in international markets as well.

The results of this analysis, which are presented in the third and fourth columns of Table 2, indicate that an inverted U-shaped relationship exists between the percentage of countries covered by a PTA and the incidence of states joining these arrangements. As shown in the final column, the estimate of COUNTRY $PTA_{t-1}$ is positive, that of COUNTRY $PTA^2_{t-1}$ is negative, and both are statistically significant. This suggests that the rate at which states join PTAs has been marked by a ceiling effect, tailing off once the percentage of countries that are parties to a PTA becomes relatively large.[19] In light of this strong quadratic relationship, the estimates derived after including COUNTRY $PTA^2_{t-1}$ in model (2) are emphasized below.

Like the results pertaining to the rate of PTA formation, waning U.S. hegemony has sparked a rise in the number of countries joining a PTA, since the estimate of $HEGEMONY_{t-1}$ is negative and significant. There is also some evidence of an upward trend in the rate at which states join PTAs and that this rate rises during global recessions. But, unlike the results based on model (1) neither the estimate of $YEAR_t$ nor that of $\Delta GNP_{t-1}$ is statistically significant. In addition, while a state's decision to join a PTA increases the probability that others will do likewise in the same year, the rate at which states join PTAs is largely unrelated from one year to the next. The estimate of the lagged endogenous variable in the fourth column of Table 2 is very small and not significant (although, as shown in the third column, it is significant when COUNTRY $PTA^2_{t-1}$ is omitted).

With these exceptions, however, the estimates in Table 2 are statistically significant, and their quantitative effects tend to be large. For example, decreasing the value of $HEGEMONY_{t-1}$ by one standard deviation yields about a 70% increase in the predicted number of PTAs that are formed and roughly a 125% increase in the predicted number of states that join a PTA, holding constant the remaining variables in models (1) and (2) at their mean values. The corresponding increase in the predicted number of PTAs established due to a rise of one standard deviation in (the instrument for) the number of PTAs formed 1 year earlier (FORM $PTA_{t-1}$) is almost 90%. But changes in global output have a less pronounced influence on commercial regionalism. Holding constant the other variables at their means, a one standard deviation reduction in the value of $\Delta GNP_{t-1}$ generates roughly a 35% increase in the predicted value of FORM $PTA_t$ and only about a 10% rise in that of JOIN $PTA_t$.

## PTA FORMATION WITHIN THE GATT

Thus far, my analysis has addressed the proliferation of all PTAs established since the conclusion of World War II. Considerable interest has been expressed in this topic, but some studies of regionalism place particular stress on the increasing number of preferential arrangements notified to the GATT/WTO under Article XXIV and the Enabling Clause during this era (e.g., Bhagwati 1993; Finger 1993; Serra et al. 1997;

19. Furthermore, there is no evidence that the number of existing PTAs influences the rate at which states join these arrangements. I included this variable ($PTA_{t-1}$) in model (2) and found no statistically significant evidence that it affects JOIN $PTA_t$.

World Trade Organization 1995). It is therefore important to determine the reasons for the rise in PTAs within the GATT; however, little empirical evidence has been accumulated on this score. In the following analysis, I examine whether the factors emphasized earlier also affect the rate at which PTAs notified to the GATT are formed and the rate at which parties to the GATT accede to these arrangements.[20] I then assess whether GATT negotiations have influenced the growth of such PTAs.

To begin, models (1) and (2) are estimated after measuring FORM $PTA_t$, JOIN $PTA_t$, the instruments for the lagged endogenous variables, $PTA_{t-1}$, and COUNTRY $PTA_{t-1}$ based solely on PTAs notified to the GATT and, in the case of the latter variable, the percentage of GATT members that are party to such an arrangement.[21] The results are reported in the first and third columns of Table 3. As in Table 2, there is no indication of a quadratic relationship between the number of existing PTAs and the rate at which PTAs form, and there is considerable evidence of a quadratic relationship between the percentage of GATT members that belong to a PTA and the frequency with which these states join preferential arrangements. Hence, neither the results derived when $PTA^2_{t-1}$ is included in model (1) nor the results when COUNTRY $PTA^2_{t-1}$ is omitted from model (2) are presented in Table 3.

Because there is little indication of positive contagion in the rate of PTA formation (i.e., the estimate of $\delta$ is not statistically significant), the parameters in model (1) are estimated using Poisson regression. The sign of each estimate in the first column of Table 3 is the same as its corresponding estimate in Table 2, and the estimates of $PTA_{t-1}$, $\Delta GNP_{t-1}$, $YEAR_t$, and FORM $PTA_{t-1}$ continue to be significant. In this regard, the factors affecting the formation of all PTAs are quite similar to those influencing the establishment of PTAs notified to the GATT. But certain differences do exist between the results in Tables 2 and 3. Except for $HEGEMONY_{t-1}$, the absolute value of each estimate in the first column of Table 3 is much larger than the corresponding estimate in Table 2. Furthermore, whereas the rate of PTA formation throughout the world has experienced a statistically significant increase during periods of hegemonic decline, the rate of PTAs notified to the GATT has not. The estimate of $HEGEMONY_{t-1}$ is negative, but its absolute value is far smaller than the estimate in Table 2 and it is not significant.

In addition, many of the factors influencing the rate at which states join PTAs are similar, regardless of whether we focus only on PTAs notified to the GATT or the broader sample analyzed earlier. Because the estimate of $\delta$ is positive and statistically significant, the parameters in model (2) are again estimated using negative binomial regression. As noted above, an inverted U-shaped relationship exists between the

20. By the GATT, I am referring to both it and the WTO.

21. To conduct this analysis, I include only those PTAs notified to the GATT under Article XXIV or the Enabling Clause and date their origin in the year the GATT lists them as entering into force. Note that this procedure yields different values of the dependent variables and $PTA_{t-1}$ than in the preceding analysis because certain PTAs included earlier were not notified to the GATT and others (e.g., the Association of Southeast Asian Nations and some African PTAs) were notified to the GATT only some time after they were established. Thus, the dates of their formation are different in the present analysis than before. Recall that COUNTRY $PTA_{t-1}$ measures the percentage of GATT members that are parties to PTAs notified to it. Members of PTAs recognized by the GATT that are not parties to the GATT itself are considered PTA members if and when they join the GATT (see note 11).

TABLE 3
Regressions of the Annual Number of PTAs That Form and Countries That Join PTAs, Based on Models (1) and (2), for PTAs Notified to the GATT, 1952-1994

| *Variable* | *Model (1)* | | *Model (2)* | |
|---|---|---|---|---|
| Intercept | –318.585*** | –243.251** | –727.741*** | –763.738*** |
| | (–2.60) | (–1.99) | (–4.81) | (–4.98) |
| Hegemony | –16.746 | –9.191 | –126.797*** | –132.239*** |
| | (–0.74) | (–0.40) | (–3.76) | (–3.98) |
| Existing PTAs | –0.221*** | –0.177** | | |
| | (–2.71) | (–2.15) | | |
| % GATT members in PTAs | | | 6.506* | 6.833** |
| | | | (1.94) | (2.04) |
| % GATT members in PTAs$^2$ | | | –23.387*** | –24.257*** |
| | | | (–4.86) | (–4.99) |
| Change in GNP | –0.254*** | –0.260*** | 0.092 | 0.091 |
| | (–3.93) | (–4.02) | (1.05) | (1.07) |
| Year | 0.164*** | 0.125** | 0.382*** | 0.401*** |
| | (2.65) | (2.02) | (4.86) | (5.03) |
| Lagged PTAs formed | 0.763*** | 0.632*** | | |
| | (4.40) | (3.41) | | |
| Lagged GATT members joining PTAs | | | –0.027 | –0.025 |
| | | | (–0.30) | (–0.28) |
| GATT | | 1.227** | | –0.371 |
| | | (2.52) | | (–1.06) |
| Log likelihood | –46.36 | –42.69 | –81.37 | –80.81 |
| $\chi^2$ | 48.83*** | 56.16*** | 33.05*** | 34.16*** |

NOTE: The parameters in model (1) are estimated using Poisson regression; those in model (2) are estimated using negative binomial regression. Figures in parentheses are $t$ statistics. For each regression, $N = 43$.
*$p < .10$; **$p < .05$; ***$p < .01$ (two-tailed).

percentage of GATT members that belong to a PTA and the frequency with which they join preferential arrangements. Like the rate for the broader sample, the rate at which parties to the GATT enter preferential arrangements notified to it therefore seems to be marked by a ceiling effect. Also consistent with the results in Table 2 is that the number of GATT members joining PTAs is unrelated to the number doing so 1 year prior and that eroding U.S. hegemony has stimulated a rise in the rate at which GATT members accede to PTAs. But, in contrast to the previous findings, there is strong evidence of an upward trend in the rate at which states join commercial unions, since the estimate of $YEAR_t$ is positive, large, and statistically significant; and the estimate of $\Delta GNP_{t-1}$ is positive, rather than negative, although it continues to have a relatively small and statistically insignificant effect on JOIN $PTA_t$.

Besides evaluating whether the variables in models (1) and (2) influence the growth of PTAs notified to the GATT, it is also important to determine whether GATT negotiations have influenced the rates at which these commercial arrangements form and states join them. There are various reasons why this may be the case. Participants in a GATT negotiating round might complete PTAs to enhance their bargaining leverage in these negotiations or as a means of ensuring that commerce will be liberalized with important trade partners should the round falter. Furthermore, a GATT round can raise issues that participants choose to address by establishing a PTA or that enhance GATT members' bargaining position in ongoing negotiations over a preferential trade initiative, thus spurring its conclusion (Whalley 1998). It is widely acknowledged, for example, that various countries manipulated issues arising during the Uruguay Round to obtain more favorable terms in negotiations over PTAs (Bhagwati and Panagariya 1996; Whalley 1998). GATT members may also establish and enter PTAs during a negotiating round to help offset anticipated multilateral reductions in trade barriers if these states face strong domestic pressures for protection, since preferential arrangements can limit the market access of third parties and are permitted under both Article XXIV of the GATT and the Enabling Clause.[22]

But, although GATT members might create and accede to PTAs more frequently during negotiating rounds than otherwise, the opposite might also be the case. For example, states that believe regional trade initiatives are likely to hamper GATT negotiations and that want to expand the scope of multilateral trade liberalization will probably have little incentive to enter PTAs during a negotiating round. More generally, preferential and multilateral trade agreements may be substitutes; if so, the rates at which countries form and enter PTAs will decline throughout the course of GATT negotiations.

To test these hypotheses, I introduce a variable, $GATT_{t-1}$, in models (1) and (2) that equals 1 if a GATT negotiating round is ongoing in year $t-1$ and 0 otherwise.[23] The results, which are shown in the second and fourth columns of Table 3, indicate that including $GATT_{t-1}$ in these models has little bearing on the sign, size, or significance level of any remaining coefficient. Moreover, an ongoing negotiating round yields a marked rise in the frequency with which PTAs notified to the GATT are formed. The estimate of $GATT_{t-1}$ based on model (1) is positive and statistically significant; and, holding constant the remaining variables at their means, the predicted number of PTAs established during a GATT round is roughly three and one half times greater than in other years. By contrast, an ongoing negotiating round seems to reduce the incidence of GATT members joining PTAs, although the estimate of $GATT_{t-1}$ based on model (2) is not significant. Although the roughness of this analysis is obvious, these findings suggest that states have formed PTAs notified to the GATT much more frequently, but have entered new and existing preferential arrangements somewhat less frequently, during GATT negotiations than at other times.[24]

22. This hypothesis is consistent with what Bhagwati (1988, 53) refers to as the "law of constant protection," which suggests that reductions in one type of protection stimulate increases in other types to compensate groups that are harmed by the initial reductions. For an analysis of this proposition, see Mansfield and Busch (1995).

23. Rounds of the GATT were conducted in 1949 (Annecy, France), 1951 (Torquay, United Kingdom), 1956 (Geneva), 1960-1961 (Geneva, the Dillon Round), 1964-1967 (Geneva, the Kennedy Round), 1973-1979 (the Tokyo Round), and 1986-1994 (the Uruguay Round) (see Jacobson 1984, 247). Note that because 1952 is the first year for which complete data exist for all variables in models (1) and (2), the Annecy Round is not included in this analysis.

24. In addition to the tests reported above, I also examined whether the preceding results are sensitive to outliers. Especially unusual is the rate at which countries joined PTAs in 1976 due to the very large number

## DISCUSSION OF THE RESULTS

The results of this study largely conform with the argument that threats to the stability of the international trading system create incentives for states to establish and join PTAs. Countries that do so safeguard access to members' markets, thereby reducing their vulnerability to any future closure of global commerce. Hegemonic decline and international recessions can place stress on the trading system, and both factors have contributed to the proliferation of PTAs. Furthermore, as states form and join PTAs at an accelerated pace, other countries tend to respond quickly in kind, perhaps to avoid being placed at a competitive disadvantage in global markets. At the same time, however, the support for this argument is also qualified. The business cycle is only weakly related to the rate at which states join PTAs; and preferential arrangements have formed frequently during GATT negotiations, which pose little threat to the stability of the international economic system unless they break down.

Echoing longstanding views about the effects of hegemony on international economic stability (Gilpin 1975; Kindleberger 1973; Krasner 1976), various contemporary observers attribute the growth in regionalism to the decline in U.S. leadership and power. Consistent with this position, analyses that are not restricted to the GATT yield strong evidence that PTAs form and states join PTAs at increasingly rapid rates as hegemony erodes. But much of the existing research pertaining to hegemonic stability theory focuses on economic relations among parties to the GATT. Whereas declining hegemony also fosters the accession of these countries to PTAs, it has a much weaker influence on the frequency with which preferential arrangements notified to the GATT are formed. These findings suggest that, within the GATT, declining hegemony is associated with the creation of PTAs that include more members than PTAs formed during periods of emerging or stable hegemony and/or that countries join existing PTAs in greater numbers as hegemony wanes. They also imply that hegemony has less influence on the rate at which preferential arrangements are established than on the rate at which states become parties to them.

In addition, global recessions stimulate the formation of PTAs but have little influence on the frequency of states joining PTAs. One explanation for the effects of economic downturns on the establishment of these arrangements is that international recessions prompt import-competing firms and other segments of society to press for protection. Governments have incentives to respond to these pressures by forging discriminatory commercial arrangements with countries whose leading industries are not chief rivals of influential domestic sectors. Doing so rather than imposing unilateral trade barriers is particularly advantageous for GATT members because such arrangements avoid breaching GATT regulations. That the quantitative effect of global

of countries that formed associations with the EEC in this year (primarily ACP countries via the Lomé Convention). In no case, however, is a dummy variable that equals 1 in 1976 and 0 otherwise statistically significant based on either model. And in all cases, the signs, sizes, and significance levels of the parameter estimates in models (1) and (2) are similar to those in Tables 2 and 3. Furthermore, it should be noted that auxiliary regressions indicate no evidence of excessive collinearity among the indepeddent variables in models (1) and (2).

recessions on the incidence of PTA formation is larger based on analyses restricted to the GATT than on those including all preferential arrangements accords with this position.

Another explanation for these findings is that states conclude PTAs during global recessions to stimulate exports. Faced with depressed global demand and the prospect of systemic closure, both governments and export-oriented firms have reason to establish commercial arrangements that guarantee preferential access to foreign markets. The benefits of doing so are likely to be especially pronounced for firms that can realize economies of scale by increasing production to service these markets.

Of course, the tests conducted here have addressed only the influence of global recessions in a preliminary manner, which may help to account for the weakness of the relationship between this factor and the incidence of states entering PTAs. For example, although the business cycle's effect on the rates at which PTAs form and states join PTAs was lagged by 1 year, negotiations leading to a PTA's creation obviously can take much longer than 1 year to conclude. Therefore, the preceding results offer little insight into whether such negotiations tend to begin during global economic downswings, and the dearth of data on their duration precludes an analysis of this topic. It is interesting, however, that the average length of time between signing a new PTA notified to the GATT and its implementation is roughly 1 year.[25] The tendency for PTAs to be concluded during global recessions seems consistent with the hypothesis advanced earlier.

There is also evidence of clustering in the frequencies with which PTAs are formed and states enter these arrangements. Both for the world as a whole and the GATT, the rate of PTA creation is directly related from one year to the next, suggesting that preferential arrangements are often initiated as strategic reactions to each other. Exemplary in this regard was the development of the European Free Trade Association (EFTA) in response to the European Economic Community's (EEC) formation. Furthermore, various preferential trade initiatives have begun taking shape in Asia and Latin America in reaction to the recent proliferation of PTAs elsewhere; and these initiatives, in turn, have prompted European Union (EU) officials to explore the possibility of establishing additional preferential arrangements with states outside of Europe (Barfield 1996, 152). In the same vein, the economic revitalization experienced by EEC members soon after its inception stimulated the creation of numerous PTAs in Latin America and Africa by countries anxious to achieve similar results, just as improved economic performance by members of the EU and NAFTA may soon spark the emulation of these PTAs by other states (Fernández 1997; Pomfret 1988, 161, 178; Yarbrough and Yarbrough 1992, 105-106).

But, although PTAs often seem to form in response to each other, this response generally does not occur in the same year. This probably reflects the time needed to organize the relevant countries, negotiate the commercial arrangement's terms, and complete the domestic legislative and procedural tasks needed to bring a new PTA to fruition.

25. This figure is based on a comparison of the dates each agreement was signed and implemented. These dates are taken from the World Trade Organization (1995, 77-91).

By contrast, if a country enters a PTA, then it increases the probability of other countries doing likewise in the same year. As noted earlier, the fact that any PTA's creation requires a joint decision by multiple states to simultaneously become members certainly contributes to this tendency. But more is probably at work here, including strategic interaction among countries competing in international markets. A state's decision to join a PTA may prompt its economic rivals to quickly follow suit rather than to be left at a competitive disadvantage. Preferential agreements that were formed between the EC and various Mediterranean countries, for example, damaged other Mediterranean countries that exported similar goods to the EC, leading them to press for and obtain comparable agreements. Furthermore, the Yaoundé Convention induced developing countries that did not have preferential access to EC markets to demand commercial preferences to offset discrimination that their goods faced in Europe (Pomfret 1988, 178).

More recently, the spate of states entering PTAs has led others—especially those in East Asia and many developing countries—to consider doing the same rather than to be left without adequate access to important foreign markets (Bhagwati and Panagariya 1996; de Melo and Panagariya 1993, 5-6; Perroni and Whalley 1996, 57; Yarbrough and Yarbrough 1992, 105-106). Illustrating these countries' concerns, President Salinas of Mexico remarked early in the NAFTA negotiations that "[w]hat we want is closer commercial ties with Canada and the United States, especially in a world in which big regional markets are being created. We don't want to be left out of any of those regional markets" (quoted in Fernández 1997, 19; see also Bhagwati 1991, 72).

Positive contagion in the rate at which countries join preferential arrangements may also stem from the tendency for existing PTAs to conclude agreements with other states contemporaneously rather than sequentially. The EEC/EC followed this pattern, signing hub-and-spoke agreements with multiple European, Middle Eastern, and African countries in particular years. So did EFTA, which (like the EC) initiated a series of preferential agreements with former Soviet republics and Eastern European countries in the early 1990s. This tendency for PTAs to introduce additional members in groups shows no sign of abating. The Association of Southeast Asian Nations, for example, was poised to admit Cambodia, Laos, and Myanmar together,[26] until the coup in Cambodia during 1997 prompted a change in these plans.

Finally, the preceding results suggest that regionalism has become increasingly pervasive over time, since a rise has occurred in the frequency with which PTAs have formed and states have joined them during the past 50 years. Moreover, this increase has been more precipitous within the GATT than for the world as a whole, especially when focusing on the incidence of countries entering PTAs. One explanation for this tendency is that the GATT's success in lowering many trade barriers over time has led participants to rely on the discriminatory instruments that it still permits—including PTAs notified to the GATT under Article XXIV or the Enabling Clause—with rising frequency. Another explanation, however, is that multilateral and regional trade initiatives are complementary (Lawrence 1996; Rodrik 1998). Progressive reductions in

26. See *The Economist*, March 1, 1997, 41-42.

protection within the GATT may have been encouraged by the growth of PTAs and also may have stimulated efforts to reinforce and deepen multilateral liberalization at the regional level via PTAs.

## CONCLUSION

Arguments that the international economy is experiencing a wave of regionalism are widespread and often based on claims about the recent spread of PTAs. Such claims, however, have not been matched by empirical analyses of the rates at which PTAs form and states join these arrangements. The purpose of this article has been to examine why these rates have fluctuated during the period since World War II.

I have argued that the specter of systemic closure can prompt countries to establish and enter PTAs, since doing so helps guarantee their access to key foreign markets if the international trading system actually fragments. Hegemonic decline and global recessions both increase the risk of closure. That these factors have contributed to the proliferation of PTAs is consistent with this argument. So is the tendency for PTAs to form and grow more rapidly soon after an increase in the number of new PTAs and states entering preferential arrangements.

More generally, my results imply that economic expansions, renewed international economic leadership by the United States, and the advent of more effective means of managing strategic interaction among both states and PTAs are likely to dampen the recent wave of regionalism. The fact that neither of the latter two developments seems to be on the horizon suggests that this wave may not yet have crested.

## REFERENCES

Aitken, Norman D. 1973. The effect of the EEC and EFTA on European Trade: A temporal and cross-section analysis. *American Economic Review* 63:881-92.

Anderson, Kym, and Richard Blackhurst. 1993. Introduction and summary. In *Regional integration and the global trading system*, edited by Kym Anderson and Richard Blackhurst. London: Harvester Wheatsheaf.

Bagwell, Kyle, and Robert Staiger. 1997. Multilateral tariff cooperation during the formation of regional free trade areas. *International Economic Review* 38:291-319.

Baldwin, Robert. 1993. Adapting the GATT to a more regionalized world: A political economy perspective. In *Regional integration and the global trading system*, edited by Kym Anderson and Richard Blackhurst. London: Harvester Wheatsheaf.

Barfield, Claude E. 1996. Regionalism and U.S. trade policy. In *The economics of preferential trade agreements*, edited by Jagdish Bhagwati and Arvind Panagariya. Washington, DC: AEI Press.

Bhagwati, Jagdish. 1988. *Protectionism*. Cambridge, MA: MIT Press.

———. 1991. *The world trading system at risk*. Princeton, NJ: Princeton University Press.

———. 1993. Regionalism and multilateralism: An overview. In *New dimensions in regional integration*, edited by Jaime de Melo and Arvind Panagariya. New York: Cambridge University Press.

Bhagwati, Jagdish, and Arvind Panagariya. 1996. Preferential trading areas and multilateralism—Strangers, friends, or foes? In *The economics of preferential trade agreements*, edited by Jagdish Bhagwati and Arvind Panagariya. Washington, DC: AEI Press.

Bond, Eric, and Costas Syropoulos. 1996. Trading blocs and the sustainability of international cooperation. In *The new transatlantic economy*, edited by Matthew B. Canzoneri, Wilfred J. Ethier, and Vittorio Grilli. Cambridge: Cambridge University Press.

Busch, Marc, and Helen V. Milner. 1994. The future of the international trading system: International firms, regionalism, and domestic politics. In *Political economy and the changing global order*, edited by Richard Stubbs and Geoffrey Underhill. New York: St. Martin's Press.

Chadwick, Richard W., and Karl W. Deutsch. 1973. International trade and economic integration: Further developments in trade matrix analysis. *Comparative Political Studies* 6:84-109.

Corden, W. Max. 1993. The revival of protection in developing countries. In *Protectionism and world welfare*, edited by Dominick Salvatore. New York: Cambridge University Press.

de Melo, Jaime, and Arvind Panagariya. 1993. Introduction. In *New dimensions in regional integration*, edited by Jaime de Melo and Arvind Panagariya. New York: Cambridge University Press.

de Melo, Jaime, Arvind Panagariya, and Dani Rodrik. 1993. The new regionalism: A country perspective. In *New dimensions in regional integration*, edited by Jaime de Melo and Arvind Panagariya. New York: Cambridge University Press.

Eichengreen, Barry, and Jeffrey A. Frankel. 1995. Economic regionalism: Evidence from two 20th century episodes. *North American Journal of Economics and Finance* 6:89-106.

Fernández, Raquel. 1997. Returns to regionalism: An evaluation of non-traditional gains from RTAs. National Bureau of Economic Research working paper no. 5970, Cambridge, MA.

Finger, J. Michael. 1993. GATT's influence on regional arrangements. In *New dimensions in regional integration*, edited by Jaime de Melo and Arvind Panagariya. New York: Cambridge University Press.

Fishlow, Albert, and Stephan Haggard. 1992. *The United States and the regionalization of the world economy*. Paris: OECD Development Center Research Project on Globalization and Regionalization.

Foroutan, Faezeh. 1993. Regional integration in sub-Saharan Africa: Past experience and future prospects. In *New dimensions in regional integration*, edited by Jaime de Melo and Arvind Panagariya. New York: Cambridge University Press.

Frankel, Jeffrey A. 1993. Is Japan creating a yen bloc in East Asia and the Pacific? In *Regionalism and rivalry: Japan and the United States in Pacific Asia*, edited by Jeffrey A. Frankel and Miles Kahler. Chicago: University of Chicago Press.

Frankel, Jeffrey A., Ernesto Stein, and Shang-Jin Wei. 1995. Trading blocs and the Americas: The natural, the unnatural, and the super-natural. *Journal of Development Economics* 47:61-95.

Frankel, Jeffrey A., and Shang-Jin Wei. 1998. Regionalization of world trade and currencies: Economics and politics. In *The regionalization of the world economy*, edited by Jeffrey A. Frankel. Chicago: University of Chicago Press.

General Agreement on Tariffs and Trade. 1986. *International trade*. Geneva: General Agreement on Tariffs and Trade.

———. 1996. *International trade*. Geneva: General Agreement on Tariffs and Trade.

Gilpin, Robert. 1975. *U.S. power and the multinational corporation: The political economy of foreign direct investment*. New York: Basic Books.

———. 1987. *The political economy of international relations*. Princeton, NJ: Princeton University Press.

Gowa, Joanne. 1994. *Allies, adversaries, and international trade*. Princeton, NJ: Princeton University Press.

Grieco, Joseph. 1997. Systemic sources of variation in regional institutionalization in Western Europe, East Asia, and the Americas. In *The political economy of regionalism*, edited by Edward D. Mansfield and Helen V. Milner. New York: Columbia University Press.

Grossman, Gene M., and Elhanan Helpman. 1995. The politics of free-trade agreements. *American Economic Review* 85:667-90.

Haggard, Stephan. 1997. Regionalism in Asia and the Americas. In *The political economy of regionalism*, edited by Edward D. Mansfield and Helen V. Milner. New York: Columbia University Press.

Hanlon, Joseph. 1986. *Beggar your neighbor*. London: Villiers.

Hartland-Thunberg, Penelope. 1980. *Trading blocs, U.S. exports, and world trade*. Boulder, CO: Westview.

Jacobson, Harold K. 1984. *Networks of interdependence: International organizations and the global political system*. 2nd ed. New York: Knopf.

Keohane, Robert O. 1984. *After hegemony: Cooperation and discord in the world political economy.* Princeton, NJ: Princeton University Press.

———. 1986. Theory of world politics: Structural realism and beyond. In *Neorealism and its critics*, edited by Robert O. Keohane. New York: Columbia University Press.

Kindleberger, Charles P. 1973. *The world in depression, 1929-1939.* Berkeley: University of California Press.

King, Gary. 1989. *Unifying political methodology: The likelihood theory of statistical inference.* New York: Cambridge University Press.

Kisanga, Eliawony J. 1991. *Industrial and trade cooperation in Eastern and Southern Africa.* Hong Kong: Avebury.

Krasner, Stephen D. 1976. State power and the structure of foreign trade. *World Politics* 28:317-47.

Krugman, Paul. 1991. The move to free trade zones. In *Policy implications of trade and currency zones*, edited by Lawrence H. Summers. Kansas City, MO: Federal Reserve Bank.

———. 1993. Regionalism versus multilateralism: Analytical notes. In *New dimensions in regional integration*, edited by Jaime de Melo and Arvind Panagariya. New York: Cambridge University Press.

Lake, David A. 1988. *Power, protectionism, and free trade: International sources of U.S. commercial strategy.* Ithaca, NY: Cornell University Press.

Lawrence, Robert Z. 1996. *Regionalism, multilateralism, and deeper integration.* Washington, DC: Brookings Institution.

Maddala, G. S. 1983. *Limited-dependent and qualitative variables in econometrics.* New York: Cambridge University Press.

Mansfield, Edward D. 1994. *Power, trade, and war.* Princeton, NJ: Princeton University Press.

Mansfield, Edward D., and Rachel Bronson. 1997. Alliances, preferential trading arrangements, and international trade. *American Political Science Review* 91:97-104.

Mansfield, Edward D., and Marc Busch. 1995. The political economy of nontariff barriers: A cross-national analysis. *International Organization* 49:723-49.

Martin, Lisa L. 1992. *Coercive cooperation: Explaining multilateral economic sanctions.* Princeton, NJ: Princeton University Press.

McKeown, Timothy J. 1991. A liberal trading order? The long-run pattern of imports to the advanced capitalist states. *International Studies Quarterly* 35:151-72.

Milner, Helen V. 1997. Industries, governments, and the creation of regional trade blocs. In *The political economy of regionalism*, edited by Edward D. Mansfield and Helen V. Milner. New York: Columbia University Press.

Olson, Mancur. 1965. *The logic of collective action: Public goods and the theory of groups.* Cambridge, MA: Harvard University Press.

Orimalade, Adeyinka, and R. E. Ubogu, eds. 1984. *Trade and development in economic community of West African states.* Delhi: Vikas.

Oye, Kenneth A. 1992. *Economic discrimination and political exchange: World political economy in the 1930s and 1980s.* Princeton, NJ: Princeton University Press.

Perroni, Carlo, and John Whalley. 1994. The new regionalism: Trade liberalization or insurance? National Bureau of Economic Research working paper no. 4626, Cambridge, MA.

———. 1996. How severe is global retaliation risk under increasing regionalism? *American Economic Review (Papers and Proceedings)* 86:57-61.

Pollins, Brian M. 1996. Global political order, economic change and armed conflict: Coevolving systems and the use of force. *American Political Science Review* 90:103-17.

Pomfret, Richard. 1988. *Unequal trade: The economics of discriminatory international trade policies.* Oxford: Basil Blackwell.

Rodrik, Dani. 1998. Comment. In *The regionalization of the world economy*, edited by Jeffrey A. Frankel. Chicago: University of Chicago Press.

Serra, Jaime, Guillermo Aguilar, Jose Cordoba, Gene Grossman, Carla Hills, John Jackson, Julius Katz, Pedro Noyola, and Michael Wilson. 1997. *Reflections on regionalism: Report of the study group on international trade.* Washington, DC: Carnegie Endowment for International Peace.

Viner, Jacob. 1950. *The customs union issue.* New York: Carnegie Endowment for International Peace.

Waltz, Kenneth. 1979. *Theory of international politics*. Reading, MA: Addison-Wesley.

Westhoff, Frank H., Beth V. Yarbrough, and Robert M. Yarbrough. 1994. Preferential trade agreements and the GATT: Can bilateralism and multilateralism coexist? *Kyklos* 47:179-95.

Whalley, John. 1998. Why do countries seek regional trade agreements? In *The regionalization of the world economy*, edited by Jeffrey A. Frankel. Chicago: University of Chicago Press.

Winters, L. Alan, and Zhen Kun Wang. 1994. *Eastern Europe's international trade*. Manchester: Manchester University Press.

World Trade Organization. 1995. *Regionalism and the world trading system*. Geneva: World Trade Organization.

Yarbrough, Beth V., and Robert M. Yarbrough. 1992. *Cooperation and governance in international trade: The strategic organizational approach*. Princeton, NJ: Princeton University Press.

———. 1997. Dispute settlement in international trade: Regionalism and procedural coordination. In *The political economy of regionalism*, edited by Edward D. Mansfield and Helen V. Milner. New York: Columbia University Press.

# Why Democracies Cooperate More: Electoral Control and International Trade Agreements

Edward D. Mansfield, Helen V. Milner, and B. Peter Rosendorff

Over the past fifty years, barriers to international trade have decreased substantially. While the decline in protectionism since World War II has stemmed partly from unilateral changes in trade policy by countries, it has also been a result of agreements among countries to liberalize commerce. In this article, we analyze the conditions under which states have concluded such agreements and, more generally, explore the domestic factors affecting interstate economic cooperation. We argue that the likelihood of states cooperating on trade policy depends crucially on their regime type: as states become more democratic, they are increasingly likely to conclude trade agreements.

Our analysis has implications for two broad areas in the field of international relations. First, a large and influential body of research has emerged on the effects of regime type on the outbreak and resolution of interstate conflict, the durability of political-military alliances, the propensity of states to join intergovernmental organizations (IGOs), and various other aspects of foreign policy.[1] Very little of this literature, however, focuses directly on the links between regime type and foreign economic policy. We conduct one of the initial analyses bearing on this important topic.

Earlier versions of this paper were presented at the 1998 Annual Meeting of the American Political Science Association, Boston; the 1999 International Economics Association World Congress, Buenos Aires; the 1999 Latin American Meetings of the Econometric Society, Cancun; the 2000 Southeastern Theory and International Economics Meeting, Houston; the 2000 Latin American and Caribbean Economic Association Annual Meetings, Rio de Janeiro; the 2000 Public Choice Society Annual Meetings, Charleston; and seminars at Brown University, the University of California, Riverside, the University of Michigan, the University of Rochester, the University of Southern California, UCLA, and Yale University. We are grateful to participants in these seminars and David Baldwin, Marc Busch, Peter Gourevitch, Joanne Gowa, David Lake, Lisa Martin, James Morrow, Jon Pevehouse, and Alastair Smith for helpful comments.

1. See, for example, Bueno de Mesquita and Lalman 1992; Bueno de Mesquita et al. 1999; Gaubatz 1996; Mansfield and Snyder 1995; Russett and Oneal 2001; and Russett, Oneal, and Davis 1998.

*International Organization* 56, 3, Summer 2002, pp. 477–513
© 2002 by The IO Foundation and the Massachusetts Institute of Technology

Second, this article joins the debate over the causes of international economic cooperation. Many studies attribute variations in cooperation to features of the global system, especially the distribution of capabilities and international institutions.[2] In contrast, much less research addresses the domestic sources of economic cooperation, and virtually none considers the influence of regime type.[3] Furthermore, the few studies that have been conducted on this topic pertain only indirectly to international trade agreements.[4] We help fill this gap in the literature by conducting one of the first direct examinations of the effects of regime type on the establishment of trade agreements. Such agreements embody cooperation among their members because they involve mutual policy adjustments, entailing the reciprocal lowering of trade barriers.

Our analysis shows how international cooperation in trade can be influenced by the control that voters exert over political leaders—a factor that varies starkly between democracies and autocracies. The regular occurrence of fair and competitive elections is fundamental to all democracies.[5] As G. Bingham Powell observes, "There is a widespread consensus that the presence of competitive elections, more than any other feature, identifies a contemporary nation-state as a democratic political system."[6] Such elections vest the public with control over government leaders that is absent in nondemocratic polities.[7] In democracies, political leaders must succeed at the polls to maintain office. To this end, they must gain the support of voters, whose attitudes toward the incumbent tend to depend heavily on their perceptions of recent economic performance.[8] In contrast, elections held in autocracies are much less free and fair; they vest the populace with much less control over public officials and place few (if any) constraints on the autocrat's policy choices. In our analysis, the superior ability of elections in democracies to constrain leaders prompts democratic rulers to be more cooperative internationally than their nondemocratic counterparts.

Elections, however, are not the only domestic constraints leaders face. In any political regime, leaders must balance the policies that enhance their electoral prospects with those that meet the demands of special interest groups.[9] In what follows, we model how this trade-off affects the optimal foreign economic strategy of political leaders operating in different regime types.

It is clear that international trade agreements may stem in part from the associated economic gains that leaders expect to derive. We do not explicitly model these gains

2. See, for example, Keohane 1984; Krasner 1976; and Milner 1992.
3. See, for example, Milner 1997; and Reinhardt 1996. For an exception, see Leeds 1999.
4. See Mansfield, Milner, and Rosendorff 2000; McGillivray and Smith 2000; Remmer 1998; and Verdier 1998.
5. See Dahl 1971, 1–5; and Schumpeter [1942] 1976, 269.
6. Powell 2000, 4.
7. Schumpeter [1942] 1976.
8. See, for example, Fiorina 1981; Kiewiet 1983; and Lewis-Beck 1988.
9. Grossman and Helpman 1994.

here since others have done so.[10] Equally important, but far more poorly understood, however, are the political gains that also motivate state leaders to cooperate in trade. The model we develop focuses on these domestic political incentives. It demonstrates that, as the fate of a government becomes more dependent on free and fair elections, its leaders derive increasing gains from trade agreements, prompting them to engage in greater cooperation with other countries on commercial issues. Hence, the probability of a country concluding an international trade agreement increases as its domestic institutions become more democratic.

This outcome occurs because trade agreements can enhance the utility of both heads of state and voters. Trade agreements convey information to voters about the activities of leaders; in turn, such information helps leaders retain office. This informational role is an important aspect of cooperative agreements, and—although more domestically-oriented—it supports the claims of Robert O. Keohane about the value of information provision in fostering international cooperation.[11]

Voters have heterogeneous preferences about trade policy. Depending on their factor endowments, some prefer higher levels of protection and others prefer freer trade. A purely vote-maximizing representative would therefore choose a tariff level that maximizes the utility of the median voter. However, trade barriers create rents for interest groups whose support policymakers may desire to win. Hence political leaders may seek to raise barriers beyond the level preferred by the median voter to create these rents. Constituents harmed by government rent seeking can threaten to remove the incumbent; politicians trade off increased rents with a decreased vote share at the next election.

Voters, however, face an informational problem in their attempt to monitor politicians; namely, they cannot distinguish perfectly between adverse economic shocks over which leaders have little control and economic adversity stemming from the extractive policies of leaders. Consequently, voters in a democracy may remove a leader from office during economic downturns, even if that individual has not engaged in rent seeking. Leaders in such situations would like to find a way to demonstrate that poor economic performance is not the result of their extractive policies.

Entering into a trade agreement with another country is one way to do so. We argue that such agreements offer a more credible means for leaders to signal voters about their policy choices than do unilateral policy declarations, which leaders may be able to quietly reverse at any time. A trade agreement is defined here as (1) a public commitment by leaders to a less protectionist policy than otherwise would be implemented, and (2) an institutional device that credibly conveys that a state's obligations have been violated in the event of unilateral abrogation. A trade agreement, then, is both a promise and an alarm. It commits each participating

10. See, for example, Bagwell and Staiger 1999.
11. Keohane 1984.

country to lower at least some trade barriers, and countries that violate their international commitments trip an alarm sounded by other participants or the organization monitoring the agreement.

Our model thus emphasizes the signaling function of international agreements. Reporting on the behavior of signatories is a key, although frequently overlooked, function of many commercial agreements. The World Trade Organization (WTO), for example, regularly issues public reports on all of its members' trade policies. These trade policy reviews are an important means by which countries' behavior can be monitored. In addition, its dispute settlement mechanism publicizes suspected violations of the agreement. The European Union (EU) also issues public summaries of the extent to which countries are adopting and implementing its directives.[12] The North American Free Trade Agreement (NAFTA)'s dispute settlement mechanism serves a similar purpose—countries can be publicly accused of violating their international commitments and forced to undergo a long, open process of defending their behavior. We do not claim that voters actually read these documents, but rather that they are more likely to hear about a foreign government's or international organization's complaints regarding their government's violations of a trade agreement than they are to learn about changes in domestic trade policy. Such international accusations of bad behavior are more newsworthy than are unilateral changes in trade policy, as many countries (such as Mexico and Canada during the negotiations over NAFTA) have realized.

Furthermore, publicly exposed cheating on trade agreements can generate domestic "audience costs" for political leaders.[13] Voters become aware that economic downturns may be attributable to leaders' overly protectionist policies and so become more likely to remove them from office. Recent public opinion research, for example, suggests that voters value commercial institutions—like the WTO—and believe they are needed to support an open trading system, implying that leaders may pay a political price for violating the rules of such institutions.[14] These audience costs tend to be higher in democracies than in other regimes because the political survival of democratic leaders hinges more on election outcomes. International economic cooperation can thus help democratic governments boost their chances of re-election, thereby providing a strong inducement for them to pursue such agreements. Autocratic leaders, however, have less reason to worry about voters and consequently face less pressure to solve the informational problems addressed in this article by concluding commercial agreements.

The model we develop demonstrates that leaders have greater political incentives to conclude trade agreements as elections grow in importance. We expect, therefore, the probability of signing an agreement to increase as a country becomes more democratic. To test this hypothesis, we examine whether the regime types of states

12. Martin 2000, chap. 7.
13. Fearon 1994.
14. Herrmann, Tetlock, and Diascro 2001.

have influenced their propensity to form and expand preferential trading arrangements (PTAs) during the period since World War II. Consistent with our model, we find that democratic countries are about twice as likely to form a PTA as autocratic countries, and that pairs of democracies are roughly four times as likely to do so as autocratic pairs. These results provide strong evidence that democracies are more commercially cooperative than other countries.

## The Model

We begin by specifying the nature of the underlying economy, which allows us to derive the trade policy preferences of voters. Then we model the structure of the polity, deriving the government's preferences over trade policy. We use an imperfect information model where there is uncertainty about the state of the world. Consequently, voters do not know exactly what policy leaders choose. The extent to which a state is democratic influences how much impact elections have on the probability that a leader retains office, given the voters' choices and the policies adopted. We first derive a Nash equilibrium for the purely domestic game between voters and the government in setting the level of trade barriers. Then we derive the Nash equilibrium for the same game, except that we allow governments to sign trade agreements with other countries. We show that allowing them to make agreements can generate gains for both governments and voters compared to the no-agreement case, and that the gains accruing to governments are directly related to the extent of democracy. Finally, we show that the model indicates that the probability of a trade agreement being signed by two countries increases as either country becomes more democratic. The appendix contains the complete formal derivation of our results.

### *The Economy*

We analyze a small, open Heckscher-Ohlin economy producing two goods with two factors of production, as the appendix further specifies. The domestic price of the imported good (in terms of the export good) in period $\tau$ is $p_\tau$, and $p_\tau = \pi_\tau(1 + t_\tau)$ where $\pi_\tau$ is the world price (in period $\tau$) and $t_\tau$ is the current period level of trade barriers, modeled here as an ad valorem tariff. Because the economy is small, the world price ($\pi_\tau$) is given and cannot be affected by states' actions. Without any loss of generality, we normalize the price such that trade ceases at $t_\tau = 1$ (that is, the tariff is prohibitive at 100 percent).

Individuals in the economy maximize the discounted sum of their one-period utilities, which depend on domestic prices and the tariff in two ways. A higher domestic price of the imported good (perhaps due to tariffs) lowers consumption of that good, but if the individual's income rises with protection, consumption (and hence utility) may rise. We can write any individual $l$'s utility as a function solely of domestic prices (which in turn depend on the tariff) as

$$U^l = \sum_{\tau=0}^{\infty} \delta^{\tau} U^l(p_{\tau}).$$

Voters differ in their ownership of capital; as such, they differ in the level of protection that each desires most. Since we assume that the imported good is labor-intensive, those individuals who own much capital prefer low or even negative tariffs, whereas those who own little but their labor prefer higher tariffs. We assume that the median voter, indexed by $m$, owns relatively little capital, and therefore prefers a positive, but moderate, level of trade barriers, denoted $t^m$.

This assumption about voters' trade preferences is entirely appropriate. In the United States, which is among the least trade-dependent countries, public opinion data show that a vast majority of elites and a majority of the mass public support relatively free trade.[15] In more trade-dependent countries, such sentiment is likely to be even stronger.

### *The Polity*

The executive (also called the incumbent or the government)—whether a democratic or autocratic leader—is a pure rent seeker unconcerned about social welfare.[16] The executive may extract rents either directly via trade tax revenues or indirectly from interest groups in exchange for trade barriers that shield these groups from foreign competition. We adopt a very general objective function for government rents, $G(t)$. It is assumed to be an increasing function of home trade barriers, $G'(t) > 0$. The executive wishes to maximize the sum of the discounted[17] rents collected by the government,

$$G = \sum_{\tau=0}^{\infty} \delta^{\tau} G(t_{\tau}).$$

The government is a pure rent seeker, and these rents rise monotonically with the level of protection. This purely venal behavior implies that any predictions we make about the limits on the extractive behavior of leaders stem from the institutional structures within which policies are chosen, rather than from the players' preferences. Furthermore, any variations in policy choice across regimes will be a consequence of institutional variation, not of variations in preferences.

15. See Chittick and Billingsley 1989; and Herrmann, Tetlock, and Diascro 2001.

16. Social or consumer welfare does not enter the government's objective function, making our claims harder to establish.

17. We assume that the discount rates of voters and the government are the same, but that their utility functions are different.

This assumption also ensures that the government will, ceteris paribus, always desire a level of tariffs higher than voters prefer. This tension between voters and leaders—with voters attempting to restrain an extractive leader—is central. Alternatively, we could specify the government's preferences as single-peaked in the tariff. For example, the government may receive a share of the tariff revenues, so that the point at which these are maximized is the preferred level of tariffs of the government. All the same results follow as long as we maintain the assumption that the government's unconstrained, ideal tariff is higher than that of the median voter.

If the government's ideal tariff were to lie below that of the median voter, the political problem facing the voters would be different. No longer would they have to restrain the rent-seeking impulses of their leaders; instead they would encourage leaders to choose higher tariffs. If voters are highly protectionist, and even more so than leaders, the decision to establish trade agreements is itself puzzling. One then has to explain why leaders would negotiate public agreements to adopt policies that are opposed not only by many special interest groups (for example, import-competing groups), but also by a majority of the populace. Our model does not deal with this ordering of preferences.

The voters' problem is informational. Voters are incompletely informed about the exact level of trade barriers, but they do know the domestic price of the goods they produce and consume.[18] We assume that the world price, $\pi_T$, is subject to exogenous shocks in each period. The distribution of these shocks is given and known to all.[19] Voters, however, cannot determine exactly how the shocks and government policy combine to affect domestic goods prices.

The sequence of events in each period of our model is as follows: the executive decides on the government's trade policy, $t_T$, and then the world economy experiences a shock to world prices, $\pi_T$. These two events together determine domestic prices, $p_T$, which are what voters observe. Prices and incomes are then established, and consumption occurs, all of which determine the voters' welfare. At the end of each period, the median voter examines its welfare, $U^m$, which determines its support for or opposition to the incumbent in the election. If the voter's welfare is above some threshold level, which is determined endogenously, then it votes to re-elect. This one-shot game is repeated ad infinitum.

The executive must commit to a trade policy before the shock has materialized. That is, the government must choose policy in the face of uncertainty about the world price that will be obtained. Once the shock materializes, its magnitude is still unknown to the voters, as is the tariff chosen. In the case of an adverse shock, voters cannot tell if the low utility they experience was caused by an exogenous shock to

18. It is not obvious that voters know the exact policy choices of their representatives. For example, United States voters are much more likely to know the domestic price of sugar than the level of the quota imposed on imported sugar by the government.

19. These shocks to the exogenous world price are identically and independently distributed (i.i.d.) in each period over a finite support.

the economy or by excessive protectionism on the part of the executive. Voters base their electoral decision only on the information available to them, implying that they may reject executives for events that are beyond the executives' control. The executive thus faces the prospect of being ousted from office in every electoral period.

The voters will choose a voting rule conditional on the observed domestic price and hence their current period utility. This simple retrospective voting rule is one in which the voters optimally choose a threshold level of utility, $\underline{U}^l$, such that voter $l$ will choose to reappoint the executive in period $\tau$ if $l$'s utility is at least as good as its threshold value, that is, if $U^l(p_\tau) \geq \underline{U}^l$.

We define the (*ex ante*) probability of the median voter recommending reappointment as the probability that actual utility (as a consequence of the policy $t_\tau$ and the shock $\pi_\tau$) is larger than the specified threshold $\underline{U}^m$. That is $\phi(t_\tau, \underline{U}^m) = \Pr[U^m(p_\tau) > \underline{U}^m]$. We assume that $\phi(1, U) = 0$ for all $U$. That is, when trade barriers are set so high that imports are prohibited, the electorate fails to vote for re-election with certainty.[20]

## *Political Regime Type*

An election is a determination by voters about whether the executive should remain in office. Both democracies and autocracies hold elections. What differs across regimes is the degree to which these contests affect the executive's fate. The more democratic a country, the more important are elections in determining whether the incumbent retains office. If the election's outcome is binding, the regime is a "pure democracy." If, on the other hand, the executive retains office irrespective of the voters' decision, the regime is a "pure autocracy."

We allow a continuum of possibilities for the role of elections and hence for the type of regime: the degree to which the election binds the executive ranges from low to high. That is, the actual probability that the executive keeps office is a weighted average of the probability in a pure democracy and the certainty of keeping office in a pure autocracy. The actual probability of keeping office in any period, $\tau$, is:

$$\rho(t_\tau, \underline{U}^m, \sigma) = \sigma\phi(t_\tau, \underline{U}^m) + (1 - \sigma) \text{ where } \sigma \in [0, 1]. \tag{1}$$

The variable, $\sigma$, indicates a country's regime type and takes on higher values in more democratic polities. In a pure democracy, $\sigma = 1$. Only the support of the voting public determines whether a leader retains office. In a pure autocracy, by

20. Equivalently, $U^l[\pi^{\min}(1 + 1)] < U$ for all $U > 0$ and for all individuals, $l$, where $\pi^{\min}$ is the minimum value in the support of $\pi$. That $\phi(1,U) = 0$ for all $U$ is a feature of the political system, not of the preferences of the government. That is, in all systems, complete rent extraction leads the electorate to recommend eviction from office.

contrast, $\sigma = 0$. The incumbent executive keeps office irrespective of the electorate's sentiments.[21]

*The Executive's Optimal Level of Trade Barriers*

Given that the economy is small, the executive can choose trade barriers without being able to affect world prices and hence other countries' policy decisions, and vice versa. Each executive will choose a level of trade barriers that balances the threat of rejection at the polls with the gains from rent seeking, independent of the foreign country's behavior. Because we are examining the behavior of all countries in the world, it is appropriate to assume that the average country lacks global market power. Very few countries ever have enough market power to affect world prices for any good, let alone for all goods in the economy.

In any period, $\tau$, after choosing domestic trade policy $t_\tau$, the executive gains $G(t_\tau)$. The value of choosing $t_\tau < 1$ at the start of any period, $\tau$, can be written (recursively) as

$$\Gamma_\tau(t_\tau) = G(t_\tau) + \delta\rho(t_\tau, \underline{U}^m, \sigma)\Gamma_{\tau+1}. \tag{2}$$

The executive chooses the current period's trade policy, taking the future play of the game as given ($\Gamma_{\tau+1}$ is the continuation value of the game). The decision reached today affects today's rents and the probability of re-election, but does not affect the level of extraction undertaken tomorrow (because the shocks are i.i.d.). Maximization of equation (2) determines the government's optimal choice of trade policy, which we label $t^\circ$. The optimal choice of trade barriers exactly balances the gains in rents from higher barriers with the reduced likelihood of re-election. We show in Lemma A.1 (in the appendix) that, as the voter's choice of the threshold level of welfare rises, the optimal tariff rate chosen by the incumbent ($t^\circ$) must decline. Voters can thus exercise control over their government.

The executive can adopt an alternative strategy, however, which we label the Leviathan strategy. In this course of action, the government maximizes its economic extraction by setting tariffs at their highest level, $t = 1$, and consequently reducing its prospects of re-election. There is still some chance that a maximally extractive government will remain in office in the next period despite the will of the voters

21. It has been suggested that a key distinction between democracies and autocracies is that democratic leaders are less patient (that is, have lower discount factors) and are only concerned about the next election, whereas autocratic leaders have a longer time horizon. See, for example, Haggard and Kaufman 1995, 152. Our model formalizes this intuition by incorporating the role of elections into leaders' decision making. If the election is substantively important, the effect of the election is, in equilibrium, to lower the implied discount factor that leaders use to calculate their future (expected) stream of rents. The leader's effective discount rate is shown endogenously to be lower the more democratic the state.

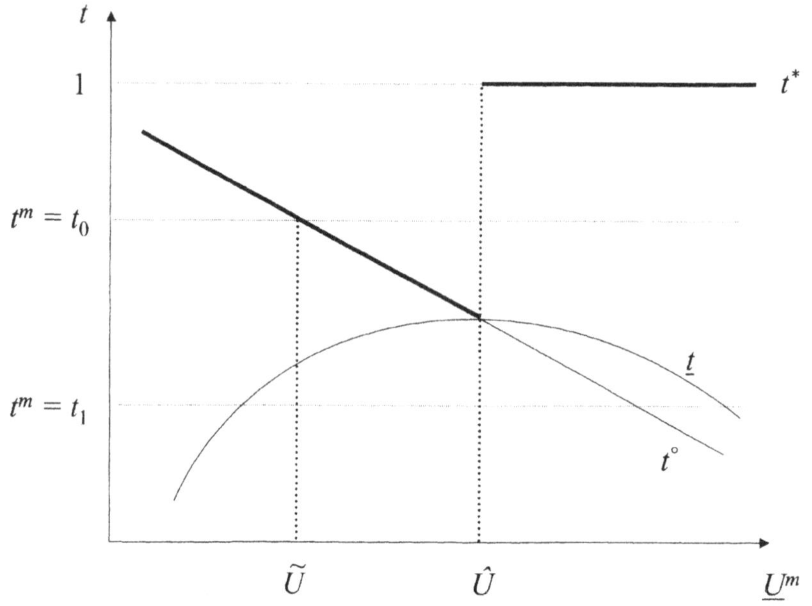


**FIGURE 1.** *The best response functions*

because the country is not a perfect democracy. This happens with probability $1 - \sigma$. A lower tariff, $t$—one that balances the rent extraction motive with re-election concerns as in $t^\circ$ above—is preferred by the incumbent over the Leviathan tariff, $t = 1$, when the executive gains more from the lower tariff than from the Leviathan policy. The incumbent's optimal choice between the maximal Leviathan tariff and the moderate tariff then depends on the voters' selection of their welfare threshold, $\underline{U}$. Setting the threshold too high requires the government to choose a very low tariff; in response, the incumbent may choose the Leviathan action, extracting the maximal amount of rents now and risking rejection in the future election. If the threshold is set too low, the government extracts as much as possible, ensuring that the low utility threshold of the voters is still satisfied. Hence the choice of tariff depends crucially on the threshold chosen by the voters. Figure 1 illustrates the government's best response function, indicated in bold.

There is some threshold ($\hat{U}$) that is the highest the incumbent will accept before resorting to the Leviathan action. And since the optimal tariff, $t^\circ$, falls with the threshold (see Lemma A.1 in the appendix), there is some minimum tariff level, $\underline{t}$, which the incumbent will accept. This tariff, $\underline{t}$, is calculated to be the lowest that the executive will accept instead of adopting the maximally extractive, Leviathan tariff;

the executive is indifferent between the Leviathan and this moderate tariff. Any attempt by the voters to restrict the tariff below this level by raising their welfare threshold induces the government to choose the Leviathan strategy. Any tariff above this minimum level is preferred to the Leviathan tariff by the government. Thus voters have some, but not complete, control over the government through the threat of elections.

*Optimizing Voter Behavior*

If the government adopts the Leviathan strategy of maximal tariffs, then there is no role for the voters regardless of their welfare threshold. If, instead, the government adopts a more moderate strategy, then the voters (who select their thresholds before the government implements its tariff policy) choose a threshold to maximize their expected utility:

$$EU(p) = EU\{\pi[1 + t^{\circ}(\underline{U}^{m},\sigma)]\}.$$

*The Nash Equilibrium*

Consider again Figure 1. In the region where $t^{\circ}$ lies above $\underline{t}$—that is, where $U < \hat{U}$—the optimal response by the government to any $U$ is $t^{\circ}$. When $U$ gets too large, the government switches to the Leviathan strategy and adopts the maximal tariff of 1.

The median voter wants a tariff that lies as close as possible to her (*ex ante*) ideal, $t^{m}$. If $t^{m}$ lies everywhere above $\underline{t}$ (as in the case where $t^{m} = t_0$ in Figure 1), then the voter sets the threshold at $\tilde{U}$ and the government responds with $t^{\circ} = t^{m}$. Alternatively, when $t^{m}$ crosses $\underline{t}$, the voter's ideal tariff lies below that which the government can be constrained to provide. Hence, the voters restrict the government to the lowest tariff possible by choosing a threshold at $\hat{U}$. We prove that this pair of strategies is a Nash equilibrium in Lemma A.3 in the appendix.

If the government is perfectly constrained by voters, then $t^{m}$ is the tariff imposed in response to the threshold of $\tilde{U}$. If, however, the government is imperfectly controlled by the voters, then the government implements a tariff of $\underline{t}(\hat{U})$ in response to $\hat{U}$. The degree of control that the voters exercise depends crucially on whether $t^{m}$ is larger or smaller than $\underline{t}(\hat{U})$. Now $t^{m}$ is exogenous; $\underline{t}(\hat{U})$, on the other hand, is the lowest tariff the executive is prepared to accept before switching to the maximally extractive, Leviathan tariff.

The value of the equilibrium tariff, $\underline{t}$, that leaves the executive indifferent between playing it or the Leviathan strategy, depends on the degree of control the voters exercise over the executive, that is, on $\sigma$, the level of democracy (see Lemma A.4 in the appendix). However, more democratic polities will not necessarily adopt lower tariffs in the equilibrium to this tariff-setting game. As the polity becomes more democratic, the benefits of the Leviathan tariff fall because the executive becomes more likely to be replaced when selecting this strategy. To maintain the indifference condition between (the payoffs from) $\underline{t}$ and the Leviathan strategy, the benefits generated by a more moderate tariff must fall as well; thus $\underline{t}$ should fall. But a lower $\underline{t}$ also increases the likelihood of re-election in the next period and hence keeps the government in office longer in expectation. This latter effect raises the long-run returns to the government, causing the indifference condition between $\underline{t}$ and the Leviathan tariff to be violated once again. The relative size of these two effects is indeterminate at our level of generality. Hence, it is not necessarily true that more democracy leads to lower unilateral tariffs.

Although the equilibrium tariff, $\underline{t}$, is determined by both the preferences of the players and the domestic institutions that govern the voters' control of the executive, it is *not* necessarily the case that, as domestic institutions become more democratic, the equilibrium tariff, $\underline{t}$, in this game falls. Democracies, in our model, are not unilaterally freer traders than other regime types.[22]

In what follows, however, we show that democracies are more likely to join PTAs than other countries. Moreover, we establish that democracies do not join PTAs solely to lower trade barriers. A more interesting and deeper result related to PTA formation grows out of the model: such arrangements can solve an informational problem that limits the head of state's credibility. In the eyes of the voters, participating in a PTA bolsters the credibility of offers made by the executive to reduce trade barriers, and enhances the leader's prospects of re-election.

In the next section we compare the gains for the executive from the unilateral policy choice described above to those reaped from signing an international trade agreement. We show that both voters and executives can be made better off with an agreement, and that this is increasingly true as a country becomes more democratic.

### *International Cooperation and Trade Agreements*

In addition to setting their own unilateral policies, executives have the capability to negotiate trade agreements with other countries. But an executive will only do so if the gains from an agreement are at least as great as those from setting policy

22. The unilateral, equilibrium tariff (under imperfect control) is the lowest tariff the executive will accept rather than adopt the maximally extractive, Leviathan action; That is, in equilibrium, the executive plays $\underline{t}$ and earns a return identical to the Leviathan payoff, $G(\underline{t})/\{1 - \delta[\sigma\phi(\underline{t},U) + (1 - \sigma)]\} = G(1)/[1 - \delta(1 - \sigma)]$. As the polity becomes more democratic (as $\sigma$ rises), the benefits of the Leviathan action fall; that is, the right-hand side falls. As the right-hand side falls, so does the left-hand side, but the left falls by less. To maintain the indifference condition, the benefits of a moderate action (the left hand side) must fall even more. A fall in the moderate tariff, $\underline{t}$, reduces the benefits to the government in any period ($G(\underline{t})$ falls). But it also increases the likelihood of re-election ($\phi(\underline{t},U)$ rises) and hence keeps the government in office longer in expectation. This might raise the discounted returns to government, violating the indifference condition. Hence it is not necessarily true that more democracy leads to lower unilateral tariffs. It depends on the particular functional form of the distribution function $\phi(\underline{t},U)$ that captures the uncertainty relative to the shape of government's objective function $G(\underline{t})$. See Lemma A.4 for the implicit differentiation of the equality above.

unilaterally. When can an executive gain from a trade agreement? An agreement is a pair of trade policies and a signaling institution. The signal may be a complaint filed by another country that is party to the agreement or a determination of non-compliance by the international institution monitoring the agreement. That is, an agreement by definition comprises a level of trade barriers lower than the executive's optimal unilateral policy, $t^C < t^*$. It also includes a mechanism for the institution or a foreign country to signal others that the home executive has cheated and raised trade barriers above the agreement level. Consequently, the agreement trips an alarm if $t > t^C$; otherwise, no signal is sent.

The agreement, then, is a level of trade barriers below the government's ideal unilateral level and an alarm mechanism that other governments or a trade institution—such as the General Agreement on Tariffs and Trade (GATT) or the WTO—can use whenever the actual trade policy of a party to the agreement deviates from the one agreed upon. A commercial agreement is public and therefore provides information that voters can use to more closely monitor the executive. In particular, monitors of the trade agreement (such as an independent agency like the WTO or even the participating governments themselves) can announce, just before each election, whether the executive in each country is in compliance with the agreement.[23]

We assume that voters can observe this signal. Moreover, voters have an incentive to pay close attention to it, since the signal improves their welfare. Equally, the trade institution and its members have an incentive to divulge this information and make sure that voters pay attention to it, since this disciplines the government. Our assertion is that voters are more likely to hear about a foreign country's or an international organization's accusations that their government violated a trade agreement than they are to know about a unilateral change in domestic trade policy. We expect that international accusations of violations will be much more newsworthy than marginal, unilateral changes in the tariff code. An international trade agreement, then, both sets policy and provides information.

Under an international trade agreement, the executive will abide by the terms of the agreement whenever the long-term gains from doing so exceed the gains from the Leviathan strategy. The voters reward a compliant executive by setting a zero threshold; that is, they always vote to re-elect the government. If the agreement is violated, the voters set an unreachable threshold and vote to reject the incumbent with certainty. Lemma A.5 establishes that this is equilibrium behavior for both the executive and the voters.

23. As noted earlier, the WTO does indeed issue such reports on all member countries periodically. Its trade policy reviews of member countries are an important aspect of monitoring, as is its dispute settlement system.

## Comparing the Regimes: Imperfect Control and Gains for the Executive

When the voters can only imperfectly control the executive, can the executive still gain from the agreement relative to the no-agreement situation? The agreement decreases the tariff below what was the lowest acceptable tariff in the absence of the agreement, that is, $t^C \in [t^m, \underline{t}]$. Since the voters prefer a tariff lower than $\underline{t}$, they obviously gain (or at least no worse off). Does the government gain?

We assume that the voting rule for individuals casting ballots adjusts to the new information the agreement provides. The probability of re-election still depends on their overall utility, but voters also make use of the information embedded in the alarm. If no alarm sounds, it is optimal for the median voter to cast a ballot for the incumbent. After all, the agreed-upon tariff is, by definition, preferred to the tariff absent the agreement. On the other hand, if the alarm sounds, the median voter rejects the incumbent, although there is still the $(1-\sigma)$ chance that the offending government manages to hold onto office.

The value of international cooperation over noncooperation for the executive is the difference between the executive's gains from cooperation and the gains from unilateral policymaking:

$$\Delta(t^C;\ \sigma) = \frac{G(t^C)}{1-\delta} - \frac{G(1)}{1-\delta(1-\sigma)}. \tag{3}$$

PROPOSITION 1: *Under imperfect voter control, for any $t^C \in [t^m, \underline{t}]$,*

a) *the agreement is preferred by governments that are sufficiently democratic and patient, that is, $\Delta(t^C, \sigma) > 0\ \forall\ \sigma > \bar{\sigma}(\delta)$;*

b) *the more democratic the polity, the greater the gains from cooperation, that is, $d\Delta/d\sigma > 0$.*

In Proposition 1, we show that the more democratic the country, the more its government prefers the international agreement. Proposition 1 also shows that the gain to the executive from cooperating increases as the state becomes more democratic. As the level of democracy, $\sigma$, rises, the probability of being removed from office grows even when the executive is not overly extractive, *ceteris paribus*. Hence, relative to an autocrat, a democratic executive (whose re-election is more dependent on the wishes of voters) has more to gain from making an agreement and thus lowering the chance of eviction from office without a legitimate cause. The executive trades off a greater degree of certainty about re-election when he cooperates in exchange for a lower level of rents because he chooses a lower level of trade barriers.

Notice that any trade agreement, $t^C \in [t^m, \underline{t}]$, yields a gain for the executive. The best possible agreement (for the executive) may be to agree to a tariff as close to $\underline{t}$

as possible. Little would be relinquished in the trade negotiations, but much would be gained in terms of the domestic polity. Recall, of course, that we have abstracted from other motivating factors that induce states to form PTAs, such as the welfare gains from trade creation and the political gains from trade diversion or from deep integration, all of which might induce an executive to lower tariffs even further. But our primary concern here has been to establish the role that an agreement can play in solving the domestic monitoring problem.

### *Comparing the Regimes: Perfect Control and Gains for the Executive*

In the case where the median voter exercises perfect control over the government (that is, $t^* = t^m$), it is also the case that the government will gain from the agreement. The extra information provided by the agreement reduces the chance that the government is unfairly evicted. Consider the case where the agreement sets tariffs equal to those favored by the median voter; that is, $t^C = t^m$. This agreement then merely formalizes pre-existing behavior. Then the gains for the executive from international cooperation relative to noncooperation now are

$$\Delta(t^m; \sigma) = \frac{G(t^m)}{1-\delta} - \frac{G(t^m)}{1-\delta[\sigma\phi(t^m, U) + (1-\sigma)]}.$$

In this case, as Proposition 2 demonstrates, the international agreement is preferred by executives in all regime types, yet it is democratic executives that have the most to gain from these agreements. The executive's gains from signing an agreement rise with the country's level of democracy.

PROPOSITION 2: *Under perfect control, for any agreement $t^C = t^m$,*

a) $\Delta(t^C; \sigma) > 0$ *for all $\sigma$;*
b) *the more democratic the polity, the greater the gains from cooperation, that is, $d\Delta/d\sigma > 0$.*

### *The Voters' Gain from the Cooperative Agreement*

Even if the government gains, we need to show that the voters gain as well from an international agreement in all situations. In the case where the government is imperfectly constrained by voters in the absence of a trade agreement, it is balancing two pressures. The first induces the incumbent to extract as much rent as possible by applying a very high tariff, while the second pushes him to limit his extraction so he does not reduce his chances of re-election too much. The net effect is to choose a tariff that is higher than that preferred by the median voter; hence, $t^* > t^m$. Thus any international agreement that lowers the actual tariff below $t^*$ and closer to the median's ideal, $t^m$, will be preferred by the median voter. As such, the median voter prefers any international agreement $t^C \in [t^m, t^*)$ to the lack of an agreement.

If the government is perfectly constrained by the voters, no improvement with respect to the voters' utility is possible from an international agreement. The agreement at the pre-existing tariff level—the median voter's ideal level—is beneficial to the government but leaves the voters indifferent. (The government will not agree to an international agreement that lowers tariffs below both its and the median voter's ideal level since this will lower its utility and spur its removal from office.) Given these conditions, the median voter weakly prefers the international agreement to the lack of one, as Proposition 3 formally proves.

PROPOSITION 3: *The median voter prefers the trade agreement regime to the no-agreement regime.*

In a world where voters cannot perfectly distinguish between a reduction in utility stemming from an adverse economic shock, on the one hand, and from excessive government rent seeking, on the other, executives and voters will both gain from international trade agreements that provide information about the executive's behavior. Thus we have our central result: the incentives for a leader to sign a trade agreement increase as the country becomes increasingly democratic. As such, the more democratic the polity, the greater the likelihood that the country will sign a trade agreement.

### *The International Game*

For any international trade agreement to be signed, at least two countries must agree. How do both (or all) countries' gains change when the home country becomes more democratic? In this model, because the countries are small, the behavior of each has no impact on the other. An increase in one country's level of democracy has no impact upon the other country's willingness to sign an agreement.

If the probability of signing a trade agreement increases in the gains from such an agreement, then the probability of an agreement depends independently on the level of democracy in each country. As one country becomes more democratic, the other countries' willingness to sign an agreement never falls. Therefore, the probability of an agreement between two or more countries always rises as the level of democracy in any one of them increases. Moreover, the model implies that, although their effects are independent, when each country is very democratic the probability of a trade agreement is highest. It is lowest when each country is very autocratic.

Let $F_i$ and $F_j$ be the probabilities that countries $i$ and $j$, respectively, sign a trade agreement. Since these probabilities are increasing in the gains from this agreement, we know from Propositions 1 and 2 that the gains from the agreement depend on the tariff levels chosen and the degree of democracy in each country. Thus we have $F_i = F[\Delta(t^C;\sigma_i)]$ and $F_j = F[\Delta(t^C;\sigma_j)]$, with $F$ being a continuous function that takes a value between 0 and 1, and rises with $\Delta$. Then the probability that a PTA forms between $i$ and $j$ is simply the product of these two probabilities: $\Pr(PTA_{ij}) = F_iF_j = F[\Delta(t^C;\sigma_i)]F[\Delta(t^C;\sigma_i)]$. Since both of these depend on the level of democracy, we have the following proposition.

PROPOSITION 4: *The probability that two countries form a PTA rises with the level of democracy in each country. That is,*

$$\frac{d\Pr(PTA_{ij})}{d\sigma_i} > 0 \quad \textit{and} \quad \frac{d\Pr(PTA_{ij})}{d\sigma_j} > 0.$$

Democracies have a greater incentive to enter into cooperative trade agreements than other polities. There are, of course, other, more standard arguments for trade agreements, especially in the small, open-economy environment assumed here. The economic costs and benefits of joining such arrangements have been extensively studied and are clearly important.[24] We, however, focus on another key determinant of the decision to form a commercial arrangement that has been the subject of remarkably little research to date, namely, the regime types of the member states.

## The Empirical Evidence

The preceding analysis indicates that a country is increasingly likely to conclude a cooperative trade agreement as it becomes more democratic and that the probability of two or more countries signing such an agreement rises with the level of democracy in each country. In the remainder of this article, we conduct some preliminary statistical tests of these propositions.

We focus on explaining agreements that establish or expand PTAs—a group of institutions that includes customs unions, common markets, free trade areas, and other commercial agreements. Reductions in reciprocal trade barriers among participants are central to all such arrangements. In fact, Article XXIV of the GATT stipulates that any PTA notified to this body must largely abolish barriers to commerce within the preferential grouping.[25] States making reciprocal trade barrier reductions are engaged in acts of economic cooperation, so it is appropriate to test our model of cooperative trade agreements by focusing on the formation and expansion of PTAs.[26] It is clear that agreements to enter into a preferential trading

24. See Anderson and Blackhurst 1993; Bhagwati 1993; de Melo and Panagariya 1993; Fernández and Portes 1998; Krueger 1999; Pomfret 1988; Panagariya 2000; and Whalley 1998.

25. See Anderson and Blackhurst 1993; Bhagwati 1993, 27; and de Melo and Panagariya 1993.

26. It is important to note that whether such trade barrier reductions adversely affect third parties has no bearing on whether the reductions constitute acts of economic cooperation among the PTA members. As Lisa L. Martin points out, "While cooperation improves the expected welfare of the cooperating states relative to the status quo *ex ante*, it is not necessarily a Pareto-improving (mutually beneficial) move for

arrangement do not constitute the entire universe of trade agreements to which this model could be applied. Nonetheless, PTAs comprise a substantial portion of the commercial agreements concluded since World War II, which is the period analyzed here. Furthermore, comprehensive data on other such agreements are not available for many countries included in our sample.

*A Statistical Model of PTAs*

Proposition 4 demonstrates that the probability of two countries signing a trade agreement is a positive function of the level of democracy in each country. To test this formal proposition, we estimate the following model of PTA formation:

$$\begin{aligned} PTA_{ij} = {} & \beta_0 + \beta_1 REG_i + \beta_2 REG_j + \beta_3 GDP_i + \beta_4 GDP_j + \beta_5 \Delta GDP_i \\ & + \beta_6 \Delta GDP_j + \beta_7 TRADE_{ij} + \beta_8 DISPUTE_{ij} + \beta_9 COL_{ij} \\ & + \beta_{10} ALLY_{ij} + \beta_{11} DISTANCE_{ij} + \beta_{12} GATT_{ij} \\ & + \beta_{13} HEGEMONY + e_{ij}. \end{aligned} \tag{4}$$

The dependent variable is the log of the odds that a pair of states, $i$ and $j$, enters a PTA in year $\tau + 1$, where we observe 1 if this occurs and 0 otherwise. We code $i$ and $j$ as entering a PTA if they—either by themselves or in combination with other countries—form a new preferential arrangement, or if one of them joins a PTA in which the other is already a member. Hence, the observed value of $PTA_{ij}$ is 1 in the year $i$ and $j$ enter a preferential arrangement, but not in years when they belong to a pre-existing arrangement. In the following analysis, however, we also briefly consider whether the variables in equation (4) help to explain the existence of a preferential grouping between $i$ and $j$. Although the PTAs included in our analysis are drawn primarily from those notified to the GATT, they also include other arrangements since there is no reason to limit our model's application to commercial agreements concluded among parties to the GATT.[27]

---

the world as a whole." Martin 2000, 13; see also Keohane 1984. It is also important to note that, although a large and influential body of literature exists on the economic effects of PTAs, the nature and strength of these effects remain subjects of fierce debate and have little bearing on our analysis. See, for example, Bhagwati 1993; Frankel, Stein, and Wei 1998; Krueger 1999; Krugman 1993; Panagariya 2000; and Pomfret 1988.

27. For a list of PTAs notified to the GATT, see World Trade Organization 1995. In addition to these PTAs—which are limited to arrangements formed by GATT and WTO members—we include the PTAs listed in Hartland-Thunberg 1980. We also include the Council on Mutual Economic Assistance (CMEA), the Southern African Customs Union, the Economic Community of West African States (ECOWAS), the Southern African Development Coordination Conference, and the Eastern and Southern African Preferential Trade Area. On these PTAs, see de Melo and Panagariya 1993; Foroutan 1993, 246–51; Hanlon 1986; Kisanga 1991; Orimalade and Ubogu 1984; and Pomfret 1988.

Each PTA is coded as starting in the year it enters into force. (Note that we do not consider agreements strengthening or superceding an existing PTA to be new preferential arrangements.) The original

LEMMA A.5: *For any international trade agreement* $t^C \in [t^m, \underline{t}]$, *the following strategies constitute a Nash equilibrium:* $t^* = \begin{cases} t^C & \text{if } \sigma > \bar{\sigma}(\delta) \\ 1 & \text{otherwise} \end{cases}$ *and* $\underline{U}^* = \begin{cases} 0 & \text{if no alarm sent} \\ \infty & \text{otherwise} \end{cases}$.

*Proof:* The optimal deviation for the government is the Leviathan action (since any tariff above $t^C$ leads to rejection by the voters). Then the equilibrium dominates defection whenever $\Delta(t^C; \sigma) > 0$ which is equivalent to the condition $\sigma > [1 - G(t^C)/G(1)](1/\delta - 1) \equiv \bar{\sigma}(\delta)$. As for the voters, once the alarm has (or has not) been sent, changing the threshold will have no effect on their payoffs; hence the equilibrium action is weakly preferred.

Along the equilibrium path, the voter knows more about the actions of the executive than in the unilateral case. However, the state of the world is still unknown—hence perfection refinements are not applicable in a non-trivial way. Nevertheless, at any information set, once reached, it remains optimal for the voters to behave according to the equilibrium strategies—that is, the equilibrium behavior is optimal conditional on the publicly available information.

*Proof of Proposition 1:* The condition that $\Delta(t^C; \sigma) > 0$ follows directly from Lemma A.5; $\partial\Delta(t^C, \sigma)/\partial\sigma = G(1)/[1 - \delta(1 - \sigma)]^2\, \delta > 0$.

*Proof of Proposition 2:* $\Delta(t^C; \sigma) = \delta G(t^C)/(1 - \delta)\ \delta\{1 - [\sigma\phi(t^C, U) + (1 - \sigma)]\}/\{1 - \delta[\sigma\phi(t^C, U) + (1 - \sigma)]\} > 0$ for all $\sigma$ and $d\Delta(t^C; \sigma)/d\sigma = \delta G(t^C)(\phi - 1)(\delta\{1 - [\sigma\phi(t^C, U) + (1 - \sigma)]\} - 1)/(1 - \delta)\{1 - \delta[\sigma\phi(t^C, U) + (1 - \sigma)]\}^2 > 0$ for all $\sigma$.

PROPOSITION 3: $U^m[\pi(1 + t^C)] \geq U^m[\pi(1 + t^*)]$ *for any* $t^C \in [t^m, \underline{t}]$.

*Proof:* $G_t > 0$ for all $t$; by inspection of equation (7), it must be that at $t = t^*$, $\phi_t(t) < 0$. Now $\phi_t(t) = 0$ at $t = t^m$ since the voter's utility is maximized, and therefore the probability of re-election is maximized. Therefore $t^* \geq t^m$. After any agreement, $t^C \in [t^m, \underline{t}]$, $\phi(t^C) \geq \phi(t^*)$ since $\phi_t(t) < 0$ for all $t > t^m$ and hence given any realization of $\pi$, $U^m[\pi(1 + t^C)] \geq U^m[\pi(1 + t^*)]$.

PROPOSITION 4: $d\text{Pr}(PTA_{ij})/d\sigma_i > 0$ *and* $d\text{Pr}(PTA_{ij})/d\sigma_j > 0$.

*Proof:* $d\text{Pr}(PTA_{ij})/d\sigma_i = FF'\ d\Delta/d\sigma_i > 0$ since $F' > 0$ by assumption, Propositions 1 and 2 establish the second term, and $F$ lies between 0 and 1. The proof for the second case is identical.

## References

Anderson, Kym, and Richard Blackhurst. 1993. Introduction and Summary. In *Regional Integration and the Global Trading System*, edited by Kym Anderson and Richard Blackhurst, 1–15. London: Harvester Wheatsheaf.

Bagwell, Kyle, and Robert Staiger. 1999. An Economic Theory of GATT. *American Economic Review* 89 (1):215–48.

Banks, Jeffrey S., and Rangarajan K. Sundaram. 1993. Adverse Selection and Moral Hazard in a Repeated Elections Model. In *Political Economy: Institutions, Information, Competition, and Representation*, edited by William A. Barnett, Melvin J. Hinich, and Norman J. Schofield, 295–312. Cambridge: Cambridge University Press.

To measure each state's regime type, identified as $\sigma$ in the formal model above, we rely on a widely used index constructed by Keith Jaggers and Ted Robert Gurr.[28] This index combines data on five factors that help to capture the institutional differences between democracies and autocracies that we emphasized earlier: the competitiveness of the process for selecting a country's chief executive, the openness of this process, the extent to which institutional constraints limit a chief executive's decision-making authority, the competitiveness of political participation within a country, and the degree to which binding rules govern political participation within it. Following Jaggers and Gurr, these data are used to create an 11-point index of each state's democratic characteristics (*DEMOC*) and an 11-point index of its autocratic characteristics (*AUTOC*). The difference between these indices, $REG = DEMOC - AUTOC$, yields a summary measure of regime type that takes on values ranging from $-10$ for a highly autocratic state to 10 for a highly democratic country.

There are three principal reasons we rely on this measure in the following analysis. First, our formal model treats regime type ($\sigma$) as a continuous variable, with the competitiveness of elections ranging from perfectly competitive to completely uncompetitive. As noted above, the index developed by Jaggers and Gurr has a range of 21 points, unlike some other measures of regime type.[29] Second, their index highlights a number of institutional dimensions of regime type that we stressed. The ability of voters to choose the chief executive, which is central to our model, is expected to rise as the process for selecting the executive becomes more competitive and more open, and political participation becomes increasingly competitive. Jaggers and Gurr's index captures each of these three institutional elements, whereas various alternative measures do not.[30] Third, their index covers more countries during the period since World War II than any other measure of regime type with which we are familiar.[31]

In equation (4), $REG_i$ is the value of Jaggers and Gurr's measure for state $i$ in year $\tau$ and $REG_j$ is the value of this measure for state $j$ in $\tau$. Which state in each pair is

members of every PTA are coded as joining it in this year. A state that enters an existing PTA is coded as having formed a preferential arrangement with each member of the arrangement in the year of its accession. In a few cases, the year when a PTA enters into force or the year a state joins an existing PTA is not available. In those cases, we rely on the year in which the negotiations leading to the arrangement's formation or expansion were completed. The GATT/WTO only lists PTAs whose members are parties to the GATT and only does so when these agreements are officially notified to it. Thus for some PTAs, the date given by the WTO as to when states enter the preferential arrangement differs from the date furnished by the other sources listed above. In these cases, we use the earliest date. For a further explanation of how we code the formation of PTAs, see Mansfield 1998.

28. See Jaggers and Gurr 1995; and Gurr, Jaggers, and Moore 1989.

29. For example, the measure developed by Przeworski et al. treats regime type as dichotomous. Przeworski et al. 2000.

30. For example, Gastil 1980 and 1990.

31. See, for example, Bollen 1980; Gasiorowski 1996; Gastil 1980 and 1990; and Przeworski et al. 2000.

$i$ and which one is $j$ is randomly determined. Recall that our model (Proposition 4) demonstrates that the probability of concluding a trade agreement increases as each participant becomes more democratic. Hence, we expect that both $\beta_1$ and $\beta_2$ will be positive and that there will be no significant difference between them.

Besides countries' regime types, other factors are likely to influence the formation of PTAs, and we account for their effects as well. As we indicated previously, a number of economic factors may condition a country's decision to join a trade agreement. The size of its domestic market is one such factor. States with larger home markets tend to depend less on trade and may therefore have less reason to conclude agreements that expand their access to foreign markets than economically smaller states. To address this possibility, we include $GDP_i$ and $GDP_j$ in equation (4). These variables are the gross domestic products (GDPs) of states $i$ and $j$ in year $\tau$. Furthermore, economic conditions may affect the probability that countries sign trade agreements. Some observers, for example, have argued that downturns in the business cycle may stimulate the formation of cooperative agreements.[32] Therefore, we analyze the effects of $\Delta GDP_i$ and $\Delta GDP_j$, which are the changes in the GDP of $i$ and $j$ from year $\tau - 1$ to $\tau$, and are used here as rough measures of the business cycle in each state.[33] Controlling for such economic factors is important so that we can establish the independent effects of domestic political institutions.

In addition to political and economic conditions within countries, relations between countries are likely to affect their willingness to form a PTA.[34] Many observers, for example, argue that the amount of economic exchange between states influences whether they enter a preferential grouping. Rising economic intercourse may increase the prospects of PTA formation by fostering the growth of coalitions with an interest in developing institutional mechanisms to promote greater economic integration and avert the breakdown of economic relations among the group's members.[35] In the same vein, increasing trade flows can heighten the susceptibility of private traders to opportunistic behavior by foreign governments, prompting firms to press for the establishment of PTAs to reduce the ability of governments to engage in such behavior.[36] We therefore include $TRADE_{ij}$, which is the flow of exports from $i$ to $j$ in year $\tau$, in equation (4).[37]

32. Mattli 1999.

33. Data on GDP and the change in GDP are taken from Summers and Heston 1991; and Maddison 1995. Note that while we measure the change in GDP from year $\tau - 1$ to year $\tau$, we also estimated equation (4) after measuring both $\Delta GDP_i$ and $\Delta GDP_j$ from $\tau$ to $\tau + 1$. These two sets of results are very similar.

34. Note that using country-pairs—rather than individual countries—as the unit of analysis allows us to control for the effects of both domestic and international influences on PTA formation.

35. Nye 1988, 239.

36. Yarbrough and Yarbrough 1992.

37. Data on trade flows are taken from the International Monetary Fund's *Direction of Foreign Trade*, various years. Note that these data and those on GDP are expressed in U.S. dollars and in real terms; they are deflated using the United States wholesale price index and producer price index.

The nature of political relations between *i* and *j* is also likely to affect their willingness to form a PTA. It is widely recognized, for example, that various countries have established trade agreements with their former colonies, partly to maintain political influence over colonial possessions once they become independent states.[38] In addition, Cold War dynamics affected international economic relations during the period analyzed here and may have contributed to the establishment of PTAs since World War II. To control for such dynamics—and security relations more generally—we analyze the effects of political-military alliances and military disputes on PTAs.

Countries may be more likely to enter PTAs with their allies than with other states. Trade liberalization yields efficiency gains that enhance the political-military capacity of participants, and alliances help to internalize these security externalities.[39] Since PTAs liberalize commerce among members, alliance politics may influence the likelihood that states will establish such an agreement. It is also important to take account of military disputes since such events obviously might discourage participants from forming a commercial agreement. We therefore include $DISPUTE_{ij}$, $COL_{ij}$, and $ALLY_{ij}$. The first of these variables equals 1 if *i* and *j* are embroiled in a military dispute in $\tau$ and 0 otherwise. The second variable equals 1 if *i* and *j* had a colonial relationship (ending after World War II) in $\tau$ and 0 otherwise. The third variable equals 1 if *i* and *j* are allies in $\tau$ and 0 otherwise.[40]

The geographical distance between states is another factor that is likely to influence their willingness to enter a PTA. One reason why states form PTAs is to guarantee and expand access to the markets of their key trade partners.[41] Frequently, a country's primary commercial partners are located in relative proximity, since as the distance between states increases, so do transportation costs and various other impediments to commerce.[42] To account for the effects of geographical proximity on the establishment and expansion of commercial agreements, we include $DISTANCE_{ij}$ in equation (4).[43] We mentioned earlier that many of the PTAs in our sample were formed under the auspices of the GATT. To analyze whether members of this organization have been more likely to establish trading arrangements than other states, we include $GATT_{ij}$. This variable equals 1 if both *i* and *j* are parties to the GATT in $\tau$ and 0 otherwise.

The factors just described pertain to conditions within countries and relations between them, but systemic conditions may affect the formation of PTAs as well. Particularly important in this regard is the influence of hegemony. Since various

38. See Grilli 1993; and Pomfret 1988, 163.

39. See Gowa 1994; and Gowa and Mansfield 1993.

40. Data on military disputes are taken from Jones, Bremer, and Singer 1996. Data on former colonial relations are taken from Kurian 1992. Data on alliances are taken from Small and Singer 1969; and the Correlates of War Project 1993.

41. Whalley 1998.

42. Frankel, Stein, and Wei 1998.

43. Data on distance are taken from Oneal and Russett 1999.

studies have concluded that waning hegemony tends to stimulate the proliferation of PTAs, we analyze *HEGEMONY*, which is the percentage of global trade accounted for by the state that conducts the greatest amount of commerce in a given year.[44] Finally, $e_{ij}$ is a stochastic error term.

Since comprehensive data on both PTAs and the independent variables described above are only available for the period after World War II, we focus our analysis on this era. More specifically, our sample includes all pairs of countries for which complete data on the variables in equation (4) are available for at least part of the period from 1951 to 1992.[45] To estimate this model, we pool the available data across time and country-pairs and then conduct a logistic regression. Following Nathaniel Beck, Jonathan N. Katz, and Richard Tucker, we account for any temporal dependence in the data by including a natural spline function (with three knots) of the number of years that have elapsed (as of year $\tau + 1$) since each pair of states, $i$ and $j$, last formed a PTA.[46] To conserve space, however, we do not present the estimates of this function.[47] In addition, the tests of statistical significance we report are based on Huber (robust) standard errors, which account for the grouped nature of the data (in the present case, by country-pairs). Recent research indicates that they are superior to logit standard errors in time-series cross-section models with a binary dependent variable.[48]

### *The Statistical Results*

The first column of Table 1 contains our initial results. Consistent with the propositions derived from our formal model, the estimated coefficients of $REG_i$ and $REG_j$ are both positive and statistically significant, indicating that the likelihood of establishing a trade agreement rises as each state in a given dyad becomes more democratic.[49] Moreover, the effects of regime type on commercial cooperation do not vary between states $i$ and $j$. Indeed, there is no statistically significant difference between the estimates of $REG_i$ and $REG_j$ ($\chi^2 = 0.26$; $p = .61$).

44. See Bhagwati 1993; Gilpin 1987; Krugman 1993; and Mansfield 1998. This measure of hegemony has been used repeatedly in studies of the international political economy. See, for example, Krasner 1976; Lake 1988; Mansfield 1998; and McKeown 1991. Note that global trade is defined as the sum of total global exports and total global imports and that, for each year analyzed below, the United States is the state having the highest percentage of global trade. Data used to construct this variable are taken from the International Monetary Fund's *International Financial Statistics*, various years.

45. Only those countries listed by Singer and Small as members of the international system are included in our sample. Singer and Small 1994.

46. See Beck and Katz 1997; and Beck and Tucker 1996.

47. Note that the base of the spline function and each of the three knots are statistically significant in all of the following analyses.

48. See Beck and Katz 1997; and Beck and Tucker 1996.

49. We also sorted these variables by their size, assigning $REG_i$ the larger annual regime score in each pair and $REG_j$ the lower score. This procedure, which accords with much of the literature on the democratic peace, yields estimates that are very similar to those reported below. See, for example, Russett and Oneal 2001; and Russett, Oneal, and Davis 1998.

**TABLE 1.** *Effects of regime type, GDP, the change in GDP, trade, military disputes, colonial relations, alliances, distance, the GATT, and hegemony on PTA formation, 1951–1992*

| *Variable* | *(1)* | *(2)* | *(3)* | *(4)* |
|---|---|---|---|---|
| *Intercept* | 7.315** | 7.223** | 6.847** | 7.212** |
| | (11.85) | (11.64) | (11.82) | (11.54) |
| $REG_i$ | 0.038** | 0.038** | 0.035** | 0.038** |
| | (8.89) | (8.80) | (8.84) | (8.93) |
| $REG_j$ | 0.035** | 0.035** | 0.032** | 0.035** |
| | (8.47) | (8.40) | (8.15) | (8.51) |
| $GDP_i$ | $-4.84 \times 10^{-10}$** | $-3.29 \times 10^{-10}$** | $-7.75 \times 10^{-10}$** | $-4.89 \times 10^{-10}$** |
| | (−3.29) | (−3.47) | (−4.26) | (−3.34) |
| $GDP_j$ | $-3.84 \times 10^{-10}$* | $-2.26 \times 10^{-10}$* | $-6.94 \times 10^{-10}$** | $-3.88 \times 10^{-10}$* |
| | (−2.39) | (−2.16) | (−4.17) | (−2.43) |
| $\Delta GDP_i$ | $4.72 \times 10^{-9}$ | | $6.41 \times 10^{-9}$ | $4.63 \times 10^{-9}$ |
| | (1.28) | | (1.55) | (1.26) |
| $\Delta GDP_j$ | $4.85 \times 10^{-9}$ | | $6.88 \times 10^{-9}$* | $4.77 \times 10^{-9}$ |
| | (1.71) | | (2.04) | (1.69) |
| $TRADE_{ij}$ | $-1.21 \times 10^{-7}$ | $-1.23 \times 10^{-7}$ | | $-1.18 \times 10^{-7}$ |
| | (−1.53) | (−1.56) | | (−1.52) |
| $DISPUTE_{ij}$ | −0.740 | −0.734 | −0.620 | |
| | (−1.91) | (−1.89) | (−1.64) | |
| $COL_{ij}$ | 1.338** | 1.327** | 1.356** | 1.324** |
| | (8.74) | (8.73) | (8.62) | (8.45) |
| $ALLY_{ij}$ | 0.665** | 0.663** | 0.645** | 0.673** |
| | (9.70) | (9.69) | (9.34) | (9.73) |
| $DISTANCE_{ij}$ | −0.731** | −0.730** | −0.681** | −0.717** |
| | (−17.51) | (−17.47) | (−20.20) | (−16.62) |
| $GATT_{ij}$ | 0.391** | 0.389** | 0.376** | 0.396** |
| | (6.05) | (6.03) | (5.79) | (6.12) |
| *HEGEMONY* | −53.75** | −53.07** | −52.29** | −53.84** |
| | (−14.92) | (−14.73) | (−14.68) | (−14.93) |
| $\chi^2$ | 1915.28** | 1906.12** | 1866.84** | 1911.48** |
| *Log likelihood* | −7146.54 | −7147.73 | −7173.51 | −7149.97 |

*Note:* These parameters are estimated using logistic regression, after including a natural spline function with three knots. Figures in parentheses are asymptotic *z*-statistics computed using Huber standard errors. In each model, $N = 223{,}568$.

**$p \leq .001$. Two-tailed tests are conducted for all estimates.

*$p \leq .05$. Two-tailed tests are conducted for all estimates.

Furthermore, the effects of regime type on PTA formation are quantitatively large. To gauge the magnitude of these effects, we derive the predicted probability of a pair of states establishing a trade agreement if both of them are highly democratic (that is, if $REG_i = REG_j = 10$), if one is highly democratic and the other is highly autocratic (that is, if $REG_i = 10$ and $REG_j = -10$), and if both are highly

**TABLE 2.** *The influence of regime type on the predicted probability of a dyad forming a PTA and the predicted number of dyads forming a PTA*

| *Regime types of i and j* | *Predicted probability of a dyad forming a PTA*[a] | *Predicted annual number of dyads forming a PTA*[b] |
|---|---|---|
| Two democracies | .0057 | 30.3 |
| One democracy and one autocracy | .0028 | 14.9 |
| Two autocracies | .0013 | 6.9 |

[a]To compute these predicted probabilities, we use the estimates in the first column of Table 1. We assume that $i$ and $j$ are not involved in a military dispute, that they do not have a prior colonial relationship, and that they are neither allies nor parties to the GATT (that is, $DISPUTE_{ij} = COL_{ij} = ALLY_{ij} = GATT_{ij} = 0$). All remaining variables are evaluated at their means.

[b]These figures are computed by multiplying the predicted probability of a dyad forming a PTA by the total number of observations in the sample (223,568) and then dividing that product by the number of years in the sample (42).

autocratic (that is, if $REG_i = REG_j = -10$).[50] Since the modal pair of states in our sample is not involved in a military dispute, did not have a colonial relationship, and is not made up of either allies or parties to the GATT, we set $DISPUTE_{ij}$, $COL_{ij}$, $ALLY_{ij}$, and $GATT_{ij}$ equal to zero to compute these probabilities. The remaining variables in equation (4) are evaluated at their means.

As Table 2 shows, on average, the probability of a democracy entering a trade agreement is roughly double the probability of an autocracy doing so. Pairs of democracies are about twice as likely to form a PTA as are pairs composed of a democracy and an autocracy. The latter pairs, in turn, are about twice as likely to engage in commercial cooperation as are autocratic pairs. Expressed in terms of the predicted number of dyads forming a PTA, our results indicate that roughly 30 democratic pairs, 15 mixed pairs, and only 7 autocratic pairs are expected to enter into a trade agreement in an average year.

Turning to the remaining variables, there is evidence that the economic size of countries affects their propensity to enter PTAs. The estimates of $GDP_i$ and $GDP_j$ are negative and statistically significant, indicating that the likelihood of a country joining a commercial agreement increases as the size of its home market declines. As expected, political relations between states also influence the likelihood that they will join a cooperative agreement. That the estimates of $COL_{ij}$, $ALLY_{ij}$, and $GATT_{ij}$ are positive and statistically significant indicates that states with a prior colonial

50. In evaluating the probability of a PTA between a democracy and an autocracy, our decision to consider the case where state $i$ is the democracy and state $j$ is the autocracy is entirely arbitrary. The predicted probability under these conditions is virtually identical to the predicted probability when $i$ is the autocracy and $j$ is the democracy.

relationship, those that are political-military allies, and those that are parties to the GATT are especially likely to enter a PTA. In addition, trade agreements tend to form between states located in proximity to each other and during periods of waning hegemony, since the estimates of $DISTANCE_{ij}$ and *HEGEMONY* are negative and significant.

Equally noteworthy is that the business cycle, trade flows, and military disputes have relatively little influence on whether or not states join the same PTA. The positive estimates of $\Delta GDP_i$ and $\Delta GDP_j$ imply that economic expansion increases the prospects that states will accede to a commercial agreement, whereas the negative estimates of $TRADE_{ij}$ and $DISPUTE_{ij}$ suggest that heightened trade flows and military disputes discourage the establishment of PTAs. None of these estimates, however, are statistically significant.

Having estimated the effects of regime type on PTA formation, it is important to assess the robustness of our results. To this end, we begin by dropping $\Delta GDP_i$, $\Delta GDP_j$, $TRADE_{ij}$, and $DISPUTE_{ij}$—the variables that are not statistically significant based on our initial findings. As the second, third, and fourth columns of Table 1 show, doing so has little bearing on the remaining estimates.

We also address whether our results depend on the use of Jaggers and Gurr's index of regime type. As noted earlier, there are important reasons to rely on this measure, given our objectives. However, Adam Przeworski, Michael E. Alvarez, José Antonio Cheibub, and Fernando Limongi have developed another measure of regime type that taps the domestic institutions emphasized in our model.[51] They code states in which "those who govern are selected through contested elections" as democratic and all other states as autocratic.[52] The data compiled by Przeworski et al. cover fewer countries and years than are included in our initial analyses, and their dichotomous measure is not as well-suited to testing our model as Jaggers and Gurr's index. But the stress they place on whether or not elections are contested in coding a state's regime type is consistent with our model.

To further assess the robustness of our results, we therefore redefine $REG_i$ and $REG_j$ as dummy variables that equal 1 if Przeworski et al. code states $i$ and $j$, respectively, as democratic in year $\tau$ and 0 otherwise. We then estimate the parameters in equation (4) again. As with the findings presented in Table 1, the estimated coefficients of both $REG_i$ and $REG_j$ are positive and statistically significant.[53] Furthermore, there continues to be no evidence of a significant difference between them. Equally important, the quantitative effects of regime type generated using Przeworski et al.'s data are much the same as those generated using Jaggers and Gurr's data. Based on Przeworski et al.'s measure of regime type, for example, a democracy is roughly three-quarters more likely to enter a PTA than an autocracy,

51. Przeworski et al. 2000.
52. Ibid., 15.
53. More specifically, the estimate of $REG_i$ is .509, the estimate of $REG_j$ is .580, and both estimates are statistically significant at the .001 level.

and democratic pairs are about three times as likely to join a trade agreement as autocratic pairs. Thus our findings are quite robust with respect to the data used to measure regime type.

Next, we include a number of additional factors in equation (4) that might influence the formation of PTAs. First, there is reason to expect that pairs of states belonging to the same PTA will have less incentive to enter (another) one than pairs that are not already party to the same arrangement. We therefore include a variable indicating whether *i* and *j* are already members of a common PTA in year $\tau$. Second, it is widely argued that, due to strategic interaction among countries competing in international markets and for other reasons, PTAs tend to form in reaction to one another.[54] This implies that states are especially likely to establish a commercial agreement soon after the creation of other agreements. As such, we include the number of PTAs formed in year $\tau - 1$.

Third, we include a variable indicating whether *i* and *j* have command economies in $\tau$. All countries marked by the existence of a command economy are nondemocratic, and such countries rarely have entered preferential groupings. Hence, we need to ensure that the observed relationship between regime type and PTA formation does not stem from the effects of command economies.[55] Fourth, we include a time trend to account for any secular changes in the global economy that might influence the establishment of PTAs. In addition, we estimate equation (4) using conditional logistic regression—a technique that is equivalent to including pair-specific fixed effects in the model—to account for any heterogeneity in the data.[56]

Regardless of whether we include the variables just described separately or together and regardless of whether equation (4) is estimated using conditional logistic regression, the estimates of $REG_i$ and $REG_j$ remain positive and statistically significant.[57] Equally, there is virtually no change in these estimates when we redefine the dependent variable in equation (4) as the existence of a PTA between *i* and *j* in year $\tau + 1$, rather than the formation of a preferential grouping between them. Recall that the observed value of $PTA_{ij}$ is 1 if a PTA forms between *i* and *j* in $\tau + 1$, and 0 otherwise. When we recode this variable as 1 in all years, $\tau + 1$,

54. See de Melo and Panagariya 1993, 5-6; Fernández and Portes 1998; Mansfield 1998; Oye 1992; and Pomfret 1988.

55. Data on command economies are taken from Kornai 1992.

56. Greene 1993, chap. 16.

57. Estimating our model using conditional logistic regression leads to the omission of roughly 85 percent of the observations in our data, since most country-pairs included in the analysis did not form a PTA during the period since World War II. Furthermore, using this estimation procedure to analyze cross-section time-series data with a binary dependent variable has serious drawbacks. See Beck and Katz 2001; and King 2001. Nonetheless, when equation (4) is estimated using this procedure, the estimate of $REG_i$ is .028, the estimate of $REG_j$ is .023, and both estimates are statistically significant at the .001 level. Of course, factors that are specific to time might also affect the formation of PTAs. A common way of addressing these factors is to include year-specific fixed effects, but these effects are perfectly correlated with *HEGEMONY*, which takes on a different value in each year we examine.

where $i$ and $j$ belong to the same PTA—regardless of whether the arrangement was formed in $\tau + 1$—the results are much the same as those reported in Table 1. In still another analysis, we eliminated all observations for a given country-pair after that pair formed a PTA. Since the probability of states forming a PTA is likely to be lower if they already belong to one than if they do not, this is another useful check on our earlier results. The results are again quite similar to those in Table 1 (although it is interesting that the size of the estimates of both $REG_i$ and $REG_j$ increase by about one-third). These analyses, then, continue to indicate the robustness of our findings.

Finally, the formation of a PTA is a rare event. Gary King and Langche Zeng have recently argued that using logistic regression to estimate the probability of rare events can yield biased results.[58] They have developed methods to correct such biases, and we use these methods to generate another set of estimates of the parameters in equation (4). The resulting estimates and standard errors are very similar to those in Table 1, demonstrating that our findings do not suffer from a rare events bias.[59]

In sum, our statistical results strongly support the propositions developed earlier—particularly the proposition that the likelihood of signing a trade agreement rises with the degree of democracy in each country. During the period since World War II, more democratic states have displayed a greater propensity to enter trade agreements than less democratic states, even after controlling for a host of other economic and political factors. Furthermore, the probability of a pair of countries forming a commercial agreement is highest if both countries are democratic and is lowest if both are autocratic.

## Conclusion

We have argued that the regime type of states can strongly affect their propensity to cooperate on economic issues. Leaders in democracies have a greater incentive to pursue international cooperation in trade than do their nondemocratic counterparts. We developed this argument using a formal model of trade policymaking emphasizing the electoral constraints faced by political leaders. Although there are many reasons why countries choose to cooperate, our analysis emphasizes how a country's regime type creates domestic political incentives for leaders that influence this choice.

Our model assumes that both democratic and autocratic leaders would like to maximize the rents stemming from trade barriers, but that both may lose office if their rent seeking becomes excessive. The problem faced by voters and leaders,

58. King and Zeng 2001.

59. This result is not unexpected, since King and Zeng point out that the influence of their methods will be most pronounced when the number of observations being analyzed is less than a few thousand. King and Zeng 2001. Our sample is obviously much larger than that size.

however, is that voters have incomplete information about their leaders' behavior: they do not know exactly what trade policy their leaders have chosen at any point in time. And domestic executives cannot credibly commit to accurately divulge this information. Hence, when exogenous shocks adversely influence the economy, an incumbent executive may be voted out of office not because the executive was too extractive, but rather because voters mistakenly assume that the executive was engaged in protectionist predation. The prospect of losing elections due to factors beyond the incumbent executive's control provides a strong incentive to find ways of reassuring voters that the government is not being too extractive. Trade agreements are one such means.

Commercial agreements can mitigate the executive's informational problem. The monitors of these agreements—either countries that are party to them or the international trade institutions themselves—can credibly signal to voters whether their leader is cheating or abiding by the agreement. Accusations of cheating against one's government by foreign countries or an international institution are newsworthy events that can alert (at least some) voters to the government's behavior. Because of this signal, executives can improve their chances of re-election. In democracies, however, voters have a greater impact on the tenure of leaders than in autocracies, since the democratic electorate can more easily turn incumbents out of office. Since autocratic leaders face fewer worries about re-election, they have fewer incentives to relinquish policy autonomy and sign trade agreements, making them less likely than more democratic leaders to seek commercial cooperation. The greater accountability of leaders to voters in democracies makes a difference. Surprisingly, this result is obtained even though democratic executives discount the future more heavily than their autocratic counterparts.

In our model, international agreements serve a domestic purpose. They allow executives to commit themselves credibly to actions that voters would otherwise find incredible. Unilateral trade barrier reductions are less credible to voters and more easily repealed than are mutually agreed-upon international reductions. Others have argued that international institutions promote cooperation by providing information, but they have been less specific about how this mechanism actually induces leaders to choose cooperation.[60] Here, we identify one mechanism by which cooperative agreements can convey information to voters about the behavior of their leaders, thus allowing voters to better judge their leaders. Other mechanisms might serve this purpose as well, but our claim is that trade agreements do so especially well. The information provided by trade agreements benefits all of the players in our analysis—voters and governments alike. Existing studies rarely acknowledge that international institutions can serve this function. The tendency for such institutions to be created with monitoring and dispute settlement mechanisms suggests their importance in disseminating information domestically as well as internationally.

60. For example, Keohane 1984.

International cooperation can thus generate domestic political benefits for leaders, making them more likely to seek cooperative agreements in the first place.

Our empirical findings strongly support the two central hypotheses stemming from the formal model. Since World War II, more democratic countries have displayed a greater likelihood of concluding trade agreement than other countries, even when holding constant various political and economic influences. Equally, pairs of democratic countries are about twice as likely to form a PTA as are pairs composed of a democracy and an autocracy and roughly four times as likely to form such cooperative agreements as are autocratic pairs. In sum, holding constant Cold War influences, economic variables, and various other factors, we find considerable evidence that democracy promotes commercial cooperation. Clearly, democracy is not alone in promoting such agreements, but our findings indicate that it is a potent impetus to cooperation.

Our study also sheds light on other hypotheses about international cooperation. First, whereas functionalist theories argue that high levels of trade between countries should promote cooperation, we find that trade flows do not have much impact on the probability of signing a commercial agreement. Second, as realist theories suggest, alliances and the existence of a stable hegemon foster cooperation in trade. Somewhat surprisingly, however, military disputes have little bearing on trade agreements. Third, we find that GATT members are especially likely to establish preferential agreements, which accords with the view of neoliberal institutionalists that international institutions can improve the ability of states to cooperate. Even when we account for the effects of these and other potential influences on commercial cooperation, however, domestic politics still affects whether states enter into trade agreements.

Scholars of international relations have displayed a longstanding interest in the sources of economic cooperation. Most research on this topic has been cast at the international level. Far less attention has been paid to the domestic influences on economic cooperation. Our results highlight the drawbacks of ignoring these influences. In addition to systemic and economic factors, the regime types of states strongly condition their likelihood of forging a trade agreement. In commercial matters, democracies are more cooperative than are other states because of the domestic political benefits that can be generated by international trade agreements.

## Appendix

In this economy, the export good is the numeraire, and the domestic price of the import good in period $\tau$ is $p_\tau = \pi_\tau (1 + t_\tau)$. Both goods require capital and labor for production, which occurs with constant returns to scale. Let the economy-wide aggregate endowment of capital ($K$) relative to labor ($L$) be $k = K/L$. Factors are perfectly mobile domestically.

Each individual, $l$, owns one unit of labor, which is paid a wage $w(p_\tau)$, and each owns $k^l$ units of capital, a unit of which is paid $r(p_\tau)$. Individual preferences for the goods are identical and homothetic in the two goods. An individual $l$'s (one-period) indirect utility can be written as

$$U^l(p_\tau) = V(p_\tau)I^l(p_\tau)$$

where the individual's income is

$$I^l(p_\tau) = w(p_\tau) + r(p_\tau)k^l + \theta^l(p_\tau - \pi_\tau)M(p_\tau)$$

and where $M(p_\tau)$ is the quantity of imports and

$$\theta^l = \frac{w + rk^l}{wL + rK}$$

as in Mayer.[61] The last term implies that tariff revenue is distributed back to individuals in proportion to each individual's share of national factor income.

Voters differ along the single dimension $k^l$. Assuming no costs to voting, the tariff preferred by the majority of voters is the ideal tariff of the individual with the median capital-labor endowment ratio. This individual, indexed $m$, is endowed with $k^m$ units of capital (and a single unit of labor). Since the importable is labor-intensive and the median individual owns more labor relative to capital than does society as a whole, that is, $k^m < k$, the median voter prefers a positive level of trade barriers. Given the realization of the world price, $\pi_\tau$, any voter, including the median voter, has an ideal tariff. Maximization of one period utility with respect to $t_\tau$ shows that the utility-maximizing tariff for the median voter, $m$, is

$$t_\tau^m = -\frac{I}{M'(p_\tau)} \frac{\partial \theta^m / \partial p}{\theta^m}$$

where $I$ is aggregate income. Note first that the quantity of imports decreases with their price, so that $M'(p_\tau) < 0$. Since the economy exports a capital-intensive good, and $k^m < k$, then $\partial \theta^m / \partial p > 0$, so the median voter prefers a positive level of trade barriers.[62]

Each individual has a vote in an election. Unlike in Mayer, where the vote is over a tariff policy in a direct democracy setting, here the voters use the election to indicate their support for the incumbent.[63]

Following Ferejohn, we are interested in equilibria where voters follow a simple retrospective voting rule,[64] in which voter $l$ will choose to reappoint the executive in period $\tau$ if their welfare is at least as good as an endogenously determined threshold value, that is, if $\underline{U}^l(p_\tau) \geq \underline{U}^l$. Banks and Sundaram have studied the repeated election game between the voter and the executive in a more general setting (they permit variations in the types of executives [adverse selection] in addition to the moral hazard we study here), and they show the existence of a sequential equilibrium of this threshold-type equilibrium, conditioned on currently available public information.[65]

61. Mayer 1984.
62. Ibid.
63. Ibid.
64. Ferejohn 1986.
65. Banks and Sundaram 1993.

As in Persson et al., we look for an equilibrium in which voters condition their voting decision on their utility in the current period and not on any previous period.[66] A history-dependent rule would require commitment across periods to be optimal; here voters re-optimize at the beginning of every period. Moreover, the action of the executive is not conditioned on any of its past actions but rather on the current state—whether the executive currently is in office or not. Hence the equilibrium strategies of interest will be Markov and stationary.

Unlike Banks and Sundaram, we consider only one type of incumbent—the preferences of the government are common knowledge.[67] An executive removed from office is never reappointed, and there is always another candidate (identical in all respects) available to take over the executive. Moreover, the government moves before the uncertainty is resolved each period. Hence there is nothing to be learned by the voters from the actions of the government.

Recall that $\phi(t_\tau, \underline{U}^m) = \Pr(U^m(p_\tau) > \underline{U}^m)$, and therefore $\phi_t < 0$ and $\phi_{\underline{U}^m} < 0$.

ASSUMPTION: $\phi(1, U) = 0$ for all $U$.

From equation (2) the executive solves:

$$\frac{\partial \Gamma}{\partial t} = G_t + \delta\sigma\phi_t\Gamma = 0 \tag{5}$$

for the optimal $t$ in any period. From equations (1) and (2) we have, in equilibrium:

$$\Gamma = \frac{G(t)}{1 - \delta[\sigma\phi(t, \underline{U}^m) + (1 - \sigma)]}. \tag{6}$$

Substituting equation (6) into equation (5), we have that the optimal trade policy $t^\circ$ for the executive satisfies:

$$G_t\{1 - \delta[\sigma\phi(t, \underline{U}^m) + (1 - \sigma)]\} + \delta\sigma\phi_t G = 0. \tag{7}$$

LEMMA A.1: *$t^\circ$ falls with $\underline{U}^m$.*

*Proof:* Totally differentiating equation (5), we have $\Gamma_{tU}dU + \Gamma_{tt}dt = 0$, or $dt^\circ/d\underline{U}^m = -(\Gamma_{t\underline{U}^m}/\Gamma_{tt})$. Now $\Gamma_{t\underline{U}^m} = \delta\sigma\phi_{t\underline{U}^m}\Gamma < 0$ since $\phi_{t\underline{U}^m} < 0$ by Leibniz's rule (the tariff and the threshold are strategic substitutes). $\Gamma_{tt} < 0$ so $dt^\circ/d\underline{U}^m < 0$.

For the Leviathan strategy, where $t = 1$, we assume that the probability that the median voter re-elects the incumbent is zero when incumbent chooses this strategy: $\phi(1,U) = 0$ for all $U > 0$. Then the gains to the incumbent executive from choosing $t_\tau = 1$ at the beginning of any period $\tau$ are $\Gamma(1) = G(1) + \delta(1 - \sigma)\Gamma$. A lower tariff $t$ is preferred by the incumbent over the Leviathan tariff when:

66. Persson, Roland, and Tabellini 1997.
67. Banks and Sundaram 1993 and 1998.

$$G(t) + \delta\rho(t, \underline{U}^m, \sigma)\Gamma(t) \geq G(1) + \delta(1 - \sigma)\Gamma(1). \tag{8}$$

Define $\underline{t}$ such that equation (8) is satisfied with equality. Then at $\underline{t} = \underline{t}(U^m,\sigma)$ the government is exactly indifferent between the lower tariff and the Leviathan strategy.

LEMMA A.2: *Define $\hat{U}$ such that $t°(\hat{U}, \sigma) = \underline{t}(\hat{U}, \sigma)$. Then $d\underline{t}/d\underline{U}^m > 0$ for $U < \hat{U}$, and $d\underline{t}/d\underline{U}^m < 0$ for $U > \hat{U}$.*

*Proof:* Implicit differentiation of equation (8) taking the continuation values as given yields $d\underline{t}/d\underline{U}^m = -\delta\sigma\Gamma\phi_{\underline{U}^m}/(G_t + \delta\sigma\Gamma\phi_t)$. Now the numerator is positive, and the denominator is positive for all $t < t°$. So for $U < \hat{U}$ we have $t < t°$ and hence $d\underline{t}/d\underline{U}^m > 0$.

LEMMA A.3: *Let $\tilde{U}$ satisfy $t^m = t°(\tilde{U}, \sigma)$. Then the following pair of strategies is a Nash Equilibrium:* $t^* = \begin{cases} t°(\underline{U}^m, \sigma) & \text{if } \underline{U}^m < \hat{U} \\ 1 & \text{otherwise} \end{cases}$ *and* $\underline{U}^* = \begin{cases} \hat{U} & \text{if } t^m \leq \underline{t}(\hat{U}, \sigma), \\ \tilde{U} & \text{otherwise} \end{cases}$.

*Proof:* Equations (7) and (8) establish that the government is playing a best response to any threshold $\underline{U}^m$. The median voter wants to get a tariff as close as possible to her (*ex ante*) ideal, $t^m$. If $t^m > \underline{t}$, then the voter sets the threshold to $\tilde{U}$, given that the government responds with $t° = t^m$. On the other hand, when $t^m$ crosses $\underline{t}$, then the voter's ideal tariff lies below that which the government can be constrained to provide. Hence the voters restrict the government to the lowest tariff possible by choosing a threshold at $\hat{U}$. Hence the voters control the executive as much as is possible; the median voter is playing a best response.

Notice that the voters' strategy here is to choose a threshold, which is effectively equivalent to deciding whether to recommend re-election or not. At the moment at which the voter chooses a threshold, a threshold chosen higher than the utility observed is a recommendation to evict; a lower one, a recommendation to re-elect.

Notice that perfection-type refinements here (such as subgame perfection) are not applicable in a non-trivial way. Subgame perfection requires that the equilibrium strategies be Nash in any proper subgame. But there are no proper subgames in this game. For instance, at the moment at which the voter must choose a threshold in any period (effectively deciding to recommend re-election or not) the voter does not know either the state of the world ($\pi$) or the actions of the executive ($t$) in that period. Hence the decision point is an information set not a single node.

There is a sense, however, that conditional on the publicly available information, the threat to evict (when experienced utility is low) is credible. Consider again the information set where the voter must choose a threshold. Suppose the payoff that period is low—such that the voter is supposed to recommend (in the equilibrium) eviction (by setting high threshold). Suppose they do not. Then in the next period, the government, aware that low payoffs do not imply eviction, will switch from then on to the Leviathan strategy. Such a failure to evict is clearly worse for the voter, and so the voter will continue to evict when called to do so.

LEMMA A.4: *The sign of $d\underline{t}/d\sigma$ is indeterminate.*

*Proof:* Implicit differentiation of equation (8) and by the definition of $\underline{t}$, we have $d\underline{t}/d\sigma = -\delta[G(1)(\phi - 1) + G(t)]/\{G_t[1 - \delta(1 - \sigma)] + \delta G(1)\sigma\phi_t\}$. Now the first term in the numerator is negative, while the second is positive. In the denominator, the first term is positive, while the second is negative.

———. 1998. Optimal Retention in Agency Problems. *Journal of Economic Theory* 82 (2):293–323.

Beck, Nathaniel, and Jonathan Katz. 1997. The Analysis of Binary Time-Series Cross-Section Data and/or the Democratic Peace. Paper presented at the 14th Annual Meeting of the Political Methodology Group, Columbus, Ohio.

———. 2001. Throwing Out the Baby with the Bath Water: A Comment on Green, Kim, and Yoon. *International Organization* 55 (2):487–95.

Beck, Nathaniel, and Richard Tucker. 1996. Conflict in Space and Time: Time-Series Cross-Section Analysis with a Binary Dependent Variable. Paper Presented at the 92nd Annual Meeting of the American Political Science Association, San Francisco, Calif.

Bhagwati, Jagdish. 1993. Regionalism and Multilateralism: An Overview. In *New Dimensions in Regional Integration*, edited by Jaime de Melo and Arvind Panagariya, 22–51. New York: Cambridge University Press.

Bollen, Kenneth A. 1980. Issues in the Comparative Measurement of Political Democracy. *American Sociological Review* 45 (3):370–90.

Bueno de Mesquita, Bruce, and David Lalman. 1992. *War and Reason: Domestic and International Imperatives*. New Haven, Conn.: Yale University Press.

Bueno de Mesquita, Bruce, James D. Morrow, Randolph M. Siverson, and Alastair Smith. 1999. An Institutional Explanation of the Democratic Peace. *American Political Science Review* 93 (4):791–808.

Chittick, William, and Keith Billingsley. 1989. The Structure of Elite Foreign Policy Beliefs. *Western Political Quarterly* 42 (2):201–24.

Correlates of War Project. 1993. Alliances Data. Unpublished data set, University of Michigan.

Coughlin, P. J. 1992. *Probabilistic Voting Theory*. Cambridge: Cambridge University Press.

Dahl, Robert. 1971. *Polyarchy: Participation and Opposition*. New Haven, Conn.: Yale University Press.

de Melo, Jaime, and Arvind Panagariya. 1993. Introduction. In *New Dimensions in Regional Integration*, edited by Jaime de Melo and Arvind Panagariya, 3–21. New York: Cambridge University Press.

Fearon, James. 1994. Domestic Audiences and the Escalation of International Disputes. *American Political Science Review* 88 (3):577–92.

Ferejohn, John. 1986. Incumbent Performance and Electoral Control. *Public Choice* 50 (2):5–25.

Fernández, Raquel, and Jonathan Portes. 1998. Returns to Regionalism: An Evaluation of Nontraditional Gains from Regional Trade Agreements. *The World Bank Economic Review* 12 (2):197–220.

Fiorina, Morris. 1981. *Retrospective Voting in American National Elections*. New Haven, Conn.: Yale University Press.

Foroutan, Faezeh. 1993. Regional Integration in Sub-Saharan Africa: Past Experience and Future Prospects. In *New Dimensions in Regional Integration*, edited by Jaime de Melo and Arvind Panagariya, 234–71. New York: Cambridge University Press.

Frankel, Jeffrey A., Ernesto Stein, and Shang-Jin Wei. 1998. Continental Trading Blocs: Are They Natural or Supernatural? In *The Regionalization of the World Economy*, edited by Jeffrey A. Frankel, 189–219. Chicago: University of Chicago Press.

Gasiorowski, Mark. 1996. An Overview of the Political Regime Change Dataset. *Comparative Political Studies* 29 (4):469–83.

Gastil, Raymond D. 1980 and 1990. *Freedom in the World: Political Rights and Civil Liberties*. New York: Freedom House.

Gaubatz, Kurt Taylor. 1996. Democratic States and Commitment in International Relations. *International Organization* 50 (1):109–39.

Gilpin, Robert. 1987. *The Political Economy of International Relations*. Princeton, N.J.: Princeton University Press.

Gowa, Joanne. 1994. *Allies, Adversaries, and International Trade*. Princeton, N.J.: Princeton University Press.

Gowa, Joanne, and Edward D. Mansfield. 1993. Power Politics and International Trade. *American Political Science Review* 87 (2):408–20.

Green, William H. 1993. *Econometric Analysis*, 2d ed. Englewood Cliffs, N.J.: Prentice Hall.

Grilli, Enzo R. 1993. *The European Community and Developing Countries*. Cambridge: Cambridge University Press.

Grossman, Gene, and Elhanan Helpman. 1994. Protection for Sale. *American Economic Review* 84 (4):833–50.

Gurr, Ted Robert, Keith Jaggers, and Will H. Moore. 1989. *Polity II: Political Structures and Regime Change, 1800–1986*. Study no. 9263. Ann Arbor, Mich.: Inter-University Consortium for Political and Social Research.

Haggard, Stephan, and Robert Kaufman. 1995. *The Political Economy of Democratic Transitions*. Princeton, N.J.: Princeton University Press.

Hanlon, Joseph. 1986. *Beggar Your Neighbor*. London: Villiers Publications.

Hartland-Thunberg, Penelope. 1980. *Trading Blocs, U.S. Exports, and World Trade*. Boulder, Colo.: Westview Press.

Herrmann, Richard K., Philip E. Tetlock, and Matthew N. Diascro. 2001. How Americans Think About Trade: Reconciling Conflicts among Money, Power, and Principles. *International Studies Quarterly* 45 (2):191–218.

International Monetary Fund. Various years. *Direction of Foreign Trade*. Washington, D.C.: IMF.

———. Various years. *International Financial Statistics*. Washington, D.C.: IMF.

Jaggers, Keith, and Ted Robert Gurr. 1995. Tracking Democracy's Third Wave with the Polity III Data. *Journal of Peace Research* 32 (4):469–82.

Jones, Daniel M., Stuart A. Bremer, and J. David Singer. 1996. Militarized Interstate Disputes, 1816–1992: Rationale, Coding Rules, and Empirical Patterns. *Conflict Management and Peace Science* 15 (2):163–213.

Keohane, Robert O. 1984. *After Hegemony: Cooperation and Discord in the World Political Economy*. Princeton, N.J.: Princeton University Press.

Kiewiet, Roderick. 1983. *Macroeconomics and Micropolitics*. Chicago: University of Chicago Press.

King, Gary. 2001. Proper Nouns and Methodological Propriety: Pooling Dyads in International Relations Data. *International Organization* 55 (2):497–507.

King, Gary, and Langche Zeng. 2001. Explaining Rare Events in International Relations. *International Organization* 55 (3):693–715.

Kisanga, Eliawony J. 1991. *Industrial and Trade Cooperation in Eastern and Southern Africa*. Hong Kong: Avebury.

Kornai, Janos. 1992. *The Socialist System: The Political Economy of Communism*. Princeton, N.J.: Princeton University Press.

Krasner, Stephen D. 1976. State Power and the Structure of Foreign Trade. *World Politics* 28 (3):317–47.

Krueger, Anne O. 1999. Are Preferential Trading Arrangements Trade-Liberalizing or Protectionist? *Journal of Economic Perspectives* 13 (4):105–24.

Krugman, Paul. 1993. Regionalism versus Multilateralism: Analytical Notes. In *New Dimensions in Regional Integration*, edited by Jaime de Melo and Arvind Panagariya, 58–79. New York: Cambridge University Press.

Kurian, George Thomas. 1992. *Encyclopedia of the Third World*. 4th ed. Vols. 1–3. New York: Facts on File.

Lake, David A. 1988. *Power, Protectionism, and Free Trade: International Sources of U.S. Commercial Strategy*. Ithaca, N.Y.: Cornell University Press.

Leeds, Brett Ashley. 1999. Domestic Political Institutions, Credible Commitments and International Cooperation. *American Journal of Political Science* 43 (4):979–1002.

Lewis-Beck, Michael S. 1988. *Economics and Elections: The Major Western Democracies*. Ann Arbor: University of Michigan Press.

Maddison, Angus. 1995. *Monitoring the World Economy, 1820–1992*. Paris: Organization for Economic Cooperation and Development.

Mansfield, Edward D. 1998. The Proliferation of Preferential Trading Arrangements. *Journal of Conflict Resolution* 42 (5):523–43.

Mansfield, Edward D., Helen V. Milner, and B. Peter Rosendorff. 2000. Free to Trade: Democracies, Autocracies, and International Trade. *American Political Science Review* 94 (2):305–21.

Mansfield, Edward D., and Jack Snyder. 1995. Democratization and the Danger of War. *International Security* 20 (1):5–38.

Martin, Lisa L. 2000. *Democratic Commitments: Legislatures and International Cooperation.* Princeton, N.J.: Princeton University Press.

Mattli, Walter. 1999. *The Logic of Regional Integration: Europe and Beyond.* New York: Cambridge University Press.

Mayer, Wolfgang. 1984. Endogenous Tariff Formation. *American Economic Review* 74 (5):970–85.

McGillivray, Fiona, and Alastair Smith. 2000. Trust and Cooperation Through Agent-Specific Punishments. *International Organization* 54 (4):809–24.

McKeown, Timothy J. 1991. A Liberal Trading Order? The Long-Run Pattern of Imports to the Advanced Capitalist States. *International Studies Quarterly* 35 (2):151–72.

Milner, Helen V. 1992. International Theories of Cooperation: Strengths and Weaknesses. *World Politics* 44 (3):466–96.

———. 1997. *Interests, Institutions, and Information: Domestic Politics and International Relations.* Princeton, N.J.: Princeton University Press.

Nye, Joseph S. 1988. Neorealism and Neoliberalism. *World Politics* 40 (2):235–51.

Oneal, John R., and Bruce Russett. 1999. Assessing the Liberal Peace with Alternative Specifications: Trade Still Reduces Conflict. *Journal of Peace Research* 36 (4):423–42.

Orimalade, Adeyinka, and R. E. Ubogu, eds. 1984. *Trade and Development in Economic Community of West African States.* Delhi: Vikas Publishing.

Oye, Kenneth A. 1992. *Economic Discrimination and Political Exchange: World Political Economy in the 1930s and 1980s.* Princeton, N.J.: Princeton University Press.

Panagariya, Arvind. 2000. Preferential Trade Liberalization: The Traditional Theory and New Developments. *Journal of Economic Literature* 38 (2):287–331.

Persson, Torsten, Gerard Roland, and Guido Tabellini. 1997. Separation of Powers and Political Accountability. *Quarterly Journal of Economics* 112 (4):1163–1202.

Pomfret, Richard. 1988. *Unequal Trade: The Economics of Discriminatory International Trade Policies.* Oxford: Basil Blackwell.

Powell, G. Bingham. 2000. *Elections as Instruments of Democracy.* New Haven, Conn.: Yale University Press.

Przeworski, Adam, Michael E. Alvarez, José Antonio Cheibub, and Fernando Limongi. 2000. *Democracy and Development: Political Institutions and Well-Being in the World, 1950–1990.* New York: Cambridge University Press.

Reinhardt, Eric. 1996. Posturing Parliaments: Ratification, Uncertainty, and International Bargaining. Ph.D. diss., Columbia University, New York.

Remmer, Karen. 1998. Does Democracy Promote Interstate Cooperation? *International Studies Quarterly* 42 (1):25–52.

Russett, Bruce, and John Oneal. 2001. *Triangulating Peace: Democracy, Interdependence, and International Organizations.* New York: Norton.

Russett, Bruce, John Oneal, and David R. Davis. 1998. The Third Leg of the Kantian Tripod for Peace. *International Organization* 52 (3):441–68.

Schumpeter, Joseph. [1942] 1976. *Capitalism, Socialism, and Democracy.* Reprint, New York: Harper Colophon.

Singer, J. David, and Melvin Small. 1994. *Correlates of War Project: International and Civil War Data, 1816–1992.* Study no. 9905. Ann Arbor, Mich.: Inter-University Consortium for Political and Social Research.

Small, Melvin, and J. David Singer. 1969. Formal Alliances, 1816–1965: An Extension of the Basic Data. *Journal of Peace Research* 6 (3):257–82.

Summers, Robert, and Alan Heston. 1991. The Penn World Table (Mark 5): An Expanded Set of International Comparisons. *Quarterly Journal of Economics* 106 (2):327–68.

Verdier, Daniel. 1998. Democratic Convergence and Free Trade. *International Studies Quarterly* 42 (1):1–24.

Whalley, John. 1998. Why Do Countries Seek Regional Trade Agreements? In *The Regionalization of the World Economy*, edited by Jeffrey A. Frankel, 63–83. Chicago: University of Chicago Press.

World Trade Organization. 1995. *Regionalism and the World Trading System*. Geneva: WTO.

Yarbrough, Beth V., and Robert M. Yarbrough. 1992. *Cooperation and Governance in International Trade: The Strategic Organizational Approach*. Princeton, N.J.: Princeton University Press.

*B.J.Pol.S.* **37**, 403–432 *Copyright © 2007 Cambridge University Press*
doi:10.1017/S0007123407000221 *Printed in the United Kingdom*

# *Vetoing Co-operation: The Impact of Veto Players on Preferential Trading Arrangements*

EDWARD D. MANSFIELD, HELEN V. MILNER AND JON C. PEVEHOUSE*

Since the Second World War, preferential trading arrangements (PTAs) have become increasingly pervasive features of the international economic system. A great deal of research has addressed the economic consequences of these arrangements, but far less effort has been made to identify the political factors leading states to enter them. In this article, the domestic political factors affecting whether countries enter PTAs are investigated, placing particular emphasis on the number of veto players within a state. It is argued that the probability of forming a PTA declines as the number of such players rises. The results, covering 194 countries from 1950 to 1999, strongly support this argument. Holding various political and economic factors constant, increasing the number of veto players within a country significantly reduces the probability of signing a PTA.

Since the Second World War, preferential trading arrangements (PTAs) have become increasingly pervasive features of the international economic system. Scores of these institutions have been formed since then and almost every country currently participates in at least one. PTAs are a broad class of international commercial agreements that include common markets, customs unions, free trade areas and economic unions, as well as other arrangements. All of these arrangements require members to adjust their trade policies towards one another (usually through domestic legislation), granting each member preferential access to the others' markets. A great deal of research has addressed the economic consequences of preferential arrangements, but far less effort has been made to identify the factors leading states to enter them, especially the domestic influences on PTA formation. Recently, a number of studies have started to fill this gap. Some have emphasized the role played by interest groups;[1] others have focused on the effects of a country's regime type.[2]

We argue, however, that the number of 'veto players' is an equally important influence on whether states enter PTAs. Preferential arrangements require countries to change their trade policies and existing theories of veto players suggest that the probability of such change depends on the number of these players, not just on interstate bargaining. Veto players are institutional or partisan actors whose consent is needed to alter policies. The

* Mansfield, Department of Political Science, University of Pennsylvania; Milner, Department of Politics, Princeton University; Pevehouse, Department of Political Science, University of Wisconsin. Earlier versions of this article were presented at the Annual Meeting of the American Political Science Association, Washington, D.C., 2006; and at the Annual Meeting of the Midwest Political Science Association, Chicago, 2005. For helpful comments, we are grateful to Regina Baker, Joanne Gowa, Witold Henisz, Robert Pahre, Robert Staiger, Ronald Rogowski, B. Peter Rosendorff, George Tsebelis, Hugh Ward, Beth Yarbrough and the anonymous referees.

[1] Giovanni Maggi and Andres Rodriguez-Clare, 'The Value of Trade Agreements in the Presence of Political Pressures', *Journal of Political Economy*, 106 (1998), 574–601; Gene M. Grossman and Elhanan Helpman, *Interest Groups and Trade Policy* (Princeton, N.J.: Princeton University Press, 2002).

[2] Edward D. Mansfield, Helen V. Milner and B. Peter Rosendorff, 'Why Democracies Cooperate More: Electoral Control and International Trade Agreements', *International Organization*, 56 (2002), 477–514.

impact of these actors on PTA formation has not been studied to date, but existing research on 'two-level games' indicates that it is difficult to forge international agreements when leaders confront an array of domestic groups with diverse preferences and the ability to block policy initiatives.[3] Much of this research has focused on divided government, a situation where the majority party in the legislature differs from the executive party. Legislatures, however, are only one type of veto player. Moreover, whereas this literature has analysed the effects of whether or not government is divided, it has not addressed variations in the extent of legislative divisions. Conceptualizing veto players along a continuum has both theoretical and empirical advantages.

Although theories of veto players have been developed to explain aspects of comparative politics and foreign policy, we show that they also add to our understanding of international co-operation.[4] All other things being equal, increasing the number of veto players never increases and usually decreases the range of agreements that countries involved in international negotiations to form a PTA will find acceptable, thereby reducing the prospect of co-operation between them. We also conduct the first systematic test of the relationship between veto players and the decision to enter preferential arrangements. The results strongly support our argument. Based on an analysis of all PTAs formed in the period 1950–99, we find that states are much less likely to enter a trade agreement as the number of veto players increases.

## DOMESTIC POLITICS AND PREFERENTIAL TRADING ARRANGEMENTS

Central to our argument is the view that domestic politics bears heavily on the prospects of states entering a PTA. Thus, we depart from much of the work on international relations that treats the state as a unitary actor. Instead, we view the state as an aggregation of actors with varying preferences who share decision-making authority. The distribution of decision-making power among these actors and the extent to which their preferences diverge define the number of veto players in a country.

Theories of veto players focus attention on those agents who, because of their institutional role or partisanship, have the ability and desire to block policy change. Their

[3] Jongryn Mo, 'The Logic of Two Level Games with Endogenous Domestic Coalitions', *Journal of Conflict Resolution*, 38 (1994), 402–22; Helen V. Milner and B. Peter Rosendorff, 'Trade Negotiations, Information, and Domestic Politics', *Economics and Politics*, 8 (1996), 145–89; Helen V. Milner, *Interests, Institutions, and Information: Domestic Politics and International Relations* (Princeton, N.J.: Princeton University Press, 1997); Ahmer Tarar, 'International Bargaining with Two-Sided Domestic Constraints', *Journal of Conflict Resolution*, 45 (2001), 320–40.

[4] George Tsebelis, 'Decision Making in Political Systems: Veto Players in Presidentialism, Parliamentarism, Multicameralism and Multipartyism', *British Journal of Political Science*, 25 (1995), 289–325; George Tsebelis, *Veto Players: How Political Institutions Work* (Princeton, N.J.: Princeton University Press, 2002); Mark Hallerberg and Scott Basinger, 'Internationalization and Changes in Tax Policy in OECD Countries: The Importance of Domestic Veto Players', *Comparative Political Studies*, 31 (1998), 321–52; Robert J. Franzese, 'The Positive Political Economy of Public Debt: An Empirical Examination of the OECD Postwar Debt Experience' (unpublished manuscript, Department of Political Science, University of Michigan, 1999); Witold J. Henisz, 'The Institutional Environment for Economic Growth', *Economics and Politics*, 12 (2000), 1–31; Witold J. Henisz, 'The Institutional Environment for Infrastructure Investment', *Industrial and Corporate Change*, 11 (2002), 355–89; Daniel Treisman, 'Decentralization and Inflation: Commitment, Collective Action or Continuity', *American Political Science Review*, 94 (2000), 837–57; Witold J. Henisz and Edward D. Mansfield, 'Votes and Vetoes: The Political Determinants of Commercial Openness', *International Studies Quarterly*, 50 (2006), 189–211.

assent is necessary to alter existing policies.[5] The existence of institutions for sharing decision-making power creates the potential for veto players. In a highly influential theory, Tsebelis has shown that the difficulties of policy making grow as the number of veto players increases, as their preferences diverge and as the internal coherence of the actors declines.[6] Policy stasis or adherence to the status quo becomes more likely as the number of veto players increases. 'The size of the winset of the status quo', Tsebelis argues, 'has specific consequences on policymaking: significant departures from the status quo are impossible when the winset is small – that is, when veto players are many – when they have significant ideological distances among them, and when they are internally cohesive.'[7]

Conceptually, regime type and veto players are distinct and we treat them as such. Veto players exist in all types of regimes. Even in non-democratic countries, domestic politics is rarely a pure hierarchy with a unitary decision maker and no veto players. In a dictatorship, the support of the professional military or a political party is frequently necessary for the leader to retain power and implement policies. These groups often exercise veto power over the executive's proposals and may help set the country's policy agenda. Indeed, the existence of these domestic groups is central to an important body of literature on democratization that argues that inter-group competition in autocracies is an impetus for political liberalization.[8] Thus, even in hierarchical states, autocrats are often unable to unilaterally dictate policy: domestic groups with varying preferences who have veto power can compete for influence over policy and dictators depend on them in making policy.

Democratic regimes are even more likely to have veto players than non-democratic regimes, although the number of such players varies considerably among democracies. In most democratic polities, the legislature and the executive vie for control over decision making. Sometimes two or more political parties or coalitions compete.[9] Domestic political institutions determine how such control is distributed among the relevant actors. For example, constitutions often assign certain powers to the executive and others to the legislature. Domestic actors may either share control over the policy process or possess distinct powers. In the United States, for instance, both the president and Congress have the authority to make certain legislative proposals. These branches share ratification power since the president can veto a bill passed by Congress. In many parliamentary systems, legislatures do not initiate proposals; only the executive does and she cannot veto a proposal once the legislature amends and ratifies it. In both cases, decision-making powers are jointly held. In the former, both players share control over the same procedures, while in the latter, the players control different aspects of the process.

In most countries, the executive branch sets the agenda in foreign affairs and has the power to initiate foreign economic policy. To negotiate international trade agreements and

[5] Tsebelis, 'Decision Making in Political Systems'; Tsebelis, *Veto Players,* p. 2.

[6] Tsebelis, 'Decision Making in Political Systems'; Tsebelis, *Veto Players,* p. 2.

[7] Tsebelis, *Veto Players,* p. 2.

[8] Robert Kaufman, 'Liberalization and Democratization in South America: Perspectives from the 1970s', in Guillermo O'Donnell, Philippe Schmitter and Lawrence Whitehead, eds, *Transitions from Authoritarian Rule: Comparative Perspectives* (Baltimore, Md.: Johns Hopkins University Press, 1986), pp. 85–107; Guillermo O'Donnell and Philippe C. Schmitter, *Transitions from Authoritarian Rule: Tentative Conclusions About Uncertain Democracies* (Baltimore, Md.: Johns Hopkins University Press, 1986); Adam Przeworski, *Democracy and the Market* (Cambridge: Cambridge University Press, 1991).

[9] In corporatist systems, three actors are important: the executive ('the state'), organized labour and organized capital. They share control over the key elements of economic policy making, setting the agenda as well as devising, amending, ratifying and implementing policies.

to implement foreign economic policy, however, the executive needs the tacit or explicit support of other domestic groups. Sometimes trade policy requires a vote of support from the legislative branch. Frequently it requires the tacit support of groups like the military. Like domestic policy, trade policy is subject to the influence of domestic veto players. Such groups must ratify the policy choices made by the executive.

Interest groups affect trade policy but they are not the focus of our attention here. Trade policy has distributional consequences and so we expect certain coalitions to favour more open trade and others to favour protectionism.[10] The composition and power of these distributional coalitions differ across countries, since states vary with respect to their comparative advantage and factor endowments. These groups are not the focus of this article for several reasons. First, in a cross-national context, it is hard to determine how to model and empirically specify the structure of interest groups in each country. We know that groups opposing and supporting trade liberalization exist in all countries, but their identity and relative influence will vary according to the specific national context. We abstract away from this diversity.

Secondly, we follow many existing models of veto player models in assuming that interest groups affect trade policy indirectly. On the one hand, these groups shape the preferences of the executive since she worries about retaining office and thus requires their support. The executive negotiates with interest groups over the choice of whether to proceed with a PTA and over its terms prior to engaging in international negotiations. Thus, the executive's position already reflects the influence of those interest groups who are important for the executive.

On the other hand, interest groups affect policy indirectly through their influence on the preferences of veto players. Trade policy creates distributional winners and losers within society, and thus generates pressure for interest groups to organize and press for their preferred policy. A primary way to do so is through political parties and their platforms. In the trade policy literature, there is a long tradition of associating parties with the trade policy preferences of different interest groups.[11] Preferences over trade policy often structure political cleavages that are represented in party systems. Hence, we expect interest groups to operate through parties, and leaders of such parties constitute the executive and legislature. In our model of veto players, the structure of the legislature and its partisan composition are key elements. In sum, interest groups are represented here indirectly by their impact on the preferences of the executive and the parties.

Consider the recent discussions over the Central American Free Trade Agreement (CAFTA). CAFTA was negotiated between the Central American countries and the United States and signed in 2004. By early 2006 it had not yet been ratified by all of its member states. Then, one of Costa Rica's presidential candidates, Otto Solis, representing the left-wing opposition Citizen's Action Party (PAC) threatened to veto CAFTA if he won,

[10] Ronald Rogowski, *Commerce and Coalitions: How Trade Affects Domestic Political Alignments* (Princeton, N.J.: Princeton University Press, 1989); Ronald Rogowski, 'Political Cleavages and Changing Exposure to Trade', *American Political Science Review*, 81 (1987), 1121–37; Helen V. Milner, 'Resisting the Protectionist Temptation', *International Organization*, 41 (1987), 339–65; Michael J. Hiscox, *International Trade and Political Conflict: Commerce, Coalitions and Mobility* (Princeton, N.J.: Princeton University Press, 2002).

[11] Rogowski, *Commerce and Coalitions;* Helen V. Milner and Benjamin Judkins, 'Partisanship, Trade Policy and Globalization: Is there a Left–Right Party Divide on Trade Policy?' *International Studies Quarterly*, 48 (2004), 95–119.

claiming that the agreement would ruin the country's agricultural sector. Solis and his party could have won enough seats in the legislature (eighteen of fifty-seven) to prevent a qualified majority needed to ratify the treaty.[12] The PAC's potential power in the legislature could make them a potent veto player.

Our model makes no claim regarding the actual preferences of veto players. We are agnostic on this score and simply assume that some of them favour while others oppose trade liberalization. Consistent with Tsebelis, we show in the model that follows that a rise in the number of veto players never increases, and in most cases lowers, the probability of an agreement.[13] Consequently, as the number of veto players increases, the space for a policy which departs from the status quo is reduced.

By definition, veto players must ratify policy change, such as joining a trade agreement. We employ a broad notion of ratification. Formally, the head of state in a democracy – whether the prime minister, president, chancellor or premier – is often required by the national constitution to obtain the approval of the legislature for international agreements, including PTAs. Hence, the chief executive must negotiate a preferential arrangement that is acceptable to a majority of the legislature, either a simple plurality or some supermajority depending on the issue-area and the country. In the United States, for example, any treaty negotiated by the president must be approved by two-thirds of the Senate. That the executive must obtain legislative approval will affect how she negotiates. Bringing home an unratifiable PTA is likely to be costly – domestically and internationally – for the executive. She will, therefore, need to anticipate the legislature's (or any other veto player's) reaction to the proposed arrangement and ensure it is domestically acceptable.

Ratification can also be less formal. In dictatorships, shifts in foreign economic policy often require the support of groups like the military or local leaders; implicitly these groups have ratified a trade agreement that is enacted if they had the ability to veto it and chose not to. Informal ratification also occurs in democracies. If a leader needs to change a domestic law, norm or practice in order to implement a PTA, even if no formal vote on the arrangement itself is required, a legislative vote on any necessary domestic change becomes a vote on the agreement.

This domestic ratification game is a central element of our argument. In the simplest case, the executive and a single veto player share power: the player must ratify the proposed PTA that the executive negotiates with a foreign country. The executive and the foreign country understand this in advance and realize that any proposed arrangement must survive this domestic test before it can be implemented. The veto player need not have the power to amend the proposed agreement. Hence, the executives bargain with each other and ultimately propose an agreement, anticipating the reaction of the veto player, which in turn accepts or rejects the PTA. Because of this ratification constraint, veto players influence international trade agreements.

## A MODEL OF INTERNATIONAL CO-OPERATION IN TRADE POLICY

Our framework for analysing co-operation on international trade is closely tied to the literature on two-level games, which analyses domestic and international bargaining in

[12] Adam Thompson, 'Costa Rican hopeful vows to obstruct Cafta', *Financial Times*, 26 February 2006.

[13] Tsebelis, 'Decision Making in Political Systems'; Tsebelis, *Veto Players*, p. 2.

tandem.[14] We advance this literature by explicitly incorporating veto players into a two-level model. Existing research on two-level games has not only explored the impact of domestic constraints on international relations, but also the impact of domestic factors on bargaining power in world politics. Some of this work has addressed the domestic conditions under which international co-operation is possible; other parts of it have been more concerned with the (dis)advantages that domestic divisions (the so-called 'Schelling conjecture') can create at the international bargaining table.

Using a model developed by Milner and Rosendorff and by Milner, we model the effects on international economic co-operation of changes in the number of veto players.[15] In this game, two chief executives – home and foreign – are joint agenda-setters; they propose an agreement over trade policy using the Nash Bargaining Solution.[16] Figure 1 shows the results of a two-player international game without any domestic politics, where P is the executive negotiating in the home country (call her the president or prime minister) and F is the foreign country. No veto players exist in either country except the executives. This game assumes complete and perfectly symmetric information. The ideal points of P and F ($p$ and $f$) are common knowledge, as is the position of the status quo ($q$). The payoffs to the players decline linearly as the distance of the outcome from each player's ideal point rises. Each executive is a unitary, rational actor. We assume P and F have no domestic political considerations that are not factored into their ideal points; these ideal points maximize their political support.[17] The horizontal axis depicts all the possible values of the status quo ($q$). The vertical axis represents a continuum of policy outcomes on a single issue. In the arena of trade policy, this could be the difference between the home country's and the foreign country's trade barriers. Negotiating a trade agreement means choosing a pair of trade barriers for each country that is different from the status quo and usually one in which the level of barriers for the members is lower than the status quo.

[14] Robert Putnam, 'Diplomacy and Domestic Politics: The Logic of Two-Level Games', *International Organization*, 42 (1988), 427–60; Peter Evans, Harold Jacobsen and Robert Putnam, eds, *Double-Edged Diplomacy* (Berkeley: University of California Press, 1993); Keisuke Iida, 'When and How Do Domestic Constraints Matter? Two Level Games with Uncertainty', *Journal of Conflict Resolution*, 37 (1993), 403–26; Mo, 'The Logic of Two Level Games with Endogenous Domestic Coalitions'; Jongryn Mo, 'Domestic Institutions and International Bargaining: The Role of Agent Veto in Two-Level Games', *American Political Science Review*, 89 (1995), 914–24; Milner and Rosendorff, 'Trade Negotiations, Information, and Domestic Politics'; Eric Reinhardt, 'Posturing Parliaments: Ratification, Uncertainty, and International Bargaining' (Department of Political Science, Columbia University, 1996); Milner, *Interests, Institutions, and Information;* Robert Pahre, 'Divided Government and International Cooperation in Austria–Hungary, Sweden–Norway, and the European Union', *European Union Politics*, 2 (2001), 131–62; Tarar, 'International Bargaining with Two-Sided Domestic Constraints'; Daniel Drezner, ed., *Locating the Proper Authorities: The Interaction of Domestic and International Politics* (Ann Arbor: University of Michigan Press, 2003).

[15] Helen V. Milner and B. Peter Rosendorff, 'Trade Negotiations, Information, and Domestic Politics', *Economics and Politics*, 8 (1996), 145–89; Helen V. Milner and B. Peter Rosendorff, chap. 2 and Appendix, in Milner, *Interests, Institutions, and Information*.

[16] See Milner and Rosendorff (as detailed in fn. 15) and Milner, *Interests, Institutions, and Information*, for a derivation of the results and discussion of the use of the Nash Bargaining Solution (NBS). We use the NBS because it imposes minimal structure on the bargaining game, which best replicates the international environment in contrast to the domestic one. In addition, when offers are made suitably fast, other bargaining games, such as Rubenstein's, converge to the NBS.

[17] We assume that the preferences of interest groups are contained in the ideal points of the political actors. These actors use the preferences of the interest groups that are important to them to construct their ideal points.

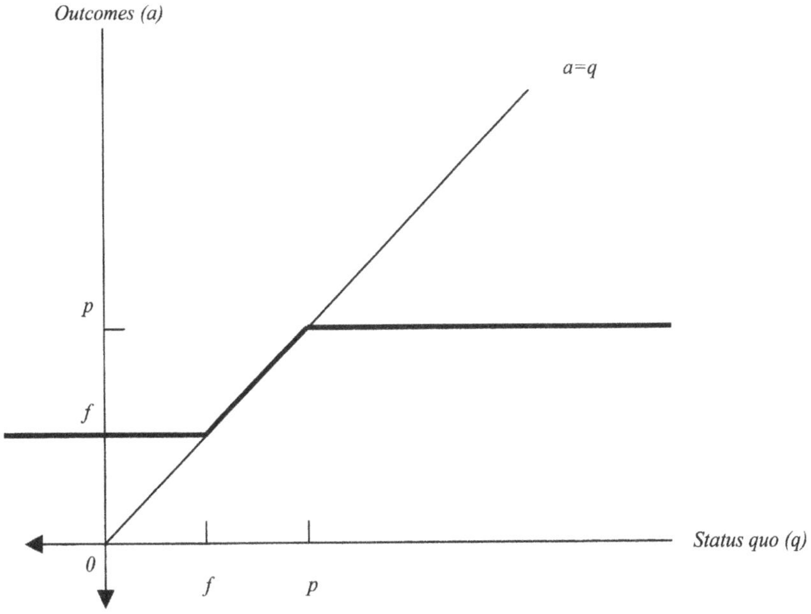


*Fig. 1. A pure international game: no domestic veto players*

The figure captures both the ideal points of the actors and the outcomes of the negotiations ($a$). The dark line represents the policies chosen given the value of the status quo, as shown along the horizontal axis. There is never a failure to agree in the complete information model analysed here. The figure is drawn to represent the outcomes of this game for all possible combinations of preferences and status quo.[18] Failure to co-operate is represented by a continuation of the status quo.

What are the outcomes of the Nash Bargaining Solution in this simple model? When $f < q < p$, the status quo is always the outcome in Figure 1. No agreement is the result because a mutually profitable bargain is not possible. When $q$ takes on any other range of values, mutually profitable bargains can be forged. This may mean, however, that one player ends up better off than the other. A rational player will accept gaining less than her counterpart if the bargain improves her position relative to the status quo. Figure 1 shows that when the status quo does not lie between $p$ and $f$, agreement is possible. It also demonstrates that the co-operative outcome will always be located between the ideal points

[18] The status quo or reversion point is assumed to be exogenous; it can lie anywhere in the policy space. This simplifying assumption turns out to be theoretically important, since veto players could also affect the status quo, as in Pahre, 'Divided Government and International Cooperation in Austria–Hungary, Sweden–Norway, and the European Union', pp. 145–53. Others, such as Kyle Bagwell and Robert W. Staiger, *The Economics of the World Trading System* (Cambridge, Mass.: MIT Press, 2002), apply a Nash equilibrium to the trade bargaining game between two executives as the sole reversion point.

of the two actors. Its exact position within this area is determined by the location of the status quo, $q$.[19]

As the difference between the countries ($p$ and $f$) grows larger, two implications follow. First, the area of no agreement becomes larger ($f < q < p$), rendering co-operation less likely. Secondly, the constraint exercised by the status quo increases. As the difference between the actors ($p - f$) rises, they must accept more extreme outcomes. When $q < p << f$, then F will accept P's ideal point, which is now much farther away. These results coincide with conventional wisdom.

Now compare the unitary actor case described above with Figure 2, where we introduce veto players into the analysis. We assume a non-unitary state by adding a ratification game. We introduce a veto player, V, who must 'ratify' any agreement negotiated internationally; that is, the veto player must tacitly or explicitly agree to accept the proposed international agreement. For example, the veto player could be a legislature, which takes some kind of vote – on a new law, budget allocation or constitutional amendment, among other things – that allows it to accept or reject the executive's proposal. The veto player has his own ideal trade policy, which maximizes his political support. As before, his utility declines linearly as the outcome moves away from his ideal point. Interest groups enter into the calculation of all the veto players' ideal points to the extent that these political actors depend on interest groups for political support. V is portrayed as a unitary actor representing the median member of the veto group. Therefore, V's 'vote' decides the outcome of the ratification contest. The veto player here must either accept the proposal negotiated by P and F, or reject it and return to the status quo. The executives jointly propose a take-it-or-leave-it policy to the veto player. V does not have amendment powers.[20] We maintain the assumption of full and symmetric information: P, V and F know each others' preferences and the nature of the proposed agreement. The veto group, which must approve the agreement, knows the preferences of P and F and the nature of the agreement. P and F likewise recognize that the agreement they negotiate must be ratified by V and they understand exactly what terms V will accept. The two executives once again are joint proposers, using the Nash Bargaining Solution to fix a proposal.

Figure 2 shows the outcome of the ratification game when the executive's preferences are located closer to those of the foreign country than are the veto player's ($f < p < v$). The veto group here is very protectionist because its ideal point is furthest from the foreign executive's. In Figure 2, the vertical axis represents the ideal points of the players and the proposed agreement. The horizontal axis is the position of the status quo. The darkened line shows the agreement reached along the vertical axis, given the position of the status quo along the horizontal one. It demonstrates when co-operation is possible if the structure of preferences is such that the veto player is the most protectionist actor. Figure 3 shows the outcomes when the structure of preferences is altered, so that the home executive is most protectionist, $f < v < p$. The structure of domestic preferences affects the ratification game and hence the co-operative outcomes. Different countries will have veto players with different preferences; here we model the situation assuming that their preferences over trade policy can take any form.

[19] If $q > p > f$, then $p$ is the outcome. Conversely, when $q < f < p$, then $f$ is the outcome. The player with the ideal point closest to the status quo, $q$, exerts greater influence. This is a fairly standard result in bargaining analysis since the actor with the best alternative to the agreement has greater leverage. See Howard Raiffa, *The Art and Science of Negotiation* (Cambridge, Mass.: Harvard University Press, 1982).

[20] We assume that the ratifier, V, plays only strategies that are not dominated and that the two international negotiators bargain using the NBS, whose structure is intentionally not modelled.

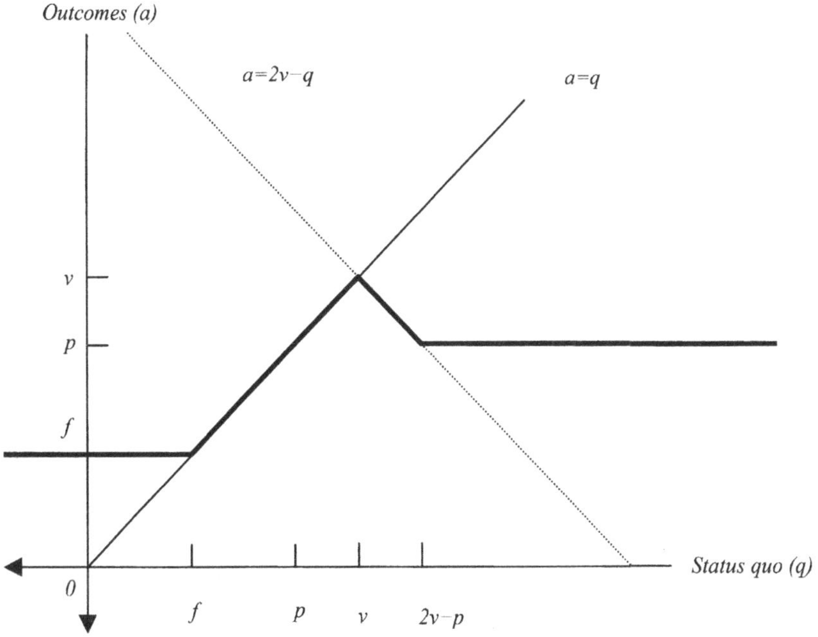


*Fig. 2. Domestic politics and one veto player, $p > v$*

When the executive is the more protectionist actor, as in Figure 3, domestic politics has no effect on international negotiations. This is evident since the outcomes in Figures 1 and 3 are exactly the same. In the domestic game, when $f < v < p$, the veto group cannot constrain the executive, even when the status quo is closest to the veto player's ideal point. The autonomy of the executive is maximized when she is very protectionist. For example, when the status quo lies between $f$ and $v$, no agreement will occur since neither V nor P will move to F's side of the status quo, and vice versa. When the status quo is between P and V ($f < v < q < p$), the veto player is still impotent, since P will never accept any proposal from which it derives less than the status quo. In this case, which might occur when the veto player represents interest groups that gain from trade liberalization, the home executive becomes the binding constraint on co-operation.

Under what conditions do veto players matter? The answer involves a comparison of Figures 1 and 2. In this game, consider what happens when the status quo is between $p$ and $v$ in Figure 2. If P and F negotiate to point $p$, V will reject such an agreement and implement the status quo, $q$, since $q$ is closer to $v$ than is $p$. Hence, for P and F to induce ratification, they must offer $q$ or better. The best ratifiable agreement, then, is $q$, which is offered and accepted. So no co-operation is the outcome in Figure 2 when the status quo lies between $p$ and $v$. P and F are unable to co-operate to realize the joint gains available under the international game. In Figure 1, the outcome in the region to the right of $p$ is a co-operative agreement at $p$. Adding a veto player to the game whose preferences lie to

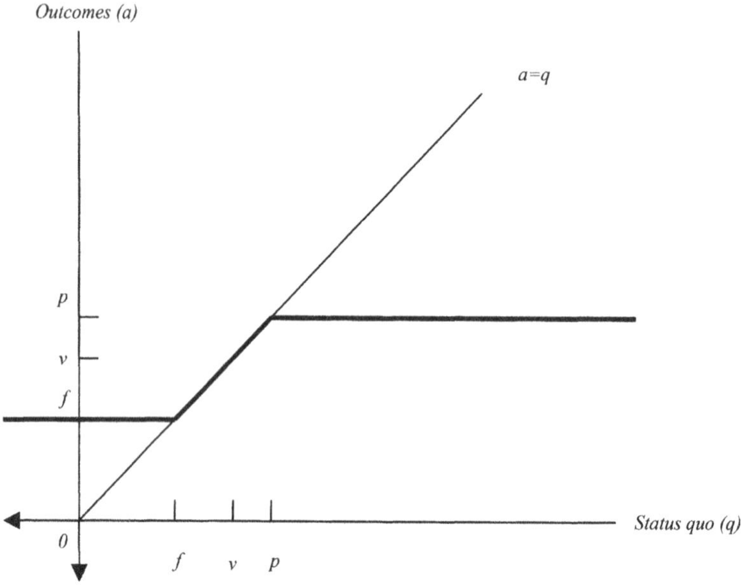


*Fig. 3. Domestic politics and one veto player, $p > v$*

the right of P and F creates a new zone of non-agreement when the status quo is also to the right of P. Holding P and F's preferences constant, then, adding a veto player – as in Figure 2 – increases the region where movement from the status quo to a co-operative agreement is impossible.[21] The range of acceptable agreements among the countries has declined as a protectionist veto player is included in the game. Note that, in this model, adding a free trade veto player has no effect on international co-operation.

Comparing the international game (Figure 1) to the domestic politics game (Figures 2 and 3) reveals the implications of introducing a single veto player. When the veto player and the executive share decision-making power in a ratification game, international agreement is never more likely, *ceteris paribus*. With this additional domestic veto player, there is a range ($p < q < v$) in Figure 2 where the status quo is the outcome, while mutual gains for the international negotiators simultaneously exist and remain unexploited. The range where $q$ is the outcome expands when the veto player and executive 'share' decision-making power. Consequently, the presence of veto players makes international co-operation less likely than in the international game. It is not just the anarchic nature of

[21] Consider also what happens in Figure 2 when the status quo is to the right of the veto group, V (that is, $f < p < v < q$), but not too extreme (that is, $v < q < 2v - q$). For every $q > v$, there is a point $(2v - q)$ to the left of $v$ that V finds indifferent to $q$. That is, the utility of the status quo for V is equal to the utility obtained at $2v - q$ (since the loss function is linear). Since V is indifferent between $q$ and $2v - q$, we allow V to accept an offer of $2v - q$ if it is made. Now P and F both prefer $2v - q$ to $q$ when $q > v$. So the executives P and F offer $2v - q$, a point that the veto group V will accept. In this region in Figure 2, domestic politics exercises a substantial constraint on the international negotiations. The negotiators will have to offer a co-operative agreement that is ratifiable, but it is one that they do not like as much as in Figure 1.

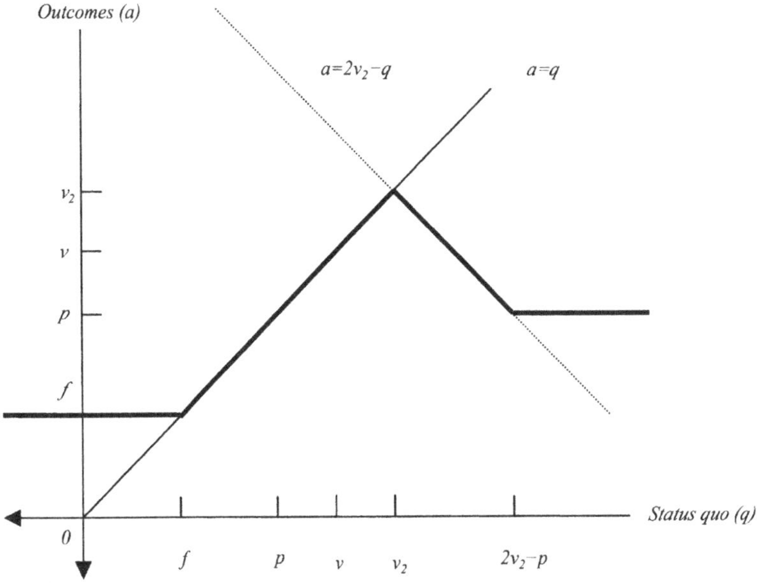


*Fig. 4. Adding a second veto player,* $p > v > v_2$

the international system, but also domestic politics, that renders co-operation difficult, suggesting that even realists may underestimate how hard it is to foster international co-operation.[22]

The precise impact of adding more veto players depends on their preferences, but in no case does such an addition increase the likelihood of agreement. This claim implies that the other veto players remain the same; that is, Figure 4 simply adds a veto player to the game depicted in Figure 2. If another veto player, $V_2$, is added to the game and its preferences lie to the right of V (that is, $f < p < v < v_2$), then as long as $q$ is to the left of V ($f < p < q < v < v_2$) the outcome is not changed. But when $q$ is between V and $V_2$, the second veto player will oppose any change to the status quo that the other players prefer and a new region of non-agreement is created. Figure 4 shows this situation. The outcome when the status quo lies between V and $V_2$ is now confined to the status quo. No co-operation is possible in this zone, whereas it was possible before the additional veto player was introduced into the game. This result is identical to moving the first veto player, V, further away from P. Adding new veto players never makes co-operation more likely and often reduces its probability.[23]

[22] See, for example, Kenneth N. Waltz, *Theory of International Politics* (Reading, Mass.: Addison-Wesley, 1979). We note that adding a veto player here is not the same as adding another country to the game. Adding a country would be captured by the results of a Nash Bargaining Solution among three players, with the three being joint agenda-setters. Adding a domestic veto player introduces the ratification game.

[23] Tsebelis, *Veto Players*, shows that this result holds in a multidimensional space. His Proposition 1.1 is equivalent to our central hypothesis. Or, as in Milner and Rosendorff, 'Trade Negotiations, Information, and Domestic Politics' and Milner, *Interests, Institutions, and Information*, it is similar to making government more divided, as the preferences of the legislature and the executive diverge.

What if the executive could offer something valuable to a veto player to change his ratification vote? If bribery is allowed – that is, if P (or F) could transfer some of their utility to the veto groups in order to buy their acquiescence – a similar result holds. P (and F) will only transfer as much utility as they get from the agreement relative to the status quo, thereby limiting their ability to bribe. As more veto players are added, at best P (and F) has to bribe no more groups if all the new veto players are free traders; but at worst (that is, if their preferences are protectionist and far to the right of P's and F's), it will have to make ever larger bribes. At some point, it will not be able to transfer enough utility to make the bribe effective. Hence, adding more veto players tends to result in paying more bribes (and never results in paying fewer bribes), reducing the probability that an executive can bribe all the veto players. Our veto player result therefore does not depend on whether bribery is allowed.[24]

Recall that failure of ratification never occurs in the variant of this model where there is complete information. Such failure only occurs in the presence of incomplete information. Our figures are drawn to represent the outcomes of this game for all possible combinations of preferences and status quos. Failure to co-operate is represented by a continuation of the status quo. The comparison across the figures, then, is between the sizes of the region where a move from the status quo to the co-operative outcome (that is, an agreement where both sides are better off) is possible with no veto players and with one veto player or more, *ceteris paribus*.

In the game where no veto players exist, this co-operative region is never smaller and usually bigger than where there is at least one veto player. Or there are more combinations of preferences and status quos in the game without veto players where co-operation results than in the game marked by one or more veto players. Since we do not know the combinations of preferences and status quos for each country (or pair of countries) at a given point in time, we assume a uniform distribution of such combinations of preferences and status quo. Hence, our results imply that the probability of drawing a country-pair with a set of preferences and status quos that leads to the conclusion of an agreement is never lower and is usually higher with no veto players than with one or more such players.

The model here makes a comparison between the outcomes possible given a prior structure of preferences and the addition of a new veto player to that structure. Adding a new veto player to an existing configuration of veto players and executives never increases the area where co-operation is possible. But our empirical analysis involves comparisons of countries at given points in time and of each country over time, where there is no equivalent comparison between a particular structure of preferences and that structure plus a new veto player. In the data, the preferences of existing actors vary as we change the number of veto players. Does changing the number of veto players without knowing the actors' preferences affect the results of our model? Is co-operation still relatively unlikely if the number of veto players increases, but the additional players' preferences are quite similar to the existing configuration of veto players? To address these questions, we run a set of simulations. We randomly generate 'countries' with different numbers and locations of veto players and then match them with all the other 'countries' to see if there

[24] Tsebelis's result that adding veto players in multidimensional issue space also reduces the ability to move from the status quo supports this claim, since bribery here is just like adding another issue dimension.

is a Nash Bargaining Solution equilibrium where co-operation occurs. We then run regressions on the simulated data to see if the probability of co-operation falls as the number of veto players increases, given that each country and pair has a randomly drawn set of preferences for its veto players and executives. The results of these regressions support our argument: the number of veto players is inversely related to the probability of co-operation even when the preferences of the players are not being held constant.[25] These findings suggest that our model might hold more generally, even if preferences are allowed to vary when making comparisons across different numbers of veto players.

The following tests of our model centre on the decision by states to enter PTAs, institutions which are prime examples of mutual policy adjustment and international co-operation. All parties to these agreements must lower their trade barriers so that the other members have improved market access. Such policy changes have domestic distributional consequences. Lowering trade barriers creates groups that gain from the policy ('winners') and groups that bear costs ('losers'). When these losing groups are not represented by a veto player(s) (even though they affect the ideal points of the political actors), co-operation may be more likely; if only the winners are represented by a veto player, then the situation most resembles Figure 3. However, when veto players exist that represent the preferences of the losers, changing policy and co-operating with other states in a PTA become much more difficult and unlikely, as in Figure 2 when compared to Figure 3. As the number of veto players rises, the probability that losers from trade liberalization are represented by one or more veto players also rises, and thus the chances of ratifying a PTA fall. Even if the winners from trade liberalization are added to the game, it may not make ratification easier. If the losers are represented by a veto player, such as $v_2$ as in Figure 4, then adding a pro-free trade veto player, such as $v$, has no effect on the likelihood of agreement.[26] Or, similarly, if the pro-free trade groups, $v$, already exist as veto players, but now the losers are added as a veto player, $v_2$, then co-operation will become less likely.

PTAs do not exhaust the trade agreements to which our argument could be applied. However, they constitute a very large portion of the commercial agreements forged over the past half-century and data on other types of these agreements are in short supply. Equally, there is widespread agreement that preferential arrangements have been quite influential, exerting a substantial impact on the global trading system. It is also important to recognize that, although economists have engaged in longstanding debates

[25] The procedure for the simulations is as follows. First, using the uniform distribution, we randomly draw a number between one and six to express the number of veto players in a country for 500 such countries. Secondly, using the uniform distribution, we randomly draw for each country each veto player's ideal point from the uniform distribution between 0 and 1 inclusive. This gives us a dataset of 500 countries with veto players ranging in number from one to six. Label the first veto player the executive. Thirdly, we pair all of the 500 countries with each other in a dyadic dataset, creating more than 124,000 observations. Fourthly, using the uniform distribution, we randomly draw a number between 0 and 1 inclusive to represent the status quo for each pair of countries. Fifthly, if the status quo falls strictly outside the range of the maximal and the minimal veto player's ideal points in each pair, then co-operation occurs by the Nash Bargaining Solution and we code a new variable labelled co-operation equal to 1. If the status quo falls inside the interval defined by the range of the minimum and maximum veto player in a pair, then co-operation fails to occur by our model and co-operation equals 0. We create this new variable for each pair. Sixthly, we run a probit model to see whether, as the number of veto players in the pair increases, the probability of co-operation falls. These results hold when using the normal distribution as well. They also hold if we allow bribery among the players within a country.

[26] If the influence of domestic groups is simply felt through the location of the executive's ideal point (that is, that as free trade groups become more active the executive shifts her ideal point to the left), then the game does change. But it is important to distinguish changes in preferences from changes in the number of veto players.

about the effect of trade barrier reductions among PTA members on third parties, this issue is of little consequence for our purposes.[27] Such reductions are significant acts of economic co-operation involving the contracting parties, even if they are trade-diverting or otherwise adversely influence states outside a PTA. As Martin points out, 'While cooperation improves the expected welfare of the cooperating states relative to the status quo *ex ante*, it is not necessarily a Pareto-improving (mutually beneficial) move for the world as a whole.'[28] Trade agreements are a form of co-operation, but they may primarily benefit the countries that are involved. Thus, a model of two-level games can be usefully extended by incorporating the theory of veto players.

## THE STATISTICAL MODEL

To test our theory, we begin by estimating the following model:

$$\begin{aligned} PTAOnset_{ij} = {} & \beta_0 + \beta_1 Veto\ Players_i + \beta_2 Veto\ Players_j + \beta_3 Regime\ Type_i + \\ & \beta_4 Regime\ Type_j + \beta_5 Trade_{ij} + \beta_6 GDP_i + \beta_7 GDP_j + \beta_8 \Delta GDP_i + \\ & \beta_9 \Delta GDP_j + \beta_{10} Dispute_{ij} + \beta_{11} Ally_{ij} + \beta_{12} Former\ Colony_{ij} + \\ & \beta_{13} Contiguity_{ij} + \beta_{14} Distance_{ij} + \beta_{15} Hegemony + \beta_{16} GATT_{ij} + \varepsilon. \end{aligned} \quad (1)$$

The dependent variable is the log of the odds that a pair of states, $i$ and $j$, enters a PTA in year $t+1$, where we observe 1 if this occurs and 0 otherwise. We focus on reciprocal arrangements, which involve policy adjustment on the part of all members, and exclude non-reciprocal arrangements. In the latter, one state unilaterally grants another country preferential access to its market. Veto players are likely to play less of a role in the formation of these arrangements than reciprocal PTAs since the countries that are granted preferences need not change their trade policy. Nonetheless, we revisit this issue when assessing the robustness of our results.

Note that the observed value of $PTAOnset_{ij}$ is 1 only when states initially join a PTA, not in subsequent years when the agreement is in force. We are interested in the initiation of co-operation, which depends on domestic ratification, and not its durability. We draw our sample of PTAs primarily from the World Trade Organization (WTO),[29] but also include arrangements that were not notified to either this organization or its predecessor, the General Agreement on Tariffs and Trade (GATT), since there is no reason to believe that veto players influence the decision to enter only those PTAs notified to these bodies.[30]

From the standpoint of testing our theory, the central independent variables in Equation 1 are *Veto Players$_i$* and *Veto Players$_j$*. These variables, measured in year $t$, indicate the extent of constitutionally mandated institutions that can exercise veto power over decisions

[27] Jacob Viner, *The Customs Union Issue* (New York: Carnegie Endowment for International Peace, 1950); Jagdish Bhagwati, 'Regionalism and Multilateralism: An Overview', in Jaime de Melo and Arvind Panagariya, eds, *New Dimensions in Regional Integration* (New York: Cambridge University Press, 1993), pp. 22–51; Richard Pomfret, *Unequal Trade: The Economics of Regional Trading Arrangements* (New York: Oxford University Press, 1997); Arvind Panagariya, 'Preferential Trade Liberalization: The Traditional Theory and New Developments', *Journal of Economic Literature*, 38 (2000), 287–331.

[28] Lisa L. Martin, *Democratic Commitments: Legislatures and International Cooperation* (Princeton, N.J.: Princeton University Press, 2000), p. 13. See also Robert O. Keohane, *After Hegemony: Cooperation and Discord in the World Political Economy* (Princeton, N.J.: Princeton University Press, 1984).

[29] World Trade Organization (WTO), *Regionalism and the World Trading System* (Geneva: WTO, 1995).

[30] We draw data on PTAs that were notified to neither GATT nor the WTO from Edward D. Mansfield and Jon C. Pevehouse, 'Trade Blocs, Trade Flows, and International Conflict', *International Organization*, 54 (2000), 775–808.

in states *i* and *j* as well as the alignment of actors' preferences between those institutions within each state. The data are taken from Henisz, who measures the presence of effective branches of government outside of the executive's control, the extent to which these branches are controlled by the same political party as the executive, and the homogeneity of preferences within these branches.[31] As he notes, the measure 'draws from recent theoretical developments in positive political theory to develop a structurally derived and internationally comparable measure of the degree of constraints on policy change using data on the number of independent veto points in the political system ... and the distribution of political preferences both across and within these branches'.[32]

Henisz's measure is well-suited to testing our theoretical model. His measure is theoretically derived from a spatial model of veto players. The theory underlying his measure is very similar to our model: it is a single dimensional, spatial model of policy choice that allows the status quo and the preferences of the actors to vary across the entire space. Since we are focused on trade policy, a single policy dimension is useful; preferences range from protectionist to free trade. His measure thus captures what our model represents as a veto player very naturally. Henisz's research reveals that:

> (1) each additional veto point (a branch of government that is both constitutionally effective and controlled by a party different from other branches) provides a positive but diminishing effect on the total level of constraints on policy change and (2) homogeneity (heterogeneity) of party preferences within an opposition (aligned) branch of government is positively correlated with constraints on policy change.[33]

The resulting measure is a continuous variable ranging from 0 to 1. When *Veto Players*$_i$ or *Veto Players*$_j$ equals 0, there is a complete absence of veto players in states *i* or *j*, respectively. Higher values indicate the presence of effective branches of government to balance the power of the executive. In cases where effective branches exist, the variables take on larger values as party control across some or all of these branches diverges from the executive's party. For example, in the United States, the value of this measure is larger during periods of divided government.[34] Because of this variable's theoretically-based construction and its attention to both domestic institutional arrangements and the preferences within those arrangements, it is especially appropriate for testing our hypothesis.[35]

[31] Henisz, 'The Institutional Environment for Infrastructure Investment'. Henisz has developed two measures of veto point, one that includes the judiciary and one that does not. We use the latter measure since there is little reason to believe that the judiciary would influence the decision to enter a PTA. However, our results are quite similar when we use the alternative measure.

[32] Henisz, 'The Institutional Environment for Economic Growth', p. 5.

[33] Henisz, 'The Institutional Environment for Infrastructure Investment', p. 363.

[34] For more details concerning this measure of veto players, see Henisz, 'The Institutional Environment for Economic Growth', and Henisz, 'The Institutional Environment for Infrastructure Investment'.

[35] Henisz's measure has some advantages compared to alternative measures of veto players. For example, Thorsten Beck, George Clarke, Alberto Groff, Philip Keefer and Patrick Walsh, 'New Tools in Comparative Political Economy: The Database of Political Institutions', *World Bank Economic Review*, 15 (2001), 165–76, have developed a measure that emphasizes the electoral rules and the degree of electoral competition in a country, as well as the degree of partisan differences across these players. This measure, however, is available for fewer countries than Henisz's measure and it only covers the period from 1975 onward. Using the Beck *et al.* measure rather than Henisz's measure cuts the size of our sample in half, which is clearly undesirable. However, there is a good deal of agreement between Henisz's measure and Beck *et al.*'s measure where those samples overlap – the correlation between a country's annual score on Henisz's measure of veto players and its score on Beck *et al.*'s measure is about 0.75, suggesting that our results are not driven by the choice of measure.

For at least two reasons, we rely on Henisz's more general measure of veto players rather than constructing a measure of veto players that is specific to trade policy. First, constructing such a measure would require a great deal of detailed information that is simply unavailable for many countries. Equally, countries not missing this information at random are likely to be those with low numbers of veto players or unstable institutions, creating a potential source of bias. Secondly, it is not clear that a measure of veto players for trade policy would look much different from one for all policy, as developed by Henisz. Most changes in trade policy must endure the same institutional hurdles and ratification processes that all other policies face. In the United States, for example, trade policy initiatives have been contested by Congress and the president; both have the ability to block policy change. Fast track, the procedure often used to move trade legislation forward, simply reduces Congress's ability to amend a trade agreement. It does not change the fact that a majority in both houses must ratify that policy change. Veto players affect the ratification of changes in policy; trade agreements tend to require changes in policy in most countries and thus to invoke the usual institutional veto players.

We also include a number of variables that previous studies have linked to the formation of PTAs to ensure that any observed effect of veto players is not due to other international or domestic factors. A number of these variables also help us to control for the general differences in preferences between pairs of countries. For instance, countries without ongoing disputes, ones that are allies or that trade extensively, or those that share similar voting profiles at the United Nations may have much smaller differences in the preferences of their executives; that is, the distance between $p$ and $f$ will be smaller. Holding these factors constant is important for testing our argument about the effect of veto players.

Past research has found that democracies tend to join PTAs at a higher rate than non-democracies.[36] Consequently, we introduce *Regime Type*$_i$ and *Regime Type*$_j$, which are 21-point indices of country $i$'s and country $j$'s regime type in year $t$. These variables are constructed using the Polity dataset. They range from 10 for the most democratic states to $-10$ for the most autocratic ones.[37] As such, we expect them to be directly related to the onset of PTAs.[38] It is essential to include these variables since they capture some of the same institutional features as *Veto Players*$_i$ and *Veto Players*$_j$ (for example, constitutionally mandated limitations on executive authority). We need to ensure that the influence of veto players is not simply an outgrowth of the effects of regime type.

Next, *Trade*$_{ij}$ is the logarithm of the total value of trade (in constant 1995 US dollars) between countries $i$ and $j$ in year $t$.[39] Various observers argue that increasing economic exchange creates incentives for domestic groups that benefit as a result to press

[36] Mansfield, Milner and Rosendorff, 'Why Democracies Cooperate More'.

[37] Keith Jaggers and Ted Robert Gurr, 'Tracking Democracy's Third Wave with the Regime Type III Data', *Journal of Peace Research*, 32 (1995), 469–82.

[38] We use Gleditsch's update of the Polity IV dataset (see Kristian Gleditsch, 'Modified Regime Type 4 Data', available online at http://weber.ucsd.edu/~kgledits/Regime Type.html, 2004). See also Monty Marshall, 'Regime Type 4 Data Set Codebook', http://www.cidcm.umd.edu/inscr/Regime Type/index.htm, 2004.

[39] We add 0.001 to all values of trade since some dyads conduct no trade in particular years and the logarithm of zero is undefined.

governments to enter PTAs, since these arrangements help to avert the possibility that trade relations will break down in the future.[40] Moreover, heightened overseas commerce can increase the susceptibility of firms to predatory behaviour by foreign governments, prompting firms to press for the establishment of PTAs that limit the ability of governments to behave opportunistically.[41]

Besides economic relations between countries, economic conditions within countries are likely to influence PTA formation. Particularly important in this regard is a state's economic size. Large states may have less incentive to seek the expanded market access afforded by PTA membership than their smaller counterparts. We therefore analyse $GDP_i$ and $GDP_j$, the logarithm of country *i*'s and country *j*'s gross domestic products (in constant 1995 US dollars) in year *t*. Moreover, fluctuations in economic growth may affect whether states enter preferential arrangements. On the one hand, some research indicates that downturns in the business cycle lead states to seek membership in such arrangements.[42] On the other hand, increased growth is likely to increase a country's demand for imports and supply of exports, creating an incentive to gain preferential access to overseas markets. To address this issue, we introduce $\Delta GDP_i$ and $\Delta GDP_j$, the change in $GDP_i$ and $GDP_j$ from $t-1$ to $t$.[43]

In addition, political relations between states may influence whether they join the same PTA, independent of their respective domestic political structures. In our model, co-operation also depends on the extent of differences in preferences between the countries' leaders. The further apart these preferences are, the less likely is co-operation. To hold these preferences constant, we include a number of variables that measure the foreign policy differences between states. Military hostilities between states signal large differences in preferences between countries and may discourage economic co-operation and thus their propensity to sign PTAs. Similarly, political–military co-operation may promote economic co-operation, as Gowa has argued.[44] $Dispute_{ij}$ is coded 1 if countries *i* and *j* are involved in a militarized interstate dispute (MID) during year *t*, 0 otherwise.[45] $Ally_{ij}$ equals 1 if countries *i* and *j* are members of a military alliance in year *t*, 0 otherwise. Since previous research on economic regionalism has found that a former colonial relationship between *i* and *j* increases the likelihood that they will enter the same PTA, we also include $Former\ Colony_{ij}$, which equals 1 if countries *i* and *j* had a colonial

[40] Joseph Nye, 'Neorealism and Neoliberalism', *World Politics*, 40 (1988), 235–51.

[41] Beth V. Yarbrough and Robert M. Yarbrough, *Cooperation and Governance in International Trade* (Princeton, N.J.: Princeton University Press, 1992). Note that we use Gleditsch's data on trade flows (Kristian Gleditsch, 'Expanded Trade and GDP Data', *Journal of Conflict Resolution*, 46 (2002), 712–24). Gleditsch draws much of his data from the International Monetary Fund's (IMF's) *Direction of Trade Statistics*. Like the IMF data, however, Gleditsch's data are in current dollars. We deflate these data using the US consumer price index.

[42] Walter Mattli, *The Logic of Regional Integration: Europe and Beyond* (New York: Cambridge University Press, 1999).

[43] Gross domestic product (GDP) data are also taken from Gleditsch, 'Expanded Trade and GDP Data' and are deflated using the US consumer price index.

[44] Joanne Gowa, *Allies, Adversaries, and International Trade* (Princeton, N.J.: Princeton University Press, 1994).

[45] For a description of the MIDs data, see Daniel Jones, Stuart Bremer and J. David Singer, 'Militarized Interstate Disputes, 1816–1992: Rationale, Coding Rules, and Empirical Patterns', *Conflict Management and Peace Science*, 15 (1996), 163–213. For a review of the updated MID data, see Faten Ghosn and Glenn Palmer, 'Codebook for the Militarized Interstate Dispute Data, Version 3.0', available online at http://cow2.la.psu.edu, 2003.

relationship that ended after the Second World War, 0 otherwise.[46] Adding these controls also allows us to hold constant to some extent the differences between the countries while focusing on the number of domestic veto players in explaining co-operation.

Geographic distance is another important influence on PTA membership. States often enter PTAs to obtain preferential access to the markets of their key trade partners. These partners tend to be located nearby, since closer proximity reduces transport costs and other impediments to trade. We introduce two variables to capture distance. $Contiguity_{ij}$ is a dummy variable that is coded 1 if countries *i* and *j* share a common border. $Distance_{ij}$ is the logarithm of the capital-to-capital distance between *i* and *j*. It is useful to include both variables since some states have distant capitals (for example, Russia and China) yet share borders, while other states do not share borders but are in relatively close proximity (for example, Benin and Ghana).[47]

In addition, systemic conditions are likely to affect the prospects of PTA formation. Many studies have found that declining hegemony contributes to the proliferation of preferential arrangements.[48] We therefore include *Hegemony*, the proportion of global GDP produced by the state with the largest GDP (in our sample, the United States for each year) in year *t*. This variable, therefore, takes on the same value for each country in *t*.

Because the GATT and the WTO recognize and attempt to govern the establishment of PTAs, members of these global institutions may also be disproportionately likely to enter preferential arrangements.[49] To account for this possibility, we introduce $GATT_{ij}$ in the model. It equals 1 if countries *i* and *j* are both members of GATT in each year, *t*, prior to 1995 or if they are both members of the WTO in years from 1995 on, and 0 otherwise.[50] Finally, $\varepsilon$ is a stochastic error term.

Descriptive statistics for all of the variables are presented in Table 1. The sample in the following analyses is comprised of all pairs of states during the period from 1950 to 1999. Which state is *i* in each pair and which one is *j* is determined by random assignment. Because the observed value of the dependent variable is dichotomous, we use logistic regression to estimate the model. To account for temporal dependence in the formation of PTAs, we include a spline function of the number of years that have elapsed (as of *t*) since each dyad last formed a PTA.[51] In the following tables, however, the estimates of this function are omitted to conserve space.

[46] Mansfield, Milner and Rosendorff, 'Why Democracies Cooperate More'. Data on former colonial relations are taken from George T. Kurian, *Encyclopedia of the Third Word*, 4th edn, Vols. 1–3 (New York: Facts on File, 1992). Data on alliances are taken from the Correlates of War Project (Douglas M. Gibler and Meredith Sarkees, 'Measuring Alliances: The Correlates of War Formal Interstate Alliance Data Set, 1816–2000'), available online at http://cow2.la.psu.edu, 2003.

[47] Data on distance and contiguity are taken from John R. Oneal and Bruce Russett, 'Assessing the Liberal Peace with Alternative Specifications: Trade Still Reduces Conflict', *Journal of Peace Research*, 36 (1999), 423–42.

[48] Bhagwati, 'Regionalism and Multilateralism'; Paul Krugman, 'Regionalism versus Multilateralism: Analytical Notes', in Jaime de Melo and Arvind Panagariya, eds, *New Dimensions in Regional Integration* (New York: Cambridge University Press, 1993), pp. 58–79; Edward D. Mansfield, 'The Proliferation of Preferential Trading Arrangements', *Journal of Conflict Resolution*, 42 (1998), 523–43.

[49] Edward D. Mansfield and Eric Reinhardt, 'Multilateral Determinants of Regionalism: The Effects of GATT/WTO on the Formation of Preferential Trading Arrangements', *International Organization*, 57 (2003), 829–62.

[50] Data are taken from the WTO web site: http://www.wto.org.

[51] Nathaniel Beck, Jonathan N. Katz and Richard Tucker, 'Taking Time Seriously: Time-Series–Cross-Section Analysis with a Binary Dependent Variable', *American Journal of Political Science*, 42 (1998), 1260–88.

TABLE 1 *Descriptive Statistics*

| Variable | Mean | Standard Dev. | Min. | Max. |
|---|---|---|---|---|
| *PTAOnset* | 0.007 | 0.081 | 0 | 1 |
| *Veto Players$_i$* | 0.175 | 0.213 | 0 | 0.674 |
| *Veto Players$_j$* | 0.177 | 0.213 | 0 | 0.708 |
| *Regime Type$_i$* | − 0.420 | 7.754 | − 10 | 10 |
| *Regime Type$_j$* | − 0.393 | 7.754 | − 10 | 10 |
| *Trade** | − 1.350 | 4.918 | − 6.908 | 12.492 |
| *GDP$_i$** | 17.178 | 1.797 | 13.099 | 22.870 |
| *GDP$_j$** | 17.182 | 1.795 | 13.099 | 22.870 |
| *$\Delta GDP_i$* | $5.56 \times 10^6$ | $2.43 \times 10^7$ | $-1.61 \times 10^8$ | $4.06 \times 10^8$ |
| *$\Delta GDP_j$* | $5.59 \times 10^6$ | $2.43 \times 10^7$ | $-1.61 \times 10^8$ | $4.06 \times 10^8$ |
| *Dispute* | 0.005 | 0.071 | 0 | 1 |
| *Ally* | 0.073 | 0.261 | 0 | 1 |
| *Former Colony* | 0.004 | 0.063 | 0 | 1 |
| *Contiguity* | 0.038 | 0.190 | 0 | 1 |
| *Distance** | 8.220 | 0.783 | 1.872 | 9.42 |
| *Hegemony* | 0.220 | 0.018 | 0.201 | 0.276 |
| *GATT* | 0.343 | 0.475 | 0 | 1 |
| *Number of PTAs* | 1,585.195 | 1,359.705 | 26 | 4,782 |
| *GDP Ratio** | 2.027 | 1.510 | 0.00003 | 9.589 |
| *Capability Ratio** | 2.015 | 1.504 | 0.00001 | 10.164 |
| *$tau_b$* | 0.189 | 0.294 | − 0.866 | 1 |

$N = 339{,}910$ for all variables except $tau_b$ ($N = 277{,}360$).
*Variables are expressed in logarithms.

## THE RESULTS

Table 2 presents the estimates of Equation 1. Consistent with our argument, the coefficient estimates of both *Veto Players$_i$* and *Veto Players$_j$* are negative, statistically significant and large, indicating that states are less likely to forge trade agreements as the number of veto players rises. Furthermore, as expected, there is virtually no difference in the size of the estimates of *Veto Players$_i$* and *Veto Players$_j$* ($\chi^2 = 0.08$; $p = 0.78$). Based on these results, an increase from the mean number of veto players in state *i* (or state *j*) to the maximum number yields more than a 50 per cent decrease in the predicted probability of PTA formation. Increasing both *Veto Players$_i$* and *Veto Players$_j$* from their respective means to their respective maximum values yields more than a 75 per cent dip in the likelihood of creating a PTA. Recall that we have held constant various factors which are likely to underlie differences in preferences between countries, improving our confidence that these results actually reflect the influence of domestic politics.

In addition to the predicted probability of PTA formation, we assess how veto players affect the predicted number of PTAs created in a given year. Figure 5 shows the predicted number of country-pairs forming a PTA annually for the observed values of *Veto Players$_i$* and *Veto Players$_j$*, based on 3,000, replications of the parameter estimates in the first column of Table 2.[52] Increasing the mean value of either of these variables to its sample

[52] This figure and the predicted probabilities have been generated using the CLARIFY program. All continuous variables are set to their sample means while the discrete variables are set at their modal category. See Gary King, Michael Tomz and Jason Wittenberg, 'Making the Most of Statistical Analyses: Improving Interpretation and Presentation', *American Journal of Political Science*, 44 (2000), 347–61.

TABLE 2 *The Effects of Veto Players on PTA Formation, 1950–99*

| Variable | Base Model | Includes Hub and Spokes | FTAs/CUs/ CMs/EUs | CUs/CMs/EUs |
|---|---|---|---|---|
| *Veto Players*$_i$ | − 1.608** | − 0.718** | − 1.538** | − 1.965** |
| | (0.244) | (0.174) | (0.252) | (0.331) |
| *Veto Players*$_j$ | − 1.698** | − 0.724** | − 1.657** | − 2.381** |
| | (0.244) | (0.170) | (0.250) | (0.320) |
| *Regime Type*$_i$ | 0.049** | 0.044** | 0.050** | 0.055** |
| | (0.006) | (0.005) | (0.006) | (0.008) |
| *Regime Type*$_j$ | 0.040** | 0.041** | 0.042** | 0.051** |
| | (0.006) | (0.004) | (0.006) | (0.007) |
| *Trade*$_{ij}$ | − 0.006 | 0.047** | − 0.007 | − 0.012 |
| | (0.008) | (0.006) | (0.008) | (0.009) |
| *GDP*$_i$ | − 0.208** | − 0.201** | − 0.215** | − 0.286** |
| | (0.020) | (0.015) | (0.020) | (0.024) |
| *GDP*$_j$ | − 0.183** | − 0.179** | − 0.199** | − 0.241** |
| | (0.019) | (0.015) | (0.020) | (0.024) |
| *ΔGDP*$_i$ | $6.94 \times 10^{-10}$ | $-1.63 \times 10^{-9}$ | $9.11 \times 10^{-10}$ | $-6.94 \times 10^{-9}$** |
| | $(1.14 \times 10^{-9})$ | $(8.87 \times 10^{-10})$ | $(1.14 \times 10^{-9})$ | $(2.26 \times 10^{-9})$ |
| *ΔGDP*$_j$ | $3.64 \times 10^{-10}$ | $-2.15 \times 10^{-9}$** | $9.42 \times 10^{-10}$ | $-6.08 \times 10^{-9}$** |
| | $(1.01 \times 10^{-9})$ | $(7.97 \times 10^{-10})$ | $(9.56 \times 10^{-10})$ | $(1.47 \times 10^{-9})$ |
| *Dispute*$_{ij}$ | − 0.484 | − 0.377 | − 0.444 | − 0.732* |
| | (0.274) | (0.248) | (0.281) | (0.337) |
| *Ally*$_{ij}$ | 1.269** | 0.726** | 1.210** | 1.203** |
| | (0.083) | (0.063) | (0.087) | (0.100) |
| *Former Colony*$_{ij}$ | − 0.813 | 0.660** | –† | –† |
| | (0.717) | (0.192) | | |
| *Contiguity*$_{ij}$ | − 0.170 | − 0.383** | − 0.231 | − 0.193 |
| | (0.119) | (0.101) | (0.124) | (0.143) |
| *Distance*$_{ij}$ | − 0.910** | − 0.819** | − 0.934** | − 0.903** |
| | (0.050) | (0.036) | (0.053) | (0.061) |
| *Hegemony* | − 18.033** | − 18.199** | − 17.852** | − 16.016** |
| | (1.989) | (1.361) | (2.103) | (2.253) |
| *GATT*$_{ij}$ | 0.326** | 0.387** | 0.389** | 0.626** |
| | (0.057) | (0.042) | (0.058) | (0.065) |
| Constant | 11.404** | 12.064** | 11.768** | 12.601** |
| | (0.842) | (0.605) | (0.884) | (0.952) |
| Log-likelihood | − 11,389.03 | − 16,869.78 | − 10,824.14 | − 7,662.21 |
| *N* | 339,910 | 341,073 | 339,774 | 339,091 |

*Note*: Parameters are estimated using logistic regression, after including a cubic spline function with no knots. Entries in parentheses are Huber standard errors clustered on the dyad. $^{**}p \leq 0.01$; $^{*}p \leq 0.05$. All tests of statistical significance are two-tailed.

†There is no case where states with a former colonial relationship formed a reciprocal FTA, CU, common market or economic union.

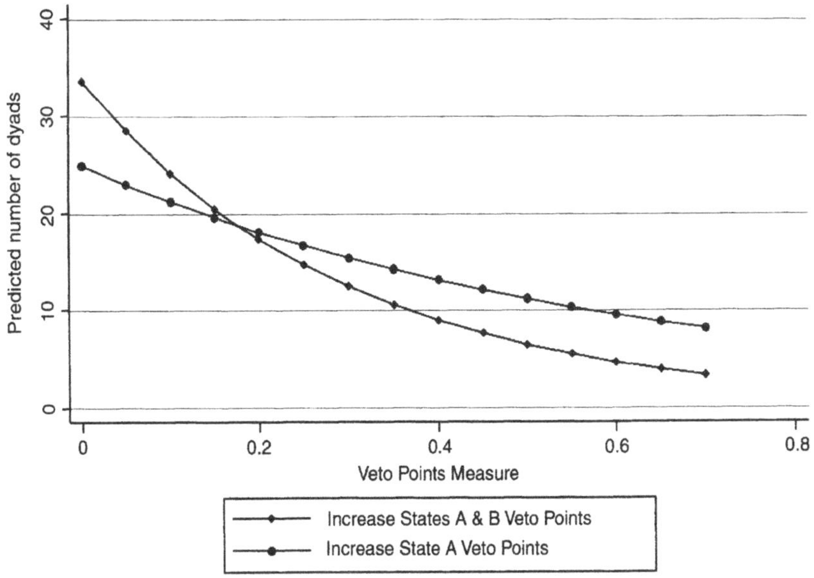


*Fig. 5. Predicted annual number of dyads forming a PTA*
*Note*: Simulated predicted probabilities based on estimates from Table 2, column 1. Simulations based on 3,000 replications of the parameter estimates using CLARIFY.

maximum yields a decrease of about ten dyadic arrangements (we show only an increase for state *i* since the coefficient estimates are virtually identical). Raising both variables simultaneously from their respective means to their maximum values reduces the number of PTAs formed each year by about fourteen. These results confirm that countries have greater difficulty engaging in international economic co-operation as the number of veto players grows.

Furthermore, the coefficient estimates for many of the control variables tend to be statistically significant and have the expected sign. First, political conditions within countries and political relations between them generally have a strong bearing on PTA formation. The positive and significant estimates of $Regime\ Type_i$ and $Regime\ Type_j$ confirm that democracies are more likely to enter such arrangements than other states. Equally, the estimate of $Ally_{ij}$ is positive and statistically significant, indicating that military allies are especially likely to accede to PTAs. Colonial relations and political disputes, however, have a weak effect on preferential arrangements. The estimates of $Dispute_{ij}$ and $Former\ Colony_{ij}$ are negative, but neither of them is statistically significant. Each of these findings, except the effect of former colonial ties, is consistent with past empirical work and we will address this exception later.

Secondly, systemic factors influence preferential arrangements. The coefficient estimate of *Hegemony* is negative, that of $GATT_{ij}$ is positive, and both are statistically significant. As hegemony wanes, states are more likely to form preferential arrangements, a finding that is consistent with existing research on economic regionalism.[53] Membership in the GATT and the WTO encourages membership in PTAs as well. Thirdly, states are more likely to enter a PTA as the distance between them declines, since the estimate of $Distance_{ij}$ is negative and significant. Controlling for the influence of distance, however, contiguity has little additional effect on the formation of preferential arrangements.

Fourthly, the coefficient estimates of $GDP_i$ and $GDP_j$ are negative and statistically significant, indicating that states with large economies are less likely to enter a trade agreement than their smaller counterparts. But neither the business cycle nor the flow of trade between states bears heavily on their prospect of joining a preferential grouping. Although the estimates of $\Delta GDP_i$, $\Delta GDP_j$ and $Trade_{ij}$ are positive, none of them are statistically significant.

## ASSESSING THE ROBUSTNESS OF THE RESULTS

Before concluding, it is important to assess the robustness of our results. First, we analyse whether our results depend on how PTAs are coded. Recall that we restrict attention to reciprocal PTAs – that is, arrangements that involve policy adjustment on the part of all members – and exclude non-reciprocal arrangements. Almost all of the latter are 'hub and spoke' arrangements, in which members of the European Community (EC)/European Union (EU) furnish certain less developed countries (LDCs) with preferential access to European markets without obtaining similar preferences in return (for example, the Lomé Convention). Excluding these arrangements is entirely appropriate for our purposes because the domestic politics underlying entry into arrangements of this sort are likely to differ from the politics underlying decisions to enter reciprocal PTAs, particularly for the LDC, which does not have to make any trade policy concessions. Nonetheless, we also estimate our model after including hub and spoke arrangements. The results in the second column of Table 2 show that the coefficient estimates of $Veto\ Players_i$ and $Veto\ Players_j$ remain negative and statistically significant, but that they are (in absolute value) less than half as large when we include such arrangements in the sample. Thus, as expected, veto players have a much more sizeable influence on the formation of reciprocal PTAs than non-reciprocal arrangements.

Most of the remaining coefficient estimates are unaffected by this change in the dependent variable. However, it is interesting that the estimate of $Former\ Colony_{ij}$ is positive and statistically significant, reflecting the fact that many hub and spoke arrangements were forged between LDCs and their past metropoles. Equally, the estimate of $Contiguity_{ij}$ is negative and significant, which probably stems from the tendency for hub and spoke arrangements to form between non-contiguous countries. Nonetheless, there is no evidence that the effects of veto players are affected in an unexpected way by our decision to exclude non-reciprocal arrangements between the EC/EU and developing countries.

Nor is there any indication that the EC/EU itself is driving our results, despite the fact that participants in these institutions have been especially active in forming PTAs. When we remove all country-pairs that belong to the EC/EU in each year, the coefficients of $Veto\ Players_i$ and $Veto\ Players_j$ remain negative, large and highly statistically significant.

[53] Mansfield, 'The Proliferation of Preferential Trading Arrangements'.

While all reciprocal PTAs aim to improve and stabilize the access that each member has to the other participants' markets, there are crucial differences among these arrangements. Some cover only a small set of products; free trade areas (FTAs) involve the substantial reduction or elimination of trade barriers on many (if not all) products; customs unions (CU) entail the elimination of trade barriers within the arrangement and the establishment of a common external tariff on the products of third parties; common markets are customs unions in which members also implement similar product regulations and permit the free flow of factors of production between members; and economic unions are common markets in which members also use a common currency. These different arrangements attempt to achieve different degrees of economic integration: those covering a small set of products are the least integrative and economic unions are the most integrative.

It is useful to determine whether our results hold when focusing on arrangements that aim to achieve greater integration. To address this issue, we re-estimate our model after eliminating all observations in which states formed a preferential arrangement that is not an FTA, a CU, a common market, or an economic union. We then estimate the model again, focusing only on the establishment of CUs, common markets and economic unions. As shown in the third column of Table 2, removing arrangements that cover only a small group of products has virtually no bearing on the coefficient estimates of veto players. As shown in the fourth column, removing these arrangements and FTAs also has no effect on the sign and statistical significance of *Veto Players*$_i$ and *Veto Players*$_j$.[54] However, the absolute value of these coefficient estimates is noticeably larger than when the dependent variable includes all PTAs. This result may reflect the tendency for more extensive integration to generate more pronounced distributional consequences within the participating countries, creating bigger gains for the distributional winners and bigger losses from the distributional losers. As the number of veto players increases, so does the likelihood that at least one such player will have a constituency that expects to suffer a loss in welfare due to a PTA. Consequently, this actor has particular incentive to block the formation of PTAs designed to achieve extensive integration.

Secondly, it is useful to examine whether our results hinge on how veto players enter the statistical model. Thus far, we have assumed that *Veto Players*$_i$ and *Veto Players*$_j$ have a linear effect on PTA formation. To analyse whether our results hold up if their effect is treated as non-monotonic, we replace *Veto Players*$_i$ and *Veto Players*$_j$ with their natural logarithms and with a logistic transformation of these variables.[55] In addition, we replace *Veto Players*$_i$ and *Veto Players*$_j$ with the sum of these variables. Finally, for each dyad-year, we include only the higher value for these two variables, a variant of the 'weak link' specification that has been used in various empirical studies of the liberal peace.[56] As reported in the first four columns of Table 3, the coefficient estimates of these variables are always negative, large and statistically significant.

In addition to the functional form of veto players, it is important to ensure that our results are not being driven by collinearity between regime type and veto players. These variables

[54] The results are unchanged if we code these observations as 0 rather than missing.

[55] There are some cases where the value of veto points is 0. Since the natural logarithm and the logistic transformation of 0 are undefined, we arbitrarily add 0.001 to each value of veto points, thereby retaining all of our original observations. Note, however, that our results are unchanged if we do not adopt this procedure.

[56] Bruce Russett and John Oneal, *Triangulating Peace: Democracy, Interdependence, and International Organization* (New York: W.W. Norton, 2001).

TABLE 3 *Alternative Ways of Modelling the Effects of Veto Players on PTA Formation, 1950–99*

| Variable | Veto Players logged | Veto Players exponential | Veto Players additive | Veto Players weak link | Veto Players residual† |
|---|---|---|---|---|---|
| *Veto Players$_i$* | − 0.076** | − 0.077** | − 1.652** | − 2.666** | − 1.587** |
| | (0.020) | (0.018) | (0.183) | (0.232) | (0.244) |
| *Veto Players$_j$* | − 0.088** | − 0.088** | – | – | − 1.679** |
| | (0.197) | (0.018) | | | (0.244) |
| *Regime Type$_i$* | 0.039** | 0.042** | 0.050** | 0.052** | 0.011** |
| | (0.008) | (0.007) | (0.005) | (0.004) | (0.003) |
| *Regime Type$_j$* | 0.032** | 0.035** | 0.040** | 0.040** | 0.000 |
| | (0.007) | (0.007) | (0.005) | (0.004) | (0.003) |
| *Trade$_{ij}$* | − 0.010 | − 0.009 | − 0.006 | − 0.007 | − 0.007 |
| | (0.008) | (0.008) | (0.008) | (0.008) | (0.008) |
| *GDP$_i$* | − 0.222** | − 0.221** | − 0.207** | − 0.210** | − 0.208** |
| | (0.020) | (0.020) | (0.020) | (0.019) | (0.020) |
| *GDP$_j$* | − 0.195** | − 0.194** | − 0.184** | − 0.187** | − 0.184** |
| | (0.020) | (0.020) | (0.020) | (0.019) | (0.019) |
| *ΔGDP$_i$* | $8.67 \times 10^{-10}$ | $8.43 \times 10^{-9}$ | $6.90 \times 10^{-10}$ | $4.25 \times 10^{-10}$ | $6.95 \times 10^{-10}$ |
| | $(1.18 \times 10^{-9})$ | $(1.17 \times 10^{-9})$ | $(1.14 \times 10^{-10})$ | $(1.14 \times 10^{-9})$ | $(1.14 \times 10^{-9})$ |
| *ΔGDP$_j$* | $4.90 \times 10^{-10}$ | $4.68 \times 10^{-9}$ | $3.66 \times 10^{-10}$ | $1.25 \times 10^{-10}$ | $3.62 \times 10^{-10}$ |
| | $(1.04 \times 10^{-9})$ | $(1.04 \times 10^{-10})$ | $(1.01 \times 10^{-10})$ | $(1.01 \times 10^{-9})$ | $(1.01 \times 10^{-9})$ |
| *Dispute$_{ij}$* | − 0.477 | − 0.478 | − 0.484 | − 0.428 | − 0.483 |
| | (0.275) | (0.275) | (0.274) | (0.273) | (0.274) |
| *Ally$_{ij}$* | 1.281** | 1.282** | 1.269** | 1.187** | 1.270** |
| | (0.084) | (0.084) | (0.083) | (0.083) | (0.083) |
| *Former Colony$_{ij}$* | − 0.763 | − 0.769 | − 0.812 | − 0.622 | − 0.814 |
| | (0.721) | (0.721) | (0.717) | (0.712) | (0.717) |
| *Contiguity$_{ij}$* | − 0.166 | − 0.167 | − 0.179 | − 0.180 | − 0.179 |
| | (0.120) | (0.119) | (0.119) | (0.117) | (0.119) |
| *Distance$_{ij}$* | − 0.901** | − 0.902** | − 0.910** | − 0.901** | − 0.910** |
| | (0.050) | (0.050) | (0.050) | (0.050) | (0.050) |
| *Hegemony* | − 18.886** | − 18.777** | − 18.033** | − 17.629** | − 18.042** |
| | (1.991) | (1.990) | (1.989) | (1.980) | (1.990) |
| *GATT$_{ij}$* | 0.302** | 0.306** | 0.326** | 0.297** | 0.326** |
| | (0.056) | (0.056) | (0.057) | (0.056) | (0.057) |
| Constant | 10.895** | 10.807** | 11.404** | 11.454** | 11.659** |
| | (0.894) | (0.888) | (0.842) | (0.824) | (0.841) |
| Log-likelihood | − 11,431.41 | − 11,426.52 | − 11,389.08 | − 11,348.19 | − 11,390.73 |
| *N* | 339,910 | 339,910 | 339,910 | 339,910 | 339,910 |

*Note*: Parameters are estimated using logistic regression, after including a cubic spline function with no knots. Entries in parentheses are Huber standard errors clustered on the dyad. $**p \leq 0.01$; $*p \leq 0.05$. All tests of statistical significance are two-tailed.

†*Veto Players$_i$* is the residual of a regression of *Veto Players$_i$* on *Regime Type$_i$*. *Veto Players$_j$* is the residual of a regression of *Veto Players$_j$* on *Regime Type$_j$*. Since the values of these variables are estimated, the standard errors of their coefficients are biased. To address this issue, the standard error of each of these coefficients is bootstrapped.

are both analytically and empirically distinct, but they are also highly correlated.[57] We therefore regress *Veto Players*$_i$ on *Regime Type*$_i$ and *Veto Players*$_j$ on *Regime Type*$_j$. The residuals of these regressions are that portion of veto players that is not explained by a state's regime type. Thus, the bivariate correlation between these residuals and regime type is virtually zero. We then replace *Veto Players*$_i$ and *Veto Players*$_j$ with these residuals and re-estimate the model. The results shown in the final column of Table 3 indicate that the coefficient estimates of these variables are negative, statistically significant and large.[58] Most of the other estimates are essentially unchanged as well. Thus, our results are not unduly influenced by collinearity between regime type and veto players.

Thirdly, we analyse whether the results are sensitive to our modelling decisions. As noted earlier, the observed value of our dependent variable is 1 in years $(t + 1)$ when states $i$ and $j$ enter a PTA, 0 otherwise. We do not remove observations after the pair signed a PTA from the dataset because many country-pairs formed more than one PTA during the period covered here. In various cases, they established a second arrangement without abolishing the first. Nonetheless, it is important to assess the implications of this modelling strategy. For any pair of states that form a PTA, we therefore eliminate all yearly observations after the arrangement is established and then re-estimate the model. As reported in the first column of Table 4, the effects of veto players do not depend in any substantial way on whether we include or exclude these observations.

To further address this issue, we rely on event history analysis, after redefining the dependent variable as the number of years until states $i$ and $j$ form a PTA.[59] Since we have no theoretical expectations concerning the shape of the baseline hazard rate, we use a Cox proportional hazard model. The results, which are in the second column of Table 4, provide additional support for our argument. The coefficient estimates of *Veto Players*$_i$ and *Veto Players*$_j$ are negative, large and statistically significant. Consequently, as the number of veto players rises, the hazard rate declines, indicating that the length of time until states $i$ and $j$ establish a PTA increases. Thus, signing a preferential arrangement is forestalled by a heightened number of veto players.

In Equation 1, the dependent variable is dyadic; it measures whether a pair of states entered the same PTA in a given year. However, many of the independent variables in the model – including veto players – are monadic. Some studies have analysed data of this sort using 'directed dyads' rather than the undirected dyads that we have examined thus far. In a directed dyad approach, each pair of states generates two observations per year – one where each state in the pair is country $i$. For example, in the case of France and Russia in 1995, there is one observation where France is country $i$ and a second observation where Russia is $i$. Each monadic variable enters Equation 1 once and corresponds to whichever state is designated as country $i$. To ensure that our results do not hinge on whether we utilize

[57] The bivariate correlation between *Veto Players*$_i$ and *Regime Type*$_i$ and between *Veto Players*$_j$ and *Regime Type*$_j$ is roughly 0.8.

[58] Because the coefficient estimates of each residual are second-stage estimates, we bootstrap the standard errors 1,500 times and add the resulting estimate of bias to the original standard error estimate.

[59] For an overview of this technique, see Janet Box-Steffensmeier and Bradford Jones, *Event History Modeling: A Guide for Social Scientists* (New York: Cambridge University Press, 2004). We start counting years at the beginning of our time series (1950).

TABLE 4 *Alternative Specifications of PTA Formation, 1950–99*

| | First PTA only | Event history | Directed dyads | BKP trade data | Eliminating zeros in trade data |
|---|---|---|---|---|---|
| *Veto Players$_i$* | −1.794** | −1.644** | −1.559** | −0.728* | −1.085** |
| | (0.299) | (0.296) | (0.149) | (0.330) | (0.280) |
| *Veto Players$_j$* | −1.892** | −1.750** | – | −1.310** | −1.219** |
| | (0.302) | (0.295) | | (0.322) | (0.279) |
| *Regime Type$_i$* | 0.050** | 0.047** | 0.040** | 0.015 | 0.031** |
| | (0.007) | (0.007) | (0.004) | (0.008) | (0.007) |
| *Regime Type$_j$* | 0.039** | 0.037** | – | 0.023** | 0.028** |
| | (0.007) | (0.007) | | (0.008) | (0.007) |
| *Trade$_{ij}$* | −0.009 | −0.016 | −0.032** | −0.006 | −0.059** |
| | (0.010) | (0.009) | (0.005) | (0.012) | (0.016) |
| *GDP$_i$* | −0.259** | −0.246** | −0.076** | −0.154** | −0.122** |
| | (0.025) | (0.024) | (0.010) | (0.025) | (0.025) |
| *GDP$_j$* | −0.246** | −0.237** | – | −0.122** | −0.120** |
| | (0.025) | (0.024) | | (0.024) | (0.025) |
| *ΔGDP$_i$* | $6.27\times10^{-10}$ | $2.58\times10^{-10}$ | $2.60\times10^{-9}$** | $-3.00\times10^{-9}$ | $-3.78\times10^{-10}$ |
| | $(1.27\times10^{-9})$ | $(1.06\times10^{-9})$ | $(6.71\times10^{-10})$ | $(2.21\times10^{-9})$ | $(1.23\times10^{-9})$ |
| *ΔGDP$_j$* | $1.23\times10^{-9}$ | $1.81\times10^{-9}$ | – | $-6.74\times10^{-9}$** | $-7.74\times10^{-11}$ |
| | $(1.10\times10^{-9})$ | $(1.02\times10^{-9})$ | | $(1.76\times10^{-9})$ | $(1.03\times10^{-9})$ |
| *Dispute$_{ij}$* | −1.013** | −0.789* | −0.197 | −0.224 | −0.285 |
| | (0.378) | (0.357) | (0.215) | (0.273) | (0.288) |
| *Ally$_{ij}$* | 1.622** | 1.515** | 1.116** | 1.313** | 1.257** |
| | (0.090) | (0.086) | (0.062) | (0.010) | (0.093) |
| *Former Colony$_{ij}$* | −0.417 | −0.252 | 0.974 | 0.685 | −0.844 |
| | (1.069) | (1.049) | (0.689) | (0.706) | (0.710) |
| *Contiguity$_{ij}$* | −0.266 | −0.386* | −0.193* | 0.087 | 0.042 |
| | (0.178) | (0.165) | (0.083) | (0.119) | (0.120) |
| *Distance$_{ij}$* | −1.112** | −1.088** | −0.791** | −0.758** | −0.809** |
| | (0.053) | (0.043) | (0.041) | (0.062) | (0.060) |
| *Hegemony* | −17.088** | −16.979** | −37.132** | −12.228** | −12.405** |
| | (2.445) | (2.326) | (1.534) | (2.248) | (2.197) |
| *GATT$_{ij}$* | 0.509** | 0.420** | 0.367** | 0.200** | 0.353** |
| | (0.074) | (0.074) | (0.043) | (0.075) | (0.066) |
| Constant | 14.289** | – | 10.982** | 7.663** | 7.284** |
| | (0.961) | | (0.523) | (0.973) | (0.969) |
| Log-likelihood | −7,774.03 | −10,660.00 | −26,211.04 | −6,170.15 | −7,927.61 |
| *N* | 302,324 | 300,473 | 781,007 | 179,508 | 211,413 |

*Note*: Parameters are estimated using logistic regression, after including a cubic spline function with no knots. Entries in parentheses are Huber standard errors clustered on the dyad. **$p \leq 0.01$; *$p \leq 0.05$. All tests of statistical significance are two-tailed.

*Vetoing Co-operation* 429

undirected or directed dyads, we re-estimate the model after reconfiguring the data as a series of directed dyads.[60]

The results presented in the third column of Table 4 indicate that our results do not hinge on this decision. The coefficient estimate of *Veto Players*$_i$ is negative and statistically significant. In addition, the estimates of the control variables do not depend much on whether we analyse directed or undirected dyads.

It is also important to consider the implications of using logistic regression to analyse PTA formation, in light of the rarity with which such arrangements are established in our sample. King and Zeng contend that using logistic regression to analyse rare events can produce biased estimates.[61] To guard against this possibility, we re-estimate Equation 1 using King and Zeng's rare event logit procedure. The resulting estimates (which are not presented to conserve space) are nearly identical to those generated by the traditional logit model. Thus, we are confident that our estimates do not suffer from a rare event bias.

Fourthly, we address whether our results depend on the trade data used in the analysis. We have used data on bilateral trade flows compiled by Gleditsch. Recently, however, a different trade dataset has been developed by Barbieri, Pollins and Keshk.[62] To begin, we re-estimate the model after using this alternative compilation. Then we remove all observations from our original dataset in which a dyad was coded as conducting no trade in a given year, since such dyads could be considered unimportant to the international trading system and particularly unlikely to form a PTA. The results shown in the final two columns of Table 4 indicate that the coefficient estimates of *Veto Players*$_i$ and *Veto Players*$_j$ remain negative, large and statistically significant.

Fifthly, we analyse a set of variables that are not included in Equation 1 but that could influence the establishment of PTAs. Because of strategic interaction among states competing in the international economy, PTAs tend to form in reaction to one another.[63] As a result, a given country-pair may be more likely to form a PTA as these arrangements become increasingly ubiquitous. To address this possibility, we include in Equation 1 the number of dyads throughout the world that are members of a PTA in year $t$ (*Number of PTAs*). In addition, power relations between states might affect their likelihood of establishing a PTA. We therefore include two variables: (1) the logarithm of the ratio of the larger state's GDP to the smaller state's GDP in each dyad-year, and (2) the logarithm of the ratio of the stronger state's military capabilities to the weaker state's capabilities. To measure each state's military capabilities, we rely on the Correlates of War Project's national military capabilities index, which is made up of total population, urban population, energy consumption, iron and steel production, military manpower and military expenditures.[64]

[60] Since including each dyad-year twice artificially depresses the standard errors in our statistical analysis, we cluster the standard errors on the undirected dyad, eliminating any efficiency gains that stem from including each observation twice.

[61] Gary King and Langche Zeng, 'Explaining Rare Events Bias in International Relations', *International Organization*, 55 (2001), 693–715.

[62] On the Gleditsch data, see fn. 41. See also Katherine Barbieri, Brian M. Pollins and Omar Keshk, 'The Correlates of War Trade Data Set: A Progress Report' (paper presented at the Annual Meeting of the Peace Science Society (International), Ann Arbor, Michigan, 2003).

[63] Raquel Fernández and Jonathan Portes, 'Returns to Regionalism: An Evaluation of Non-traditional Gains From RTAs', *World Bank Economic Review*, 12 (1998), 197–220; Mansfield, 'The Proliferation of Preferential Trading Arrangements'.

[64] J. David Singer, Stuart Bremer and John Stuckey, 'Capability Distribution, Uncertainty, and Major Power War, 1820–1965', in Bruce Russett, ed., *Peace, War, and Numbers* (Beverly Hills, Calif.: Sage Publications, 1972), pp. 37–74; J. David Singer and Melvin Small, 'National Material Capabilities Dataset', Study No. 9903 (Ann Arbor: Inter-University Consortium for Political and Social Research, 1993).

TABLE 5 *The Effects of Potentially Omitted Variables on PTA Formation, 1950–99*

| | Num. global PTAs | GDP ratio | Capability ratio | Tau-B | Country fixed effects |
|---|---|---|---|---|---|
| *Veto Players$_i$* | −1.636** | −1.598** | −1.619** | −1.757** | −0.656** |
| | (0.232) | (0.242) | (0.244) | (0.276) | (0.234) |
| *Veto Players$_j$* | −1.708** | −1.689** | −1.708** | −1.911** | −0.723** |
| | (0.232) | (0.241) | (0.243) | (0.277) | (0.232) |
| *Regime Type$_i$* | 0.045** | 0.050** | 0.050** | 0.053** | 0.082** |
| | (0.006) | (0.006) | (0.006) | (0.007) | (0.007) |
| *Regime Type$_j$* | 0.035** | 0.041** | 0.041** | 0.043** | 0.072** |
| | (0.006) | (0.006) | (0.006) | (0.006) | (0.006) |
| *Trade$_{ij}$* | 0.000 | −0.006** | −0.007 | −0.024** | 0.036** |
| | (0.008) | (0.008) | (0.008) | (0.009) | (0.009) |
| *GDP$_i$* | −0.214** | −0.203** | −0.206** | −0.244** | 0.073 |
| | (0.019) | (0.021) | (0.020) | (0.022) | (0.073) |
| *GDP$_j$* | −0.191** | −0.176** | −0.181** | −0.198** | 0.104 |
| | (0.019) | (0.020) | (0.020) | (0.021) | (0.072) |
| *ΔGDP$_i$* | $5.08\times10^{-10}$ | $2.31\times10^{-9}$ | $1.16\times10^{-9}$ | $3.17\times10^{-10}$ | $2.17\times10^{-9}$ |
| | $(1.08\times10^{-9})$ | $(1.13\times10^{-9})$ | $(1.15\times10^{-9})$ | $(2.40\times10^{-9})$ | $(1.64\times10^{-9})$ |
| *ΔGDP$_j$* | $3.48\times10^{-10}$ | $1.97\times10^{-9}$ | $8.30\times10^{-10}$ | $-3.54\times10^{-9}$ | $1.32\times10^{-9}$ |
| | $(9.49\times10^{-10})$ | $(9.86\times10^{-10})$ | $(1.01\times10^{-9})$ | $(2.00\times10^{-9})$ | $(1.63\times10^{-9})$ |
| *Dispute$_{ij}$* | −0.471 | −0.473 | −0.486 | −0.052 | −0.183 |
| | (0.272) | (0.272) | (0.273) | (0.271) | (0.262) |
| *Ally$_{ij}$* | 1.256** | 1.243** | 1.259** | 0.889** | 2.008** |
| | (0.083) | (0.082) | (0.082) | (0.082) | (0.089) |
| *Former Colony$_{ij}$* | −0.798 | −0.609 | −0.776 | 0.360 | −1.792* |
| | (0.716) | (0.713) | (0.716) | (0.716) | (0.854) |
| *Contiguity$_{ij}$* | −0.182 | −0.179 | −0.180 | −0.126 | −0.611** |
| | (0.117) | (0.117) | (0.118) | (0.126) | (0.100) |
| *Distance$_{ij}$* | −0.910** | −0.896** | −0.905** | −0.880** | −1.161** |
| | (0.050) | (0.048) | (0.050) | (0.051) | (0.048) |
| *Hegemony* | −8.159** | −18.710** | −18.107** | −24.333** | 27.375** |
| | (2.026) | (1.998) | (1.987) | (2.115) | (3.054) |
| *GATT$_{ij}$* | 0.295** | 0.315** | 0.324** | 0.271** | −0.186* |
| | (0.056) | (0.056) | (0.056) | (0.062) | (0.073) |
| *Constant* | 9.254** | 11.459** | 11.384** | 12.833** | −18.376** |
| | (0.858) | (0.841) | (0.840) | (0.839) | (3.750) |
| *Number of PTAs* | 0.0002** | – | – | – | – |
| | (0.0001) | | | | |
| *GDP Ratio* | – | −0.125** | – | – | – |
| | | (0.022) | | | |
| *Capability Ratio* | – | – | −0.038 | – | – |
| | | | (0.021) | | |
| *Tau$_b$* | – | – | – | 2.047** | – |
| | | | | (0.102) | |
| Log-likelihood | −11,322.85 | −11,364.19 | −11,386.61 | −9,449.17 | −9,729.16 |
| *N* | 339,910 | 339,910 | 339,910 | 277,360 | 309,917 |

*Note*: Parameters are estimated using logistic regression, after including a cubic spline function with no knots. Entries in parentheses are Huber standard errors clustered on the dyad. $^{**}p \leq 0.01$; $^{*}p \leq 0.05$. All tests of statistical significance are two-tailed.

In addition, we would like to account for the similarity of states' and leaders' (P and F in our spatial model) foreign policy preferences, since similar preferences of this sort may promote international economic co-operation, regardless of domestic politics. Recall that to address this issue, we included in Equation 1 a number of variables that are likely to tap the similarity of such preferences, especially alliance relations and political-military conflict. Although more direct measures of foreign policy preferences are notoriously difficult to construct, we also follow a number of previous studies in using the $tau_b$ correlation between the United Nations (UN) voting patterns of states $i$ and $j$ in year $t$ for this purpose.[65] This variable can range from $-1$ to 1 and increases as states' voting records become increasingly similar.[66]

As shown in Table 5, three of the four aforementioned variables strongly influence PTA formation. Country-pairs are more likely to enter a preferential arrangement if a large number of other dyads have recently formed such an arrangement, if their national incomes are asymmetrically distributed, and if they have similar UN voting records. These relationships, however, have no bearing on the effects of veto players, which continue to affect the creation of PTAs strongly.

Finally, there are various historical, political and economic factors that are specific to the countries in our sample that are not included in our model, but which could influence whether the states opt to enter a PTA. One way to account for any unmeasured heterogeneity of this sort is to include country-specific or pair-specific fixed effects in the model. Various observers argue that in situations like ours, where the dependent variable is dichotomous and has a highly skewed distribution, a fixed-effects specification introduces more problems than it resolves.[67] However, these observers maintain that if researchers are committed to estimating a fixed-effects model when analysing such a dependent variable, it is preferable to include country-specific rather than pair-specific effects. To assess the robustness of our results, we therefore re-estimate Equation 1 after including country-specific fixed effects.

The results presented in the final column of Table 5 show that the coefficient estimates of *Veto Players*$_i$ and *Veto Players*$_j$ continue to be negative and statistically significant. Equally, these estimates are only marginally smaller (in absolute value) when a fixed-effects specification is used. Taken together, the results in this section therefore demonstrate that our earlier findings are quite robust.

## CONCLUSIONS

The recent proliferation of PTAs has stimulated rising interest in the consequences of these arrangements. Far less effort has been made to assess the factors prompting states to enter PTAs, especially factors operating in the domestic political arena. In this article, we have addressed this issue by incorporating domestic veto players into a model of two-level

[65] Erik Gartzke, 'Kant We All Just Get Along? Opportunity, Willingness, and the Origins of the Democratic Peace', *American Journal of Political Science*, 42 (1998), 1–27.

[66] Data for this variable are taken from Gartzke, 'Kant We All Just Get Along?' Some studies of international relations have recently begun to use a different measure of preference similarity, referred to as *S*. See Curtis S. Signorino and Jeffrey M. Ritter, 'Tau-b or Not Tau-b: Measuring the Similarity of Foreign Policy Positions', *International Studies Quarterly*, 43 (1999), 115–44. Our results do not depend on which measure is used.

[67] See, for example, Nathaniel Beck and Jonathan N. Katz, 'Throwing Out the Baby With the Bath Water: A Comment on Green, Kim, and Yoon', *International Organization*, 55 (2001), 487–95.

games. Our model suggests that it becomes increasing difficult for states to forge PTAs as the number of veto players rises. A series of empirical tests, based on an analysis of PTA membership from 1950 to 1999, support our argument. Countries are much less likely to sign trade agreements as the number of veto players increases.

These results are substantively as well as statistically significant. An increase in the number of domestic veto players can cut the probability of forming a PTA by as much as 50 per cent. Moreover, these results do not stem from the effects of regime type on PTA formation. We find that democracies are more likely to sign trade agreements than other countries, but that the number of veto players exerts an independent influence on the prospects of establishing a preferential arrangement. Neglecting any of these domestic factors in studies of PTAs is, therefore, a risky strategy.

Although our focus has been on the formation of PTAs, our argument has implications for the duration of PTAs as well. More specifically, heightened veto points inhibit policy change. Hence, while veto players reduce the likelihood of entering a PTA, they also are likely to enhance the durability of any PTA in which a state participates. This topic could be fruitfully addressed in future research.

Furthermore, our results bear on various other issue-areas in the field of international relations, particularly the politics of international co-operation. PTAs are simply one type of international co-operation, involving the mutual adjustment of trade policy. Our results thus imply that international co-operation of any type becomes harder to achieve when the number of veto players rises in the participating countries. In addition, the number of domestic veto players may also affect the likelihood of international conflict. Our findings accord with earlier research indicating, for example, that divided government influences trade policy,[68] the escalation of military disputes,[69] and in the US context, the use of military force abroad.[70] More generally, they imply that domestic politics may exert a strong influence on the decision to co-operate. Indeed, domestic politics may be a greater obstacle to international co-operation than political or military relations among states.[71] It has certainly been a more neglected influence. Although we provide only one empirical test of this proposition, the strong association between domestic veto players and PTA formation supports our hypothesis and points to the promise of future research in this area. Extending theories of international politics by including domestic variables like veto players can be a fruitful exercise; we have shown that theories of two-level games can be usefully expanded by incorporating a theory of veto players.

[68] Susanne Lohmann and Sharyn O'Halloran, 'Divided Government and US Trade Policy: Theory and Evidence', *International Organization*, 48 (1994), 595–632; Richard Sherman, 'Delegation, Ratification, and US Trade Policy: Why Divided Government Causes Lower Tariffs', *Comparative Political Studies*, 35 (2002), 1171–97.

[69] Paul Huth and Todd Allee, *The Democratic Peace and Territorial Conflict in the Twentieth Century* (Cambridge: Cambridge University Press, 2003).

[70] William G. Howell and Jon C. Pevehouse, 'Presidents, Congress, and the Use of Force', *International Organization*, 59 (2005), 209–32.

[71] Milner, *Interests, Institutions, and Information*.

# Multilateral Determinants of Regionalism: The Effects of GATT/WTO on the Formation of Preferential Trading Arrangements

Edward D. Mansfield and Eric Reinhardt

**Abstract** Preferential trading arrangements (PTAs) have spread widely over the past fifty years. During the same era, multilateral openness has grown to unprecedented heights, spurred by the General Agreement on Tariffs and Trade (GATT) and its successor, the World Trade Organization (WTO). If the cornerstone of the manifestly successful multilateral regime is nondiscrimination, why have its members increasingly resorted to preferential liberalization? We argue that developments at the heart of GATT/WTO encourage its members to form PTAs as devices to obtain bargaining leverage within the multilateral regime. Specifically, the growth in GATT/WTO membership, the periodic multilateral trade negotiation rounds, as well as participation and, especially, losses in formal GATT/WTO disputes, have led its members to seek entrance into PTAs. Conducting the first statistical tests on the subject, we find strong evidence in support of this argument.

*What are the problems of the GATT that lead countries to turn to their neighborhood instead?*

Paul Krugman (1993, 73)

During the past fifty years, the international trading system has been marked by the rapid proliferation of preferential trading arrangements (PTAs). During the same era, multilateral openness has grown to unprecedented heights, spurred by the General Agreement on Tariffs and Trade (GATT) and its successor, the World Trade Organization (WTO). That these developments have occurred in tandem is somewhat surprising. Whereas the norm of nondiscrimination in trade is the corner-

For helpful comments, we are grateful to Marc Busch, Peter Gourevitch, David Lake, Lisa Martin, Joy Mazumdar, Helen Milner, Thomas Oatley, Çaglar Özden, Francisco Parodi, Jon Pevehouse, Jay Smith, Jeffrey Stacey, Chris Zorn, and two anonymous reviewers. For research assistance, we thank Yoram Haftel, Jesse Hamner, and Jon Pevehouse. Earlier versions of this article were presented at the 2000 Annual Meeting of the American Political Science Association, Washington, D.C.; the 2001 Annual Meeting of the Midwest Political Science Association, Chicago; and seminars at Emory University, the University of Chicago (PIPES), the University of Illinois, and the University of Wisconsin.

*International Organization* 57, Fall 2003, pp. 829–862
© 2003 by The IO Foundation.
DOI: 10.1017/S0020818303574069

stone of GATT/WTO, PTAs vest each member with preferential access to the other participants' markets. Equally surprising is that most preferential groupings are composed of GATT/WTO members. It is not clear why states form preferential economic blocs when they belong to a successful multilateral regime. How the spread of PTAs will affect the GATT/WTO system has been widely studied and fiercely debated.[1] Remarkably little research, however, has addressed how, if at all, the multilateral regime has conditioned the spread of PTAs.

We argue that GATT/WTO has played a large role in stimulating the formation of PTAs. A central reason why states enter PTAs is to increase their bargaining power. Preferential arrangements serve this purpose by furnishing states with insurance against the emergence of conditions within GATT/WTO that could threaten their economic interests, as well as by giving states a greater voice in multilateral trade talks and increasing their market power. Developments within the multilateral regime can create incentives for states to enhance their bargaining power, thereby triggering the establishment of preferential groupings. These developments include the growth of GATT/WTO membership, which has reduced each participant's leverage over the pace and path of multilateral liberalization. Such growth has also heightened collective action problems within the regime, making it progressively more difficult to conclude new multilateral agreements, monitor members' behavior, and enforce the regime's rules. Forming a PTA composed of a small group of members with similar economic interests can help states insure against the adverse consequences stemming from these problems.

In addition, the central vehicles used to promote an open global trading system—the periodic multilateral trade negotiations (MTNs) sponsored by GATT/WTO—can prompt members to enter PTAs as a means of guaranteeing they will not be left behind if the MTN stalls and of boosting their bargaining position in the multilateral talks. Therefore, states have reasons to establish a PTA during multilateral negotiating rounds. Trade disputes among GATT/WTO members are also likely to influence whether and when states accede to a preferential arrangement. A country embroiled in a GATT/WTO dispute may seek PTAs with third parties in the hopes of improving its leverage in the conflict. Likewise, losing a GATT/WTO dispute can impel a state to form preferential arrangements with third parties to obtain countervailing market access, insurance against future GATT/WTO enforcement failures, or additional bargaining leverage.

To test these arguments, we conduct one of the first systematic analyses of PTA formation within GATT/WTO. The evidence strongly supports our claims. Countries are more likely to form a PTA when (1) GATT/WTO membership rises, (2) a multilateral negotiating round is taking place, and (3) they have recently participated in a GATT/WTO dispute, especially when (4) they obtained an unsatisfactory outcome in the dispute. More generally, our results indicate that while

1. See Bhagwati 1993; Bhagwati and Panagariya 1996; Krugman 1993; Lawrence 1996; Mansfield and Milner 1999; Oye 1992; Pomfret 1997; and WTO 1995a.

GATT/WTO has made considerable headway in liberalizing foreign trade, it has also had various unintended consequences. Particularly important is that developments and institutional features associated with the growth of multilateral liberalization—such as rising GATT/WTO membership, MTNs, and active dispute settlement—create incentives for states to seek bilateral commercial arrangements in hopes of obtaining the greatest possible benefits from the multilateral regime.

## Discrimination in a 'Nondiscriminatory' System

The central feature of all PTAs is the special market access that each member grants the other participants. Members set lower trade barriers on goods produced within the preferential grouping than on those produced elsewhere. These institutions—which include agreements that partially liberalize commerce, free trade areas (FTAs), customs unions, and common markets—have dotted the international landscape for centuries, but they have become increasingly pervasive in the past fifty years. Dozens have formed since the conclusion of World War II, and the concentration of trade flows has risen substantially within many PTAs, leading to widespread agreement that these groupings have become key elements of the international political economy.[2]

Because PTAs are generally made up of countries located in the same geographical region, the spread of these arrangements has led many observers to conclude that commercial regionalism is on the rise. As shown in Figure 1, two distinct waves of regionalism took place during the second half of the twentieth century.[3] The first occurred from the late 1950s through the 1970s; the second occurred in the 1990s.

Most PTAs formed since World War II have been composed of parties to GATT and the WTO; and, at present, virtually every WTO member belongs to some type of preferential arrangement.[4] From its inception, GATT attempted to regulate these arrangements.[5] Article XXIV of the 1947 General Agreement on Tariffs and Trade—GATT's founding document—stipulates that member-states are permitted to form a PTA only if it eliminates barriers to "substantially all the trade" among its mem-

2. Serra et al. 1997, 8.
3. See Bhagwati 1993; and Mansfield and Milner 1999.
4. WTO 1995a. In this article, we are only concerned with "reciprocal" PTAs. Nonreciprocal agreements, such as the Generalized System of Preferences, are ones in which advanced industrial states unilaterally grant preferential market access to developing countries without requiring any trade concessions in return. The consequences for the trading regime are profoundly different than when preferences are reciprocal. Özden and Reinhardt 2003. While virtually every party to the WTO belongs to some PTA, only about half of them belong to a reciprocal PTA, as shown in Figure 2.
5. Provisions for forming PTAs were made at the time of GATT's establishment because it was apparent that this body would be hard pressed to forbid states from doing so. In addition, some decision makers seemed to believe that Article XXIV's requirement that PTAs remove all trade barriers among members would complement GATT initiatives to promote multilateral openness. Bhagwati 1993, 35–36.

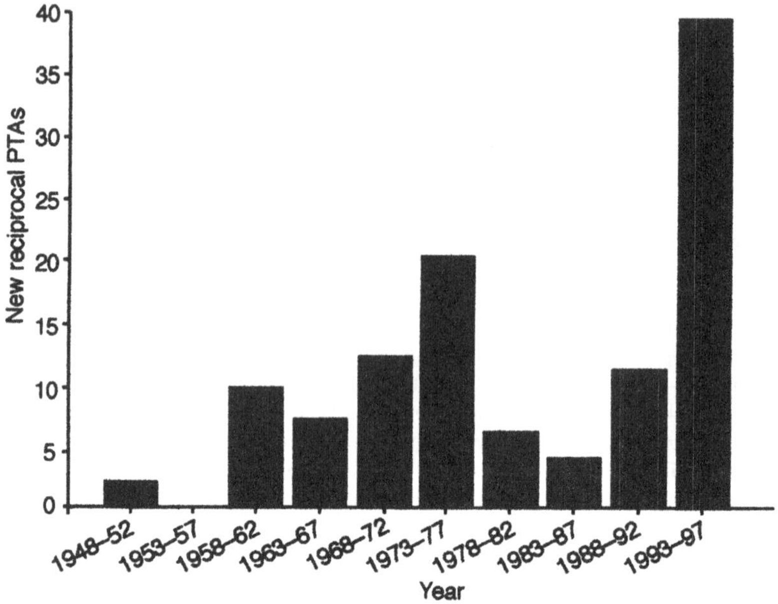


*Note:* Year indicates the date that PTAS entered.

**FIGURE 1.** *Number of new reciprocal PTAs notified to GATT/WTO, 1948–98*

bers and does not "on the whole" increase protectionism against nonmembers.[6] Further, the Enabling Clause, which was adopted by GATT in 1979, permits developing countries to furnish preferences to one another through the creation of PTAs that do not adhere to Article XXIV.[7]

These efforts to regulate the formation of PTAs, however, have met with little success. As Jagdish Bhagwati points out, with respect to such arrangements, the multilateral regime "is so full of holes in its discipline that almost anything goes."[8] Members have been required to notify new preferential groupings to GATT working parties (before 1995) and to the WTO's Committee on Regional Trade Agreements (since 1995). These bodies—which assess the degree of compliance by PTAs with GATT/WTO rules—have failed to reach judgment on all but one of the 118 PTAs submitted for review, mostly because of differences among members about

6. See Bhagwati 1993; and WTO 1995b, 791.
7. WTO 1995a, 18–19.
8. Bhagwati 1993, 44.

what constitutes compliance.[9] As a WTO staff member observes, "history has proved this to be one of the most unsatisfactory of all GATT procedures."[10] Consequently, a former GATT Deputy Director General concluded, "Of all the GATT articles, this [Article XXIV] is one of the most abused. [New PTA members] have little fear that they will be embarrassed by some GATT body finding them in violation of their international obligations and commitments and recommending that they abandon or alter what they are about to do."[11]

In fact, GATT/WTO members joining a PTA routinely violate Article XXIV. Trade barriers within preferential arrangements are almost never completely eliminated and members frequently raise trade barriers on nonmembers' products. Germany's average tariff on third parties, for example, nearly doubled after its accession to the European Economic Community in 1958.[12] To align with the European Union's (EU) textile and apparel import regime, Turkey increased its quantitative restrictions against outside states after signing an FTA with the EU in 1995.[13] Similarly, Mexico, Israel, and the members of the *Mercado Común del Cono Sur* (Mercosur) increased their external trade barriers after joining PTAs.[14] Even preferential groupings whose members have not raised their external trade barriers often inflict some damage on third parties, if for no other reason than because the preferential access granted to members' products degrades the competitiveness of nonmembers' products within the PTA.[15]

To be clear, we are not claiming that PTAs generally have been economically harmful. Although the available evidence indicates that some PTAs—especially those composed of developing countries—have had adverse economic consequences, various studies conclude that other arrangements—particularly those formed in recent years—have promoted economic welfare.[16] Regardless, the welfare implications of PTAs do not directly bear on the issues addressed here.

Nonetheless, the fact that GATT/WTO has been unable to prevent PTAs from enacting policies that place third parties at a competitive disadvantage in international markets suggests that, contrary to the view of some observers, GATT/WTO has not "made the world safe for regionalism."[17] Rather, we argue that

9. See Crawford and Laird 2001; Sampson 1996, 90; and WTO 1995a, 63, and 1999a.
10. Sampson 1996, 90.
11. WTO 1995a, 63.
12. Ibid., 47.
13. Hudec and Southwick 1999, 72–74.
14. Panagariya 2000, 317.
15. See Frankel 1997, 112–13; Freund and McLaren 1999; Sapir 2001; and Winters and Chang 2000.
16. See Bhagwati 1993; Bhagwati and Panagariya 1996; Frankel 1997; Panagariya 2000; and Pomfret 1997. Central to assessing the global welfare implications of a PTA is whether it creates more trade among members than it diverts from efficient producers located outside the arrangement. Viner 1950. However, it should be noted that in addition to this factor, PTAs affect members' welfare by influencing foreign direct investment, the governance of international economic relations, and other issues. See Lawrence 1996; and Yarbrough and Yarbrough 1992.
17. *New York Times*, 19 December 1993, D4.

Business School
Campus de Rouen
1, rue du Maréchal Juin
BP 215 - Cedex
76825 Mont Saint Aignan
Tél : 02 32 82 57 00

states form PTAs to ensure the greatest possible gains from the multilateral regime itself.

## How the Multilateral Trade Regime Induces PTA Formation

Much research concludes that states form PTAs to obtain the economic gains stemming from preferential access to members' markets (although it is worth reiterating that whether states actually benefit from such arrangements remains the subject of substantial controversy). A growing body of literature, however, focuses on the incentives for states to establish PTAs as a means of increasing their bargaining power within the multilateral regime.[18] We focus on two ways that states entering preferential groupings enhance such power.

First, establishing a preferential arrangement can strengthen a state's bargaining position vis-à-vis nonmembers by furnishing it with insurance against developments within the multilateral regime that threaten its interests. Developments such as the failure to reach agreement in multilateral trade talks become less costly because the state has already secured open access to its PTA partners' markets. An Australian government official illustrated this point nicely. Speaking about two proposed FTAs, he remarked that "Australia's clout in the WTO talks depends on holding the line in our bilateral trade negotiations with Japan [and] the U.S. . . ."[19]

Safeguarding access to crucial overseas markets by forming a PTA is particularly useful if the enforcement mechanisms in the multilateral trade regime, designed to minimize discrimination and new protectionism, prove weak.[20] Under these conditions, a preferential arrangement furnishes members with insurance against the prospect of their key trade partners unilaterally raising trade barriers in the future. Even if GATT/WTO enforcement mechanisms are strong, however, halting progress in achieving multilateral liberalization can stimulate fears of losing competitiveness in international markets, especially on the part of smaller states. For instance, at a time when the Uruguay Round had stalled and was threatening to end in failure, an Inter-American Development Bank official declared, "The Caribbean is in danger of becoming a backwater. Small countries will be wiped out unless they integrate."[21] Referring to the unsuccessful efforts to jumpstart multilateral liberalization at the WTO's 1999 Seattle Ministerial meeting and China's looming accession to the WTO, Singapore's Foreign Minister expressed concerns

18. See, for example, Bhagwati 1993; Bhagwati and Panagariya 1996; Fernández and Portes 1998; Krueger 1999; Krugman 1993; Ludema 1996; Mansfield 1998; Oye 1992; Perroni and Whalley 2000; and Whalley 1998.

19. *Australian*, 29 April 2002, 4.

20. Bagwell and Staiger 2001, 321.

21. *Journal of Commerce*, 3 September 1991, 5A.

that Southeast Asia was "being left behind economically while North Asian countries raced ahead."[22]

By insuring states against the loss of competitiveness in international markets and any future disruption in trade that developments within the multilateral regime could precipitate, PTAs promote the bargaining power of their members. The claim that preferential arrangements vest states with insurance against shocks to the international trading system has gained increasing currency in recent years.[23] To date, however, no effort has been made to analyze how events within GATT/WTO might lead member-states to seek the insurance that PTAs provide. This gap in the literature is surprising because it is widely acknowledged that even the United States has considered using PTAs to help offset the effects of any failures at the multilateral level.[24] In 1993, for example, U.S. Trade Representative Mickey Kantor explicitly argued that trade liberalization within the Asia-Pacific Economic Cooperation (APEC) and the proposed Free Trade Agreement of the Americas (FTAA) would be viable means to expand U.S. market access in the event that the Uruguay Round faltered.[25]

Second, PTAs may also boost bargaining power by giving states a greater voice in international trade forums and enhancing their market power. Many developing countries have considerable difficulty maintaining sufficient expertise on the multitude of covered issues and policies to participate effectively in multilateral trade negotiations. In fact, many of them have no delegation at the WTO whatsoever.[26] To help resolve these problems, various PTAs pool members' resources to improve how they research, articulate, and represent their common interests in trade talks with nonmembers. For example, observers agree that a primary goal of the Caribbean Community and Common Market (CARICOM) was to "strengthen the region's external position through the coordination of member states' [trade] policies."[27] Indeed, CARICOM has sometimes negotiated as a group at the WTO.[28] Likewise, Prime Minister Said Musa of Belize justified the proposed Central American-Caribbean FTA by saying, "we need to establish a common strategy so that we can obtain special treatment in international trade negotiations."[29] Even larger countries have incentives to use PTAs to coordinate on the best ways to pursue their mutual interests vis-à-vis third parties. For instance, Malaysian Prime Minister Mahathir Mohamad's 2002 proposal for an East Asian Economic Group,

22. *Financial Times*, 25 July 2000, 10.
23. See Fernández and Portes 1998; Mansfield 1998; Perroni and Whalley 2000; Whalley 1998; and Yarbrough and Yarbrough 1992.
24. Whalley 1998.
25. *Irish Times*, 29 October 1993, 14.
26. See Michalopoulos 1999; and Reinhardt 2002.
27. IADB 2000, 31; see also Andriamananjara and Schiff 2001.
28. WTO 2001.
29. James Canute, "Caribbean and Central America Press for Co-Operation," *Financial Times*. Available at ⟨www.ft.com⟩. Accessed 12 February 2002.

a revival of a Uruguay Round-era plan, was intended to help its potential members "be more effective in protecting their collective interests." [30]

Further, PTAs may increase leverage by accumulating the market power of individual members, giving them a greater ability to influence their terms of trade and to negotiate favorable settlements with outsiders.[31] On this score, Pascal Lamy—the EU's Commissioner for External Trade—conceded that "consolidating Mercosur will give Brazil and its partners . . . more political weight in international negotiations." [32] Anticipating the formation of Mercosur, a Brazilian official similarly remarked, "Dealing directly with the U.S. on international trade issues is like getting into a cage with a tiger. Only if we have others in with us do we stand a better chance of getting some satisfactory results." [33]

The ability of a PTA to heighten the market power of members is especially pronounced for states in a customs union—such as the European Community (EC) and Mercosur—because these institutions erect a common external tariff (CET) and thus bargain over tariff levels with third parties as a unit.[34] However, states need not form a customs union to enhance their negotiating position. It is widely argued that states have tried to influence the outcome of multilateral negotiations by threatening to form or actually establishing various types of PTAs.[35] Further, regardless of whether a PTA imposes a CET, its members accrue bargaining power insofar as the arrangement improves their reversion point in negotiations with third parties and promotes collective action among them. In any case, Rodney Ludema has identified a fairly broad set of conditions under which the external bargaining power of customs unions and other PTAs is quite similar.[36] Hence, we focus on PTAs as a group, rather than distinguishing among different types of them, in the following analysis.

Central to our argument is that developments within GATT/WTO have influenced when member-states have sought the bargaining power offered by PTAs. As we explain below, the existence of a GATT/WTO multilateral negotiating round, fluctuations in its membership, and its mechanisms to settle commercial disputes between members are particularly important in this regard.

### *Multilateral Trade Negotiations*

Since its creation, GATT/WTO has sponsored eight rounds of MTNs: Geneva (1947), Annecy (1949), Torquay (1950–51), Geneva (1955–56), Dillon (1961–62),

30. *Business Times (Malaysia)*, 23 May 2002, 2.
31. See Fernández and Portes 1998, 201; Krugman 1993, 73; Lawrence 1996, 37; and Oye 1992.
32. European Commission, Trade DG, Information Unit, 10 July 2001.
33. *Financial Times*, 2 July 1985, 5. See also Lawrence 1996, 37.
34. However, FTAs routinely level asymmetries in external tariffs using rules of origin. WTO 1995a, 48–49.
35. See Fernández and Portes 1998; Krueger 1999; and Whalley 1998.
36. Ludema 1996.

Kennedy (1963–67), Tokyo (1973–79), and Uruguay (1986–94), plus the Doha Development Agenda, launched in November 2001. Participants in MTNs that enter a PTA may be able to strengthen their bargaining position in these negotiations.[37] Heightened market power enhances the ability of members to use protectionist instruments to improve their terms of trade, thereby dampening their incentive to liberalize trade and bolstering their bargaining position in multilateral negotiations.[38] Further, by vesting each member with preferential access to the markets of other participants, PTAs can help firms in member-states to achieve economies of scale. States entering a preferential grouping thus face a reduced need for multilateral liberalization to generate such economies, bolstering their leverage in multilateral negotiations.[39] In this vein, it is noteworthy that the definitive accounting shows that countries such as Bolivia, India, Australia, South Africa, and Ecuador were granted significantly fewer Uruguay Round market access concessions than, respectively, Uruguay, Brazil, Austria, Turkey, and Honduras.[40] At the time, the latter five countries were members of more preferential arrangements than the former five, suggesting that participation in these arrangements did indeed increase their bargaining power in the Uruguay Round. If PTAs boost bargaining power in MTNs, as this illustrative evidence suggests, then MTNs should provide an impetus for states to enter PTAs.

Moreover, by forming a PTA with key trade partners during a multilateral negotiating round, parties to GATT/WTO can obtain insurance against the round stalling or failing to produce results in the specific areas they deem most important.[41] A deadlocked MTN would place pressure on the multilateral regime and could threaten the stability of commercial relations between important trade partners. Such partners can minimize the severity of this threat by entering a PTA, because the grouping liberalizes commerce among members and limits their ability to raise trade barriers in the future. In addition, entering a PTA helps a state attract foreign investment: overseas firms are often drawn to the expanded market access offered by preferential groupings, especially when the outcome of multilateral talks is uncertain or delayed.

Although each of the eight MTNs sponsored by GATT/WTO yielded accords that liberalized global trade, nearly every MTN has been marked by intense disagreement while being fashioned. Ministers and observers often asserted that the round was in a state of crisis and teetering on the brink of failure until the final text was inked. The desire for insurance and bargaining power more generally is thus paramount throughout an MTN. We therefore hypothesize that PTAs are more likely to form during an MTN than when no such negotiation is underway.

37. See Bhagwati and Panagariya 1996; and Whalley 1998.
38. See Mansfield 1998, 527; and Oye 1992.
39. See Bhagwati 1993; and Fernández and Portes 1998, 201–2.
40. Finger, Ingco, and Reincke 1996, 201.
41. See Fernández and Portes 1998, 212; Krugman 1993, 74; Mansfield 1998, 535–36; Perroni and Whalley 2000; Whalley 1998; and WTO 1995a, 52.

Anecdotal evidence is consistent with this hypothesis. The WTO, for example, officially attributed the wave of regionalism during the past decade to events in the Uruguay Round, such as the failed Brussels Ministerial meeting in December 1990.[42] In the same vein, economic ministers of the Association of Southeast Asian Nations (ASEAN) launched an FTA in 1993, an initiative that was widely viewed as "a sign [of] . . . concern about the inability to achieve a successful conclusion to the Uruguay Round."[43] Equally, many observers point to the stalled multilateral negotiations as a critical catalyst for the U.S.-Canada FTA, arguing that the United States conceived of this arrangement as "a prod to recalcitrant nations to join in the GATT effort to make sure they weren't cut out of the action."[44] More recently, the United States has proposed an extensive series of bilateral trade accords, with the explicit purpose of leveraging more concessions from nonmembers during the Doha round of WTO talks.[45]

### *Growing GATT/WTO Membership*

Membership in GATT/WTO has grown more than sixfold since its inception, from twenty-two states in 1948 to 137 in 2000.[46] It is widely recognized that as the multilateral system adds members, each member's leverage declines.[47] Especially for smaller states, which have relatively little bargaining power to begin with, there are clear incentives to respond to a decrease in leverage by banding together to enhance their influence through the formation of a PTA. Consistent with this hypothesis, a number of formal models have shown that rising GATT/WTO membership decreases the leverage of each participant and stimulates the establishment of preferential groupings.[48] To date, however, this issue has not received much systematic empirical scrutiny.

There are a number of related reasons to expect growth in the size of GATT/WTO to precipitate PTA formation. As the number of parties to the multilateral regime has increased, so have the severity of collective action problems and the heterogeneity of preferences within the institution.[49] An expanded membership reduces each participant's ability to monitor the trade practices of its counterparts. States also face rising incentives to cheat: because the actions of any single mem-

42. See Dryden 1995, 370; and WTO 1995a, 54.
43. *Far Eastern Economic Review*, 5 November 1992, 50.
44. Dryden 1995, 340; see also Preeg 1995, 80.
45. For example, upon the completion of the U.S.-Singapore FTA negotiations, U.S. Trade Representative Robert Zoellick declared, "I firmly believe that a process of . . . competitive liberalization will enhance our ability to get Doha done." See *Washington Post*, 20 November 2002, E3; and *Financial Times*, 1 November 2002, 14.
46. Chile signed the 1947 GATT agreement but did not accede formally until 1949. WTO 1995b, 1136.
47. See, for example, Koremenos, Lipson, and Snidal 2001, 791–92; and McCalman 2002, 154.
48. See Freund 2000, 373–74; and McCalman 2002, 154.
49. See Fernández and Portes 1998, 205; and Krugman 1993, 74.

ber are likely to have relatively little bearing on the performance of the multilateral regime, cheating is less likely to weaken the GATT system.[50]

Further, increased membership tends to introduce greater heterogeneity of preferences, as well as trade and business practices, within GATT/WTO. For example, when there are more negotiating partners, trade liberalization tends to influence more goods and adversely affect a greater number of potent interest groups.[51] Adding developing countries to the multilateral regime creates further complications, because the trade barriers these states most want removed (for example, those on textiles and agriculture) have long been the sacred cows of protectionist interests in the advanced industrial states. The accession of developing states to GATT/WTO also has intensified North-South divisions on intellectual property and labor and environmental standards. The WTO Director General admitted after the failed Seattle Ministerial meeting in 1999 that "the reason we had problems was the diversity of our members."[52] Even the addition of a single member can hamper efforts to promote multilateral liberalization. For example, the EU Trade Commissioner recently stated that "a round with China in is going to be much more difficult than a round without China in."[53] Because of China's WTO accession, Prime Minister Junichiro Koizumi has proposed a dramatic shift away from Japan's historical aversion to regionalism, starting with a PTA involving Singapore.[54]

Faced with heightened difficulty arriving at any overarching agreement on economic matters as the number of members grows,[55] parties to GATT/WTO may find it advantageous to form smaller, preferential arrangements composed of states with common interests on trade policy.[56] Such arrangements provide insurance against future disruptions of trade that might occur if multilateral negotiations buckle under the weight of a large number of participants with disparate commercial preferences, thereby enhancing the members' bargaining power within the regime.

### *GATT/WTO Disputes*

While MTNs and membership growth are two of the most obvious achievements of the multilateral regime, the daily business—indeed, the "jewel"[57] or

50. Krugman 1993, 74.
51. Ethier 1999, 136.
52. *New Straits Times (Malaysia)*, 30 January 2000, 19.
53. *Financial Times*, 25 May 2000, 14.
54. See *International Trade Reporter*, 6 September 2001, 1389; and *Australian Financial Review*, 24 April 2002, 4.
55. The first MTN, in 1947, took six months to complete, whereas the last one took nine years.
56. See Ethier 1999; and Westhoff, Yarbrough, and Yarbrough 1994. In the same vein, Downs, Rocke, and Barsoom argue that PTAs have an easier time achieving deep integration than GATT/WTO because they generally have a more homogeneous set of members. Downs, Rocke, and Barsoom 1998.
57. Hudec 1993, 9.

"backbone"[58]—of the GATT/WTO system is settling commercial disputes among its members.[59] Formal GATT/WTO disputes occur with striking frequency and are another factor likely to affect the establishment of PTAs.[60] In a dispute, one state—the "complainant"—notifies GATT of its objections to trade practices of a counterpart—the "defendant." The disputants consult bilaterally and may request an independent legal judgment by a GATT/WTO-appointed panel of experts. Enforcement, however, is left to the complainant alone. Accordingly, a disputant is more likely to prevail—that is, to induce concessions from a defendant or withstand a complainant's retaliatory threats, as appropriate—if it possesses significant market power.[61] Because PTAs possess more market power than any constituent member, states may enhance their leverage in trade disputes by entering a preferential grouping.[62]

Of course, the stakes involved in any single dispute—while often surprisingly large—are small compared to those involved in forming a PTA.[63] It is therefore unlikely that, by itself, participating in a single GATT/WTO dispute would be sufficient to prompt a state to seek a preferential arrangement. Involvement in a dispute, however, dramatically raises a state's chances of participating in other future disputes.[64] Consequently, the costs of forming a PTA are at least partially offset by what are likely to be a long stream of improved dispute outcomes.

Further, many disputes concern policies, such as export subsidies, aimed at increasing competitiveness in a third party's market. An unsatisfied disputant may seek a PTA with that third party as a way of bypassing the dispute process. For instance, one of Argentina's primary motives for entering and deepening its commitment to Mercosur was to secure preferential access to the Brazilian wheat market. Brazil was Argentina's leading export market for wheat, and its competitiveness in that market was threatened by Canadian and U.S. export subsidy programs, which Argentina had challenged ineffectually in a GATT dispute.[65] In some disputes, third parties also face the possibility that disputants will arrive at a settlement that discriminates against them, thereby increasing the incentives for third parties to form a PTA with either disputant (separately) to ensure that their market access is not jeopardized.[66] Thus, we hypothesize that if either of a pair of countries has recently participated in a GATT/WTO dispute with a third party, the two will be more likely to form a PTA with each other.[67]

58. Moore 2000.
59. Reinhardt forthcoming, chap. 1.
60. From 1948 through 1998 there were over 600 GATT/WTO trade disputes.
61. See Hudec 1993, 318, 324, 326; and Mavroidis 2000.
62. See Bagwell and Staiger 2001; and WTO 1995a, 53.
63. On the size of the stakes involved in GATT/WTO disputes, see Reinhardt forthcoming.
64. Busch and Reinhardt 2002.
65. See *Los Angeles Times*, 9 December 1994, D3; and GATT 1994, 24.
66. Busch and Reinhardt 2002.
67. A good part of the U.S. emerging interest in regionalism in the 1980s derived from its frequent GATT disputes (often incompletely resolved) with the EU. Indeed, in February 1988, Treasury Secretary James Baker publicly chastised the EC's recalcitrance on several outstanding disputes and threat-

The incentives to form a PTA are greater still if a state ends up losing its dispute as well. Whether a state "wins" or "loses" a dispute is not defined by any multilateral legal judgment, but rather by practical policy consequences. A complainant loses for our purposes if it fails to induce the target to change the disputed policies fully; a defendant loses if it fails to maintain the status quo (protectionist) policy in the face of foreign pressure. Losing a dispute constitutes a proven bargaining failure. For a complainant, a loss is firsthand evidence that GATT's enforcement system is weak. The lesson may be that market access for its exports is best insured through bilateral rather than multilateral means. For a defendant, a loss is proof of its weakness, which is particularly galling when other states are sometimes able to resist foreign challenges against their protectionist practices. The lesson may be that the reciprocity underpinning the regime is only enforced at the convenience of more powerful members. Hence, we hypothesize that a state that has lost a recent GATT/WTO dispute will be especially likely to enter a preferential arrangement with a third party, to insure itself against future defeats and to bolster its position henceforth in such conflicts.

## Research Design

Despite the widespread interest expressed in commercial regionalism, little systematic empirical research has analyzed the influences on PTA formation, let alone the role of GATT/WTO.[68] To address the hypotheses advanced earlier, we examine each pair of GATT/WTO members, *i* and *j*, that do not already share a PTA in every year, *t*, from GATT's creation in 1948 until 1998.[69] Our dependent variable, PTA, is the log of the odds that *i* and *j* form a PTA entering into force in *t*, given that the pair did not belong to the same PTA in year $t - 1$. We observe 1 if this occurs and 0 otherwise. We consider all PTAs (that is, partially-liberalizing agreements, FTAs, customs unions, and common markets) formally notified to GATT/WTO, as long as they are "reciprocal," meaning that each party grants the others preferential market access.[70] The annual number of GATT/WTO members entering reciprocal PTAs is shown in Figure 2. Out of all pairs of GATT/WTO members not already in the same PTA, a little more than 6 percent joined together in new PTAs at some point from 1948 through 1998.

ened that the United States was considering FTA talks with Japan, South Korea, and Taiwan, which took shape later as APEC. See Hudec 1993; and Preeg 1995, 80.

68. For some exceptions, see Mansfield 1998; and Mansfield, Milner, and Rosendorff 2002.

69. A state is included in the sample during year *t* if it was a member of GATT/WTO on any day in that year. The EC/EU is the only PTA that itself is a member of GATT/WTO; we do not include it but do count its member states. See Jackson 1969, 898–900; GATT 1990, 139; and WTO 1998.

70. See Smith 2000, 151; and WTO 1995a, 77–91 and 1999b. Note that PTA "upgrades" (for example, Sweden, Finland, and Austria, were in an FTA with the EU and then acceded to the EU proper in 1995) are not included in the following analysis, because the participants were already PTA members in $t - 1$.

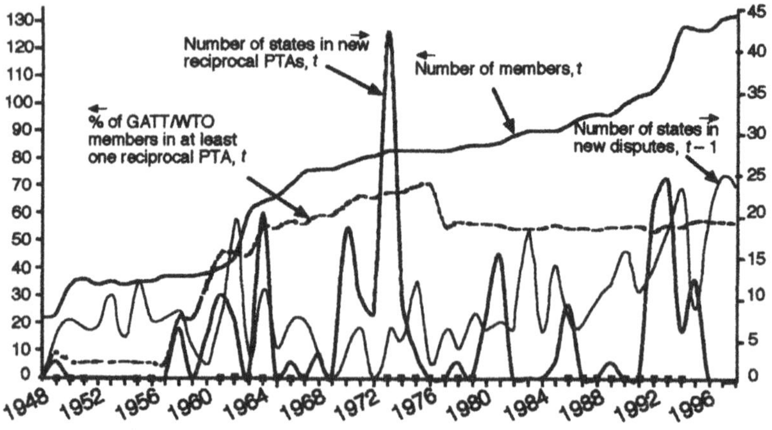


*Note:* Small arrows point to relevant vertical axis. Squares on horizontal axis show years in which an MTN was underway. "Number of states in new disputes" counts EU as one state.

**FIGURE 2.** *Trends in GATT/WTO membership, disputes, and reciprocal PTAs, 1948–98*

*Explanatory Variables*

To test our arguments, we focus on four explanatory variables. First, NUMBER OF MEMBERS is the number of contracting parties to GATT/WTO in $t - 1$.[71] Second, MTN ROUND UNDERWAY equals 1 if a formal multilateral trade negotiation occurred in $t$, 0 otherwise. Third, NEW DISPUTE WITH THIRD PARTY equals 1 if either $i$ or $j$ participated as a complainant or defendant in a GATT/WTO dispute with a third party in $t - 1$ (not counting third parties in PTAs with the other state in the pair), 0 otherwise.[72] Based on the arguments advanced earlier, we expect to find positive associations between PTA formation, on the one hand, and NUMBER OF MEMBERS, MTN ROUND UNDERWAY, and NEW DISPUTE WITH THIRD PARTY, on the other. Trends in these variables are shown in Figure 2. For the full population of GATT/WTO member-pairs, MTN ROUND UNDERWAY and NEW DISPUTE WITH THIRD PARTY equal 1 in 53 percent and 31 percent of the observations, respectively.

The final explanatory variable, DISPUTE LOSS WITH THIRD PARTY, indicates the performance of $i$ and $j$ in GATT/WTO disputes with third parties. It draws on an

71. The EC itself is not included in this count.

72. We include all complaints formally filed, not just those in which GATT/WTO adjudication panels were established or issued rulings. Disputes lodged against or by the EC/EU are assigned to every one of its contemporary members. The list of disputes is from Busch and Reinhardt 2002, which draws on Hudec 1993; and WTO 1995b, 620, 623–28, 772–87, and 1999c.

existing measure of the extent of concessions—none, partial, or full—made by a defendant to the initial demands of the complainant in a GATT/WTO dispute, regardless of whether a ruling was ultimately issued.[73] We define a participant as "losing" if it fails to meet its primary objectives in the conflict. The complainant loses if it fails to induce full concessions from the defendant; the defendant loses if it makes any concessions. DISPUTE LOSS WITH THIRD PARTY equals 1 if either $i$ or $j$ lost a dispute with a third party (again, excluding disputes where the third party belongs to a PTA with the other state in the pair) that started in year $t - 3$, 0 otherwise. We lag the effects of this variable by three years because the average length of GATT disputes is roughly two to three years. This variable equals 1 in 20 percent of the population of GATT/WTO dyad-years. We anticipate a positive relationship between DISPUTE LOSS WITH THIRD PARTY and PTA formation.

### *Control Variables*

To adequately assess the effects of these explanatory variables, it is important to control for various other factors that previous studies have identified as likely influences on PTA formation. First, open trade generates efficiency gains that can be used to enhance states' political-military capability. Preferential trading arrangements—all of which liberalize commerce among participants—thereby generate a security externality. States can help internalize this externality by trading more freely with political-military allies than with neutral countries or adversaries.[74] As such, PTAs are more likely to form between allies than between other states.[75] Hence, we analyze ALLIANCE, which equals 1 if $i$ and $j$ maintained a formal military alliance in $t - 1$, 0 otherwise.[76]

Second, it is widely recognized that PTAs tend to form among states located in close geographical proximity to one another. A state's primary trade partners tend to be neighbors because of the reduction in transportation and transaction costs stemming from close proximity.[77] We therefore assess the effects of DISTANCE, which is the mileage (in thousands) between the capital cities of $i$ and $j$, set to 0 if the pair is contiguous.[78] Third, recent research indicates that the likelihood of $i$ and $j$ forming a PTA rises as each country becomes more democratic.[79] We thus include DEMOCRACY, a 21-point measure of each state's regime type in $t - 1$ that ranges from $-10$ for highly autocratic countries to 10 for highly democratic ones.[80]

Fourth, as a state's domestic market grows larger, it typically depends less on foreign trade and has less need to increase its market power for bargaining pur-

73. See Busch and Reinhardt 2002 and 2003; Hudec 1993; and Reinhardt 2001 and forthcoming.
74. See Gowa 1994; and Gowa and Mansfield 1993.
75. See Mansfield 1993; and Mansfield and Milner 1999.
76. Data on alliances are taken from Correlates of War Project 1993; and Lai and Reiter 2000.
77. See Deardorff 1998; and Frankel 1997, chap. 3.
78. Data on distance are obtained from Bennett and Stam 1999.
79. Mansfield, Milner, and Rosendorff 2002.
80. Data for this variable are found in Gurr and Jaggers 1999.

poses. Further, the expanded market access furnished by PTAs can help firms in member-states to realize economies of scale, but the corresponding gains tend to be greater for firms located in small countries. Hence, we expect the probability of PTA formation to be greater for economically small states than for their larger counterparts. To address this hypothesis, we analyze the gross domestic product (GDP) (in trillions of constant 1995 international dollars, expressed in terms of purchasing power parity) of each state in $t - 1$. Fifth, because many observers have noted that rich states tend to form PTAs more frequently than poor ones, we control for both states' PER CAPITA GDP (in thousands of constant 1995 international dollars, expressed in terms of purchasing power parity) in year $t - 1$. Sixth, it has been argued that downturns in the business cycle can prompt states to enter PTAs.[81] Because PTAs discriminate against third parties, joining a preferential grouping is one way that governments can respond to the domestic pressures for protection that often accompany recessions without contravening GATT/WTO rules. Joining a PTA also attends to a country's export-oriented firms, which have particular reason to press for preferential access to foreign markets in the face of depressed demand for their products. We therefore include GROWTH, the annual percentage change in each state's real GDP for year $t - 1$.[82]

We have argued that strategic interaction guides the formation of PTAs, as states seek to augment their bargaining position within GATT/WTO. Moreover, we have argued that developments within GATT/WTO influence the nature of strategic interaction across dyads and across time, thereby affecting which states form PTAs and when states do so. However, it is obvious that other factors also influence strategic interaction in the international trading system. These factors, too, are likely to affect the establishment of preferential groupings, and it is therefore important to account for them in our analysis.

To this end, we include TRADE, which is the sum of $i$'s imports from and exports to $j$ (in trillions of constant 1995 U.S. dollars) in $t - 1$.[83] Because preferential arrangements provide states with insurance against being locked out of the participants' markets, we expect GATT/WTO members to form PTAs with their most important trade partners. PTAs liberalize commerce among members and restrict their ability to increase trade barriers in the future, creating an incentive for those economic partners that would suffer most if commerce was disrupted to create such groupings.[84]

81. See Mansfield 1998, 526; and Mattli 1999, 81.

82. Data on GDP, per capita GDP, and growth are taken from IMF 1998b; Summers and Heston 1991; and World Bank 2001.

83. Data on bilateral trade flows are obtained from IMF 1999a. Nominal values of trade are adjusted by changes in the U.S. producer price index, which is found in United States 2000.

84. Furthermore, as neofunctionalists have long argued, international commerce promotes the development of coalitions with an interest in creating institutional mechanisms to increase economic integration and avert the breakdown of economic relations between the trade partners. Integration also increases the vulnerability of private traders to opportunistic behavior by foreign governments, which in turn gives them a motive to constrain governments' behavior using a PTA. See Mattli 1999, 23–28, 46–50; and Yarbrough and Yarbrough 1992.

Not only do we expect GATT members to establish PTAs with their most important trade partners, we also expect them to form PTAs with states that belong to the same preferential groupings as these partners. Doing so further reduces the prospect of being closed out of vital foreign markets, for example, if groupings involving a state's key commercial partners—but excluding this state itself—raise trade barriers against third parties. As such, we include TRADE PARTNER PTA COVERAGE. This variable is the proportion of *i*'s top ten GATT/WTO trade partners, exclusive of *j*, which maintained a reciprocal PTA with *j* in $t - 1$.

Within GATT/WTO, preferential groupings often form in reaction to each other.[85] As an increasing number of GATT/WTO members establish PTAs, those states left uncovered by an arrangement have a growing incentive to join one. Such states have reason to fear that they will be placed at a competitive disadvantage vis-à-vis participants in PTAs, generating pressure on them to enter a trade bloc. Furthermore, the perception that PTAs are spreading because participants are reaping economic benefits can prompt states that do not belong to a preferential grouping to join one.[86] Equally, existing PTAs can provide templates for states that are considering forming one, furnishing "institutional models" that can be duplicated or altered and thereby decreasing the costs associated with establishing such an arrangement.[87] Consequently, as PTAs proliferate, it may become easier to set up new groupings.

In addition, we mentioned earlier that PTAs generally are vested with greater bargaining power than their constituent members. As the number of states covered by a PTA grows larger, the bargaining power of states that remain uncovered by such an arrangement degrades. Thus, states that do not belong to a preferential grouping have reason to enter one as PTAs spread. We therefore include PTA DENSITY—the portion of GATT/WTO dyads that belong to a reciprocal PTA in $t - 1$, excluding those in which either *i* or *j* is a member.

We also consider the possibility that the relationship between PTA DENSITY and the likelihood of PTA formation is characterized by a saturation or ceiling effect.[88] When enough dyads belong to preferential groupings, it is likely that relatively few pairs with an interest in forming a PTA will be left uncovered by one. If so, there may be a quadratic relationship between PTA DENSITY and the likelihood of PTA formation. To address this possibility, we add PTA DENSITY$^2$.

Two of our four key explanatory variables concern participation in and the outcomes of *i*'s and *j*'s GATT/WTO disputes with third parties. To verify that the effects of these two variables do not stem from the bilateral dispute record between *i* and *j*, we add a dummy variable, NEW DISPUTE BETWEEN *i* AND *j*, which equals 1 if either state filed a GATT/WTO dispute against the other in year $t - 1$. Our argument does not speak to the likely impact of this variable on PTA forma-

85. See Pomfret 1997; and Serra et al. 1997.
86. See Pomfret 1997; and Yarbrough and Yarbrough 1992.
87. Yarbrough and Yarbrough 1997, 158.
88. Mansfield 1998.

tion. A record of disputes may, on the one hand, indicate intense conflicts of interest that reduce the probability of *i* and *j* forming a PTA. On the other hand, *i* and *j* may seek to avoid the costs of these confrontations by embedding a solution in a new joint PTA, much as Canada sought with the U.S.-Canada FTA to tie the hands of the United States on a series of unfair trade actions (on lumber, etc.) recently disputed under GATT. Finally, we include YEAR, which is *t*, to capture any secular trend in PTA formation between GATT/WTO members.

## *Statistical Models*

A number of the aforementioned control variables—DEMOCRACY, GDP, PER CAPITA GDP, GROWTH, and TRADE PARTNER PTA COVERAGE—are "monadic," meaning that they measure properties of each state in a pair, not the pair itself. Thus, each of these variables should be entered in the model twice, with one variable corresponding to country *i* and a second variable corresponding to country *j*. Yet arbitrarily determining which state in a pair is *i* and which one is *j* could influence our results, so we estimate a "directed dyad" model in which each dyad-year is analyzed twice. For example, in the case of the U.S.-Canada dyad in 1990, we include one observation where the United States is *i* and Canada is *j*, and a second observation where Canada is *i* and the United States is *j*. Each monadic variable is included in this model only once, for the country listed as *i* in each particular observation. Of course, analyzing directed dyads doubles the number of observations in the sample, thereby producing standard errors that are too small. To correct this problem, we cluster the standard errors over the *un*directed dyad. As a result, this test is more conservative than one based on the 151,912 undirected dyad-years in the population. Rather than doubling the sample size, clustering the standard errors over the undirected dyad effectively reduces it by a factor of 17 (to 8,799 dyads), yielding estimated standard errors that are about four times larger than would otherwise be the case.

Nevertheless, for comparison, we also estimate a more typical undirected dyad model that includes each monadic variable twice. Which state is *i* and which one is *j* is determined by random assignment. Descriptive statistics for the variables included in the basic directed dyad and undirected dyad models—labeled models (1) and (3) and models (4) and (6), respectively—are shown in Table 1.

Because a number of independent variables are missing a considerable amount of data, these models include a little less than half the universe of the yearly dyadic observations from 1948 to 1998. To assess whether our results are sensitive to these missing data, we also estimate directed and undirected dyad models (labeled (2) and (5), respectively) without GROWTH, ALLIANCE, and TRADE, raising the sample size to about 85 percent of the population (for directed dyads). Whereas our initial analyses exclude the first and last few years of the sample due to missing data, omitting these variables allows us to analyze the entire period from 1948 to 1998.

Table 1. Descriptive statistics

| Variable | Directed dyad years Models 1 and 3 | | | | Undirected dyad years Models 4 and 6 | | | |
|---|---|---|---|---|---|---|---|---|
| | *Mean* | *SD* | *Min.* | *Max.* | *Mean* | *SD* | *Min.* | *Max.* |
| PTA, $t$ | 0.006 | 0.076 | 0 | 1 | 0.006 | 0.077 | 0 | 1 |
| NUMBER OF MEMBERS, $t-1$ | 85.255 | 14.823 | 23 | 105 | 86.195 | 13.406 | 23 | 105 |
| DETRENDED # OF MEMBERS, $t-1$ | −2.104 | 7.070 | −10.573 | 12.446 | −2.177 | 7.074 | −10.574 | 12.446 |
| MTN ROUND UNDERWAY, $t$ | 0.652 | 0.476 | 0 | 1 | 0.656 | 0.475 | 0 | 1 |
| NEW DISPUTE WITH 3RD PARTY, $t-1$ | 0.381 | 0.485 | 0 | 1 | 0.394 | 0.489 | 0 | 1 |
| DISPUTE LOSS WITH 3RD PARTY, $t-3$ | 0.302 | 0.459 | 0 | 1 | 0.315 | 0.465 | 0 | 1 |
| NEW DISPUTE BETWEEN $i$ AND $j$, $t-1$ | 0.016 | 0.124 | 0 | 1 | 0.017 | 0.131 | 0 | 1 |
| ALLIANCE, $t-1$ | 0.094 | 0.292 | 0 | 1 | 0.098 | 0.297 | 0 | 1 |
| DISTANCE, $t$ | 4.866 | 2.701 | 0 | 12.363 | 4.932 | 2.687 | 0 | 12.363 |
| TRADE, $t-1$ | 0.0004 | 0.0032 | 0 | 0.1878 | 0.0004 | 0.0034 | 0 | 0.1790 |
| PTA DENSITY, $t-1$ | 0.004 | 0.032 | −0.075 | 0.080 | 0.004 | 0.031 | −0.075 | 0.080 |
| PTA DENSITY$^2$, $t-1$ | 0.001 | 0.002 | 0 | 0.006 | 0.001 | 0.002 | 0 | 0.006 |
| DEMOCRACY $i$, $t-1$ | 2.423 | 7.755 | −10 | 10 | 2.236 | 7.782 | −10 | 10 |
| DEMOCRACY $j$, $t-1$ | — | — | — | — | 2.165 | 7.777 | −10 | 10 |
| GDP $i$, $t-1$ | 0.250 | 0.770 | 0.0001 | 6.440 | 0.251 | 0.782 | 0.0001 | 6.440 |
| GDP $j$, $t-1$ | — | — | — | — | 0.242 | 0.758 | 0.0001 | 6.440 |
| PER CAPTIA GDP $i$, $t-1$ | 7.438 | 9.156 | 0.114 | 45.951 | 7.349 | 9.157 | 0.114 | 45.951 |
| PER CAPTIA GDP $j$, $t-1$ | — | — | — | — | 7.267 | 9.173 | 0.114 | 45.951 |
| GROWTH $i$, $t-1$ | 3.564 | 4.846 | −24.049 | 39.487 | 3.513 | 4.893 | −24.049 | 39.487 |
| GROWTH $j$, $t-1$ | — | — | — | — | 3.570 | 4.870 | −24.049 | 39.487 |
| TRADE PARTNER PTA COVERAGE $i$, $t-1$ | 0.132 | 0.233 | 0 | 0.9 | 0.140 | 0.238 | 0 | 0.9 |
| TRADE PARTNER PTA COVERAGE $j$, $t-1$ | — | — | — | — | 0.140 | 0.237 | 0 | 0.9 |
| YEAR, $t$ | 1980.42 | 9.473 | 1950 | 1993 | 1980.93 | 8.969 | 1950 | 1993 |
| POSTCOMMUNIST, $t$ | 0.025 | 0.157 | 0 | 1 | 0.025 | 0.155 | 0 | 1 |
| FORMER COLONIAL RELATIONSHIP, $t$ | 0.029 | 0.169 | 0 | 1 | 0.032 | 0.177 | 0 | 1 |
| Number of observations | 149,308 | | | | 65,153 | | | |

*Note*: Shaded rows identify the variables that are cental to our argument. SD = standard deviation.

## Results

Because the observed value of the dependent variable is dichotomous, we use a logit specification to estimate these models. To account for any duration dependence in the data, we include a natural cubic spline function of the number of years *i* and *j* have been without a PTA, as of *t*.[89]

As reported in Tables 2 and 3, the models fit the data well.[90] Further, the results of these analyses strongly support our argument about the impact of the multilateral regime on PTA formation. The estimates of NUMBER OF MEMBERS, MTN ROUND UNDERWAY, NEW DISPUTE WITH THIRD PARTY, and DISPUTE LOSS WITH THIRD PARTY are positive as well as both statistically (at the .001 level) and substantively significant.[91] Equally, the coefficient estimates are quite similar regardless of whether we use the directed or undirected dyad approach—see models (1) and (4)—or whether we use the larger-sample specification without ALLIANCE, GROWTH, and TRADE—see models (2) and (5).

To address the substantive effects of these factors as well as some selected control variables, Figure 3 reports the "relative risk" of states *i* and *j* forming a PTA, based on the results in model (1). For each dummy variable shown in Figure 3, this risk is the probability of establishing an arrangement when the variable equals 1 divided by the probability when it equals 0 (since the coefficient estimate of each dummy variable in the figure is positive), holding constant the remaining variables in the model. For every other variable with a positive (negative) coefficient estimate in model (1), the relative risk is the predicted probability of PTA formation when the variable is one standard deviation above its mean (at the mean) divided by this probability when the variable is evaluated at its mean (one standard deviation above the mean).

Our results clearly indicate that rising GATT/WTO membership has increased the probability of states creating a PTA. Figure 3 shows that shifting NUMBER OF MEMBERS from its sample mean by one standard deviation yields more than a forty-fold increase in the predicted probability of PTA formation, a far larger impact than any other variable considered here. In addition, during a multilateral trade negotiation, the likelihood of any two states establishing a preferential grouping increases by roughly a factor of six. If either state in the pair participated in a new GATT/WTO dispute with a third party in $t - 1$, the prospect of entering a PTA

89. Beck, Katz, and Tucker 1998, 1270–71. Wald tests of the joint significance of the terms in this spline function (which yield $p < .001$ for all models) confirm that they should be included.

90. Estimates were produced using *Stata* 7.0's *logit, robust cluster* command. Note that there is little evidence of collinearity in this analysis. The exceptions include PER CAPITA GDP with DEMOCRACY, DISTANCE with YEAR and NUMBER OF MEMBERS, and PTA DENSITY with its square, which all exhibit no more than moderate ($r < .6$) bivariate correlations. Only NUMBER OF MEMBERS and YEAR are highly correlated. Their estimates are nonetheless statistically significant.

91. Wald tests lead us to reject the null hypothesis that NUMBER OF MEMBERS, MTN ROUND UNDERWAY, NEW DISPUTE WITH THIRD PARTY, and DISPUTE LOSS WITH THIRD PARTY jointly equal zero, with $p < .001$ for all models.

| Variable | Model 1 (1950–93) | | Model 2 (1948–98) | | Model 3 (1950–93) | |
|---|---|---|---|---|---|---|
| Prob (PTA) = 1 | *Coefficient* | *SE* | *Coefficient* | *SE* | *Coefficient* | *SE* |
| NUMBER OF MEMBERS, $t-1$ | 0.251** | 0.0030 | 0.155** | 0.012 | — | — |
| DETRENDED # OF MEMBERS, $t-1$ | — | — | — | — | 0.235** | 0.024 |
| MTN ROUND UNDERWAY, $t$ | 1.848* | 0.154 | 1.900** | 0.155 | 1.730** | 0.159 |
| NEW DISPUTE WITH 3RD PARTY, $t-1$ | 0.527** | 0.133 | 0.629** | 0.118 | 0.587** | 0.133 |
| DISPUTE LOSS WITH 3RD PARTY, $t-3$ | 1.183** | 0.115 | 1.073** | 0.102 | 1.270** | 0.114 |
| NEW DISPUTE BETWEEN $i$ AND $j$, $t-1$ | −0.933 | 0.643 | −0.922 | 0.619 | −0.809 | 0.640 |
| ALLIANCE, $t-1$ | 0.270* | 0.116 | — | — | 0.453** | 0.117 |
| DISTANCE, $t$ | −0.627** | 0.027 | −0.665** | 0.026 | −0.545 | 0.027 |
| TRADE, $t-1$ | 14.304** | 3.129 | — | — | 16.826** | 3.459 |
| PTA DENSITY, $t-1$ | −37.658** | 3.971 | −23.331** | 2.636 | −32.651** | 3.263 |
| PTA DENSITY$^2$, $t-1$ | −364.91** | 83.59 | −690.87** | 70.01 | −455.14** | 82.62 |
| DEMOCRACY $t-1$ | 0.065** | 0.006 | 0.047** | 0.005 | 0.059** | 0.005 |
| GDP, $t-1$ | −0.273** | 0.059 | −0.133* | 0.054 | −0.311** | 0.061 |
| PER CAPTIA GDP $t-1$ | 0.010* | 0.004 | 0.016** | 0.004 | 0.018** | 0.004 |
| GROWTH $t-1$ | −0.022** | 0.008 | — | — | 0.006 | 0.008 |
| TRADE PARTNER PTA COVERAGE $t-1$ | 3.040** | 0.135 | 2.765** | 0.128 | 3.073** | 0.142 |
| YEAR, $t$ | −0.503** | 0.042 | −0.395** | 0.025 | −0.040** | 0.018 |
| POSTCOMMUNIST, $t$ | — | — | — | — | 2.772** | 0.209 |
| FORMER COLONIAL RELATIONSHIP, $t$ | — | — | — | — | 1.511** | 0.197 |
| CONSTANT | 968.966** | 79.678 | 763.259** | 48.358 | 73.128** | 35.361 |
| Number of observations | 149,308 | | 259,267 | | 149,308 | |
| Model $\chi^2$ | 2661.9**, 22 d.o.f. | | 3069.4**, 19 d.o.f. | | 2768.6**, 24 d.o.f. | |
| Pseudo-$R^2$ | 0.390 | | 0.360 | | 0.414 | |

*Note*: Shaded rows identify the variables that are cental to our argument. Two-tailed tests are conducted for all estimates. Robust standard errors (SEs) clustered over dyads. Six duration dependence splines omitted from table. PTA DENSITY is "centered" by subtracting .075 to reduce collinearity without other effects. d. o. f. = degrees of freedom.

$^{**}p < .01$.

$^{*}p < .05$.

Table 3. Duration dependent logit models of PTA formation, undirected dyads.

| *Variable* | *Model 4 (1950–93)* | | *Model 5 (1948–98)* | | *Model 6 (1950–93)* | |
|---|---|---|---|---|---|---|
| Prob (PTA) = 1 | *Coefficient* | *SE* | *Coefficient* | *SE* | *Coefficient* | *SE* |
| NUMBER OF MEMBERS, $t-1$ | 0.289** | 0.046 | 0.142** | 0.012 | — | — |
| DETRENDED # OF MEMBERS, $t-1$ | — | — | — | — | 0.258** | 0.034 |
| MTN ROUND UNDERWAY, $t$ | 1.911* | 0.179 | 1.827** | 0.160 | 1.652** | 0.181 |
| NEW DISPUTE WITH 3RD PARTY, $t-1$ | 0.546** | 0.161 | 0.573** | 0.127 | 0.595** | 0.159 |
| DISPUTE LOSS WITH 3RD PARTY, $t-3$ | 1.415** | 0.146 | 1.098** | 0.112 | 1.534** | 0.145 |
| NEW DISPUTE BETWEEN $i$ AND $j$, $t-1$ | −0.700 | 0.739 | −0.920 | 0.633 | −0.492 | 0.735 |
| ALLIANCE, $t-1$ | 0.170 | 0.138 | — | — | 0.434** | 0.145 |
| DISTANCE, $t$ | −0.566** | 0.037 | −0.605** | 0.031 | −0.431** | 0.036 |
| TRADE, $t-1$ | 33.070** | 5.482 | — | — | 43.086** | 5.980 |
| PTA DENSITY, $t-1$ | −45.103** | 5.833 | −22.836** | 2.971 | −38.741** | 4.364 |
| PTA DENSITY$^2$, $t-1$ | 203.29** | 93.98 | −621.78** | 69.53 | −281.46** | 85.06 |
| DEMOCRACY i, $t-1$ | −0.063** | 0.010 | −0.039* | 0.009 | −0.059** | 0.009 |
| DEMOCRACY j, $t-1$ | 0.041* | 0.010 | 0.027** | 0.009 | 0.038** | 0.010 |
| GDP i, $t-1$ | −0.171 | 0.119 | 0.020 | 0.118 | −0.301* | 0.136 |
| GDP j, $t-1$ | −0.188 | 0.193 | −0.021 | 0.101 | −0.311* | 0.220 |
| PER CAPTIA GDP $i$, $t-1$ | −0.31** | 0.007 | −0.009 | 0.006 | −0.024** | 0.007 |
| PER CAPTIA GDP $j$, $t-1$ | −0.007 | 0.007 | 0.006 | 0.006 | −0.002 | 0.007 |
| GROWTH i, $t-1$ | −0.045** | 0.015 | — | — | −0.017 | 0.014 |
| GROWTH j, $t-1$ | 0.042** | 0.014 | — | — | −0.019 | 0.014 |
| TRADE PARTNER PTA COVERAGE i, $t-1$ | 3.458** | 0.248 | −2.591** | 0.192 | 3.907** | 0.260 |
| TRADE PARTNER PTA COVERAGE j, $t-1$ | 3.528** | 0.244 | 2.673** | 0.202 | 4.007** | 0.261 |
| YEAR, $t$ | −0.573** | 0.064 | −0.374** | 0.026 | −0.049* | 0.023 |
| POSTCOMMUNIST, $t$ | — | — | — | — | 3.088** | 0.225 |
| FORMER COLONIAL RELATIONSHIP, $t$ | — | — | — | — | −2.030** | 0.255 |
| CONSTANT | 1103.07** | 121.91 | 723.037** | 50.786 | 89.410 | 46.433 |
| Number of observations | 65,153 | | 115,846 | | 65,153 | |
| Model $\chi^2$ | 1414.0**, 27 d.o.f. | | 2276.0**, 23 d.o.f. | | 1449.2**, 29 d.o.f. | |
| Pseudo-$R^2$ | 0.465 | | 0.388 | | 0.493 | |

*Note*: Shaded rows identify the variables that are cental to our argument. Two-tailed tests are conducted for all estimates. Robust standard errors (SEs) clustered over dyads. Six duration dependence splines omitted from table. PTA DENSITY is "centered" by subtracting .075 to reduce collinearity without other effects. d. o. f. = degrees of freedom.

$^{**}p < .01$.

$^{*}p < .05$.

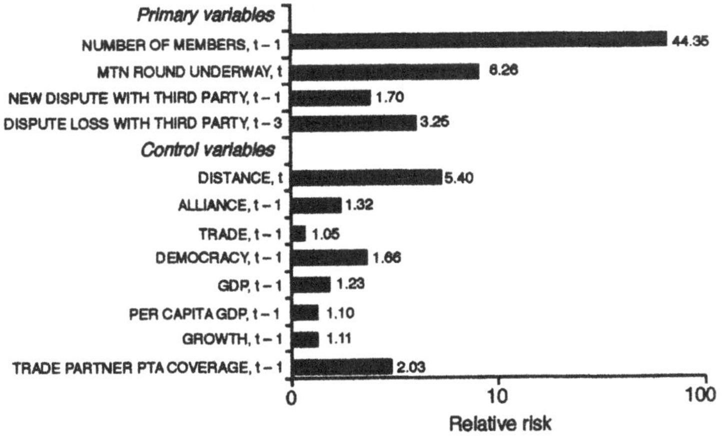


*Note:* Horizontal axis is in logarthmic scale. For all variables that are not dichotomous and that have a positive (negative) coefficient, "relative risk" is the predicted probability of PTA formation when the variable in question equals its sample mean plus one standard deviation (sample mean), divided by the predicted probability of PTA formation when it equals its sample mean (sample mean plus one standard deviation) holding other variables at their sample means. For dichotomus variables, the comparison is between values of 1 and 0. (The ratios are inverted for GDP and DISTANCE, whose coefficients are negative.)

**FIGURE 3.** *Estimated substantive significance of selected variables in model (1), in terms of relative risk*

almost doubles. If either state recently lost a GATT/WTO dispute with a third party, the probability of a new preferential grouping between them more than triples. Even if none of these variables add more than 0.1 percent to the chance of any two states entering a PTA, as many as eight additional bilateral PTAs would form in a single year as a result (since there were more than 8,000 GATT/WTO dyads by the end of the period we analyze). Clearly, the multilateral trading system has played a substantively important role in shaping PTA formation.

Moreover, these results are quite robust. For instance, as shown in models (2) and (5), the reduction in sample size that occurs when ALLIANCE, GROWTH, and TRADE are included has little discernible effect on the estimates of the variables pertaining to the multilateral trading regime. Nor do these estimates change if we add a number of omitted variables that seem likely to influence the formation of PTAs. For example, we include a measure of hegemony in the international trading system,[92] a variable indicating whether $i$ and $j$ were antagonists in a milita-

92. Gilpin 1987.

rized interstate dispute in year $t - 1$,[93] a measure of trade dependence between $i$ and $j$, and country-specific fixed effects.[94] Finally, we exclude all observations including the United States, an outlier in terms of GATT/WTO dispute participation,[95] or the founding members of the EC, which are outliers in terms of PTA formation. Each of these analyses yields estimates quite similar to those in Tables 2 and 3.

A related issue that merits consideration is whether our findings about the effects of the multilateral regime might really stem from the wave of postcolonialism in the 1960s or the wave of postcommunism in the 1990s. Members of the same imperial system are probably more likely to establish PTAs than other states once colonialism ends, and the states of Eastern Europe have demonstrated a remarkable zeal for regional trade arrangements since the Berlin Wall's collapse. Also, it is well known that the waves of postcolonialism and postcommunism took place at roughly the same time as the two waves of regionalism we discussed earlier. Likewise, how much of the proliferation in PTAs can we attribute to heightened GATT/WTO membership given that its growth is highly correlated with time? To address these issues, we add one dummy variable to the model that equals 1 if either $i$ or $j$ has transitioned from a communist regime (POSTCOMMUNIST) and another indicating whether both states were members of the same colonial system at some point after World War II (FORMER COLONIAL RELATIONSHIP). We also detrend NUMBER OF MEMBERS, replacing this variable with the residuals of a regression of NUMBER OF MEMBERS on YEAR.

The results are reported in the columns labeled models (3) and (6) in Tables 2 and 3, respectively. Not surprisingly, the results show that postcommunist states and those that were in the same imperial system are much more likely to form PTAs than other countries. Particularly important for present purposes, however, is that the estimates of our four key variables (with NUMBER OF MEMBERS now detrended) are virtually identical to those in models (1) and (4), still positive and statistically significant.[96] Thus, we continue to find strong evidence that develop-

93. Jones, Bremer, and Singer 1996.

94. We measure hegemony two ways: (1) using the U.S. portion of total world imports plus exports, based on data taken from IMF 1999a, and (2) using the ratio of U.S. GDP to the GATT/WTO member with the next highest GDP in year $t - 1$. We measure trade dependence using the value of bilateral trade divided by the GDP of $i$ and $j$, respectively.

95. Reinhardt forthcoming.

96. We conducted a number of additional robustness tests as well. PTA formation is a rare event. King and Zeng have recently argued that using a logit model to analyze rare events can yield biased results. King and Zeng 2001. We therefore estimate models (1) and (4) using a method they developed to correct such bias. The results are virtually identical to those in Tables 2 and 3, indicating that our findings are not undermined by any rare-events bias. If we reestimate the models coding TRADE as 0 when the IMF records an annual trade flow as missing, the results are effectively identical. The same is true if we use the natural log of GDP, PER CAPITA GDP, DISTANCE, and TRADE (substituting the minimum non-zero sample value of DISTANCE and TRADE when they are exactly 0). Further, the coefficients of our key variables remain positive and significant even if we (1) estimate heteroskedastic probit variants of models (1) and (4) (*Stata* 7.0's *hetprob, robust*) with variance functions conditioned

ments within the multilateral regime are important forces shaping the proliferation of PTAs.[97]

It is important to reiterate that the pronounced effect of the GATT/WTO system on PTA formation is observed even after accounting for the influence of alliances, market size, national income, the business cycle, regime type, distance, the flow of trade, and various other factors shaping strategic interaction in the international trading system. The effects of these control variables largely accord with our expectations, although a few of them depend on the model's specification. For example, economically larger states are less likely to join PTAs than their smaller counterparts, but this influence is much stronger when we focus on directed rather than undirected dyads. In addition, preferential groupings are unlikely to form between countries that are geographically distant, poor, or enjoy high levels of economic growth. Again, though, the effects of economic development and growth depend somewhat on which model is considered. Democracies tend to form PTAs, as do allies and states that trade extensively. PTAs are also a product of "bandwagoning" insofar as a country is more likely to enter a preferential arrangement with other states that already belong to groupings with its primary trade partners. Finally, there is evidence of a saturation or ceiling effect in the formation of preferential arrangements. Because we "centered" PTA DENSITY to reduce collinearity, the negative and statistically significant estimates of PTA DENSITY and PTA DENSITY$^2$ indicate that there is an inverted U-shaped relationship between the proportion of country-pairs in preferential groupings and the odds of a given pair of states establishing a new PTA.

It is also important to point out that the features of the GATT/WTO system that we have emphasized tend to have larger substantive effects on PTA formation than the control variables in our model. As shown in Figure 3, the effects of DISTANCE, TRADE PARTNER PTA COVERAGE, and DEMOCRACY are relatively sizeable, ranging from about a fivefold decrease in the predicted probability of forming a PTA if the mean distance between states $i$ and $j$ rises by one standard deviation to a two-thirds increase in this probability if the average regime score experiences a similar rise. The remaining control variables, however, have much smaller effects on the likelihood of entering a preferential grouping.

on TRADE, GDP, YEAR, DISTANCE, NUMBER OF MEMBERS, and TRADE PARTNER PTA COVERAGE; or (2) use a nonproportional hazards specification by including the interaction of all variables with the (logged) number of years the pair has gone without a PTA.

97. Still another possibility is that our findings about the strong direct effects of GATT/WTO membership might stem from an underlying demand for greater trade, stimulating participation in all international trade organizations, both preferential and multilateral. However, we have controlled for many of the economic factors that are likely to influence such demand, including GDP, growth, and per capita income. We also controlled for time, which may proxy for any secular increase in the demand for greater foreign commerce. Finally, we took account of the flow of trade as well as various features of the international trading system (for example, the existence of a multilateral negotiating round and the portion of GATT/WTO dyads that belong to a PTA), additional factors that are likely to be related to the demand for trade. Consequently, there is little reason to worry that our findings reflect the influence of such demands.

## Interpretation of the Results

One of our core findings is that participation and undesirable outcomes in GATT/WTO disputes induce countries to seek PTAs with third parties. Once formed, do PTAs actually insure against future losses and improve a state's bargaining position in such conflicts, as our argument implies? Leaders seem to believe so. For example, Malaysian Prime Minister Mahathir's reaction to the U.S. steel safeguard tariffs, which were imposed in spring 2002 and subsequently challenged under WTO dispute rules, was to renew his push for trade integration in Southeast Asia.[98] No statistical study has yet examined the impact of PTA membership on GATT/WTO dispute outcomes. However, we can offer some preliminary evidence on this score by adding our data on each disputant's participation in PTAs to an existing statistical model of GATT dispute outcomes.[99]

Specifically, to tap the bargaining power and insurance provided by preferential groupings for any given state, we sum the GDP of all its PTA partners with its own national income. The logged value of this variable is statistically significant for both state $i$ and state $j$ when we include it in the model of dispute outcomes, indicating that greater GDP increases the likelihood of a favorable outcome.[100] If, however, we subtract the PTA partners' GDPs from this variable, leaving just the disputant's GDP, it is no longer significant.[101] For a small complainant (say, with a GDP of $10 billion), joining a PTA with partners possessing $500 billion of GDP boosts its ability to leverage full concessions from a typical GATT/WTO defendant by a third (increasing the predicted probability from 0.27 to 0.36). The effect of such a change would of course be compounded over numerous future disputes. What is more, this finding is not driven by PTAs with a common external tariff, because the sample includes few customs union members.[102] Instead, the bargaining benefits of PTAs in GATT/WTO disputes are due almost entirely to FTAs, which make up most of the groupings considered here. It is thus quite plausible to attribute the finding that GATT/WTO disputes are associated with PTA formation to states' motivation to seek extra insurance and bargaining power because of such disputes.

As a more specific illustration of the links between GATT disputes and PTA formation, consider Venezuela's free trade areas with Mexico and Colombia. These preferential arrangements were formed in 1995, on the heels of Venezuela's first

98. *Business Times (Malaysia)*, 23 May 2002, 2.

99. To this end, we use model (2) from Reinhardt 2001, 178, and the updated data from Reinhardt forthcoming.

100. This model controls for whether a GATT panel is formed, how the panel rules (if at all), and several features of the measure in dispute.

101. Results available on request. The correlation between a disputant's GDP and the sum of its PTA partners' GDP plus its own is too high to include both in the same model.

102. Because the EC, by far the most frequent customs union disputant, acted as a unit in GATT disputes, its GDP is already counted as the sum of its members' GDP. Our variable thus only contributes the GDPs from the EC's external PTA partners, which did not share the same external tariff.

experiences as a GATT complainant in disputes against the EU and United States. Further, the United States and Canada both were involved in rapidly increasing numbers of GATT/WTO disputes, many against the EU, in the years immediately preceding the establishment of their free trade area. Chile participated in just five disputes between 1949 and 1987, but was embroiled in thirteen high-stakes conflicts with the United States and the EU from 1988 to 1997. It is no coincidence that Chile completed (separate) talks aimed at creating free trade areas with Mexico, Canada, Mercosur, Bolivia, Colombia, Ecuador, and Venezuela in the second half of the 1990s.[103] In a similar vein, all of the ASEAN members together participated in just one GATT dispute before 1987. By contrast, they participated in seven during the years leading up to the 1993 AFTA accord, which the prime ministers of Singapore and Malaysia claimed would "give ASEAN a bigger voice . . . in talks with the European Community."[104] This evidence is obviously anecdotal, but—consistent with our quantitative results—it suggests that the GATT/WTO dispute settlement system has contributed to the proliferation of PTAs.

Anecdotal evidence also lends support to our hypothesis that multilateral trade negotiations induce PTA formation. For instance, in the midst of the Uruguay Round, the difficulty of reaching agreement among such a heterogeneous group of countries prompted Singapore's foreign minister to "question the usefulness" of GATT and to endorse an ASEAN-based free trade area.[105] APEC ministers resolved to "use their combined strength as leverage against Europe" to bring a quick end to the Uruguay Round in 1993.[106] Equally, the Caribbean states formed the Caribbean Free Trade Association (CARIFTA) during the Kennedy Round and then CARICOM during the Tokyo Round at least partly to boost their collective negotiating leverage in these multilateral trade negotiations.[107]

## Conclusions

Central to the GATT/WTO system are efforts to liberalize trade on a multilateral basis, expand the number of parties to this organization, and enforce compliance with its rules through a reliable dispute settlement procedure. GATT/WTO has been remarkably successful in meeting these objectives. At the same time, however, such efforts have contributed greatly to the rise of PTAs, institutions that pose a challenge to GATT/WTO's principle of nondiscrimination. Although it is widely recognized that PTAs have proliferated rapidly among GATT/WTO members, there has been little systematic research addressing how developments within the multilateral regime have contributed to their spread.

103. Smith 2000, 152.
104. *Straits Times*, 23 October 1993, 1.
105. *Daily Telegraph*, 10 February 1993, 13.
106. *Straits Times*, 3 November 1993, 4.
107. Andriamananjara and Schiff 2001.

We argue that GATT/WTO members form preferential groupings to improve their bargaining position in trade negotiations with third parties. Heightened bargaining power is especially useful during multilateral trade negotiations, when GATT/WTO adds members, and during commercial disputes. Specifically, adding members to the MTN regime reduces each participant's leverage, creating incentives for states to pool their influence by establishing a PTA. Increasing the regime's size can also render multilateral negotiations more contentious and harder to conclude by expanding the range of interests that need to be accommodated. Faced with greater difficulty arriving at any multilateral solution to commercial issues as the size of GATT/WTO grows, its members may find it useful to enter smaller, preferential groupings composed of states with common economic interests.

In the same vein, preferential arrangements also provide participants with insurance against future disruptions of commerce that might arise if multilateral negotiations stall or the system weakens as a growing number of states with heterogeneous commercial preferences accede to GATT/WTO. Furthermore, in the course of striking MTNs or resolving ongoing disputes, states may enter PTAs to solidify important trade relations or to bolster their market power in the hopes of leveraging greater concessions from third parties. States also look to the success of the MTN regime's enforcement system for cues. If too many disputes end in nascent trade wars, members lose confidence in the multilateral trading system. To secure their market access and to obtain the greatest possible benefits from the multilateral regime, states have reason to lock open key markets by forming PTAs with crucial trade partners. Our results, therefore, indicate that not only have GATT/WTO rules done little to constrain the emergence of PTAs, developments within the multilateral trade regime have actually contributed to the rise of these arrangements.

Our findings have implications for the study of both economic regionalism and international relations. Scholars of international relations have devoted considerable attention to identifying the factors leading to the establishment of multilateral institutions. Far less effort, however, has been devoted to addressing whether and, if so, how these institutions influence state behavior.[108] In addition, too little effort has been made to address how changes within multilateral institutions affect the actions of members. Our analysis bears heavily on these issues. That GATT/WTO has influenced the behavior of its members is no surprise. After all, it is widely understood that this institution has generated substantial trade liberalization. More surprising, though, is that developments within it have systematically contributed to the formation of discriminatory commercial groupings. In ways not previously recognized, core features of the multilateral trading regime—such as its growing membership, dispute settlement system, and periodic negotiating rounds—have prompted states to enter preferential arrangements that clash with the regime's fundamental norm of nondiscrimination.

108. See Keohane 1984; and Martin and Simmons 1998, 743.

Of course, this situation does not imply that PTAs are welfare-degrading or that they will undermine the multilateral trading system. On the one hand, parties to GATT/WTO with protectionist interests may set up PTAs to countervail multilateral trade liberalization. Unlike unilateral measures such as raising tariffs, forming a preferential grouping allows states to discriminate against third parties without breaching GATT/WTO rules.[109] On the other hand, however, parties to GATT/WTO with an especially liberal orientation may set up PTAs because doing so allows them to achieve greater openness than could otherwise be realized in a multilateral setting.[110] Either possibility is consistent with our analysis, which is silent on the global welfare implications of preferential groupings.

During the past decade, a considerable amount of interest has been expressed in whether PTAs will be "building blocks" or "stumbling blocks" to greater multilateral liberalization.[111] Regardless of whether PTAs will bolster or undermine the WTO, our results point out the problems associated with ignoring the reverse line of causation, namely, how multilateral liberalization bears on the formation of PTAs. Furthermore, many studies have analyzed the conditions influencing whether states choose multilateral or bilateral strategies.[112] Our analysis suggests some conditions under which a multilateral approach is likely to grow less attractive, prompting states to pursue PTAs with greater intensity. But whereas existing studies often assume that states choose either bilateral or multilateral strategies, our findings also indicate that these strategies are not mutually exclusive. States frequently rely on both types of strategies simultaneously, for example, engaging in multilateral trade negotiations and establishing a PTA at the same time.[113]

In addition, the preceding results show that the determinants of PTA formation are not limited to developments within GATT/WTO. For instance, there is considerable evidence that the creation of preferential groupings is guided by strategic interaction.[114] As more country-pairs become covered by these groupings, the odds increase that those pairs that do not belong to the same PTA will establish one in response. As Alan Winters puts it, PTAs resemble street gangs: "you may not like them, but if they are in your neighborhood, it is safer to be in one."[115] PTA formation, however, is also marked by a saturation or ceiling effect. Once most dyads that could benefit by creating a preferential grouping have done so,

109. Pomfret 1997.

110. See Kahler 1992; and Westhoff, Yarbrough, and Yarbrough 1994. Westhoff, Yarbrough, and Yarbrough present a framework that helps to explain why PTAs might allow subsets of GATT/WTO members to generate more trade liberalization than is possible in the GATT/WTO setting, especially as the preferences of its members become more heterogeneous.

111. See Bhagwati 1993; and Lawrence 1996.

112. Yarbrough and Yarbrough 1992.

113. Kahler 1992. In U.S. Trade Representative Zoellick's words, "We can walk and chew gum at the same time." *Washington Post*, 20 November 2002, E3.

114. See Baldwin 1997; Fernández and Portes 1998; Mansfield 1998; Oye 1992; Pomfret 1997; and Yarbrough and Yarbrough 1992.

115. Quoted in Crawford and Laird 2001, 201.

the likelihood of PTA formation declines. Further, allies are more likely to enter into a PTA than other states, which accords with the argument that alliances help to internalize the security externalities stemming from arrangements that liberalize trade among participants. We also find some support for functionalist claims that international economic institutions tend to form in response to increasing interdependence and rising levels of economic exchange. The flow of trade is directly related to the establishment of PTAs, although its effect is substantively small.

Finally, domestic conditions influence whether states enter preferential arrangements. Democracies are more likely to join such arrangements than autocracies, economically smaller states are generally more likely to do so than their larger counterparts, and economic downturns tend to promote PTA formation. These findings highlight the obvious, but important, point that preferential trading arrangements are caused by various factors operating at different levels of analysis. As such, no single theoretical approach will suffice to explain their proliferation fully.

While our results shed new light on the links between the multilateral trade regime and PTAs, they also raise various questions for future research. For example, the form, trajectories, and duration of preferential trading agreements vary widely.[116] What determines the institutional form of a PTA—particularly whether it is a common market, a customs union, an FTA, or a different type of arrangement? Why are some PTAs—such as the Latin American Free Trade Association—never fully implemented, while others—like Mercosur—experience rapid consolidation?[117] Why do some FTAs ultimately evolve into customs unions (such as when former EFTA members joined the EU), while others do not? What explains whether a PTA "broadens" by adding new members, "deepens" its scope by covering policies and issues not previously included (such as labor or capital mobility, monetary policy, etc.), strengthens its implementation and enforcement mechanisms, or simply dies a quiet death? Answering these questions is sure to promote an improved understanding of regionalism, as well as the international political economy.

During the past half-century, GATT/WTO has met with considerable success in fostering multilateral trade liberalization. At the same time, however, its success has had various unintended consequences.[118] Here, we have identified one especially important consequence that has been largely overlooked. The very instruments of GATT/WTO's progress—its growing membership, active dispute settlement, and frequent trade negotiations—encourage states to seek bilateral options to secure the greatest possible benefits from the multilateral regime.

116. Smith 2000.

117. WTO 1995a, 34–35.

118. For discussion of the unintended—and often unwelcome—consequences of international institutions, see Martin and Simmons 1998, 749–51; and Barnett and Finnemore 1999.

## References

Andriamananjara, Soamiely, and Maurice Schiff. 2001. Regional Cooperation Among Microstates. *Review of International Economics* 9 (1):42–51.

Bagwell, Kyle, and Robert W. Staiger. 2001. Reciprocity, Non-Discrimination, and Preferential Agreements in the Multilateral Trading System. *European Journal of Political Economy* 17 (2):281–325.

Baldwin, Richard E. 1997. The Causes of Regionalism. *World Economy* 20 (7):865–88.

Barnett, Michael N., and Martha Finnemore. 1999. The Politics, Power, and Pathologies of International Organizations. *International Organization* 53 (4):699–732.

Beck, Nathaniel, Jonathan N. Katz, and Richard Tucker. 1998. Taking Time Seriously: Time-Series–Cross-Section Analysis with a Binary Dependent Variable. *American Journal of Political Science* 42 (4):1260–88.

Bennett, D. Scott, Jr., and Allan C. Stam, III. 1999. *EUGene: Expected Utility Generation and Data Management Program*, version 1.18. Pennsylvania State University. Available at ⟨www.eugenesoftware.org⟩.

Bhagwati, Jagdish. 1993. Regionalism and Multilateralism: An Overview. In *New Dimensions in Regional Integration*, edited by Jaime de Melo and Arvind Panagariya, 22–51. New York: Cambridge University Press.

Bhagwati, Jagdish, and Arvind Panagariya. 1996. Preferential Trading Areas and Multilateralism—Strangers, Friends, or Foes? In *The Economics of Preferential Trade Agreements*, edited by Jagdish Bhagwati and Arvind Panagariya, 1–78. Washington, D.C.: AEI Press.

Bowles, Paul. 1997. ASEAN, AFTA and the "New Regionalism." *Pacific Affairs* 70 (2):219–33.

Busch, Marc L., and Eric Reinhardt. 2002. Testing International Trade Law: Empirical Studies of GATT/WTO Dispute Settlement. In *The Political Economy of International Trade Law: Essays in Honor of Robert E. Hudec*, edited by Daniel L. M. Kennedy and James D. Southwick, 457–81. New York: Cambridge University Press.

———. 2003. Transatlantic Trade Conflicts and GATT/WTO Dispute Settlement. In *Dispute Prevention and Dispute Settlement in the Transatlantic Partnership*, edited by Ernst-Ulrich Petersmann and Mark Pollack. New York: Oxford University Press.

Correlates of War Project. 1993. Alliances Data. Unpublished manuscript, University of Michigan, Ann Arbor.

Crawford, Jo-Ann, and Sam Laird. 2001. Regional Trade Agreements and the WTO. *North American Journal of Economics and Finance* 12 (2):193–211.

Deardorff, Alan V. 1998. Determinants of Bilateral Trade: Does Gravity Work in a Neoclassical World? In *The Regionalization of the World Economy*, edited by Jeffrey A. Frankel, 7–22. Chicago: University of Chicago Press.

Downs, George W., David M. Rocke, and Peter N. Barsoom. 1998. Managing the Evolution of Multilateralism. *International Organization* 52 (2):397–419.

Dryden, Steve. 1995. *Trade Warriors: USTR and the American Crusade for Free Trade*. New York: Oxford University Press.

Ethier, Wilfred J. 1998. Regionalism in a Multilateral World. *Journal of Political Economy* 106 (6):1214–45.

———. 1999. Multilateral Roads to Liberalization. In *International Trade Policy and the Pacific Rim*, edited by John Piggott and Alan Woodland, 131–52. New York: St. Martin's.

Fernández, Raquel, and Jonathan Portes. 1998. Returns to Regionalism: An Evaluation of Nontraditional Gains from RTAs. *World Bank Economic Review* 12 (2):197–220.

Finger, J. Michael, Merlinda D. Ingco, and Ulrich Reincke. 1996. *The Uruguay Round: Statistics on Tariff Concessions Given and Received*. Washington, D.C.: World Bank.

Frankel, Jeffrey A. 1997. *Regional Trading Blocs in the World Economic System*. Washington, D.C.: Institute for International Economics.

Freund, Caroline L. 2000. Multilateralism and the Endogenous Formation of Preferential Trade Agreements. *Journal of International Economics* 52 (2):359–76.

Freund, Caroline L., and John McLaren. 1999. On the Dynamics of Trade Diversion: Evidence from Four Trade Blocs. International Finance Discussion Paper 637. Washington, D.C.: Board of Governors of the Federal Reserve System.

General Agreement on Tariffs and Trade (GATT). 1990. *GATT Activities, 1989: An Annual Review of the Work of the GATT*. Geneva: General Agreement on Tariffs and Trade.

———. 1994. Council of Representatives—Held in the Centre William Rappard on December 17, 1993. C/M/268. Geneva: General Agreement on Tariffs and Trade.

Gilpin, Robert. 1987. *The Political Economy of International Relations*. Princeton, N.J.: Princeton University Press.

Gowa, Joanne. 1994. *Allies, Adversaries, and International Trade*. Princeton, N.J.: Princeton University Press.

Gowa, Joanne, and Edward D. Mansfield. 1993. Power Politics and International Trade. *American Political Science Review* 87 (2):408–20.

Gurr, Ted Robert, and Keith Jaggers. 1999. *Polity 98: Regime Characteristics, 1800–1998*. Center for International Development and Conflict Management. College Park, Md.: University of Maryland. Available at ⟨www.cidcm.umd.edu/inscr/polity/⟩. Accessed 7 July 2003.

Hudec, Robert E. 1993. *Enforcing International Trade Law: The Evolution of the Modern GATT Legal System*. Salem, N.H.: Butterworth Legal Publishers.

Hudec, Robert E., and James D. Southwick. 1999. Regionalism and WTO Rules: Problems in the Fine Art of Discriminating Fairly. In *Trade Rules in the Making: Challenges in Regional and Multilateral Negotiations*, edited by Miguel Rodríguez Mendoza, Patrick Low, and Barbara Kotschwar, 47–80. Washington, D.C.: Organization of American States and Brookings Institution Press.

Inter-American Development Bank (IADB). 2000. *Periodic Note on Integration and Trade in the Americas*. Washington, D.C.: Inter-American Development Bank.

International Monetary Fund (IMF). 1998a. *Direction of Trade Statistics*. Washington, D.C.: IMF.

———. 1998b. *International Financial Statistics*. Washington, D.C.: IMF.

Jackson, John H. 1969. *World Trade and the Law of GATT*. Indianapolis: Bobbs-Merrill.

Jones, Daniel M., Stuart A. Bremer, and J. David Singer. 1996. Militarized Interstate Disputes, 1816–1992: Rationale, Coding Rules, and Empirical Patterns. *Conflict Management and Peace Science* 15 (2):163–213.

Kahler, Miles. 1992. Multilateralism with Small and Large Numbers. *International Organization* 46 (3):681–708.

Keohane, Robert O. 1984. *After Hegemony: Cooperation and Discord in the World Political Economy*. Princeton, N.J.: Princeton University Press.

King, Gary, and Langche Zeng. 2001. Explaining Rare Events in International Relations. *International Organization* 55 (3):693–715.

Koremenos, Barbara, Charles Lipson, and Duncan Snidal. 2001. The Rational Design of International Institutions. *International Organization* 55 (4):761–99.

Krugman, Paul. 1993. Regionalism Versus Multilateralism: Analytical Notes. In *New Dimensions in Regional Integration*, edited by Jaime de Melo and Arvind Panagariya, 58–79. New York: Cambridge University Press.

Lai, Brian, and Dan Reiter. 2000. Democracy, Political Similarity, and International Alliances, 1816–1992. *Journal of Conflict Resolution* 44 (2):203–27.

Lawrence, Robert Z. 1996. *Regionalism, Multilateralism, and Deeper Integration*. Washington, D.C.: Brookings Institution.

Ludema, Rodney D. 1996. On the Value of Preferential Trade Agreements in Multilateral Negotiations. Working Paper 97-22. Washington, D.C.: Georgetown University.

Mansfield, Edward D. 1993. Effects of International Politics on Regionalism in International Trade. In *Regional Integration and the Global Trading System*, edited by Kym Anderson and Richard Blackhurst, 199–217. New York: Harvester Wheatsheaf.

———. 1998. The Proliferation of Preferential Trading Arrangements. *Journal of Conflict Resolution* 42 (5):523–43.

Mansfield, Edward D., and Helen V. Milner. 1999. The New Wave of Regionalism. *International Organization* 53 (3):589–627.

Mansfield, Edward D., Helen V. Milner, and B. Peter Rosendorff. 2002. Why Democracies Cooperate More: Electoral Control and International Trade Agreements. *International Organization* 56 (3):477–513.

Martin, Lisa L., and Beth A. Simmons. 1998. Theories and Empirical Studies of International Institutions. *International Organization* 52 (4):729–57.

Mattli, Walter. 1999. *The Logic of Regional Integration: Europe and Beyond.* New York: Cambridge University Press.

Mavroidis, Petros C. 2000. Remedies in the WTO Legal System: Between a Rock and a Hard Place. *European Journal of International Law* 11 (4):763–813.

McCalman, Phillip. 2002. Multi-Lateral Trade Negotiations and the Most Favored Nation Clause. *Journal of International Economics* 57 (1):151–76.

Michalopoulos, Constantine. 1999. The Developing Countries in the WTO. *World Economy* 22 (1): 117–43.

Moore, Michael. 2000. WTO's Unique System of Settling Disputes Nears 200 Cases in 2000. PRESS/ 180. Geneva: World Trade Organization.

Oye, Kenneth A. 1992. *Economic Discrimination and Political Exchange: World Political Economy in the 1930s and 1980s.* Princeton, N.J.: Princeton University Press.

Özden, Çaglar, and Eric Reinhardt. 2003. The Perversity of Preferences: GSP and Developing Country Trade Policies, 1976–2000. Working Paper No. 2955. Washington, D.C.: World Bank.

Panagariya, Arvind. 2000. Preferential Trade Liberalization: The Traditional Theory and New Developments. *Journal of Economic Literature* 38 (2):287–331.

Perroni, Carlo, and John Whalley. 2000. The New Regionalism: Trade Liberalization or Insurance? *Canadian Journal of Economics* 33 (1):1–24.

Pomfret, Richard. 1997. *Unequal Trade: The Economics of Regional Trading Arrangements.* New York: Oxford University Press.

Preeg, Ernest H. 1995. *Traders in a Brave New World.* Chicago: University of Chicago Press.

Reinhardt, Eric. 2001. Adjudication Without Enforcement in GATT Disputes. *Journal of Conflict Resolution* 45 (2):174–95.

———. 2002. Tying Hands Without a Rope: Rational Domestic Response to International Institutional Constraints. In *Locating the Proper Authorities*, edited by Daniel Drezner, 75–102. Ann Arbor: University of Michigan Press.

———. Forthcoming. *Legislative Politics and GATT Trade Disputes, 1948–1994.* New York: Cambridge University Press.

Sampson, Gary P. 1996. Compatibility of Regional and Multilateral Trading Agreements: Reforming the WTO Process. *American Economic Review (Papers and Proceedings)* 86 (2):88–92.

Sapir, André. 2001. Domino Effects in Western European Regional Trade, 1960–1992. *European Journal of Political Economy* 17 (2):377–88.

Serra, Jaime, Guillermo Aguilar, José Córdoba, Gene Grossman, Carla Hills, John Jackson, Julius Katz, Pedro Noyola, and Michael Wilson. 1997. *Reflections on Regionalism: Report of the Study Group on International Trade.* Washington, D.C.: Carnegie Endowment for International Peace.

Smith, James McCall. 2000. The Politics of Dispute Settlement Design: Explaining Legalism in Regional Trade Pacts. *International Organization* 54 (1):137–80.

Summers, Robert, and Alan Heston. 1991. The Penn World Tables (Mark 5): An Expanded Set of International Comparisons, 1950–1988. *Quarterly Journal of Economics* 106 (2):327–68.

United States. 2000. *Economic Report of the President.* Washington, D.C.: Government Printing Office.

Viner, Jacob. 1950. *The Customs Union Issue.* New York: Carnegie Endowment for International Peace.

Westhoff, Frank H., Beth V. Yarbrough, and Robert M. Yarbrough. 1994. Preferential Trade Arrangements and the GATT: Can Bilateralism and Multilateralism Coexist? *Kyklos* 47 (2):179–95.

Whalley, John. 1998. Why Do Countries Seek Regional Trade Agreements? In *The Regionalization of the World Economy*, edited by Jeffrey A. Frankel, 63–83. Chicago: University of Chicago Press.

Winters, L. Alan, and Won Chang. 2000. Regional Integration and Import Prices: An Empirical Investigation. *Journal of International Economics* 51 (2):363–77.
World Bank. 2001. *World Development Indicators 2001 CD-ROM*. Washington, D.C.: World Bank.
World Trade Organization (WTO). 1995a. *Regionalism and the World Trading System*. Geneva: WTO.
———. 1995b. *Guide to GATT Law and Practice*, vol. 2. Geneva: WTO.
———. 1998. Membership of the World Trade Organization. WT/INF/6/Rev.4. Geneva: WTO.
———. 1999a. Report (1999) of the Committee on Regional Trade Agreements to the General Council. WT/REG/8. Geneva: WTO.
———. 1999b. Regional Trade Agreements Notified to the GATT/WTO and in Force in April 1999. Geneva: WTO.
———. 1999c. Overview of the State-of-Play of WTO Disputes. Geneva: WTO. Available at ⟨www.wto.org/english/tratop_e/dispu_e/stplay_e.doc⟩. Accessed 7 July 2003.
———. 2001. Negotiating Proposal on Behalf of Members of the Caribbean Community (CARICOM). G/AG/NG/W/100. Geneva: WTO.
Yarbrough, Beth V., and Robert M. Yarbrough. 1992. *Cooperation and Governance in International Trade: The Strategic Organizational Approach*. Princeton, N.J.: Princeton University Press.
———. 1997. Dispute Settlement in International Trade: Regionalism and Procedural Coordination. In *The Political Economy of Regionalism*, edited by Edward D. Mansfield and Helen V. Milner, 134–63. New York: Columbia University Press.

# The Expansion of Preferential Trading Arrangements

EDWARD D. MANSFIELD
*University of Pennsylvania*

AND

JON C.W. PEVEHOUSE
*University of Wisconsin*

The growing number of preferential trading arrangements (PTAs) since World War II has generated substantial interest in their economic and political effects. It has also prompted interest in the factors that give rise to PTAs, but very little research has been conducted on the growth of extant PTAs. To address this shortcoming, we analyze why some arrangements expand, whereas others do not. We find strong evidence that expansion is most likely when the existing members of a PTA display a high degree of trade openness and when the size distribution of these members is fairly uniform. We also find that PTAs that add new members are likely to do so again in the near future and that, throughout the global system, PTAs tend to expand in clusters. Equally, there is some indication that the market size of a PTA affects its odds of expansion. Finally, we investigate which states join enlarging PTAs. We find that PTAs expand by taking on new members that are economically and politically similar to existing members.

Since the conclusion of World War II, there has been tremendous growth in both the number of preferential trading arrangements (PTAs) and the number of countries that are party to them. This development has generated substantial interest in the effects of PTAs on the welfare of states and the stability of the international trading system. It has also prompted interest in the factors that give rise to PTAs. Almost all of the latter research examines why new PTAs form or why states elect to enter such arrangements. Yet, much of the growth of PTAs stems from existing arrangements taking on additional members. Except for the literature addressing the enlargement of the European Union (EU), however, very little research has focused on the growth of extant PTAs. The purpose of this paper is to help fill this gap by analyzing why some PTAs expand, while others do not.

The paper proceeds in three parts. Initially, we assess whether any general patterns exist in the formation and expansion of PTAs during the period since World War II. PTAs are institutions that grant each member preferential access to the other participants' markets and that are designed to foster economic integration among member-states. We find that bilateral arrangements (i.e., those comprised of two members that grant each other reciprocal preferences) and "hub and spoke" agreements (i.e., those in which one state or set of states grants unilateral preferences to other members that are not reciprocated) almost never expand. By contrast, over half of the multilateral PTAs (i.e., those comprised of more than two members, all of which grant the other participants reciprocal preferences) formed during this era have taken on additional members after their inception.

Second, we analyze the factors influencing which multilateral PTAs expand and when they do so. We find strong evidence that enlargement is most likely when the existing members display a high degree of trade openness and when the size distribution of these members is fairly uniform. We also find that PTAs that add new members are likely to do so again in the near future and that, throughout the global system, PTAs tend to expand in clusters. Equally, there is some indication that the market size of a PTA affects its odds of expansion: economically large arrangements are more likely to grow than smaller ones, although this result is less robust than the others. Finally, we investigate which states join enlarging PTAs. We find that these arrangements tend to expand by adding members that are economically and politically similar to existing participants.

### Patterns of PTA Formation

Although all PTAs grant member-states preferential market access, they differ in various respects (Pomfret 1988; de Melo and Panagariya 1993). Some—which we refer to as partial arrangements—grant preferential access to only select segments of members' markets. Free trade areas (FTA) eliminate trade barriers on many, if not all, products within the arrangement. Customs unions eliminate trade barriers on the participants' goods and erect a common external tariff (CET) on imports from third parties. Common markets are customs unions marked by similar product regulations and the free flow of factors of production among members. Economic unions are common markets in which members also coordinate fiscal and monetary policies (Balassa 1961).

As shown in Figure 1, PTAs have proliferated rapidly over the past 60 years. During this era, hundreds of these institutions have formed and by the turn of the twenty-first century, almost every country participated in at least one. Since World War II, there have been two waves of

*Authors' note:* Earlier versions of this paper were presented at a conference on "The Politics of Preferential Trade Agreements," held at Princeton University, April 30-May 1, 2010, the World Congress of the International Political Science Association, Madrid, July 8–12, 2012, and a seminar at the University of Virginia. We are grateful to the participants at these events, two anonymous reviewers, and Christina Davis, Lisa Martin, and William Thompson for useful comments and suggestions. The data used in this article are available from the authors or from the *ISQ* data archive.

Mansfield, Edward D. and Jon C.W. Pevehouse. (2013) The Expansion of Preferential Trading Arrangements. *International Studies Quarterly*, doi: 10.1111/isqu.12064
© 2013 International Studies Association

PTAs (Bhagwati 1993; Mansfield and Milner 1999). The first wave began during the late 1950s and lasted roughly two decades; the second began during the late 1980s and early 1990s.

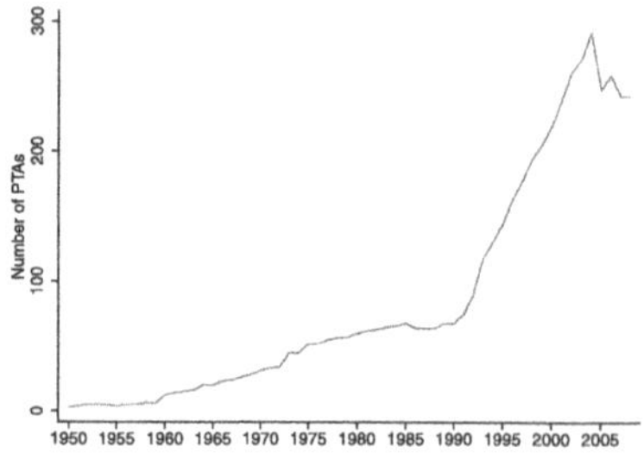


FIG 1. The Distribution of PTAs over Time, 1950–2007.

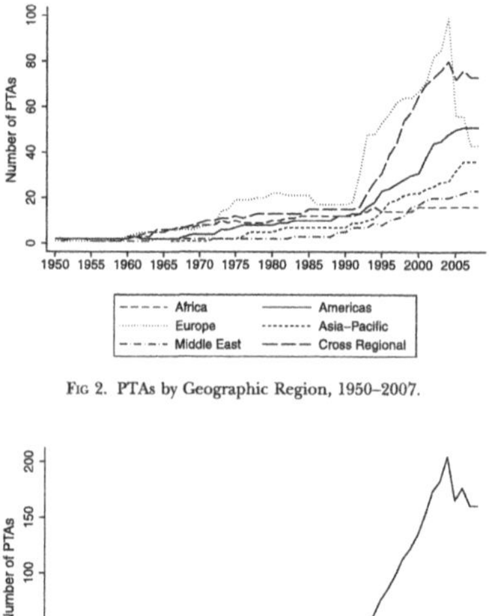


FIG 2. PTAs by Geographic Region, 1950–2007.

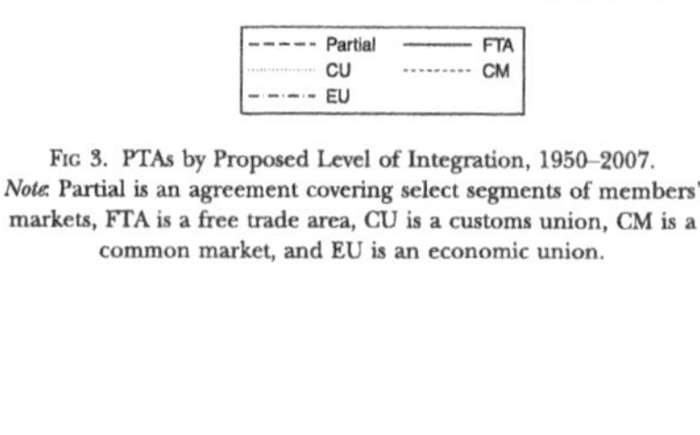


FIG 3. PTAs by Proposed Level of Integration, 1950–2007.
*Note*: Partial is an agreement covering select segments of members' markets, FTA is a free trade area, CU is a customs union, CM is a common market, and EU is an economic union.

Figure 2 indicates that every region of the world has experienced an increase in the number of PTAs over time. The number of cross-regional arrangements has risen as well. However, different types of arrangements have proliferated at different rates. As shown in Figure 3, there has been a steady increase in the number of customs unions, common markets, and economic unions. The number of partial arrangements has grown at a more rapid clip. Most dramatic, however, has been the spike in FTAs over the past two decades.

In Figure 4, we distinguish among PTAs by whether they are bilateral, multilateral, or hub and spoke agreements. Both multilateral PTAs and hub and spoke agreements display a fairly gentle upward slope. Bilateral PTAs, by contrast, experienced a substantial jump beginning around 1990. Their numbers peaked soon after the turn of the century and then declined slightly over the past 5 years.

Taken together, Figures 3 and 4 reveal that there has been a dramatic rise in bilateral FTAs over the past 20 years. This development has been fueled in large measure by the collapse of the Berlin Wall and the decision by the United States to start negotiating preferential arrangements (Lawrence 1996; Mansfield and Milner 1999). The end of the Cold War and the demise of the Soviet Union created a large number of former communist countries that aimed to become more fully integrated into the world economy. They also feared being frozen out of key markets, as countries throughout Europe rushed to establish preferential groupings (Baldwin 1995a). The result was a spate of PTA formation involving (and, in many cases, between) states that were former Soviet republics or former Soviet allies.

At the same time, the United States changed its position on PTAs. Whereas the United States had long eschewed entering these arrangements, protracted and deep-seated difficulties concluding the Uruguay Round convinced the George H. W. Bush Administration that establishing some PTAs would increase its bargaining power in the General Agreement on Tariffs and Trade (GATT) negotiations and create a safety net if the round collapsed (Hufbauer and Schott 2005). Equally, the United States began to consider preferential arrangements as

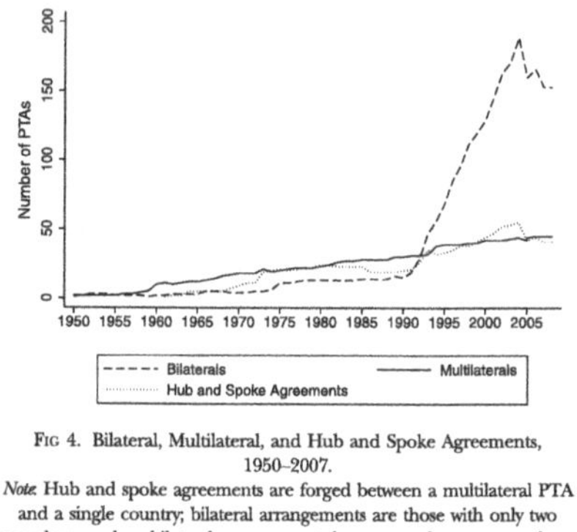


FIG 4. Bilateral, Multilateral, and Hub and Spoke Agreements, 1950–2007.
*Note*: Hub and spoke agreements are forged between a multilateral PTA and a single country; bilateral arrangements are those with only two members; and multilateral arrangements have more than two members (excluding hub and spoke agreements).

vehicles to reward politically valuable countries, especially in the Middle East. These views continued to hold sway in the administrations of Bill Clinton and George W. Bush.

Most of the groupings concluded as a result of both the Cold War's end and the US decision to pursue PTAs were bilateral FTAs. For states that had been in the Soviet orbit, there was a pressing need to form such arrangements quickly. It was easier for pairs of countries to strike deals than for larger groups of states to do so. Moreover, FTAs are self-enforcing agreements that do not require the contracting parties to establish much institutional infrastructure, set a CET, or coordinate a wide range of economic policies. For the United States, entering bilateral rather than multilateral agreements enhanced its influence over the other participating countries (Hufbauer and Schott 2005:6). In exchange for preferential access to the large, lucrative US market, it could negotiate favorable terms, especially if it bargained with countries sequentially, rather than in groups. Equally, entering FTAs rather than customs unions, common markets, or economic unions allowed the United States to avoid coordinating internationally on economic issues other than trade policy.

The recent decline in bilateral FTAs (see Figures 3 and 4) has stemmed from the EU's expansion. Many of the same central European states that rushed to form bilateral FTAs after the fall of the Soviet Union (e.g., Poland, Hungary, the Czech Republic, and Slovakia) were either forced to dissolve those arrangements as a condition of EU accession or replaced them with EU membership. Thus, while bilateral groupings and FTAs remain much more common than other types of PTAs, EU expansion accounts for their recent decline.

### The Expansion of PTAs

Hundreds of PTAs have formed over the past 60 years. Some have expanded by taking on additional members, although most have not. A number of studies have advanced arguments about why and how PTA enlargement occurs (Baldwin 1995a; Downs, Rocke, and Barsoom 1998; Mattli 1999). Most of the work on this topic, however, has focused on the European Community (EC) and the EU (Pahre 1995; Moravcsik and Vachudova 2003; Schimmelfennig and Sedelmeier 2005; Vachudova 2005). We are unaware of any systemic analyses of which PTAs expand, an important gap that this paper should help to fill.

To begin, we address whether there are discernable patterns in the expansion of PTAs across either the region in which member-states are located or the type of arrangement. As we show more fully later, there is no strong tendency for expansion to vary across either geographic regions or the depth of integration that the arrangement aims to achieve (i.e., whether it is a partial arrangement, an FTA, a customs union, a common market, or an economic union).

By contrast, there is a striking tendency for neither bilateral nor hub and spoke agreements to grow. There are only one or two instances of a bilateral PTA taking on a new member. The Mano River Union, formed by Liberia and Sierra Leone in 1973, added Guinea in 1980. Canada and the United States, which had formed the Canada–United States Free Trade Agreement (CUFTA) in 1988, joined with Mexico to establish the North American Free Trade Agreement (NAFTA) in 1994. The latter agreement superseded the former, although there is some disagreement about whether NAFTA was an outgrowth of CUFTA. Regardless, there are no other instances of a bilateral PTA expanding. Similarly, the Lomé Convention was formed in 1976 by the EC and various African, Caribbean, and Pacific countries. This agreement has been renegotiated several times since then, adding various members each time.[1] Nonetheless, it is the only hub and spoke agreements that expanded. Most of these arrangements are negotiated in a manner similar to bilateral arrangements: the existing PTA bargains with a single country over what market access will be granted to this "spoke."

There are various reasons why these PTAs rarely expand. As we mentioned earlier, hub and spoke arrangements involve a state or group of states granting unilateral preferences to another state or group of states. Frequently, these are countries that had a colonial relationship. Hub and spoke arrangements are usually highly specific, covering a very narrow range of goods and services and are often designed to reinforce trade relations and solidify the metropole's influence after its colony gains independence. Consequently, such arrangements tend to be customized to serve the very particular trade relationship of the original signatories. These states are unlikely to have much interest in adding spokes, and states outside the arrangements are unlikely to view membership in an existing hub and spoke arrangement as attractive.

Like hub and spoke arrangements, bilateral PTAs are established for reasons that limit the prospects of expansion. Some of these arrangements are set up by a large power and a smaller state. The United States, as we mentioned earlier, has formed a series of bilateral PTAs over the past few decades. Frequently, bilateralism allows the large member to increase its influence over the smaller member by exploiting the smaller state's economic dependence and hence its interest in gaining preferential and stable access to a sizable market (Kahler 1992). When bilateral PTAs are set up for this purpose, the larger member will have little interest in adding members to an existing grouping, preferring instead to establish new bilateral arrangements with prospective PTA partners. More common, however, are bilateral PTAs that do not involve a major power. These institutions rarely, if ever, have a formal organizational structure (Koremenos, Lipson, and Snidal 2001:762; Gray 2010). Instead, they are self-enforcing agreements that rely on "economic 'hostages', reciprocity, and issue linkages" (Yarbrough and Yarbrough 1992:68). This very sparse institutional structure limits the specter of expansion. For a self-enforcing agreement to hold, each party must conclude that the expected value of compliance exceeds the expected value of violating the agreement. As the number of members increases, the odds that each party will arrive at this conclusion decrease. More generally, taking on additional members increases distributional problems and the need for monitoring within the PTA. Lacking the institutional infrastructure needed to address these problems, bilateral PTAs are unlikely to expand (Yarbrough and Yarbrough 1992).

Multilateral PTAs, in contrast, do not face the same impediments to enlargement as hub and spoke arrangements or bilateral PTAs, and they have expanded with

[1] The Lomé Convention is currently referred to as the Contonou Agreement.

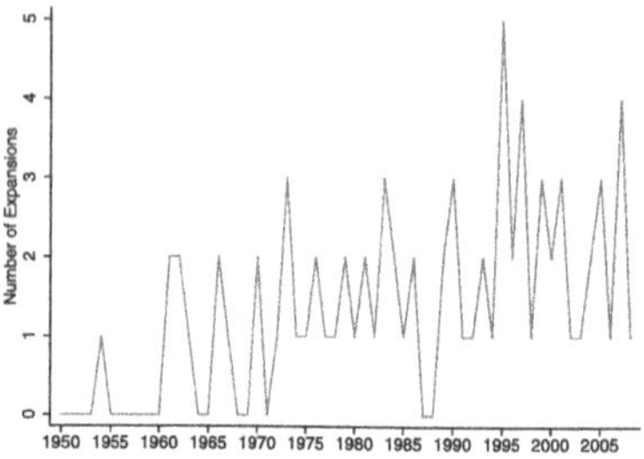


FIG 5. The Number of Multilateral PTA Expansions over Time, 1950–2007.

much greater frequency. In fact, of the 63 multilateral arrangements that formed after World War II, 37 have expanded at least once and 15 of them have taken on new members at least twice. As shown in Figure 5, there is little evidence of any trend over time in this process. What explains the growth of multilateral PTAs? In this paper, we focus on four factors: (i) the PTA's market size, (ii) its members' trade openness, (iii) the size distribution of its members, and (iv) whether other multilateral PTAs throughout the global system have recently expanded.

First, various economic studies conclude that PTAs form to enlarge the size of the market over which members have preferential access. A larger market creates advantages for firms in member-states, expanding their export opportunities, allowing them to realize economies of scale in production, and promoting competition (Balassa 1961:36–38; Pomfret 1988; de Melo and Panagariya 1993). It also bolsters the economic power of participants, improving their terms of trade vis-á-vis third parties and their influence in multilateral trade negotiations (Lawrence 1996; Fernández and Portes 1998; Whalley 1998).

Likewise, PTAs may expand in an effort to increase the market size and economic power of the constituent states. For PTAs covering a small market, taking on an additional member may be attractive, but doing so is unlikely to generate much additional economic and bargaining power unless the new party is quite large. PTAs with a relatively large market, by contrast, already possess some influence in the world economy. The existing members may view expansion as a means of becoming even more influential, helping to shape the global trading system and wielding power in their relations with third parties. In a similar vein, PTAs can provide members with insurance in the event of a global trade war or the erosion of the multilateral trading system (Whalley 1998). By increasing the size of the market covered by the PTA, taking on new members can augment the extent of that insurance.

Further, prospective members are likely to be drawn to PTAs covering a larger market. Indeed, this claim is at the heart of Baldwin's (1995a, 2008) "domino theory" of regionalism. Baldwin argues that remaining outside a large PTA is especially costly for exporters because they have restricted access to the grouping's sizable market and firms located in member-states experience efficiency gains as the result of competing in this market. As the PTA grows larger, so do the costs stemming from being a third party. Consequently, we expect countries to express a particular interest in entering PTAs with bigger internal markets. PTAs covering a larger aggregate market are therefore more likely to expand than their smaller counterparts.

Second, we expect that PTAs made up of states that are open with respect to trade will be more likely to expand than those comprised of states that are closed. If one purpose of expanding a PTA is to increase the commercial opportunities for member-states, then PTAs composed of countries that already trade extensively and depend on overseas commerce are more likely to expand than those where the participants are relatively closed. More generally, Pahre (2008: chapter 8) argues that states marked by lower trade barriers and extensive openness are especially likely to enter trade agreements and to cooperate on overseas commerce. This logic implies that such states may also be likely to expand those agreements to which they are already a party. Further, Pahre suggests that agreements among commercially open states tend to be quite stable. This and the fact that commercially open PTA members are generally better and more reliable trade partners than closed members is likely to spur states considering entry into a preferential arrangement to select one characterized by extensive openness.

Third, the size distribution of members is likely to affect whether a PTA expands. Previous research has found that the size distribution of participants affects how effectively these groupings function. In particular, some studies have argued that an asymmetric distribution of economic power within PTAs helps to solve collective action problems because the largest member-state is better able to act as a privileged group and provide public goods for the arrangement (Deutsch, Burrell, Kann, Lee, Lichterman, Lindgren, Lowenheim, and Van Wagenen 1957; Russett 1967). But doing so is expensive for the large state, and these costs increase as the size of the PTA —and thus the amount of the public good that is required—increases, unless the grouping adds a member that is big enough to help share the burden of public goods provision. If a new participant is sufficiently large, however, then it may challenge the existing leader, seeking to alter the PTA in a way that serves its interests and threatens those of the leader. Consequently, in PTAs marked by a high concentration of power, the leading state(s) has reason to oppose expansion. Arrangements in which members are more uniformly sized are more likely to expand.

Fourth, various studies have argued that PTA formation and expansion are guided by strategic interdependence. More specifically, there is reason to expect that PTAs take on new members in reaction to each other, giving rise to positive contagion in PTA expansion (e.g., Pomfret 1988; Yarbrough and Yarbrough 1992; Baldwin 1995a; Fernández and Portes 1998; Baldwin and Jaimovich 2010; Mansfield and Milner 2012). A PTA's growth, for example, may prompt fears by third parties that the enlarged arrangement will degrade their competitiveness, thereby leading them to apply for entry into a rival bloc. In the same vein, a state joining a PTA may generate concern by its economic competitors (outside the bloc) that this state's preferential access to an expanded market will furnish it with a competitive advantage, prompting its rivals to join other PTAs to obtain similar benefits. Furthermore, PTAs may expand in reaction to each other because adding members enhances a preferential arrangement's market power and bargaining power, thereby eroding the power of PTAs that do not expand and states that remain outside of these groupings.

## The Empirical Analysis

To test these arguments, we estimate the following model:

$$\begin{aligned}\text{PTA E}{\small\text{XPANSION}}_i = {} & \beta_0 + \beta_1 \text{M}{\small\text{ARKET}}\ \text{S}{\small\text{IZE}}_i + \beta_2 \text{O}{\small\text{PENNESS}}_i \\ & + \beta_3 \text{C}{\small\text{ONCENTRATION}}_i \\ & + \beta_4 \text{S}{\small\text{YSTEM}}\ \text{E}{\small\text{XPANSION}}_i \\ & + \beta_5 \text{T}{\small\text{IME}}\ \text{S}{\small\text{INCE}}\ \text{E}{\small\text{XPANSION}}_i + \varepsilon_i \end{aligned} \tag{1}$$

In this model, PTA Expansion$_i$ is the log of the odds of the $i^{th}$ multilateral PTA expanding in year $t + 1$, where we observe 1 if expansion occurs and 0 otherwise.[2] Our unit of analysis is the PTA year. This marks a departure from previous studies of PTA membership, which tend to focus on state-level decisions to join these groupings.

Among the independent variables, Market Size$_i$ is the total gross domestic product (GDP) in real terms of the countries comprising the $i^{th}$ PTA in year $t$; Openness$_i$ is the average openness—defined as the ratio of the sum of exports and imports to GDP—of the states in the $i^{th}$ PTA in year $t$; and System Expansion$_i$ is the number of instances of multilateral PTA expansion throughout the global system in year $t$, excluding any expansions involving the $i^{th}$ PTA.[3] To measure Concentration$_i$, we rely on a widely used index (Singer, Bremer, and Stuckey 1972; Mansfield 1994):

$$\text{C}{\small\text{ONCENTRATION}}_i = \sqrt{\frac{\sum_{i=1}^{N_i}(S_{ij}^2) - \frac{1}{N_i}}{1 - \frac{1}{N_i}}} \tag{2}$$

In equation (2), $S_{ij}$ is the proportion of the aggregate GDP in the $i^{th}$ PTA that member-state $j$ possesses and $N_i$ is the number of members in this PTA in year $t$. Finally, $\varepsilon_i$ is a stochastic error term.

This analysis covers the period from 1950 to 2007, since most empirical research on PTAs has focused on the post-World War II era. Because the observed value of our dependent variable is dichotomous, we use logistic regression to estimate model (1). To account for any temporal dependence in the data, we include the base of a spline function in the model (Beck, Katz, and Tucker 1998).[4] More specifically, Time Since Expansion$_i$ is the length of time since the $i^{th}$ PTA last expanded, as of year $t$.[5] To conduct tests of statistical significance, we rely on standard errors that are clustered by PTA to account for the grouped nature of the data.

Table 1. Descriptive Statistics

| *Variable* | *N* | *Mean* | *Standard Dev.* | *Min.* | *Max.* |
|---|---|---|---|---|---|
| PTA Expansion | 1242 | 0.058 | 0.234 | 0 | 1 |
| Time Since Expansion | 1242 | 9.599 | 10.248 | 0 | 57 |
| Concentration | 1242 | 0.451 | 0.187 | 0.273 | 0.986 |
| Market Size | 1242 | 1.302 | 2.521 | 0.002 | 18.283 |
| Openness | 1242 | 0.076 | 0.029 | 0.023 | 0.211 |
| System Expansion | 1242 | 1.771 | 1.208 | 0 | 5 |
| Africa | 1242 | 0.348 | 0.476 | 0 | 1 |
| Americas | 1242 | 0.210 | 0.408 | 0 | 1 |
| Europe | 1242 | 0.149 | 0.356 | 0 | 1 |
| Asia-Pacific | 1242 | 0.093 | 0.290 | 0 | 1 |
| Middle East | 1242 | 0.112 | 0.315 | 0 | 1 |
| Free Trade Area | 1242 | 0.169 | 0.375 | 0 | 1 |
| Customs Union | 1242 | 0.239 | 0.427 | 0 | 1 |
| Common Market | 1242 | 0.326 | 0.469 | 0 | 1 |
| Economic Union | 1242 | 0.020 | 0.140 | 0 | 1 |
| $V_i$ | 1242 | 1.036 | 0.442 | 0.039 | 2.648 |
| $\sqrt{N_i - 1}$ | 1242 | 2.427 | 0.957 | 1 | 7.141 |
| Age | 1242 | 16.475 | 12.584 | 1 | 58 |
| Currency Union | 1228 | 0.102 | 0.257 | 0 | 1 |
| Allies | 1078 | 0.649 | 0.423 | 0 | 1 |
| System States | 1242 | 0.864 | 0.145 | 0.173 | 0.974 |
| Joining System States | 1242 | 0.159 | 0.100 | 0 | 0.396 |
| Major Powers | 1242 | 0.138 | 0.345 | 0 | 1 |
| GATT Round | 1242 | 0.387 | 0.487 | 0 | 1 |
| ΔGATT Size | 1184 | 2.212 | 4.195 | 0 | 20 |
| Post-Cold War | 1242 | 0.505 | 0.500 | 0 | 1 |
| Hegemony | 1242 | 0.227 | 0.033 | 0.187 | 0.417 |
| Democracy | 1215 | 0.383 | 6.338 | −9.667 | 10 |
| MIDs | 1242 | 0.333 | 0.842 | 0 | 11 |
| Development | 1242 | 8657.705 | 8950.945 | 670.377 | 48650.56 |
| Trade | 1170 | 1735.973 | 11037.0 | 0 | 132156.4 |
| States Contiguous | 1228 | 0.410 | 0.273 | 0 | 1 |
| Legalism | 1073 | 1.809 | 1.829 | 0 | 5 |
| Number of Prior Expansions | 1242 | 0.970 | 1.349 | 0 | 7 |

Descriptive statistics for the variables in model (1) and the other variables that we analyze later are shown in Table 1. Our initial results, which are reported in the first column of Table 2, indicate that each of the four independent variables in this model has a strong effect on PTA expansion. The coefficient estimates of Market Size$_i$ and Openness$_i$ are positive, those of Concentration$_i$, System Expansion$_i$, and Time Since Expansion$_i$ are negative,

[2] Data on multilateral PTAs are taken from Mansfield and Milner (2012).

[3] Data on openness are taken from the Penn World Table (Heston, Summers, and Aten 2009). Data on GDP are taken from the World Bank's *World Development Indicators* (2009).

[4] Although the inclusion of the base of the spline function (i.e., Time Since Expansion$_i$) mimics an event history model, we also formally re-estimate the baseline model as both a Cox proportional hazard model and a Weibull model. In both cases, the results are substantively identical to those presented below.

[5] Such analyses typically include both the base of the spline function and a set of (usually three) knots. However, we found no evidence that any of the knots affect PTA expansion.

TABLE 2. Determinants of PTA Expansion, 1950–2007.

| | *Model 1* | *Model 2* | *Model 3* | *Model 4* | *Model 5* | *Model 6* | *Model 7* | *Model 8* |
|---|---|---|---|---|---|---|---|---|
| Market Size | 0.070 (0.031) ** | 0.078 (0.034) ** | 0.046 (0.035) | 0.102 (0.026) *** | 0.096 (0.056)* | 0.021 (0.058) | 0.053 (0.039) | 0.065 (0.031) ** |
| Openness | 11.271 (3.779) *** | 10.882 (3.409) *** | 11.627 (4.081) *** | 11.573 (3.724) *** | 13.195 (4.619) *** | 11.791 (4.097) *** | 10.993 (3.892) ** | 11.288 (4.054) ** |
| Concentration | −2.132 (0.663) *** | −2.014 (0.742) *** | −2.110 (0.672) *** | −2.044 (0.834) ** | −2.260 (0.664) *** | −1.826 (0.803) ** | −1.986 (0.639) *** | – |
| Time Since Expansion | −0.073 (0.027) *** | −0.068 (0.025) ** | −0.077 (0.029) *** | −0.073 (0.026) *** | −0.067 (0.027) ** | −0.078 (0.027) *** | −0.085 (0.028) *** | −0.075 (0.028) *** |
| System Expansion | −0.282 (0.126) ** | −0.301 (0.125) ** | −0.186 (0.114) | −0.248 (0.124) ** | −0.355 (0.391) | −0.254 (0.132)* | −0.255 (0.131)* | −0.278 (0.128) ** |
| Free Trade Agreement | – | 0.561 (0.420) | – | – | – | – | – | – |
| Customs Union | – | 0.060 (0.344) | – | – | – | – | – | – |
| Common Market | – | 0.443 (0.301) | – | – | – | – | – | – |
| European Union | – | 0.371 (0.283) | – | – | – | – | – | – |
| Legalism | – | – | 0.024 (0.072) | – | – | – | – | – |
| Trade | – | – | – | 0.00002 (0.000016) | – | – | – | – |
| Africa | – | – | – | – | – | −0.397 (0.369) | – | – |
| Americas | – | – | – | – | – | −0.018 (0.421) | – | – |
| Europe | – | – | – | – | – | 0.494 (0.579) | – | – |
| Asia—Pacific | – | – | – | – | – | −0.348 (0.427) | – | – |
| Middle East | – | – | – | – | – | −0.200 (0.427) | – | – |
| $V_i$ | – | – | – | – | – | – | – | −0.920 (0.127) *** |
| $\sqrt{N_i - 1}$ | – | – | – | – | – | – | – | 0.296 (0.127) ** |
| Constant | −1.934 (0.406) *** | −2.267 (0.531) *** | −2.108 (0.488) *** | −2.078 (0.431) *** | −2.656 (1.813) *** | −1.970 (0.557) *** | −1.945 (0.427) *** | −2.638 (0.447) *** |
| N | 1242 | 1242 | 1073 | 1170 | 1040 | 1242 | 1192 | 1242 |

(*Note.* Entries are logistic regression estimates with robust standard errors in parentheses. Standard errors are clustered on the PTA. Column 5 contains year-specific fixed effects, which are omitted from the table to save space. Column 7 excludes the EC/EU. Statistical significance is indicated as follows: ***$p < .01$; **$p < .05$; *$p < .10$. All tests of statistical significance are two-tailed.)

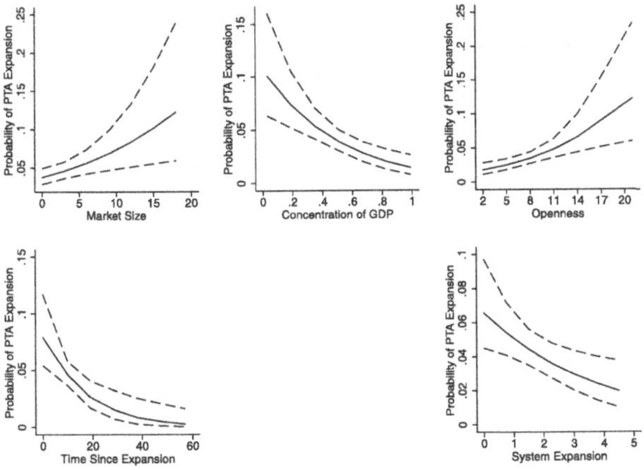


FIG 6. Predicted Probability of PTA Expansion.

*Note:* Each graph presents the predicted probability of a multilateral PTA expanding, based on the results in the first column of Table 2. Probabilities are calculated over the range of values observed in the data for each of the five independent variables. Dashed lines represent 95% confidence intervals.

and all five estimates are statistically significant. Furthermore, the effects of these variables are fairly sizable.

Figure 6 presents five graphs containing the predicted probabilities (along with 95% confidence intervals) of PTA expansion, calculated over the range of values of our independent variables. For each graph, the baseline probability of a PTA expanding in year $t + 1$ is 0.04. The upper left graph shows the predicted probability of PTA expansion in a given year as the value of MARKET SIZE$_i$ increases (measured in trillions of constant US dollars). Initially, the probability rises gradually; it then grows more rapidly once MARKET SIZE$_i$ exceeds \$10 trillion. Increasing the mean value of MARKET SIZE$_i$ by one standard deviation yields about a 20% spike in the probability of a PTA taking on a new member.[6]

The upper right graph shows the effect of trade openness within a PTA. Like MARKET SIZE$_i$, the effect of OPENNESS$_i$ becomes more marked as this variable grows larger. However, its influence is even more sizable. A one standard deviation increase in the mean value of OPENNESS$_i$ generates nearly a 40% jump in the predicted probability of PTA expansion.

The remaining three graphs show the influence of CONCENTRATION$_i$, SYSTEM EXPANSION$_i$, and TIME SINCE EXPANSION$_i$ on the probability of enlarging a PTA. As GDP concentration declines, creating a more uniform distribution, the probability of PTA expansion rises. A one standard deviation increase in the mean of this variable, generating a more asymmetric distribution, leads to about one-third drop in the predicted probability of expansion. Similarly, we find considerable evidence that PTA expansions tend to cluster together in certain years, suggesting that these groupings take on new members in reaction to each other. The more enlargements that occur throughout the international system in 1 year, the lower the odds that any given PTA will grow in the subsequent year. A one standard deviation increase in the mean number of PTA expansions occurring in year $t$ yields a 30% reduction in the predicted probability that PTA $i$ will add a member in year $t + 1$. Finally, in the first 3 years after a given PTA adds a member, the probability of its further expansion roughly doubles, indicating that these arrangements tend to enlarge quickly when they do expand. This effect falls off rapidly, however. By about 12 years after taking on a new member, the probability of future expansion falls below the baseline probability of PTA growth.

More generally, PTAs that expand once tend to do so again in the near future. This may reflect a tendency for certain groupings to appear particularly attractive to prospective members or for the founding members of certain arrangements to have an ongoing interest in enlarging the institution. It is also consistent with Baldwin's domino theory. As he points out, once a new member is added, "the PTA enlargement implies that discrimination facing the remaining nonmembers expands and this again heightens the pro-membership political economy forces in outsiders, potentially producing a membership application from an outsider that previously found it politically optimal to stay out. The cycle repeats itself until a new political equilibrium membership in the PTA obtains" (Baldwin 2008:34).

### The Effects of Institutional Characteristics of PTAs

PTAs are a broad class of trade agreements marked by substantial institutional diversity. One key source of such variation is the depth of cooperation and integration among members. Some observers have argued that deeper PTAs are less likely to expand than shallower arrange-

[6] This and other marginal effects we report are calculated after holding the remaining variables in the model at their mean values.

ments. Deeper arrangements cover a wider variety of issues, increasing the complexity of the process of acceding to the PTA and the range of policies to which candidates for membership must agree to adhere (Baldwin 1995b; Kahler 1995). Other observers, however, maintain that deep PTAs promote expansion by reducing the competitiveness of shallower arrangements and thereby attracting prospective members (Baldwin 1995a; Pahre 1995).[7] To address this issue, we analyze three indicators of PTA depth: (i) the extent of integration that the preferential grouping aims to achieve, (ii) whether the grouping is marked by a formal dispute settlement mechanism (DSM), and (iii) the volume of trade among the grouping's members.

The degree of proposed integration among PTA members is lowest in partial arrangements and grows progressively greater in FTAs, customs unions, common markets, and economic unions, respectively. To address whether the likelihood of PTA expansion depends on the degree of proposed integration, we define variables indicating whether each arrangement was designed to grant partial preferences, to be an FTA, a customs union, a common market, or an economic union. We arbitrarily designate partial arrangements as the reference category. As shown in the second column of Table 2, none of the estimated coefficients of these variables are statistically significant and a likelihood ratio test provides no evidence that we should include these variables as a group ($\chi^2 = 3.11$; $p = .54$). Furthermore, pairwise tests indicate that no individual coefficient estimate pertaining to the level of proposed integration is statistically distinct from any other individual estimate of this sort. As such, the likelihood of expansion does not seem to depend on the extent to which a PTA aims to promote integration among member-states.

Nor is the likelihood of expansion affected by whether PTAs are marked by a formal DSM that can help to adjudicate economic conflicts between members and enforce the terms on which these disputes are settled. To address this institutional feature, we include LEGALISM$_i$, a six-point index that ranges from 0 to 5 and that is constructed using McCall Smith's (2000) criteria for measuring DSMs within these arrangements, where higher values of this index reflect more fully developed and institutionalized dispute settlement procedures. The results, shown in the third column of Table 2, indicate that LEGALISM$_i$ has a very weak effect on PTA expansion. The estimated coefficient of this variable is positive, but it is relatively small and far from statistically significant.

Finally, we consider the effects of TRADE$_{it}$, which is the mean volume of dyadic trade within a PTA in year $t$.[8] Previous empirical work has used the volume of trade to measure the depth of cooperation within a preferential grouping (Downs, Rocker, and Barsoom 1998).[9] As shown in the fourth column of Table 2, the estimated coefficient of this variable is negative. But like the other measures of PTA depth, it is neither sizable nor statistically significant. Consequently, we find little evidence that the depth of a PTA affects its likelihood of expansion. Moreover, except for the effect of MARKET SIZE$_i$ when LEGALISM$_i$ is analyzed, introducing these factors in the model has little bearing on our original estimates.

**Robustness Checks**

Having generated some initial estimates of our model, we now address the effects of a battery of factors that are omitted from equation (1) and that might account for our earlier results. First, we estimate our model after including year-specific fixed effects to account for shocks felt throughout the global system at a given point in time (e.g., the global business cycle, declining or rising hegemony, or worldwide patterns of PTA formation) that may provide incentives for PTAs to expand and that could also be correlated with the independent variables in our model. The results are in the fifth column of Table 2. All of the estimated coefficients remain statistically significant, and all of them have the same sign and are roughly the same size as our initial estimates. Equally, a likelihood ratio test does not allow us to reject the null hypothesis that the model should be estimated without the year-specific effects ($\chi^2 = 44.27$; $p = .22$). Thus, system-wide shocks do not account for our findings.

Second, region-specific factors—such as waves of newly independent states entering the international system after decolonization or economic shocks (e.g., the Asian economic crisis)—might influence whether PTAs composed of states located in a given area expand. To account for these factors, we add dummy variables indicating whether the members of each PTA are located solely in Africa, the Americas, Europe, Asia-Pacific, the Middle East, or whether the members inhabit more than one of these regions.[10] The reference category in this analysis is an arrangement composed of members located in more than one region. As shown in the sixth column of Table 2, these region-specific fixed effects are neither individually nor jointly significant ($\chi^2 = 5.38$; $p = .37$), which demonstrates that PTA expansion does not vary in any systematic way across different geographical areas.[11] Indeed, the only noticeable effect of including these variables is to substantially attenuate the impact of MARKET SIZE$_i$.

Third, the EC/EU has enlarged at various points over the past three decades. Indeed, what little literature exists on PTA expansion focuses almost exclusively on this institution, which initially added new members in 1973 with the inclusion of Great Britain, Denmark, and Ireland, and which grew for the sixth time in 2007 with the accession of Romania and Bulgaria. We want to ensure that our findings are not driven by these various episodes. To this end, we re-estimate our original model after excluding the EC/EU. The results are reported in the seventh column of Table 2. That the coefficient estimate of MARKET SIZE$_i$ is no longer statistically significant indicates that the European observations help to account for the observed relationship between a PTA's aggregate GDP and the likelihood of it expanding. However, the remaining results are unchanged, indicating that the effects of openness, concentration, the expansion of PTAs system-wide, and the length of time since a prior expansion occurred owe little to the EC/EU.

Finally, it is useful to address the effects of concentration on PTA expansion in more detail. Prior research has

[7] For an overview of this issue, see Downs, Rocker, and Barsoom (1998).

[8] Data are taken from Barbieri, Keshk, and Pollins (2009).

[9] Adding the sum (rather than the mean) of trade, the first difference of the mean level of trade, or the logarithm of the mean of trade has no bearing on our findings.

[10] We define regions based on the Correlates of War Project's (2008) categories.

[11] Furthermore, there are no statistically significant differences between any of these regional variables.

shown that CONCENTRATION$_i$ can be expressed as follows (Mansfield 1994:104):

$$\text{CONCENTRATION}_i = \frac{V_i}{\sqrt{N_i - 1}} \quad (3)$$

Equation (3) allows us to disentangle two key constituent features of concentration: $N_i$, which is the number of member-states in the $i^{th}$ PTA, and $V_i$, which is the coefficient of variation (standard deviation divided by the mean) of $S_{ij}$ in equation (2). Recall that $S_{ij}$ is the proportion of the aggregate GDP in the $i^{th}$ PTA that member-state $j$ possesses in year $t$. As such, $V_i$ is a measure of the size distribution of the member-states comprising the $i^{th}$ PTA, where higher (lower) values indicate a more skewed (uniform) distribution and hence greater (less) inequality among the participants.

In the eighth column of Table 2, we replace CONCENTRATION$_i$ with $V_i$ and $\sqrt{N_i - 1}$.[12] Both factors have a strong bearing on PTA expansion. The estimated coefficient of $V_i$ is negative, that of $\sqrt{N_i - 1}$ is positive, and both of them are statistically significant. Thus, PTAs are particularly likely to expand when member-states are more equally sized and when the number of participants is relatively large. The latter result is consistent with the argument that PTAs aim to promote cooperation among members and that, as Pahre (1995:132) notes, cooperation within an international institution is "more resistant to defections by individual states as the number of actors increases."

### Additional Determinants of PTA Expansion

The preceding analysis indicates that, except for MARKET SIZE$_{it}$, the effects of the variables in our model are quite robust. However, there are a wide variety of factors that might be expected to influence PTA expansion and that are omitted from our model. In this section, we examine many of these factors, including some that have been featured in studies of PTA formation and membership. None of them have a statistically significant influence on the probability of PTA expansion.

Table 3 presents the battery of additional variables added one at a time to the baseline model. The first column lists these variables, the second column shows the *p*-value associated with each variable's estimated coefficient, and the third column reports any change to the estimated coefficients of the remaining independent variables.

First, we add AGE$_{it}$, the number of years that the $i^{th}$ PTA has been in existence as of year $t$. It is possible that newer PTAs may try to enhance their influence in the global trading system by taking on additional members. Conversely, PTAs may wait until some time has passed to admit new members so that any issues in the operation of the agreement can be ironed out before growing.[13] Second, we analyze whether PTAs in which members cooperate on other economic and political issues are more or less likely to enlarge. Trade institutions in which members also coordinate currency policies, for example, may be particularly likely to expand. We therefore include CURRENCY UNION$_{it}$, which is the percentage of country-pairs in each PTA that maintain a currency union with each other in year $t$.[14] Equally, political–military cooperation among member-states could make a PTA especially attractive to potential members. We thus include ALLIES$_{it}$, which is the percentage of dyads in each PTA that are political–military allies in year $t$.[15]

TABLE 3. Alternative Specifications

| *Variable* | *p* | *Effects on Other Independent Variables* |
|---|---|---|
| Age | .284 | None |
| Currency Union (% members) | .656 | MARKET SIZE$_i$ not significant |
| Allies (% members) | .959 | None |
| System States (%) | .868 | None |
| Joining System States (%) | .401 | None |
| Great Powers | .165 | MARKET SIZE$_i$ not significant |
| GATT Round | .661 | None |
| ΔGATT Size | .474 | None |
| Post-Cold War | .623 | None |
| Hegemony | .910 | None |
| Democracy | .574 | None |
| MIDs | .979 | None |
| Development | .491 | None |
| States Contiguous | .303 | MARKET SIZE$_i$ not significant |
| Number of Prior Expansions | .950 | None |

Third, we examine whether features of the international system provide an impetus to PTA expansion. We include the percentage of states throughout the global system that are parties to at least one PTA in year $t$. This variable, SYSTEM STATES, helps to capture any process of contagion or diffusion that might prompt PTA expansion. As more states become members of these arrangements, PTAs may race to add states that remain outside these groupings. Next, we add the percentage of states in the international system joining a PTA in year $t$. This variable, JOINING STATES, is intended to capture the possibility that a large number of states entering PTAs worldwide will prompt other countries to rapidly seek membership in existing PTAs.

Our third systemic variable is HEGEMONY, which is the percentage of global GDP generated by the state with the largest national income in year $t$ (for the purposes of this study, the United States).[16] We also add a variable that equals 1 if there is a GATT/WTO negotiating round occurring in year $t$ and 0 otherwise.[17] PTAs may seek to expand during GATT/WTO rounds as a means of enhancing their bargaining power in the multilateral negotiations (Mansfield and Reinhardt 2003).[18] We include another variable that measures the year-to-year change in GATT/WTO membership (Δ GATT SIZE). An increase in the ranks of the GATT/WTO may indicate that states have confidence in, and are committed to, the multilateral regime and therefore have less interest in

[12] Note that the results are very similar if we replace $\sqrt{N_i - 1}$ with $N_i$.

[13] Note that we also analyzed whether there was a quadratic relationship between PTA expansion and both $N_i$ and AGE$_i$, but found no evidence of this sort.

[14] Data are taken from Goldstein, Rivers, and Tomz (2007). For currency unions and alliances (discussed below), we measure the percentage of all dyads in the PTA that maintain a currency union or alliance.

[15] Data are taken from the ATOP project (Leeds, Ritter, Mitchell, and Long 2002).

[16] This variable is computed using the World Bank's *World Development Indicators* (2009).

[17] Data are taken from Mansfield and Reinhardt (2003).

[18] We also included the number of years since the beginning of the GATT/WTO negotiating round. This alternative measure was not statistically significant.

entering preferential arrangements. Alternatively, the decision by some states to enter the GATT/WTO may lead their competitors that are not members of the multilateral regime to press for entry into preferential arrangements. Further, we address whether the end of the Cold War stimulated the expansion of PTAs. As we discussed earlier, the conclusion of the Cold War precipitated a rapid increase in the number of PTAs. It is possible that this episode also led PTAs to take on additional members (Lawrence 1996). To address this issue, we include POST-COLD WAR, a variable which equals 0 in all years prior to 1989 and 1 in all years thereafter.

Fourth, we address the effects of member-state characteristics and relations on the prospects of PTA expansion. To begin, DEMOCRACY$_i$ is the mean regime score for all members in the $i^{th}$ arrangement at year $t$.[19] We follow the standard practice of calculating this score using the Polity Project's 21-point index, which ranges from −10 to 10, where higher (lower) values correspond to more democratic (autocratic) regimes (Jaggers and Gurr 1995). We average this score over all members in year $t$. Given that more democratic states are particularly likely to join PTAs (Mansfield, Milner, and Rosendorff 2002; Mansfield and Milner 2012), it may be the case that arrangements with a high proportion of democracies tend to admit additional members.

Similarly, we account for the presence or absence of major powers in each arrangement by creating an indicator variable (GREAT POWER$_i$) coded as 1 if any member of PTA $i$ in year $t$ is considered a great power by the Correlates of War Project (2008). Admitting new members may be expensive or require coordination among the participants. Due to their size and strength, great powers may help to bear these costs and facilitate such coordination. Next, we consider the effects of political–military conflict. Institutions beset by military disputes between members may be ill-prepared to take on new members and unattractive to prospective participants. MIDs$_i$ is the count of militarized interstate disputes initiated between pairs of states in the $i^{th}$ PTA in year $t$.[20] We also analyze whether the economic development of member-states influences the likelihood of PTA enlargement by including the mean per capita GDP of the $i^{th}$ PTA's members in year $t$.[21]

Fifth, some PTAs may have difficulty expanding because they are designed to be regional or subregional and all or most of the potential members already participate. To address this issue, we define STATES CONTIGUOUS$_i$. For each PTA member in year $t$, we calculate the percentage of contiguous countries (either sharing a border or within 50 miles separated by water) that belong to the same PTA. Then, we take the average of these percentages to create a single metric for each PTA in each year. The higher the value of this variable, the larger the percentage of nearby countries that already belong to the arrangement, which could impede expansion if it is regional or subregional in scope.

Finally, it may be that the number of times a PTA has expanded as of year $t$ affects the odds of it expanding in year $t + 1$. Perhaps some PTAs are generally more open to adding new members or are considered more successful and attractive. If so, the arrangements that expand repeatedly should be more likely to add members again. Note that this variable, NUMBER OF PRIOR EXPANSIONS$_i$, differs from TIME SINCE EXPANSION$_i$, which is the length of time since the $i^{th}$ grouping last enlarged. In contrast, NUMBER OF PRIOR EXPANSIONS$_i$ is a count of the number of previous expansions, regardless of when they occurred.

However, of the fifteen variables that we have described in this section and that are listed in Table 3, not a single one has a statistically significant influence on PTA expansion. By chance alone, we would have expected one to have a significant effect. More important for our purpose is that including these variables has no bearing on the effects of OPENNESS$_i$, CONCENTRATION$_i$, or SYSTEM EXPANSION$_i$. Somewhat less robust is the influence of MARKET SIZE$_i$. In three of these fifteen cases, adding a variable attenuates the strength of the relationship between MARKET SIZE$_i$ and PTA expansion, a result that is consistent with our findings in Table 2.

**Who Joins? Characteristics of New PTA Members**

The preceding results reveal that certain features play a key role in determining whether multilateral trade institutions expand. However, it is also important to gain an understanding of which states are joining the expanding PTAs. There is a burgeoning literature on the country characteristics that stimulate accession to PTAs (e.g., Mansfield et al. 2002; Mansfield, Milner, and Pevehouse 2007; Mansfield, Milner, and Rosendorf 2012). Here, we draw on this literature to offer a preliminary assessment of whether states tend to enter groupings comprised of members that have characteristics similar to their own.

Various studies have concluded that PTAs comprised of states that are relatively homogeneous politically and economically function more smoothly and effectively than heterogeneous arrangements. First, we analyze whether PTAs tend to take on new members with regimes types that are similar to the existing membership. Hurrell (1995:69), for example, suggests that part of the EU's success can be traced to "common democratic institutions," among other factors. Similarly, in their pioneering work on regional arrangements, Haas and Schmitter (1969:711–12; see also Katzenstein 1997:23) hypothesized that a membership marked by "pluralism" in their respective polities augurs well for the success of an arrangement. Of course, some arrangements (e.g., the EU and Mercosur) have demanded that all members have strong democratic credentials, which provides further reason to suspect that PTAs that expand may eschew potential entrants that differ politically from existing member-states.

Second, we assess whether enlarging PTAs add members with similar market sizes and development levels as existing members. Earlier, we found that PTAs composed of equally sized states were particularly likely to expand. This implies that new members should be roughly the same size as existing members. Previous research indicates that arrangements comprised of states with very different market sizes and development levels are prone to "backwash effects" (Myrdal 1957; Balassa 1961:201–2). These effects lead smaller and less developed states to suffer from integration with larger and more developed economies, raising the specter of a breakdown in cooperation within the PTA. Thus, smaller states may avoid arrangements made up of states with larger economies and groups of small states may choose not to extend

[19] We use Gleditsch's (2008) update of the Polity IV data to construct this variable.

[20] Data are taken from Ghosn, Palmer, and Bremer (2004).

[21] Data are taken from the Penn World Table (Heston, Summers, and Aten 2009).

membership invitations to larger economies. It is likely, then, that expanding PTAs will add states that are of a similar size and development level as existing members.

Finally, we address whether growing PTAs take on new members with similar degrees of trade openness as existing members. Some observers point to similarity among key economic policies as a marker of a PTA's success (e.g., Nogues and Quantanilla 1993:285). Trade policy is particularly important in this regard. Trade openness is a crude indicator of trade policy because it could reflect various factors other than policy decisions (Leamer 1988). Nonetheless, alternative measures of trade policy cover only a fraction of the countries in our sample, and trade openness has been widely used as such a measure. Furthermore, Downs, Rocker, and Barsoom (1998) have shown that deep economic integration is most easily achieved if a relatively small group of states committed to extensive integration form a PTA and then add new members. A highly integrated group of states is likely to be marked by a high level of trade openness. It stands to reason that such a group will select new members who are already committed to open trade.

In a preliminary attempt to address whether states tend to enter groupings comprised of members that have characteristics similar to their own, we therefore analyze four variables: regime type, GDP, per capita GDP, and trade openness. More specifically, for each episode of PTA expansion, we compute the mean level of each variable (based on the data sources discussed earlier) for the existing members of the PTA in the year when new members enter the arrangement. We then compare these averages to the average of each variable for the new members.

Table 4 shows the results of these two sample *t*-tests. In the case of regime type, market size, and economic development, there are no systematic differences between existing members and new participants. In the case of trade openness, there is a marginally significant ($p = .10$) difference; but the lower panel of this table indicates that this difference is due to the EC/EU. The results of these tests therefore provide considerable evidence that PTAs tend to expand by taking on members who are similar to existing ones. This could be due to a preadmission process in which states that wish to accede are required to make certain political or economic changes, or it may simply reflect a particular type of selectivity in choosing new members. Regardless, while these tests are somewhat crude and a more systematic analysis is necessary before drawing firm conclusions, multilateral PTAs do not seem to "stretch" very much by admitting member-states with very different domestic characteristics than existing members.[22]

TABLE 4. Two Sample *t*-tests Comparing Characteristics of Current PTA Members with New Members

| | *Regime Type* | *GDP* | *Per Capita GDP* | *Openness* |
|---|---|---|---|---|
| All Cases | | | | |
| Existing Members | 0.993 | $1.89 \times 10^8$ | 10158.02 | 0.082 |
| New Member(s) | 1.048 | $1.92 \times 10^8$ | 11333.08 | 0.077 |
| $H_0$: Mean difference = 0 (*t*-statistic) | 0.101 | 0.033 | 0.673 | −1.671 |
| *p* | 0.92 | 0.97 | 0.50 | 0.10 |
| *N* | 66 | 69 | 69 | 67 |
| Excluding EU Cases | | | | |
| Existing Members | 0.049 | $1.47 \times 10^8$ | 8765.55 | 0.082 |
| New Member(s) | −0.048 | $1.61 \times 10^8$ | 10691.84 | 0.078 |
| $H_0$: Mean difference = 0 (*t*-statistic) | 0.157 | 0.177 | 1.011 | −1.344 |
| *p* | 0.88 | 0.86 | 0.32 | 0.18 |
| *N* | 59 | 62 | 62 | 62 |

## Conclusion

Over the past six decades, there has been a tremendous proliferation of PTAs. Much of this activity has stemmed from states forming new preferential arrangements. However, PTAs have also become increasingly important features of the international political economy because many of them have expanded, taking on additional member-states. Very little attention has been focused on why some PTAs expand, while others do not, and the purpose of this paper has been to shed light on this important topic.

We find that bilateral PTAs and hub and spoke agreements almost never grow. Multilateral PTAs, by contrast, often enlarge. The latter arrangements are most likely to take on additional members when the existing members are especially open with respect to trade and when the size distribution among them is relatively uniform. Furthermore, the addition of new members exhibits temporal clustering. PTAs that add a new member tend to do so again in the near future. Equally, PTAs throughout the global system tend to expand at roughly the same time. There is also some evidence that PTAs covering a large market are more likely to expand than smaller arrangements, although this result is less robust than the others. Finally, it seems that PTAs expand with an eye toward maintaining a certain amount of economic and political uniformity among members. The regime type, market size, economic development, and trade openness of new entrants are very similar to that of existing PTA participants.

The results of this study also suggest various avenues for future research. First, while our focus has been on PTAs, too little effort has been focused on explaining the expansion of international institutions more generally (Downs, Rocker, and Barsoom 1998). Why, for example, have some political-military alliances or human rights agreements expanded while many have not? Future research is needed to determine whether the results of this analysis are confined to PTAs or whether they help to explain the expansion of a wider range of institutions. Some of the more general factors that we have analyzed may well guide the expansion of various institutions, including strategic interaction among PTAs and among countries, the length of time since a PTA last expanded, and the size distribution of members. Moreover, the finding that bilateral PTAs rarely expand is not limited to economic institutions. For example, based on an analysis of the ATOP data (Leeds, Ritter, Mitchell, and Long 2002), we find that fewer than 2% of bilateral alliances have expanded over the past two

[22] Ideally, one could use data on applications for admission to a PTA to conduct a more fine-grained analysis of which states are admitted or rejected. While data on applications for large PTAs often are available, such data tend to be very difficult to locate for smaller PTAs, those PTAs that are not notified to the GATT/WTO, and those involving developing countries.

centuries, whereas almost a third of multilateral alliances have added members. Our analysis of the Correlates of War data on alliances (Gibler and Sarkees 2004) yields very similar results: only 3% of bilateral alliances have expanded since the end of the Napoleonic Wars, while nearly 30% of multilateral alliances have grown in size. Nonetheless, a number of the factors that guide PTA expansion—especially trade openness and, to a lesser extent, market size—seem better suited to explaining international trade institutions than other types.

Second, whereas PTAs have become particularly prominent features of the international economic landscape since World War II, this is hardly the first era in which these arrangements played an important role. Indeed, PTAs have existed for hundreds of years (Mansfield and Milner 1999; Pahre 2008), and it would be useful to determine whether the factors that explain expansion in the current era help to explain expansion in past eras as well. Finally, we have only engaged in a preliminary analysis of which states enter the arrangements that expand. A better sense is needed of what types of states are entering which PTAs, what distinguishes the founding members of a PTA from those that accede to it at a later date, the relationship between new and existing members, and other related issues.

## References

BALASSA, BELA. (1961) *Theory of Economic Integration*. Homewood, IL: R.D. Irwin.

BALDWIN, RICHARD. (1995a) A Domino Theory of Regionalism. In *Expanding Membership of the European Union*, edited by Richard Baldwin, Pertti Haaparanta, and Jaako Kiander. Cambridge: Cambridge University Press.

BALDWIN, RICHARD. (1995b) The Eastern Enlargement of the European Union. *European Economic Review* 39: 474–481.

BALDWIN, RICHARD. (2008) Big Think Regionalism: A Critical Survey. In *Regional Rules in the Global Trading System*, edited by Antoni Estevadeordal, Kati Suominen, and Robert Teh. New York: Cambridge University Press.

BALDWIN, RICHARD, AND DANY JAIMOVICH. (2010) Are Free Trade Agreements Contagious? National Bureau of Economic Research Working Paper No. 16084. Cambridge, MA: National Bureau of Economic Research.

BARBIERI, KATHERINE, M. G. OMAR KESHK, AND BRIAN POLLINS. (2009) TRADING DATA: Evaluating our Assumptions and Coding Rules. *Conflict Management and Peace Science* 26: 471–491.

BECK, NATHANIEL, JONATHAN KATZ, AND RICHARD TUCKER. (1998) Taking Time Seriously: Time-Series Cross-Sectional Analysis with a Binary Dependent Variable. *American Journal of Political Science* 42: 1260–1288.

BHAGWATI, JADISH. (1993) Regionalism and Multilateralism: An Overview. In *New Dimensions of Regional Integration*, edited by Jamie de Melo and Arvind Panagariya. New York: Cambridge University Press.

CORRELATES OF WAR PROJECT. (2008) State System Membership List, v2008.1. Available at http://correlatesofwar.org. (Accessed May 18, 2012.)

DEUTSCH, KARL W., SIDNEY A. BURRELL, ROBERT A. KANN, MAURICE LEE, JR., MARTIN LICHTERMAN, RAYMOND LINDGREN, FRANCIS L. LOWENHEIM, AND RICHARD W. VAN WAGENEN. (1957) *Political Community and the North Atlantic Area: International Organization in the Light of Historical Experience*. Princeton, NJ: Princeton University Press.

DOWNS, GEORGE W., DAVID M. ROCKE, AND PETER N. BARSOOM. (1998) Managing the Evolution of Multilateralism. *International Organization* 52: 397–419.

FERNÁNDEZ, RAQUEL, AND JONATHAN PORTES. (1998) Returns to Regionalism: An Analysis of Nontraditional Gains from Regional Trade Agreements. *World Bank Economic Review* 12: 197–220.

GHOSN, FATEN, GLENN PALMER, AND STUART BREMER. (2004) The MID3 Data Set, 1993–2001: Procedures, Coding Rules, and Description. *Conflict Management and Peace Science* 21: 133–154.

GIBLER, DOUGLAS M., AND MEREDITH SARKEES. (2004) Measuring Alliances: The Correlates of War Formal Interstate Alliance Data set, 1816–2000. *Journal of Peace Research* 41: 211–222.

GLEDITSCH, KRISTIAN. (2008) Modified Regime Type 4 Data. Available at http://weber.ucsd.edu/~kgledits/Regime Type.html. (Accessed May 18, 2012.)

GOLDSTEIN, JUDITH, DOUGLAS RIVERS, AND MICHAEL TOMZ. (2007) Institutions in International Relations: Understanding the Effects of the GATT and the WTO on World Trade. *International Organization* 61: 37–67.

GRAY, JULIA. (2010) Politics and Patronage: The Function of Disfunctional Regional Trade Agreements. Paper presented at a conference on The Politics of Preferential Trade Agreements: Theory, Measurement, and Empirical Applications. Princeton University, April 30-May 1.

HAAS, ERNST, AND PHILIPPE SCHMITTER. (1969) Economics and Differential Patterns of Political Integration: Projections about Unity in Latin America. *International Organization* 18: 705–737.

HESTON, ALAN, ROBERT SUMMERS, AND BETTINA ATEN. (2009) Penn World Table Version 6.3. Center for International Comparisons of Production, Income and Prices. University of Pennsylvania.

HUFBAUER, GARY C., AND JEFFREY SCHOTT. (2005) *NAFTA Revisited: Achievements and Challenges*. Washington, DC: Institute for International Economics.

HURRELL, ANDREW. (1995) Regionalism in Theoretical Perspective. In *Regionalism in World Politics: Regional Organization and International Order*, edited by Louise Fawcett and Andrew Hurrell. New York: Oxford University Press.

JAGGERS, KEITH, AND TED ROBERT GURR. (1995) Tracking Democracy's Third Wave with the Polity III Data. *Journal of Peace Research* 32: 469–482.

KAHLER, MILES. (1992) Multilateralism with Small and Large Numbers. *International Organization* 46: 681–708.

KAHLER, MILES. (1995) *International Institutions and the Political Economy of Integration*. Washington, DC: Brookings Institution.

KATZENSTEIN, PETER. (1997) Introduction: Asian Regionalism in Comparative Perspective. In *Network Power: Japan and Asia*, edited by Peter Katzenstein and Takashi Shiraishi. Ithaca, NY: Cornell University Press.

KOREMENOS, BARBARA, CHARLES LIPSON, AND DUNCAN SNIDAL. (2001) The Rational Design of International Institutions. *International Organization* 55: 761–799.

LAWRENCE, ROBERT Z. (1996) *Regionalism, Multilateralism, and Deeper Integration*. Washington, DC: Brookings Institution.

LEAMER, EDWARD R. (1988) Measures of Openness. In *Trade Policy Issues and Empirical Analysis*, edited by Robert E. Baldwin. Chicago: University of Chicago Press.

LEEDS, BRETT ASHLEY, JEFFREY M. RITTER, SARA MCLAUGHLIN MITCHELL, AND ANDREW G. LONG. (2002) Alliance Treaty Obligations and Provisions, 1815–1994. *International Interactions* 28: 237–260.

MANSFIELD, EDWARD D. (1994) *Power, Trade, and War*. Princeton, NJ: Princeton University Press.

MANSFIELD, EDWARD D., AND HELEN V. MILNER. (1999) The New Wave of Regionalism. *International Organization* 53: 589–627.

MANSFIELD, EDWARD D., AND HELEN V. MILNER. (2012) *Votes, Vetoes, and the Political Economy of International Trade Agreements*. Princeton, NJ: Princeton University Press.

MANSFIELD, EDWARD D., AND ERIC REINHARDT. (2003) The Multilateral Determinants of Regionalism: The Effects of the GATT/WTO on the Formation of Preferential Trading Arrangements. *International Organization* 57: 826–862.

MANSFIELD, EDWARD D., HELEN V. MILNER, AND B. PETER ROSENDORFF. (2002) Why Democracies Cooperate More: Electoral Control and Preferential Trade Agreements. *International Organization* 56: 477–513.

MANSFIELD, EDWARD D., HELEN V. MILNER, AND JON C. PEVEHOUSE. (2007) Vetoing Cooperation: The Impact of Veto Players on Preferential Trading Arrangements. *British Journal of Political Science* 37: 403–432.

MATTLI, WALTER. (1999) *The Logic of Regional Integration: Europe and Beyond.* New York: Cambridge University Press.

MCCALL SMITH, JAMES. (2000) The Politics of Dispute Settlement Design: Explaining Legalism in Regional Trade Pacts. *International Organization* 54: 137–180.

DE MELO, JAIME, AND ARVIND PANAGARIYA. (1993) Introduction. In *New Dimensions in Regional Integration*, edited by Jaime de Melo and Arvind Panagariya. New York: Cambridge University Press.

MORAVCSIK, ANDREW, AND MILADA ANNA VACHUDOVA. (2003) National Interests, State Power, and EU Enlargement. *East European Politics and Societies* 17: 42–57.

MYRDAL, GUNNAR. (1957) *Economic Theory and Under-Developed Regions.* London: Duckworth.

NOGUES, JULI J., AND ROSALINDA QUANTANILLA. (1993) Latin America's Integration and the Multilateral Trading System.. In *New Dimensions in Regional Integration*, edited by Jaime de Melo and Arvind Panagariya. New York: Cambridge University Press.

PAHRE, ROBERT. (1995) Wider and Deeper: The Links between Expansion and Integration in the European Union. In *Towards A New Europe: Stops and Starts in European Integration*, edited by Gerald Schneider, Patricia Weitsman, and Thomas Bernauer. Westport, CT: Praeger.

PAHRE, ROBERT. (2008) *Politics and Trade Cooperation in the Nineteenth Century: The "Agreeable Customs" of 1815–1914.* New York: Cambridge University Press.

POMFRET, RICHART W. T. (1988) *Unequal Trade: The Economics of Discriminatory International Trade Policies.* Oxford: Basil Blackwell.

RUSSETT, BRUCE. (1967) *International Regions and the International System: A Study in Political Ecology.* Chicago: Rand-McNally.

SCHIMMELFENNIG, FRANK, AND ULRICH SEDELMEIER, Eds. (2005) *The Politics of European Union Enlargement: Theoretical Approaches.* New York: Routledge.

SINGER, J. DAVID, STUART BREMER, AND JOHN STUCKEY. (1972) Capability Distribution, Uncertainty, and Major Power War, 1820–1965. In *Peace, War, and Numbers*, edited by Bruce Russett. Beverly Hills, CA: Sage Publications.

VACHUDOVA, MILADA ANNA. (2005) *Europe Undivided: Democracy, Leverage, and Integration After Communism.* New York: Oxford University Press.

WHALLEY, JOHN. (1998) Why Do States Seek Regional Trade Agreements? In *The Regionalization of the World Economy*, edited by Jeffrey Frankel. Chicago: University of Chicago Press.

WORLD BANK. (2009) *World Development Indicators.* Washington, DC: World Bank Group. Available at http://data.worldbank.org/data-catalog/world-development-indicators/wdi-2012. (Accessed June 1, 2012.)

YARBROUGH, BETH V., AND ROBERT M. YARBROUGH. (1992) *Cooperation and Governance in International Trade: The Strategic Organizational Approach.* Princeton, NJ: Princeton University Press.

# Index

**A**

adversaries, xiv, 37, 39, 39, 52, 60. *See also specific topics*

Africa, 79, 331

alliances, xiv, xv, 134, 137; bilateral trade and, xv, 51–64 (*see also* bilateralism; *specific countries*); exports and, xv, 43, 44, 57, 60 (*see also* exports); free trade and, 37–49 (*see also* free trade); major powers and (*see* major powers); multipolarity and, xiv, 29, 37, 40, 47n16; political-military alliances, 37–49, 47n18; PTAs and, xv, 51–64 (*see also* preferential trading arrangements); security and (*see* security externalities); World War II and, 40

anarchic systems, xii; free trade and, 38, 45; international system, 37–49, 51; major powers and, 14; security externalities and, 51; supranatural authority, 37

APEC. *See* Asia-Pacific Economic Cooperation

ARCH-in-mean model, 79–90, 88

Argentina, 306

Arusha Accords, 79

ASEAN. *See* Association of Southeast Asian Nations

Asia-Pacific Economic Cooperation (APEC), 301, 321

Association of Southeast Asian Nations (ASEAN), 221, 304, 321

Australia, 69, 71, 300

Austria, 91

autarkic systems, 148

autocracies, xix–xx, 129, 234; cooperation and, 253; democracies and, xx, xxv, 128, 134, 140, 141; international trade and, 127–143; macroeconomics and, 149; mixed pairs and, 127, 140, 141; PTAs and, xxv, xxvi, 250 (*see also* preferential trading arrangements); ratification and, xxvi; trade barriers and, xx, 131; *See also specific countries, topics*

autonomy, 105, 106

**B**

basic force models, 21

Berlin Wall, 330

bilateralism, xiv, 51–64, 91; alliances and, 41, 45, 46, 54; bipolar systems, xii, xiv, 29, 37–49, 47n16; dyads and, 291, 310–313, 319, 336; FTAs and, 331; GNP and, 41 (*see also* gross domestic product); gravity models and, xiv, xv, 41, 54, 62, 134; mixed pairs, xx; multilateral agreements and (*see* multilateralism); PTAs and, 51, 53, 61, 331, 339 (*see also* preferential trading arrangements); trade barriers and, 134; volatility and, 74; *See also specific countries*

Bolivia, 321

Brazil, 152, 302, 306

Bronson, R., xv, 51–64

Bulgaria, 336
Busch, M. L., xviii, xix, 99–125
Bush, G. H. W., 330
business cycles, xxiv, 17, 207–208

C

CAFTA. *See* Central America Free Trade Agreement
Canada, 68, 72, 172, 221, 230, 304, 306, 312–313, 321, 331
Canada-United States Free Trade Agreement (CUFTA), 172, 331
Caribbean Community and Common Market (CARICOM), 301
Caribbean Free Trade Association (CARIFTA), 321
CARICOM. *See* Caribbean Community and Common Market
CARIFTA. *See* Caribbean Free Trade Association
causality, 159
Central America Free Trade Agreement (CAFTA), 268
CET. *See* common external tariff
Chile, 60, 71, 149, 321
Chile-European Union (EU) Association Agreement, 69
China, 71, 129, 305
CMEA. *See* Council for Mutual Economic Assistance
coalition governments, 152
COCOM. *See* Coordinating Committee for Multilateral Export Controls
Cold War, 46, 61, 140, 148, 247, 255, 330, 338
collective action, 5, 31. *See also specific topics*
Colombia, 321
colonial relations, 55, 56, 61, 135, 137, 247, 281–282, 286
COMECON. *See* Council for Mutual Economic Assistance
command economies, 55, 56, 61, 135, 137, 252
common external tariff (CET), 302, 329
common markets, xxiii, 206, 265, 287, 297, 324, 329, 336
communications, 17
communism, 210. *See also* Cold War
complete information system, 271
concentration of capabilities, 3, 34; distribution of, 28–29, 34; factors in, 10; global leader, xxiv; hegemony and, 12, 36 (*see also* hegemony); index of, 9; major powers and, 9 (*see also* major powers); McKeown model, 11n31; military and, 12, 20; openess and, xiii (*see also* openness, of trade); polarity and, 29; population and, 20; power and, xxi, 21; PTAs and, 337; shares of, 34; systemic analyses, 33; tariff levels and, 14; trade and, 11n31, 14–15, 27–29; U-shaped relationship, 15; war and, 11n31, 20
consumer price index (CPI), 162
cooperation, 270; autocracies and, 253 (*see also* autocracies); democracies and, 253, 255 (*see also* democracies); economic institutions, 65–96, 92; hegemony and, 255 (*see also* hegemony); information and, 229; PTAs and, 92, 294 (*see also* preferential trading arrangements); regime type and, 253; trade agreements and, 238–239; trade policy and, 269–278; veto players (*see* veto players); *See also specific agreements, topics*
Coordinating Committee for Multilateral Export Controls (COCOM), 52, 61
Correlates of War Project (COW), 45, 53, 54, 62, 136, 291
cosmopolitanism, 195
Council for Mutual Economic Assistance (COMECON), 61, 153
CPI. *See* consumer price index

Cuba, 182
CUFTA. *See* Canada-United States Free Trade Agreement
currencies, 109
customs unions, xv, xxiii, 41, 68, 206, 265, 287, 297, 324, 329, 336
Czech Republic, 331

**D**

democracies, xix–xx, 234; autocracies and, xx, xxv, 128, 134, 140, 141 (*see also* autocracies); cooperation and, 227–263 (*see also* cooperation); elections and, xxv, 149, 228, 230 (*see also* elections); executive branch, xxv, xxvi (*see also* executive); fragmentation and, 146; interest groups (*see* interest groups); international trade and, xx, 127–143, 145; legislature and, 128, 131, 140, 141; macroeconomics and, 149, 164; mixed pairs, 127, 140, 141; non-democratic countries and, 267; party systems, 268–269; PTAs and, xxv, xxvi, 250, 338; public officials and, xix, xx; ratification and, xxvi, 267, 269; trade barriers and, xx, 131; unemployment and, xxi; veto points and, xxi, 164, 267 (*see also* veto players); voters and, xxv
Denmark, 336
depression, xii, 4, 17
developing countries, 210, 286–293, 299. *See also specific countries, topics*
discount factor, 40, 46n12
distance, 134, 137, 309; contiguity and, 282, 286; exports and, 41, 43, 44, 56, 59; gravity models, xiv, 41, 54, 62, 134
Doha Development Agenda, 303, 304
domestic institutions, xix, xx, 105–108, 123, 145. *See also specific types, topics*
domino theory, 332
Durbin-Watson statistics, 22, 24
dyads, 291, 310–313, 319, 336. *See also* bilateralism

**E**

East Asian Economic Group, 301
EC. *See* European Community
economic unions, xv, xxiii, 265, 287, 329, 336. *See also specific agreements*
economies of scale, 54
Ecuador, 321
education, 173, 182, 188, 190, 193, 196–197
EEC. *See* European Economic Community
efficiency, xiv, 37
EFTA. *See* European Free Trade Association
elections, xxv, 102, 149, 230; democracies and, xxv (*see also* democracies); districts, 106; executive and, 233, 234, 238 (*see also* executive); information and, 229, 233; interest groups (*see* interest groups); Japan and, 121; pocketbook voting, 177; protectionism and, 254; self-interest and, 177; trade agreements and, 230; U.S. and, 121; vetoes and, 145–146; voters and, 149, 230, 233, 254
environment, xxiii, 71
ethnocentrism, xxii, 171, 180, 194, 196, 198
EU. *See* European Union
European Community (EC), 55, 68, 79, 286–293, 302, 321
European Economic Community (EEC), 45, 55, 220, 221, 299
European Free Trade Association (EFTA), 220, 221, 324
European Union (EU), 230, 286–293, 299, 329, 338
exchange rate: NTBs and, xviii, 114; protectionism and, xviii; societal

theories and, 122; trade policy and, xviii; unemployment and, 101–103; U.S. and, 119
executive, 232; action of, 256–258; chief executive, xx, xxv, 127, 152; divided government, 266; elections and, 233, 234, 238; gains for, 240–243; informational problem, 254; protectionism and, 254, 273; ratification and, 267, 269; trade barriers and, 235–236; trade policy and, 233–234, 235–236, 254, 273; types of (*see* regime types); veto players and, 266 (*see also* veto players)
exports: alliances and, 43, 44, 57, 78–79 (*see also* alliances); colonial ties and, 56 (*see also* colonial relations); command economies and, 56; distance and, 43, 44, 56; GATT and (*see* General Agreement on Tariffs and Trade); GDP and, 56; GNP and, 43, 44; major powers and, 57 (*see also* major powers); population and, 43, 56; PTAs and, 57, 78–79, 87, 220 (*see also* preferential trading arrangements); ratio of, 17; volatility and, 65, 87 (*see also* volatility); warfare and, 43, 56 (*see also* war)

**F**

factor endowments model. *See* Heckscher-Ohlin model
family financial conditions, 180
FDI. *See* foreign direct investment
Finland, 91
Folk theorem, 46n10
foreign direct investment (FDI), xxiii, 73, 180
foreign policy attitudes, 171
fragmentation, xxi, 146. *See also specific topics*
France, 41, 152, 289
free trade, 169, 206, 265, 297; alliances and, 37–49; anarchic system and, 38, 45; as beneficial, 45, 169; bilateralism and, 331; education and, 193; FTAs, xxiii, 41, 206, 265, 297, 324, 329, 331, 336; hegemony and, 5, 15 (*see also* hegemony); income and, 37; international institutions and, xv; isolationism and, 171; openness and (*see* openness); protectionism and, 192; PTAs and, 41, 336; security and, 37–49; Soviet Union and, 31; suboptimal, 45; trade preferences and, 192, 193; veto points and, 148; *See also specific agreements, topics*
Free Trade Agreement of the Americas (FTAA), 301
Freedom House, 153

**G**

game theory, 46n11, 130, 141, 266, 269, 271, 294, 37049. *See also specific types, topics*
GATT. *See* General Agreement on Tariffs and Trade
GDP. *See* gross domestic product
gender, 174, 188
General Agreement on Tariffs and Trade (GATT), xvi, 54, 56, 100, 105, 135, 137, 140, 162, 281, 339; Article XXIV, 215–216, 297, 299; dispute settlement, 305–307, 321; Doha Round and, 303, 304; Enabling Clause, 215–216, 221, 298; exports and, 56, 87; hegemony and, 219; industrial nations, 86; liberalization and, 295; membership data, 60, 61, 62–63; multilateralism and, xxvii, 295, 296, 302, 322; nondiscrimination, 321; nontariff barriers, 46n6; NTBs and, 100; protectionism and, 110, 298; PTAs and, xxvii, xxviii, 55, 208, 215–221, 247, 255, 295–329; reciprocal agreements, 74; regionalism and, 299–300; tariffs and, 39, 100, 110, 298; Uruguay Round, 68, 300–301;

volatility and, xvi, 74, 84–87, 91; WTO and (*see* World Trade Organization)
Generalized System of Preferences, 79
Germany, 41, 55, 58, 91, 120, 152, 299
globalization, 175, 180
GNP. *See* gross national product
Gowa, J., xiii, xiv, 5, 15, 37–49
Granger casuality, 159
gravity models, xiv, 41, 54, 62, 134, 134n14
Great Britain, xii, 4, 7, 30, 41, 336
gross domestic product (GDP), 20, 105. *See also specific countries, topics*
gross national product (GNP), 13–14, 41, 43, 44. *See also specific countries, topics*

**H**

Heckscher-Ohlin model, xxii, 46, 169–173, 195, 231
hegemonic stability theory, xii, xiii, xxiv; concentration and, 21, 32 (*see also* concentration of capabilities); empirical evidence and, 6–9; free trade and, 5; global markets and, 3, 12, 16–17; limitations of, 5; major powers and (*see* major powers); power and, 3, 7, 13; relative inequality and, 13, 32; systemic outcomes and, 8; U-shaped model and, 32; war and, 3; *See also* hegemony
hegemony: business cycles and, 17, 207–208; classifications of, xiii, 19–28; concentration and, 9–12, 34, 36 (*see also* concentration of capabilities); cooperation and, 255 (*see also* concentration); declining, xxiv, 282; definition, xiii, 7, 8, 19–28, 30; free trade and, 4, 15, 207 (*see also* free trade); GATT and, 219 (*see also* General Agreement on Tariffs and Trade); Gilpin classifications, 22, 23, 24, 36; Great Britain and, 7, 30, 41; hegemonic stability (*see* hegemonic stability theory); import levels and, 6; international systems and, 3, 9 (*see also* specific topics); major powers and (*see* major powers); measurement of, 7, 8, 30; openness and, 4, 207; power and, xiii, 8; PTAs and, xxiv, 214, 219, 247, 282; recession and, xxv; regionalism and, 207; stability and (*see* hegemonic stability theory); tariff levels and, 5, 6 (*see also* tariffs); Wallerstein classifications, 23, 24, 36
Henisz, W. H., xx, 145–167
Hirschman-Herfindahl index, xiv, 11, 12
Hong Kong, 75
hub and spoke agreements, xxviii, 331, 339
human rights, xxiii, 195
Hungary, 331

**I**

IGOs. *See* intergovernmental organizations
IMF. *See* International Monetary Fund
imperfect competition, 134
import levels, 6, 101, 105, 157. *See also specific countries, topics*
income: demand elasticity and, 17–18; free trade and, 37; GDP and, 20, 105; gravity model and, 134n14; per-capita, 134n14; power and, 37; self-interest and, xxii (*see also* self-interest); trade and, 18–28
India, 152
industry: GATT membership and, 86; intrafirm trade, 18, 52n4; policy preferences and, 170; sensitivity of, 109; volatility and, 86; *See also specific topics*
information, 272; collective level, 176, 190; complete information, 271;

cooperation and, 229; elections and, 229, 233; media and, 175; preferences and, 175; trade agreements and, 229
institutions, xix, 106, 109. *See also specific types, topics*
Inter-American Development Bank, 300
interest groups, 106, 129, 164, 165; democracies and, 146 (*see also* democracies); domestic institutions and, 145; fragmentation and, 146; liberalization and, 273; party systems, 268–269; pressure from, xvii, 103, 106, 108, 111, 123; PTAs and, 265; trade barriers and, 228, 229; trade policy and, xxi, 268
intergovernmental organizations (IGOs), 227
International Monetary Fund (IMF), 62
Ireland, 336
isolationism, xxii, 171, 174, 182, 194, 195, 198
Israel, 206n3, 299
Italy, 41

**J**
Japan, 41, 47, 47n26, 58, 62, 69, 120–121
Japanese-United States Security Treaty, 47n26

**K**
Kenya, 79
Knowledge Networks (KN) survey, 178–195

**L**
labor force: factor endowments, 173; retirees, 174; skill level, 174; SOC systems, 175, 176, 180; unemployment and, 172, 176; unions and, 175
Latin America Free Trade Association, 324
law of constant protection, 110
LDCs. *See* less developed countries
leaders, xviii. *See also* regime types; *specific topics*
legislatures, 127; democracies and, 128, 131, 140 (*see also* democracies); median voter models, 129; parliamentary systems, 111, 152, 267; protectionism and, 140; *See also specific countries, topics*
less developed countries (LDCs), 210, 286–293, 299. *See also specific countries, topics*
Leviathan strategy, 235–237, 238n22
liberalization, 65, 195, 227, 297; alliances and, 53 (*see also* alliances); autocracies and, 127 (*see also* autocracies); democracies and, 102, 127 (*see also* democracies); hegemony and, 4; interest groups and, 273; multilateralism and, 305; protectionism and, 102, 140; security externalities and, xiv; U.S. and, 32
Lomé Convention, 55, 79, 286–293, 331

**M**
Macao, 75
macroeconomics: autocracy and, 149 (*see also* autocracies); democracies and, 149 (*see also* democracies); downturns and, 109; factors in, 122, 162; NTBs and, 123; openness and, 146; preferences and, xxi; protectionism and, xx, 123, 164; statecraft and, 37; veto points and, 145, 146; *See also specific topics*
major powers, 135, 137, 338; alliances and, xv, 53, 60; anarchic system and, 14; concentration and, 9, 10; definition of, 58; exports and, 57; hegemony and, 5; power and, xii, 3, 10; PTAs and, 53; relative inequalities, 13; tariffs and, xv, 31;

war and, 24, 34; *See also specific countries, topics*
Malaysia, 69, 321
Mansfield, E. D., vii–xxxi
mass opinion surveys, xvii, xxi–xxii. *See also specific surveys, topics*
media, 175, 197
Mediterranean countries, 221
Mercosur, 302, 306, 321, 324, 338
Mexico, 69, 208, 221, 230, 299, 321, 331
Mexico-European Free Trade Area, 69
MFN. *See* most favored nation
military, xiii, 20, 37, 39; alliances and, xiv, 51, 281; concentration and, 12; conflicts and, 281 (*see also* war); COW Project (*see* Correlates of War Project); political-military cooperation, 281; PTAs and, 294, 338; security externalities and, 37; *See also specific countries, conflicts*
Milner, H., xx, xxv, xxvi, 127–143, 227–294
mixed pairs, 127, 140, 141, 152
monopoly, 53
most favored nation (MFN), 208
Multifibre Arrangement, 111
multilateralism, 65; bilateralism and, xxii, xxviii, 331 (*see also* bilateralism); GATT/WTO and, xvi, xxvii, 295, 296, 302, 322 (*see also* General Agreement on Tariffs and Trade; World Trade Organization); liberalization and, 295, 305; MTNs, 296, 300–307; PTAs and, xxv, xxviii, 296, 300–307, 322, 323, 332; regionalism and, 295–329; U.S. and, 331; volatility and, 91; *See also specific countries, topics*
multinational corporations, 109
multipolar systems, xiv, 29, 37, 40, 47n16
Mutz, D. C., xxii, 169–201

**N**

National Annenberg Election Survey (NAES), 178–195, 227
NAES. *See* National Annenberg Election Survey
NAFTA. *See* North American Free Trade Agreement
Napoleonic Wars, 340
Nash equilibrium, 130, 231, 237–238, 270, 271, 277
national interest, 99, 103, 104, 121–123, 171
nationalism, 180, 182, 194
natural resources, 17
New Zealand, 68, 113
nontariff barriers (NTBs), xviii, 99, 122; domestic institutions and, 123; exchange rate and, 114; GATT and, 100 (*see also* General Agreement on Tariffs and Trade); Japan and, 120; macroeconomics and, 123; measurement of, 124; model of, 111–112; national interest and, 123; parliamentary systems and, 114; proportional representation and, 114, 116–117; protection and, 108; public officials and, xix; societal models and, xix, 122, 123; statist approaches and, 104, 105, 122; tariffs and, 99–125; UNCTAD ratios, 111; unemployment and, 108, 114, 120; U.S. and, 119; West Germany and, 120; WTO and, 100 (*see also* World Trade Organization)
North American Free Trade Agreement (NAFTA), 72, 180, 208, 221, 230, 331
North Atlantic Treaty Organization, 135
North Korea, 61
NTBs. *See* nontariff barriers

## O

openness, of trade, xxii; concentration and, xiii; hegemony and, 4, 207; international markets, 30, 37–49; macroeconomic conditions and, 146; protectionist sentiment and, 145; PTA members and, 332; security externalities and, 51; trade barriers and, 332; unemployment and, 149, 157
Organization of Petroleum Exporting Countries (OPEC), 153
out-groups. *See* ethnocentrism

## P

Pakistan, 152
Pareto frontier, 46n7, 130, 141
parliamentary systems, 111, 114, 152, 267
Penn World Table, 62
Peru, 149
Pevehouse, J., xxvi, xxviii, 265–294, 329–341
pluralist models. *See* societal models
Poland, 331
policy preferences, 130, 175, 178
Polity Project index, 338
Pollins, B., 16n48
population, 20, 41, 43, 54, 56, 56, 137
Powell, R., 39
power: basic force models, 21; capabilities and, 21; concentration and, xii, xiii, xxi, 9, 10, 13, 21, 33 (*see also* concentration of capabilities); fragmentation and, xxi; hegemony and, 7, 8, 13 (*see also* hegemony); income and, 37; major powers and, xii, 3, 10 (*see also* major powers); market/political power, 13n39; security externalities and, 37; tariffs and, 37–43 (*see also specific topics*; tariffs); trade and, 18–28
PR. *See* proportional representation systems
preferential trading arrangements (PTAs), xv, xvi, xxiii, 137, 140, 153, 331; alliances and, xv, 57–58, 61, 62 (*see also* alliances); autocracies and, xxv, xxvi, 250 (*see also* autocracies); bilateralism and, xxviii, 41, 51, 53, 61, 331, 339; business cycles and, xxiv; closure and, 222; Cold War and, 247, 338; combination, xv; common markets and, 206; concentration and, 337 (*see also* concentration); CUs and, 41, 206, 287; democracies and, xxv, xxvi, 250, 338 (*see also* democracies); disputes, 306; domestic politics and, 266–269; DSMs, 336; dyads and, 293, 310; economic size and, 250–251, 281; effects of, xv; environment and, xxiii; expansion of, xxvii, xxviii, 205–226, 329–341; exports and, 57, 87, 220; foreign investment and, xxiii; formation of, 91, 205–207, 247–253; FTAs and, 41, 68, 206, 336 (*see also* free trade); GATT and (*see* General Agreement on Tariffs and Trade); hegemony and, xxiv, 214, 219, 247, 282 (*see also* hegemony); history of, 340; hub and spoke agreements, xxviii, 331, 339; human rights and, xxiii; incentives for, 205; institutional characteristics, 335–336; interest groups and, 265 (*see also* interest groups); internal markets, 332; international system and, xxiv, 205–225, 294; legislatures and, xxvi; major powers and, 52, 53, 61 (*see also* major powers; specific countries); military and, 338 (*see also* military); multilateralism and, xxv, xxviii, 296, 300–307, 322, 323, 332; nondiscrimination and, 295–298, 321; openness and, 332; opportunism and, 52; peace and, xxiii; protection and, xxiv (*see also*

protectionism); ratification, xxvi; recessions and, xxv, 208, 214, 219, 220, 222; reciprocal agreements, xxviii, 74; regime types and, xxvi, 249–250, 265, 338 (*see also* regime types); regionalism and, 206, 222, 338; relation-specific investments and, 208; security and (*see* security externalities); size and, 281; strategic interaction and, xxiv, 209–210; trade barriers and, 53 (*see also specific topics*; trade barriers); types of, xxiii; veto players and, xxvi, 265–294 (*see also* veto players); volatility and, xvi, 65–96, 84 (*see also* volatility); welfare and, xxiii, 210; World War II and, 247, 340; WTO and (*see* World Trade Organization); *See also specific agreements, topics*

pressure groups, 103, 106, 108, 123

prisoner's dilemma, 37–49, 39, 40

private agents, 52, 52n6

proportional representation (PR) systems, 107, 114, 116–117, 152

protectionism, xviii, xxiv, 17, 70, 129, 233; constant protection, law of, 110; decline in, 227; domestic institutions and, 99; exchange rate and, xviii; executive and, 254, 273; free trade and, 192 (*see also* free trade); GATT and, 110, 298; gender and, 174, 188; import penetration and, 157; interest groups and, 164; legislatures and, 140; liberalization and, 102, 140; macroeconomics and, xx, 123, 164; national interest and, 99; NTBs and, 108 (*see also* nontariff barriers); openness and, 145; recessions and, 219; societal theories and, 99, 100, 148; specific factor model, xxii, 171, 173, 180, 192, 195; state-society literature and, 123; tariff equivalents, 72; trade barriers and (*see* trade barriers); unemployment and, xviii, 101–103, 147, 148, 164; voters and, 254 (*see also* voting); women and, 174–175, 188; *See also specific countries, topics*

PTAs. *See* preferential trading arrangements

public goods, 5, 6

public officials, xviii, xix, xx, 104, 108. *See also* regime types; *specific topics*

public opinion, xxii, 188, 230

**R**

race, 184, 192, 195

ratification, 267, 269, 274, 276

recessions: business cycles and, 208; hegemony and, xxv; protectionism and, 219; PTAs and, xxv, 208, 214, 219–222; trade agreements and, 229

reciprocal agreements, xxviii, 74

regime types, xix–xx, xxv, 137, 138, 231–235; autocracies (*see* autocracies); cooperation and, 253; democracies (*see* democracies); executive (*see also* executive); Gurr index, 134–135; imperfect control and, 240–243; interstate conflict, 227, 228; Jaggers-Gurr index, 251; Polity Project index, 338; PTAs and, 249–250, 265, 338; trade barriers and, 132–134; trade policy and, 145, 149–150; veto players and, 267, 287–288; *See also specific types, topics*

regionalism, 205, 215, 281, 286; domino theory and, 332; GATT and, 299–300; growth of, 206; hegemony and, 207; multilateralism and, 295–329; PTAs and, 206, 222, 338; regionalization, 206n3; strategic interdependence and, 210; U.S. and, 219

Reinhardt, E., xvi, xxvii, 65–96, 295–329

relation-specific investments, 52, 53, 208
relative inequality, of capabilities, 13, 34
religion, 192
Ricardo-Viner model, xxii, 169–201
Romania, 336
Rosendorff, B. P., xx, xxv, 127–143, 227–263
Russian Civil War, 47n26

S

second best, theory of, 46n7
security externalities, xiv, 31; adversaries and, xiv, 60; alliances and, xiv; defined, 51n2; free trade agreements and, 37–49; international system and, 51; military and, 37; negative, 51; open trade and, xiv, 51; power politics and, 37
self-interest, xxii, 169, 173, 181–182; elections and, 177; factor endowments and, 171; groups and (*see* interest groups); income and, xxii (*see also* income); policy preferences and, 175; specific factors model and, 171, 192; trade policy and, 170, 175; welfare and, 177
shocks, external, 65, 233. *See also specific types, topics*
Singapore, 69, 321
Singapore-Australia FTA, 69
size, xix, 31, 281, 332
Slovakia, 331
small group theory, 5, 6, 30, 31
SOC. *See* Standard Occupational Classification
social welfare, 103, 232
societal approaches, xvii, xxi, 100–103, 107–109, 122; institutions and, xix, xx, 145; NTBs and, xix, 122, 123; protection and, 99, 100, 148; statist approaches and, 99, 103–107, 122; trade policy and, xvii, xix, 146–147; unemployment, 122
sociotropic models, xxii, 169, 171, 176, 190, 196
South Africa, 62
South Korea, 60
Soviet Union, xiii, 31, 41–44, 61, 153, 330, 331
specific factors model, 169–201
Standard Occupational Classification (SOC), 175, 176, 180
statist approaches, 107–109; NTBs and, 105, 122; pressure groups and, 123; societal approaches, 99, 103–107, 122; trade policy and, 103–107
strategic interdependence, 208–210
Sweden, 91
Switzerland, 152
systemic analyses, 8, 33. *See also specific types, topics*

T

take-it-or-leave-it (TILI), 130, 141
Tanzania, 79
tariffs, 5; allies and, 40; business cycles and, 17; concentration and, 14; CU and, 287; endogenous theory, xvii; equivalents, 72; free trade and (*see* free trade); game theory and, 38–41, 46n11; GATT and, 100; hegemony and, 6 (*see* hegemony); major powers and, xv, 31; MFN and, 208; NTBs and, 46n6, 99–125; optimal, 5, 38–41; power and, 37–43; prisoner's dilemma and, 38–41; prosperity and, 17; protection and (*see* protectionism); relative inequality, 13; trade barriers and, 13; WTO and, 100; *See also specific countries, topics*
technological advance, 17, 29
Thailand, 69
Tit for Tat, 46n11

trade barriers, 5, 13; autocracies and, xx, 131; democracies and, xx, 131; executive and, 235–236; GATT, xvi; institutions and, 65–96; interest groups and, 229; Nash equilibrium and, 129; NTBs and, 46n6; openness and, 332; optimal level of, 235–236; protectionism (*see* protectionism); PTAs and, xvi, 53; regime types and, 132–134; tariff equivalents, 72; trade flows and, 47n19; *See also specific topics*; tariffs

trade policy, xviii, xxv, 196, 229; cooperation and, 269–278; democracy and, xx (*see also* democracies); domestic institutions and, xix; executive and, 233–234; interest groups and, xvii, 268 (*see also* interest groups); mass attitudes, xxi–xxii; openness and, 339; policy and, 175; preferences and, xvii, 173, 175; protectionism and, 129; regime types and, 145, 149–150; self-interest and, 170, 175; societal approaches, xvii, xix, 107–109, 146–147; statist approaches and, 103–109; unemployment and, 165, 170; veto points and, 147–148, 165, 280 (*see also* veto players); *See also specific countries, topics*

trade preferences, 170; education and, 173, 174, 182, 190; factor endowments and, 195; free trade and, 192, 193; information and, 175; national interest and, 171; origins of, 171–178; race and, 192; religion and, 192; Ricardo-Viner model, 195; trade policies and, 170, 173; union membership and, 190; urban-rural residence and, 192; U.S. and, 170, 232

transportation costs, 17

Turkey, 152

two-level games, 266, 269, 270, 294

**U**

Uganda, 79

UN. *See* United Nations

UNCTAD. *See* United Nations Conference on Trade and Development

unemployment, 101, 109; democracy and, xxi; exchange rate and, 101–103; factor endowment and, 172; import penetration and, 157; labor force and, 172, 176; NTBs and, 108, 114, 120; openness and, 149, 157; protectionism and, xviii, 101–103, 147, 148, 164; societal theories and, 122; trade policy and, 165, 170; unions and, 175, 188, 190; West Germany and, 120

union membership, 175, 188, 190

United Nations Conference on Trade and Development (UNCTAD), 111

United Nations (UN), 111, 182, 293

United States, xii, xiii, 152, 306, 312–313, 321; Canada and, 304, 312–313; education and, 182, 195, 196, 197; electoral system, 121; ethnocentrism and, 184; exchange rates and, 119; factor endowments and, 171; FTAs and, 206n3, 304, 312, 313, 331 (*see also specific countries, agreements*); globalization and, 180; information and, 176; interest groups (*see* interest groups); isolationism and, xxii; Israel and, 206n3; Japan and, 62, 120, 121; labor force, 170, 171; liberalization and, 32; military force, 294; multilateral agreements, 331 (*see also specific countries, agreements*); NAFTA and, 72, 180, 208, 221, 230, 331; national interest and, 121; NATO and, 135; NTBs and, 119; party system, 184, 188; preferences in, 109, 169–201, 232, 280; protectionism and, xxii, 188 (*see also* protectionism); PTAs and, 330 (*see also* preferential

trading arrangements); public attitudes, xxii; ratification and, 267; Reagan administration, 119; regionalism and, 219; South Korea and, 60; specific factors approach, 170; World War II and, 4; *See also agreements, specific topics*
urban-rural residence, 192
Uruguay Round, 68, 69, 72, 300, 301

**V**
Venezuela, 320, 321
veto players, xxi, xxv, 165, 279, 280; addition of, 275, 276; centralized government and, 146; cooperation and, 265–294; democracies and, xxi, 145–147, 164, 165, 267; executive and, 266; free trade and, 277; hegemony and (*see* hegemony); macroeconomics, 145, 146; major powers (*see* major powers); Nash equilibrium and, 270; PTAs and, xxvi, 265–294; ratification and, 269, 274, 276; regime types and, 267, 287–288; spatial models, 279; stability and, 147; trade policy and, 145, 147–148; two-level games and, 294
volatility, xxiii, 18, 87; ARCH-in-mean model, 88; bilateralism and, 74; GATT and, 74, 91; industrial nations and, 86; international trade levels, xvi, 65–96; measures of, 76, 77, 91; multilateralism and, 91; PTAs and, xvi, 65–96, 84; reciprocal agreements and, 74; as tax, 88; WTO and, 65, 84

**W**
Wallerstein, I., xiii, 9
Waltz, K., xii, 14, 29
war, 33, 39, 55, 127–143, 137, 227, 281; concentration and, 11n31; COW Project and (*see* Correlates of War Project); defense pacts, 47n26; exports and, 43, 56; major powers and, 24, 34; peace, xxiii, 47n26; trade and, 15–29; World War I, 30; *See* World War II
Warsaw Pact, 61, 135
welfare, xxiii, 130, 177, 182, 210, 299–300
West Germany, 55, 58, 120
winner-take-all systems, 107
women, policy and, 174–175, 188
World Trade Organization (WTO), xvi, xxviii, 100, 222, 295–329; DFI and, 180; dispute settlement and, 70, 71; Doha Round, 303, 304; DSU of, 68; exports and, 55, 56; GATT and (*see* General Agreement on Tariffs and Trade); NTBs and, 100; openness and, xxvii; PTAs and, 205, 208, 215–221, 247, 255; public reports, 230; Regional Trade Agreements, 298; Seattle meeting, 305; tariffs and, 100; Uruguay Round, 68, 69, 72, 300, 301; U.S. and, 71; volatility and, 65, 84
World War I, 30
World War II, xii, xiii, 4, 29, 40, 53, 135, 247, 340

**Y**
Yaoundé Convention, 221

Lightning Source UK Ltd.
Milton Keynes UK
UKOW06n1506270715

255896UK00004B/118/P

... School
Campus de Rouen
1 rue du Maréchal Juin
BP 215 - Cedex
76825 Mont Saint Aignan
Tél : 02 32 82 57 00

9 789814 644280

## A RETOURNER

| | | | |
|---|---|---|---|
| 12/10/23 | | | |
| | | | |
| | | | |
| | | | |
| | | | |
| | | | |
| | | | |
| | | | |
| | | | |
| | | | |
| | | | |
| | | | |
| | | | |
| | | | |
| | | | |
| | | | |
| | | | |

DEMCO, INC.